W9-BTG-406

THE LETTERS OF

RALPH WALDO EMERSON

Facsimile Pages of Letter to William Emerson
November 10, 1814

Con——— November 10

Brother,

offend if attempt *

erogl phics; I lately of the Duke

of York's them, it was give Sa-

rah by ff Bradford; have t k

y from t . I li Con—

very much. I go school here

li it every d . W is t

song by G. B. t prom send me the

d we mov send it s soon as .

Mrs cam Summer St. b

have spend thanksgiving at

* I-C, non est litera

37

her . I have Patronage
yet. O soon enjoy the hap-
ess of ing here. Charles send
Charles than he X . Send me
Your Collectanea M nor 1st time
. reg ics t up too
much time , so pr X qqs
m short
Yours

Ralph.

Wm Emerson.

THE LETTERS OF

RALPH WALDO EMERSON

IN SIX VOLUMES

EDITED BY

RALPH L. RUSK

VOLUME ONE

NEW YORK AND LONDON

COLUMBIA UNIVERSITY PRESS

First printing 1939
Second printing 1966

PUBLICATION OF THIS WORK WAS MADE POSSIBLE
THROUGH THE AID OF THE ALBERT H. WIGGIN FUND

Printed in the United States of America

Preface

The letters of Emerson have been in course of publication since his " brief parting word " to the Second Church was printed by I. R. Butts, presumably in December, 1832, or in the following January. Within a few years they began to appear, usually one or two at a time, in newspapers and books; and in this irregular manner a number became known during the lifetime of their author. After his death, others found their way into the periodical press or into biographies of him or of his correspondents. Among the biographies, *A Memoir,* by J. E. Cabot, is noteworthy for its extracts from letters.

But the first fruits of a serious interest in the epistolary record were C. E. Norton's editions of *The Correspondence of Thomas Carlyle and Ralph Waldo Emerson;* and these were followed by five volumes which, though mostly small, are still important – E. W. Emerson's *A Correspondence between John Sterling and Ralph Waldo Emerson,* Norton's *Letters from Ralph Waldo Emerson to a Friend,* F. W. Holls's *Correspondence between Ralph Waldo Emerson and Herman Grimm,* H. H. Furness's *Records of a Lifelong Friendship* (the first approach to a literal text), and H. F. Lowry and R. L. Rusk's *Emerson–Clough Letters.* Altogether, the six collections contain full or partial texts of more than two hundred letters of Emerson.

Obviously no complete record can ever be made, though fresh manuscripts will doubtless continue to come to light in considerable numbers. The present edition includes the new letters of Emerson known to me that are available for publication, together with some that have hitherto been printed only in fragmentary form. It also includes a calendar of others, published and unpublished.

I have tried to print a literal text, with no interpolated corrections or apologies. The original manuscripts, and, next to them, the photostats or photographs of them in the Columbia University Library, must remain important as the final authorities to which appeal can be made. Unfortunately the originals deteriorate, and many of them pass from one owner to another and drop out of sight; and the reproductions, though they have special virtues of their own, may sometimes prove deceptive. The best that can be done, however, is to make all these sources as easily accessible as possible. The ownership of the Emerson letters I have used is fully recorded. Other manuscripts mentioned or quoted in the footnotes or index without any indication of ownership are the property of the Ralph Waldo Emerson Memorial Association.

A number of letters are known only through copies, mostly made, presumably, in the 1880's, by or for J. E. Cabot, Emerson's first literary executor, and now owned by the Memorial Association. These copies are printed here without revision and are described in the notes; and a few letters the originals of which are accessible but cannot conveniently be reproduced photographically are printed from longhand copies I have made or have checked. But with these exceptions, and some eight or ten others, also duly noted, no copies other than photostats or photographs of the originals have been used as sources of the text.

In the introduction I have discussed some aspects of the letters, making free use of Emerson's own words. If numerous brief borrowed passages appear without any formal acknowledgment, they are not far to seek in the letters themselves.

My greatest debt is to the members of the Ralph Waldo Emerson Memorial Association for the use of their rich collection of manuscripts and for permission to print all hitherto unpublished Emerson letters contained in this edition – permission which they finally granted, I ought to acknowledge, in spite of their feeling that many of the letters about business affairs or of a very private and personal nature might better remain unpublished. Members of the Association have, besides, given indispensable aid at almost every stage in the long progress of this work, and the warmest thanks are due to Mr. Edward Waldo Forbes, Mr. W. Cameron Forbes, Mr. Raymond Emerson, and Professor K. G. T. Webster. My colleague Dr. Haven Emerson put at my disposal his extensive file of family correspondence. Officials of the Harvard College Library allowed me to make full use of the collection of Emerson letters which is second in importance only to that of the Memorial Association. Professor Bliss Perry gave his friendly and powerful aid when it was most needed.

Special acknowledgments for permission to use valuable collections or for aid in discovering widely scattered manuscripts must be made to Mr. W. T. H. Howe, Mr. Owen D. Young, Dr. Nicholas Murray Butler, Mrs. Mildred Conway Sawyer, Mr. Carroll A. Wilson, Mr. Oliver R. Barrett, Dr. James I. Wyer, Mrs. Charles W. Andrews, Dr. H. W. L. Dana, Mrs. Humphreys Johnstone, Dr. Charles C. Williamson, Mr. Roger Howson, Professor Isadore Gilbert Mudge, Mr. James F. Clarke, Professor Townsend Scudder, Mr. Edward Gookin, Miss Frances Plimpton, Dr. Arthur E. Christy, Mr. F. W. Pratt, Professor Odell Shepard, Dr. Frederic I. Carpenter, Dr. Max Farrand, Professor Ralph Barton Perry, Dr. Robert Forsythe, Mr. John H. Birss, Mr. Edward G. Bernard, Dr. Edward S. Parsons, Mr. Allen French, Miss Sarah Bartlett, Dr. Viola C. White, and Mr. William H. M. Adams. Many dealers in manuscripts also gave generous aid, but particularly Goodspeed's Book Shop, of Boston, and the late Thomas F. Madigan, of New York.

My thanks are likewise due to the heirs or executors who have granted permission to publish letters to Emerson from various correspondents, or other manuscript material — to Professor Arnold Whitridge for the letters of Matthew Arnold, to Mme Hubert Dussy for the letter of Jean Baptiste François Baille, to Mr. James A. S. Barrett for the letters of Thomas Carlyle, to Mr. Arthur Clough (through Professor Howard F. Lowry) for the letters of Arthur Hugh Clough, to Mrs. Mildred Conway Sawyer for the MSS of Moncure D. Conway, to Mr. Frederick G. Corning for the letter of J. L. Corning, to the Memorial Association and to Dr. Haven Emerson for the letters of various members of the Emerson family, to the heirs of Annie Adams Fields for excerpts from her diaries, to Mrs. Arthur B. Nichols for the letters of Margaret Fuller, to Mrs. Frank M. Clendenin for the letters of Horace Greeley, to Mr. Manning Hawthorne for the letters of Nathaniel Hawthorne, to Miss Mildred Howells for the letters of William Dean Howells, to Mr. Alleyne Ireland for the letters of Alexander Ireland, to Mr. Henry James for the letter of William James, to the Trustees of the Longfellow House in Cambridge for the letters of Henry Wadsworth Longfellow, to Mr. William F. Badè for the letters of John Muir, to Miss Edith Guerrier for the letter of Daniel Ricketson, to Mrs. John W. Ames for the letters of Dr. Ezra Ripley and Samuel Ripley, to Mr. F. B. Sanborn for the letters of Franklin Benjamin Sanborn, and to Dr. James I. Wyer for the letter of Mary Elizabeth Wyer. The late Justice Holmes authorized the publication of the letters of his father, Oliver Wendell Holmes.

Permission to publish passages of correspondence that are already in print has been granted by the heirs of Annie Adams Fields for her volume entitled *Authors and Friends,* by the Appleton-Century Company for *The Century Illustrated Monthly Magazine,* by Dr. Richard C. Cabot and the Houghton Mifflin Company for J. E. Cabot's *A Memoir of Ralph Waldo Emerson,* by Mrs. Mildred Conway Sawyer for Moncure

D. Conway's *Emerson at Home and Abroad* and *Autobiography,* and by the Emerson heirs for the various books of which they own the copyrights.

Necessary financial aid has been made available through the kindness of the President, Provost, and other officials of Columbia University and by the University's Council on Research in the Humanities. And no less necessary has been the assistance which many persons, but chiefly my wife, have given me in gathering editorial materials, in preparing the manuscript for the press, and in reading the proofs.

R. L. R.

New York
April, 1938

Note to the Second Printing

For this reprinting, the few original misprints and errors of fact have been corrected from notes provided by Professor Rusk and Professor Eleanor M. Tilton of Barnard College. There has been no editing to bring the volumes up to date. For example, notes of the location of manuscripts have not been revised although a good many letters have changed hands since 1939. Letters formerly owned by W. T. H. Howe and Owen D. Young are now in the New York Public Library (Henry W. and Albert A. Berg Collection); the Furness correspondence has been acquired by the University of Pennsylvania; the Clough letters are now in the Bodleian; letters to James Freeman Clarke, Henry James, Sr., Oliver Wendell Holmes, James Russell Lowell, and others are in the Houghton Library, Harvard University. Other letters, formerly in private hands, have been acquired by the University of Virginia (C. Waller Barrett Collection), Henry E. Huntington Library, and the Morgan Library.

Contents

VOLUME V

VOLUME VI

Introduction

I

In the early 1840's dependable John Stacy presided over the village post office conveniently established in his bindery and bookstore on the Mill Dam, and all classes of the citizenry came to his door. The men to be seen there were mostly farmers, with a few tradesmen, physicians, lawyers, teachers, and preachers. One frequent customer, however, refused to fit into any such easy division of society — a gentleman of more than the average height, with narrow, sloping shoulders, finely poised head, and bold features, who was officially listed as Charge No. 29 but was already known to some readers in America and in England as the author of *Nature* and *Essays* and as a contributor to *The Dial* and, presently, its editor. Fortunate enough to live only a few steps from the Lexington road, he had more than one means of access to the mails. Between trips to the post office he could stop the stagecoach as it rattled along the foot of Revolutionary Ridge to Coolidge Castle, like a ghost of the past which was doomed to vanish forever before the onset of the locomotive puffing its way out further and further every month from Charlestown toward Concord. The stage drivers still obligingly accepted mail and parcels for a price. Besides, friendly neighbors setting out for New York or other distant cities were in the habit of inquiring for a letter to carry.

It was well that there were so many channels to the outside world. The little magazine required a deal of correspondence, and the friends the books had stirred up accounted for more. Altogether No. 29 was hard put to it to keep up his end and was having to apologize, very graciously. A letter, he had discovered, could make an ugly bracket in one's afternoon, it being neither study nor exercise. To people over the water, or to people of genius who could not speak, one must submit to apply this organ; but to all cisatlantics whose tongues played to their souls, the seldomer the better. Yet his own appetite for letters had grown capacious as the sea. For the first time in his life, a circle of friends and disciples had laid siege to him and broken down his reserves and reticences. Had he always been a hermit, unable to approach his fellow men, and did the social divinities suddenly offer him a roomful of friends? Well, please God, he would not be wanting to his fortune but would eat his pomegranate — seed, stem, and leaves — with thankfulness and would be known as a writer of letters and sonnets.

There were important compensations for the trouble and the loss of good hours of which he complained. He had long ago come to the conclusion that letters had a vast superiority over conversation as a medium of ideas. Men said (heaven help their poor wits) that they had rather have ten words *viva voce* than volumes of letters for getting opinions. But the fact was that communication through an interpreter would be better than the ordinary conversation. Politeness ruined conversation, and you got nothing but the scum and surface of opinions. Instead of holding to the old verse " Speak that I may know thee," it were better to admonish a man, " Speak, that I may suspect thee; write, that I may *know* thee." After additional years of experience he could hardly have changed his opinion, though he had not ceased to experiment. He had tried for hours at a time, and even day after day, to learn the minds of his friends through conversation; but at every trial the temperature dropped sooner or later, and in the end there was likely to be blank disappointment.

He could have made a still stronger plea for letters as the best preservative of that fine spiritual essence, the personality of the writer. He might have served as his own most apt example, for he was at his worst in familiar conversation. The reports that have come down to us are conclusive on this point. No amount of Boswellizing would have sufficed, and no table talk. The letters were destined to be the most satisfactory record of the personality of Emerson.

It is true that even in them he sometimes felt hampered by the too constrictive social conventions of his time. What a misfortune to live among the civilized when all personalities were indecorus! Montaigne and Saadi, he remembered, told all that befell them with the name and date, and it was counted unto them for fame; but now people were sent to Coventry for such frankness. Yet he was no easy prey to intellectual anemia of any sort and could, on proper occasion, forget the danger of Coventry. When he began work on the memoir of Margaret Fuller, he told his friend Ward that the personalities must be left in the book, that to leave them out would be to leave out Margaret. Letters, too, were biography, or autobiography, and must keep this invigorating sap. His own letters flowed on for decades, and if they seldom transgressed the rules that threatened reprisals, they were commonly bold enough in asserting the individuality of their author.

His experience in the writing of letters went back a long way. Even before he began scribbling in the diaries of which we know, the endless almanacs that marked the days and seasons of his mental life, he had commenced this more general and more informal record. When he was eleven, and the family purse so low that every scrap of paper must have been precious, he was already practicing the epistolary art, though for some years he made little progress in it. He fell into the habit of beginning with only the slightest notion of a subject. He would stretch a slender thread of thought to the breaking point and still doggedly persevere in the hope of stumbling upon an inspiration, or he would write against time when he learned tardily of an " opportunity " in the person of a relative or friend who happened to be traveling in the right direction. Until he was nearly eighteen, when his Aunt Mary announced her discovery of his new-born dignity of style, he wrote in a regrettably juvenile manner, like the mere boy he was. But there were momentary gleams of qualities that were to become characteristic during his middle life.

II

Humor, which few readers of the essays and lectures would dream of discovering in Emerson, but which is a delightful part of his familiar letters, was already recognizable in the somewhat laborious literary acrobatics he attempted for the entertainment of his brothers in early years. He was lavish with puns, satirical epithets, and mock-heroics. For a time he even achieved repute as the family wit. In the rollicking miscellanies of news and general criticism which he mailed to classmates shortly after graduation from college, his sense of humor was indubitable, though still youthful and in a state of transition.

Then came a series of events that carried him more rapidly toward emotional maturity. During a period of some ten years beginning in 1826, he suffered repeated blows of outrageous fortune — disease which threatened to cripple him permanently, his young wife's illness and death, the crisis of his ministry at the Second Church, the deaths of his brothers Edward and Charles. When he had partly recovered from these shocks and had definitely begun his literary career with comfortable headquarters in Concord, the humor, which had never been long out of sight, reappeared, like water cooled and improved by running a little while underground. It kept only the slightest satirical tang. Far from uproarious, it had very little resemblance of any kind to the frontier type commonly proclaimed as nineteenth-century American. It was hardly laughter at all, only the temperate mirth of a cultured, philosophical man who was, however, no pedant but fully aware of the commonplace world in which he lived.

Thus the letters detail the news of the household with some exaggeration for the sake of the fun. They publish the health and prospects of the dog and the kittens. The old gentleman in the study, we hear, wastes much good time — dips a pen in ink and affects to write a little from upper dictation, but presently falls to copying old, musty papers, then to reading a little in Plato and in the Vedas; picks his pea vines or waters his melons or thins his carrots; then walks a little and talks a little — and the marvelous day has fled. While he still considered with due solemnity the advisability of yielding to the determined persuasion of the associationists and transplanting himself to Brook Farm, he amused Elizabeth Hoar with the objection that after so many social ages it was time for one lonely age, with Tom Wyman at Walden Pond, and none of your Alcotts or Owens, as its saint and pattern. Zimmerman's treatise on solitude, he declared, should be the only book. He thought of occupying the Concord monument as a stylite and admonished his correspondent to hurry home and hear his last words before he should be perched. Lidian Emerson's devotion to her native Plymouth from the days of their courtship and her habit of revisiting the place are the subjects of many humorous observations in his letters to her. He upheld the honor of Concord by sending her the best pears from the home lot, but finding that she was at the same moment sending him pears from Plymouth, concluded that it was hardly worth while for them to pelt each other with fruit across sixty miles. He commented to his daughter Ellen on the cumbrous baggage that the Plymouth expeditions required and thought it passed wonder that her mother had left behind the shower bath and the calf. In writing to recommend a laborer, he enumerated the latter's virtues, as his delight in horses and his care of the cows, but had to admit also one vice; namely, a rare indulgence in drink — " of which he is vastly ashamed, & thinks if I will only hide it, he shall never let it be known again." Was it possible, he asked, that there was employment for so many virtues and such a small, disappearing vice?

Many letters show that he could even survive with credit the supreme ordeal and laugh at his own philosophy. He was frequently surprised and amused by the seriousness with which conservatives and practical men looked upon his heresies. On his last voyage to Europe he wrote home to assure his wife that his well-known orthodoxy was walled round, on shipboard, by whole families of missionaries and that he had heard two sermons and the English service, together with many hymns. But, he added, the liberal ocean sang louder and made one church of all.

The courtesy which pervades the letters is so Emersonian that no other term can describe it. It has its undeniable charm, and its weakness, since it necessarily implies certain negations. It is too individual to reduce writing to dull formality, but it must suppress some of that liberty and raciness that are so admirable in Montaigne and Saadi. The politeness that spoils conversation sometimes threatens the sister art. One finds here little of the genius for repartee and broad jest that belongs to many a notable writer of letters. The delight in malicious gossip, the cleverness, and the air of the man of the world that make Horace Walpole refreshing to most readers are lacking. Emerson is too near to the Puritans, whose conscience he has inherited, though he escapes their religion, and his native courtesy is too strong and genuine, to allow him to navigate waters beyond Suez where the commandments can be safely forgotten. His description of Plato would fit his own case: he is a great, uniform gentleman, and nothing is more characteristic of him than his good breeding. And for such a distinction one must make sacrifices.

But if malice was not a Puritan virtue, anger might be on occasion. Emerson, to be sure, had no constitutional fondness for disputation, whether carried on by tongue or by pen. The apology he wrote to Ware for failure to accept a challenge to debate through the mails was characteristic. Nor did he wish to have anybody take up the cudgels on his behalf. He was consistent when he acknowledged John Chapman's efforts to answer unfriendly critics of the second series of essays. He had long ago settled it, he said, that it was best not to set up any defense at all but simply to go on affirming. He could tolerate any amount of vituperation aimed at him because of his radical views. And yet there were occasions when what seemed a flagrant injustice of quite another kind roused anger that got free expression. Dishonesty, or even what he sometimes mistook for it, in the conduct of those with whom he had business dealings could stir him to epistolary wrath. There were inky encounters with publishers he challenged on behalf of his friend Carlyle, whose literary property he was determined to protect from American pirating. Usually the provocation was ample; but perhaps the longest duel of the sort he ever fought turned out to be quite quixotic, through Carlyle's own fault. Emerson kept himself screwed up to a bellicose mood for months, only to find, after much correspondence, that Carlyle had heedlessly thrown away his own rights. There were, he concluded, limits even to the charms of wrath, and he forthwith turned round and proposed that the offending publisher be rewarded for his eagerness by being made the accredited American agent for all of Carlyle's books. He resented the journalistic bootlegging which endangered his own income as a lecturer, an income necessary, as he explained, to pay for his bread. Many an enterprising editor received a reprimand for printing lengthy quotations from lectures which had to be repeated in towns where his newspaper was read. But Emerson was most effective as a belligerent when he championed the victims of social or political injustice. The growing passion of the debate over slavery embittered some of his letters, and during the clash of arms that followed the wordy war he was swept momentarily out of his philosophical calm into partisan hatred. A more admirable example and perhaps the most elaborate of his angry protests was that addressed to President Van Buren on behalf of the defrauded Cherokees.

Confessions of coldness and restraint are common and are sometimes justified. Much depended on the correspondent. Henry James, Sr., had some grounds for his complaint, though he wrote it in illness and depression. The letters to him are prim, bloodless, and maidenly enough. Some to persons with whom Emerson was on terms of respect rather than of intimacy are so guarded that they seem pale and insipid. There was, indeed, as he was wont to declare, a certain lack of emotional vitality in him. He found it difficult to be a photometer and a stove at the same time. In the letters to Ellen Tucker, which are unfortunately lost, he must have been freer than at any other time in his life from emotional reticence. But with her death, one suspects, the old inhibitions were strengthened and, in some respects, became permanent. The letters to Lydia Jackson were written by a mature man, who was at the same time writing a philosophical treatise on nature, and not by a young lover. After a dozen or more years of married life he wrote apologetically from abroad that the letter for which his wife asked and which was always due remained unwritten.

Yet these deficiencies are easy to overestimate, and the whole body of Emerson's correspondence goes to prove that he was capable of much more warmth and enthusiasm in his friendships, as well as in his domestic relations, than has been supposed. It is impossible to discover the complete stoic in him. If he confessed to the fact of cold and imperfect intercourse, he still denied any deficiency of affection. He counted and weighed but loved also. He could not tell how warm and glad the mere naming of his friends made his solitude. He was resolved never to go back to his old arctic habits. His friends were sacred, and even a new one could take him by storm. Anna Barker's unique gentleness at once unbarred all doors, so that no brother or sister or father or mother or lifelong acquaintance ever seemed to arrive quite so near. Many years later he bewailed the chasms of time and space and religious faith that had come to separate him from this friend. But what if she did stay away and hide herself still farther away in the seclusion of opinion? She remained an endeared and enshrined person, with generous and happy influence. From England he addressed his new friend Edward Bangs without any formality, " For you must allow me an affectionate expression — me so far off & you so young . . ." And hardly had the Civil War come to an end before he was writing, as tenderly as Walt Whitman could have done, to his old classmate and late enemy Robert Barnwell, one of the leaders of the South which had been pillaged by Northern troops. Barnwell must know that distance, politics, war, even, had not been able to efface in any manner the high, affectionate regard which his college contemporaries had firmly held for their avowed chief in days when boys give a romantic value to that distinction such as they can never give again.

Letters about his children, or to them, add more than enough evidence to put an end to the legend of the stoic. He supplies his wife with copious details of the doings of the nursery in her absence. He begins under some difficulties, with young Waldo jogging his elbow and courteously offering a broken cocoa shell and back again presently to interrupt with his as yet untranslatable Sanskrit. At New York the lecturer, in his hotel, is not so far off but that he can still see Ellen and the boy — " my little creeper with a shawl over her shoulders, blessed shoulders I should have said, & head erect as a turtle's making great eyes to the door to know what this parting ado might mean, & Waldo surveying the stage horses." And a few days later, on the eve of a journey to Providence for more lectures, he writes to Waldo: " I do not think I shall see you until you have gone to bed thirteen or fourteen times, & waked up again just as many mornings." Two years after the boy's death he confesses in a letter to Margaret Fuller that he is as unreconciled as when the calamity was new; and he recalls Ben Jonson's vision of his dead son, adding, "That same preternatural maturity did my beautiful statue assume the day after death . . ."

The letters in general are written in the tone of optimism that has mistakenly been regarded as constant in Emerson. In this respect, however, many of them correct the essays and poems. He wrote that his brother Charles, already doomed to premature death, was despondent and found his fate hard; but, he added, this hard fate belonged to the race rather than to any individual. It was possible to get used to being poor, for the first and happiest men of earth had been so, but it was not so easy to away with pain and disease. On hearing of a death, he had no plea to make for universal optimism. No, life was sad in every corner; this much one learned once more. To Sophia Hawthorne he had nothing better to write when he heard that Louisa was drowned. Who knew, he asked, what was the shortest and most excellent way out of the calamities of the present world? Yet this is not the dominant note. Confession of his misadventures in search of the Sangreal by no means prevented him from persisting in the affirmation that it did exist and must be had, and that every contrary opinion and rumor came from the kitchen.

Writing to intimate friends, he was at perfect ease, happily suspending current rules of punctuation and, on occasion, quite ignoring the mechanics of composition in all its branches, hurrying on with his thought and caring nothing for revision. Why should not Concord emulate the glorious freedom of the Elizabethans? A message of importance to some stranger across seas might be a different matter, or advice to Alcott on that friend's unfortunate experiments in authorship, when the least offensive-looking word might turn out to be barbed. Then there might be painstaking drafts, with numerous erasures and revisions. But in general what Emerson thought of the drudgery of correcting a book was doubtless at least equally apropos to the revision of letters. It was disgraceful when you thought you had done your writing to waste your time in parsing and spelling and punctuating, repairing rotten metaphors, bringing tropes safe into port, and other such tinkering arts. The chapters might eventually get some attention. But the letters should not. One was not writing them, at least, for a future generation. There could hardly be any concern with the chance that they might prove to be as important as most of the essays and poems; and who could guess that the cool Englishman Matthew Arnold would one day hazard the opinion that even Thomas Carlyle might live, in the long run, not by his shelf full of essays and histories but " by such an invaluable record as that correspondence between him and Emerson "?

But many a metaphor was sound, nevertheless, and whole fleets of tropes got safely into port. It was hard for Emerson to write either verse or prose without injecting poetry, his thoughts so readily became objects. He was a good practitioner of the principles of composition he had set down in the chapter on language in his first volume. It is easy to detect the poet at play — never at work — discovering unexpected similarities and identities, and multiplying them together to produce those astronomical sums which only the arithmetic of the imagination can afford. It is usually possible to gauge the degree of his intimacy with a correspondent by the exuberance of the imagery. He had a boyish zest for this kind of extravagance. If he supposed himself quite incompetent to do Margaret Fuller any justice, he thought that in some moment of power he would roll up her letters in cloth of asbestos, and shooting across the lunar and solar sphere, alight on the star of Lyra or on the shoulder of Orion and there, in some grotto of light, meditate on her genius until he had computed its orbit and parallax, its influence, its friend, and its enemy. Or the same exuberant imagination would result in a racy census of mid-century America, whose people by no means perished, though they had no vision: the roads were full of all manner of hale teamsters and riders, cattle and tantivy; the farms, of stout men dispersed at proper distances, planting, fencing, and ditching; and the towns, of manufacturers, bankers, runners, and miscellaneous red and swarthy eaters, knowing little and caring less for the pale Unitarians and philosophers who spied them from their churches and corners and damned them for nobodies.

Descriptive and narrative passages of some power are likely to turn up in letters pretty obviously guiltless of any conscious attempt at literary effect. Emerson returned home over the Middlesex hills " with the dodging moon now up, now down, then high again, as I rode high or low." At Nantasket Beach it was not only his reading but the gentle July sea that drew ancient Greece to him. Every hour of the day had a certain serenity and amplitude from the always visible blue sea line, over which little white columnar sails fled into the invisible, like the pretty trifles we call men and women, with each his own poise, compass, and errand. Now and then there was a more imposing pilgrim, as the

English steamer coming in and, a few hours afterward, going out. The hundred-gun ship " Ohio " went by like some burlier individual, a noisy Webster or Napoleon or Luther, plowing along our main of time, gazed after by all eyes and all spyglasses from all other craft. But these too passed, being only fugitive; and nothing but the broad, blue line endured. Within a few days he was back in Concord, making new prayers to the local or universal muse. Under the soft moon kissing the trees over the bones of his ancestors, he still seemed to hear David's psalter on the cadences of the evening wind. The potent Hebraism of his ministerial ancestry had quite dissipated the Hellenic dreams at the seashore.

But he could lift himself entirely out of his mood of nature worship and describe a city with almost as much fervor. New York, which he had already hated and loved, was a symbol of abundant life. A few months after the reverie in his ancestral village he was in the city of magnificence and of steam, where everything seemed irrevocably destined for a national, for an imperial, prosperity. What a bay! What a river! What climate! What men! What ample interior domain — lake, mountain, forest! What manners, what histories and poetry should rapidly arise and for how long — for an endless date, it seemed! His cabin, indeed, fitted him better, perhaps only because of a certain poorness of spirit. In his next transmigration he would choose New York.

As he extended his travels, the letters were freighted with a rich variety of places, incidents, and persons. In December of the same year, he, with six insides, was dumped unceremoniously into a snowbank in Maine. The accident, he wrote, produced some slight wounds and some sudden developments of character in the ladies, who emerged successively (one of them cursing and swearing without stint) from the bowels of the coach. After they had passed Alfred, in many a mile there was nothing but snow and stars and pine trees, and in traveling it was sometimes possible to have a superfluity of these fine objects. The villages were few and cold as the Tobolsks and Irkutsks of Siberia; and he bethought himself, as he stared into the white night, whether he had not committed a misdemeanor against some Czar and, while he dreamed of Maine, was bound a thousand versts into arctic Asia. Journeys to the West, beginning in 1850, resulted in numerous passages of equal virtue. Mammoth Cave, the Indians at Faribault, a steel furnace at Pittsburgh are celebrated. Descriptions of persons abound, from the briefest summary of intellectual characteristics to the elaborate portraits of Carlyle.

III

The letters, with their changing moods and temperamental varieties of style, give us, no doubt, the most valuable glimpses we can hope to have of the essential personality of Emerson. But they are perhaps equally important for the light they throw on the events of his life, the genesis of his ideas, and the slow growth of his addresses, essays, and poems.

Such early letters to his Aunt Mary as survive form an illuminating introductory chapter to the story of those mental adventures which were, indeed, the most exciting events of his life. The fragmentary evidence is enough to show the surprising vigor of his debate with her over the doctrines with which he expected, some day, to be concerned in the pulpit, and the beginnings of his liberalism. The discussion went on for years and left him, certainly, in no orthodox frame of mind. In 1826, when he was at last on the verge of the ministry, he had, he professed, no objection to the step; but life was queer, and the only proper humor seemed to be quiet astonishment. Presently he was carrying on an epistolary examination of relative and absolute truth. To grow wise, he concluded, was to grow doubtful.

While the battle of the mind continued with varying fortune, the fight for the body was also in progress. A few days after his manifesto of philosophical and religious doubts, he told of the lung complaints which threatened him as he stood on the threshold of his profession. Soon he had resigned his understanding into the hands of his doctors and would journey. A voyage to South Carolina and Florida failed to end his forebodings. Then a period of half-hearted supply preaching at his father's old church was cut short for lack of health, and he thought of abdicating his ministry before it had fairly commenced and already considered turning author. He reported from the towns of western Massachusetts the ill success of his plan to preach there as a substitute in order that he might benefit by the inland air and find time for writing sermons. A somewhat similar tour of irregular service took him to New Hampshire, where he met Ellen Tucker, enthusiastic accounts of whom were presently dispatched to New York for his brother William.

Letters to the Second Church in Boston record the main events of his only regular pastorate, interrupted by more journeys in search of health, this time for Ellen, whom he married in September, 1829. The correspondence of his brothers throws new light on this period from beginning to end — the ordination, the preaching, the pastoral labors. Some incidents were comical. The young minister, we hear, made long calls, kindly and affectionate, on families that had no other claim to his attentions than that of bearing the same name with his parishioners. There is much equally intimate detail.

Ellen's death made it easier to follow the natural course and part from the church. She was beyond misfortune, Emerson wrote, and he would not invite any others to penury and disappointment if he was doomed. A little more than a year after her death the break was all but certain. A committee declared their undiminished respect for their pastor but refused to agree with his novel notions. The ostensible point at issue seemed, in later years, paltry enough, and he would have great difficulty in remembering the grounds of his objections to the orthodox views. But other vastly more important causes had been long at work, as the correspondence shows. Letters of his own and of Charles to William record the final hesitating act of separation. The repairing of the church gave him a chance to travel to Waterford for consultation with the wise aunt, whose wisdom did not, however, quite suffice for such a crisis as this. She had long since settled her opinions and had pleaded with him to remain in the ministry, as his ancestors had done, and leave a name to be "enrolled with the Mathers & Sewalls of that venerable City" of Boston. Her influence had now drawn him again straight to her, but he made his own decision. Her intellectual tutelage was at an end; and her faint hope that he would return in time to the truth of dogmatic theology, as she wrote him, was vain. In her estimation, he had suffered a decisive defeat and his career was ruined. "I can only do my work well," he replied, "by abjuring the opinions & customs of all others & adhering strictly to the divine plan a few dim inches of whose outline I faintly discern in my breast." On September 9, 1832, he preached his apology. On the 11th he wrote his letter of resignation. If the parish had been polled then, Charles told William, probably three-fourths would have voted to keep their minister; but those in authority avoided any such danger. Even so, the parish committee painstakingly canvassed the possibilities of settling the dispute; but on October 28 the proprietors, not the parish, voted, by a small majority, for dismission.

The letter of resignation contained no startling proclamation. Yet while the apologetic sermon was being prepared a new direction of life was being vaguely marked out. One who was afterwards to stand among a select group of men as the representative writer, no cleric to be enrolled among the Mathers and Sewalls of any city, but a liberal who was more liberal than the young minister knew, seemed to point the way. Emerson wrote to the aunt who foresaw the ruin of his career and bade him " Farewell, if for aye ": " I am entering into acquaintance with Goethe . . . The Germans think there have been but three men of genius — Homer, Shakspear, & Goethe. If I go into the country to books, I shall know him well . . ."

Then comes the remarkable series of letters in which the traveler sets down his itinerary, describes at length the cities and countries he visits, and comments on the people he encounters, but at the same time stanchly holds by the thesis, later written into the essays for all the world to quote, that traveling is a fool's paradise. Before he went to the country to books, he not only healed himself of his physical ails by this first voyage to Europe but he initiated himself into the fraternity of living makers of books by seeking out Landor in Italy and Coleridge, Carlyle, and Wordsworth in Britain. It was comforting to meet a man of genius like Carlyle because he was above the meanness of pretending to knowledge which he did not have. Tradition and authoritarianism vanished a little farther into the discarded past.

The correspondence of 1835 tells pretty fully the story of the historical discourse at Concord, the first of the pamphlets Emerson published and remarkable as showing better than any other writing his ability to carry on painstaking research in printed and manuscript sources. For the moment, and by accident, he was a scholar in the narrower sense; and the record is full enough to include a bibliography and even an account of an attempt to allay the fears of the local historian, who thought his own literary property in danger. Before this address was under weigh, however, a large part of *Nature* was done. Its author afterwards recalled that it was mostly written in the Old Manse, but the ideas from which it grew are scattered through many letters over a long period of time. The same sources also throw new light on other literary landmarks. A vast difference appears between the shallow conception of " the Age of the American Scholar " in a letter of June, 1818, and what we know as *The American Scholar.* The beginnings of that address can be traced far back through the letters as well as the journals. Yet it finally came into being, in August, 1837, by the narrowest margin of chance. On June 19 of that year Emerson wrote his brother William of feeble health and the prospect of a long journey or a voyage, and on the same day Dr. Ezra Ripley provided a letter of introduction for the "late pastor of the second church . . . travelling in hope of regaining his health." Had there not been a quick change for the better, the late pastor might have been sailing tropical seas by August. Moreover, he was only an honorary member of Phi Beta Kappa; and his address, the most famous ever delivered for that society, was only a stopgap. Felton, who wrote him the invitation just three days after Ripley had penned the introduction for the intending traveler, explained that the Reverend Dr. Wainwright, who had been engaged for the occasion, had left the committee in the lurch, having declined within a few days. Finally, as the letters show, there was a dearth of inspiration until a short time before the event. As late as August 7 the toiling substitute orator wrote that he could not get any word from Olympus, any Periclean word, for Phi Beta Kappa. On the 31st, however, every Olympic and Periclean word was in its place and was soon thereafter preserved in the type of James Munroe's little eighteen-cent pamphlet so that no mischance could henceforth obscure the voice that spoke on that day. Carlyle heard it in England and had no longer any doubt about his young friend. And at that time Carlyle's assent must have been sufficient to convince Emerson himself. It would not be long until he could cut the last threads that bound him, as he said, to that prized gown and band, the symbols black and white of old and distant Judah, and could turn author in earnest.

Some of the fundamental doctrines of his Divinity School address, for which the way was by this time cleared, were discussed through the mails a dozen years before they were spoken to the graduating class at Cambridge. So early, as his correspondence shows, he was aware of the fateful proposition (though perhaps not yet entirely convinced of its truth) which was to become a central pillar in his own teachings — it was "one of the *feelings* of modern philosophy, that it is wrong to regard ourselves so much in a *historical* light as we do, putting Time between God & us; and that it were fitter to account every moment of the existence of the Universe as a new Creation, and *all* as a revelation proceeding each moment from the Divinity to the mind of the observer." This might be sophistry, but it was precisely the reasoning which, under one or another color, men used when they united mysticism to the profession of Christianity.

By December of 1828, shortly before he was elected junior pastor of the Second Church, Emerson was already writing the most conciliatory of replies to the objections of Henry Ware, Jr.; the final break and the exchange of letters which has long since been partly published were still some years in the future. He confessed that he had affected generally a mode of illustration rather bolder than the usage of preaching warranted. He had done this on the principle that religion was nothing limited or partial, but of universal application, and interested in all that interests man. He could, however, readily suppose that he had erred in failing to add to his positions the authority of Scripture quotation. A few months after his ordination, he wrote another apology to the same adviser: he was distressed to learn that his audience thought he did not look to the Scriptures with the same respect as others. The withdrawal from the Second Church occurred some three years later, and the correspondence of another half-dozen years throws further light on the long foreground of the Divinity School address.

Not all of the students who wrote the formal invitation in March of 1838 could have been ignorant that Emerson was far from orthodox. But their letter asked only for " the customary discourse," and to the audience in general the thing that actually happened on the evening of July 15 was like the explosion of a bombshell in a peaceful countryside. No wonder the students disagreed as to whether the address should be offered to a larger public and finally proposed that though three hundred copies should be printed, none should be published. Ware, whose earlier fears were now justified, issued an unmistakable reprimand to his former colleague. Young Nathan Hale, Lowell's friend, was not alone in the opinion that the affair would be Emerson's ruin. Even the liberal-minded and loyal half uncle, Samuel Ripley, urged that any further publicity be avoided: " When I heard that you intended to publish it I positively denied the fact. . . . I don't want to see you classed with Kneeland, Paine &c, bespattered & belied." In the excitement of the moment, Emerson yielded to admonishments that there must at least be careful revision before printing; yet the virtue did not go out of the address. Before the end of August it was both printed and published, and plenty of attacks followed. Even Aunt Mary, long since grieved because of her nephew's growing radicalism, could never forgive this pamphlet. Apparently as late as 1853, she referred to it as a thing " w'h should be oblivion's, as under the influence of some malign demon." Her nephew was not much perturbed. " They say the world is somewhat vexed with us on account of our wicked writings," he wrote to his brother a couple of months after the address was delivered. "I trust it will recover its composure."

Scarcely one of the essays that went into the volume of 1841 is without an antecedent here. Back of some is the early correspondence with Aunt Mary. There are paragraphs in "Friendship" which echo the long debate, by way of the Concord mail, with Margaret Fuller, Caroline Sturgis, and Samuel Gray Ward. Some of the poems of the 1847 volume can also be traced in the same way. There is proof of bardic ambitions even in the letters written in boyhood, when verse and nonsense were sometimes nearly the same thing. In 1834 there had been a period of creative power. In February of the next year Emerson wrote to Lydia Jackson that though his singing was husky and mostly in prose, poetry was his vocation. The correspondence with James Freeman Clarke tells the story of the first important verses to get into print, and a letter to another friend in later years seems to show that it was Elizabeth Hoar who persuaded the reticent poet to allow "Each and All" and the three companion pieces to go to Clarke's magazine, *The Western Messenger*. Publication there may have inspired new efforts. Soon, at all events, Emerson reported to Margaret Fuller how much he pined to write verses that did not quite come. The wind, the water, the ferns all but coined themselves into rimes before him; yet the last step of the alchemy failed. "Monadnoc" was at least vaguely incipient as early as September, 1839, when he wrote of the New Hampshire highlands, where the dignity of the landscape made the traveler more sensible of the meanness and mud of the population at the taverns, untempered by so much as a spark of the true fire. In the letters written immediately after the death of his son Waldo are phrases that mark the unconscious beginnings of "Threnody." The boy was the world's wonderful child; but the sun rose and set, and the winds blew, and Nature seemed to forget that she had crushed her sweetest creation. Two years later Margaret Fuller wrote to ask a copy of the unfinished verses. Numerous other pieces are described from time to time as in the making; and some can be redated from the letters, which also show the growth of the projects for the first and second volumes of poems. "Days," perhaps better known than anything else in the second volume, appears in a new light, with a history going back to about 1840, when Emerson wrote that "Heaven walks among us ordinarily muffled in such triple or tenfold disguises that the wisest are deceived & no one suspects the days to be gods." Having got at last distilled into pure verse and having passed through the columns of *The Atlantic* with no ill effects, it suffered an evil fate in the volume of 1867. The poet, as he wrote to Cabot, read with amazement the opening line. "Damsels" had somehow slipped in, but "Daughters" was right and should be.

The lectures in *Representative Men* became chapters only after a long epistolary history. Emerson fully realized the temerity of his attempts to reveal the significance of the greatest minds, which he reassessed in terms of spiritual values. Who dared print, being unlearned, an account of Plato or of Swedenborg, or, being uninspired, of Shakespeare? Yet there was no telling what rowdy Americans, whose name was Dare, might do. The author of those lecture-chapters was never confident that he had completed even the most elementary preparations for so huge a task. Nearly two years after their publication he wrote to Ward of Swedenborg: "You are right in taxing me with ignorance of his mind. I would read him if I could, but it is one of his demerits, it is part of his fate, that I cannot." The full letters of the second English visit contributed much, with the journals of that period, to the making of *English Traits,* after they had served, to some extent, as a quarry for lectures. The book was long delayed, partly, again, because of Emerson's distrust of his mastery of the subject. He wrote to Clough, who was then considering migration to America if the means of livelihood could be assured, and invited him to be a guest at Concord for two or three months and act as expert consultant to "answer a catechism of details touching England, revise my notes on that country, & sponge out my blunders."

As years passed, the letters revealed more and more an inevitable change. Interest was turning gradually from new ideas, and creative power of every kind was ebbing. Even much earlier there had been times when the art of writing seemed disappointing. The mind's grasp was never quite equal to its reach. There were not many greater misfortunes to peace of mind, Emerson had written to Hedge, than to have keen susceptibility to the beautiful in composition and just to lack that additional wit which suffices to create it. A few decades later and that difficulty was beginning to be a harsh reality, softened only by the lessening desire to write. Correspondence with Conway and others showed the increasing distress which too urgent publishers caused the aging writer. Composition came to be more and more a matter of collaboration. Old materials were collected and rearranged with the greatest difficulty. The last drop of fortitude, as well as the help of the two most dependable collaborators, was required for the completion of a few pages.

Meantime, for many years, the career of author had been paralleled by that of lecturer. The author of the essays and poems could not expect to live by them. Lectures had to be got together, sometimes in great haste, when he found it necessary to eke out the too modest income supplied by the estate his first wife had left. By the early 1840's the lyceums as far south as New York and Philadelphia were ready to hear him. Then his geography expanded rapidly. As a letter of 1850 shows, he first went beyond the Appalachians in response to a request signed by a hundred men — his reputation had traveled before him.

Curiously enough, however, the author of *The American Scholar* got to the Ohio and the Mississippi by way of Europe. The provincialism he had deplored had not vanished. Before Cincinnati realized that she must hear him, he had been heard by miscellaneous mechanics' institutions and athenaeums in northern England and Scotland and, finally, by the aristocracy in London. And so it happened that our record became cosmopolitan a second time before it began to celebrate the forests and prairies in the heart of America. The letters from abroad in 1847–1848 contained, on the whole, the most detailed account of his contacts with other men that Emerson was ever to give. He was, as he wrote home, reconciled to the clatter and routine of lecturing because of the excellent opportunity to see England and the best people there — the merchants, the manufacturers, the scholars, and the thinkers. He saw Wordsworth, Carlyle, Tennyson, Dickens, Macaulay, Thackeray, De Quincey, John Bright, Cobden, Jeffrey, Crabb Robinson, Hallam, Milnes, Lady Byron, Lyell, Stephenson. He studied the antiquities of the British Museum with Sir Charles Fellows, Kew Gardens with Sir William Hooker, the Hunterian collection with Richard Owen. For good measure he crossed the Channel to revolutionary France, witnessed an abortive uprising in Paris, and heard Lamartine make his great speech on Poland in the National Assembly. The lecture seasons on both sides of the Atlantic paid dividends that were not all noted in the ledgers at the Boston and Concord banks.

These professional tours, especially in this country, always involved a good deal of preliminary correspondence to arrange places, dates, and subjects. Then, for the benefit of the family at home, came the copious recitals of adventures and accidents that befell the wayfaring man. At

Niagara Falls he narrowly escaped from a burning hotel. On Lake Erie his steamer was afire and threatened with destruction before she could reach the harbor of Cleveland. At St. Louis he was in the same house with people who were dying of the cholera. He traveled over the frozen prairie in the snow, and he crossed the Mississippi on the ice. At Lafayette, Indiana, he was compelled to charter a special train in order to reach Chicago in time for his lecture. At Fairhaven, Vermont, he had his pockets picked, it seems, and borrowed money to pay his railroad fare. Landslides, floods, and belated trains made life uncertain but added zest to his letters. It was all a little wearing, too. He resolved to take in sail before it was time to be old. In February of 1867 he wrote home that he meant never to come to the West again. The resolution was premature, but within a few years he began to withdraw from lyceums even in the East. Near the end, he achieved, under the management of his publisher, an impressive financial success, the net receipts for a course of six lectures being, as he wrote Fields, over sixteen hundred dollars, "which is by much the largest sum I ever received for work of this kind." And about the same time he made a surprisingly satisfactory experiment with informal readings, mostly from the poets.

He was now a familiar figure to audiences in many cities and towns; and the local critics, though they said much the same things of him year after year, have contributed a valuable supplement to the information given in the letters. In Boston he was an institution as firmly based as the State House. Everywhere he made less and less effort to hold the attention of his audiences. When he gave a few lectures at San Francisco, in 1871, during his only visit to the Far West, a reporter described him in paragraphs that might almost have been drawn from other newspapers in many parts of the country. The audience, we hear, would not dream that the lecturer had said anything the whole evening which he thought particularly worthy of being said. A bulky manuscript lay before him, which he fingered backwards and forwards, as if at a loss whether to commence at the first page or in the middle. Finally selecting a good starting point, he began in a conventional tone to read, but did not confine himself closely to the manuscript, with which he was very familiar. It was refreshing to look upon this tall, straight man, in spite of his suit of black. But the difference between hearing him read his works and reading them for oneself was all in favor of the latter. He impressed a Chicago reporter in the following November, when he last crossed the Appalachians, as belonging to an earlier age. His clothes were clerical still, without wrinkle; his hair was long, white, and thin, and was combed close to his head, as was the custom in early Colonial days; his manner was slightly stiff and awkward but that of the true gentleman.

After the strenuous lecturing days were over there was one more extensive journey — this time with his daughter Ellen to Europe and to Egypt. There are not many echoes in the letters. In England he found old and new friends, but his curiosity for new persons and things was waning. He describes briefly his third visit to Paris, which he saw after the Prussian storm had blown over and after the terrible destruction during the days of the commune — " The injuries done to the great city were insignificant to our eyes in its splendor today." A few sentences picture Nice with her gardens, palm trees, and pepper trees; and other cities of France and Italy get as little attention from the tired traveler, glad to let his daughter take over the office of scribe. From Cairo he wrote of the mob of all colors and costumes and of no costume at all — Turk, Copt, Arab, Nubian, Italian, German, English, and American men and women filling the narrow, unpaved streets and lanes — and of the carriages of the rich whose servants ran ahead to clear the way, the boys with their donkeys at every corner, and the heavily-burdened camels in every street. He breakfasted with the khedive, whose son, fresh from Oxford, had much to say of boating, and knew only a little of Pusey and Ruskin (the latter now Emerson's prime favorite). But his energy flagged as he described the voyage on the Nile through clear, hot days, under rich skies, past shores lined with palm groves and inhabited by innumerable birds — the ibis, the hawk, and the eagle, with vast flights of geese and ducks and flocks of little birds of sparrow size which flew in a rolling globe, whirling around and returning again every minute. The pen grew heavier, and the Nile letter was not completed till Emerson had reached Keswick, in the Lake Country of England, the following May. And only a few notes were written on the journey out of Egypt, back through the Continent, England, and Scotland, and across the Atlantic.

Many more letters, however, were to come from Concord, marking the unspectacular events of the remaining years until Emerson had grown so old that he found it hard to remember how to spell even the simplest words and would sometimes work from a draft provided by his daughter Ellen. On July 1, 1881, he ended, so far as this record shows, with a single sentence of acknowledgment and good wishes to a society named in his honor.

IV

Emerson's scholar was man thinking, whose reading was only for idle times. But the letters contain plentiful evidence of acquaintance with many books, from ancient poetry and history to accounts of scientific discoveries in the second half of the nineteenth century.

In youth Emerson apparently acquired only a little more than the average contemporary schoolboy's knowledge of the classics. His Greek and Latin quotations, which diminish rapidly until they have almost completely disappeared in later years, testify to a love, not of grammar, but of ideas or, at the worst, of rhetoric. They may well be a little inaccurate — as most of his borrowings even from English books are likely to be — but they are pretty certain to suit his need exactly. By the time he was eleven years old, as the correspondence shows, Sarah Alden Bradford was luring him to classical studies, of which she herself had no mean mastery. Such first aids as Dalzel's Greek anthologies gave him an introduction to a variety of writers, in their native language, though usually, at the first good opportunity, he deserted the ancient texts for English translations.

Among the poets, he mentions Homer most frequently; and Homer is mainly the *Iliad,* which he quotes once or twice in the original. The great dramatists have only a minor place. After the first enthusiasm for academic studies had died down he seems to have been incited to some renewal of interest by his brother Charles, who, as a letter of 1836 says, " was an excellent Greek scholar and has recently read with me, more properly, *to* me, a dialogue of Plato & the Electra of Sophocles." Both Socrates and Plato were of the highest importance, but they belong with the philosophers. Herodotus and Plutarch were the favorite historian and biographer. There is early mention of Beloe's Herodotus, and Smith's Thucydides, besides some English versions of Xenophon. Plutarch, in spite of a later start, far outdistanced these. A moralist, not only in his works whose general title announces that character, but in the *Lives* as well, he was sure of high esteem. In 1828, when Emerson acknowledged the receipt of one of these prized volumes, he remarked that he had seen most of it before, in French. As soon as he set foot in Sicily, his mind turned to Plutarch and his heroes. When he was supervising the education of young Hillman Sampson, he saw to it that the favorite biographies were on the boy's reading list. In 1841 he wrote to his brother William: " Do you never read Plutarch? I can never have done with him. Only yesterday I read the life of Cleomenes & of the

Gracchi & Demosthenes: and I keep the ' Morals ' always near me. They are admirable Prayer Books." It is not surprising to find that this patron saint shed his influence on many an essay and lecture.

The letters also give evidence that Emerson had some acquaintance with nearly all the great Latin writers and that he could read them in the original. It is true that Lucretius, in some ways nearest to him in philosophical outlook, gets only passing notice. Cicero, Vergil, Horace, Livy, and Caesar are more frequently mentioned than any other Latins. Yet it is a striking fact that little is heard of even these most popular of the Roman classics after the middle years. For the rest, we have a few echoes of Ovid; of the historians Sallust and Tacitus, both apparently known to some extent in the original; of Seneca, Persius, Juvenal, the Plinys. The flowers of rhetoric faded. A few memorable ideas or events learned from the old pages sometimes recurred to the reader. The mastery of English achieved with the help of a Latin vocabulary remained, no doubt, a very great but imponderable result. The diction of the letters, however, leans heavily in the direction of plain Anglo-Saxon.

V

The ancient masterpieces, though never shorn of all their glory, are soon secondary in interest to more modern writings. English literature, a much larger fraction of the American cultural heritage in the nineteenth century than now, easily ranks first, though the one work in the language which is quoted most frequently is that library translated from foreign tongues which we know as the English *Bible*. There are about a hundred passages that are definitely Biblical (besides many that have at least a vague Scriptural quality). It is not surprising that the larger number are from the *Old Testament,* which is several times as long as the *New. Genesis,* with its epic story, seems to be the favorite of all the books, with *Psalms* next. A calendar of borrowings would show some significant facts. During school and college years, when literary allusions are numerous, the *Bible* seldom appears. The highest point of its influence is naturally reached in the decade 1823–1832, mainly spent in preparation for the ministry and in preaching. In the following decade Scriptural quotations and allusions are not half so many in proportion to the bulk of the writing, and the decline continues until they are almost entirely absent.

Next to the *Bible* is Shakespeare. Some twenty of the plays are quoted, mentioned, or alluded to, though there is apparently no evidence of any interest of the sort till after college. In 1865 Emerson wrote in reply to an inquiry that he was not much of an expert in editions and had contented himself these forty years with the plain duodecimos of the Isaac Reed edition, London, 1820. This was doubtless a set which bore the signature of his brother Charles, with the date 1822; and it is probable that significant first-hand acquaintance with Shakespeare did not begin much earlier. But in that same year the praises of the great dramatist are sung for Withington. In 1823 *Twelfth Night* is quoted, and about 1824 the " fine play " on Henry VIII is recommended to a young reader. Soon thereafter quotations and allusions show a familiarity with many works by the same author. For a time there is almost impartial devotion to comedies and tragedies; but in the end Emerson belies his reputation as a confirmed optimist and gives his vote decidedly for the tragedies, putting *Hamlet* in first place by a wide margin. In search of barbed arrows of thought to carry his own meaning, he turns more often to Shakespeare than to any other author; but his interest is not confined to borrowings. A letter to Christopher Gore Ripley in 1841 gives impressive evidence of familiarity with Shakespeare scholarship. Written apparently almost on the spur of the moment and at a beach, where there could hardly have been a library to consult on such matters, it contains a summary of sources that would do credit to a candidate for a degree in English literature.

Next to Shakespeare stand Milton and Wordsworth. Like Shakespeare, Milton was not a quantity to be determined, but rather a measuring stick to be applied to other poets. Emerson knew at least something about him through Johnson's *Lives,* by 1815. In 1822 we hear of the reading of Milton during a walking tour through the Massachusetts hills. Shut in his cabin by stormy weather on his first voyage to Europe, the miserable traveler could piece together nearly all of " Lycidas " from memory, as he recalled, it seems, in a letter written some thirty years later. *Paradise Lost* was, however, the favorite source of quotations; and there are also allusions to its companion epic, to various minor poems, and even to the letters.

Wordsworth had at first stirred the boy Emerson's ire, as a hitherto unpublished entry in the diary testifies — and it was a common experience for older and wiser judges than he. But he hardly mentioned the much-maligned poet in the early letters. It was in 1826 that he unburdened himself, perhaps to Aunt Mary, about those " mystic and unmeaning verses," written " on a theory," though he already knew there were good passages to be had for the searching. In the following September she challenged him with her comment on Sampson Reed's *Observations on the Growth of the Mind.* The rare things in that pamphlet, she declared, were simply borrowed from Wordsworth. Presently Emerson showed a change of heart. But it was frequently the more austere poems, and not, curiously enough, those of extreme mystical quality, that drew his praise in the letters, though one remembers the famous dictum in *English Traits* that the great ode was the high-water mark of the contemporary intellect. He recommended " Dion," as well as the sonnets, to his brother Edward " when you want a sermon." In Sicily he regretted that he could discover little associated with the hero of that poem, and as late as 1869 we find him describing it as grand. He quotes from " Laodamia." Twice he was a pilgrim to the Wordsworth shrine at Rydal Mount. Neither occasion left a wholly favorable impression; but as a letter of 1833 shows, the poet appeared for a moment in true character as he repeated sonnets from the series on Staffa, and the American visitor's admiration survived even the less satisfactory interview of 1848. Meantime Emerson read the volume of 1842 — valuable, he wrote to Margaret Fuller, because here were genuine poems, while most that pretended to be were not. Within a few weeks he had read " that pauper poem " with the contentment and quiet applause which one gave to conversation of eminent good sense. Surely these eyes saw, these ears heard, this brain thought; and therefore one might well listen to this voice. And he added a judgment which was startling for its insight, as it was more than half a century in advance of the discoveries of Harper and Legouis — " the tragedy " seemed to give new tidings of the man Wordsworth, that he had sometime seriously queried with himself whether a brave sin might not stimulate his intellect and so pay its way. Thus Emerson, as many passages of both correspondence and journals confirm, fluctuated between something near disgust and something not far from veneration as he turned from the mere verse exercises by a theorist to the indubitable evidence of the great poems. On the whole, he would have to give Wordsworth a high place. As late as 1871 he told Forster of his delight in reading Crabb Robinson's reply to Landor's attack on the poet. Robinson cared little what a man was not but much what he was, and Wordsworth was the author of a hundred poems the least of which could not be sacrificed to give the openness of heart Landor would make an unconditional requirement.

For the rest, the letters mention a large number of English writers from the fourteenth century on. In answer to a criticism of his own meter, Emerson commends his critic to Chaucer. He remembers more than one dramatist among Shakespeare's contemporaries. He is fond of Ben Jonson. He mentions Spenser infrequently, but, as a boy, was delighted with *The Faerie Queene*. In 1820 he cited Bacon, who was to make a deep impression upon him. He was early curious about Donne, who, however, has no such important place as the reader of Emerson's own poetry might expect. Vaughan, too, is little noticed, and the references to Herbert are mostly late, though a letter of 1829 is enthusiastic and we hear from W. H. Furness of an old commonplace book, presumably belonging to school days, which contained some lines of Herbert's written in Emerson's hand. Dryden is no great favorite, and Pope is less honored than others of his century.

Thomson's " A Hymn on the Seasons " was threadbare by 1817, and forty years afterwards Emerson could remember a dozen lines of " Spring " with unusual accuracy. Gray is echoed and Cowper is quoted in boyhood letters. Hume and Gibbon were both of considerable interest. Johnson was beginner's guide to the poets, and in 1817 *The Rambler* was brought home. Some two years later, however, the young student confessed that, though reading Boswell, he had not got half through Johnson's own works. Burke, a little known even before the end of the Latin school days, was described for Aunt Mary as an improved Cicero and was one of the wise masters mentioned in the correspondence with Lydia Jackson. The Ossianic distemper naturally left a few marks. References to Burns are surprisingly tardy. Southey, whose *Joan of Arc* is reviewed in a letter of 1816, gets little attention thereafter.

Among the major Romantic writers, Scott is mentioned or quoted more frequently than any but Wordsworth. *The Vision of Don Roderick,* read in 1816, was reported as nothing important, but soon there were plenty of enthusiastic comments on other poems. Letters to Withington praised the novels and boldly prophesied that posterity would regard their author as the greatest of writers with the single exception of Shakespeare. Doubtless Emerson read more from Scott than from any other novelist, and we come upon sufficient evidence that he remembered both novels and poems. Unlike Shakespeare, Scott and Byron appealed mainly in early years, and this was especially true of Byron. At fifteen one was only too likely to rate the third canto of *Childe Harold's Pilgrimage* as the best of poetry and could hardly climb a hill without thinking of Manfred or some other Byronic hero or else of Scott's Bertram in *Rokeby*. But the Byronic fever, which ran its course through that generation of readers, died out early in Emerson, and we seldom hear of the old literary idol after 1833.

Coleridge, benefactor and teacher of the young intellectuals of his time, was read chiefly in precisely those years when Emerson was developing most rapidly his peculiar mental bias. At the college library, by 1826, a charge-book witnessed the borrowing of *Biographia Literaria;* and correspondence with Aunt Mary in 1829 recorded the discovery of *The Friend.* A few weeks later *The Friend* was still a powerful attraction, but *Aids to Reflection* was in even higher favor. The three works proved to be among the most influential that Emerson ever read. In 1833 he sent a note to their author and followed it up with a visit at Highgate. But no amount of garrulous talk could shake the allegiance of the young man who had known those books. He carried back to America a copy of *Fraser's Magazine* because it contained a capital print which would serve as a memorial of the meeting. Next year the battered old oracle was gone from his perch; and Emerson wrote to Benjamin Hunt that since Coleridge was dead, Carlyle was the best thinker of the age.

Carlyle, like several of his contemporaries, had the status of friend and correspondent; and the personal element in the relationship was so weighty that it will not do to compare his importance with that of earlier writers. His works are not frequently quoted, but they are much discussed; and he, of all literary men, has the most prominent place here. The question of when Emerson first became a reader of the anonymous magazine articles may be impossible to answer, but the evidence of the letters definitely carries the date back as far as 1827. In October of that year he called his brother William's attention to the essay on Richter in *The Edinburgh Review.* He was struck by the fact that the description of Richter's style exactly fitted Aunt Mary's. Before half a dozen years had passed he had found his man at Craigenputtock and was prepared to cling to him pretty faithfully over the uneven course of a long friendship, which was mainly epistolary. Generally, throughout the later years, Carlyle reigns a great favorite; but many comments on him or even to him show Emerson willing to see the faults of his Scottish Jupiter. These are, however, too many acres to walk around in one day.

As for Shelley and Keats, they fare no better than in the journals. There is not much about either of them until 1840, when Emerson, with the encouragement of Margaret Fuller, discovered some good words in "your demoniacal Shelley." On first looking into "The Defence of Poetry" he got little satisfaction, finding it stiff and academical, with nothing that was not long ago the property of the whole forum. But he read a little more, with more love, and concluded that perceptions of particular facts were clear enough, though the whole mind wanted liquidity and expansion. As late as 1868, in a remarkable letter to James Hutchison Stirling, there is devastating judgment of Shelley as a writer and only mild enthusiasm for Keats: "But Shelley, — was he the poet? He was a man in whom the spirit of the Age was poured, — man of aspiration, heroic character; but poet? Excepting a few well known lines about a cloud & a skylark, I could never read one of his hundreds of pages, and, though surprised by your estimate, despair of a re-attempt. Keats *had* poetic genius, though I could well spare the whole Endymion."

There are only two or three letters to Landor, whom Emerson met at Florence during the first Italian visit, but many which mention him or even contain generous appraisals of the imaginary conversations. When, however, an American edition of selected conversations was proposed, a closer examination revealed unsuspected imperfections. On the subject of the fiery commentary which was inspired by certain passages in *English Traits,* Emerson seems to have remained wisely silent. Craving bread as well as beauty, he could love Charles Lamb and yet not be content with him, and did not read him again. This Benvenuto Cellini of writers, he told Furness, added nothing to one's stock with all his enchasing. Tennyson was known and valued early, but we soon hear of a lack of serious matter. The poems of 1842 were good and bad. They were a godsend indeed but wanting in rude truth, the form being too much elaborated and the matter still not sufficiently vital. So wrote the old Puritan in Emerson, though he closed with a blessing, wishing all laurels for such benefactors. Half a dozen years later came the meeting in England. The man satisfied; and the poet, henceforth less discussed, continued to keep the niche he had won. Emerson obviously cared little for the novels of Dickens, whom he also came to know personally. The author of *American Notes* was promptly set down as slight, exaggerating, and fabulous, and the book itself as lively rattle, readable enough, and very quotable into the philanthropic papers. It would have been hard for any reasonable person to say a better word on these two subjects. But in general the lack of enthusiasm for Dickens, and for Thackeray too, was to be expected in a reader who, in spite of an early flare for Scott, cared little enough for fiction of any kind.

Clough received hearty applause for his poetry and some frank criticism that was not so favorable. The meetings of 1848 had, however, made the two men close personal friends; and judgments have to be read in the light of that important fact. There was a lesser correspondence with Matthew Arnold. Emerson had also met him in England, but Clough served as a link between the two men. A copy of the last words on Homer was dispatched to Concord, as the author explained, " because of the passage about Clough at the end of them, which I wished you, as a valued friend of his, to see." But by the time he made this explanation he was able to announce the approach of *A French Eton,* and this was not the last book of his sending. In 1876 he added this acknowledgment: " Your writings have given me and continue to give me so much pleasure and stimulus, that I consider myself almost bound to make an offering to you of any production at all considerable which comes from me; since you are sure to have had some part in it." Emerson wrote his opinions of the Englishman's productions to various friends. The final lecture on translating Homer, he told his son, was the most amiable of books. He informed Carlyle of his delight in Arnold's fine criticism. There are evidences of the usual passing about of the fortunate discoveries from friend to friend. *Essays in Criticism* was welcomed as a treasure. " Thyrsis " was read with delight, as a letter to Mrs. Clough testifies. It was in his journals that Emerson distinguished between the excellence of the critical works and what he regarded as the poverty of the verse.

Many other English writers get little more than honorable mention. Ruskin, almost the last to rise into favor, was early of some interest for his theories of architecture, which, as Emerson believed, the American Greenough had anticipated. But it was the reading of *The Two Paths* that aroused strong enthusiasm. In 1871 Ellen wrote that her father was praising the book at every meal. Ruskin, she said, was the man he wished to see in England. When Emerson was there not long afterwards, he told Max Müller more than once of his desire to hear the Slade Professor lecture at Oxford, and the matter was arranged. He rejoiced like a boy in the prospect; but, it is clear from the journals, disappointment followed, and he had soon heard more than enough of doleful opinions on the state of contemporary society. He had found it difficult to excuse the Jeremiah in Carlyle. Another ordeal of the sort was out of the question at this late date.

VI

The letters show no great interest in early American writers, and comment on contemporary Americans is often restrained. The Colonials obviously aroused mainly an antiquarian curiosity and had their brief hour of importance when the address on Concord history was in the making. The orator of the second centennial celebration went to the trouble to search out reprints or original editions of " Mourt," the elder John Winthrop, Edward Johnson, William Hubbard, Francis Higginson, John Underhill, Thomas Shepard, Cotton Mather, Thomas Hutchinson, and even John Josselyn. But little else is heard of them. There is evidence of respect for the chief statesmen of Revolutionary times, though not of acquaintance with many of their writings. Such shepherds of Apollo's flock as Kettell and Griswold were known personally or as correspondents; but their folds sheltered too many black sheep to be worthy of painstaking inspection. There is hardly an echo of American song before Bryant, and there seems to be no mention of him till long after his appearance at Phi Beta Kappa in the year of Emerson's graduation from college. Ellen Tucker's delight in the poet and her imitation of his style may have spurred appreciation on the part of her husband, who was presently, however, lamenting Bryant's folly in leaving poetry for the chance of earning bread. Later letters stick to the theme of unfaithfulness to the high calling. The poet was sinking ingloriously into the business man and politician – not a violet left, but the field all stiff with the thistles and teazels of politics. Meetings with him in New York inspired further severe comment. Seen at close range, he turned out a very ordinary mortal – gentlemanlike, good, easy, and dull.

At seventeen or thereabouts Emerson watched the rising star of Irving with some admiration and a good deal of doubt, as new evidence from the diaries shows. The youthful critic looked for the salvation of American literature through moral and didactic works like the essays of Johnson in *The Rambler,* over which he had lately been brooding. Writings of an ephemeral nature like *The Sketch-book* would not help. One loved the picturesque glitter but would willingly exchange it for instruction and improvement. The letters, which have little to add, are hardly more flattering. *Bracebridge Hall* seemed merely to make matters worse. A few extracts were enough to show that its author had left his fine *Sketch-book* style for the deplorable Dutch wit of Knickerbocker. Cooper got little more notice than Irving. There was a discouraging verdict on *The Spy*. An incomplete reading did not disclose any ground for comparison with Scott. *The Pioneers* was early liked without reservation, and a letter to Griswold about a Cooper memorial meeting once more singles it out; but there is little other evidence of acquaintance with any of the novels. Scott's romances would be nearly enough of that kind of entertainment. Even Hawthorne, who is frequently mentioned, was judged a better critic than story writer, and existed principally as a personality well worthy of exploration, if one could compass it.

A number of lesser writers belong among close friends or disciples of Emerson, and have their own peculiar passports to a kind of immortality. Their shades are not to be met, doubtless, in the literary acre of the Elysian Fields, but still wander along the lanes and beside the ponds of Concord. The resonant and tireless voice of Alcott too often died away in inarticulate murmurs when he sat in the presence of pen and ink. The Transcendental schoolteacher is the honored subject of many a letter, but his writings receive for the most part ingeniously phrased yet unmistakable disapproval. The younger William Ellery Channing, whose uncle of the same name is shown due respect but leaves a surprisingly small mark on the correspondence, came to Emerson at a fortunate time, sponsored by mutual friends. The master seemed determined to discover a poet in him and to make the world agree. He put his candidate bodily into *The Dial,* he attended to the publishers when it was time to bring out a volume of poems, he did his best to find a few readers for the volume by reviewing it promptly, and he raised funds to send his poet abroad in search of new inspiration. The long epistolary record of this brave endeavor is at least a notable proof of generosity. Jones Very, of Salem, whom many thought merely a madman, was prized for his spiritual insight; and his poems and essays were also helped through the press. There was, after all, a kind of sanity in this unhappy person of which the world seemed to stand very much in need.

Thoreau and Whitman were authentic discoveries. Searching tirelessly for genius, Emerson followed down many false trails; but two such successes were enough to pay for all the mistakes. He found Thoreau first and remained more consistently loyal to him. The most remarkable thing about this discovery was that Thoreau was not only a contemporary but a fellow townsman, and that any one had the audacity to look for genius at home. Emerson joyfully exhibited his prodigy, too, in *The Dial.* Against Margaret Fuller's judgment, not to mention Theodore Parker's, he continued his steady praise, apologizing now and then, to be sure, for disappointments. If the latest poem was not quite equal to expectation, he could still admire this perennial threatening, though he had already lived long enough to see many threats incarnated which delayed to strike and finally never struck at all. It was Emerson who carried the first book to the publishers and pleaded vainly for the acceptance of this seven days' voyage in as many chapters, pastoral as Izaak Walton, spicy as flagroot, broad and deep as Menu. Next year he wrote confidently to an English correspondent of the young writer's future in this country " & I think in yours also." Thoreau and Emerson, being endowed with distinct personalities, could never wholly accept each other. But this limitation did not in the least affect personal loyalty. Emerson even constituted himself a guardian of his friend's posthumous fame. When a reviewer of *Letters to Various Persons* pounded hard on the favorite theory of Thoreau's dependence on his master and praised the master more than the disciple, the Concord mail brought back a protest — " it is long since I, and I think all who knew him, felt that he was the most independent of men in thought & in action." When he was about to ship the manuscript journals to Blake for preservation, Emerson wrote that he understood how Thoreau could vex tender persons with his conversation, but that the writings must and would find a multitude of readers. Later he told the same correspondent of his hope that " your reading formerly, & now that you have all his rich manuscripts in your study, — will justify & increase your old affection & estimation of his genius." Shortly before Emerson's death Blake began to bring out his volumes of excerpts.

The letter of July 21, 1855, about *Leaves of Grass,* doubtless speaks the highest praise that Emerson ever addressed to any poet. Within a few weeks he was writing to Cabot about " the American Poem," whose author was " a Mirabeau of a man, with such insight & equal expression, but hurt by hard life & too animal experience," and to Furness about " that wonderful book "; but before confiding his discovery to the none too merciful Carlyle he waited for the results of other experiments. The experiments were not very satisfactory, and it was nearly a year before he mentioned the subject to the Scot, with ample apology. In 1857 he wrote to Caroline Tappan that Whitman was choked by titanic abdomen but was nevertheless one of the two producers that America had yielded in ten years. There was less of this poet in the later correspondence, though enough to show that Emerson did not fully repent his early enthusiasm, however much conventional-minded friends might be amazed at it.

The only other " producer " was, curiously enough, Delia Bacon. It is not surprising that such a census of native genius should include neither Poe nor Melville, both of whom are ignored. The reasons for incompatibility are obvious. Richard Henry Dana is commended for his *Two Years before the Mast* – " He was my scholar once, but he never learned this of me: more's the pity." The personal relationship may have helped the good opinion of the book, but voyages and travels that had the indubitable marks of genuineness about them were much to Emerson's taste. Longfellow, Holmes, and Lowell all came quickly to enjoy the special privileges of personal friends and correspondents, who, whatever their obvious faults might be, were hardly fit subjects for censure. Longfellow's books are mentioned chiefly in the letters to their author, with courteous, measured applause. Holmes as man and as writer meant much less than Longfellow. The latter was a literary celebrity so well known on both sides of the ocean that transatlantic visitors could be referred to him with pride and satisfaction. There is evidence of strong approval of Lowell as a partisan in war time. But of the many letters to him, perhaps only one or two make any serious attempt to fix his literary magnitude. A paragraph written in September, 1865, is specific and positive. It lauds sufficiently the " admirable Ode," a " national poem," and particularly its " eighth Strophe, with its passion & its vision." It also affirms, against any previous judgments, that success in comic verse has in no wise hindered command of all the resources of the serious muse; but it advises the dropping of needless reminders of Tennyson before recent poems are gathered into a volume. An unfinished letter of perhaps some five years later bears witness to the continually growing scope of Lowell's verse: " I think you are bent on winning every prize in the games . . ." Of the critical essays there is likewise some hearty approval.

Whittier and Theodore Parker, both hard-fisted crusaders in the reform movements of the time, appealed for direct action a little too impatiently and insistently to suit Emerson's philosophical mood. But as the issue of slavery became sharply defined and Emerson himself was forced into action, he found such men more congenial. In spite of misunderstandings and temperamental antagonisms, he came to value Parker highly. The historian of Massachusetts, he thought, would discover in these discourses, with their realism, their power of local and homely illustration, their courage and vigor, and their masterly sarcasm, the means of knowing how the lamp of reform was fed. Harriet Beecher Stowe, it is plain, was viewed from Concord as another propagandist rather than as a novelist.

Writers who began to be known after the War were too late to matter a great deal. Mark Twain's extravagant repentance, after his unsuccessful attempt to upset the dignity of the literary Olympians at the Whittier dinner, was uncalled for so far as it concerned Emerson, who did not quite hear the speech, even when it was read to him, and easily forgot it. Not he but his daughter Ellen replied to the apology which was hastily sent. His old age made him indifferent, and his good sense would probably have been a sufficient reliance if the event had occurred earlier. Bret Harte once came to Concord, and his visit partly explains what slight interest is shown in him. There seems to be no sign of readings from Eggleston, though we know that some attempt was made to draw Emerson's attention to him. The early commendation of the stories of the younger Henry James was written to the elder. The novels, which came later, could hardly have won so favorable a reception. Howells was known as editor of *The Atlantic,* and the letters record some routine dealings with him, as well as dissent from his judgment of certain poems by Emma Lazarus, but have nothing to say about his books.

VII

In his thirteenth year Emerson was studying French, as he wrote to his brother William, to whom he presently offered a translation as evidence. Some months later, after more preliminary practice with selected readings, he issued another epistolary bulletin on his progress, showing that he could now manage the fiction of Madame de Genlis. Reading other foreign languages might continue to be as laborious as swimming the Charles River, and he would prefer to go over the convenient bridge of English translation when he could; but French soon offered only minor difficulties. It was, moreover, the one foreign language which he seriously tried to learn to speak, with just what results it is not quite clear. He must have attempted some conversation when he first visited Paris, and the letters tell of his attendance on lectures at that time. In preparation for his next visit, he worked hard to polish up his French. He told Parker of going to town twice a week to pronounce a little with Dr. Arnoult. Presently the *Courrier des Etats-Unis* was duly arriving from

New York to serve as one of his professors. A letter from Manchester shows that he intended to resume the filing of his French tongue in London. Face to face with the Parisians, he wrote only vaguely of his linguistic achievements, confessing that his French was far from being as good as Madame de Staël's. He continued, however, to regard the spoken language as an important part of a liberal education; and a few years later he instructed Ellen, away at school, that she must by all means master it. He had been on the point of sending her to a convent in Montreal for no other purpose, though he was well aware that no French man or woman ever set foot in Concord.

But if the letters offer no evidence that Emerson was ever proficient in French conversation, they show plainly his acquaintance with French literature, often in the original texts. In 1816 he reported that he had started *Les Aventures de Télémaque,* for generations a classic for American youth, who doubtless usually knew it in the easily available English versions. He was reading the original. Some two years later he was in *Gil Blas.* At the same time he was well along with Racine's *Phèdre.* As yet he read this by dint of hard labor over Nugent's pocket dictionary and surely with little pleasure. But he was destined to be rewarded when, after many years, he sat in the Théâtre de la République while Rachel gave life to the lines of that old play, and again when he saw her in *Mithridate.*

His knowledge of French literature, though never profound, extended in some manner over a long span of its history. In 1843 he wrote that he had *Le Roman de la rose,* apparently a French edition of the thirteenth-century work, and recorded his first reading of Montaigne's Italian journey and then of the story of the last days of the admirable Étienne de la Boétie. His joy was not spoiled by Hazlitt's translation. With the essays, which he found the most valuable of all French books, he had long been acquainted. A memorable passage in *Representative Men* tells how the single odd volume lay long neglected until, when he was newly escaped from college, he read it and procured the rest. Four years after he graduated, but more than thirty years before the lecture was published, that lone volume duly made its appearance in the correspondence. Sterling's *Westminster* article which honored " my old gossip Montaigne " found a welcome. Many a young disciple had the praises of the Frenchman from Emerson's lips or from his pen. Two or three hours with William Tappan in New York, and everything but Montaigne and Michelangelo was forgotten. Walter Langdon, remembering the enthusiasm of his friend for such reading, was one day to send him a sumptuous edition of the original text in three quartos, from Joseph Bonaparte's library. Meantime, the great essayist was definitely elected one of the world's representative men.

Perhaps the only recognizable trace of Molière is a parody of some lines from an old song used in *Le Misanthrope,* and other early French writers are seldom mentioned. When Emerson prepared a reading list for a cousin who had been his pupil in Boston, he was brief on French literature, vaguely advising " some more " of the masterpieces – " and Telemachus & La Bruyere if you can find them, are entertaining and instructive." Saint-Simon's memoirs, though they belonged a century in the past, had been published in a reasonably adequate version only a few years before Emerson explored them. There are signs of some familiarity with Fontenelle. Bayle was apparently known only by reputation till 1868, when a copy of his book which had belonged to William was sent to Concord. The Bayle, said a letter of acknowledgment, was a great treasure, at least in renown. A good many pages had been promptly examined and a good many more would be. It should stand with Wood's *Athenæ Oxonienses* and with Landino's Dante, the gifts of Thomas and John Carlyle. Montesquieu has equally slight importance.

As a boy Emerson thought of French as the language of Voltaire. Later he quoted *Socrate* and gave its author rank with Gibbon, Newton, and Edward Everett, which was, at the moment, a high distinction, not at all lessened by the addition of the third name or by the satirical tone of the passage. There is also evidence of reading in various other volumes of the great liberal, and in Noël's biography. Rousseau is early honored with Milton and Newton. Another allusion to him suggests that the " contemptuous chapter " in *Émile* " upon the Slavery of the Sick " may have had something to do with Emerson's own impatience of ill health. Aunt Mary's quickness to detect an error in sentiment was a reminder of Rousseau. His repute, however, does not keep an even course through the correspondence. At one time he is rated, with Byron, as ill company, but next year is a fine genius. Or he is the sublime of whimsicality and, once more, is bracketed with Aunt Mary. It is noteworthy that the *Confessions* is praised.

The letters show that Emerson was at least aware of Alembert. He wrote to Margaret Fuller, whose estimate of Maistre was enthusiastic, that he had never read that author. She and Samuel Gray Ward were plainly responsible for a brief flurry of interest in Béranger, which did not yield much pleasure. Madame de Staël seems a familiar figure but is mentioned only casually. In 1848 we naturally hear of a number of French authors of that time, a few of whom Emerson saw in Paris. He heard Lamartine and could in some measure judge his prowess as a political orator. He attended a lecture by Michelet. He reported a meeting with Tocqueville, friend of Americans, and with the Comtesse d'Agoult, but saw almost no private society. He was, as he wrote home, to have seen Quinet, Lamennais, and others, but turned his back and hastened to London for his lecture engagements. Quinet was already an Emersonian.

Vigny's place here is clearly due to Margaret Fuller, who likewise performed friendly service for George Sand, about the same time. Emerson dipped into the works of the latter and found a fervid eloquence, sometimes authentic revelations of human nature, but also ridiculous improbabilities. He was still a little obsessed with the notion that the French intellect was sick. He would not compare such an author, a mere Parisian Corinna, with Bettina, that sublime German original. Margaret Fuller was distressed because he had begun with the wrong novels. He tried again, discovering wonderful opulence of mind in *Spiridion,* which, though too long, was brilliant and inventive. Later she saw the Parisian Corinna in the flesh, talked to her, and even ventured, it seems, to give her a copy of the badly-printed London edition of his poems. When he himself next visited Paris, in the midst of political upheaval, he failed to meet George Sand; but he did not lose all interest in her, and in due time we find him in temporary possession of a part of the *Histoire de ma vie,* which Clough had recommended.

Another French novelist arrived at an inopportune time. It was during a sick spell that Emerson lost a week in the house with Eugène Sue, as good as another fever on top of the natural one. There was some reading in Paul de Kock, Balzac, and Victor Hugo. The evidence as to the elder Dumas is vague. There is a record of the borrowing of *Causeries du lundi;* and when one of the occasional schemes for an international periodical was afoot, Emerson confessed that his fancy was piqued by the idea of appearing in the same magazine with its author. He wrote to Mrs. Botta that he thought her visit to Paris could not but be gratifying when Sainte-Beuve was of the party. The next year he grieved that the great Frenchman was dead. He directed youthful Emma Lazarus, who was seeking literary advice, to a chapter in Taine's *Nouveaux essais,* then only a few years old. During his last European visit he presumably met Taine at the home of the Laugels, in whose care an inscribed copy of the history of English literature, which is still to be seen at Concord, was apparently sent.

VIII

It is probable that Emerson had some guidance in the study of Italian before he sailed on his first voyage to Europe. He may have had lessons, sometime during his undergraduate years, from an Italian resident of Boston or Cambridge, possibly from the Perodi mentioned in letters of February, 1820. Or, during his residence at Divinity Hall, he could have studied under Bachi, who joined the college faculty in 1826. At any rate, it is clear that he had made an effort to learn the spoken language and that even more than the usual difficulties beset him when he tried to make practical use of it. What a comedy all tuition in a foreign tongue seemed to the traveler newly arrived in Sicily! He had overestimated his knowledge of Italian and the ease of speaking it, he confessed to his brother William. Besides, these Sicilians had not only an accent but a dialect of their own and printed books in it. He might as well meet Arabs for conversation, yet he hoped for better speed when he reached the mainland. From Florence he wrote that he was laboring a little with Italian. The evidence, however, is meager. Years later there are letters that add something more definite to the record: his small stock of linguistic knowledge was strained to the utmost when the *Vita nuova* had to be conquered.

Though readings in Italian literature did not depend altogether on mastery of the language, it seems clear that Emerson, whose serious interest began with Dante, never got far beyond that poet. When he was a boy of fifteen, he sent his brother Edward a copy of a passage from Cary's translation of the *Inferno* printed in *The Edinburgh Review*. But he was only vaguely aware of the source from which it came. Some years afterwards he had a copy of Dante, apparently received as a gift. Unfortunately, we do not hear what use he made of it. Letters from Italy, which mention the poet several times, prove little. In Paris, Emerson attended lectures at the Sorbonne and could perhaps have heard Fauriel on Dante. Then, in London, as he wrote to William, he went to the British Museum armed with an introduction to the librarian, who was Cary, the translator. But whatever these earlier faint traces of acquaintance with the subject may signify, the correspondence shows pretty conclusively that the chief period of his interest in the great Florentine was the early years of the friendship with Margaret Fuller. Her influence, at that time, on his reading of Continental literatures was greater than we have hitherto known. In January, 1839, he reported his first excursion into the *Vita nuova,* having used, doubtless, a text she had lent for the purpose. In February he promised her that he would try the book again. Some two years later he wrote his wife that a visit to Boston had yielded good books, including the *Vita nuova* once more. Next year he was pleading vainly with Margaret Fuller to undertake the translation of the little bible of love. She refused, finally, on the ground that her knowledge of the language was not equal to so delicate a task, whereupon, piqued by some disparaging remark of hers about his failure to comprehend the book, he proceeded to do the thing himself by main force and awkwardness. With a copy supplied by George Bancroft, he set to work, announcing in July, 1843, that he had done the whole into English, the ruggedest grammar English that could be, keeping lock-step with the original. He showed his sheets to Ellery Channing, who turned at least some of the prose sonnets and canzoni into verse. Margaret commented: " Where there is a will, there is a way *surely*." When *The Massachusetts Quarterly Review* was being projected, Emerson suggested to Theodore Parker that this translation might make two instalments. But apparently it never appeared anywhere. Presently the translator was much more interested in John Carlyle's version of the *Inferno,* and we hear of vigorous efforts on behalf of its American edition. There are, for the rest, a considerable number of more casual references to Dante, who was always alluring, at once the most outward and inward of bards. Norton's work as translator and critic and probably Fauriel's *Dante et les origines* helped to keep up the reader's interest. Norton, it seems, gradually sent to Concord a standard iconography of Dante; and a copy of the Bargello portrait still hangs in the Emerson house. *The New Life* as translated by the same scholar inspired the dictum, in keeping with earlier judgments, that though the prodigies were all in the *Commedia,* the humanity was still in the lesser book.

But on the evidence of the letters, no other Italian author compares with Dante. An early reference to the coronation of Petrarch and the report, years later, of the copy of Ugo Foscolo's essays on that poet discovered in Boston do not prove or disprove serious reading. Ward's article in *The Dial* on Boccaccio was welcomed, and there is mention of a copy of Ariosto. Michelangelo, fervently admired, is usually the mighty painter and sculptor, not the poet. But soon after the first visit to Italy there is a request for the loan of the *Rime* from the college library — preparations were afoot for the lecture which presently became a magazine article. This practical issue of the studies, it should be added, did not mean the end of interest in the subject. Some years later the books by Quatremère de Quincy and Richard Duppa were explored and judgment pronounced emphatically in favor of Duppa. Tasso was honored at the time of the first Italian tour and was later seen through Landor's eyes. Alfieri is at least mentioned.

IX

Apparently Emerson did not emulate his two brothers who learned to read and write the Spanish language. Nor did he go far into Spanish literature in translation. He tells of reading the *Chronicle of the Cid,* doubtless Southey's version, with joy. There are some allusions to Cervantes, and Montesquieu's gibe about the one good book which ridicules all the rest is repeated. So far as the letters are concerned, *Don Quixote* does indeed stand in almost solitary grandeur as the representative of Spanish literature.

X

When Emerson was at college the fame of the new German philosophy, poetry, and scholarship had already begun to be heard across the Atlantic. Göttingen, Berlin, and Heidelberg were attracting adventurous American youth. Edward Everett returned in 1819, and his name runs like a refrain through the next ten years. There was talk of sending Edward Emerson to a German university; and presently William set out for Göttingen, whence he wrote with the enthusiasm of a neophyte. He urged his brother Waldo to make all haste to follow him, and we hear how carefully the matter was weighed at home. If it was every way advisable, indisputably, absolutely important, young Emerson would go. But funds were scarce, and he decided to buy his schooling in divinity at the cheapest stall and make haste to enter his profession. The German towns were but castles in the air for him. The future author of America's second declaration of independence had perhaps been turned back by his good angel. And yet he had not quite settled it to his own satisfaction whether either German or Hebrew was worth the trouble of reading anyhow. He hated cordially to study them but resolved that he would the moment he could see the necessity. Thereupon the Hebrew naturally sank out of sight once and for all. German was a ghost that would not be laid, and within a few years it looked very substantial.

In December of 1828 Emerson reported from New Hampshire that no line was yet read from the German book in his luggage – probably the volume of Goethe borrowed from the college library five days earlier. Presumably he had already been at work on the needful grammar, but the time for putting any such knowledge to practical use was still to come. It was not until he was about to leave the ministry that he began to be acquainted with Goethe, who had just died. It is very doubtful whether he seriously considered the possibility of visiting Germany when he went abroad a few months later, and he could have spent only the briefest time in the German-speaking part of Switzerland. Yet he announced before he traveled northward from Florence that he was laboring with the language a little, and for a few years after his return home he doubtless read somewhat in it. The question of a more determined effort must have been raised when, as the correspondence of 1836 shows, Hermann Bokum spent a day with him. Soon thereafter this teacher wrote that he would be very happy to assist in acquiring a thorough knowledge of the German language – " unless you have followed my advice & become a pupil of Miss Hoar."

Whether or not Emerson took any lessons of either Bokum or Elizabeth Hoar, it is clear that the first visit of Margaret Fuller to Concord greatly encouraged German studies. The same letter that reports her visit tells of the purchase of fifteen volumes of *Goethe's nachgelassene Werke*. Goethe was a wonderful man, wrote Emerson; " I read little else than his books lately." Margaret Fuller obviously deserved a good share of the credit along with Carlyle, and she was busy sowing the foreign seeds in other quarters at the same time. The Harvard trio of Bokum, Sales, and Bachi sent word through Emerson that they stood ready to teach the pronunciation of German, French, and Italian to any ladies who might read those languages with her the ensuing winter. The missionary of transatlantic cultures was marching forward with strong allies. Next year there were extensive German readings in progress at Concord, and Margaret was back again, giving Emerson – against his will, yet much to his present satisfaction – the lessons mentioned in the journals. He had at least taken his first steps and got his sense of direction, though his victory was never to be complete. He was destined to struggle through many a volume of German, but to the end of his days he found the spoken language a mystery. As he confessed to Grimm in 1872, he could only read in silence, never speaking a word.

In spite of such handicaps, however, he succeeded in getting most of what he cared for from German authors, though obviously an effective first-hand acquaintance with systematic philosophers, like Kant, was quite out of the question, and he did not read very widely even in general literature. From first to last, his enthusiasm for the Germans, which was much influenced by Carlyle, aimed mainly at Goethe; but this was not the whole story.

Among earlier writers at least one was known and admired. The name of Luther must have been a household word, but it took on new significance in 1834 and 1835. We hear the praise of this right royal soul who stood upright with all his might, let who would kneel, shuffle, or cringe. It is easy to understand this admiration for the man who, in his day, had also had the courage to follow his own convictions. Presently he was pressed into service as one of the first company of representative men whom Emerson assembled for exhibition on the lecture platform. The table-talk was read, but naturally the main concern was with biographical accounts of the Protestant hero. By 1824 William recommended Herder, and soon afterwards Edward asked for an English edition of the work on the philosophy of history. A dozen years later, when Emerson opened the *Briefe an Johann Heinrich Merck,* he found Wieland the charm of the book.

But it was chiefly Goethe for whose sake he explored both Merck and Zelter. A letter of 1830 shows that by that time he had read the first part of *Faust* in Gower's translation and that he also knew Shelley's fragmentary version. He was not very favorably impressed. The drama was bold and varied, but grotesque, out of nature, and wide of Shakespeare. Until the late 1840's, however, there is much about the great German, who, in spite of shortcomings on the side of moral insight, was now pretty consistently accepted as the literary man of the age. The objections set forth to Carlyle in 1834 were by no means so fatal as they seemed. Nothing but the strongest conviction of Goethe's worth could have kept up the reader's courage through those discouragingly numerous little volumes of the Cotta edition. Presently there were fifty-five of them on Emerson's shelf, and he could report to Carlyle that he had contrived to read almost every one. It must be a very strong or a very weak man, he told Convers Francis, who could read these books with impunity and without feeling their influence on all his own speculation. There was something gigantic about Goethe, measure him how you would. Emerson busied himself in behalf of an English version of Eckermann. Margaret Fuller made and published one. A letter records the discovery that Goethe seems to speak of nothing so wisely as of art. Within a few years, Emerson's friend Samuel Gray Ward duly published a translation of the essays on art. Margaret Fuller was comforted by commendations of her project for a life of Goethe (which she never completed). And we hear of the new American edition of *Faust,* of the article on Goethe for *The Dial,* of the lecture on Goethe, of poems, novels, plays, and essays by Goethe. These epistolary echoes continue for many years, but the placing of his bust in that private hall of fame called *Representative Men* practically closed the discussion. The matter was simply settled by that time, as were the estimates of many other literary figures. Yet in 1871, when Emerson acknowledged Grimm's gift of a copy of the conversations with Müller, he remarked that he thought he had always an ascending regard for Goethe and added that he had kept the new book close by him as a treasure and had only now sent it to a friend with advice to translate it.

The German gallery does not quite end here. Schiller is early quoted more than once, though he is of slight importance in the long run. The history of the Thirty Years' War did not compare with the account of the Battle of Lützen in *The Harleian Miscellany.* We learn of the borrowing of an unpublished translation of *Maria Stuart.* Emerson told Furness, the translator of " Das Lied von der Glocke," that he did not like the poem and thought it owed some of its currency to illustrations and music. Richter was an amazing spectacle, not to be greatly admired. With all his manliness, insight, outsight, oversight and undersight, the good Jean Paul soon made one weary and nervous. There was perpetual emphasis, perpetual superlative. The Schlegels, Platen, and Tieck are mentioned; and there is evidence of familiarity with Fouqué's *Undine.* There was a meeting with Freiligrath, Longfellow's friend, in London. The life and letters of Niebuhr were known in Susanna Winkworth's translation. Heeren's works on ancient history were a delight. Many years later, some of the volumes of Varnhagen von Ense's diaries were good reading. Something of Mundt's was sent from Germany by

Charles Stearns Wheeler, who, during the brief time left to him, did his best to give Emerson full information and gossip on German scholars and writers.

But aside from Goethe, curiously enough, the now discredited Bettina von Arnim was of all German writers most heartily acclaimed, though only for a few years. At first there was a good deal of caution in spite of Margaret Fuller's great enthusiasm. Bettina was wonderful, but these creatures all wing and without reserve made genius cheap and offended our cold Anglo-Saxon constitution. There was a prompt apology, however, after the first adequate reading; and the faint praise was retracted. In Germany one would wish only to see her. She possessed numerous exceptional virtues. She seemed the only formidable test that was applied to Goethe. Her genius was indeed purer than his. Emerson circulated her correspondence among his friends, and he lent a copy to Bixby to print the American edition from. Even when Aunt Mary contemptuously rejected the book, her nephew remained firm in his opinion. Writing to Heath, in Germany, he increased the number of contemporary worthies in that country only by two, admitting Schelling and Humboldt as deserving of curiosity along with Bettina. It was true that some returning travelers did not much distinguish her in their memories, but the world owed to her the most remarkable book ever made by a woman. In 1858 he assured Gisela von Arnim that he had for fifteen years been an admirer of her mother; yet it had been as long a time since Bettina had played an important part in the letters.

XI

Few great literary men have cared less than Emerson did for the systematic philosophers. He soon wearied of observing these incredibly patient workmen as they fitted their neat little intellectual bricks together, painstakingly filling every chink with the mortar of logic. This pedestrian exercise of what he was accustomed to call the Understanding interested him little more than the boresome and endless arguments of the religious controversialists, of which he had long since had his fill. The mature Emerson read for lusters, for gleams of insight. A systematic, logical structure of thought seemed mainly a waste of energy. The idle times of the scholar were those when he failed to gain any light through his own intuition; and the books best for such times were the records of other men's intuitions, not mere exhibitions of Understanding, that subordinate faculty which was nearly always busy to some degree in all men.

Yet the letters show acquaintance with many of the world's great thinkers from the Greeks to nineteenth-century contemporaries. One of the Zenos is cited. For Pythagoras, we hear of the fragments and of the life by Iamblichus. But Socrates and Plato dwarf the rest of the ancients. Neither was without honor even in the college years. The former was the subject of a prize essay and so had special claims on the loyalty of its author. In Italy, it seems, Emerson was annoyed by Landor's ridicule of his hero; and in Scotland he was surprised because Carlyle had little admiration for " the glory of the Greek world." He wrote to Elizabeth Peabody the most enthusiastic eulogy, showing his faith still unshaken: Jesus, though supreme as an ethical teacher, was only an exclusive and partial development of the moral element; but Socrates was a complete, universal man. To another friend he praised the social talent of the Greek, who moved among men at his ease, safe in his impenetrable armor of witty courtesy.

But as Emerson explained to Withington in 1822, it was difficult to distinguish Socrates from his disciple. In a book on Socrates, Plato was likely to appear as a Boswell to be ransacked for information; but when Plato was the hero of the tale, poor Socrates became a theoretic personage or the mere mouth of his disciple. The young student's own knowledge was very limited, but he took Plato's philosophy to be, he added, not too profound for easy comprehension, mixed and softened with a proportion of imagination and poetry. Indeed it was Plato, poet in spite of the banishment of poets from his ideal republic, whom he chose in times of need as his chief guide through the dark jungle of the human mind.

It is interesting to find, half a dozen years later, some comment on his means of knowing this mentor. In the first place, he confesses profound ignorance of the Greek text – he was thus an easy prey to all the multitude of misunderstandings that are inevitable in the translation of a subtle thinker, in addition to the many difficulties that would stand in the way of even a skillful reader of the original. Taylor's translation was the standard but was very faulty, inasmuch as it was Greek indeed. An English version made from Dacier's French was more intelligible but full of vulgarisms. Sydenham's part of Taylor's volumes was, however, in good repute, according to a professor at college. The upshot of the whole matter was, so far as it concerned Emerson, that for many years the Sydenham and Taylor volumes of 1804, together, doubtless, with something from Victor Cousin, were Plato for all practical purposes, but that the Neoplatonic writers, with their abundant information or misinformation about the master, were very important additional lights.

Plato reigned long as a prime favorite in the library. That daily routine of reading in 1840 – a little in Plato, a little in the Vedas, before the tour of duty in the garden – was not imaginary. Next year the same old gentleman, in his study or out of it, was still "poring on some pedantic nonsense of Plato or Company," as several letters attest, and dropping finally into a serious paean of praise for the great thinker who was never pedantic but united wisdom and poetry, acuteness and humanity, into a golden average. Another year and a reading of the *Protagoras* brought the conclusion that Plato was indeed no dreamer but trod the cliffs and pinnacles of Parnassus as if he walked in the street, and came down again into the street as if he lived there. In 1845, Emerson entertained "all summer, if no longer" the project of a lecture on Plato. But when, after some years, the time came for him to print and to give the philosopher his definite niche, he felt many doubts about his own scholarship. He read on and on in the dialogues, which still seemed quite worthy of their fame – the best thing in Boston was the love of these. When the lecture finally became a chapter it had a postscript on the readings of the Bohn edition, and long afterwards there was a letter acknowledging the gift of Jowett's version with "its superiority to all our old translations." Emerson now recalled the pitiful inadequacy of the Englished Dacier, a translation of a translation, which had been his first approach to the great philosopher, and of the Taylor, its successor, the whole edition of which, he thought, must have come to America.

Plato had brought in his train the Neoplatonists, not to mention the English Platonists. Both groups of camp followers were discussed with correspondents. The Neoplatonists were welcomed with acclaim, and yet with distrust. These dazzling Alexandrians had none of Plato's air of facts and society about them. The judgment showed the hard head of a Yankee once more rising clearly out of Transcendental mists. As early as 1839, it seems, there was a letter which had something to say about Plotinus, and the next year, one that probably alludes to that author. Later we hear of a book by Iamblichus that is to be read. Proclus and Porphyry show themselves at about the same time, and Proclus went to Nantasket Beach in the soft summer days when *The Method of Nature* was taking form. Thereafter a lull came in the excitement over these writers, so far as our record shows; and five years later there was the regretful admission that they seemed to require a race of more longevity and leisure than mankind to sound all their depths, which yet did not pretend to be the sea but only the swimming school.

Other Greek philosophers, unless we reckon Plutarch among them, are rarely mentioned. It is not surprising that Aristotle is hardly more than a name. Epicurus is quoted, perhaps indirectly.

The earliest English thinkers likewise play minor parts. Roger Bacon is left a mere shadow. Francis Bacon, though one of Emerson's Olympians, is chiefly valued for other writings than the formal philosophical treatises. The English Platonists get most attention about the same time with the Alexandrians. Both Cudworth, notable for his influence, and More are mentioned in the year of the latter's appearance, sponsored by Alcott, as a belated contributor to *The Dial*. There is news of a volume of Norris, which came to Concord with Alcott and Lane. Again, we hear of the *Effigies* (translated from Waryng) as a gift to Convers Francis. Plainly the letters offer very inadequate evidence as to the importance of these Englishmen.

But the philosophical writers from the seventeenth to the nineteenth century who appear in the correspondence are of various nationalities. Spinoza is hardly mentioned, though there are some noteworthy remarks about an admirable contribution on this subject which Cabot sent too late for the expiring *Dial* to publish. Emerson read the tardy paper three or four times and still had by no means exhausted its interest. He thought, when he had finished, that whatever he himself might write would be a plagiarism from it. Leibnitz has an unimportant rôle. In 1827 some things in Locke were deep, serene sense; but there is not much about this English thinker, against whom the main current of the young American's own thought was soon definitely set. Some forty years later Emerson advised his nephew that Locke was and always would be a respectable name, though now little and less read. Berkeley, on the other hand, was a positive force in the development of Transcendental thought. A little essay called " Ideal Theory " may have been an enclosure in an early letter, or even a part of the letter itself. Elsewhere in the correspondence we come upon a " sweet tissue " of speculations touching idealism. The warp, we are told, is from Pyrrho and the woof from Berkeley. By this time, indeed, Emerson must have drawn heavily on the Bishop. At any rate he was to write to Margaret Fuller that he knew but one solution to his nature and relations, and that he found this solution in remembering the joy with which, in boyhood, he caught the first hint of the Berkeleian philosophy. Hume's historical works are noticed early; and there are some records of a debate with Aunt Mary over his ideas, showing no great love for him but admiration. Where was the accomplished stripling to be found who could cut off the Scotch Goliath's metaphysical head? He who would confound this uncircumcised must have an adroiter wit than all his forebears. But Emerson could not listen long to a sayer of No. By 1832 he was looking to Goethe, whom, he said, the Germans regarded as the restorer of faith and love after the desolations of Hume and the French.

Kant was on the side of Emerson in this conflict so far as certain fundamental ideas were concerned, but as different from him as possible in method. The "painful speculations" of the German, which were acknowledged in 1826 to be undeniably beneficial in the long run to the mass of humanity, could make little appeal to the mature mystic, who had no faith in the wearisome piling up of logical Ossas on logical Pelions as a means of getting at truth. The kingdom of God was, after all, within. It now seems clear that for Emerson the main stream of German influence was filtered through the poetical minds of Coleridge, Wordsworth, and Carlyle; and the thought of the American had a far more ancient spring in Greece. It is true that he accepted Cabot's paper on Kant for *The Dial*. In 1870, too, as he wrote Harris, he thought it good that Cabot was reading lectures on Kant at Harvard. But the letters offer no evidence that he read much of Kant himself or was greatly influenced directly by him.

Almost the last letter to Grimm describes Schleiermacher as "never one of my high names." There is some scattering comment on Schelling, Fichte, and Hegel. To Heath, in Germany, Emerson wrote that the most firmly-rooted philosopher might be tempted from his home to hear Schelling, and confessed "more curiosity in respect to his opinions than to those of any living psychologist." The grandeur of the attempt to unite natural and moral philosophy made that writer a sort of hero. Hedge was urged to translate the introductory Berlin lecture of 1841 for *The Dial*. We hear also of Cabot's manuscript translation, apparently of the old "Philosophische Untersuchungen über das Wesen der menschlichen Freyheit." Emerson wrote his praise: "This admirable

Schelling, which I have never fairly engaged with until the last week, demands the 'lamp' & the 'lonely tower' and a lustrum of silence. I delight in his steady inevitable eye, and the breadth of his march including & disposing of so many objects of mark." But in the same paragraph he confessed that " this subtlety & strictness of dialectic in which you & your tutors Spinoza & Schelling delight, is at first as difficult & repulsive to me as logarithms." A few weeks later he added, " Schelling continues to interest me, but I am so ill a reader of these subtle dialectics, that I let them lie a long while near me, as if in hope of an atmospheric influence when the Understanding refuses his task." Nothing could reveal better Emerson's habitual attitude toward writings woven out of formal logic. The following year he wrote that he had concluded to let the Schelling translation alone: it was one of those books that require too long a time for mortal man. He contented himself, it seems, by vainly endeavoring to help Cabot find a publisher.

Hegel was known by reputation, at least, from the time when young Wheeler tried to chart for the editor of *The Dial* the currents of contemporary thought in Germany. But this was already more than a decade after the philosopher's death, and the letters do not indicate any serious attempt on Hegelian doctrines till long afterwards. Then, urged on by Cabot it seems, Emerson set out on this new adventure with little enthusiasm. Presently he reported that he did not find his way into Hegel as readily as he had hoped and was not so richly rewarded as better scholars probably had been. But he was not allowed to leave off these distasteful studies permanently. In the 'sixties William T. Harris shone on the western horizon as chief luminary of the St. Louis school of Hegelians. Emerson gave a hearty welcome to *The Journal of Speculative Philosophy* and professed his willingness to be made acquainted with the true value and performance of the German thinker, who at first sight was not engaging, nor at second sight satisfying. Such immense fame, he conceded, could not be a mistake, and he would read and wait. These Fabian tactics had small results; but about the same time, another Hegelian of commanding ability swam into his ken in the person of James Hutchison Stirling, author of *The Secret of Hegel.* An acknowledgment of this book, with generous praise, began another notable correspondence. But the relationship was, as with Harris, largely personal; and it can hardly be said that there is proof of any great interest in Hegel on Emerson's part.

Meantime, the Frenchmen Cousin, Jouffroy, and Gérando had

long since appeared in the letters. When Emerson was first in Paris he had at least a glimpse of Jouffroy. He heard lectures, but apparently not by Cousin, who, he wrote home, had unfortunately quit Plato since the Three Glorious Days. Though he concluded to reject eclecticism utterly, he received many useful hints from its foremost teacher that led to other writers and philosophers, or even got information from him that saved the trouble of investigating them at first hand. Gérando's place is disappointingly small.

Had Herbert Spencer succeeded in his efforts to attract the attention of Emerson and to establish satisfactory relations with him, as he wished to do, there might have been a significant story to tell here of the intercommunity of American and English thought in the second half of the nineteenth century. But we have only the evidence of what might have been, and nothing further need be said either of Spencer or of any of his contemporaries.

XII

But there remains an important group of philosophers, religious teachers, and poets who, though widely separated in geography and in cultural lineage from Europe and America, were destined to leave a deep impress on Western thought. These were the wise men from India, Persia, and China who, almost to the exclusion of Bombay, Calcutta, and Canton merchants, were, for Emerson, the Orient. In a letter of 1873, to Max Müller, he reviewed the history of his acquaintance with the Hindu sages, his memory still mainly accurate except as to the name of one translator. "All my interest in the Aryan," he wrote, "is old reading of Marsh's Menu, then Wilkins's Bhagavat Geeta; Burnouf's Bhagavat Purana; & Wilson's Vishnu Purana, — yes & a few other translations. I remember I owed my first taste for this fruit to Cousin's sketch, in his first Lectures, of the Dialogue between Krishna & Arjoon, & I still prize the first chapters of that Bhagavat as wonderful . . ." Everywhere in this literature, he admitted, passages of grandeur were followed closely by passages of commonplace superstition, which must have been interpolated by foolish hands. But yet what books! He counted them all potential corrections of our old narrow history of religions and supposed their effect would appear more conspicuously in America than in England, as the state does not here back up the creed.

A year or so after writing thus to Max Müller, Emerson published in *Parnassus* some lines from "A Hymn to Narayena" which seem to mark both the inception and the end of his Eastern studies. If these verses were not a translation from the Sanskrit, as he must have supposed them to be, they were nevertheless a genuine incarnation of the Hindu spirit. They were the same that his Aunt Mary had copied and sent to him in 1822. He had transcribed them forthwith into his diary and replied to her that he was curious to read her Hindu mythologies. He was already dreaming on the possible contents of pages as dark to him as the characters on the seal of Solomon. It is true that there is some evidence of his earlier but vague consciousness of these things. He had already listed a memoir of Sir William Jones in his diary, but only among "*Books Inquirenda.*" A hitherto unpublished entry, possibly of 1820 or the following year, but presumably of 1822, shows that he had at least some indirect knowledge of the laws of Menu. He had read a little, we hear, in the *Christian Register* about Rommohun Roy, the "Hindoo convert," who was just then a welcome ally of the Unitarians in their disputes with the Trinitarians; but he seems not to have been so much impressed as his aunt had been. The real beginning of the Orient for him was pretty obviously in that exchange of letters with her.

In spite of this prodding, it was to be a long time before he reported his reading of lectures in Volume I of Cousin's "Philosophy," with which he was delighted. The letter of May 24, 1831, seems to throw an interesting light on the little history afterwards sent to Max Müller. It was this first volume of Cousin which contained the sketch of the *Bhagavadgita*. In 1832 Emerson wrote of Linberg's translation of the same volume, which he acquired for his library then or later. All this was before the earliest publication of his own characteristic doctrines; and "Brahma" was far in the future.

The Eastern fever gradually grew. In June of 1845 Emerson was writing to Elizabeth Hoar about a new enthusiasm. The real *Bhagavadgita,* which he had never before held in his hands, had, he announced, arrived in Concord — doubtless sent there by Cabot. Hitherto he had admired only extracts. He was not even yet sure of his bearings in the realm of Hindu literature and supposed his treasure was a "much renowned book of Buddhism." By August he could report a further acquisition: "The 'Purana' I carried with me to Vermont, & read with wonder in the mountains. Nothing in theology is so subtle as this & the Bhagavat." Once equipped with his own copy of the latter work, which he had long since ordered from London, he lost no time in propagating the little gospel among his friends, and several letters relate to its comings and goings. But when he received a suggestion for an American edition, he sent a negative reply. As he wrote to Alger a few years later, it would not do to publish our prayers in the daily paper and students who were ripe for this Oriental bible would rather take a little pains and search for it than find it on the pavement.

Meantime, allusions to Eastern literature had become common. There was, for example, the business of getting ethnical scriptures into *The Dial.* John B. Hill, an old classmate, had to be supplied with the newly rediscovered lore; and as the *Bhagavadgita,* one of the desired sources, was not available at the moment, Emerson, as he writes, tore "from a commonplace book this fine French sketch of Cousin, which you must put together & read." In other years there were other seekers after the wisdom of India who likewise found refreshment at the Concord fountain.

Zoroaster was, at an early date, among the dark names awaiting an exploration which is not recorded in the correspondence. Letters to Margaret Fuller and Thoreau announced *The Gulistan,* in English, which was lent and eventually lost for a long time. But Emerson had not done with it, and there are further signs of his interest before he sponsored an American edition. *The Desatir* was likewise a book to lend to one's friends. Readings of Hafiz, in Hammer-Purgstall's German, and the lecture on "The Superlative" testified to a growing interest in Persian literature. Afterwards came the discovery that Hammer had omitted many treasures. Mewlana Dschelaleddin and Feridoddin Attar were also deep men. They knew as much of the soul and of ethics as any Greek or Englishman, and yet the libraries were stuffed with dull books by third-rate writers. This *Blüthensammlung,* which Tholuck had gleaned after Hammer's harvest, was a delight.

A number of Chinese books appear in the letters. In 1843 Confucius was an old story; but Mencius was wholly new, and his quiet sunshine proved to be a dangerous foil to Carlyle's storm lights in *Past and Present.* There were some dealings with Anson Burlingame, representative of the American government at Peking. Sumner sent the official papers relating to China that had been published by the Senate. We hear also of the "Chinese Banquet" in Boston, which was stately and interesting — "I sat next to Fung, who speaks English very well, & we were good neighbors." Thus did relations with both old and new China flourish.

XIII

The authors about whom Emerson wrote to his friends are of such number and variety that they cannot all be mentioned here even in the most casual manner; but there is one more shelf in his library that is too important to be ignored. The correspondence shows a great curiosity about physical science. Sometimes there is no hint of metaphysical implications; but a fit background against which to read most of the passages on this subject that belong to the mature years is a letter of 1835 to Benjamin Hunt. Emerson wondered whether his old pupil, borne along by the tide of the time, was amazed by those laws of terrible beauty which took the souls of Newton and Laplace and Humboldt. As for himself, he added, he found the best charm of natural laws to be " their correspondence with Spiritual laws of which they seem but symbols & prophecies." Tracing such analogies, he even dreamed of making ethics an orderly branch of knowledge.

The record, however, begins earlier and spans a long period of his life. As a boy of thirteen, he wrote of his visits to the humble museum of the Linnæan Society in Boston, and some years later he was recommending scientific dialogues (with theological leanings) for the use of a young lady. The reading of J. F. W. Herschel on the character and advantages of such studies fired him with enthusiasm. It was a noble enough book, he wrote, to tempt a man to leave all and find out natural science. He dreamed of a telescope, a laboratory, and a battery. Visits to the museums in Europe were a new revelation to him. Returning home, he took to drafting lectures on natural history, meantime exploring whatever he could find about geology, chemistry, and physics. He praised the works of Playfair and Cuvier as well as the popular lucubrations of the Reverend Dionysius Lardner. Cuvier seemed to write as if he had the planet on a table before him, turning it round and boring in with his corkscrew wherever he wished. What a refreshment to escape from Antimasonry, Jacksonism, and Bankism to the phenomena of the polar regions or the habits of the oak or the geographical problem of the Niger!

Galileo, Kepler, Newton, and many other leaders of scientific thought are familiar figures in the letters, though this need not mean that they were well known through their own writings. On the one hand, there are evidences of acquaintance with some of the pious-intentioned Bridgewater treatises; and on the other, there are enthusiastic comments on Robert Chambers's *Vestiges,* which was so liberal for its time that the author found it wise to conceal his identity. Humboldt is celebrated as the Napoleon of travelers, an encyclopedia of science, a man who knew more of nature than any other one in it. Emerson would some day speak his praise for a larger audience, gathered for the centennial in Boston. At the Royal Institution, he heard Faraday, reckoned the best lecturer in London. Later, at Clough's suggestion, he read the lecture on the conservation of force. The second visit to England had meantime afforded the best opportunity he was ever to have to visit museums, attend the meetings of the scientific societies, and know the scientists themselves. America had no such display of talent as this which he duly recorded.

Yet even his own brother-in-law, Charles T. Jackson, was a chemist and geologist of note, and we hear many echoes of the long battle with Morton for recognition as the discoverer of the surgical use of ether. Letters to Charles Sumner and others testify to a firm conviction that Jackson deserved full credit and that Morton's claims were false. Agassiz had left Europe for good and was an American too. His liking for scientific pursuits on a grand scale and his daring imagination – not quite daring enough to accept the new theory of evolution – made a strong appeal to his friend and fellow member of the Saturday Club. As man's knowledge of the physical world made its spectacular advance during the third quarter of the nineteenth century, Emerson was a fascinated spectator, though the epistolary history of his studies in that direction is far from satisfactory. A few weeks after the appearance of *On the Origin of Species,* he wanted it for a road book, on his lecture tour, but was unable to obtain a copy in the benighted regions he had penetrated. By 1869, he was writing to Mrs. Botta of his reading in Darwin as if it were extensive. In a letter of 1872 he told of a conversation with a scientist on " Darwin, Agassiz, &c." He acknowledged the fame of Huxley but confessed a lesser acquaintance with him than with Owen, Tyndall, or Darwin. He was aware of the debate between Huxley and his own correspondent Stirling on protoplasm as the physical basis of life, and seems to have helped to draw attention to it. But nothing shows better his respect for science than an opinion he wrote to Mrs. Botta: Natural science was indeed the point of interest now, and, he thought, was dimming and extinguishing a good deal that was called poetry. Those sublime and all-reconciling revelations of nature would exact of poetry a correspondent height and scope or else put an end to it.

XIV

It would be easy to overestimate the extent of the reading Emerson did in the books of which he wrote and equally easy to exaggerate the influence of what he actually read. The oracle he praised today he might doubt or discard tomorrow. He had strong defenses against encroachments upon his ideas and clung to the belief that one's private revelation of truth must be respected first. It was, he wrote to a friend, a high compliment to any man to make him the avowed subject of our study; and for himself, when he paid such dangerous homage he was quick to seek remuneration in a double self-trust.

Yet after all reasonable subtractions from their value, the letters are important to our knowledge of his adventures as an explorer of other minds. And they are invaluable for the new light they throw upon the growth of his own mind and personality. Mysteries enough remain even in one who may seem to the casual observer the most transparent of men. But with the aid of essays, lectures, poems, and journals and, now, of these letters, we can know Emerson as well, perhaps, as we know any of his contemporaries and better than any of them knew him.

Explanatory Note

The following arbitrary titles and abbreviations are used in the notes to the letters:

Bluebook List . . . . MS calendar of letters, in several small notebooks owned by the Memorial Association. It was apparently made for the use of J. E. Cabot and is valuable for its evidence of letters that I have been unable to find — evidence which, however, must be used with caution, as there are some errors in dates.

c. . . . . copyright.

c. . . . . *circa.*

Cabot . . . . James Elliot Cabot, *A Memoir of Ralph Waldo Emerson,* 2 vols., Boston and New York, 1887.

C–E Corr. . . . . *The Correspondence of Thomas Carlyle and Ralph Waldo Emerson,* ed. Charles Eliot Norton, 2 vols., Boston, 1883; supplementary letters published separately, but under the same title, Boston, 1886; the supplementary letters arranged with those of the first edition, 1888.

Cent. Ed. . . . . *Centenary Edition The Complete Works of Ralph Waldo Emerson,* ed. Edward Waldo Emerson, 12 vols., Boston and New York, n. d. (1903–1904).

CUL . . . . Columbia University Library.

HCL . . . . Harvard College Library.

Journals . . . . *Journals of Ralph Waldo Emerson,* ed. Edward Waldo Emerson and Waldo Emerson Forbes, 10 vols., Boston and New York, 1909–1914. These volumes contain a large part — but by no means all — of what is to be found in the extant MS originals.

MS *Journals* . . . . The originals, owned by the Ralph Waldo Emerson Memorial Association.

MS memorandum books . . Twenty-nine small volumes, owned by the Memorial Association. They contain divisions for daily memoranda and are mostly described on their printed title pages as pocket books or diaries. They were used by Emerson chiefly for listing his lecture engagements. The years for which the printers labeled them are 1833, 1848, 1853–1861, and 1863–1880; but a number have important jottings for more than one year. In a few of the latest, entries were made by Ellen as well as by her father.

ph. .... photostat (or photograph).

RWEMA .... Ralph Waldo Emerson Memorial Association.

typescript *Journals* ...... Copies made from the MS *Journals.* These copies, which are now nearly complete, attempt to supply a literal text, with no omissions. They are owned by the Memorial Association.

WmE List .... William Emerson List, a MS calendar similar to the Bluebook List and apparently made for the same purpose; also owned by the Memorial Association.

It should be added that catalogues of auction companies and autograph dealers are not mentioned by title but simply by name of company or dealer and by date of sale or of catalogue.

Roman numerals are used to indicate passages of two or more words in the text which are already in print, but excerpts given only in catalogues of auction companies and dealers are disregarded.

In a few cases, particularly in the text of early letters, I have merely italicized words which, in the manuscripts, are underscored more than once. In such cases the italics seem to give the emphasis intended by the author.

THE LETTERS OF

RALPH WALDO EMERSON

1813–1835

1813

To Mary Moody Emerson, Boston? *c.* March? 1813

[Mentioned in Apr. 16, 1813: "I have sent a letter to you in a Packet bound to Portland, which I suppose you have not received, as you made no mention of it in your letter to mamma." Perhaps there were earlier letters which have disappeared, leaving no trace.]

To Mary Moody Emerson, Boston, April 16, 1813

[Parts of this letter, the MS of which I have not been able to discover, are printed in James Elliot Cabot's "A Glimpse of Emerson's Boyhood," *The Atlantic,* LIX, 662–663 (May, 1887); and the same extracts reappear in Cabot, I, 35–37. In *The Bookman,* XXIV, 92–94 (June, 1903), Edward Waldo Emerson reprinted portions of what *The Atlantic* and Cabot had published and added part, but apparently not all, of what they had omitted.]

To Mary Moody Emerson, Boston? June? 1813

[The first of two letters, "very near together," acknowledged in Mary Moody Emerson, June 21, 1813.]

To Mary Moody Emerson, Boston? June? 1813

[The second of the two letters mentioned in the preceding note.]

To Mary Moody Emerson, Boston? July? 1813

[Mary Moody Emerson, June 21, 1813, is endorsed "Answered."]

1814

To Sarah Alden Bradford, Boston? May 6, 1814 [1]

Friday ¹May 6th 1814.¹

My Friend

Your favor [2] I receiv'd of late
But know that I cannot like you translate
But yet my humble efforts I will make
Not in the Greek 'tis verse I undertake.

1. MS owned by Professor James B. Thayer; ph. in CUL. Excerpts I–II are printed, with minor changes, in *Worthy Women of our First Century,* ed. Wister and Irwin, 1877, pp. 129–130. Sarah Alden Bradford, notable among women of her day for her learning, had early attracted the attention of Mary Moody Emerson and soon became intimate with the other members of the Emerson family. In later letters she appears as the wife of Samuel Ripley, half brother of Mary Moody Emerson, and as his associate in his school at Waltham. The best account of her is by Elizabeth Hoar, in *Worthy Women,* pp. 113–227; but Emerson's own notices, especially one in the letter of Jan. 25 and 27, 1819, are of much interest.

2. Probably the young scholar had recently sent Miss Bradford a translation of the first eighteen lines of Vergil's fifth eclogue, for in a letter partly printed in *Worthy Women,* p. 129 (where it is dated simply 1814), she urges him to " continue this versification," suggests a letter in Latin or Greek, and inquires what in Rollin and what stories of Vergil interest him most. She hints at the special charm of the episode of Nisus and Euryalus. She very cleverly lures him on to further efforts at an epistolary display of learning: " Only think of how much importance I shall feel in the literary world."

At least a part of an 1805 edition of *The Ancient History,* bearing the bookplate of William Emerson, is still in the Emerson library at the Antiquarian House, in Concord; and the letter of Apr. 16, 1813, seems to show that in the Emerson household Rollin was read aloud, each boy taking his turn. Years later the book remained an unpleasant memory, if we may take at their face value the passage in the *Journals* (VI, 122) about the insistence of " Aunt Betsey and Uncle Gulliver " upon Rollin and the allusion to the " obsolete history " in " The Transcendentalist " (*Cent. Ed.,* I, 356). As for the Vergil, Emerson had begun it at school as early as 1813 (letter of Apr. 16, 1813).

Perhaps the version of the present letter here printed was not the first written, as only a few emendations appear in the manuscript. The only considerable change was made in the fourth line from the end. Here the translator first wrote " As standing the verdant "; then he inserted " corn " after " standing "; and finally he

You ask in Rollin what I like the best
Under whose banners I myself enlist?
Tis Athens bravery which does me delight
I follow her in peace and in the fight.
I wish that Rollin in his history brought
The wars of Troy to every reader's thought,
The burning city, and Æneas' flight
With great Anchises on that fatal night.
You mention Nisus and Euryalus too
Those youthful heroes and those friends so true,
With you I like that charming history well
Both in an act of friendship nobly fell
But to your fifth Bucolic I proceed
And here young Mopsus tunes his slender reed.

Fifth Bucolic from the 19th to the 36th line.

[11]Mopsus. Turn now O youth from your long speech away
The bower we've reach'd recluse from sunny ray
The Nymphs with pomp have mourn'd for Daphnis dead
The Hazels witness'd and the rivers fled
The wretched mother clasp'd her lifeless child
And Gods and stars invok'd with accents wild.
Daphnis! the cows are not now led to streams
Where the bright sun upon the water gleams,
Neither do herds the cooling river drink
Nor crop the grass upon the verdant brink;
O Daphnis! both the mountains and the woods
And Punic lions and the raging floods
All mourn for thee – thou first did hold
In chariot reins the spotted tiger bold:
Daphnis the Bacchanalian chorus lead
He plac'd himself at the mad dancers head.
Twas Daphnis who with beauteous fingers wove

---

crossed out all but " corn," which he doubtless also intended to cancel, and rewrote the line as printed. In later letters discarded words or phrases are not noted unless they are significant.

Various examples of Emerson's early verse are already well known, but a pair of hitherto unpublished poems of this period, both dated, are valuable as showing the youthful poet's attempts to deal with serious subjects. They are printed below, VI, 329–332.

The stems of leaves he gathered from the grove.
As the great beauty of a tree is seen,
From vines entwining round its pleasant green;
As vines themselves in grapes their beauty find,
As the fair Bull of all the lowing kind,
As standing corn does grace the verdant fields
So to thy beauty every rival yeilds[II];
Since from our arms by fate thou hast been took
Phœbus and Pales have our fields forsook.

Ralph, Waldo, Emerson.

Miss Sarah, A. Bradford.

To Sarah Alden Bradford, Boston, July 14, 1814[3]

Boston July 14 1814

My Friend

I hope you will forgive my long delay
In writing you but I no longer stay
The cause of my not writing Ill not tell
You know the reason and you know too well.
I saw the New York Museum * monday night.
Beasts birds and pictures do compose the sight
Great men and women and poor Bonaparte
Done in wax figures well compose a part
There still as night the infant in her hands
The Virgin Mary with a friar stands
You would be pleas'd to see the infants face
Gilt rays of glory the small image grace
Smiling it lies upon its mothers arm
The little figure seems to fear no harm.
The martyr Rogers who was burnt I saw
With other preachers near the museum door
Walking along another view I had
Of various birds in various vestures clad

* Independence

3. MS owned by Professor James B. Thayer; ph. in CUL. The museum here described seems to have been more properly the Columbian Museum, which had its origin, many years earlier, in the New York Museum (*Proc. Mass. Hist. Soc.*, 2d series, XIX, 8). The *Boston Patriot*, July 2, 1814, advertised that this Columbian Museum would be open and brilliantly illuminated on the Fourth.

Two Eagles there with their wide wings display'd
One male one female both in black array'd,
I saw amid the party-color'd throng
They stood conspicuous as I pass'd along.
Stretchd at its length with aspect grim and rude
A Bellows Fish upon the floor I view'd
With sharpest teeth and jaws extended wide
He seem'd as if all others he defy'd.
Here stopping though much more I might relate
I leave these lines in their unfinish'd state
Though few they are and many faults you see
Pardon them all and quickly write to me.

Ralph W Emerson

To Miss S. A. Bradford.

To William Emerson, Concord, November 10, 1814

[MS owned by RWEMA; ph. in CUL. The year 1814 is given in the endorsement by a contemporary hand, apparently William Emerson's. The facsimile of this picture letter which appears as the frontispiece to this volume does not indicate the liberal use of colors on the original, sometimes significant, as in the two blurs standing for the word "read." With the aid of the colors, William Emerson probably read the letter thus:

Concord November 10

Dear Brother,

I hope you will not be offended if I attempt * a letter in hieroglyphics; I lately read a letter of the Duke of York's in them, it was given to Aunt Sarah by Sheriff Bradford; I have taken many from that. I like Concord very much. I go to school here and I like it more and more every day. Where is that song by G. B. that you promised to send me the day we moved send it as soon as you can. Mrs William Smith in Summer St. begs to have you spend thanksgiving at her house. Have you read Patronage yet. I hope you will soon enjoy the happiness of being here. Aunt and Charles send love Charles more than he can express. Send me your Collectanea Minora 1st time you can. Hieroglyphics take up too much time and paper; so pray excuse my shortness

Yours in love

Ralph.

Wm Emerson.

* H, non est litera

This is the earliest of the several hundred letters to Emerson's oldest brother which are printed in these volumes. For Samuel Bradford, Sheriff of Suffolk County, see the letter of Sept. 9, 1818. "G. B." is probably George Partridge Bradford, a younger brother of Sarah Alden Bradford. He became a school teacher and appears often in later letters as one of Emerson's most intimate friends. *The Boston Directory* of 1816 lists a Hannah Smith, widow of William Smith, living on Summer St., near the old home of the Emersons. Mention of Maria Edgeworth's *Patronage,* the four volumes of which were first published in 1814, seems to show some acquaintance with the popular fiction of the day about the time Scott's novels began to appear. The third American edition of Andreas Dalzel's Ἀνάλεκτα Ἑλληνικὰ Ἥσσονα. *Sive Collectanea Græca Minora* was printed at the Harvard press in 1813.]

1815

To William Emerson, Concord, February 24, 1815[1]

ᴵConcord February 24

My dear Brother,

What a change has taken place in the times since I saw you last & how happy is the change — But a little while since, and the cry of war was heard in every place but now —

Fair Peace triumphant blooms on golden wings
And War no more of all his victory sings.

When the news reached this place[2] a smile was on every face, and joy in every heart.ᴵ I hope you was in Boston on Wednesday and enjoyed the Celebration of Peace; if you were, do write where you staid, and what you saw, how all our friends there, do, and whatever you know that is new. ᴵᴵOn the 22d instant the steeple of the court-house here, was illuminated and appeared very brilliant from this house. When I came to see you, you did not pack up your Cicero's Orations in the bundle, and I should like to have you send it the first opportunity in your bundle of clothes. Today I got through the Incredibilibus in Collectanea.[3]

1. MS owned by RWEMA; ph. in CUL. Excerpts I–II are printed, with some errors, in *The Atlantic,* LIX, 666 (May, 1887), and in Cabot, I, 46. The MS is dated simply Feb. 24, but William Emerson's endorsement shows that this letter was received Feb. 25, 1815, and answered two days later. William's pretty regular endorsements over a period of more than fifty years are almost always accurate.

2. According to the *Boston Daily Advertiser,* Feb. 14, 1815, news of the peace reached Boston on the 13th of that month. A paragraph in a letter from William Emerson to his mother, written from Cambridge on the 27th, two weeks after the news arrived, probably reflects the sentiment, and perhaps illustrates the rhetoric, of the college boys:

"What glorious events have transpired since I saw you. Joy thrills through every vein, hope beats in every breast, pleasure beams in every countenance. Peace! O glorious, enrapturing sound! The very thought sets the secret springs of every soul in motion, gives to indolence itself, reanimation; we seem to tread a new earth, and magic seems to work before our enchanted eyes. The dark clouds of a moonless night have passed away, and the first rays of a springlike sun awaken our souls from their lethargy, and incite them to energy and action." (MS owned by Dr. Haven Emerson.)

3. *Cf.* Nov. 10, 1814.

And now dear William with a rhyme I'll close
For you are tir'd, I may well suppose,
Besides we soon shall hear the nightly bell
For prayers, so now Farewell!

Y'rs affectionately,

William Emerson. Ralph.[II]

Inclosed you will find the billet from your cousin which accompanied the books you loaned her.

To William Emerson, Boston, June 2 and 3, 1815[4]

Boston June 2nd. 1815

My Dear Brother

Yesterday afternoon I went to see mrs Charles Bradford when I left you; I saw little Russell & was told that he weighed 21 pounds and is 6 months old – I held him up to Sam and he had the impudence to box his ears.

Today I went to Riding School with Sarah Bradford & was much pleased. Mr Roulstone has 8 or 12 horses which he uses in the school all of which have their names as General, Venus, Charley, Holley, Noble, Favourite, & others; General I think is the handsomest – Venus the strongest – each have different parts in which they excel; Mr Frothingham was not there as I expected.

This afternoon I began to read Johnson's lives of the Poets and have read Cowley, Denham, and began Milton: I like it very much for Johnson intersperses it with his own wit. In criticising on Cowley's poems he brings in 4 lines from Donne and says " on reading the following lines the reader may cry out Confusion worse confounded "

Here lies a she-sun and a he-moon there
She gives the best light to his sphere
Or each is both and all and so
They unto one another nothing owe Donne –

This is old fashioned Poetry – I should like to see the Poem it was taken from. I dont like Cowley for his uneven measure or rather no

4. MS owned by RWEMA; ph. in CUL. William Emerson was now in the latter half of his freshman year at Harvard, and this letter was sent to him there. In the MS each of the passages now set off by a single pair of quotation marks has these marks at the beginning of every line. Comment on Corbett Owen's poem in the *Musæ Anglicanæ* is to be found in G. B. Hill's edition of *Lives of the English Poets*.

measure at all; Johnson says, "He takes the liberty of using in any place a verse of any length from two syllables to twelve." Cowley wrote a translation of Pindar in which his "endeavour was not to shew precisely what Pindar spoke but his manner of speaking" he thinks it "the highest and noblest kind of writing in verse" but Johnson do'nt like it on account of the looseness of the measure he says "this lax and lawless versification so much concealed the deficiencies of the vulgar, and flattered the laziness of the idle, that it immediately overspread our books with poetry; all the boys and girls caught the pleasing fashion, & they that could do nothing else could write like Pindar!! The rights of antiquity were invaded and disorder tried to break into the Latin a Poem on the Sheldonian Theatre in which all kinds of verse were shaken together is unhappily inserted in the Musæ Anglicanæ. &c. &c.

Saturday Morning. Did you arrive safe at Cambridge? Do write soon & tell me how you do – if you have got settled –

Yesterday the Apple tree was rocked by the wind & we thought it would blow over it rocked the tree so much that it cracked the ground all around it – Edward has not got home yet therefore I am alone. But I have written a long letter. Mother sends love. Y'rs affectionately

Ralph.

W[il]liam [5] Emerson.

To William Emerson, Boston, December 21, 1815 [6]

Boston Dec 21st

Dear William

Three Heroes have undertaken the charge successively of your shoes of which the writer is the last Tis now after 8 o clock

5. Two letters have been torn away by the opening of the seal.

6. MS owned by RWEMA; ph. in CUL. The year is clearly 1815, for the superscription shows that William Emerson was in 14 Hollis Hall, a room which, according to the Harvard catalogues, he occupied only in the year beginning Oct., 1815. Miss Sales, the teacher of French mentioned here and later, may have been, I conjecture, related to Francis Sales, instructor in Spanish and French at Harvard, 1816–1854. This Francis Sales, celebrated as the jovial but infinitely courteous "S." in Lowell's "Cambridge Thirty Years Ago," was, as his early pupil George Ticknor recalled, from the South of France and had difficulties of his own in mastering the French language (*Life, Letters, and Journals of George Ticknor*, 1909, I, 7). Many letters testify to Emerson's interest in the study of French and to his reading of books in that language.

A. M. and Mother told me this morning to see that they went today — Charles yesterday and Edward day before took care of them.

Please to bring with you (if you have one) a French Grammar as Edward and myself go to Miss Sales' to school every Monday Wednesday and Friday.

We hope tomorrow to see you not as a spectre as you came last time but clad in flesh and blood. If you can possibly send home that table Mother requests you would — if the Stageman comes home empty. Love from all

Vale

R W Emerson

To his Honor Bill Emerson

P. S. No news! N. B. Bring Rollin.

R W E.

1816

To William Emerson, Boston, January 9, 1816[1]

Boston Jan 9th 1816

I can not help observing to you, Mon cher frere how much I was offended as a 'man of honour' as I profess to be, in your writing to Charle the youngest in the family first and omitting to write to me the 'Man of the House' 'Generalissimo' &c. &c. But no more ceremony as Uncle goes now. Edward & I have begun a new french Book given by Miss Sales to us for a New Year's Present named Recueil Choisi. It contains very entertaining Stories. You ask about Mrs Parker's accounts of her Husband. She has recieved a letter 4 days after his arrival of 22 days in the Galen. But I have no time — Uncle waits.

Yours &c

Ralph.

W. Emerson.

To William Emerson, Boston, January 12, 1816[2]

Boston Jan 12th 1816

Dear Willm,

Pursuant to your request in Charles' letter to keep letters ready at all times I have begun to write though I do not know any opportunity at present. You know there was a reason why I did not write you a longer letter on the 9th, for I had begun a letter of one

1. MS owned by RWEMA; ph. in CUL. Numerous *Recueils* were popular early in the nineteenth century, but I have not been able to identify the *Recueil choisi* mentioned here and quoted from memory, in English translation, in the letter of Jan. 12, 1816. According to the *Boston Daily Advertiser,* Oct. 14 and 23, 1815, Daniel P. Parker sailed from Boston on the "Galen," bound for London, late in Oct., 1815. *The Boston Directory,* 1818, shows he was a merchant residing on Beacon St. The name "Charles" was left incomplete for lack of room at the edge of the MS.

2. MS owned by RWEMA; ph. in CUL. Doubtless William was helping in the school of his half uncle Samuel Ripley, who must be the "Uncle" of this and the preceding letter.

half sheet thinking that Uncle would spend the night here; but when he came down [and was][3] going immediately I was obliged to cut short. But [is there] any excuse for you to write a *note?* when I recieved it [I] was so angry I could have torn it to pieces to see a card-party billet (as I should thought from its form) instead of the letter I expected. Oh! now I remember when I first had it in the rage of the moment I was going to run & write on a peice of paper I am much obliged to you for the *note* but soon expect to recieve the *letter;* but hurry prevented me — In cooler blood I sat down this evening but Oh mirabile dictu I know not what to say! Let me see I will think — well as nothing occurs I will write a translation of the first Anecdote in Recueil Choisi which if you have read before in English will sadly disappoint me — well then "The Emperor Aurelien arriving before the city of Tyane and finding the gates shut swore in his anger he would not leave even a dog alive in the city. However the city being taken by storm & the soldiers entreating him to keep his resolution (hoping thereby to obtain great booty) he said, Soldiers! I shall keep my resolution You may therefore if you wish kill all the *dogs* but I forbid anyone doing any harm to the inhabitants." This is not literal for I have not the book by me but from memory. But enough paper shortens — Mother wishes you if you can write to Cambridge and get your black waistcot. Ralph.

Friday Evening Jan 12 1816

P. S. I began with a quarter of a sheet from views of economy but I found as you see pretty scant room; and as it is written so fine (which perhaps I ought not to have done) it must pass for a *Letter*. Charles sends love — Edward wants to write but knows not what to say — 'All's well' But before I close please remember to send me a Sallust if you can for I have reviewed Cicero & Coll.[4] pretty nearly through.

Write a *long* answer

Yrs

Ralph W Emerso

Willm. Emerson.

3. The MS was mutilated when the seal was opened. These two words are doubtfully legible, and those in the two pairs of brackets following are wholly conjectural. The incomplete signature in the postscript is written close to the edge of the sheet.

4. Apparently the *Collectanea* of the letters of Nov. 10, 1814, and Feb. 24, 1815.

To William Emerson, Boston, January 13 and 15, 1816[5]

Boston Jan 13 1815

Again, dear brother, I have commenced a letter. It is now after 2 and Mother is at dinner, Edward & Charles are gone of an errand; all is quiet, or in dialect Poetice[6] –

Here Silence holds her reign & all is quiet
Save where the wintry wind howls hoarse without
And enters at the chink –

But I forgot you do not like My Lisping Muse why then should she be called from her slumbers to give entertainment to one who will only answer her with reproofs and say 'Ralph don't make poetry till you have gone through Algebra.'

On Monday (day after tomorrow) I begin to study Geography at Latin School[7] with Cummings' Geography,[8] 2 beautiful Globes, An Orrery, and a large Atlas. You will say that if I begin with such great advantages I ought certainly to make great improvement; it is true and I hope I shall. I should think it would appear to us almost a vacation week it certainly will be a relaxation from hard study.

Monday Jan 15 1816 I was obliged for all the quiet on Saturday noon to leave my letter and you and go for the lamp at the brass-founder's and have not been able to resume it till now; it is now evening – " past 7 o'clock and alls well." I studied Geography today and lied[9] the manner much – in all the famous places we pass Mr Gould[10] relates what they are famous for such as speaking of the deserts of Africa, one asked if men could not pass over them, Mr Gould told them Bonaparte passed over part of them with his army he then shewed them his march and told some incidents happening at that time &c. &c.

Today one was asked by Mr Gould where about in the world Kamt-

5. MS owned by RWEMA; ph. in CUL. Saturday was the 13th and Monday the 15th of January in 1816, not 1815; and the mention of Lathrop's death is conclusive evidence that the second date given in the letter is correct.

6. Apparently reminiscent of Gray's " Elegy."

7. Emerson had entered the Boston Public Latin School in 1812 (Henry F. Jenks, *Catalogue of the Boston Public Latin School,* 1886, p. 151).

8. The second edition of Jacob A. Cummings's *An Introduction to Ancient and Modern Geography* had been published at Boston in 1814.

9. A letter was omitted in dividing the word between lines.

10. Benjamin Apthorp Gould was headmaster of the Boston Public Latin School, 1814–1828. Under his direction it is said to have advanced rapidly in repute as well as in numbers. (Jenks, p. 8.)

chatka was? looking on the Map the boy answered *at the two corners;* sed ego ut homo probitatis non memorabo nominem alicujus.

Yesterday Mr Holley[11] preached in the morning and Mr Frothingham[12] in the afternoon at the First Church the latter from Genesis *And he asked them saying Is your father yet alive is he well? and they answered he is well*[13] – It was a funeral sermon on account of Dr Lathrop's death – we thought it a very ingenious text.

Barren of all information or news I am obliged to

Leave, dear William in unfinish'd state
This sorry letter to its dreaded fate

Oh! I dread your displeasure to see at two different time my uncultivated Muse, muse did I say, my – – I know not what to call her, has stuck in her head nay thrice for see spite of all my commands she says

Forgive, dear Wm Oh forgive my tongue
That fain would usher in a little song
But – cruel fortune – wonderful to tell
My Master bids me give a last
Farewell –

Yrs affectionately
Ralph.

P. S. Edward says he would fain write
Sed eheu
Mirabile dictu
* Vox hæsit faucibus[14]

Ralph

N. B.

Expectatur in lingua vernacular vel latina litera ab Emerson – tui[15]

R.

* I may have alarmed you but truth! he is not dumb in the house

R –

11. Horace Holley, pastor of the Hollis Street Church, later known as the president of Transylvania University.

12. Nathaniel Langdon Frothingham (1793–1870), Unitarian pastor in Boston 1815–1850, was Emerson's friend during many years and appears frequently in later letters.

13. *Genesis,* 43:27–28. Probably Emerson quoted from memory, as he habitually did in later years. John Lathrop, pastor of the Second Church in Boston, had died Jan. 4, according to the *Boston Daily Advertiser,* Jan. 6 and 8, 1816.

14. The last phrase seems to be from the *Aeneid,* III, 48.

15. Obviously young Emerson's own Latin.

To William Emerson, Boston? January? 20? 1816? [16]

Saturday =

Dear William,

I fear you will think no better of me for the miserable scrawl that accompanies this and I do not think I should send it only that it would be considerable time and paper wasted if I did not – and, besides, when vexed with school business a good-natured letter from home even if it be nonsense is not I suppose in the highest degree unpleasant – So you must *forgive* offensive parts and remember it comes from one not *always* though *often silly* We are all well and hope the same for you –

Good-night –

Yrs afft–ly

Ralph –

W. E.

" Don't view me with a critick's eye
But pass my imperfections by." – [17]

To Edward Bliss Emerson, Boston, October 15 and 16? 1816 [18]

Boston Oct 15 1816

Dear Edward

It is now the second evening since you left us,[19] yet as [I]mother says you are likely to be dull during the first days of your stay[I] in your new abode. But perhaps this letter will not reach you before you

16. MS owned by RWEMA; ph. in CUL. This note is written on both sides of a small scrap of paper now attached to the letter of Jan. 13 and 15, 1816, which it may well describe. The Saturday following Jan. 15 that year was the 20th. The mention of William as " vexed with school business " fits this date, as the letter of Jan. 13 and 15 is addressed to him at Waltham.

17. Emerson might have read David Everett's " Lines Spoken at a School-exhibition, by a Little Boy Seven Years Old " in *The Columbian Orator,* the seventeenth edition of which appeared at Boston in 1814. But doubtless the piece was familiar to most schoolboys in 1816.

18. MS owned by RWEMA; ph. in CUL. Excerpts III–V were printed in *The Atlantic,* LIX, 667 (May, 1887), and I–V, in Cabot, I, 47–48. In both printed versions alterations were made to suit the context. That this letter was not finished till Oct. 16 seems to be pretty conclusively shown by the first sentence in Oct. *c.* 23, 1816.

19. The *Biographical Catalogue of . . . Phillips Academy Andover, 1778–1830,* 1903, p. 80, shows that Edward Bliss Emerson, 12, of Boston, entered in 1816 and left in 1818, and that he at first lived in the home of Mrs. Phebe Abbot, " the venerable Mrs Abbott " of the present letter.

are acquainted with your new associates and do not need it; but I do not doubt but that at any time, tidings from home will be acceptable and especially from a person of so much consequence as his honor R. W. Andover, for the first week I suppose, even Andover, the seat of so much learning, of the Muses, the Arts, and Sciences, will appear irksome to the august traveller who has entered the town and has honored the roof of the venerable Mrs Abbott by his abode – I am afraid that as it was so wet and muddy the good people of Andover did not come out into the street to pay their salutation as you entered the town – but as I profess to be Poet [II]I suppose you expect me to write " Poetice "[II] accordingly I will write the method on the next page (as the page lessens) how you should have entered Andover had I been Master of Ceremonies

[But stop I must puzzle my muse now][20]

And now arrives the chariot of state
That bears with regal pomp Ned, Bliss the great
See from afar arise a dusty cloud
And see approaching fast the gathering crowd
See yonder rank of learned sages come
Like reverend fathers of majestic Rome
Down from their aged heads their hats they bend
On either hand the bowing lines extend
While thro' the midst with elevated mein
Stalks " Edward Emerson the great " between
Hark the loud clangor of the sounding bell
To Andoveria's college hails thee well
(&c &c &c

But the Muse begins to lag and I cannot go on but suffice it to say the train moves on to the town and give a dinner to E B E Esqr A B C d F R S D D A M &c But you see fancy a little overstepped the reality for instead of a Chariot of state I believe your Excellency rode in to the town in so humble vehicle as a Chaise! and instead of four neighing steeds a menial horse more like an ass than like " the generous horse " but enough of this nonsense –

[III]Aunts only message is " be brave " [21] i.e. Do not be cast down by

20. The brackets are Emerson's own.

21. The brilliant, if eccentric, Mary Moody Emerson appears frequently in the family correspondence as the intellectual mentor of her youthful nephews, a rôle in which she delighted and which she may well have regarded as a duty after the death of her brother. Emerson himself has given the best accounts of her in his letters, in the *Journals,* and in the sketch now included in *Lectures and Biographical Sketches.*

thoughts of home[III] — but I must get another pen — I have not gotten out of my confinement yet and as you know that the prospect from the great Basement [22] is not the most ample I have nothing great to delight my powers of vision from this room therefore if you are dull remember that I can sympathise a little with you. I think that if you are as little homesick as Jarvis [23] was when he came here you will do very well — As I sit mostly at one window I will endeavor to make you acquainted with what I see as I suppose you had no opportunity to take a minute survey but

" The wide unbounded prospect lies before me "
Imprimis then, a dirty yard
[IV]By boards and dirt and rubbish marr'd[IV]
Pil'd up aloft a mountain steep
Of broken Chairs and beams a heap
But rising higher you explore
In this fair prospect wonders more
[V]Upon the right a wicket grate
The left appears a jail of State
Before the view all boundless spreads
And 5 tall Chimnies lift their lofty heads[V] —

I cannot write any more except that Mother Aunt and Charles &c send love and Mother got home safely — Do not shew this to any one mother said it was likely you would —

Yours affectionately

Ralph

P. S. The doctor says I must have a blister on —

But a good deal of information, particularly about her eccentricities of behavior and opinion, is to be found in George Tolman's *Mary Moody Emerson,* privately printed, n. d. (preface dated 1929).

22. The death of the pastor of the First Church meant poverty for his family. The view described was not from Ruth Emerson's boarding house in Beacon St. (*The Boston Directory,* 1816) but from her next one, in Hancock St., near by. This would still fit the suggestion in Cabot (I, 48) that the gate (or "grate," to use the word that actually appears in the letter) was that of the Granary Burying Ground and the "jail of State" the County Jail in Court St. Charles Shaw, in *A Topographical and Historical Description of Boston,* 1817, pp. 226–227, described the antiquated jail as a stone building, 90 by 23 feet, standing between the old and new court houses. The five fireplaces he mentioned as the special equipment of the third floor tally with the "5 tall Chimnies" of the verses.

23. Possibly the C. Jarvis of the letter of Oct. *c.* 24, 1817, who was pretty clearly Emerson's classmate Charles Jarvis, remembered in *Journals,* VI, 38, for his admiration of Edward Everett.

To Edward Bliss Emerson, Boston, October *c.* 23, 1816 [24]

Dear brother

Perhaps you have not received any letter from home so soon as you had a right to expect but it has not been from any neglect on our part; I began a letter to you the same evening mother came home and finished it the next morning; [25] but no chance came till Sunday evening by Dr Woods [26] I hope you have not been homesick. If you remember when you was at home you boasted and " knew " you should not be: you now can tell best and I hope will soon tell us by letter how you like Andover " the seat of the Muses, Knowledge," and so forth.

Andover, I fear, with all its attractions in gloomy weather as it has been does not look as pleasant as home to you not accustomed to the voices or house of Strangers –

In my last if you remember I drew you off in great style as E. B. E. the great, entering the town of Andover but now begging your honor's pardon I will point out (be not offended) one of your honor's failings – viz – sometime before you went I beleive it was while you expected to go to Exeter you told me that I was to have the whole museum while you was gone but when you was just going you resigned your whole part to Charles which did not please me much I confess as I am not willing to keep a Museum with him and the handsomest things are " in common " and furthermore I think I had some little right to be consulted and therefore I cannot that half the museum is legally the Property of aforesaid Charles – but enough – we must leave it to some Arbiter at another time – thus I have finished the Law business.

24. MS owned by RWEMA; ph. in CUL. Though this letter bears no date, it clearly follows that of Oct. 15 and 16? and falls somewhere between the 20th and the 26th of that month. According to the letter of Oct. 15 and 16? 1816, Edward had left for Andover on the 14th. The Sunday mentioned in the first paragraph of the present letter must have been the 20th, so that the date is later than that. But as the ten-day period prescribed by the doctor, which began on Oct. 15 or 16 – probably 16 – was not yet up, the date is earlier than the 26th.

25. This apparently was the letter I have dated Oct. 15 and 16? 1816. But it is barely possible that Emerson intended a period after " evening " and meant " mother," in spite of its small initial letter, to begin a new sentence. If so, the reference would be to a lost letter of Oct. 14, and the letter of Oct. 15 and 16? would have to be dated simply Oct. 15, as in Emerson's own heading.

26. Probably Dr. Leonard Woods, professor of theology at Andover. *Cf.* Nov. 17, 1816.

Mother wishes you to ask some gentleman whether it be as cheap for you to buy your quills and other Stationary at Andover as it would be for her to buy it here and send it you.

The day I wrote to you Dr Warren [27] called here and told Mother I must have a blister on for ten days; that time has not expired yet and therefore I am kept home (as the Irishman said) sick ten days after I was well.

This letter as almost all mine contains little else than nonsense; I hope no more will be like it in that respect. Mother says that our letters should be improving to both, that we ought to write what strikes us in our reading particularly thereby improving each with the reading of the other. During my stay at home I have read "Whelpeley's Historical Compend" that Mary Ladd [28] has lent me – I have finished that and Joan of Arc and the "Vision of Don Roderick" which book William bought me at auction. "Joan of Arc" is a poem by Southey – This woman was famous in the time of one of the Henry's of England (I beleive the 5th) [29] when he invaded France he obtained several victories over Charles King of France and took many of the towns and laid seige to Orleans – This woman beleiving herself inspired to be the savior of France went to Chinon where Charles was obtained from him an army and immediately went to Orleans where she conquered the English army in several battles and continuing her course went to Rheims where she crow[ned Char]les [30] before assembled France – On this the Poem is though of course he exaggerates and makes her really inspired – She afterwards fell into the hands of the English who murdered her – but the Poet takes good care not to have his heroine degraded so much as that and therefore closes it at the coronation of Charles.

The vision of Don Roderick is a short poem of W. Scott's but not any thing great. Whelepeley's History is a brief survey of the history of every nation on earth; and as you now know what I have been reading

27. Apparently John C. Warren, listed as a physician in *The Boston Directory,* 1816, and doubtless the same Dr. Warren who reappears in many later letters.

28. Doubtless Emerson's cousin, born 1797, daughter of William Ladd and Mary Haskins (Warren Ladd, *The Ladd Family,* 1890, p. 291).

29. Emerson's memory was not quite accurate either in the number of his Henry or in his reference to the English king as the besieger of Orléans.

30. The portions of words here printed in brackets were torn away with the seal. In the following sentence a word or words are missing for the same reason.

I beleive I must close as the paper shortens. Dr Moody [31] (self stiled) is very anxious about the health of Ned Bliss: all send love

Yrs &c

Ralph

P. S. William promised to write to you; perhaps you have received his letter — when you write tell what hours the Academy keeps &c

Ralph W Emerson

To Edward Bliss Emerson, Boston, November 3 and 4, 1816 [32]

Sunday Evening November 3d

Dear Edward,

We have received your two letters for Mother & Aunt and I read them with great pleasure especially Mother's — I was glad you said nothing of having been attacked with a certain disease called by some " Homesickness " —

Most likely you have not heard of Aunt Ripley's [33] arrival from Waterford. She arrived here a week from Friday and went to Concord on Monday last. Perhaps you have heard of the fire which has been raging in Maine for many weeks or months for many miles around the country destroying the woods fences houses &c — Even Waterford's sublime and awful " cloud-capt " hills enchanting vales [34] were not exempted from the flame; Aunt Ripley says that the fire ran along the feilds as fast as a horse could trot — for three days and nights the Meeting-House was in danger and as there was no engine in the town they were obliged to " fight " the fire as they call it by digging trenches having wet boughs and other such precautions — Aunt says that she rode out at eleven o'clock at night to see the fire turn round the bend of the mountain upon the top and that it was one of the sublimest sights she ever saw.

Mr Joy [35] has written a reply to the " Statement of facts " which you read and if what he relates is true the Messrs Barrells are as much to

31. Mary Moody Emerson, no doubt.

32. MS owned by RWEMA; ph. in CUL. Nov. 3 fell on Sunday in 1816, and the references to Edward's recent departure to Andover, to the study of French, and to the fires in the District of Maine all confirm that year. The *Independent Chronicle*, Boston, Oct. 7 and 17, 1816, describes the recent great fires in Oxford County.

33. For Emerson's aunt Phebe Emerson, wife of Lincoln Ripley, see Dec. 22, 1839.

34. Here Emerson added the words " and deep blue lakes," but doubtless realizing the incongruity, canceled them.

35. Perhaps the Benjamin Joy who had built the new meeting house and parsonage for the First Church when William Emerson was pastor (*cf.* Cabot, I, 2). It

blame as we thought he must be — I sincerely hope that his Pamphlet is as he has intitled it " A *true* Statement."

I have begun to read a French Novel by Madame de Genlis called " Chevaliers de la cygne "[36] (Knights of the Swan) and I find, as it is easy French, I can read it fast enough to make it interesting. It is one which Sarah Alden has lent me and is in 2 Vols.

Aunt met Miss Sales the other day and told her that you had gone to Andover upon which she offered to have Charles come with me; I have not been since you went but expect to go tomorrow with Charles who will begin at our old acquaintance " Le prince."

You need not attend to a former foolish sentence about the Museum for it is settled: William gave me yesterday a half penny token — it is a Halifax coin and very pretty.

E. G. Loring[37] Esq[r] has gotten the Medal for speaking at our School — It was Silver about half the size of the one given by the Committee: on the one side was " Latina Schola, Bostonia, 1816." on the other " Palma Eloquentiae E. G. Loring data." — The other was given to J. G. Stevenson with the same inscription except the name — I was very sorry that I was not at school at the time. They were at Mr Gould's expense, but given out by Mr Holley —

This week I have read very little and consequently nothing of that kind to write about — I hear you have letters for us at Mr Cummings'[38] Store and I hope one of them is for me — Mother and all of us were very glad to hear you had prayers in the family where you are — but I must close for the evening — Good Night —

Monday morn.g. and all's well — Today I go to Miss Sales but have not written my exercise yet; and as I have many errands to go, I cannot devote much time to letter writing — I think you would laugh at me if you were to see how often I stop writing, and hold up my head, and pen to think what to write next — For as I have no news to relate and you well know the poor feeble brain of R W has nothing original

---

may be that the Barrells referred to were Henry F. Barrell, who had a counting house in Cornhill, and Samuel B. Barrell, an attorney at the same address (*The Boston Directory,* 1816).

36. Various editions of the popular *Les Chevaliers du cygne,* both in French and in translation, were obtainable before 1816. The Sarah Alden who provided the copy here referred to was doubtless Sarah Alden Bradford.

37. For the full names of these and of other pupils or officers of the Boston Public Latin School mentioned in later letters, see the index, where all such names are given as they appear in the *Catalogue* of 1886.

38. Jacob A. Cummings was a partner in the firm of Cummings & Hilliard, booksellers in Cornhill (*The Boston Directory,* 1816).

to produce I am very soon at a stand — — but stop. . . .[39] Oh I have got a peice of very important intelligence to communicate which I had well nigh forgot Fidel is in health and prospers — with this closes the Nonsense of your affectionate brother

Ralph Waldo

To Edward B Emerson Esq[r] residing at Andover.

P. S. You see I almost always have to write Postscripts to my letters — I am just such a forgetful sort of a being — All this is written for is to tell that Bulkeley and Charles send their love to you and Charles says the he has forgotten that you are his naughty brother and wishes you to come home.

* R. W. EMERSON.

* This was done with a stamp of Mothers but I put on the first R

To Edward Bliss Emerson, Boston, November 10, 1816 [40]

Sunday Ev.g Nov 10

My dear " brother Emerson,"

Sunday Evening is the time I generally can best devote to letter-writing, and though my time this evening is pretty short yet I shall devote it to you. We have recieved your three letters and I was very much pleased with mine: Mother thought that you must feel rather old, on being addressed as " Brother Emerson " — I hope it is not fashionable for boys to wear wigs at Andover yet — Last night I read " The Grave " a Poem by Robert Blair, which William bought for me. It is a short, serious Poem in blank verse, & is esteemed as excellent; but in one place even the heedless R. W. E. found a great fault. It was a simile which I thought to be a very great fall from sublimity after speaking of the body he says — " Like a disabled pitcher out of use " [41] — You will see, no doubt, that I have to fill up my letters with every thing I can pick up. I heard a very good transposition the other day — I was given " new door " and told to make one word of it; I took it in the common sense and tried to make out a word but gave it up, when Gardner took it up and pointed out new door. [234 7156] ¹I have begun

39. The points are Emerson's.

40. MS owned by RWEMA; ph. CUL. Excerpts I–II were printed with part of the letter of Oct. 15 and 16? 1816, in *The Atlantic,* LIX, 667 (May, 1887), and in Cabot, I, 48. Nov. 10 fell on Sunday in 1816, and the allusions to the study of French and to Edward's residence at Andover fit that year, if they do not prove it to be correct.

41. *The Grave,* London and Edinburgh, 1813, p. 19.

Telemachus in French at Miss Sales' and at home I am reading Priestley's Lectures on History –

But as even Nonsense sounds good if cloth'd in the dress of Poetry I believe I must resort to that as my last expedient[I] Now then –

" Procul oh Procul este Profani "

Virgil[42]

Far hence ignoble prose! my letter fly!
Nor longer soil the page beneath my eye –
But come ye Nine your kind assistance lend
And me poor feeble bard for once befriend –
The lays of Friendship shall my Song inspire
And Edward's name shall wake the dormant lyre –
Cold were my heart and reft of ev'ry flame
If it not kindled at thy mighty name
Yes at thy voice my feeble lyre shall rise
And draw the muses from the lofty skies!
Long on the willow branch that harp had hung
Cover'd with leaves, neglected and unstrung
Till Edward's merits call'd the stranger forth
And tun'd the aged strings to sing thy worth
x x x x x x x
But oh Urania at thy shrine I bow
And ask thy pardon for digression now!
The Song of Bard of other time to name
Minstrel of worth and not unknown to fame

Song of the Bard of other time

" [II]So erst two brethren climb'd the cloud capp'd hill
" Ill fated Jack and long-lamented Jill
" Snatch'd from the chrystal font its lucid store
" And in full pails the precious treasure bore "

But –

But ah! by dull forgetfullness oppress'd
(Forgive me Edward) Ive forgot the rest!

Yours

Ralph.[II] [43]

Edward Bliss Emerson.

42. The phrase is not quite correctly quoted from the *Aeneid,* VI, 258. The curious mélange that follows seems to be a conscious attempt to parody the English heroic style of the school of Pope, Ossian, the nursery rime, and Gray's " Elegy."

43. This letter is followed, on the same sheet, by a brief note signed " Charles C.

To Edward Bliss Emerson, Boston, November 17, 1816 [44]

Boston — Sunday even. Nov 17

Dear Edward,

I cannot begin with that sublime expression " I now take this opportunity " because I do not know of any and besides I have another letter a week old, to send to you which as it contains no news may be as good when old as new — I expect, however, that Mrs Cooper will know of some opportunity — 4 minutes after — Thomas has just come to say that Dr Woods has come to preach the Park Street Lecture therefore I must write my letter so that he can bring it to you [45] — We have in the house Jebb's Sermons [46] which are a new book from England — I like them very much indeed. There are two Sermons on the Sabbath from this text Isaiah 58 –13, 14. " If thou turn away thy foot from the sabbath, from doing thy pleasure on my holy day; and call the Sabbath a delight, the holy of the Lord, honourable; and shalt honour him, not doing thine own ways, nor finding thine own Pleasure, nor speaking thine own words; then shall thou delight thyself in the Lord." I think it a most beautiful text and wonder I have not seen it before and I mean to read the Volume through — Mr. Frothingham on the Sunday before last requested the assembly to stand during singing as being a more proper position — but left it to themselves to judge — and now the generality of the audience stand during singing Today Mr Frothingham read the Governour's Proclamation [47] and I liked it very much

At Latin School your classmates Withington, Paine, Hubbard, and Winslow still remain but are in the same class with Child &c studying Greek Testament — You are (according to your account) very busy in your *lectiones;* but there I can sympathise with you because that long morning lessons, with French besides fill up my time —

Emerson," then by the words " Finis Literarum," and finally by the sentence " Mother thinks you had better try to borrow Charles 12 or some other history to amuse you during vacation also to go on with French — " This last sentence is partly quoted in *The Atlantic* and in Cabot as Emerson's, but I believe the hand to be that of his brother Charles.

44. MS owned by RWEMA; ph. in CUL. Nov. 17 fell on Sunday in 1816; and the reference to the Latin School, as if Emerson were still a pupil there, indicates 1816 rather than a later date during Edward's residence at Andover.

45. The superscription is to Edward at Andover, " Politeness of Rev. Dr. Woods."

46. John Jebb's *Sermons on Subjects chiefly Practical* had first appeared, it seems, at London, in 1815.

47. See a note on Nov. 27, 1816.

Yesterday I went down upon Long Wharf and was surprised to see how changed the Central or New Wharf appeared to be in so short a time — It was but a little time ago, you remember, when there was nothing but water to be seen there; and now, a long block of about 30 stores fill up the place. New Cornhill is much the same: one of the Stores is already occupied —

Do you know why a tallow-chandler is the most wretched of all beings? because that he deals in *wicked* works and his wicked works are brought to *light!* — My letters in general you see are a strange medley of every thing and any thing — Whatever comes first I put in, if I think it will interest or amuse you at all: and when I have exhausted my brain I then go and end it with flattery or rhyme sometimes with both — (oh mirabile dictu!) But I have worn both of those threadbare and therefore dare not try them again. So you must excuse me from writing any more or *Poetice* from writing any more excuse

Your

Waldo

All send love to

To E. B. Emerson — A. B. C. D. E. F.

N. B. No Postscript this time!!

To Edward Bliss Emerson, Boston? November 24, 1816

[The letter of Nov. 27, 1816, describes this as "relating to Linnean Society, Thanksgiving &c." Probably it contained "the poetry of Ralph about Thanksgiving" which, Charles Emerson writes Edward on Nov. 26, 1816, "I hope you will like." The Linnæan Society of New-England had held its first anniversary meeting some seventeen months earlier; and that occasion had seemed important enough to the editor of *The North-American Review,* a still more recent sign of Boston's cultural awakening, to deserve a dozen or so pages (Sept., 1815).]

To Edward Bliss Emerson, Boston? November 27, 1816 [48]

Afternoon before thanksgiving

Dear Edward

You desire me to date my letters. I had not recieved that letter of yours when I wrote last Sunday night. The date should have been Nov 24th (to the letter relating to Linnean Society, Thanksgiv-

48. MS owned by RWEMA; ph. in CUL. Excerpts I–II are in *The Atlantic,* LIX, 666 (May, 1887), and in Cabot, I, 45. The date is clear, as the letter follows, on the

ing &c) I suppose that it will be pleasant to you to recieve a letter from home Thanksgiving day at which time I suppose you will recieve this.

Cicero calls letterwriting " mutuus absentuum sermo " [49] " *the mutual discourse of absent friends."*

[I]The other day while scouring knives I began to hum away that verse

Harp of Memnon sweetly strung[I]
To the music of the spheres
While the Heroe's dirge is sung
Breathe enchantment to our ears [50]

[II]But I really did not think that the harsh melody of the knives sounded quite so sweet as the Harp

Melodious knife! and thou harmonious sand
Tuned by the Poet scourer's rugged hand
When swift ye glide along the scouring board
With music's notes your happy bard reward[II]

But hence thou nonsense!

Bulkeley is very sorry he cant send you his turnover and regrets not seeing you – All send love

And alll are well
And so farewel

To Edward
yours

E B Emerson
Esqr —— **Ralph**

Excuse this hurried flurried badly written letter

Ralph

---

same sheet, one from Charles to Edward dated Boston, Nov. 26, 1816, and the *Columbian Centinel,* Boston, Oct. 9, 1816, prints the proclamation of Governor John Brooks appointing Thursday, Nov. 28, as Thanksgiving Day.

49. The sentiment, if not the grammar, would fit well enough into Cicero's epistles, where, however, I have not found it. As in many of his letters, the young writer was obviously making an effort to be literary, mindful, perhaps, of his mother's advice (*cf.* Oct. *c.* 23, 1816).

50. The opening lines of " The Battle of Alexandria " (*The Wanderer of Switzerland, The West Indies, and Other Poems,* Philadelphia, 1811, p. 80). In the letter of July 20 and 21, 1818, Emerson refers to the same poem of the then popular James Montgomery.

To Edward Bliss Emerson, Boston, December 3, 1816 [51]

Boston Dec.3d. 1816.
Boston, December, 3d. 1816.
Now you cant mistake the date!
Ralph

ago Mr Gould asked me if we had heard from you and if you were accepted – I told him you were on trial for two months &c – Well, said he, is he not sure of being accepted? I told him you hoped to be – Why he is the best scholar in his class here, said Mr Gould – as I thought this would be acceptable to you, I determined not to forget to place it first in my letter.

On Saturday Mr G. told the boys in the first two classes that hereafter he wished us [to] write one theme every week; but for the first time we might [write] each a letter on any subject we chose. I wrote mine on Astronomy and gave it up this morning (tis now noon) at which time we were all to give them up. – Did you ever see any Asbestos? Mr G. as I told you in my other letter gave me a peice of Jaspar – I scraped it, and there came off a sort of powder that looked like fine wool, which is asbestos.[52] Of it the ancients were used to make napkins etc. resembling cloth – and when they were dirty from use they threw them in the fire which purged without burning them. But at present Asbestos is so rare that it is only valued as a curiosity; Strange that cloth should be made from stone! Bulkeley desires me not to forget to tell you he is in the first class.[53]

Yours &c

Ralph

Again – Boston Dec. 3d. 1816.

E. B. Emerson.

51. MS owned by RWEMA; ph. in CUL. The upper left corner of the sheet has been torn away. The bracketed words printed in the second paragraph are conjectural, as that part of the MS was mutilated by the opening of the seal.

52. In old age Emerson recalled his boyhood enthusiasm for such experiments (*Journals,* X, 381), an enthusiasm significant in view of his later love of science and the probable influence of the new scientific thought in freeing him from orthodox restraints.

53. Bulkeley's mind remained undeveloped, and there are many allusions in later letters to arrangements made by his brothers for his care.

TO EDWARD BLISS EMERSON, BOSTON, DECEMBER 11, 1816 [54]

Boston December 11th 1816

Dear Edward,

This letter is my first on *business;* the former have all been frivolity; but of this R. T. Paine [55] is the theme. Miss Mary Paine has been here to have me write to you to ask the questions, to wit, If Robert comes to Andover can he be fitted for College next Commencement? Can he board with Mrs Abbott and on the same terms that you do? What are the lowest terms that he can be taken upon in the neighborhood if she cannot take him? Ask the Preceptor of the Academy how soon you, or a boy of your standing can be made ready for College — Miss Paine is very anxious to know these things and as soon as possible: therefore wishes you as soon as you have made the inquiries to answer them by mail and you may answer them in either a letter to her or to myself. She says she should be very happy to have a letter from Edward and so would Ralph. Do you think that you should like Paine for a chum if you do have him pray assist him in keeping his Logbook, Let not the scoffing insults of any meddling schoolfellow, deter him from noting in those records State, the interesting phenomena of nature, as the 2 inch snow the one inch mud &c What a loss to the world if by any unforseen unlucky accident the Annotations and Memoranda of a Paine should never come to press! But I forbear, I lose myself in the vast subject of his more vast more astonishing genius.

Samuel Bradford is in town and I have spent this afternoon with him — Mr Gould went to Inaugaration at Cambridge [56] therefore I had the day today (Wednesday) Mrs Bradford and the young ladies and Samuel all desired to have their love sent in the next letter I wrote to you and think you must have passed the vacation rather unpleasantly. Mother sends love with the rest.

I have the honor to be
Your most Obedient
& most humble Servant
Ralph W. Emerson

54. MS owned by RWEMA; ph. in CUL.

55. The young Robert Treat Paine must have enjoyed some prominence among his companions as the son of the poet and grandson of the signer; and he appears later on in the letters as an amateur astronomer. Mary Paine was doubtless his aunt, who, in 1825, married Elisha Clap, or Clapp. (See Sarah Cushing Paine, *Paine Ancestry,* 1912, p. 51; and Ebenezer Clapp, *The Clapp Memorial,* 1876, pp. 257–258.)

56. Of Professors John Gorham and Jacob Bigelow. The *Boston Daily Advertiser,* Dec. 11, 1816, announces the ceremony.

*M*r E. B. Emerson.

Mother says that if your old pantaloons have grown very thin you had better wear your new ones as soon as it is cold every day as they are warm

I am &c

R

The " Essay on Flattery " is in press but has not come out yet i. e. in the press of my thick cloggy brain heavy as a dozen pounds of Lead therefore I may well say *in press*

Yrs

Its intended author

1817

To Edward Bliss Emerson, Boston, January 5, 1817 [1]

Boston Jan. 5th 1817.

Dear Edward

It is a long time now, since we interchang-[2] letters, for I have neither written nor recieved one since you left home, (no thanks to me I suppose;) but however I have enough to fill my letter, concerning Mr Ogilvie, &c. A week from yesterday (Saturday) Mr Gould told Mr Ogilvie that as Saturday was our usual day of Declamation he should be very happy to see him at school to see us — Mr O. accepted the invitation and offered to speak himself after the boys: accordingly Mr Gould selected 12 or 13 boys to speak and told me that as my " poem " spoken at Exhibition was to the subject he should like to have me speak that — but when I came home I could not find any complete copy and so was obliged to make a new end in the evening to speak the next day — Miss Urania, luckily, being propitious it was finished, approved etc. After the boys had spoken, Mr Ogilvie said a little *de oratore* — he told us, that it was as easy to teach youth dancing by diagrams as Eloquence by lecture; but that it was to be learnt by constant practice — He then went on to the stage and spoke M'clure's peice of " the dismal swamp," " fire fly lamp &c." [3] and he spoke it as if he was indeed the actor that he described; he spoke also a peice from Burke and read much from Marmion, but nothing original — We had the parents of the boys both ladies & gentlemen there, and a great many others — Mother was there. At Cambridge, the collegians subscribed to make Mr O. a present of the ancient Greek Orators bound in twelve Volumes, 5 dolls per Vol, therefore 60 Dolls. for the whole. We have the

1. MS owned by RWEMA; ph. in CUL.

2. Emerson wrote a hyphen at the end of the line but failed to finish the word.

3. The piece was apparently Thomas Moore's " A Ballad. The Lake of the Dismal Swamp." The *Boston Daily Advertiser,* Dec. 31, 1816, advertised the oratorical exhibitions Ogilvie was to give in Boston; and, on Jan. 7, 1817, the same paper recorded the presentation by the Harvard students, in appreciation of his exhibitions in Cambridge.

pleasure now, to have William, more properly his *juniorship,* in the house, but his *business* only allows him to be here in the evenings.

I suppose you think me highly favored for I have been to the Linnæan Museum [4] again and all alone too; Mr Ward a friend of the above mentioned junior lent him his *permit* to go from Mr W. S. Shaw and Will: not feeling inclined to go I took it and went *solus;* staid as long as I wanted, and then, (mirabile dictu!) came away!

But now, alas, my cup of intelligence is exhausted and lo! nothing remaineth – the " grey goose quill " [5] hath performed its office; it hath transmitted to Edward the news of Waldo, and now it shall rest with the quills of other geese

" So ends my catechism "

Yours

– Waldo –

E. B. Emerson.

Charge – Fly, letter, swiftly fly to the dark mansion of Edward chief of – – – the – fair white hair.

Ossianulus.

To Edward Bliss Emerson, Boston, January 8, 1817 [6]

Boston Jan 8th. 1816.

Dear Edward,

Vulcan (lame rascally blacksmith) has dared to attack the fane, the sacred fane of The Muses, the cradle of Science and the Arts, I mean the Latin School – Last Evening the fire was left, not well covered up in Mr Bradford's room and late in the night fire broke out and was discovered but not till much damage had been done. This

4. *The Boston Directory,* 1816, mentions the Society's Room in Boylston Hall and shows that a William S. Shaw was district clerk at the United States Court House.

5. Doubtless borrowed from Byron (*English Bards,* l. 7). The Ossianic passage at the end recalls another current enthusiasm (*cf.* also the letter of Nov. 10, 1816), which might have reached Emerson through Byron's own verse but was too common to be escaped.

6. MS owned by RWEMA; ph. in CUL. Emerson's " 1816 " is an example of the common error in January date lines. The fire in the rooms occupied by the Latin School occurred in the early morning of Jan. 8, 1817, and is recorded in the *Columbian Centinel* of that date and in the *Independent Chronicle* of the following day. It may also be noted that Jan. 8 fell on Wednesday – the day named in the letter – in 1817. For a picture of the building on School St. which housed the Latin School at this time, see Jenks, opposite p. 93.

morning I went to see if my books were safe and found a melancholy picture of desolation where but yesterday I was busy with the rest in pursuing Science &c: the ceiling between Mr Bradfords room and ours was burnt through and I stood and looked down through a chasm of 2 yards width — The whole school was soaking then with water — my books though all there, were touched as I thought, by Neptune or else some of his water gods had been studying them, in no *dry* room, I assure you So you see that by carelessness of Mr Davis (for he was in that room the afternoon and looked to the fire) the B. P. L. G. S. was attacked and damaged by Vulcan.

We boys have gotten a small vacation while it is repairing — all the injury is inside for the outside, except the door (which was burst open) looks just as before. Next Monday (it is now Wednesday) we shall go to school again

Ralph

Mark well! Mother has put into the roll that accompanies this, your two handkerchiefs

I have the honor to be
your excellency's
most obedient
and faithful
Servant
Ralph W. Emerson.

Master Edward B Emerson.
resident at Andover
at M^rs^ H Abbotts!

N. B. Will not the Gods, think you, punish Mr Vulcanus for having hurt *templum Musarum* You know he has got one lame leg *already* for having misdemeaned himself in Coelum and now he'll get another for doing the same in Terra — however I think my letter is a great deal Vulcan*ed* by his elegant name [7]

Yours
Mithologicus
Good bye
R. W. E.
Finis Literarum
Flattery has not come out yet [8]

7. The word is almost illegible.
8. See Dec. 11, 1816.

To Edward Bliss Emerson, Boston, March 7, 1817 [9]

Boston March 7th 1817

Dear Edward,

Today was our Examination and to the joy of us all it is finished at last: we got through it tolerably well " I say it and I think I am something of a judge " for so said the squire's lady in a country town on a matter of opinion Leverett concluded the ceremonies of the day by a *very appropriate discourse* into which were introduced a *few* only of the sentences that graced Young's farewel Oration which you remember were the occasion of those *sublime* lines

* " The first speech of the Exhibition
" Will be spoke by Young the Rhetoricia [10]

Enough of this however. Mother wishes you to write to us whether you are well &c and inform Dr Moody as to the state of your health — But I forgot something in its place — Leverett said in his Sermo that the best scholar in a class was the one loved & esteemed by all — I thought an example very à propos to this was the *affection* existing between Curtis (the best schollar in Class) and myself and for another the great affection existing between the Orator himself and the rest of the school. I fear as it was so stormy a day when you went up that the People of Andover did not come out to meet your Excellency and perform the honours due to your highness and to a member of the " family of Emerson " Be it as it may, when you went up first the sky wept rain at your departure but this time, (owing to the season of the year) it wept snow.

I hope you're well and at Mrs Abbotts, how do all do
For I am very well indeed, and my name is

Waldo

P. S. Mother says that if you do not find a chance to write how your cold does and other things you must write by mail

Ralph W. Emerson

Wont you burn this immediately after reading it that none may see our family pride & oblige goody

brother Ralph.

* Curtis

9. MS owned by RWEMA; ph. in CUL.
10. At the edge of the MS, with no room for the final letter.

To Edward Bliss Emerson, Boston, March 12, 1817[11]

Boston March 1 1817
Wednesday Evening

Dear Edward

I have just recieved your letter by Mrs Abbott, but she has not been here. Tomorrow Morning I shall carry this letter, and what you desire me to send, & see if Mrs A. is to be found. I am reading Pliny's letters translated from Latin by W. Melmoth Esqr. and they are very entertaining. Mr Parkman lent them to me. One of the notes is rather pleasant. It says the Roman Orators were some of them so violent in their gesture that they would walk backwards & forward[s at a] great rate and Flavius Virginius once asked one of these *walking* Orators *Quot millia passuum declamasset* How many *miles* he had delaimed? [12] –

Curtis today with his usual *queer*ness of translating construed Haerebat nebulo,[13] " he stuck in a cloud," whereas it should have been " remained in doubt." Have you found out my transposition for Hellespontus You can make 4 words of the word Amen [14] –

– No news –

– Love as usual –

Vale *   If you transpose Vale you'll make
R W Emerson   a peice of meat

E. B. E.

11. MS owned by RWEMA; ph. in CUL. It is clear, I think, that Emerson intended " 12 " instead of " 1 " in the date line. The first two Wednesdays of Mar., 1817, were the 5th and the 12th, and the first paragraph of the letter of Mar. 19, 1817, refers pretty definitely to the present letter as " written a week ago." The manuscript is slightly mutilated, and I have printed in brackets what was probably torn away with the seal.

12. *The Letters of Pliny the Consul,* Boston, 1809, I, 110–111. The volumes may have been lent to Emerson by the Rev. Francis Parkman, father of the historian and at this time pastor of the New North Church in Boston (*cf.* C. H. Farnham, *A Life of Francis Parkman,* Boston, 1901, p. 3).

13. Cicero, *Philippics,* II, xxix, 74.

14. Various transpositions of " amen " are added in a different hand, probably Edward's.

To Edward Bliss Emerson, Boston? March 19, 1817[15]

March 19 1817

Dear Edward

I send you the enclosed letter as it was written a week ago, when I recieved your letter by Mrs Abbott who did not call here but sent the letter here which did not come here till after she had gone home.

I send you a riddle which you may guess upon for a week or two, for by that time I will send you the Answer if you can not find it out. In studying Greek this week, I put together a sentence which rather abounds in πs I think, it was this — Πολλυκιος/επολεμιζε/πολεμον/και πολλαων/πολιων/απολεσε/καρηνα/.[16] I suppose you can English it without a translation. Now for my Transposition as usual. There is a word in English which transposed bodes no good to your friend: for transposed it is — " Necet Evans," he kills Evans: [17] you must make an English adjective of it. But adieu

Yours

Waldo

E. B. Emerson

To Edward Bliss Emerson, Boston, March 31, 1817[18]

Boston March 31. 1817.

Dear Edward

I have not sent letters for a great while not having had opportunity, though I think I have not been deficient in writing. Thomas Haskins,[19] and Jarvis were here last night (Sunday) and Thomas sends you the enclosed knife. If you please accept the Lady of

15. MS owned by RWEMA; ph. in CUL.

16. The sentence is, of course, striking for the recurrence not only of π but of the syllable πολ. This and the few other Greek sentences or phrases which appear in later letters are reproduced as Emerson wrote them, without accents or breathings and, sometimes, without distinction between the forms of sigma.

17. Edward's friend was doubtless Nathaniel Evans, who entered at Andover in 1816 and left in 1817 (*Biographical Catalogue of . . . Phillips Academy Andover,* 1903, p. 80 and index).

18. MS owned by RWEMA; ph. in CUL.

19. Probably Thomas Waldo Haskins (b. 1801), son of Emerson's maternal uncle Robert Haskins and of his paternal aunt Rebecca Emerson (*cf.* Benjamin Kendall Emerson, *The Ipswich Emersons,* 1900, p. 180).

the lake from me for Aunt T. Haskins [20] has given me another. So theres two presents in one letter I meant to write you a long letter in small hand but time as well as materials fail me so excuse me. All send love for that is very cheap. I wish I could say all send *gold!* that to be sure would be worth havin[g.] [21] But that article is rather scarce at present.

I have the honor to be
Dear Edward
your brothership's
most obedient
and most
excellent brother
E. B. E. Ralph W Emer [22]

P. S. Mother says that if your sickness is gone, before you reach *the-long-ago-sent* powders you may put them away till Mr Sickness calls again.

Yrs &c
R.

To Edward Bliss Emerson, Boston, July 3, 1817 [23]

Boston July 3d 1817

Dear Edward

I suppose you have wondered why I have not written for so long a time; I believe, the want of news, and natural indolence, must be the only excuses I can plead, but now I *must* write since neither of these, I believe, can prove valid. I am very sorry on your account, that

20. For Elizabeth Foxcroft, wife of Emerson's uncle Thomas Haskins, see Sept. 25, 1849.

21. Here a fragment has been torn away with the seal.

22. The name was left unfinished, for lack of room at the edge of the sheet.

23. MS owned by RWEMA; ph. in CUL. The *Columbian Centinel* of July 5, 1817, and *A Narrative of a Tour of Observation, Made during the Summer of 1817, by James Monroe, President of the United States,* Philadelphia, 1818, pp. 94 ff., both give enthusiastic accounts of the great occasion, but young Emerson's narrative is more personal and more frank. He was proud enough to stand for two or three hours in the place of honor allotted to the blue-and-white-clad boys of the Latin School and he takes care to note that " the President made his first bow to our school "; but he seems to have shared the doubts of " most people " about the propriety of participation by a group of schoolgirls, placed opposite the boys, and he ends by confessing what the *Centinel* and *A Narrative* failed to mention – that " People are not so pleased with J. Munroe as they expected."

you cannot see the President, but I suppose you *know* every thing that I *see* relative to him. We have been expecting him for a great while till at last he arrived *yesterday:* Then at sunrise, the American flag was raised at Liberty pole at the Gunhouses and on the top of the State House: at nine the cavalcade met and begun their march to meet his – *Excellency* shall I say or *Presidency*? At the same hour the members of the B. P. L. G. S. met at their *Hall* in School St. drest in blue coats and white trousers and forming two and two according to height, after recieving as a badge of the school an artificial *rose,* half red and half white we attended to the directions of Mr Gould. This rose each of us wore in the left buttonhole of the coat. We then marched off under the direction of the Hon. Marshals, Leverett, Curtis, Loring, and Gardner, who each carried the *scroll* of *office,* tied with red and white ribbands, in conformity to the red and white roses. We then went to the *common* where on one side all the boys of the other schools were arranged, in general drest alike, and we took the *Place* of *Honor* appointed for our school, by the Committee of Arrangements, by the gunhouse with police Officers and Constables behind and side of us. Opposite to the line of boys, (which reached from the Sea Fencible's Gunhouse,[24] to the other end of the Common by Park Street Church) was a line of Girls though not so many most people thought it improper to have girls but there were only the girls of the town schools and one or two private. After being thus arranged we waited *two or three hours* standing up all the time, till after one, when we heard the cannon of the 74 [25] and of the forts giving the signal that the " long expected had come at last " no! not quite *come* but had crossed the line between Boston and Roxbury – The bells rung and having waited some time longer we saw to our great joy the plume of the Captain of the Hussars! While the Hussars and Light Horse, at the head of the Cavalcade, entered the Common the Artillery fired their salute of 18 guns [26] from the hill. When the two horse Companies had entered the common the President and Suite halted and one of the Gentlemen a Marshal I believe, said something to him after which he took off his hat and made a bow which the ladies in the windows and piazzas around answered by curtsies,

24. This seems to have been the old gun house erected on the Common in 1814 and ordered removed soon after the date of this letter (*A Volume of Records Relating to the Early History of Boston,* 1908, pp. 122, 247–248, and 257–258).

25. The " Independence," according to *A Narrative,* p. 96.

26. If *A Narrative* is correct, the number of guns fired as a presidential salute was not the same at each town visited.

waving their handkerchiefs &c and the crowd by waving their hats huzzaing &c &c Then they entered the Common and the President made his first bow to our school who all took off their hats and cheered with the [27] He was mounted on an elegant horse which belo[nged to the] Circus sent to him by the Committee of Arr. [An im]mense cavalcade followed with chaise and carriages behind. He went through the Com. to the Exchange [28] where after the addresses were delivered the company dined at *six* – People are not so pleased with J. Munroe as they expected but you will be tired if I scrawl any longer so I must bid you good bye with love from all. Yrs with affection

Ralph.

E. B. Emerson Esqr

To William Emerson, Boston, September 13, 1817 [29]

Boston September 13th 1817 –

Dear Will.$^{\underline{m}}$

I was so much inclined to ruffle your prosaical temper, by writing to you in *verse,* that I begun a letter in *rugged rhyme,*[30] but still enough *poetical,* to put the *Parson* a-scolding at the inapplicant, time-wasting Ralph: but upon maturer deliberation, and in a more charitable mood, I determined to disturb you with only an *extract,* or perhaps *prospectus* of the contemplated *evil; which* will follow. In pursuance, however, of one of your parting requests just to show you that I respected you a *little,* I took the Rambler out of the Library, yesterday, but whether I *read* it or not, still is a subject of doubt. I took at the same time, "Continuation of Russell's Modern Europe," by Coote; [31] this as I took it out for my own edification, and by my own recommendation, I think more likely to be read, than the other. I begun it last night and have read a quarter of it, though a large work. There are

27. Portions of the text have been torn away with the seal. The words in brackets below are conjectural for the same reason.

28. The Exchange Coffee House (*A Narrative,* p. 96).

29. MS owned by RWEMA; ph. in CUL.

30. "Extract from the rhyming letter" follows, according to promise, but I have not found the earlier version. Apparently these verses did not go entirely unappreciated, for this notation appears on the back: "Judgment of Mr. Ripley, 'Oh! that Ralph's a clever fellow, a clever fellow!'" The superscription contains the direction "Care of Rev. S. Ripley," the uncle in whose school William Emerson was teaching.

31. Emerson may have read this in Vol. V of *The History of Modern Europe* as published at Philadelphia in 1815.

400 French books added to the library [32] and 300 English – probably on account *of my patronage!* –

Oh I forgot to say anything about your letter, but now that I *do* think of it I believe it is of *no consequence,* and for a man of my avocations to waste a line on what was of *no consequence* would be very absurd – Edward had gone to Andover before it reached me –

And now I suppose your eyes begin to turn from the paper as you see the following " Extract from the rhyming letter or letter in rhyme, which was begun to be written, or inscribed on paper, to W. E. assistant *Schoolmaster* in Waltham, County of – " I forget what.

William does thy frigid soul,
The charms of poetry deny,
And think thy heart beyond controul,
Of each Parnassian Deity?

— —

This I suspect from that cold look,
Quenching like ice Apollo's fire,
With which each vagrant verse you took,
When offer'd from my humble lyre.

———

* Not that in truth I mean to say,
I ever had a lyre – not I –
Rhymers you know have got a way,
To Tell a *bumper,* alias *lie.* –

– I love quotations – Dr Gibbs [33] –
Or some one else perhaps – has said,
– Poets have leave to publish fibs,
And t'is a portion of their trade –

— —

But to return – ti's wrong to say,
That I should not have leave to write,
My maxim is – write while it's day, –
For soon, forsooth it will be night,

———

* The digression which begins here does not end in this " Extract "

32. Presumably this was the Boston Athenæum, which Emerson's father had helped to found. A somewhat detailed account of the libraries in Boston and Cambridge at this time is to be found in *The North American Review* for Sept., 1817.

33. Perhaps the name means nothing, though Emerson may have had in mind the Dr. James Gibbs whose translations from *Psalms* Swift had ridiculed (*Swiftiana,* London, n.d., II, 219–221).

That is – poor Ralph must versify,
Through College * *like a thousand dru[ms]*
But when well *through* then then oh [my][34]
The dark dull *night* of *Business* comes

While this my letter you peruse,
Frown no long-faced *apostrophe,*
Dare not to blame the wayward muse,
Nor scowl the *scrof'lous* brow at me –

x x x x x x

I think I'll torment you no more with bad rhyme, bad sense &c especially as my paper does not promise to support me through another verse, and my pen is none of the best – So I leave you to your cogitations, only asking you if you read as far as this, to burn immediately this nonsense, from your *truly* affectionate brother,

Ralph =

* An apt similee, *quoted* you know!

To Edward Bliss Emerson, Boston, September 24, 1817[35]

Boston Sept. 24th 1817.

Dear Ned, I promis'd some time since,[36] you know,
That my next letter should all *news* forego,
And wholly fill'd by " sentiment " and *taste*
On *common* stuff should, no *black fluid,* waste:
Then why should not Apollo fill the sheet
And I repair to his Castalian seat?
Yes, I'm resolved, in measur'd verse to write –
But stop – the subject? – any thing that's right.

Now search the world of feeling and of Worth,
Friendship, or Thought, Wit, Solitude,[37] or Mirth, –
What shall my subject be = Ah, one bright form –
Comes dancing forth, while gathers round the storm

34. The bracketed portions of this stanza are conjectural, as the manuscript has been mutilated by the opening of the seal.

35. MS owned by RWEMA; ph. in CUL.

36. Perhaps in a letter now lost.

37. Emerson seems to have written somewhat earlier a poem on " Solitude," and in after years he recalled the commendatory verses it won from the usher (*Journals,* VIII, 442).

Yes t'is sweet *Hope* [38] — I know her by the smiles
That banish doubt and each sad fear beguiles
Though o'er her head the Tempest-Genius lowers,
And Mirth affrighted leaves her fragrant bowers
Yet where the clouds of mis'ry thickest rise,
Thither lov'd Hope all fair & fearless flies
And points her finger upwards to the sky,
And tells of bliss above the storm's dark mystery
Yes, Edward, we shall find as on we go,
In life's all-varying scenes of Joy, and woe,
That when the clouds of Sorrow and Distress
The thickest join in Life's dull wilderness,
Then Hope is strongest — as the stars of Heaven,
Which brighter grow, as darker grows, the even:
Thus Providence ordains its wise decrees;
And each reflecting mind its wisdom sees
For without Hope, what comfort could we feel
When stern Affliction darts its angry steel;
Without Hopes constant unremitting ray,
That breaks the clouds and gives a glimpse of day.
And they who mark the passions of the mind,
That Hope clings fondest, always they will find,
When every other inmate, stands aghast,
As swans sing sweetest when they breathe their last.

And in the Christian's breast what hope so strong,
As that which animates the martyr's song?
The hope of life *eternal*. Good or ill —
Whate'er his prospects, — *this* upholds him still,
This bears him up beneath Oppression's rod,
With this strong faith he dares to die for God.
Were Hope excluded from the breast of man
Oh where is he would dare the Roman ban *?

* Alluding to the thousands who have suffered death for daring not to agree with Pope and other leaders of Roman superstition

38. What follows owes something, I think, to Thomas Campbell, though there are not many verbal resemblances. According to Cabot, I, 44, William H. Furness remembered that a favorite piece of Emerson's for declamation at the Latin School was "The Pleasures of Hope." There seem to be also some echoes of Pope's *An Essay on Man.*

Where will you search for him, whose daring soul,
Could rise superior to man's proud control,
And dare (uninfluenc'd by hope) defy,
Death's pointed dart, and Superstition's eye?
Yet such there *have been* – It was Hope within,
That bade them die, ere they'd commit a sin:
They knew that *they* who raging sought their life,
Could only kill the body in the strife,
That when their souls the feeble frame had fled,
* Their arm was powerless, and their vengeance dead.
Thus on they went regardless what befel,
So [tha]t [39] they kept the path of duty well;
In this conviction firm, they onward sped,
Thro' fears, and fields with kindred slaughter red.

Then let us hail fair Hope and though Despair,
In placid frenzy tear her demon hair,
Yet hope all kind at distance still appears,
And bids new joy smile thro' the glistening tears.

Edward, farewell; my theme in verse is done,
And though in clouds still hides his beams, the Sun
Yet I will sit and hope a better day,
When some kind friend this letter will convey
to you from your afft brother
Waldo.

Dr Kast and family [40] are on the way from Europe in the Galen. My vacation is lengthened to the 10th of October. Write soon *your* " sentimental " In this I see one fault already in the grammar, but remember I have not written any copy of it beforehand. Waldo to Edward.

* " Their " in this line refers to the persecutors

39. The letters in brackets were almost completely torn away with the seal.
40. See the letter of Oct. 1 and 5 following.

To Edward Bliss Emerson, Boston, October 1 and 5, 1817 [41]

Boston October 1st 1817

Dear brother,

By my date I *see* & by my feelings I *know* that warm weather is leaving us fast; and the cold frosts of Autumn are preparing the way for the dreary reign of Winter!!! Ah cold winter! Today is almost as cold as December.

Yesterday I recieved your epistolary couplet,[42] the one Sept 19th and the other 21st; Mother and the family think that you did no great honour to your *filial politeness,* by writing the *first* letter, after your arrival, and then the *second,* both to your *brother;* whilst your *mother was only mentioned, by way of filling up, in the PostScript.* We could not forbear this stricture notwithstanding all praised the goodness of the *writing* as well as ease of the letter dated 19th You know, Edward, (as I read last night) the cup of pleasure is always mixed with wormwood — oh Sad! — // //

October 5th. — Sabbath Eve. I yesterday recieved a long letter from the Senior from Waltham [43] and it is so humorous (though you stare at my saying *humorous* from his Deaconship) that I wish I could shew it to you — But I have forgot to answer your letter; as to the "Sentimental" you, no doubt, have recd *mine* but let me tell you, sir, I am in no way disposed to dispense with *yours* as I expect from it a fund of ideas enough to overstock *my* brain for a great while — but stop — in real earnest I wish to hear very much from you in the "sentimental" line for the improvement of both yourself and me. As to writing you some of the

41. MS owned by RWEMA; ph. in CUL. Excerpts I–II are in *The Atlantic,* LIX, 667 (May, 1887), and in Cabot, I, 48–49.

42. Edward, as a younger brother, seems to have been willing to admire Emerson's experiments in verse and to try his own hand now and then at epistolary couplets. On this same Oct. 1 Edward again wrote in verse — this time an account of a typical day of his life at Andover.

43. William, about to enter upon his senior year at Harvard, was probably helping again in the Ripley school, while, as his letter to his mother dated Waltham, Oct. 3, 1817, shows (MS owned by Dr. Haven Emerson), he was looking for a school of his own. No doubt it was partly because of the responsibility he felt as the oldest son of a widow that he was serious and conscientious beyond his years. It is clear from a number of the letters that he was wont to reprove Ralph for wasting time in composing what must have seemed very unprofitable verses. For some years the letters show a good deal of impatience with such admonishments, but the young poet evens the score by aiming at his critic such epithets as "his Deaconship," "Parson," and "Grand Mogul."

"*long* old fashioned letters with *poetry*" part of that request I am now granting by thinning my lines to write a long letter but as to interspersing it with poetry alias nonsense I have given you enough in my last letter to prevent the necessity of my troubling you with any more. The Grammar we want *very much* : twice you have given intelligence of your *intent* to send it, but the Gentleman himself has not yet made his appearance no more than Uncle Kast [44] and family = an apt similee! # Wm Farnham [45] has returned from his voyage to Russia. All the time he was there it was day nor did the Sun once go down as you know is usual in those *very* northern Regions all the summer. — As to intelligence, we have none here but what is *melancholy* [46] — Mr Prentiss, the minister so lately ordained at Charlestown, is *dead* of the Typhus Fever and prevailing disorder — Dr McKean is going a voyage for health from which it is very much feared he will *never return:* — and Mr Thatcher was spoken of today in prayer as if it were doubtful if he be *yet alive* — Mr Lowell and Mr Channing are both feeble especially the *former.* These melancholy prospects among the ministry together with the deaths and sicknesses everywhere make a gloomy appearance in Massachusetts ~~~~~~~ but cold weather brings with its evils the truly comfortable hopes of relief from this distressing calamity — So that I shall wish the approach of the cold weather I was so bitterly apostrophising in the commencement of my letter — but my letter is long enough and written at times *different* enough for me to change my opinion in the course of it # But now to close my mournful Catalogue of evil Mother has heard

44. Dr. Thomas Kast was the husband of Emerson's aunt Hannah Haskins. He was now expected to become a boarder in the Emerson home (*cf.* Oct. *c.* 24, 1817).

45. Probably either Emerson's uncle William Farnham, widower of Hannah Bliss Emerson, or the son of that William Farnham, born in 1799 and named after his father (*Vital Records of Newburyport Massachusetts,* 1911, I, 135). *The Boston Directory,* 1818, lists a William Farnham, mariner.

46. According to the *New-England Palladium,* Oct. 7, 1817, Thomas Prentiss, pastor of the Second Congregational Church in Charlestown, died on the morning of Oct. 5, 1817. Joseph McKean, the Harvard professor of rhetoric and oratory, voyaged vainly in search of health, dying at Havana in the following March (*Coll. Mass. Hist. Soc.,* 2d series, VIII, 164). *The Boston Directory,* 1816, names Samuel C. Thacher as pastor of the New South Church, and the *Columbian Centinel* of Sept. 20, 1817, tells of his sickness and foreign travels. Charles Lowell, father of the poet and critic, was pastor of West Church in Boston; and William Ellery Channing, forerunner of the Transcendentalists, was at the Federal Street Church. It is not strange that the son of a Boston preacher and the descendant of a long line of New England preachers who was himself looking toward the ministry should have recorded in his letters the ordinations, marriages, and deaths — and sometimes even the sermons — of the ministers whose names must have been familiar to all members of the family.

that Uncle Robert has *broken* his *wrist* # and Mother has no boarders # There I have put enough of misfortune to sink my letter, though of paper, any where; but now [unhappily][47] I cannot remember any *pleasant* news to balance it. [Ce]rtainly I know not where to look for any thing containing [i]ntelligence pleasant enough to raise spirits so much depressed by melancholy events. [I]Next Friday, you know my College life begins " Deo volente," [48] and I hope and trust will begin with determined and ardent pursuit of real knowledge that will raise me high in the Class while in Coll. and qualify me well for stations of future usefulness = Aunt Betsey is very much grieved she says that I go to *Cambridge* instead of *Providence* – you guess the reason[I] = Eliza Haskins is at our house a week who with Mother and boys join in love to you # [II]I hope going to *Cambridge* will not prevent some future time my being as good a minister as if I came all *Andovered* from *Providence* [II] So burn up this letter but remember its aff^t^ writer Ralph –

I am not at all satisfied with this letter, so renew my request to burn it; but write to *Mother,* and *then* to me and though I shall not expect to recieve the *first* letter, yet hope for *one,* and you doubtless will have a long letter soon, dated Cambridge, from

Ralph # Mater dixit, send down the greenish
Edward B Emerson = clothes for your *eccentrick* brother Robert

To fill up my epistle I believe I will just put words down so as to say wrote a *full letter* and so if you are a mind to read loud you will find it as the poet says " Sonum sine sensu " but my purpose is fulfilled by seeing my letters touch the bottom R W E –

To Edward Bliss Emerson, Cambridge, October *c.* 24, 1817 [49]

Cambridge October 24th or 5 or 6

Dear Edward,

I have but a few moments to write since C Jarvis has just come in to tell me that there is a person going from his room

47. Conjectural. One or two words have been mutilated by the seal, and the bracketed letters in the following sentence are missing for the same reason.

48. The broadside *Catalogue of the Officers and Students of Harvard University, Cambridge, October, 1817,* duly lists Ralph W. Emerson as a freshman residing at " The President's."

49. MS owned by RWEMA; ph. in CUL. The contrast of the college day with the Boston day makes it probable that this letter was written soon after Emerson first entered Harvard; and the superscription to Edward at Andover could not have been written, I think, as late as October 24, 1818. The day of the month could not have been the 26th, as there would have been no classes on Sunday. Friday, the 24th, seems the most likely day.

immediately after Commons and now, we have been to prayers and I am only waiting for the Recitation bell to go in to Prof. Brazer. My studies, (of which you know I promised not to be as silent as [some][50] folks, and am now going to plague you with the rehears[al h] ot & heavy) are in Latin Livy,[51] Grotius, &c in Greek, Majora, and in English, History and Rhetorick. The College day [52] seems about the fifth part

50. The bracketed portions of this paragraph are conjectural. A part of the manuscript has been torn away with the seal.

51. That Livy made some impression on the young reader may be gathered from Dec. 30, 1826. Grotius's *De Veritate Religionis Christianae* is given as a freshman text in the Harvard catalogue of 1820, the first, at least during Emerson's time, to give the course of instruction. An edition had appeared in Boston in 1809, and it is clear from William Emerson's letter quoted below that the *De Veritate* was assigned to freshmen in 1814. The " Majora " was doubtless the Ἀνάλεκτα Ἑλληνικὰ Μείζονα. *Sive Collectanea Græca Majora,* with notes by Andreas Dalzel. The second American edition was published at Cambridge in 1811. The catalogue of 1820 shows that the third Cambridge edition of this work was then used by the freshman class.

52. Some further light on the kind of adventures that were likely to fill a freshman's day at Harvard about this time may be had from a letter written by Emerson's brother William to his mother on Oct. 1, 2, 3, and 4, 1814 (MS owned by Dr. Haven Emerson):

" Cambridge, October 1, 1814, at N? *3* Hollis.

" My dear mother,

Being now pretty thoroughly settled, I sit down to give you a circumstantial account of the 2 or 3 first days of my College life. I arrived here about 10 o'clock yesterday morning, and found that the furniture of the last occupants was still in the room Indeed it was 3 o'clock before the room was cleared, and I could get into my study. About half past 12 o'clock, the dinner bell rung, and we were ushered into a hall in the new chapel, where we had the pleasure to see others eating, for some time, before we ourselves were employed. At last, however, having obtained some food, we made a very good dinner upon roast-beef and potatoes, (which, by the bye, we were obliged to peal ourselves,) with boiled rice and moderate sauce. After dinner I settled my things, but was obliged to put my Pembroke table into the study, because my other was too wide for the door. At 6 o'clock in the afternoon, we went to Prayers, where the President made a short prayer, then read a chapter in the bible, and closed the service by a long prayer. Immediately after, we went to supper, where we had 8 young men to a table, a biscuit apiece, two Coffee-pots to a table, a bowl of sugar, pitcher of milk, and half a lump of butter. About 8 o'clock in the evening, (for the Sophomores always attempt to trick the Freshmen,) some of the Sophomores dressed themselves in cloaks and surtouts, went into a room round a large table, darkened it by a shade to the lamp, that their faces might not be recognized, sent their messengers all round to the Freshmen, to deceive them. A recital of my adventures will be a good sample of the rest. James Blanchard and myself went to see W D Lamb a few minutes; we were scarcely seated, when some one knocked at the door, and enquired if Mr. Lamb was at home: being answered in the affirmative, he said, that the government had sent, and were waiting, for him. Lamb rose, hesitated, at length took his hat, and walking to the door, looked at the fellow, and asked him, " What government is this "? The Sophomore,

of a Boston day! because it is so cut up in parcels = at six in the morning the bell rings for prayers, (at which, by the way, I did not get up this morng till after the second bell had begun to toll,) then about half an hour after prayers the bell rings for Recitation, which bell I am

---

finding we knew the trick, bowed and retired. Upon returning from Lamb's room, Jenks called me, and told me the government wished me to follow him directly to them: I looked as calmly at him as I could, and asked, " Who personates the President? " He smiled, and went off.

" We went to bed about 9 o'clock, but there was such a continual passing up and down stairs, that I was kept awake till about half past 10 o'clock, when, as we were nearly asleep, we were very much terrified by hearing our windows break by wholesale, as we ascertained in the morning that there were 8 panes broken, and 2 cracked. A pint of water was poured into the crack of our door, when we went to lock it for the night; and our door was kicked at, about a dozen times every quarter of an hour. This morning I obtained an order for them to be mended from Mr. Cogswell, our particular tutor.

" Sunday Evening, Oct. 2.

" My troubles are not over yet. Last night, after I was asleep, there were two more windows broken: But James B. was sadly treated. He lent his hammer a minute, and wanting it again, went for it; when he returned, he was just entering the room, when he received the entire contents of a pail of water from the top of the stairs; so thoroughly was he wet, that he was obliged to change every article of his clothing. Today and yesterday we attended commons in the morning, and fared the same as at the supper mentioned above.

" We attended Dr. Holmes' meeting today, and he preached this morning . . . Today I had a lesson set me in " Grotius on the truth of the Christian Religion. He in the first place, proves that there is a God, and answers objections to this truth; secondly, that there can be but one God; 3d, that all perfection resides in him; 4th, that he is an infinite being, 5th, that he is eternal, omnipotent, omniscient, and supremely good; which is the end of my exercise. His arguments are weighty, and he writes in elegant Latin.

" Monday Evening.

" I recited my lesson in Grotius this morning. We attended Mr. Frothingham at 8 o'clock this morning, and were divided for the purpose of studying rhetoric. At 11, we attended Mr. Phillips, who set an Exercise in Mathematics. This afternoon we recited from Livy's Rom[an] History. This preface is the hardest piece of latin [I] ever met with.

" Tuesday mor[ning]

" Last night there were 2 pitchers of water poured through my broken windows. I am in a great hurry as Blanchard sets off immediately. Love to aunt, Ralph, Edward, whom I expect Thursday, and Charles. Please send up 25 cts. as a fee to Regents freshman, with a pair of scissors to trim my Lamp; and a letter would be very acceptable.

" Your affectionate and
respectful son,
W Emerson "

Interesting testimony by a classmate, relating to Emerson's own life at Harvard, is to be found in William Bancroft Hill, " Emerson's College Days," *The Literary World,* XI, 180–181 (May 22, 1880).

now expecting then Commons and the bearer goes directly after so I must cut short by telling you Uncle Kast boards with Mother all are well I have rec,[d] the Grammar and will write again soon as sure as my name is Ralph –

To Edward Bliss Emerson, Cambridge, December *c.* 20? 1817 [53]

Cambridge Dec 1817 –

Dear Edward

Only think of my condescension! Here am I a son of Alma Mater &c addressing a — — a what? Why a member of an academy – oh wonderful I admire my humility!!! # Enough of this – I have been wondering at the great Series of events which have carried W[m] to Kennebunk and of course the name took the attention of a rhymer and the melodious harmony of it induced me to try it in song e.g.

W[m] has ta'en his box & trunk
And set off by land for Kennebunk
He went not in a chinese junk
So probably will not be sunk
In former times a travelling Monk
Would take with him a brown-bread hunk
Bill, in politer times has slunk
(With lesser crusts but greater spunk)
Off to thy town sweet Kennebunk!
and I may add
Remarkable as bloody Bunk-
er hill in Charleston fair!

The muse, you see, makes poor work; but still it may set your reasoning powers to work to discover how it is possible W[m] should not be sunk, on *dry land.* I'm going to write to the subject of the ten lines above, as soon as I can – to whom at this moment perhaps some little lisping

53. MS owned by RWEMA; ph. in CUL. The date is apparently either a little earlier than that of the following letter or the same, as Emerson's assertion "I'm going to write to the subject of the ten lines above, as soon as I can" seems to refer to the letter of Dec. 23, apparently his first to William at Kennebunk. I do not know the date of William's arrival at Kennebunk; but his letter of Jan. 1 and 10, 1818, addressed to his mother (MS owned by Dr. Haven Emerson), was pretty clearly not the first to be dispatched homeward, though it may have been begun first. The word "Kennebunk" has been written on the present letter between the heading and the salutation, apparently by another hand, probably Edward's; and "K" appears several times in the margins.

stripling is approaching with "Mr Emerson may I go out I want to[54] !" – "By no means" exclaims the *fantastic* pedagogue –

And now, friend, I should have divers matters to tell thee of if – if – I knew of any thing or sundry things that were worth telling and moreover as you requested me to burn, I mean, to beg you to burn each miserable scrawl I send please do it to this poor thing the only recommendation is that is short and brings love from

R W E

to

E B E #

I shall try to send Playfairs Geometry[55] with this tedious epistle –

And so!

R W E

To William Emerson, Cambridge, December 23, 1817[56]

Cambridge Dec 23rd 1817 –

Dear Wm

Your letters, if you have written any, had not reached Boston last Saturday and Mother was very anxious to hear from her son of School-keeping-memory – Charles went to the Post Office while I was there – in vain. It may be that all wish to take observations on Nature since all appear to be interested in the first essay of the Kennebunk Pedagogue – However that may be your good chum[57] does not appear less solicitous than the rest since he exclaims "By grace" and "the deuce" when I told him we had not heard; – by the way, Mr Goddard was scraped very handsomely the other Friday at short intervals along through the melancholy thread-bare – "These as they change" &c of which he spoke the whole – My feet were still.

There is one thing I have been treasuring up this long while to tell you in my first letter, that is, an instance of the good spirit of the Fresh-

54. Word mutilated; all but what seems to be a part of one letter has been torn out of the MS.

55. The second American edition of John Playfair's *Elements of Geometry* was published at Boston in 1814.

56. MS owned by RWEMA; ph. in CUL.

57. Warren Goddard is listed in the catalogue of Oct., 1817, as William Emerson's classmate and roommate. The scraping doubtless signified vigorous disapproval of Goddard's recitation of Thomson's "A Hymn on the Seasons," lines which must have been too familiar to the college boys of that time.

man Class – Dinsmore [58] had a new plaid cloke when he returned from Thanksgiving which was stolen two days afterward. As he could ill afford it the next day he found a note in his room pinned on his Geometry begging him to accept twenty Dollars from his classmates to repair his loss – A much greater sum would have been subscribed if the paper had been carried more about for only about 20 knew of it till after it was over. So you must not speak disrespectfully of the Freshman Class – Mother says she fears you will lose your cloke before you return. // How suit the *cool shades* of Ken. with your warmer soul? Among the many sympathies arising upon you all I fear is to see you soon packing "bock agen" hissed or snowballed out of town perhaps, without pleasure & what's more without *pay*. These are my fears not my wishes but "I've heard say" that many a poor youth has been stript of his school by refusing to speak out of school to those scholars older than himself # You see I love to advise my young friends. I hope the "Prize Dissertation" [59] goes on and flourishes on Homer & Virgil – I still have a turn of the venturesome, I have written a couple of pages Ergo, Beware,. However I've wished often that the subject was Virgil's first Æneid as that must be easier –

All are well as usual not excepting the Doctor who grunts a little at Cold Weather

Remember us & write soon to

Ralph

To

Wm Emerson Esqr

A B Cedarian – Kennebunk

To Mary Moody Emerson, Boston, *c.* 1817 [60]

To Miss M. M. [Emers]on residing at the Mansion of Rev. Dr. Ripley in Concord, Mass. –

58. Othniel Dinsmore, who graduated in 1822, had entered college with Emerson in 1817 (MS *Records of the College Faculty*, IX, 121–122, in HCL).

59. Probably an essay to be submitted for a Bowdoin prize.

60. MS owned by RWEMA; ph. in CUL. The introductory sentence, the inside address, the verses, and all the names at the end seem to be in the same hand, which I believe to be Emerson's of late 1817 or early 1818. During his school terms, Edward would have been absent at Andover, so that his name would naturally not appear; and William, who might well have been at Waltham or, early in 1818, at Kennebunk, would probably not have joined in such a juvenile enterprise even had he been at home. L. Farnham is doubtless Emerson's cousin Louisa, who married Orville Dewey in 1820; and S. Bradford was probably young Samuel Bradford, mentioned earlier. The order of the names and the fact that Emerson often wrote similar rimed letters

This petition humbly sheweth
That we the signers undersigned
Sound both in body and in mind
Write this petition unto you
And may it meet your kind review.
And first beg leave the case to state
And Lawer [61]-like the facts relate —
Then, first, we find your keen survey
Is wanting to begin the day
For much we need your wakeful eyes
To see that we by *seven* rise
And when *well up* we need your care
To take the Moderaters chair
And with your peace-commanding voice
To still the children's *morning* noise.
But needless it would be to tell
These reasons which you know so well
In short your presence much we need
Our whole concerns and things to speed —
This being then our true condition
We briefly show the short petition
That you would now from Concord come
And in the mail stage hasten home
Your humble petitioners
are, Madam your most obt servants
R. W. Emerson
R. B. Emerson
C. C. Emerson
L. Farnham
S. Bradford

---

make it probable that he was sole author. At the top of the sheet is this: "I thought you would like to see the following lines which I found in one of Aunts drawers —" Obviously this introductory sentence was written after — though I think not long after — the letter proper. The superscription to Miss Rebecca Haskins, Waterford, Me., through which heavy lines have been drawn, may indicate that the sheet of paper was a discarded wrapper. "Miss MME" appears in larger hand above the Haskins address, and across the end of the superscription Mary Moody Emerson herself has written a somewhat cryptic endorsement, which I transcribe thus: "Mori memento Let those who in life's prime do not foresee the useless day!" The bracketed letters in the first line were torn from the original MS with the seal.

61. The misspelling is surprising in a letter obviously composed with more than common effort.

1818

To William Emerson, Boston, January *c.* 2, 1818 [1]

Boston Jan 1817 –

Dear W$^{\underline{m}}$

If I were aunt Mary, I should tell you how auspicious an omen it was to your future happiness that you had commenced the year 1818 in the " delightful task – &c," in the mind-expanding air, & piety-inspiring regions of Kennebunk – but being as I am less enthusiastic less scientifick Ralph I am glad to find that the year commences with M^{r} W$^{\underline{m}}$'s *earning an honest livelihood* by turning village school-master " the wonder of the swains " " that one small head could carry all he knew – " [2] You see how humble my ideas are in comparison with those of – what Uncle Daniel [3] calls " the etherial incorporeal supernatural immortal soul " of aunt Mary who says in her letter to mother speaking of K. " there repose the ashes of some of my honoured ancestors [4] – who died triumphing in the faith." —//— I am going to commence *petty* school-master, at Waltham honoured by having called forth the first school-keeping genius of yourself) on the 7th for the remaining 5 weeks. # yesterday I carried your boots to the brig Hesper for Kennebunk, directed to H McCulloch Esqr so that if you do not recieve them before this arrives you had better inquire for them.

1. MS owned by RWEMA; ph. in CUL. The correct year is given in the first sentence, and there is much other evidence of both the year and the approximate day of the month. A note by Emerson's mother which follows on the same sheet is dated Feb. 2, 1818, and explains that Ralph left this unfinished and that she would have sent it earlier if she had seen it. Emerson's statement that he is to begin teaching at Waltham on the 7th shows the date is very early in January; and the reference to the brig " Hesper," which cleared for Kennebunk on Jan. 3 (*Boston Patriot,* Jan. 5, 1818), seems to leave only the first three days of that month as possible dates. The letters of Jan. 20, and Feb. 6? 1818, give accounts of his teaching and of his earnings during this college vacation, which was to end " 3 weeks from the 24th, of January."

2. Goldsmith, *The Deserted Village,* ll. 214–216.

3. Daniel Bliss Ripley, who appears in later letters.

4. The Moodys lived at what is now Kennebunkport (Charles C. P. Moody, *Biographical Sketches,* 1847, pp. 129 ff.).

To Edward Bliss Emerson, Waltham, Massachusetts, January 20, 1818 [5]

Waltham Jan 20th 1818

Dear Edward,

I forget whether I have told you I was going to Waltham to keep Uncle's School – but even so it is – & here I am surrounded by my 14 disciples, (Pythagoras &c called their scholars disciples I believe, & modesty forbids me to say how far superiour I think myself to Pythagoras) every little while calling out, Silence! for school is just begun ie. ½ after 8 – but stop I must hear them read – Hem –

Well I have done hearing them and will therefore continue my *epistle.* It is one of the finest days of this fine winter and puts me all in tune for one of my writing fits, or else I should not be scribbling at this rate = Last friday I recieved your letter & the enclosed *memoranda* – Did I ever recieve a letter from you without five or six inclosed lines on as many peices of paper for which too, there is almost always room on the main letter You know my natural inclination to scold & so must excuse me for picking oddities. As to your list of letters I believe ad [6] of which you have made 34 – I send you my list & you will see if you pursue it *systematically* you will find more and discover them easier than by a mixed irregular *anyhow* way of transposing. And now you wish me to send you a poem you have not read what is it that has inclined you lately so much to the poetick ≡ I suppose it is like some other diseases contagious. I will try to send you the third Canto of Childe Harolde which though you have seen I doubt if you have read = but is the most beautiful poetry in my humble opinion that I ever read instance the Stanza " The sky is changed " [7] – &c You have probably heard of the domestic circumstances of Lord Byron that he has separated from his wife &c though he probably was much attached to her yet being a great libertine he introduced it is said two *mistresses* to his table, which Lady Byron could not endure, nor is it strange that she should immediately have ordered her carriage, as she did, & left him for her fathers house = since that, they have not met on which account he wrote that beautiful peice – " Fare thee well – & if forever – " &c which if you can obtain – certainly read. And now that I have tired you out

5. MS owned by RWEMA; ph. in CUL.

6. Left blank in the MS.

7. Stanza xcii.

with my poetical bloterature [8] please to excuse my not complying with your requests as readily as I could wish on account of being at Waltham from whence I have no advantages to send to Andover except *via* Boston — a roundabout course — my Vacation ends 3 weeks from the 24th, of January at which time I *must* have the Geometry as I cannot do without it = by one of the Collegians, as Osgood, if possible if not, by the stage.* I will try borrow Clarke's Homer [9] of Uncle or of some classmate. I will remember the dictionary = Uncle & Aunt Robert Haskins are in Boston = I have not seen them. [10] now I have nearly filled my paper but your request so please burn my letter — but if you burn this testimonial of his affection still remember your affectionate brother —

Ralph

Edward B Emerson

* Pathetick! [11]

To William Emerson, Waltham, Massachusetts, February 6? 1818 [12]

[I]Waltham, Feb. 7th, 1818

Well, my dear brother, I am *here* safe & sound as yet unmuzzled & unsnowballed[I] — It is Friday night and I have just recieved verbal message from mother that if I can get a letter to her, before Monday, she will send it to you — desirable object! — Boys are gone to bed — I am tired — let this be my excuse for sending thin half sheet again. — When in Boston I begun a long letter to you, but came here before I could finish it.[13] Thank you for your kind, scolding, long, letter — thank you kindly — to pay you in some weak measure for which I am " setting *to* " head & foot, heart & hand to fill up my three pages with — — no matter what, if not nonsense [II]Since I have been here I have learned to skate,

8. That is, perhaps, " blaterature," coined from " blateration " or " blatter," in contrast with " literature."

9. The first twelve books of *Homeri Ilias Græce et Latine,* London, 1729, were edited by Samuel Clarke, and the remaining twelve by his son of the same name.

10. The two gaps in this sentence are due to mutilation caused, as often, by the opening of the seal.

11. It is possible that the somewhat equivocal mark I have printed as an asterisk in the body of the letter was not so intended. Perhaps there was an asterisk on one of the fragments torn away with the seal.

12. MS owned by RWEMA; ph. in CUL. Feb. 7 fell on Saturday in 1818, so that Friday was the 6th. Excerpts I–V appear, with some changes, in Cabot, I, 67–69.

13. The letter of Jan. *c.* 2, 1818.

rhymed, written & read, besides my staple commodity — schoolkeeping & have earned me a new coat![II] Ah my boy! that's the dasher!!! [III]wear it tomorrow to Mr Gore's to dinner by invitation from King[14][III] — his birthday — Oh W^m^ what makes you grin now? — have not I guessed right? Now I'll be sober on the next page —

[IV]I did hope to have my " merces " in cash — I envied you bringing your 5 Doll. Bills to mother; but Mr R said I needed a coat & sent me to the tailor's though I should rather have worn my old coat out first & had the *money* — mean-minded me! — Just before I came from Boston Mr Frothingham sent Mother a note containing 20 Dolls. given him by a *" common friend "* for her with a promise of continuing to her 10$ Quarterly for the use of her sons in College; [15] not stipulating the *time* of continuance At this time this assistance was peculiarly acceptable, you know. It is in this manner, from the charity of others, Mother never *has,* — & from our future exertions I hope never *will be in want.* — It appears to me the happiest earthly moment my most sanguine hopes can picture, if it should ever arrive, to have a home, comfortable & pleasant, to offer to mother, in some feeble degree to repay her the cares & woes & inconveniences she has so often been subject to on our account alone.[IV] In this you *doubtless* sympathize as I often have heard you express your *intentions* on that subject though I think more & better than you will find realized.

I think your present adventure would have been far more profitable if you had a less expensive distance to go. [V]To be sure, after talking at this rate I have done nothing myself — but then I've less faculty and age than most poor collegians — But when I am out of College I will (Deo volente) study divinity & keep school at the same time try to be a minister & have a house (I'll promise no further[V] —) —

People are watching for the intended bride of their minister in [the][16] good town of Waltham [17] — He appears in a hurry for he has workmen in his house night as well as day & advises people to go to church early rainy sundays = to hear —

14. Christopher Gore, known as governor and senator and, later, as benefactor of Harvard, was living in retirement at Waltham, in luxury that astonished New Englanders of that day. Frederick Gore King was Emerson's classmate at Harvard.

15. *Cf.* the letter of Feb. 14, 15, and 20, 1819.

16. A piece of the manuscript has been torn away with the seal. It is possible that a word is also missing after " watching " in the same sentence.

17. On June 12, 1817, Sarah Alden Bradford was about to be engaged to Samuel Ripley and confided the news to Mary Moody Emerson (*Worthy Women,* p. 139). For the wedding, see a note on Sept. 16, 1818.

But my hands are so cold I cannot scribble any longer with ease & must therefore, since my paper is short, say Finis —

Your brother
Ralph

Wm Emerson

To Edward Bliss Emerson, Cambridge, March 14 and 15, 1818 [18]

Cambridge March 14th 1818

Edward I am going to write you a curious letter — I am going to follow my mood exactly — to write Poetry or Prose as I go along " sans ceremonie."

Now to begin
As sure as I sin
I'll send you this letter
For want of a better

Bravo! I did not think I should make out so well ex tempore But I hear you are probably homesick, having gone off in a dull state of mind, though you had reasoned yourself into it, as a duty; — this is the sum of what I heard at home about your honor. Ah here comes the muse

Yes it is I aver —
Better than to say, " I swear "
That is swearing you know
What wicked people do
Oh yes oh yes oh yes oh yes
So they do I guess! —

Ah Bravissimo! why I astonish myself — Stop a minute. I had my hair cut to day — I want to scratch it — — — * After a long pause — now faith if here isn't the muse again — only just turn over [19] & you shall have its " fine frenzy " " like a house a fire "

Look here!!! Poetry is my delight
Exceedingly bright

* Only imagine such an awful scene at this pause — No, it will overwhelm you

18. MS owned by RWEMA; ph. in CUL.

19. The verses which follow are written in a small hand at the top of the left half of the second page, and are set off by a semicircular line from the prose text, which continues on the right. For the last rime, the poet seems to have drawn upon his Latin vocabulary.

My desire to write
It in the night
On paper white
And imagine a sprite
All robed in white
That doth invite
To share its flight
The rhyming wight
And flies out of sight
Just like a kite
So fair & *inclite*

Oh dear I must not waste paper in rhyme & so I will fill one side at least tho' with nonsense — These scraps that I transcribe, these ebullitions of the genius of Poetry are the exuberance of a fine imagination or to speak emphatically indicate the writer to be a man of vast sense & greatness. I have too much modesty after this to tell you, though it really is the case, that I wrote them myself.

But enough of this nonsensical gibberish — I have the book I told about for you, I mean Childe Harolde III Canto, & if possible shall send it you with this — It is William's — a gift — If you have my Waltham letter with you please look at the passages I mentioned — March 15th

I have been thinking, Edward that this Spring comes on rather too rapidly for our future good. If the warm weather continues the trees will get so forward that the frost will come to nip them in their prime — Though it may be for future evil yet certainly the season is abundantly fitted for present enjoyment. — I have had some beautiful walks over mountain field & grove within a few days

I suppose it draws you out of your hermit cell where you spend your days & nights poring over the wisdom of Ulysses, the fire of Achilles &c) into the the warm & beautifully calm air we have had

When it grows steadily warm I would advise you to follow *Concord Mr Sewall's* romantick example by taking your book forth into the green (now brown) plains & by some melodious grove, pebbly brook or tall shadowy pinnacle, try if you cannot charm nature with Homer — Perhaps (for I am always full of fancies) you might teach some listening thrush or magpie to say one of the lines in the Iliad — & rapturously sing Δειvη τε κλαγγη γενετ' αργυρεοιο βιοιο[20] or some other such harmonical soft breathing verse of the sweet Grecian Bard.

20. *Iliad*, I, 49.

It is strange how one idea associates itself with others — I ne[ver][21] go up a hill now but I think of Manfred or some of [Lord] Byrons heroes or else of Scotts Bertram in Rokeby [22] & though very vain sometimes, often forget that I am nothing more than your simple, though

affectionate brother

Ralph

N. B. Mother desires you to send that French Novel home if you have it — All were well yesterday — R. W. E.

To William Emerson, Waltham, Massachusetts, May 19, 1818 [23]

Waltham May 19th 1818

Dear William,

A long preliminary discourse to a letter, as to my health, situation, &c is I suppose wholly unnecessary, since every thing is as it should be.

My motive for writing *you* first is merely to renew my request and entreaty that you would devote your time & talents to that Miltonian Dissertation.[24] — Perhaps you will laugh at me for asking so urgently & so often; but you *must* know it is of some importance as well to yourself as to Mother & friends. Only weigh in an even balance, its advantages & obstacles & it is evident which side will preponderate; in the first place, Your improvement in that accomplishment, which you must acknowledge you possess in some degree — fine writing — besides the unacquired learning of the Poet that you gain to qualify yourself for an Essayist & which in a humbler degree your poor brother is gaining in another branch [25] & then the last & brilliant prospect of the fame & *money* that attend success. And success you must have if you will but afford to the subject a few hours where Labour will answer the purpose of Genius & Inspiration. As to the obstacles, all that you can reasonably present are Indolence & self-stiled Inability which one vigorous effort would easily sacrifice at the altar of literary distinction. Foster, you remember, says " A resolute mind is omnipotent," [26] which though it be an expression

21. A fragment torn away with the seal probably contained the bracketed portions of this sentence.

22. The *Rokeby* allusion, perhaps less obvious than that to *Manfred*, is probably to stanzas xiv and xv of the second canto.

23. MS owned by RWEMA; ph. in CUL.

24. Perhaps this subject had now been chosen by William for a Bowdoin dissertation instead of the " Homer & Virgil " mentioned in the letter of Dec. 23, 1817.

25. Verse-writing?

26. John Foster, *Essays in a Series of Letters to a Friend,* 3d ed., London, 1806, I,

scarcely admissible within the bounds of truth, only believe it, & reconcile it to your mind by some metaphysical argument and *dissertative* ability will not be wanting. Consider too the character of Milton as Johnson gives it, at the conclusion of his life " Milton was born for all that was great & arduous; Difficulty retired at his touch." [27] I do not know that I have the words exactly it is the sense however. But if your breast be callous to all desire of fame & your heart hard to all the calls of literary Glory, then I would appeal to your natural *affections* & there you cannot be *null & void.* If you gain a prize only consider how much honour it would reflect on mother & with what pleasure a purse so earned would be recieved. And as probably a long period will elapse before our family will be independent of the assistance of Society our Benefactors might encouraged by a gleam of hope darted *from underneath the locks of the " Scrof'lous "* [28] and thus inclined to assist the " other brother " by some faint expectations, never alas to be realized that he would be enabled at some future time to *dissert* like his predecessor in favour. But this low motive instead of natural affection is an appeal to the family purse.

You like the Edinburgh Reviews; by only reading one solid dissertation there, where the finest ideas are ornamented with the utmost polish & refinement of language you will feel some enthusiasm to turn your own steps into a *new* path of the field of belles lettres – Believe me I had rather you would get a prize than myself if I try,[29] since it is of more importance to you as it is your last & my first chance.

I will not trouble you with details of my own progress as it may be uninteresting & is unimportant in comparison with yours = Please to give & recieve love & my best wishes for your success in poetical pursuits.

Your affectionate brother

Ralph

W Emerson.

129: " Other men have done much greater things; a resolute mind is omnipotent; difficulty is a stimulus and a triumph to a strong spirit; ' the joys of conquest are the joys of man.' What need I care about people's opinion? " Foster's " Essay II. On Decision of Character," which contains this passage and fills pp. 125–230 of his first volume, deserves some notice, I think, as feebly suggesting " Self-reliance." Though commonplace throughout in style and in ideas, it may well have helped plant in Emerson's mind a text worthy of a better sermon.

27. On the original MS the quotation marks are repeated at the beginning of each line.

28. Apparently some allusion that was familiar in the family. *Cf.* Sept. 13, 1817.

29. The letter of June 12 and 17, 1818, records Emerson's first attempt at a Bowdoin prize.

To Edward Bliss Emerson, Cambridge, June 2, 1818 [30]

Cambridge June 2 1818

Dear Edward,

In a very sentimental [31] mood, with a warm evening in a cool room, I suppose I may venture to address a few prosaic lines to my dearly beloved brother, wrapt probably in philosophick meditation on the grandeur, beauty and magnificence of Nature as displayed in the woodland scenery of Andover. Unreproved by the urgency of lessons & unoccupied by the pressure of business, a summer evening like this, is one of the pleasantest enjoyments of the Cambridge Student. If his pen is good and [his] [32] inclination thitherward, he may amuse himself like *me,* by endeavouring to impart some of his agreeable sensations to his literary brothers in Andover and like me write a letter just long enough not to tire himself or his reader. Your next letter — pray let it be a flashy sentimental — Gaze on the stars, till you get asleep and then dash off a letter about " vast concave " [33] &c in ten minutes or so! Tell how they glare, with unremitting stare, on the sons of wickedness & sloth; then turn your address to Jupiter, (who has been sick lately as I understand,) or some other bright luminary & ask him if he will be kind enough to guard your slumbers & don't forget to ask him about your brother Ralph —

Uncle Ripley is engaged to S. A. B.[34] " by the way."

To Edward Bliss Emerson, Cambridge, June 12, and Boston, June 17, 1818 [35]

Cambridge, June 12th 1818 —

Dear Edward,

If long letters suit your taste, I believe I can gratify it now; for I just recieved this paper as a present, and have one of those

30. MS owned by RWEMA; ph. in CUL.

31. The word " sentimental " has been repeated just above the line, possibly by Edward.

32. Perhaps this word was on the piece of MS torn away with the seal.

33. It is barely possible that Emerson had seen the phrase in Edward Nicklin's *Pride and Ignorance* or even in the passage quoted from that book in *The Monthly Review,* XLII, 406 (May, 1770).

34. This seems to have been old news at least to some members of the family. See a note on Feb. 6? 1818.

35. MS owned by RWEMA; ph. in CUL.

ruled papers under it. Let me see – I believe it was you that I asked to find me a motto, but I recieved none. You need not trouble yourself now, for I am not in want; I mentioned it to season my kindness in giving you a whole sheet of Letter-paper – oh present unprecedented in the annals of nations! the 6 last words are so often found in the Essay that I have just *finished* that I cannot resist their frequent repetition. I am engaged in copying off my work at present – I was going to say for the press but I fear for the *fire,* so that if it turns out prizeless, I will say it was unjust, for the flame of human genius never *blazed brighter.* Nor shall I become a love-lorn, disconsolate, solitary eremite, even if the Government think fit to light their cigars with my *elaborate* production. "Nil desperandum"[36] I will say, and then go immediately to work – to prepare another somniferous dissertation for next year, & if that succeeds no better than its elder brother, I'll put them to sleep each succeeding year with one,[37] till they, tired out by my Morphean draughts, give me the long-expected prize. "Oh how sweet is revenge" but thus it shall be, if I live &c But you must never whisper a syllable about it to any person or admit any one to my *arcana* & to that end please burn up this letter after perusal. I don't write poetry when at Cambridge or I would give a specimen of it since you like to have my letters bring the muse with them as you said.

Were it my fortune to be in a situation like Lord Byron & some other British Poets, I think I would cultivate Poetry & endeavour to propitiate the muses To have nothing to do but mount the heights of Parnassus & enjoy the feasts of polite literature must necessarily be a very pleasing employment But in this country where every one is obliged to study his profession for assistance in living & where so little encouragement is given to Poets &c it is a pretty poor trade.[38] Yes I believe both epithets are true in their literal sense, so that I have not the least thought of determination to follow it. I am going some night to the top of Parnassus

36. Horace, *Odes,* I, vii, 27.

37. There are several references in later letters to Emerson's interest in the Bowdoin prizes, and he was successful in his junior and senior years. The original MSS of *A Dissertation on the Character of Socrates,* submitted in July, 1820, and his *Dissertation on the Present State of Ethical Philosophy,* of July, 1821, are included in the bound volumes of Bowdoin dissertations still preserved in HCL. Both the Emerson MSS have been printed in *Two Unpublished Essays,* ed. Edward Everett Hale, 1896.

38. Freneau's complaint in "An Author's Soliloquy" of thirty years earlier was still valid; and other young men of Emerson's generation who were to win fame as writers shared these fears and, for the most part, found them justified.

— (any other hill will do as well) & there I will bid them farewell in some tender elegiac stanza and so pathetick that I shall hear some voice issuing out of a blasted oak, or dark cavern, that will perhaps utter those words of enchantment, on the mystick seal of Solomon, — " Dont go " — and I, warm with enthusiasm, will respond — " I must " & then awe-struck will commence my departure, yet still " will cast one longing, ling'ring look behind." [39] But you are wearied, per adventure, by my poetick powers of description, wherefore, I will cease, howsomdoever, I cease with regret, for you know I am one of those that love to wander " Round the vast top of some gigantick height." [40] &c

Boston — June 17th

Here I am at home having got my name out for sickness; I have about me an unpleasant friend named a Sore Throat, but I am fast getting well. I recieved yesterday morning your pleasant letter and am now proceeding to answer it. As to your present happiness, I congratulate you, as to your love of Solitude, I sympathize with you, as to your prospects of diligence, I wish you well. You are going to write many letters, and ask me for subjects. Can you " walk forth to meditate at even tide " [41] and want a subject? can you absorb yourself in contemplation of classick lore, in the Works of Homer Virgil & Cicero and yet want a subject for epistolary correspondence? or nearer home can you read a letter of Aunt Mary's, an enthusiast in rural pleasures, and yet want a subject.

There is a theme, which has been the subject of many college Orations, which would wake you to the pen I think since you love study so well, I mean " Senectute literis ornata " " Otium dignitatis " [42] &c You might write a long letter embellished with all the ornaments of Rhetorick on the Age of the American Scholar.[43] Imagine to yourself all the gratifications of taste and riches to form his library, philosophy room &c

39. The same stanza of the " Elegy " is echoed in the letter of Nov. 10, 1816.

40. So far as I know, this line may be Emerson's own, though it suggests the enthusiastic nature descriptions of such poets as Beattie, Akenside, and Joseph Warton.

41. Cowper, *The Task,* VI, 949. Further evidence of Emerson's early acquaintance with this poem is to be found in *Journals,* I, 72.

42. Perhaps Emerson was thinking vaguely of Cicero's " cum dignitate otium " (*Oratio pro P. Sextio,* chap. xlv).

43. Another curious suggestion of later writings, though the subject was one that attracted many orators before 1837. But probably Emerson was thinking here of the old theme celebrated in what may be called " The Choice " poems of the eighteenth century.

and take what is excellent out of Mr Gore,[44] Mr Vaughan,[45] Thos. Jefferson, and others of our distinguished countrymen. Perhaps the muses enraptured by the beauty of your prose ideas will fly to your assistance and give you a friendly hand to help you to the summit of Parnassus; but prose suits your taste better so why cannot you write me a theme-letter on this or some other equally refined subject? and if [you] like it you may write in Latin, the language of Literature, or Greek the tongue of Herodotus &c or Gallic the language of Voltaire or vernacular the language of ourselves.[46] I am fast getting well by the enlivening air & scenery of the town. Mother and brothers are well & send love.

Ralph. Send Sarah's French book, with Goldsmith.[47] R W E —

Edward B. Emerson. —

To William Emerson, Cambridge, July 20 and 21, 1818 [48]

Cambridge, July 20th 1818

Dear William,

My motives for writing to you now, are rather selfish, as I am scribbling to fill up some leisure time, as well as to draw some lines from *you* before a great while. I sent your Kennebunk letter, & mother as well as myself are quite anxious to know its contents.[49] — — Has St. Cecilia descended yet from " the seventh Heaven " to help your pen over the smoothly white expanse of writing paper? You must go & see Miss Lowell & whilst her ladyship is singing to you, imagine that it is St. C. & then go home on the strength of it & write about " Musick of the Spheres " &c. &c. & tell your audience at Commencement of some lay

44. Perhaps the " Manlius " papers of Christopher Gore are meant.

45. Probably the Anglo-American Benjamin Vaughan, Franklin's friend.

46. In the MS the word " ourselves " is repeated between the lines. The bracketed " you " was probably on the fragment torn away with the seal.

47. The French book may have been Sarah Alden Bradford's (*cf.* the letter of Nov. 3 and 4, 1816). As for Goldsmith, Edward had written a few days before (June 7, 1818) that he had finished the second volume of *The History of England* and had begun *The Citizen of the World.*

48. MS owned by RWEMA; ph. in CUL. Excerpt I appears in Edward Waldo Emerson's " Memoir of Ralph Waldo Emerson," *Memoirs of Members of the Social Circle in Concord,* 2d series, 2d part, privately printed, 1888, pp. 23–24, and again in his *Emerson in Concord,* 1889, pp. 23–24.

49. On July 23, 1818, William Emerson wrote to his mother from Waltham (MS owned by Dr. Haven Emerson) that he had just received an offer of $420 a year — apparently in addition to board and lodging — to return to Kennebunk.

more sweetly melancholy than that which echoes from the mountain harp of Scotland, tuned by the unearthly maiden that warns, the ill-fated traveller who passes her impenetrable grove, of approaching dissolution, singing sadly & melodiously! = Imitate in some degree Everett's "fabled spirit of the North, who is fairer than all the daughters of the Earth, & the rose is in her cheek, & the fire in her eye – but that rose was never crimsoned by a blush & a heart never throbbed beneath that marble bosom to the sounds of icy coldness = I will not go any further for I cannot give his own expressions & since I heard it I have been constantly wishing – sometimes for his memory to recall his words and at others, for the exalted genius that could compose such exalted language & sentiments – "And now, my classmates, the bark is ready, the masts are up, the sails are spread – and away to the dark blue sea!" [50] = I never was better pleased in my life & never expect to be = I wish however in this particular my expectations might be agreeably disappointed at Commencement when the *First Conference* [51] is announced. In six weeks, moderate talents might effect a great deal; and your subject is very poetical – you may tell them some strange tale about Memnon's Harp [52] – or read Walter Scotts superstitious innumerables – & conjure up

The fishers have heard the water-sprite [53] –

into some heavenly harmony more delightful to the pensive Soul than the blast of expiring Autumnus reechoed through the leafless forest.* July 21st We have begun Lowth's Grammar; [54] and consequently I have much more leisure than usual, having just finished my first lesson, and therefore continue to scribble, but with a better pen.

* This you see is a mere repetition of the sentimentality on the first page of this harping epistle.

50. Probably the quoted passages are from a college oration by John Everett, William Emerson's classmate. Dr. John Pierce, the indefatigable chronicler of Harvard commencements, was a witness to the oratorical ability of John Everett, who, he said, outshone the whole class in his harangue on the character of Byron at the commencement a few weeks later (*Proc. Mass. Hist. Soc.*, 2d series, V, 184). Edward Everett did not return from his four years abroad until 1819.

51. The official program of the commencement of Aug. 26, 1818, shows that William Emerson was one of four graduates to take part in "A Conference – 'Upon architecture, painting, poetry, and music, as tending to produce and perpetuate religious impressions.'"

52. *Cf.* Nov. 27, 1816.

53. Scott, *The Lay of the Last Minstrel,* VI, 362.

54. Robert Lowth's *A Short Introduction to English Grammar* had been a standard schoolbook for half a century.

[I]I shall chum next year with Dorr,[55] and he appears to be perfectly disposed to study hard. But, to tell the truth, I do not think it necessary to understand Mathematicks & Greek thoroughly, to be a good, useful, or even *great* man. Aunt Mary would certainly tell you so, and I think you yourself believe it, if you did not think it a dangerous doctrine to tell a Freshman. But do not be afraid, for I do mean to study them, though not with an equal interest to the other studies.[I] Apropos, you owe Dorr 50 Cts — On Saturday I saw Edward at home. He had come in the morning and went away while I was there; was well and in as high spirits as usual.

I believe you do not love walking as well as I, but if you do, I think the walk to Mr Lovejoy's Factory was the most beautiful that I found in Waltham; but perhaps, far more congenial to your benevolent feelings is the employment of *teaching the young idea how to shoot,*[56] and you are contemplating in your little band, the future statesmen & heroes who are to elevate Columbian glory! Success to you in your endeavours to that end. But now that I have seen my third page, and have exhibited specimens of various kinds of writing — viz. poetical scribble — stiff regularity, & a mixture of both,[57] you will be as willing as myself to view the close. After you have given my respects to Mr Ripley and my " desired to be remembered " to Mrs Upham & family you may sit down & write a long letter to your brother

Ralph.

Mr William Emerson

The Seniors remaining here, mope about, as soberly and steadily as the Graduates themselves, not excepting even Hathaway himself.

To William Emerson, Cambridge, July 23, 1818 [58]

Cambridge July 23d
8 o'clock ev'g

Dear William,

I am sincerely sorry that I cannot exclaim with Archimedes Ευρηκα Ευρηκα for I went to your room & the socks were not there

55. Doubtless Emerson's classmate William Bradley Dorr.

56. James Thomson, *The Seasons* (" Spring," l. 1153).

57. This letter exhibits several styles of handwriting, obviously achieved with a good deal of effort.

58. MS owned by RWEMA; ph. in CUL. The reference to William as a senior agrees with other evidence that the year is 1818.

in any part of the study without they were locked up in the desk. Then slowly & sadly I went to the Library & there was told that " Florian's [59] complete works " do not belong & only one or two of them Numa Pompilius inclusive; all others were out so I have nothing but this paltry epistle to send except its formal companion. For this duplicate misfortune you must console yourself by all the comforts of Philosophy. Take down Plato's works in the original Greek for instance – but you can choose for yourself. Thank you for your fable – worthy of Æsop – is it original – it displays the blaze of genius if it is – if not – no matter The above is one of Tacitus' elliptical sentences – By the way – came to a fine sentence in Tacitus today – Galba –– fatigabat alieni jam imperii deos [60] – Mr Brazers Translation – " Wearied the gods of an empire no longer his own " " by prayers " understood You recollect the poor wretch who lost his empire before he knew it, & Rome too!

But stop – At what a rate I am scribbling & talking to a Senior too, as if he did not understand latin as well as puissant self – but I am very hot – just fresh from an errand – pardon me. –

The day is done – its cares pleasures & duties – vanished with its sun, the toils of the laborer, the studies of the scholar the interests of the merchant all lie hidden in the darkness that overhangs nature Placidly & quietly as the stars that roll over us we are – hark – hark – – By and By –

The students & townspeople to the number of about 70 I think have just been engaged in a conflict a great deal of noise swearing &c [61] The President has been over to stop it – has succeeded pretty well – the combatants are retiring muttering but did not give me time to finish my dashy sentence – Ralph. –

[62] I sent your Kennebunk Letter on Saturday last R W E

To Mary Moody Emerson, Cambridge? July? 1818

[Acknowledged in Mary Moody Emerson, July 26, 1818.]

59. On the same day, July 23, 1818, William wrote to his mother (MS owned by Dr. Haven Emerson) that he was reading Florian with the greatest pleasure.

60. *Histories,* I, xxix.

61. This sentence was followed by another which was canceled but is still legible: " It first arose from Ned Loring as usual (dont say so to Uncle) ."

62. This afterthought was written above the salutation and is separated from it and the heading by two heavy lines.

To William Emerson, Cambridge? August? 6? 1818 [63]

Thursday Morn.g

Dear Wm,

As to the room, if you can get intelligence to Green & Tufts they appear to be the most able to lend their's. The Freshmen who do not lend their rooms expect to occupy them on the day Still there is Emerson & Bartlett, & Adams & Miller, but they are gone away and inaccessible to me. If all fail there is still a resource in *my* room, wh. with the removal of the bed placing chairs, & adorning with pictures greens &c (not to mention *eatables*) will make a tolerable retreat from the Meeting house.[64]

Why did you not stay Tues. Ev.g. I went to Stimpson's in vain for I wished to see you to speak of what we mentioned in the morn.g; but when I returned & found not only my handkerchief but *pears* & clothes & even my key wh. I left in the drawer, After all this, I say, I was very *cheerful!* and consoling myself with the kindness of Mother forgot you almost, whilst eating some fine fruit &c! Next Tuesday is my Examination Thursday probably I shall visit Waltham.

Your brother

Ralph

W Emerson

P S. I have not been to Plympton yet but am going today. Remember when you go to Boston to ask Uncles to see that a relation of ours be kept quietly in B. on Commencement day or else he will certainly be here as he asked very particularly about your part &c of me when he visited me last

R. W. E.

Adams sings my song [65] Ex. evening

63. MS owned by RWEMA; ph. in CUL. The endorsement "RWE July 1818" is in a hand that I cannot identify. The references to William's commencement, which occurred on Aug. 26, 1818, show that the letter was written a short time before that event. But the MS *Records of the College Faculty* (in HCL), IX, 146–147, shows Aug. 8 (Saturday) and not a Tuesday as the date set for the freshman examination in 1818. The Thursday preceding was Aug. 6. But the day of the letter remains doubtful.

64. The exercises were for many years held in the meetinghouse near the campus. The full names of Harvard students mentioned here and in later letters are to be found in the college catalogues of these years, if not in recent, easily available, quinquennial catalogues, and are printed in the index of these letters. The pairs of roommates here named and the Plympton of the postscript were all members of the class of 1818, to which William Emerson belonged.

65. This song, which was apparently to have been sung on the evening following

To Edward Bliss Emerson, Waltham, Massachusetts, September *c.* 6, 1818 [66]

Waltham, September 1818 –

Dear & honoured brother Edward,

You have written me for the sole purpose, it seems of enforcing on my negligent pen the obligation of writing to you; now to tell you the truth there are three or four different moods in which I write to three or four different persons; & in the following order. When I think I should like to write a letter & yet feel sufficiently sober to keep all my nonsense down, then I begin my letter with " My dear Mother " [67] but when I think I can write a grammatically correct epistle or any thing that I am sure can raise the risible muscles of gravity itself, *then* I address my fastidious brother – Bachelor – When in a very *compositorial rhetorical* mood, I send to an uncle in the Alibama [68] – and last of all when I want to scribble I know not why, & care not what, & moreover have leisure & rhyme at command, and peradventure want to amuse myself, *then* as *now* the pen flies over the lines to my semi-Andover semi-Boston brother Ned. In short I write to you when I am in a serio-ludrico tragico-comico miscellany of feelings. If the paper is filled it matters not how. The old proverb is Circumstances alter cases; & now that your horizon is so essentially changed; from the dark murky clouds of misanthropy, fanaticism, & error that encircle Andover to the careless noisy scenes of Boston (two equally dreaded extremes) I suppose I must begin to vary my epistolary efforts – for more than once, whilst you have been at Andover, genuine compassion (I do not know if you will thank me for it) has dictated my letter; but now you are in the very centre of the frolicsome lively busy town you

---

the freshman examination, was, I conjecture, the same uninspired set of verses copied by Josiah Quincy into his commonplace book and printed by Tremaine McDowell in *PMLA,* XLV, 326–329, as " A Freshman Poem by Emerson." The catalogue of Oct., 1817, lists four students named " Adams "; but presumably Emerson refers to John R. Adams, who is certainly the one meant in the first paragraph.

66. MS owned by RWEMA; ph. in CUL. The date is not later than the 7th, for Edward endorsed the letter as received on that day. According to the superscription, it was carried by " Mr. Ripley " (Samuel Ripley of Waltham, no doubt) to Edward in Boston.

67. *Cf.* a note on Sept. 9, 1818.

68. This seems to show that Emerson had written some letters to his half uncle Daniel Bliss Ripley, who was married this year in Alabama, and who died there, at St. Stephens, a few years later (James Harris Fitts, *Genealogy of the Fitts or Fitz Family in America,* 1897, p. 73). As the Territory of Alabama had come into existence only in 1817, the spelling in the letter is not surprising.

must impart some of its gaiety to your out-of-town friends whilst I must sober & season my letters with moral scientifick economical &c sentiments; especially when I am as sure that they will be shown to all my friends as that you will get them. Put your secret-keeping power to the test by shutting up this in your own pocketbook or in the flames — 'tis immaterial which — but unseen by all eyes save your own. I suppose when you left Andover, on the principle that " habit is a second nat[ure] " [69] you made some pathetick " loud lament," perh[aps] addressing its fields as Farewell my own dear land! or the like — I hope you did not get naturalized. By the way I have transcribed the enclosed from the Edinburgh Review. Ugolino describes the starvation of his family to the last line but three; his own actions there related is most horrid of all. This is translation from the Italian I believe.[70]

With love to all

Your affectionate brother

Edw. B. Emerson Esq[r]. Ralph.

To Ruth Haskins Emerson, Waltham, Massachusetts, September 9, 1818 [71]

Waltham Sept. 9th 1818 —

My dear Mother,

I had deferred writing you for various reasons, till now an event too calamitous to pass over in silence, compels me to address you. I did not know till yesterday afternoon of the death of the Sheriff [72] — of our greatest earthly benefactor — kindest friend. Though I knew from what you said to me before that it was possible & even probable he would not live long yet I was scarcely ever more surprised than when Uncle told me he was dead.

69. Probably from Cicero, *De Finibus,* V, 25. The last word and the word " perhaps " below have been mutilated by the seal.

70. Emerson must have inclosed some lines from Cary's translation of Dante's *Inferno,* XXXIII, quoted in *The Edinburgh Review,* XXIX, 473–474 (Feb., 1818). Later letters show admiration for the *Vita nuova* but not much liking for the *Divina commedia.*

71. MS owned by RWEMA; ph. in CUL. Probably there were earlier letters from Emerson to his mother which are now lost. The reference in Sept. *c.* 6, 1818, to beginning " my letter with ' My dear Mother ' " is evidence of such correspondence but inconclusive.

72. For Sheriff Samuel Bradford, father of Emerson's lifelong friend Samuel Bradford, see the latter's book, *Some Incidents,* privately printed, 1880. The *New-England Palladium,* Sept. 8, 1818, reports the Sheriff's death on Sept. 5 and agrees with the account here given of the practical nature of his religion.

You once spoke of the probable state of his family in case of his death. I am afraid that your gloomiest surmises will prove true. Accustomed to all the delicate attentions & possessions of opulence perhaps they are to feel sensibly the wants they have so often relieved in others. I suppose it is fortunate for Sam. that he chose the store instead of college. May we hope that if ever they need the charities they have conferred that at some future we may be in a situation to show our gratitude for constant kindness hitherto. The ministers of First Church have always shared his kindness. He was a man paid attention to all those little delicacies of life which form the gentleman. In giving he would not hurt the feelings of the reciever. As a publick man, he was necessarily to a considerable degree the Man of the world. We do not intimately know his private character. Some who would have religion displayed in a devotional outside might say he was not strictly religious; but according to the scriptures, Charity is the most powerful of all the graces. It is not the province of mortals to judge their fellow-creatures & we leave him to a Merciful Father. I shall not attempt to poetize; the subject is too serious. William's entrance into action for himself, at this time,[73] carries with it many different feelings — of sober joy — of hope — of pain. —

The rain has thrown glad[ness][74] over the features of all who are im[media]tely interested in the cares & anxieties of the husbandman — Mingled draughts of judgement & mercy —

Love to all —

Your affectionate son

Ralph —

To Edward Bliss Emerson, Waltham, Massachusetts, September 16, 1818 [75]

Waltham, Sept., 16th 1818 —

Dear Edward,

I was just now thinking that it befitted me to write homeward by the weekly Thursday post but having my purpose set, my eyes on this precious bit of paper, I wrote the English of " carus " & then stopped to consider to whom I should apply that term of affec-

73. William had left for his school at Kennebunk two days before (William Emerson to his mother, Oct. 18, 1818, owned by Dr. Haven Emerson).

74. Mutilated by the seal; another word or words in the following line of the MS are partly illegible for the same reason.

75. MS owned by RWEMA; ph. in CUL.

tion: first I thought of Mother, but I am in school, unable, consequently to write well; then of W^m. (via Boston) but some insuperable objection occurred; lastly, of course, of you, (last thoughts always best) as a handy, intermediate sort of a being, to write to whom I might be in any sort of a mood, as I said last letter; & sure that whatever tidings my letter might tell, of importance, or not, your kind tongue would be as ready as any in the house save B's alone to publish the contents & remembering withal that the last mortal being who has thought me for good in the epistolary way was yourself. All the above enumerated reasons, & more, confirmed my determination, & I scribbled accordingly as outrageously as you see.

You must not attribute such writing or matter as this, to any want of feeling on the subject of your last letter — By no means — But in school I have so much to perplex me I am glad to mingle my constant frowning positive orders for silence, study &c with some relaxation & self-entertainment. I am very much obliged for your interesting particulars relative to that event Let me beg pardon when I mention I thought one place in your letter a little *affected* (you may use the same freedom with my letters with the gratitude of the writer.) When you see Samuel [76] tell him —— all that you think at the time I ought to say to him — for such things depending more on circumstances — I will leave intirely to your good sense. After this miscellaneous oblation to your vanity, volubility & good sense permit me to subscribe myself

Your truly affectionate brother

Ralph

Edw B Emerson Esqr

With my love & respect to mother, tell her I shall be obliged at the end of my vacation to draw pretty heavily on her *purse* for these particulars, viz — paying the woman for W^m, my last bill, & moving my furniture wh. last will I suppose be about a dollar — about the Cambridge Woman, I suppose W^m told Mother her wages for he told me he would write to me & inform me but has not.

Good bye —

R W E.

Miscellaneous —

I am reading Leo X. in four Vols [77] — am in the third & proceed at the humble rate of a Vol. a week — have read as usual a great deal in Edin-

76. Samuel Bradford, son of the Sheriff.

77. Perhaps the four-volume edition of William Roscoe, *The Life and Pontificate of Leo the Tenth,* Philadelphia, 1805–1806.

burgh Reviews – Mr Frothingham's poem before Φ. B K in [78] on Genius besides having reached the top of Prospect Hill on Saturday last – written *lots* of poetry, visited a little, contemplated as much – & regularly kept school from half past 5 A: M: till 8 P M. every day this vacation commencement & Φ B K day only excepted. Sarah Bradford was here last week – Mr Ripley was published on Sunday last for the first time.[79] " Once more I bid adieu "

R. W. E.

To William Emerson, Cambridge? October 12, 1818

[Mentioned in William Emerson, Dec. 18, 1818, as referring to an " Introductory Fraternity," apparently at college.]

To William Emerson, Cambridge? November 16, 1818

[Described *ibid.* as a note of twenty words promising a letter.]

To William Emerson, Cambridge? November *c.* 23, 1818

[Referred to in William Emerson to Ruth Haskins Emerson, Nov. 29, 1818 (owned by Dr. Haven Emerson), as a letter received " Last night " and containing an account of " that unhappy fracas "; and described in William Emerson, Dec. 18, 1818, as a " motley epistle, of half a dozen dates, closing with a history of your very praiseworthy resistance to lawful authority." The rebellion of the sophomore class, which was apparently recorded in this letter, is mentioned in Cabot, I, 61. The official account, which may be read in MS *Records of the College Faculty* (HCL), IX, 168 ff., shows that the disturbance began on Nov. 1 and that negotiations between the faculty and the class continued for some weeks. Emerson is not named.]

To William Emerson, Cambridge? December 1, 1818

[William Emerson, Dec. 18, 1818, describes this as a " piece of a letter," accompanying some books.]

78. The year 1813 followed but was canceled. W. H. Tillinghast, *The Orators and Poets of Phi Beta Kappa, Alpha of Massachusetts,* 1891, p. 4, mentions Nathaniel Langdon Frothingham as poet in 1813, but gives no other information.

79. The *New-England Palladium,* Oct. 13, 1818, and the *Columbian Centinel* of the following day reported the marriage of Samuel Ripley to Sarah Alden Bradford, both giving Ripley's name as " Daniel " (the name of his brother). William Emerson, writing on the twentieth of the same month to Edward (MS owned by Dr. Haven Emerson), noted the error in the *Palladium.*

1819

To William Emerson, Waltham, Massachusetts, January 25 and 27, 1819 [1]

Waltham, Jan. 25th 1818.

Dear William,

Last Friday (Jan 22d) I recieved your letter of Dec. 18th & its enclosed $3 for which I thank you. It has been a month in Cambridge Post Office & Mr Ripley took it out. You did not tell me what I wanted to know whether my purchases suited you or not. I suppose you feel anxious to know something of your old tabernacles in an official capacity in its regenerated state. The captain-general [2] is unaltered. The new inhabitant by far the finest woman I ever saw; (our *own* friends alone excepted) She has lost all that reserve to strangers that she used to have; knows just as much & more in Literature; still cleans lamps & makes puddings; never hurts any one's feelings, & yet appears to feel a superiority for all out of her own immediate circle. When no one is reading to her, at leisure moments you will find her reading a German critic or something of the kind sometimes Reid on Light or Optics.[3] As to her knowledge talk on what you will she can always give you a new idea — ask her any philosophical question, she will always enlighten you by her answer. She is never cross or any thing like coldness; is very fond of *him* as *he* of *her*. In short I must end where I begun, that she is the finest woman I ever saw. Mr Daniel Bradford thinks of coming to Waltham to practise law.[4]

1. MS owned by Professor James B. Thayer; ph. in CUL. The references to Jan. 22 as Friday, to the captain-general and the new inhabitant, and to Kirkland's visit to Washington all show that the year was not 1818 but 1819.

2. The captain-general was Samuel Ripley, head of the Waltham school in which the Emerson brothers had been helping from time to time; and the new inhabitant was his wife, the Sarah Alden Bradford of earlier letters. For their marriage, see a note on Sept. 16, 1818.

3. Possibly Thomas Reid's *An Inquiry into the Human Mind,* the principal chapter of which is entitled " Of Seeing." There were numerous editions before 1819.

4. He went to Kentucky instead (*Worthy Women,* p. 140).

In my rapturous description at my first attempt at describing character I suppose you think I have almost lost myself, but (Jan 27th) I am not. Our good President [5] has gone to Washington by invitation of James Munroe the Stupid. Should you not like to see the two dignitaries meet? Mr Everett is expected to return by next commencement so that our class will have all the good of his lectures that they would were he here now.[6] As to Bowdoins [7] you may send me as much intelligence as you choose on Dr Johnsons literary character My chance is not as good as it was last year, yet still there is nothing like perseverance.

Folks at Waltham ask about you Miss Duncan & others — *They* say you are *very* fond of one name Olive [8] which no one else is pleased with so they think you must something particularly interesting there, more than at other places. I am very tired of my miserable pen & feelings so bid you Good bye

Your truly affectionate

Ralph

Wm Emerson

To William Emerson, Cambridge, February 14 and 15, and Boston, February 20, 1819 [9]

[I]Cambridge Feb. 14th 1819

Dear William[I]

I have recieved your letter & enclosements of the 10th ult. by Moody [10] — & hasten to express my thanks and returns before I

5. John Thornton Kirkland. For his visit to Washington, see Feb. 14, 15, and 20, 1819.

6. For a number of years the letters show this enthusiasm for Edward Everett, which was rising even before he returned from abroad. The Harvard catalogue of Oct., 1819, gives no information on courses; but that for Oct., 1820, shows that Everett's lectures were for seniors only, though he may have had courses of a different kind for others.

7. *Cf.* the letters of June 12 and 17, 1818; Feb. 14, 15, and 20, 1819; and Apr. 1 and 10, 1819.

8. Emerson's second cousin Olivia, or Olive, was the sister of the noted teacher George Barrell Emerson often mentioned in the letters (*The Ipswich Emersons,* p. 154; and Edward E. Bourne, *The History of Wells and Kennebunk,* 1875, p. 751). William Emerson mentions her in letters to his mother dated Kennebunk, Sept. 11 and 24, 1818 (owned by Dr. Haven Emerson).

9. MS owned by RWEMA; ph. in CUL. Excerpts I–VIII are in Cabot, I, 51–52.

10. Apparently Emerson's classmate George Barrell Moody, of Kennebunk, Me.

forget, lest by procrastination, I shoud again lay myself open to those severe epistolary rebukes with which I have been so often favored of late. As to my own letter there is little to answer, as I have before mentioned my reciept of your Dec.[11] letter with the enclosed $4; but perhaps *that* letter, which I wrote from Waltham [12] is still in Boston. For the French Books,[13] you know when they *must* be returned – sometime in August; nor will they, as you apprehend, subject me to inconvenience, for I took them on Mr Ripley's name. But you gave me leave to read Mother's & Ned's letters, so I suppose I may say something about *them*. [II]You speak of Mother's pecuniary exigencies at present; though pressing they are not distressful quite yet, though she is relying considerably on your assistance,[II] for rent &c.; she has only paid Mr Bruce $50 on his last Quarter & I believe is waiting for you to pay the rest. [III]I brought twenty Dollars from Waltham day before yesterday, besides your $3.50. The quarterly ten dollar present from " the unknown friend " has been discontinued 2 quarters which confirms mothers suspicions of Sheriff Bradford's being the source. The deacons, at the beginning of Jan. sent their compliments with a twenty dollar bill for mother: [III] – this last I suppose you have heard before. So much for pecuniary embarrassment relief & expectation.

I suppose Edward has told you of Mr Frothingham's "mercies recieved " & the contemplated name of this eighth wonder of the world, little beauty, uncommon child, &c. viz Thomas Bumstead. I give him my good wishes.

[IV]As to Cambridge news,[14] the Presidents absence & attentions are

11. The day of the month, perhaps "10th," which followed, has been scratched out.

12. Apparently the letter of Jan. 25 and 27, 1819.

13. See the letter of Apr. 23 and 24, 1819.

14. Emerson's information about professional promotions, and about public events in general, was extensive and usually accurate. The *New-England Palladium* records, on Feb. 5, 1819, the honors done to President Kirkland at Washington, where he was invited to stay at the White House; and, on Apr. 16, reports the ordination of John Pierpont as pastor of the Hollis Street Church (where Horace Holley had officiated before he went to Kentucky to become president of Transylvania University). Convers Francis, who later encouraged Emerson in his German studies, was ordained at Watertown on June 23, 1819, as successor to Richard Rosewell Eliot, who had died in 1818 (Convers Francis, *An Historical Sketch of Watertown*, 1830, pp. 121 and 124). Charles Briggs was ordained as pastor of the First Church at Lexington on Apr. 28, 1819, succeeding Avery Williams (Charles Hudson, *History of the Town of Lexington*, 1913, I, 333, and II, 757). Samuel Gilman, who is mentioned in the letter of Apr. 23 and 24, 1819, as a tutor at Harvard, and who reappears in these letters at the time of Emerson's Southern journey, was actually settled in

principal;[IV] then, Mr Francis will probably be settled at Watertown vice Mr Elliott, Mr Briggs at Lexington vice Mr Williams & Mr Pierpont at Mr Holley's; Mr Gilman is preaching in expectation of a call at *Taunton,* I believe. George Emerson is expected to be tutor here, instead of Mr Sparks.

Mr, I mean *Dr* Everett is coming home next August so that our class will profit by him. [V]Should you not like to have been witness of the meeting of the two Presidents at Washington? People appear to think that our Prest will do himself as much honour as a man of the world as he will as a literary character. & that Mr Munroe in appearance is little more than a comfortable ploughman.[V]

You laugh at my letters as being of a dozen dates; & now that I have a whole page to fill up, & have the credit of such an epistolary character I will avail myself of its privileges & date this again when I have more to say —

Monday Morn. [VI]Feb 15th

This morng I recieved the *very important intelligence* that I was appointed waiter; (for the first time, you know.) I am to wait in the Junior Hall; I do like it & yet I do not like it for which sentiments you can easily guess the reason.[VI] The President is to be absent a fortnight longer & in the opinion of the students Dr Ware [15] is *very important* in his high dignity of presidency pro tem. [VII]Today, we begin the studies [16] of the term — Languages in the morng; Blair at noon & Algebra in the afternoon.[VII] I am [17] this forenoon because we have a lesson set us at

I am reading Gil Blas in French & get along swimmingly I finished

---

1819 as Unitarian minister in Charleston, S. C. (*The Year-book of the Unitarian Congregational Churches, for 1858,* p. 20). Jared Sparks, later president of Harvard, was at this time tutor in mathematics and natural philosophy there but left his post to become Unitarian minister in Baltimore; and George Barrell Emerson duly appeared in the catalogue of Oct., 1819, as tutor in geometry, natural philosophy, and astronomy. Edward Everett landed in New York, on his return from Europe, Oct. 7, 1819, according to *The New-York Evening Post* of the same day.

15. Henry Ware, father of the Henry Ware of the letters of 1838, was professor of theology.

16. According to the catalogue of 1820, the sophomore class finished *Collectanea Græca Majora, Excerpta Latina,* and Legendre's geometry, all of which had been begun in the freshman year, and commenced, among other subjects, Cicero's *De Oratore,* analytic geometry, and Blair. Hugh Blair's *Lectures on Rhetoric and Belles Lettres,* 1783, had gone through many editions by 1819. The French reading mentioned later in this letter was apparently not done in the required college course.

17. Parts of this sentence were torn away with the seal.

3 acts of one of Racine's tragedies — Phedre, in the vacation by dint of hard labour at first over Nugent's[18] leaves. VIII I shall try to write on Johnson VIII You must remember your agreement relative to that[19] I may wish to add a Postscript & therefore here subscribe myself Your very affectionate brother Ralph

Mr William Emerson. Boston Feb 20th

Dear Will I have brought your letters to Mother & she is very much disappointed in not recg. the cash. Have you not enterprise or humility enough to apply to him sick or well? R W E.

To William Emerson, Cambridge, April 1 and 10, 1819[20]

Cambridge, I April 1st I 1819.

Dear William,

I cannot possibly find those books for sale, which I am trying to get for you; it has become very fashionable indeed to study French so that there are very few books for sale. I have advertised but cannot get them yet — April 10th 1819 — Still my search is vain, so that I think I must send a letter unaccompanied by books. You must not think me negligent in writing for I should have written a long time ago had I not waited to make my purchase. I shall still, however, endeavour to obtain them unless you send me word, *not* — You do not know how much Aunt Mary has enriched us in intelligence from you; she appears to have been very much pleased with her visit — has imparted all the opinions of the Kennebunkians with regard to *the Preceptor* — viz — a profound scholar, a *small eater* &c &c. I rather think you have raised yourself considerably in Aunt's opinion, for formerly, if you recollect, you did not always agree, and now I don't know of any think she likes to talk of better than Wm's modesty & Wm's — but I see you blush, I will have regard to your delicacy —

But I forgot a determination I made when I saw your *fat* letter a little while since; for I resolved that as a *trait* of such singular excellence in character required the highest strains of panegyrick I must

18. The second American edition of Thomas Nugent's *The New Pocket Dictionary of the French and English Languages* had appeared in New York in 1817. There were numerous London and Paris editions.

19. *Cf.* the letter of Jan. 25 and 27, 1819. William Emerson, Dec. 18, 1818, had promised advice upon whatever Bowdoin subject his brother should attempt.

20. MS owned by RWEMA; ph. in CUL. Excerpts I–V are printed in Cabot, I, 52–53.

write an eulogy to Ken.[21] That [II]letter made several faces shine and when I came humbly plodding home Saturday and carried a sum to the bank to change I believe I held up my head 6 inches higher than before — Mother and Aunt were afraid you had not left yourself enough to subsist upon.[22] Have you?

I told you I was waiter last quarter, and now I am this — You wonder why I was not appointed in the first quarter — it was because I did not petition, which was owing to ignorance when to go — I went a little while since to get my name out & the Prest was very gracious — told me I had grown & said he hoped *intellectually* as well as *physically* & told me (better than all) when my next bill comes out to bring it to him as I had never recieved the Saltonstall benefit [23] promised me before I entered College.[II] My next bill has not come out yet but I think I shall be inclined to remember *that.* [III]My criticism (a theme) on Guillaume le Conqurant [24] had two marks on the back, which distinction only six of the class obtained. Mathematics I hate[III] — In Greek I have been taken up every time but one this week (now Saturday) and have only been corrected in επειτοι, which for me is doing well. And now [IV]as to Bowdoin [25] I am very doubtful about writing this year for though reading Boswell I have not read half of Johnson's works;[IV] & probably a great many will try for it. [V]Do you not think I should do better to be a year writing the Character of Socrates?[V] I have not yet begun any thing. Your chum boards at Mr Wyeth's where you did; & has been to my room lately. Dickinson [26] has a private school in Cambridgeport of 30 scholars; boards at Dr Chaplin's; has been to see me too & asks after you as also does Mr James Farnsworth — I do not know whether I have

21. The letter is addressed to William at Kennebunk.

22. Many years later Emerson recalled that his brother had given up even a trip to Portland to save for the family and had actually been able to bring his mother $400 of the $420 he had received, apparently in addition to board and lodging, as his salary at Kennebunk (see June 27, 1830).

23. The income of Mary Saltonstall's legacy of 1730 was, according to her will, to be "Improved for the assistance of two persons who shall by ye overseers be esteemed of bright parts & good diligence (allways a Dissenter) to fit them for ye Service of ye Church of Christ" (*Pub. Col. Soc. Mass.*, XVI, 845). *Cf.* the letter of Apr. 23 and 24, 1819.

24. It is not quite clear whether Emerson intended "Conqurant" or "Conqierant," but, in either case, the spelling is incorrect.

25. *Cf.* the letter of June 12 and 17, 1818.

26. The catalogue of Oct., 1819, lists Edwards Dickinson, A.B., as a medical student, rooming at Dr. Chaplin's, and gives James D. Farnsworth, A.B., as a theological student.

told you that Farnsworth is engaged to a Cambridge old maid named Munroe. " I have done." I have nothing more to say that I can think of except apologies for scrawling which are cheap. I will carry this letter to Boston & if I have any thing further to add will add it there. Your second North American has been sent.[27]

All well. — Ralph —

Boston Apr 10th

All are well & send love Charles particularly & has got into Greek Grammar You did not comply with a request I formerly made that you would name when you sent for books a price which you think reasonable for the whole. Tell me [when][28] you write again what books you are likely to [need &] I will purchase them at Auctions — Mother desires you to write as quick as possible.

Ralph

To William Emerson, Cambridge, April 23, and Cambridge and Boston, April 24, 1819 [29]

Cambridge, I Apr. 23d I 1819

Dear William,

After all my tardiness & your expectations this letter accompanies but a lame bundle. The Nugent is considerably deficient in its leaves — The Bibliotheque & Wanostrocht's [30] utterly wanting I have endeavoured to supply these defects temporarily by sending you my 'Recueil' which I studied whilst with Miss Sales & my " French Con-

27. William Emerson had suggested in a letter to his mother, Oct. 20, 1818 (owned by Dr. Haven Emerson), that they subscribe for *The North American Review,* which could be read first by the family in Boston and then sent on to him.

28. This and the bracketed words below are conjectural. The MS has been mutilated by the opening of the seal.

29. MS owned by RWEMA; ph. in CUL. Excerpts I–III are in Cabot, I, 53; excerpt IV is in *Memoirs of Members of the Social Circle,* 2d series, 2d part (reissued as *Emerson in Concord*), pp. 25–26.

30. *Bibliothèques,* containing miscellanies of literary and historical matter, sometimes of such bulk that they were quite worthy of the name, had long been favorite ventures with French publishers. The first twelve volumes of a *Bibliothèque historique,* for example, appeared at Paris in 1818 and 1819. Nicolas Wanostrocht's textbook, also a popular aid to students, had achieved a second American edition at Boston in 1810, under the title *A Grammar of the French Language.* For the *Recueil,* see Jan. 9, 1816. The book of French conversations may well have been John Perrin's *The Elements of French and English Conversation,* one edition of which was dated Philadelphia, 1807.

versations " both which you may sell or lend as agreeable; if you sell, make your own price — There is another Recueil at home and I do not know that I shall ever want the other book. When at Miss Sales' I never studied Bibliotheque; I do not know why your scholars may not do as well without. As to French Grammar I have no substitute. In the mean time I am trying to get the deficient books; for these are merely assistances to drive away care till I perform my commission. [II]I went to the president today with my bills & he gave me an order to the steward for credit for 64 Dols. on Saltonstall legacy, & told me I should have more in June.[II] Your chum says he is waiting for a letter from you as he is oldest; says every body expects him to write to them, visit them, &c &c " because he has nothing to do "; but he is staying here at 5 or 600 Dols. a year — for " nothing to do." [III]The Government have just made a new law that no student shall go to the Theatre on penalty of 10 Dols. fine at first offence and other punishment afterwards.[31] I am reading 2d Vol of Boswell — 3d Vol of Spenser's Faery Queen with which I am *delighted* (a girl's word.) [III] Scott has published a third series Tales [32] in England & they are shortly expected here.

[IV]If you could see me now, by benefit of Merlin's mirror, or other assistance, you would pity me. The hour is soon after 5 o'clock A. M., at which time, by the way I get up every morn g, and some times at half past four, — well at this hour in Hollis 5, standing at your old desk twisting & turning endeavouring to collect thoughts or intelligence enough to fill the dreary blank of a page & a third more. Add to my relative situation, my chum asleep very near me.

Saturday 24th I am going to Boston to see Aunt Mary who has returned from her Concord & Waltham visits. = Our next theme is Avarice — Mr Willard always gives us these trite simple subjects con-

31. Both this regulation and one governing the taking of meals outside the college are excellent examples of the academic paternalism of the time: " No scholar shall go into any tavern or victualling house in Cambridge, to eat and drink there, unless in the presence of his parent or guardian, without leave from the President, a Professor, or Tutor, under a penalty, not exceeding fifty cents. . . . No undergraduate shall be an actor, or in any way a partaker, in any stage plays, interludes, masquerades, or theatrical entertainments, in the town of Cambridge, or a spectator at the same; under a penalty not exceeding two dollars. Nor shall he attend theatrical amusements in any other place in term time, under the penalty of ten dollars for the first offence; and if it be repeated, such other College punishment as the Immediate Government may judge adequate to rendering the prohibition effectual." (*Laws of Harvard College*, 1820, pp. 20 and 21.)

32. The third series of *Tales of my Landlord*, published in 1819, included *The Bride of Lammermoor* and *A Legend of Montrose*.

tained in one word. Mr Gilman gives the juniors a motto & generally a very ingenious one with more uncommon subjects.[IV]

Been looking through a glass darkly [33] this morning to see the Eclipse; — I am biting my nails and twisting to find something in the intellectual world to tell you but alas! all, all necessario absunt.

Boston, Noon —

The French Dict. costs a shilling — Mother sends love & says Mr Gould thought this week there was no probability of a vacancy in ushership.[34] Mr Frothingham is a School committeeman & I am going to ask him

Your affectionate brother

Mr Wm. Emerson Ralph.

To William Emerson, Cambridge, June 14, 17, and 20, and Boston, June 20, 1819 [35]

Cambridge, June 14th 1819.

Dear Wm,

I have nothing to interest you, no news to tell, no business to transact, no sentiment or poetry to communicate, no important questions to ask, & yet with all these negatives I am presumptuous enough to put so much trust in the workings of my own barren brain as to sit down with the intention of writing a letter of respectable length to your most serene sobriety. But, (to use a vulgar but expressive phrase) I shall take it fair & easy, and as usual shall not regard a month or two's difference in the commencing & concluding dates; only you will remember it was begun Monday June 14th in the year of our Lord 1819.

But let me not forget to record in the first article of my gazette that the Sophomore Class & their unworthy member your very humble servt have commenced the notorious & important study of Logic. I am getting and am intending to get *my* "lessons *verbatim* and the rest word for word" Spirit of Metaphysicks! (my pen trembles [36] with reverential awe while I write) oh smile on thy pupil & graciously hear his

33. *I Corinthians*, 13:12. *The Massachusetts Register and United States Calendar* for 1819 notes "a small eclipse of the Sun, April 24th," lasting an hour and 39 minutes.

34. At the Latin School.

35. MS owned by RWEMA; ph. in CUL.

36. Young Emerson made the most of his jest by writing this word in a trembling hand.

petitions for preeminence among thy sons! Oh by the way Ticknor [37] has got home and Everett is expected in August and therefore they will most probably have an inauguration next term — What a noble address Everett will make! so much is expected of him & he has had so long time to prepare, that I think expectation will not be disappointed. A very fine subject — Grecian Literature, (I'm soliloquizing now) why yes! I dont know but I would like it myself. —

You know there was one of the Faculty in Boston, one Dr Kast & family who boarded with mother; well they go today to housekeeping unless they lied last Saturday when I visited the family; this you see puts us out of order again & brings toil on trouble for us to procure a *boarding* reinforcement. I shall have to save my ink now by using blacking when I write to you & keep the ink to write advertisements & other similar state papers. Moreover to descend to the rules of economy still further I must let my nails grow long to make pens of and — but that is going far enough to shew you how necessity would give acumen to my already well-known-admirable powers.

It is contemplated to build the new Episcopal Church [38] in Boston of *white marble* like the city hall in New York since some proprietor or proprietors of a quarry have offered to supply them with materials at reduced prices, out of pure love to the Episcopal cause. You know its site is to be opposite the old Mall between Washington Gardens & Winter St.

June 17th I went into Boston last night & heard that the Kasts had removed yesterday & while I was there Mr & Mrs Whitman made an agreement with Mother; they are to come Friday or Saturday so that Mother is not to be two days without some boarders; at present she wants two more persons & then she will be full, & certainly with a dozen more she could not feel more anxiety than she did with four by whom the house has been — blessed, (I was going to say *infested*).

June 20th

Mr Emerson has told our class to furnish ourselves with Enfield tomorrow when we shall finish Legendre [39] — What think

37. George Ticknor, like Edward Everett, was important as an early American apostle of the new German learning. After four years abroad and much travel in various countries, he had reached home on June 6, 1819 (*Life, Letters, and Journals of George Ticknor*, I, 315).

38. St. Paul's, which still stands opposite the Common, on Tremont St., was in process of construction in 1820 (*cf.* Robert M. Lawrence, *The Site of Saint Paul's Cathedral, Boston*, 1916).

39. For George Barrell Emerson, see the letter of Feb. 14, 15, and 20, 1819. Both

you? Sophomore class such a fine one that they have Enfield put into their hands two terms sooner than other classes, besides their loss of a full fortnight sometime since,[40] as you may recollect – The other day I was chosen into the Pythologian Club [41] which has been formed since you graduated – It contains the fifteen smartest fellows in each of the two classes Junior & Soph. its object, extemporaneous discussion – Some of its members in the Junior are – Bowie, Gannett, Davis, Tucker 1st, Hall 1st,[42] Stewart, Deering, &c, in our class Otis first, King, Gourdin, Lyon,

---

William Enfield's *Institutes of Natural Philosophy* and A. M. Legendre's *Elements of Geometry* (translated from the French) had been published at Boston or Cambridge in editions especially designed for use at Harvard College.

40. See Nov. *c.* 23, 1818.

41. The information here given obviously does not fit the club which is described as probably the Pythologian, and whose records are quoted at considerable length, by the editors in *Journals,* I, 34–51. The MS there quoted is a booklet containing 72 numbered pages, some of which are left blank. The front cover bears the legends, obviously added later, " ? Pythologian " and, in different ink, " Journal of a College Society of which R. W. E. was for a time secretary. 1819–21." Aside from the entries printed in *Journals,* there are a few of some importance, unpublished so far as I know, that concern Emerson's activities as a member. At an early meeting, it is recorded, Emerson was to take part in a discussion of " Which the strongest passion Friendship or Hatred? " (p. 8) ; on May 16, 1819, he was made a member of a committee on themes; on June 13 following he debated " Whether poetry has been beneficial to morality? "; on July 5 he read an " essay upon Sentimental Feeling," described in the minutes as *" elegant & highly entertaining "*; on Aug. 2 he again took part in a discussion; on Oct. 12 he was appointed to debate " Whether the conduct of the United States towards the Indians can be reconciled to the principles of justice and humanity "; on Oct. 25 he was selected to discuss " In which state of society, the civilized or the savage, is the greatest degree of happiness to be found "; on Feb. 21, 1820, he began to act as secretary, taking down the minutes for that date as well as for some later meetings recorded in *Journals;* on May 15, 1820, he wrote down his valedictory as secretary; and, finally, at a meeting reported without date, he was one of those appointed to debate " Whether the invention of gunpowder has been an injury or advantage to the world " (p. 40) .

But the club recorded in these minutes, which seems to have been formed on April 24, 1819, at a meeting which Emerson attended, and to have consisted entirely of sophomores, could not well have been the club described in this letter – a club to which Emerson was " chosen," instead of belonging as a charter member; of which he became a member, apparently, in June, not in April; and which was composed of fifteen juniors and a like number of sophomores instead of being limited to twelve members, all of whom were sophomores. I have been unable to find any official records that I believe to belong to the Pythologian Club. But there is mention of Emerson's Pythologian poem both in the *Journals* and in the letter of Apr. 21, 1820.

42. In the college *Catalogue* of Oct., 1818, David P. and Edward B. Hall, like Charles C. and Gideon Tucker, are listed alphabetically among members of the junior class; but in the sophomore class William F. precedes George A. Otis. It is not clear whether this arrangement indicates the relative rank of classmates with the same surnames.

&c — and a very fine set they are — It is a publick club & patronized by Government though I believe its objects are meant to be secret —

Lord Byron has published a new tale [in][43] prose called the Vampyre [44] about 44 little pages — he is of course who walks in the tombs, gnaws sculls, & other equally delicious viands; but perhaps you have read it — which is more than I have though some one told me about it.

I have written a poetical theme about fancy & fairy land & enthusiasm & the like — an eccentrick though *inspired* medley of such matters.[45]

June 20th.[46]

I have just come to Boston & found your letters to *me* & the rest & have to say in answer to the Library Businesses that I will renew what you desire at one, but cannot send " Cours " [47] &c from the other by Mr McKulloch since he goes home today

But by the way, I am &c

Ralph W Emerson

43. This word, presumably, and one or more words in the following line of the manuscript were torn away with the seal.

44. *The Vampyre; a Tale,* London, 1819 (entered March 27), p. xvi, contained a statement implying that Byron was the author. Byron's denial is printed in *The Works . . . Letters and Journals,* ed. Prothero, London, 1900, IV, 286–288.

45. Doubtless the sixty-one untitled and unpublished lines (almost entirely in couplets) the " 2d copy " of which Emerson entered in his diary over the date June 15, 1819 (typescript *Journals*):

" Oh there are times when the celestial muse
Will bless the dull with inspiration's dews, —
Will bid the clowns gross sluggish soul expand
And catch one rapturous glimpse of Fairy Land
Tis when descending fancy, from the bowers
Of blest Elysium seeks this world of ours

. . .

Th enthusiast pauses as he musing stalks
In the far wild-wood's melancholy walks."

. . .

46. It is barely possible that this is to be read " 26th."

47. Perhaps J. F. Laharpe's *Lycée ou cours de littérature ancienne et moderne,* Paris, 4 vols., 1817 and 1818, as Emerson probably remembered the running head. *Cf.* July 3, 1819. The McKulloch named below is presumably the H. McCulloch of Jan. *c.* 2, 1818.

To William Emerson, Boston, July 3, 1819 [48]

Boston July 3[d] 1819

Dear W[m]

I have just come to Boston & recieved intelligence of the opportunity per Mr Sewall & read my commission with a black face for by some strange neglect for which I cannot account I have not got the French book at the College library which I ought & as to the list of French books at Boston Lib. I have — lost it — A comet appeared last night [49] for the first time probably to denounce to mankind this terrible calamity

The company under Gray yesterday came to Boston & I understand made a most splendid appearance & were entertained with a sumptuous dinner in Gray's garden.[50] This morning the parts came out [51] — & Gannett has the English Oration (Reed is not here) & I believe, Harrison, the salutatory, & in our class Barnwell & Upham have a Latin Dialogue Kingsbury Withington & Bulfinch the Greek & Coffin & Adams the English — The last contrary to all expectation. Your own brother you see is not blessed but he does really begin to concieve hopes —

As to the "wherewith" to get along in this life with, we are still in the lurch & rather more so than usual. Mother has only those two boarders that I told you of & one is in the country a few weeks now which takes away half the value even of that; So that Mother wishes me to ask you if possible to take up another quarter's salary to pay our rent August 8th. Mother does not wish to put you to any inconvenience but does not at present know how to meet that demand. In all these difficulties it is a comfort to remember that we are growing older & I don't

48. MS owned by RWEMA; ph. in CUL.

49. The *New-England Palladium,* July 6, 1819, reports that this brilliant comet has been seen for several evenings.

50. The *Palladium* of July 2 announces the march of Captain Gray's Harvard company, to occur that morning, and the entertainment "at the mansion of the family of the Commander, in Summer-street."

51. The reference to the march of the college company proves that the letter is correctly dated, and it is not probable that Emerson wrote the following sentence a day later; but the MS *Records of the College Faculty* (HCL), IX, 196–197, states that the parts for the exhibition were given out on July 4. The official order of performances for the exhibition of Aug. 19, 1819, shows that Emerson's list of parts was correct. Ezra Stiles Gannett's coveted part was "An Oration in English, 'On Mental Inaction,'" and W. B. Harrison, as salutatorian, gave a Latin oration, "De Attico."

doubt that the good taste of mankind will soon discover the talents which now like

Full many a gem of &c [52]

I am going to Cambridge again & shall obtain this La Harpe [53] of which you talk so familiarly & send him by the packet You know when all college books must be returned; — is it not before August? I send you 1 Volume of Montolieu's Works,[54] which I just obtained by returning Fontaine.[55] The book I endeavoured to get you was one of Mad. de Genlis' was not in —

Love from Mother & brothers particularly from your very affectionate

Ralph —

52. The "Elegy" is more than once echoed in earlier letters.

53. *Cf.* the letter of June 14, 17, and 20, 1819.

54. Possibly a volume of *Recueil de contes, par Mad. Isabelle de Montolieu,* of which an edition of three volumes was published at Geneva in 1803.

55. Probably this was the La Fontaine of the stories and fables, or it may have been, I suppose, Pierre François Léonard Fontaine, the writer on architecture.

1820

To Edward Bliss Emerson, Boston, January 31, 1820[1]

Boston Jan. 31st. 1819.

Dear Edward,

I am not going to trouble you with all the long apologies of letterwriters young and old when they have been negligent for after using a few pages of their epistle in this excusing & excusable introduction it generally amounts after all to nothing more or higher than mine, — laziness & procrastination.

So to begin. I have been here all this vacation reading & writing & talking & walking & contemplating & running errands & in short doing all & every thing which a mock-Poetick Junior might be expected to perform. I have been listening to " the thunders of the senate," the forensick quibbles of the bar, the high converse of the parlour and all the various chitchat of human life in Boston!!! I have been poetizing a little, dissertationising more. But I had almost forgot — I heard Mr Everett a few Sabbaths ago preach all day at Mr Palfrey's a new year's Sermon from the text " Brethren, the time is short."[2] I will give you from memory a few fine sentences — " and in another life when Goodness & Happiness, those stranger sisters, shall meet together & know each other, where we shall stand upon the confines of another world & see creation on creation sweeping by to their doom, then we shall behold that time indeed is short then we shall learn to pity little *man* piling up his monuments of marble & calling it *fame* — " this is a broken

1. MS owned by RWEMA; ph. in CUL. It is clear from internal evidence that the year 1819 is another "January" error, though unusually late in the month. Moreover, the endorsement has "31st Jan/17 March, 1820," and Edward Emerson writes from Alexandria, D. C. (now Va.), on Mar. 23, 1820, "I received your letter dated 31st Jan on the 17th of this month."

2. *I Corinthians,* 7:29. Evidently the same sermon preached in the Capitol at Washington in the following February, a sermon which seems to have been much admired (*cf.* Allibone, *A Critical Dictionary,* 1874, I, 569). John Gorham Palfrey, the historian, had become pastor of the Brattle Street Church in Boston in 1818.

passage you see from the middle of the discourse. Again speaking of the necessity of warning our friends of their eternal danger he says " and if they will not repent then *let* the passing bell wail from steeple to steeple & when you weep you will not weep alone; the angels will weep with you & *he* will weep with who shed his blood[2] for man[1] whose costly outpourings we celebrate today, (Communion day) & the recording angel in heaven will exclaim with the voice of destiny " a soul is lost, seal up! " "

When speaking of the mutability of every thing here he said Look along the pews of the church, — are none of their inhabitants changed & look at this pulpit & mark well if the same voice which now addresses you addressed you ten — twenty, — thirty years ago. These are mere scraps of the long discourse which was an hour long in the morning & as long in the afternoon; but if you read them as slow as Everett & with his manner you can well concieve of the eloquence which almost ravished the audience. I could say half the sermon the night after it. Thus far I have told you of me & my experiences & hearings &c two long pages excellently well appropriated! Now for others. Mother is well but has been too busy to write. William has twenty scholars at his schoolroom [3] beside the Tildens' Do you not congratulate him on his unexampled unexpected success? Dr Coffin presented him with a ticket to his Lectures on Physical Education [4] for himself & family & we have been — already to two. Aunt Mary is & has been here for some weeks. Miss Stearns is still alive but only so.

I hope you keep that Journal of yours faithfully regularly & largely.[5] Do hear the Missouri question if possible agitated debated or decided in the supreme Legislature of the United States. What an opportunity! I am very sorry you do not live 8 miles nearer then you might dwell in the Senate house. Give me some idea of the Capitol's external & in-

3. Ruth Haskins Emerson wrote to Edward, Apr. 9 and 16, 1820, that the school continued to be full; and there is abundant evidence in the later letters and in the miscellaneous correspondence of the family that William's years as a teacher in Boston were very successful. The school was a private enterprise, but I have found no advertisements, such as commonly appeared, in the Boston papers. A few later letters tell something about Emerson's own part in it as assistant to William.

4. The *Columbian Centinel*, Jan. 19, 1820, advertises Dr. Coffin's course of lectures on physical education.

5. In the letter of Dec. 11, 1816, Emerson had spoken on the subject of keeping a " Logbook " in a not very laudatory tone; but as early as 1819, and perhaps earlier, he was keeping journals himself. Bacon's advice, alluded to below, was doubtless remembered from the essay " Of Travaile."

ternal appearance. Webst[er has][6] gone to Washington to plead before the Supreme cou[rt] I believe. Hear Hear. You see I would have you hear & see all that is to be heard & seen at Washington & away all in one moment! Write letters three times as long for you easily can by condensing or collecting your scrawling hand. Do you hear? I shall send you now or sometime Lord Bacons rules for a traveller; the first is to keep a journal. All send love & particular remembrance to Mr & Mrs Ladd & William.

With affection &c

Mr Edward B. Emerson. Ralph

P. S. Mother will soon write to you & was very much obliged to Mr Ladd [7] for his speedy communication of your arrival & is only waiting for communication by water to write often. Waldo.

To William Emerson, Cambridge, February 12? 1820 [8]

Saturday Morn.[g]

Dear Wm

All who can tell me of Perodi are still in Boston having come out merely to enter their names & returned. I am bewailing it in sorrow of soul which knows no remedy but the hope of Monday [9]

What was my agony, think you, to find on my return that my Geometry was & is *not* in my bookshelves – the geometry which I promised Daniel F.[10] should be sent to him today. Alas! alas.

Whether I have lent or lost it I am ignorant. It is possible that Edward

6. This and the following pair of brackets contain portions of the text presumably torn away with the seal.

7. John Haskins Ladd, of Alexandria, in whose care this letter was addressed, was Emerson's cousin (Warren Ladd, p. 291).

8. MS owned by RWEMA; ph. in CUL. Endorsed " R.W.E. 1816," but obviously written about the same time as the letter of Feb. 14, 1820, and probably preceding it by only two days. Apparently the present letter was not sent, or else Emerson repeated himself unconsciously in the letter of the 14th, which was certainly sent.

9. Monday, Feb. 14, continues the same subject. I have not been able to identify Perodi, though he may have been the P. Perodi whose *Memoirs of the Reign of Murat* bears a Boston imprint dated 1818. The author of this pamphlet, who described himself as a cavalry officer and a member of Murat's staff, was, according to the copyright entry, resident in Massachusetts.

10. The Daniel Farnham of the letter of Feb. 14. He was Emerson's cousin, brother of the Louisa (Catherine Louisa) who appears here and in the following letter, as well as in *c.* 1817. For the Farnhams, see especially *Vital Records of Newburyport,* 1911, I, 135.

has it. Of this let him be assured that I shall make diligent search & inquiry to the end that I may find it. Will you not give orders that Lowths Lectures [11] which Miss Savage [12] has, may be carried to Cousin Louisa Aunt [13] took the book from the Vestry for her Do all things go on in their proper order in my absence? If not send me word & I shall make some exertions to divide my busy time between you & C.[14]

Love & veneration to all

Waldo [15]

To William Emerson, Cambridge, February 14, 1820 [16]

Cambridge Feb. 11th 1820
Monday Morn

Dear William

When I began to make inquiries on Friday about Mr Perodi (which is the name of the man) I found that all the few who could inform me were in Boston nor could I find any one till Saturday night who could tell me that the Italian lived last summer (& probably now) in Suffolk place near Dr Geo. Hayward which turns out of Newbury St on the right as you go from Essex St.

But oh William you may judge the agony of grief disappointment anger & despair &c &c which seized me on looking along my shelves & not finding the Promised procrastinated Playfairs Geometry.

Make my lamentations & respects to Mr Daniel Farnham & tell him I do not know whether I have lent or lost it but shall endeavour immediately to find it & transmit the same.

Aunt Mary borrowed Lowths Lectures from the vestry for *Louisa* will you not be so good as to give *orders* in my name that the book be sent to her. Miss Savage had when I came away.

Tell mother that the June bill was to be paid. & the reason that it was not on assessment was because the December bill came out so late

11. Robert Lowth's *Prælectiones* had long since been translated into English as *Lectures on the Sacred Poetry of the Hebrews.*

12. Perhaps the schoolmistress of that name listed in *The Boston Directory,* 1820.

13. Mary Moody Emerson, as the following letter shows.

14. Cambridge.

15. Not the first occurrence of this signature, but it was still experimental and did not become established till a little later.

16. MS owned by RWEMA; ph. in CUL. The Monday morning nearest the 11th of Feb., 1820, was the 14th, and the postmaster at Cambridge wrote the date Feb. 14 on the outside of the letter. Since the letter is brief and was mailed, it is not at all probable that it was kept several days before it was sent.

in last term. The whole sum I paid to College for the two bills was $39. 43.

Do all things & persons go on in proper order in my absence? If not send me word & I may make some exertion to divide my time between you & Cam. Till then I shall trust to your face & fidelity to keep order.

Love & veneration to all

Waldo

Mr William Emerson

To Edward Bliss Emerson, Cambridge, April 21, 1820 [17]

Cambridge April 21st 1820 =

Dear Edward,

I am going as usual to dispense with all fashionable apologies for not writing earlier or oftener, & as to this letter, if it arrives in Alexandria before you leave the city, I shall be perfectly satisfied. For though all these particularities &c answer very well like this of mine for a preface yet if a letter contains nothing of more importance at one time than another it is just as good a month as a year [18] after its date. As to news at College I may assure you that when the Senior class leaves college you will be better pleased with the performances than last year. Reed is appointed orator, Kent, the Poet; [19] — & this last gentleman is unquestionably the greatest poet that is or has been in college for a long time back. Last night I delivered a poem before the Pythologian Society [20] which I told you a long time ago that I was appointed to write. The subject — though nominally "Improvement," yet *actually* seemed to waver between that & *The course of Empire*. Having given you the subject & informing you that it contained 250 lines no doubt your own imagination will supply the rest but if you should be unwilling to get a copy of it in such a speculative way & lest also the midnight labours of the poor poet should be consigned to mature oblivion I shall endeavour to send you the performance if there be any large

17. MS owned by RWEMA; ph. in CUL.

18. Emerson probably either slipped in his logic or meant to be humorous. The word "day," written between the lines, may be a correction inserted by Edward.

19. William G. Read and Benjamin Kent were both members of the class of 1820, but only Kent appeared on the commencement program of that year.

20. For this society, see the letter of June 14, 17, and 20, 1819. The poem is mentioned in *Journals,* I, 31. It occupies a number of pages in an unpublished section of the diaries, where its heroic couplets are interrupted at intervals by unrelated entries (typescript *Journals,* No. XVII, 1820).

ship going capacious enough to hold it. But be sure if I send it to select the neatest lack-a-daisy passages you can find & satisfy the demands of my Alexandria friends who have honoured me with their requests for such lumber. And always observe the rules of decorum due from poet to patron; — make a long preface on presentation, about the abject, prostrate, *down*-to-the-*ground* humility of a luckless rhymer; tell of the unpropitious regards of the muses, the freezing glance of Apollo of the scornful, horrificable *irrefrangefrackability* of the world; — & then, make a low bow & forthwith produce the Poem — This is the best & most approved way now practised in England. — Now perhaps you are very angry & impatient to have me waste your time & my paper in haranguing nonsense about my poetry. I have therefore only to entreat your patience & pardon, for really I do not know if I have any thing else to write about. If however you want sympathy for some of those huge domestic distresses that have grown up into your path I most heartily hope & desire that the Shoemaker *will* sole your boots that the Congress *will* gratify your senses & that Mr Blagge [21] will not overthrow the world nor break up the barriers of society but will come with treasures of Coromandel & lay down his dollar at your feet. Nevertheless even should he not, be not disheartened but lay it to the charge of " the cruel fates." Perhaps you have remarked that amid all this farrago I have shewn myself profoundly ignorant of your journal; whether you have or not I must confess that I have only read the one written on board the ship. And my excuse is that on the first Saturday that I saw it in town Mr Moody & Mr Frost [22] (Wm's Collego-Kennebunko friends) so fascinated & overwhelmed me with the charms of their conversation, that — if ever you have seen either or both of them — you can easily conceive I was unable to read; — the next Saturday Aunt Mary was in town & my poem was correcting & some things going on that it was impossible — Tomorrow however I go to town & depend on reading & admiring. If the boys have written to you I suppose you know that Mother is going to move to Franklin street.[23] I do not know the merits of the house

21. Perhaps Samuel Blagge, the notary mentioned in the letter of Oct. 8, 1823, and listed in *The Boston Directory*, 1820, as " Swedish Consul, notary public." The Blagge mentioned in the present letter is certainly the same who appears in May *c.* 16, 1820.

22. Like George Barrell Moody, John Frost, of the class of 1822, was from Kennebunk.

23. *The Boston Directory*, 1820, gives the address of Mrs. Ruth Emerson as still 60 Essex St.; but, according to her letter to Edward dated Apr. 9 and 16, 1820, she was to move her household at once to 24 Franklin Place, and the move had certainly been made by Jan. 1, 1821, as Emerson's letter of that date shows.

from its situation for I have not been there. Indeed [I do not][24] know how any advantages of house or situation can [com]pensate the irreparable loss we sustain in forfieting the society & neighbourhood & protection of Mr Bruce! It requires a mightier muse than mine to conceive in adequate strains the greatness of the calamity — I shall not therefore attempt an elegy. What if you exercise your muse, if she is not dead, (she has manifested no signs of life lately that I have known) in eulogising the worth of character & the grandeur of scenery of which we are about to be deprived by a removal. I know it must be less painful to your feelings at the distance you stand than if you were present. But I will stop here after bidding you give my compliments to Mr & Mrs Ladd & to Wm if near you.

Yours. With affection &c &c &c

Ralph.

Mr Edward B Emerson —

To Edward Bliss Emerson, Boston, April 22, 1820 [25]

Boston April 22d 1820

Dear Edward,

I have just come to town from Cambridge [&] find a letter to me from you (date Apr. 4th) & letters to Mo[ther][26] & boys. In answer to your Quaker speech — it is a fine [sen]sible opinion finely & sensibly expressed, (in my humble opinion). As to the request for poetry, herewith I shall send you a pamphlet with my poem [27] but on second thoughts you must not put any of it in the paper [28] because the paper I

24. These words, I conjecture, were torn away with the seal, together with a part of the word just below. It is barely possible that a word immediately following "house" in the preceding sentence was also torn away.

25. MS owned by RWEMA; ph. in CUL. This letter follows, on the same sheet, a letter from Ruth Haskins Emerson to Edward dated Apr. 9 and 16, 1820.

26. This word and "sensible," which began below it in the original manuscript, were mutilated by the opening of the seal. The "&" of the line above is wholly conjectural.

27. Apparently the Pythologian poem mentioned in Apr. 21, 1820.

28. Edward, in a letter dated Alexandria, Jan. 17, 1819 (*i.e.*, 1820), had reminded Emerson of his promise to send some verse and had added, as an inducement, that a paper "entitled the telescope" was published there and would be a fine thing for his brother to try his fortune in. Files of this paper are owned by the Library of Congress and by Mrs. Louis S. Scott, of Alexandria, Va., but both Mrs. Scott and Miss Mary E. Lloyd have searched all the issues in vain for such a poem as Emerson describes. Presumably his request was heeded. And the *Columbian Telescope & Literary Compiler* ceased publication a few weeks later.

believe comes to some of my classmates & should the poetry be recognized there might be doubts entertained as to the originality of that confessedly mine. You must be careful not to lose or lend the poem because the copy I send you belongs to Aunt Mary & must be brought back. We send you likewise the French Grammar — & Mother says you did not acknowledge the receipt of letters by the Industry [29] — hope you recieved them. We talk about your return Regards & respects to all.

Ralph.

To Edward Bliss Emerson, Cambridge, May *c.* 16, 1820 [30]

Cambridge May 1820

Dear Edward,

I recieved last Saturday (May 13th), when in Boston, your very long & instructive letter dated April 20th. You may judge of the delightful feelings wakened in a heart sensible as mine at the praise it contained, conscious as I was that it proceeded from sincerity. To be sure I had some self complacency when I called to mind the labours I had undergone in producing those "numerous & pleasant letters" which you so gratefully mention. Fearful however that I might be overwhelmed with undeserved flattery I have determined to add *one* to their multitude which you must be sensible will just *double* their number. With regard, however, to the subject of this letter & which should be worthy of the sublime Prolegomena with which it has been ushered in, I have not yet determined whether to astonish you with elaborate displays of erudition, or give you a dissertation on the moral offices, or descend to the playful gambols of the Muse, or lastly to witch you with a narration of the news, (advertisements & all,) or beguile you with apologies of the most profound unmeaningness.

I shall inform you of my decision on the next page.

Seventhly. We come now to consider Literature at large, as an *imitative* animal; and here we must take occasion to observe, that it is a fine

29. In the *New-England Palladium* of Feb. 29, 1820, the schooner "Industry" was advertised to leave Boston for Alexandria on the first of March.

30. MS owned by RWEMA; ph. in CUL. As the "last Saturday" was May 13, the date of writing falls somewhere in the week May 14–20, but probably not on the 14th, for Emerson would very likely have remained at home over Sunday. I conjecture that he carried the letter home from Cambridge the following week end, for his mother added a postscript of her own, dated Boston, May 22, in the margin of the superscription, explaining that she had opened the letter to do so. According to the postmark, the letter was finally mailed at Boston on May 23.

child, grows greatly, & looks exactly like its mother. I must digress from the main subject of my story to ask you how they all do in Alexandria — because I may forget it. Have you been to see Lee? [31] If you have not you must go as soon as possible & note down all that he says, ad verbum, as if he were the Delphian oracle itself. When you come home I shall look up to you with envying admiration Only think of it for a moment — A young gentleman who has just returned from his *travels* & has recently left the seat of government Why a jaunt to Grand Cairo is nothing to it! I shall comfort myself however [with][32] my unalterable determination to go into a far country hereafter & make a voyage either to El Dorado or to the territories of Gloriana.[33] " But really now " do people eat drink & sleep walk ride & run in Alexandria as in other places? It is a land so very *rarely* visited (probably through terrour of wild beasts) that you will have a most tempting opportunity when you return to magnify every miracle & twist every story to the amazement of millions of auditors staring & listening with speechless credulity.

(" Carried over " —) — — [34]

For instance you may tell them that in this same fearful region of Alexandria the barbarous inhabitants imprison every body who comes there whose name begins with B & rob every one whose name begins with a vowel &c &c.; for you know Mr Blagge aye the illustrious Mr Blagge was imprisoned & Mr Emerson had his money borrowed of him — This certainly renders the assertion very probable [f]or [35] would any gentleman be so uncivil as to doubt of it.

As the learned Pherecydes of Syros observes in his book on Mineralogy,[36]

To call on thoughts when thoughts are not at home,
To try to rhyme & find you only roam;
This is like fumbling empty pockets o'er
For a spent ninepence, — fifty times & more.

In direct pursuance of which hortatory lines I have advanced thus far

31. Edward Emerson, Alexandria, Mar. 23, 1820, says he was introduced to Lee at a party and was invited to visit him. The Harvard catalogue of Oct., 1818, shows that Charles C. Lee, then a senior, was from Alexandria.

32. At least one word has been almost completely torn away with the seal.

33. In the letter of Apr. 23 and 24, 1819, Emerson reported that he was reading *The Faerie Queene* and was delighted with it.

34. Added at the end of the page, apparently for humorous effect.

35. The bracketed letter is conjectural. The MS is slightly mutilated.

36. So far as I am able to discover, the whole passage, with the exception of the name of the Greek writer, is Emerson's own invention.

without — a ninepence. Seriously, (for the first time in the letter,) I have no news to impart of consequence & am therefore hastening, as fast as the paper will diminish, to a close. Mr Everett gives lectures on Greek literature &c once a week to the Senior class & consequently I do not hear them. John Everett has returned to Cambridge from Transylvania Univ.[37] & is going to study law here. I am glad, my dear to percieve that you improve fast in writing — My pen trembles [38] for its — throne,

from you very aff^{t} brother Ralph.

Wont you be so good as to give my love & compliments to my friends in the wonderful town of Alexandria

37. He was tutor there, 1818–1820 (*A Catalogue of . . . Transylvania University . . . July, 1826,* p. 6).

38. The word is written as if by a very unsteady hand.

1821

To John Sales, Boston, January 1, 1821

[MS owned by Mr. Owen D. Young; ph. in CUL. Printed in F. B. Sanborn, *Recollections of Seventy Years,* 1909, II, 458, where it is complete except for the name repeated at the end: " John Sales Esqr."]

To Mary Moody Emerson, February? 1821

[Mary Moody Emerson, Feb. 24, 1821, praises his " letters," which she could not help reading before she went to bed. Apparently she had just received more than one letter from him; but much allowance must be made for her highly individual manner. It is quite possible that the " letters " were variously dated sections of the same MS. Her comment seems to show that he had discussed the mythology of northern Europe and, perhaps, the subject of philosophy.]

To Mary Moody Emerson, Boston, April 7, 1821 [1]

Boston Saturday Apr. 7th 1821

My dear Aunt

Mother directed me to write a note to you signifying the utter discrepancy of opinion which exists between you & herself with regard to Waldo's Exhibition, & my object is to convert you to our views. Now you must be aware that if all reasoned like you the luckless performers would speak their well-conned exercises to bare walls. And if I may be allowed to be impudent I shall suggest the fact that not twenty present will know that your proud ladyship is related to the despised & ragged poet. You are wont to say that the spectacle of this world's splendour amuses you and if it will gratify you I am very confident the company of the day will be the leaders of the fashion as the sons of senators &c have parts on that day. Furthermore if you would wish your bashful nephew to do well & claim the ground his own vanity aims to reach, you must encourage him with your presence on Tuesday, 24th April [2] – My

1. MS owned by RWEMA; ph. in CUL.

2. Emerson's poem " Indian Superstition " is listed in *University in Cambridge. Order of Performances for Exhibition. Tuesday, April 24, 1821,* 1821, p. 4. This is notable as apparently his only appearance on an exhibition program during his col-

room is No 9 Hollis. Should you come from Hamilton[3] you must not ask for Waldo the Poet — he is better known by the name of Emerson the Senior —

Mother says she cannot write herself for Bulkeley is sick but insists upon your coming to Boston & thence to Cambridge with her & agrees with you that a refusal would be a whim engendered of *Solitude.* I could say more in scandal of this last dame were I not her sworn defender, by my oath to the muses. Professor Everett has preached a fine Fast Sermon at Mr Frothingham's church & elsewhere. You must recollect your large promises of correspondence to your moste affectionate

Waldo.

Miss M. M. Emerson.

Inhabitant of Hamilton, (or rather the World.)

To Sarah Ripley, Boston, August 22, 1821[4]

Boston, August 22^d^ 1821

My dear Aunt,

Aunt Mary bids me write some gossip, which she wishes to communicate — And in the first place, your friend Miss Sally Ingersoll is about to be married to a man of great wealth — Mr Hooper of Marblehead.[5] Secondly, a cousin of yours and Aunt Mary's, Horace Bliss, was in Boston last week with the West Point Cadets.[6] We did not know he was one of them till they had been here some days, when we found him with some difficulty and brought him to our house, to shew him the pictures of his grandparents &c &c. He was very affectionate and said he was sorry that the March would not carry the Cadets through Concord. He is a lieutenant in the corps and a high scholar.

---

lege years. According to MS *Records of the College Faculty* (in HCL), IX, 248 (Mar. 7, 1821), the assignment specified that the poem should be one hundred lines in length.

3. The letter is addressed to Hamilton, Mass., one of the numerous temporary residences of the volatile aunt.

4. MS owned by RWEMA; ph. in CUL. Sarah Ripley (1781–1826) was a sister of Samuel Ripley, who kept the school at Waltham. She and her brother were the children of Emerson's grandmother Phebe Bliss by her second husband, Dr. Ezra Ripley (*The Ipswich Emersons*, p. 126).

5. Sarah Ingersoll was married to Nathaniel Hooper on Nov. 20, 1821 (Charles Pope and Thomas Hooper, *Hooper Genealogy*, 1908, p. 129).

6. Horace Bliss, nephew of Emerson's grandmother Phebe Bliss, was a cadet at West Point from 1817 to 1822 (John H. Bliss, *Genealogy of the Bliss Family*, 1881, pp. 53 and 84). On the march referred to, the cadets visited Boston Aug. 7–18 (*Boston Daily Advertiser*, Aug. 8–18, 1821).

Commencement is a week from today, on the 29th — I shall not have a dinner and have not asked any body — for a conference [7] is a stupid thing — There will be some good *parts,* though we are disappointed of John Everett's, and if you think of coming we shall be very happy to see you; Mother and Aunt and a host of brothers will be there. My room is No 9 Hollis.

I suppose you have not heard from Providence.[8] I do not yet know whether they will give me an ushership at the Latin School. Give my respects to Grandfather and Grandmother and remember me to the young ladies

Your affectionate nephew
Waldo

Miss Sarah Ripley —

Mother has gone to Newton with Bulkeley to spend a week with Mrs Greenough [9] —

To George Champlin Shepard, Boston, September 3, 1821 [10]

Boston, Sept 3d 1821

Dear Sir

I am sorry to be obliged to trouble your politeness again, but when I returned home I discovered that I had left a linen shirt at Chap-

7. The *Order of Exercises for Commencement, XXIX August, MDCCCXXI* listed "A Conference, 'On the Character of John Knox, William Penn, and John Wesley'" to be given by Emerson, Amos Gordon Goodwin, and William Pope. According to the *Columbian Centinel,* Sept. 1, 1821, and the *New-England Palladium* of Aug. 31, this exercise was somewhat altered because Pope failed to appear. Dr. John Pierce (*Proc. Mass. Hist. Soc.,* 2d series, V, 188) took no note of this part of the program but praised Upham and Barnwell. John Everett, whose oratory is admired in the letter of July 20 and 21, 1818, received a Master's degree at the commencement of 1821 but did not appear on the program as a speaker. Emerson makes no mention of William Cullen Bryant, who was to be the ΦBK poet on the day following the graduating exercises. Parke Godwin said he found "notes of introduction, etc.," from Emerson to Bryant written "not long afterward" and so thought the two must have met on this occasion (*A Biography,* 1883, I, 174). But Emerson was only a boy of eighteen, and the conjecture seems extremely doubtful. I have no proof of any letters or notes to Bryant until much later.

8. The letter of Sept. 3, 1821, shows that Emerson made a trip to Providence at that time — perhaps in quest of a school. He did not receive a place in the Boston Public Latin School, to which the following passage seems to refer.

9. Doubtless Lydia Haskins Greenough, sister of Ruth Haskins Emerson (see D. G. Haskins, *Ralph Waldo Emerson his Maternal Ancestors,* 1887, p. 147).

10. MS owned by Fanny Haskins Boltwood and Elvira Wright Boltwood; ph. in CUL. The superscription describes Shepard as a member of the sophomore class at

polin's, — and my mother, who is an excellent economist, and fortunately knows the value of a shirt better than I, says that her careless son must write a note to his cousins, and ask them to call at the hotel and send the article by Mr Ladd, if he comes through the town, or by the stage. It was marked with my name and left I think in No 23. I am very sorry to give you any trouble, if you do not find it readily, do not look any farther —

Your affectionate cousin
R Waldo Emerson.

Mr George C Shepard.

To Mary Moody Emerson and Robert Bulkeley Emerson, Boston, November 8, 1821 [11]

Boston, Nov 8th 1821.

My dear Aunt,

The winds and rains have combined to wet your delightful ramble and to disappoint the schemes which the love of nature planned. I hardly think you have wandered in wood or grove by

Providence, R. I.; and the *Historical Catalogue of Brown University 1764–1914,* 1914, p. 437 and index, shows that he was a student there but graduated at Amherst in 1824. He was the son of Emerson's maternal aunt Deborah Haskins Shepard. He became a minister of the Protestant Episcopal Church, and he married Emerson's cousin — and his own cousin — Sally Kast. (D. G. Haskins, pp. 62–63; and *The New-England Historical & Genealogical Register,* XXIII, 230–231.)

11. MS owned by RWEMA; ph. in CUL. Excerpt I is freely quoted in Cabot, I, 69. This letter is remarkable as an example of the new mastery of style and the new maturity of mind that now begin to make themselves felt. Probably a few earlier letters, now lost, showed something of this same change, for on Feb. 24, 1821, Mary Moody Emerson remarked upon the " new born dignity of your style " and suggested Everett's influence. The " little loghouse on the mountains " was, I conjecture, a figure of speech which might probably be made clear if all of Mary Moody Emerson's letters were extant. The " fatal *Gehenna* " seems to refer to the beginning of Emerson's brief career as a regular schoolteacher. But in his MS *Autobiography,* containing some chronological outlines mostly written many years after the events recorded, Emerson notes that he entered William's school as assistant in Oct., 1821. " *The drama* " was pretty definitely an essay or series of essays Emerson was writing (*cf. Journals,* I, 54–59, 106–108, 147–150, 166–167, 169–170 — entries of 1820 and 1822). In an unpublished portion of the diaries, under date of Oct. 21, 1821, there is what purports to be an address to an editor (probably imaginary), asking him to admit into his columns " some papers on the Drama which I shall successively send you." This address is followed by a number of instalments, usually labeled as letters and numbered. (See typescript *Journals.*) Considerable parts of this commentary are to be found in the printed version I have cited as dated 1820.

lake or lawn through the three dismal days last past. Nature willing to atone for your wretched entertainment has hung out the moon in this transparent sky to cheer you with its brilliant beams. But to a dull mortal like myself whom the fates have condemned to school-keeping, it is entirely indifferent what planet rules — Venus or dogstar the warm solar Mercury, or cold and solitary Mars who shone on me all last winter [1]in my little loghouse on the mountains.[1] Notwithstanding my abhorrence of midnight or morning vigils I did once think that there was something lofty something sublime in the watchfulness which claimed to itself the shining host in their solemn and silent revolution & something honourable in the solitude which mingled with such pure society. The Assyrian shepherds have inherited a spotless fame who have written their names and fancies in the stars to be read as long as language lasts. I suppose you are tired of the stars but I am one who mourn the destruction of Astrology.

Mother sends her love and wishes to hear; also of the boy Bulkeley Is he not a great deal of trouble? — but I ask pardon; that would implicate the wisdom and skill of your ladyships administration. If you stay longer I must beg the favour of letters. I am not yet in the fatal *Gehenna* and will not alarm you by by naming the doleful day. *The drama* crawls on but clamours for inspiration. Dr Sam. Clarke is read; indeed I have nothing in the world to tell you and must close. Desolate hall hath grown doubly desolate and Charles complains of your absence. Though we have not the slightest apprehension of any real intention on your part to withdraw in earnest from the town, yet we are willing to tell you what a blank is percieved. Theological controversy is all over; brilliant repartee hath vanished also; — we all wish to see you none more so than

Your nephew

Waldo

Miss M M Emerson

Dear Bulkeley, I hope you are a very good boy and very happy in the country. Mother and all send their love to you. Give our love to Grandmother Grandfather Aunt Sarah and Aunt Mary.

Your affectionate brother

Waldo

R Bulkeley

To Mary Moody Emerson, Boston? November? 1821? [12]

The Muse ceases to own her name when she is not prone & fond to assert her rectitude assailed. Were it only to hear herself talk she must reply. Ever since the fatal entrance to Gehenna she hath been awake — " But there was a pride " True, there was a pride, but it was kindled elsewhere than is supposed. Friend, thou thinkst mine hour is passed, the waters of self-annihilation and contempt are already settling calmly over me and expanding their muddy sheet between my name, and *light* forever. The child's dream was blest by some faint glimpses of strange light & strange worlds, — but the child looked at his bauble and played again with his bauble and the light was withdrawn. Now if such light had been imparted, there was *one* of whom the boy was taught the nature and advantage of the visions but when his weak nature & strong fates began to darken them — will instructer & friend alike forsake him? Joy brightens, they say, the edge of the cloud where is grief; but joy is not mine for I dislike events; grief is not mine for the spirits & the blood will circulate in some so that they shall be too silly to be sad. Pride works a little but cannot supply the place of encouragement, and the being on whom you throw your gentle execrations would rejoice to find in himself a little more of the lion for a recoil — upon a long train of woes mustered by thy predictions. Will the Nine be shamed by the company of their sex? Did they shun Corinna and abhor de Stael Have such things shed dreary clouds about the Aonian hill and put far away the templed heights of Parnassus and the silver fountain of the Pierides. These were rich thoughts which have been nourished as long and as ardently as a weak & unpoetical temperament could keep them and I do not yet know that the second sight of Cassandra or the robes of later prophecy shall shroud them all behind its dark drapery. But you speak of holier Muse. Thy

12. MS owned by RWEMA; ph. in CUL. The penciled date, " Nov 1821," at the beginning and again at the end of the letter, and incomplete superscription, " Miss M M Emerson," may both have been added later but seem to be Emerson's own. The date is probably correct, for this letter pretty clearly follows closely that of Nov. 8, 1821. A letter from Mary Moody Emerson dated only with days of the week, Friday to Tuesday, but presumably written about Nov., 1821, contains passages which throw some light on both the present letter and that of Nov. 8. She asserts that she does not think teaching is degrading but that she does have a lower opinion of women than of men (her nephew was beginning, or about to begin, teaching in his brother's school for girls). She wants to know what he could mean by connecting " those things " in his school with Parnassus. If he is awakened, let him write, but let him offer nothing to her. She asks the favor of being remembered as a dead Cassandra, not prophesying but praying for his welfare.

stern spirit would, I presume, refuse the pages of Clarke to so humble and unworthy hands; but if I am in the very jaws of peril I need a shield more. Then perhaps it will be profanation to look further; to read what Clarke hath written is wholesome but to dare hereafter to write myself — you think it wrong, while I think it to be a just & sublime employment. I do not understand the grounds of your reason and we can therefore speak no more upon it —

Your letter is as Cassandra's should be, dark, and not entirely intelligible. I write not because it was necessary but that it is a pleasure. You will say I *prove nothing* — I know it but it was in reply to a letter of *sentiment*. Thy kinsman, Waldo.

To Mary Moody Emerson, Boston? December? 1821? [13]

I ought to have answered your letter sooner which contained quite a stream of moral sentiment. I wonder how you can ever have linked a hope to the wayward destinies of a thing like me, to my dream-like anticipations of greatness. Not many indulge this prophecying vein, and yet there is something noble & striking in the attempting of a man to concieve the bent of his fortunes which begin here, and nowhere & never end; it is putting out an arm into the unseen world, and when some have done it they have felt the reaching and beckoning of somewhat unearthly. But this is denied to the multitude. = Your imagination is fond of recurring to the poor reptiles and I give you joy of the worm!

I intended to have written a long answer to your letter but the spirit is not upon me

Caduceus [14] — An emblem of wisdom used by Mercury to guide the souls of the dead to the shades.

R. Waldo E.

13. MS owned by RWEMA; ph. in CUL. This undated scrap bears the superscription "Miss M.M.E," and internal evidence makes it doubly certain that it was written to Mary Moody Emerson. The date 1821 has been added at the top of the sheet, and the text is in Emerson's hand of about 1821. This seems to follow what we may call the "Gehenna" letter of Nov.? 1821? It is possible that an undated and unpublished entry in the diaries headed "Tnamurya" and beginning "You are right It was a most uninteresting lecture" is an incomplete draft or copy of another letter to the same correspondent belonging to the end of this or the early part of the following year. It stands between entries dated Oct. 21, 1821, and Feb. 21, 1822. (Typescript *Journals*.) But it is not the only one of its kind which I have omitted because of its uncertain status.

14. In her letter of Friday to Tuesday (*c.* Nov.? 1821?) already quoted, Mary Moody Emerson had said her nephew might never choose "to 'exchange the Lyre for the Caduceus.'"

1822

To William Withington, Boston? *c.* February? 1822?

[Described in Mar. 12, 1822, as written to "Lord Withington" but lost after the messenger had failed to call for it.]

To John Boynton Hill, Boston, March 12, 1822[1]

I Boston March 12th 1822

My dear Classmate,I

You are perhaps somewhat astonished at so late an answer to your epistle — I am not the less so myself, — but my apologies are so desperately poor, that I shall e'en go on without them. I was much amused with your travels in search of your kingdom, & truly delighted to see a letter, & find myself remembered by one of my class. II I am (I wish I was otherwise) keeping a school & assisting my venerable brother lift the truncheon against the fair-haired daughters of this raw city. It is but fair that those condemned to the 'delightful task,' should have free leave to waste their wits, if they will, in decrying & abominating the same. To judge from my own happy feelings, I am fain to think that since Commencement, a hundred angry pens have been daily dashed into the sable flood to deplore & curse the destiny of those who *teach*. Poor, wretched, hungry, starving souls! How my heart bleeds for you! better tug at the oar, dig the mine, or saw wood; better sow hemp, or hang with it, than sow the seeds of instruction.II But I am indeed quite weary of complaining & hasten to relieve you from my sympathy.

What is Garrison Forest? If your benevolence will overlook my negli-

1. MS copy, in the hand of James Elliot Cabot, owned by RWEMA; ph. in CUL. I have not seen the original letter and have not discovered its present ownership. Excerpts I–VI are printed in Cabot, I, 86–87. John Boynton Hill was Emerson's classmate at Harvard, and the letters to him contrast in their easy familiarity with the more serious epistolary debates Emerson was carrying on about the same time with his aunt. Hill, like Emerson, was at this time a teacher; and the letter was addressed to Garrison Forest Academy, Baltimore. Mr. L. H. Dielman informs me that the Academy was advertised in the *Federal Gazette* of July 1, 1822, and was there described as located nine and one-half miles from Baltimore.

gence, [III]wont you sit down immediately, & entertain a poor brother of the School Militant, with some account of yourself & your region. Write sentiment, geography, statistics, latin, any thing, in short, in the wide world, but mathematics. For I am truly ambitious of writing letters & burn to say that I correspond with the reverend the honourable the wise members of the – Conventicle – if nothing else.[III] I made an effort to write to Lord Withington, but fate was averse, the messenger forgot to call, the letter was lost.[2] [IV]What kind of people are the Southerners in your vicinity?[IV] Have they legs & eyes? Do they walk & eat? [V]You know our idea of an accomplished Southerner – to wit – as ignorant as a bear, as irascible & nettled as any porcupine, as polite as a troubadour, & a very John Randolph in character & address.[V] I suppose as you approach the centre of the system, you become more warmed & influenced by the rays issuing from the wisdom & eloquence of Congress; & have probably taken sides with the fury of an Italian politician. How many duels have you fought, how many rebellions have you kindled?

I have nothing to tell you of politics, literature or college. I have darkened upon Cambridge but once since Commencement, my love for it was so wonderful, passing the love of women.[3] My reading is neither very large or very various, "multum non multa." [4] [VI]Perhaps you have seen "Europe"? [5] the most considerable American book that has been published, the most removed from our business-like habits, the most like Burke. Its author is Alexander Everett, the professor's brother at the Hague. You would mistrust the authenticity of a letter coming from me that had not this name in it.[VI] No matter, my admiration is not shaken, only my respect is, by this fierce pursuit of Plutus. To the purpose – they report that New England husbands are a great article of speculation at the South, & that hundreds of thousands of dollars are *thus* to be had for the gathering. – I trust no caution is needful to bid you be wise, for the days are evil, & the good are poor

Upham has had an offer of two thousand dollars to become a private tutor at some place in Kentucky – he has written to inquire if 2000 are to be paid in Southern bills? What at the South & cannot you get rich?

2. The only proof of this lost letter, which, I conjecture, may have been written *c.* Feb., 1822. A number of other letters to William Withington, who, like Hill, was a college classmate, were to follow. For the Conventicle Club, see Cabot, I, 61.

3. *II Samuel,* 1:26.

4. Perhaps a condensation of the advice of Pliny the Younger, *Epistolae,* VII, 9.

5. *Europe: or a General Survey,* Boston, 1822, was published anonymously and seems never to have excited much interest.

Why may not a school master as well as a slave — strike his weary foot upon another Potosi. Do but wander into the forests & try. You have heard the old rhyme which is said to have circulated in England some centuries since

> "I see a rich country far o'er the sea
> Where Gold, God, & Freedom are hid from the ee:
> Who findeth the first shall be tortured & slain
> But merry live they who discover the twain.

Who findeth all must perforce be happy. If you will come to Boston again I will promise you somewhat more hearty than the dismal hospitality which welcomed you last in our house.

Your friend & classmate

R Waldo Emerson.

To Mellish Irving Motte? Concord? April *c.* 16? 1822 [6]

I trust to your own good feelings to pardon the liberty I have taken in addressing myself to you — unasked, though to my elder. My object is simply to solicit a correspondence; and I have sufficient reasons to back my request These are; I am heartily sick of seeing & hearing mine own name; I am tired of most of my amusements & employments and next the opinion which I have entertained of you makes me desirous of learning from you, your occupations & views. If it were necessary to say more, I might add that the peculiar & striking distinctions which we see at Cambridge separating our Northern & Southern Countrymen have always urged my curiosity to inquiries somewhat deeper & more general than

6. MS, an unpublished part of Emerson's diaries, owned by RWEMA; printed from typescript *Journals*. This entry follows shortly after one dated Apr. 16 (1822) and precedes others dated Apr., 1822, and Apr. 20. Emerson's heading labels it as the copy of a letter " To ——," but according to a bracketed note, apparently by Edward Waldo Emerson, Motte was the person addressed. He was from Charleston, S. C., but other classmates, some of whom were also older than Emerson, were from the same state (MS *Records of the College Faculty,* IX, 121–122, in HCL). The probability that the present letter was to Motte is, however, greatly strengthened by the reference in Jan. 3 following to his sickness.

George McDuffie had been a congressman from South Carolina since 1821. James Gates Percival, much better known for his verses then than now, had actually sailed from Charleston on his return to the North at the end of Mar., 1822. News traveled slowly. " L " was doubtless Henry Little, listed as Emerson's classmate in the catalogue of Oct., 1819, but not in that of a year later. The letter of Mar. 12, 1822, shows Emerson eager to begin correspondence with some of his college mates and particularly interested in Southern characteristics.

common conversation allows; and I should be glad of any hints upon your manner of education which may occur to you.

Our frigid latitude can seldom supply you with topics of much moment. A stern NorthEasterly storm and a following fierce sun are the daily news which most interest the Yankees. An earthquake, a hurricane, or a City and Mayoralty are rare and improbable phenomena here, and must be looked for only once, perhaps, in a Century. It is nevertheless true that you may indulge a hope of learning at intervals of the Sea Serpent — Not that I intend to compromise with you and give up our guest — Not at all I am a Yankee & a firm believer. — But you see I have run over already all which I can hope to tell, or rather cannot hope to tell. But upon your side, you have but to brandish your pen and a less fluent gift than your own could summon up in unpremeditated lays — Pirates, Slaves, Fevers, Poems, Congress, Mr Mc.Duffie, Mr Percival, &c &c ad libitum. In short, it seems to me that I can thus dictate twenty topics to your fertile pen while I count one for mine own. I will not trouble you with the common-places upon the value and utility derived from epistolary correspondence; — these are to be found in the spelling book; I shall content myself with saying that if it will suit with your studies, a letter now and then would gratify me, very much.

You remember L. who left the Class in our Junior year. I am told he has been very ill of consumptive complaints and was given over by the physicians; but he told his friends there was no use in crying about it, for he should certainly get well — and has recovered. You recollect Dr Jackson's estimate of deaths — reckoned among the young men about 1 in 70 or 80 each year. It is somewhat remarkable that in our Class in the space of 5 years there should be no loss not even among those who have left the class. I rejoice that you are not the first exception to the long forbearance of the grim tyrant as from the severity of your sickness much was feared. Long life and happiness follow your fortune, prays Your friend & classmate.

To William Withington, Boston, April 27, 1822

[MS in the Library of Congress; ph. in CUL. Printed in " Early Letters of Emerson," ed. Mary S. Withington, *The Century,* XXVI, 454 (July, 1883). A few omissions and some minor emendations occur in the printed text. The date line, " Boston, 27 April, 1822," is not formally given. " Withington " in the salutation is given as " W * * *." The two omitted passages indicated by points in the printed version are, in order, " Here was a ' Christian Disciple,' came out with its meek motto — ' Speaking the truth in love,' — and a most bitter christian sarcasm, & terrible christian contempt launches out against poor Dr Mason for his equally apostolic exhortation "; and " and Mr Frye told me he could send a letter to you, any time so I thought proper to gratify myself by writing." Finally, *The Century* text omits the " W. Withington, A.B." at the end of the letter. " Lord " Withington, Emerson's classmate at Harvard, was now a theological student at Andover. Enoch Frye, also a member of the class of 1821, is listed in the catalogue of 1820 as from Andover and appears in *The Boston Directory*, 1822, as a schoolteacher. *The Christian Disciple and Theological Review* for Mar. and Apr., 1822, contains the article relating to the Rev. John M. Mason, of New York.]

To John Boynton Hill, Boston, May 11, 1822[7]

Boston May 11,th 1822.

My dear Hill,

I am infinitely obliged for the last letter, but as to writing sentiment & common sense &c — you sha'n't do it. I've a kind of despotic little caprice in my head, that ordains, and will not have its ordinances disputed. You shall hear what it saith — By the help of the stars I spy a man walking in Garrison Forest — a short man and a thick — but with a long head, & long sighted in the ways of this world both before & behind, and in a score of years he hath read books & men. — I determine & declare that such an one hath no business to write a good, amusing, epistolary kind of a letter; it is fit that such an one be *oracular*, — I ordain that he write a letter, which shall be no letter at all, but a treatise; which shall embody his most profound views of Plato, of Greece, of Rome; of national or local condition; of philosophy, of (even) statistics; of books, measures, men. — ' Fol de rol,' saith Mr Hill, ' and what have you to balance these extravagant demands? ' Why, saith Caprice, we will contrive to scrape up somewhat of special entertainment for Mr H's literary appetite; we can steal perhaps an odd paragraph from the North American, &c. &c. A man of expedients will always thrive.

Now, [I]by way of trying my pen, I am going to give you an insight into our city-politics,[I] which must be vastly interesting to you — no matter — when Ive got something better, you shall have it. [II]The inhabitants divide themselves[II] here, as every where else, [III]into three great classes; first, the aristocracy of wealth & talents; next, the great multitude of mechanics & merchants and the good sort of people who are for the most

7. MS owned by Professor William Bancroft Hill; ph. in CUL. Excerpts I–X are in Cabot, I, 87–90, doubtless quoted from the MS copy of the letter now owned by RWEMA (ph. in CUL).

part content to be governed without aspiring to have a share of power; lastly, the lowest order of day labourers & outcasts of every description, including schoolmasters. In this goodly assemblage, until the union of parties, at the election of Pres^t Monroe, there was no division of factions, except the giant ones of Federalist & Democrat. But when these died away, the town became so tiresomely quiet, peaceful, & prosperous that it became necessary at once, for decent variety, to introduce some new distinctions, some semblance of discord. A parcel of demagogues, ambitious, I suppose, of being known, or hoping for places as *partisans* which they could never attain as citizens — set themselves down to devise mischief. Hence it has followed, that, within a twelvemonth, the words "Aristocracy," "Nabob," &c have begun to be muttered. The very natural circumstance, that the very best men should be uniformly chosen to represent them in the legislature, is begun to be called a formal conspiracy to deprive them of their rights & to keep the power entirely in the hands of a few. Lately, this band of murmurers have actually become an organized party calling themselves "the Middling Interest,"[8] & have made themselves conspicuous by two or three troublesome ebullitions of a bad spirit at the town meetings. For the purpose of looking into their neighbours' concerns, they called a Town Meeting where they appeared in sufficient numbers to secure a majority, and there voted to[III] publish & [IV]distribute a kind of Doomsday Book, to wit, a statement of every mans property & tax from the assessor's books. This you may easily conceive, in a money getting town, where every one conceals his coppers, must be a very obnoxious measure. Another more important proceeding at the same meeting was the vote that the Selectmen be directed to instruct the Representatives to obtain from the Legislature leave to erect Wooden Buildings, which has long been against law. You know, nobody ever goes to a town meeting who is not personally interested; these votes, therefore, though easily passed, excited a general indignation when known, and a remonstrance was sent to the legislature by the whole respectable portion of the town, and the Bill was in consequence rejected. By dint of management, the other party have contrived to persuade the Mechanics & most of the Second

8. Some echoes of the doings of the Middling Interest, much as Emerson here describes them, are to be found in the *Independent Chronicle and Boston Patriot,* especially Mar. 9, Apr. 13 and 27, and May 4, 1822. As for the elections, this paper reported on Apr. 10 the indecisive balloting in which Josiah Quincy and Harrison Gray Otis were the principal candidates, and on Apr. 17 recorded the election of John Phillips, the only candidate then in nomination.

Class, that it is their interest to have Wooden Buildings, & part of a plan to deny them, & that they are oppressed &c &c, and they have succeeded in obtaining 26 hundred subscribers to a second petition to legislature, which will be offered at the next session. In a new Senatorial ticket they interfered, but did not succeed; and lastly they have been very pernicious to our interests in the election of Mayor. (By the way, did you ever see a live Mayor?) Mr Otis was nominated, and is, you know, our first citizen; his was the only public nomination and it was considered certain that he would succeed; but the Mid-Interest fixed upon Quincy, and on the day of Election, no choice was made, & both Candidates then withdrew their names. By this ingenious device the parties were reduced to take the third best, & acquiesce in the appointment of our present sublime Mayor, with the mortifying reflection that, Boston had many a worthier son than he. Such is our party history, and among our staid countrymen, we shall scarcely have a Guelf & Ghibelin controversy, though this be an ill-managed, poor-spirited party, and promises little good to our civil welfare.[IV] A *mob* is a thing which could hardly take place here; — I wish I could say as much for Baltimore.[9] And as to your sparing me the description of the City, it is the very thing you should not have spared; I wait a full & ample history of it, outside & inside, although legendary relics from Garrison forest, would I confess please the poetic vein better, & tickle the inner poetic man. Thank you much for your description of life & manners there; it is quite comprehensive, but vastly too sketchy. You recollect Marot, the "tyrant of words & syllables," [10] — be it known to you I have constituted myself — no matter by what right — an awful Censor upon the epistles of all who any word dare write to me. In the elation of my dignity I trample upon the silly insinuation that my reforming labours will be limited to a little correspondence. What! will not all nations flock to obtain a share in the advantages of my transcendant instructions? I shall have letters from Germany, Greece, China, Iceland & Siam — from the King of Hayti, & from the poet Ung [11] — who singeth on the banks of the Yel-

9. Emerson could not foresee the Boston riots during the years of excitement over slavery, but he could probably recall stories of mob violence in Baltimore during the War of 1812.

10. The epithet occurs in the tenth discourse of J. L. Guez de Balzac's *Socrate chrestien* (p. 267 in the edition of Paris, 1652), where, however, it is meant for Malherbe.

11. Perhaps the name is borrowed from Chinese geography for a poet of Emerson's own creation.

low Sea. And even on the desperate supposition, that unforeseen obstacles should prevent their arrival – I shall still write resolutely on – at such sleepy length as this same letter of mine. Here I can favour you with a beautiful morsel – from the very pen, perhaps of the Oriental poet last named. – – Ding dong, ding dong, said the bells of St Giles, as the poor Madge Groateon was carried by in a cart for to be hanged. And she cried, "Ring on, ye kind bells, for nobody has mourned for me, but you." And the bells of St Giles answered – Ding dong, ding dong.[12]

[V]I think, Mr Hill, we rather improve in the book line. Washington Irving is just about to publish a book called "Bracebridge hall"[V] which he has sold to a London bookseller for 1000 guineas. Alexander Everett's Europe is a popular book in England. [VI]N. A. Review grows better, & travels further.[VI] Wm Tudor, who wrote Letters on Eastern States is going to publish here, in the summer, a Life of James Otis[13] of which great h[ope is] entertained; [VII]and though we are inundated with silly poetry, w[e][VII] [14] to [VIII]improve.[VIII] Then, books are growing *cheaper* because they [are] imp[orted] from France. I bought a Quintilian in 3 Vols, quite a handsome book for 2.50; La Fontaine, in 2 Vols, for 62 cts. &c &c [IX]Here too I may add as testimony of our liberal spirit that the Town voted 2500 dollars to George B Emerson to procure a philosophical apparatus for the Classical School. He has just recieved part of his instruments which are the most beautiful in the country. – Bancroft[15] is expected to return from Europe in July and it is supposed that he will become the successor of Mr Greenwood in the New South Church.[IX] And now I believe I have exhausted all & more than will be interesting to you of news, jests, criticism, &c; and, Soul of Caesar! upon looking back, this is what I call a *vasty* letter. Tell me, when you write,

12. The bells of various London churches are celebrated in popular rimes and the ancient significance of St. Giles-in-the-Fields to the criminal on his way to Tyburn is well known; but I do not know the source of Emerson's Madge Groateon, if she had any source other than his own imagination.

13. *The Life of James Otis* had been announced in the *Christian Register,* Apr. 19, 1822, for publication during the following summer but did not appear till 1823 (see a note on Feb. 28 and Apr.? *c.* 8? 1823).

14. Probably from three to five letters have been torn away with the seal, besides portions of the text, as I conjecture it to have stood, that are included in the four pairs of brackets.

15. George Bancroft, like Ticknor and Everett, returned home full of the new German learning. After a brief experiment as a preacher, he quit the ministry. He appears in many later letters as teacher, as historian, and as diplomat.

how long you propose to honour Maryland with your instructions. Sit down & write a long letter to

Your friend & Classmate
R. Waldo Emerson

[x]Recollect that I have altered my name from Ralph to Waldo, so be sure & drop the first — It is quite a marrying time among our ministers; if it were not for postage, I would send you a piece of Everett's[16] Wedding Cake.[x] —

To Ruth? Haskins? Emerson, Northboro? Massachusetts, May c. 30, 1822

[Possibly to some other member of the family, but probably to the mother. See William Emerson to Ruth Haskins Emerson, May 31 and June 3, 1822, as quoted in a note on the letter of June 10 following.]

To Edward Bliss Emerson, Northboro? Massachusetts, May c. 30, 1822

[Described *ibid.* as sent "immediately on our arrival here."]

To Mary Moody Emerson, Boston, June 10, 1822[17]

[I]Boston, June 10, 1822.

My dear Aunt,[I] I have just recieved your letters by Dr Parish,[18] and am sorry I was not in town to recieve him as you wished. [II]Wm & I have been making a pilgrimage on foot, this vacation, (a fortnight), and went as far as Northborough, where we found a very pretty farmhouse, and they easily consented to board us for a week. We passed our time in a manner exceedingly pleasant,[19] and drank as deeply of those delights

16. Edward Everett was married May 8, 1822 (Paul Revere Frothingham, *Edward Everett,* 1925, p. 75).

17. MS owned by RWEMA; ph. in CUL. Excerpts I–VII are printed in Cabot, I, 78–82.

18. The superscription is to Mary Moody Emerson at the Rev. Dr. Parish's, Byfield, Mass. Elijah Parish had long been pastor there and had received the degree of D.D. in 1807 (John L. Ewell, *The Story of Byfield,* 1904, pp. 161 ff.).

19. William Emerson, in a letter to his mother, Northboro, May 31 and June 3, 1822 (MS owned by Dr. Haven Emerson), gives further details of this journey and mentions other letters written by his brother. " Waldo has forestalled me," he begins, " in his account of our arrival here, and our heroic adventures on the way have been said and sung by the same poetical personage for your future perusal; so that nothing remains for me to tell, but that there is sometimes dull weather in Northborough, as

for which Vertumnus is celebrated, as might be permitted to degraded uninitiated cits. I cannot tell, but it seemed to me that Cambridge would be a better place to study than the woodlands. I thought I understood a little of that *intoxication,* which you have spoken of; but its tendency was directly opposed to the slightest effort of mind or body; it was a soft animal luxury, the combined result of the beauty which fed the eye; the exhilarating Paradise *air,* which fanned & dilated the sense; the novel melody, which warbled from the trees. Its first charm passed away rapidly with a longer acquaintance, but not once, during our stay, was I in any fit mood to take my pen, " and rattle out the battles of my thoughts," as Ben Jonson saith well.[20] We dwelt near a pond which bore the name of " Little Chauncey," and often crossed it in a boat, then tied our bark to a tree on the opposite shore and plunged into the pathless woods, into forests silent since the birth of time, and lounged on the grass, with Bacon's Essays, or Milton, for hours. Perhaps in the Autumn, which I hold to be the finest season in the year, and in a longer abode the mind might, as you term it, return upon itself; but for a year, without books it would become intolerable. Do not think, however, that I rejoiced to get home; When our visions were interrupted by a sight of the State house, on the road returning, I averted my face as did the Greek from the fane of the Furies. I made a journal as we went, and have not read it over myself, but apprehend it hath too many *jokes* to please you; it was written for a more terrestrial meridian. I have to thank you for your letter, and its literature, but you should have filled the sheet; you sent me two pages of blank paper and I would have you remember that I have more at home than I can fill. I am a little surprised that a lady of your erudition should have forgotten that John-

well as in Boston — witness, today — a damp east wind has covered the hills and woodland with a thick mist. Notwithstanding, Waldo has gone out upon Little Chauncy to fish, and I, being too squeamish to enter willingly into such murderous designs, gladly resigned my paddle to a couple of worthy tillers of the soil, whom we found upon the shore of the pond, burning for slaughter. Here it comes into my head that I came away from B. without Milton, which you remember I intended to take; I shortly discovered my negligence, but would not return, and went sorrowing on to Newton where Mr. G. lent me one, which I have since read through. Monday.

" Edward came to see us on Saturday, in consequence of a letter Waldo sent him immediately on our arrival here. . . . Waldo went to Worcester with him and walked back yesterday morning. We walked very soberly to meeting, and after meeting walked as soberly to the tavern, it being customary with the good people in this part of Northborough not to return till after evening service, as the distance is 2½ miles. . . ."

20. *The Case is Altered,* III, i. The quotation is almost exact.

son's Poem [21] is professedly an Imitation of the 10th Satire of Juvenal; It proceeds upon the same plan as do many of Pope's Satires which are nothing but an ingenious adaptation of an ancient poem to modern manners and a better philosophy. Perhaps it lessens your respect or idolatry of the poet, considered personally; but independently of this, and as far as regards the mere sum of good reading, it is a laudable plan; for it submits the faults of one poet, to the revision of another, whom, the distance of centuries makes an impartial critic. Then the common reader is spared the difficulty of obtaining or the mortification of wanting, the original; while the classical reader enjoys a double pleasure in this improved translation; first, that of the sentiments; next, the skill & wit displayed in the application of the old to the new; as of a compliment addressed to Mecaenas, 2000 years ago, newly applied, with a lucky exactness, to Bolingbroke or Dorset. I am curious to read your Hindu mythologies.[22] One is apt to lament over indolence and ignorance, when we read some of those sanguine students of the Eastern antiquities, who seem to think that all the books of knowledge, and all the wisdom of

21. *The Vanity of Human Wishes in Imitation of the Tenth Satire of Juvenal.*

22. In her letter dated Byfield, May 24 (1822), Mary Moody Emerson relates her good fortune in finding there " this week " a visitor from India, who showed her " fine representations of the incarnation of Vishnoo," which reminded her of Greek fable and of the doctrine of transmigration. Writing from the same town under date of June 26 following, she copies in her exceedingly difficult hand what she calls " a sweet morsel of Hindu poetry," whose philosophy she thinks is, as it respects matter, the same as Berkeley's. She begins, characteristically, in the middle of a sentence:

" Of dew bespangled leaves & blossoms bright
Hence! vanish from my sight!
Delusive pictures! unsubstantial shows!
My soul absorbed one only being knows
Of all perceptions one abundant source,
Hence every object every moment flows;
Suns hence derive their force,
Hence planets learn their course
But sun and fading worlds I view no more
God only I perceive God only I adore! "

That this letter from his aunt is an important document in the story of Emerson's interest in Oriental thought (in spite of the meager evidence of the *Journals* for years to come) seems the more probable in the light of the note he wrote at the bottom of the last page: " This letter is a most beautiful monument of kindness and highminded but partial affection. Would I were worthy of it. Reread Dec. 1822 R. Waldo E." For the verses which his aunt had somehow got, not quite accurately, from Sir William Jones (see " A Hymn to Narayena," *The Works of Sir William Jones,* 1807, XIII, 308–309), Emerson presently copied them into his diary, where they now appear without any notice of her agency (*Journals,* I, 157). In old age he still remembered them and included them among his favorites in *Parnassus.*

Europe twice told, lie hidden in the treasures of the Bramins & the volumes of Zoroaster. When I lie dreaming on the possible contents of pages, as dark to me as the characters on the Seal of Solomon, I console myself with calling it learning's El Dorado. Every man has a Fairy land just beyond the compass of his horizon; the natural philosopher yearned after his Stone; the moral philosopher for his Utopia; the merchant for some South Sea speculation; the mechanic for perpetual motion; the poet for — all unearthly things; and it is very natural that literature at large, should look for some fanciful stores of mind which surpassed example and possibility.[II] You may remember the supposed number of tales printed in the Arabian age of learning, — I have forgotten, but it was incredible. Nevertheless I have high reverence for what has actually been discovered, and it teaches us the economy of mind which is established by commerce and communication between land & land. For, in two sundered hemispheres, all that vast series of efforts, which are necessary to found and finish civilization & science, were separately & independently made; whereas, but *one* progress were necessary, if the intercourse could have been previous, and the superfluous genius should have expended itself in gigantic advances beyond our present limit. [III]I know not any more about your Hindoo convert than I have seen in the Christian Register,[23] and am truly rejoiced that the Unitarians have one trophy to build up on the plain where the zealous Trinitarians have builded a thousand. There are two rising stars in our horizon which we hope shall shed a benign influence from the sources of Religion & Genius — I mean Upham & Bancroft. The second is expected to return from Europe in July, and may very probably succeed Greenwood. He is an indefatigable scholar, and an accomplished orator.[III] You are perhaps acquainted with his family, and can judge of his education. Edward has seen at Worcester a part of his library which he has been collecting in Italy & Germany. He is at Gottingen, a doctor of Philosophy. [IV]Doctor Warren tells Edward he had better voyage, and it is possible he may go to Germany and thank his sickness for an European education; [24] at least we have had some rambling conversation about such a project.[IV] Upham is exceedingly diligent and called upon me the other day. He learns 5 languages, and gave up his South-

23. The well-known story of Rammohun Roy is pretty fully told in the *Christian Register,* Nov. 23, 1821, and May 17 and June 7, 1822, but there are numerous other references to him in the same paper.

24. This project was abandoned by Edward, but later letters tell at length the story of William Emerson's residence at Göttingen.

ern School as an interruption to his studies, which, besides, would not be so profitable as to make him much less dependent. George B. E. has just returned from a fine journey to New York & Philadelphia in company with his friends, Mrs Farrar, Mr Sullivan, &c &c.[25]

[V]I must beg you to write to me, and see no reason why you should excuse yourself,[V] since it will be no effort to you, to fill a sheet to me. At least tear out a loose sheet from some manuscript, & superscribe it to me. [VI]If you cannot write now I shall be prone to inquire where are those boasted virtues of hill and dale, that you wot of? I have read lately much history — am amazed at the insipidity of Mosheim.[26] Italian history is very eventful; vastly more so, than any other, I believe. There seems to be no slumber, no peace. All men's energies are awake stirring the elements of society; and so rapid is the succession of political events, that you are not acquainted with any line of policy long enough to become deeply interested; and the chronicles become as tiresome from their variety & *flutter,* — as others do from their monotony.[VI] One circumstance has struck me forcibly every where, — that the counsels of Florence were uniformly marked by a high minded wise & patriotic policy far above the spirit displayed by any other state; and, on the contrary, that Venice is ever jealous, narrow, & perfidious; faithless on a system, it would seem, to her friends, — and most ungrateful to her benefactors This is a fault which cannot be forgiven; all her porphyry pillars, her shining throng of the master pieces of art, and all the majesty of the Adriatic can never atone for the disgraceful murder of her best & bravest sons. A dreadful retribution hath come upon her, "And silent rows the songless gondolier." [27] It has strangely disappointed & shattered my old veneration for this Queen of the isles, to learn her misdeeds. I could not read some lines on the outside of your letter but spelt out " trunk " & " books." Is it important? I see & hear nothing of Hentz. That family have just returned from a delightful visit to Waterford, and represent them all as *doing very well* there. Thayer is coming away having got tired of solitude. It is good for Thos,

25. When he taught mathematics at Harvard, George Barrell Emerson would naturally have become well acquainted with Professor John Farrar and his first wife, Lucy Buckminster. For the Hon. William Sullivan, another early friend, who is probably the person here referred to, see G. B. Emerson, *Reminiscences of an Old Teacher,* 1878, p. 64.

26. Doubtless Emerson was reading Maclaine's translation, entitled *An Ecclesiastical History, Antient and Modern.*

27. *Childe Harold's Pilgrimage,* IV, 20.

who has had the advantage of his capital. Charles studies very well indeed and will go to *George,* at Commencement.[28] No one sees his letters, but would shew them to me I suppose. We hope he will gain prizes in three weeks. Wm speaks often of writing to you, but it is a task to him. Wideworlds [29] are at your discretion but I was anxious to inform you that in the all grasping appetite of Vanity I am yet entirely indifferent to the exhibition of those; in seeking for the reason, the very natural one occurs, that they contained nothing worth shewing. [VII]Your affectionate nephew — Waldo.[VII]

One thing of main importance I would not forget. Mrs Bradford has recovered so much of her just property as to be able to pay the creditors to the full amount without calling on the bondsmen, and is delighted Sam has been very sick

To John Boynton Hill, Boston, July 3 and 6, 1822 [30]

Boston [I]July 3' 1822[I]

My dear Sir,

I am happy when I am allowed to follow the dictates of my own caprice, & as this is the very first moment in which I have been in mood for writing since I recieved your letter I shall make no apology for delaying to write. I have just been to see the Athenæum recently removed to the new house,[31] & it is royally fitted up for elegance & comfort. Mr Thorndike has presented the institution with a beautiful collection of casts of the ancient statues, which attract the eye in every corner from the tedious joys of writing & reading. The beholder in-

28. According to Jenks, p. 156, Charles Emerson had entered the Latin School in 1817. Presumably he was still there, but was to be sent to George Barrell Emerson for further schooling. I am not certain, however, of the identity of this George; and the Hentz, Thayer, and Thomas mentioned above remain unexplained.

29. In her letter of July 25 and 26 (endorsed 1822), Mary Moody Emerson says she is returning "Wide worlds." For printed portions of "Wide worlds" written about this time, see *Journals,* I, 95 ff. A number of undated scraps, filed with the Emerson letters owned by RWEMA, may have been originally parts of these journals, but were more probably intended merely as disjointed postscripts to letters to Mary Moody Emerson. All these scraps pretty obviously belong to this period, and probably either to 1822 or to 1821. They are recorded below, VI, 333–338.

30. MS copy, in Cabot's hand, owned by RWEMA; ph. in CUL. Excerpts I–IX were printed in Cabot, I, 90–92, apparently from this MS copy.

31. The new house of the Boston Athenæum in Pearl St. and the casts given by Augustus Thorndike are described in the *Columbian Centinel,* Dec. 29, 1821. The same paper, July 3, 1822, records the opening of the "superb edifice."

stantly feels the spirit of the connoisseur stealing over him, &, ere he can exorcise it, rubs up his Latin & Italian lore, & among the gazers, you may see the scholar, at pains to show his acquaintance with the lordly strangers, & his disdain of the ' ignobile vulgus ' who stare & stare, & are never the wiser. ‖You may see by my date that we are upon the eve of our great national anniversary. Does it produce much excitement in your quarter? I wish it may never rise in storms, but I find myself a little prone to croaking of late, partly because my books warn me of the instability of human greatness, & I hold, that *government* never subsisted in such perfection, as here. Except in the newspapers, & the titles of office, no being could be more remote, no sound so strange. Indeed the only time when Government can be said to make itself seen & felt, is on festivals, when it bears the form of a kind of General Committee for popular amusements. In this merry time, & with real substantial happiness above any known nation, I think we Yankees have marched on since the Revolution, to strength, to honour, & at last to ennui. It is most true that the people (of the City, at least,) are actually tired of hearing Aristides called the just — & it demonstrates a sad caprice, when they hesitate about putting on their vote, such names as, Daniel Webster, & Sullivan, & Prescott [32] & only distinguish them by a small majority over bad & doubtful men.‖ This is the first ' partly ' of the causes of my croaking. The second is, that, good men have recently been alarmed by certain overt acts of mischief, which they regard as the signs of more. It is very possible you have heard of the transactions at our Navy Yard,[33] but the public complain that Capt. Shaw & Lieut. Abbott have been punished with flagrant injustice, by a partial & tyrannical Court Martial, in which his *accuser* sat as *judge;* that the Secretary of the Navy is *un oie* under the influence of Capt. Porter; that from this judgment there is no appeal & that it is a final decision, that power may even in this country, triumph & trample over right. My knowledge of the affair is yet so limited that I cannot pretend to say if this be as repre-

32. As Hill was from New Hampshire, Emerson may mean George Sullivan, then attorney-general of that state and William Prescott, a legislator there. But the reference is doubtful. William Prescott, father of the historian, is quite as likely as the New Hampshire politician. Emerson may have read in Plutarch's life of Aristides the story of the citizen who was tired of hearing that statesman called " the Just " and so voted to ostracize him.

33. The official documents in the case of Capt. David Porter *vs.* Lieut. Joel Abbot, who was accused of defaming Capt. Isaac Hull, are printed in the *Independent Chronicle and Boston Patriot,* May 29, 1822. One of the charges against Abbot involved Capt. John Shaw.

sented; if so it is the first triumph of power that has occurred in the Heart of Good principles, & is a dismal foreboding to warrant a croak on the fourth of July. [III]Will it not be dreadful to discover that this experiment made by America, to ascertain if men can govern themselves — does not succeed? that too much knowledge, & too much liberty makes them mad.[III] Still we ourselves shall have the melancholy consolation of that magnanimous proverb — "The world will last our day," & also, in that prophetic glory familiar to our countrymen, [IV]we will seek to believe that its[IV] corruption & [V]decay shall be splendid with literature & the arts, to the latest time — splendid as the late day of Athens & Rome.[V] Tomorrow is the birthday of our pride: our self complacent orators stand on tiptoe when the day is named, [VI]& a century hence, if the orator lives too late to boast of liberty, he may[VI] drop our famed figure of *anticipation,* & yet [VII]brag of past renown & present muses.[VII] So you see by a kind of instinct, for the poor purpose of gleaning relief to fear, I obey the propensity of my nation & rake praises out of futurity. In my case however the fraud was pious, for as my comfort was prophetic, so was my affliction. O me miserum! What a pity Mr John C. Gray cannot cull from this epistle wherewith to furnish his harangue tomorrow![34] I shall leave him to his eloquence, & retire to certain cherry trees of the country. Do you have as fine fruit in Maryland as we? I trow not. I shall expend my patriotism in banqueting upon Mother Nature.

Saturday. Probably you know the story of French & Upton[35] which has been noised in the papers, & clamoured in the town. I mean the story of the man who signed a contract for 19,000 dollars with *spittle,* & covered it with *sand,* & escaped from the store before the fraud was discovered. Upton has printed some copies of a triumphant exposition of the villany, but which none of the newspapers have dared to publish; & F. is already prosecuting him for a libel. F. is esteemed worth 300,000 dollars, & I regret to say is Director of a Bank, & a member of our Common Council. This ruins him with all the world per force.

And now I have said my gossip, I must make haste to write my name, & wipe my pen, lest his volubility weary. First, however I will seek to answer your interrogatories — [VIII]We citizens venture to deny the Pirate

34. The *Independent Chronicle,* July 6, 1822, reports the celebration, at which Gray was the orator.

35. John French was, according to *The Boston Directory,* 1822, a bank director; and both he and Samuel Upton, probably the other person mentioned, were merchants at Central Wharf.

a little of reverence we have accorded to his predecessors, & are divided upon the subject of the Spy; many preferring it to the last book. which opinion I personally spurn.[VIII] I have not read but parts of it & they did not seem to approach any comparison with Scott, in any of those remarkable characteristics of the Caledonian tales. [IX]Our economical citizens have been quite dead to Bracebridge Hall, since its price was known, & I have neither read it, nor seen a single individual who has read it. The extracts which I have met with, have disappointed me much,[36] as he has left his fine Sketchbook style, for the deplorable Dutch wit of Knickerbocker, which to me is very tedious.[IX] But I fear my criticisms are somewhat sleepy, for I must quickly shut up my two luminaries to entertain the god of dreams. You slighted my commands & wrote me no treatise, therefore if the letter be dreamily dull, never think to blame

Your friend & servt.
R Waldo Emerson

I meet George Otis sometimes, he appears to be well. I saw Cheney [37] the other day at Framingham who says that at Commencement, he shall give his scholars a vacation of some years.

To Mary Moody Emerson, Boston? July? *c.* 10? 1822

[Mentioned in Mary Moody Emerson, July 25 and 26 (1822), as reread on July 26. It apparently contained some philosophical discussion and some comment on Edward Bliss Emerson. Just possibly it was the same letter which Mary Moody Emerson discussed in hers of Friday, July 19 (1822, I conjecture, though the endorsement says 1821), where she accused him of talking artfully of the history of the universe in order to rouse her from her tranquillity and spoke unflatteringly of his knowledge of metaphysics, adding that he wrote " sneaking short letters."]

36. This opinion may have been influenced by Mary Moody Emerson, who had written on June 14 that she could not bear " Brace-Hall." An unpublished passage in the diaries dated June 22 and apparently belonging to 1820 shows that Emerson had a better opinion of earlier writings of Irving but thought that moral and didactic works like *The Rambler* were much more wanted to make American literature useful and respected. " Books of an ephemeral nature like the sketch-book will not remedy the evil Although we feel the beauty of his description although we love the picturesque glitter of a summer morning's landscape as much as any yet we would willingly exchange the transient pleasure for those of active & salutary effect whose tendency is to instruct & improve rather than to entertain." (Typescript *Journals.*)

37. Both Otis and John Milton Cheney were classmates of Emerson and Hill.

TO WILLIAM WITHINGTON, BOSTON, JULY 27, 1822

[MS in Library of Congress; ph. in CUL. Printed in *The Century,* XXVI, 455–456 (July, 1883), where, besides several minor omissions, the following passage just preceding the signature is left out: "I am impatient to read my letter, but you will not ther[e]fore delay to write again to your

friend & classmate."

I supply the bracketed letter where the MS is slightly mutilated.]

TO JOHN BOYNTON HILL, BOSTON, NOVEMBER 12, 1822 [38]

[I]Boston, November 12, 1822[I]

Your last letter found me in the rabble at Commencement and contained a seasonable request for the news of the day; but since nothing very memorable occurred on that occasion, and since a respectable portion of a year has already intervened, I have thought it improper to indulge your curiosity. So that I have little left to fill my paper except Bancroft's return from Europe, which you must have heard of long ago, and the disputed succession of King Peck's dominion,[39] which is equally old. For the first, it need only be said, that he hath sadly disappointed great expectations, and for the present has done preaching. For the last; it is probable Dr Bigelow will have a speedy offer of the crown, and as probable that he will decline an honour that will better his worldly condition not a whit. *The* Professor has almost disappeared from the world, since his Matrimony, and has not once, or not but once, preached; but has issued one or two North-Americans — indifferent good — and a Greek Grammar from his elysian hermitage.[40] For the rest of the world, there is little difference in it since Mr Hill was here; the sun shines every day; the moon comes once a month, or oftener; we eat and drink and sleep, and die and are buried.

[II]By dint of much electioneering the good cause has succeeded and we are sending our Giant down among you false Southrons. We are proudly anticipating the triumph of a Northern Interest to be begun

38. MS owned by Professor William Bancroft Hill; ph. in CUL. Excerpts I–IX are printed in Cabot, I, 92–93, apparently from the MS copy owned by RWEMA (ph. in CUL).

39. William Dandridge Peck was a professor of natural history at Harvard till 1822. The title of Bigelow, the Rumford Professor, remained unchanged for some years.

40. His *Greek Grammar, Translated from the German of Philip Buttmann,* was published at Boston in 1822. Everett had become editor of *The North American Review* in 1820 (*Edward Everett,* 1925, p. 67).

or to be achieved by Mr Webster.[II] It is a curious fact that when it was announced in Taunton, that the city had elected Mr W. the Hotel was illuminated at the request of the inhabitants. Principles at Taunton are stronger than water, which you remember is " so weak, it will not run down hill." [III]I think I recorded in a former letter the rise of the Middling Interest.[III] The stir about Wooden buildings, which that respectable party made, has proved, as was expected, a mere watchword. For it is now six months since they obtained by clamour and numbers a full permission, and there is not, nor has been, to my knowledge, a single Wooden building going up in Boston. It has likewise appeared that [IV]this party only unites the old Democratic party under a new name; for this last regularly hold a mock Caucus, and agree to support the Candidate whom the M. I. have nominated. I think Webster had about two thirds of the whole number of votes.[IV]

I hope by this time Garrison Forest hath given birth to some wild adventure worth the while of a Forest — to break the dull monotony which its Teacher deplores. For my part, I fancy Mr Hill ambitious of the fame of his brother of Gandercleugh,[41] and already collecting in his Southern sojourn, the materials of twenty volumes. I see you reading the dusty faces of the urchins, finding features there, which are mere genealogical trees, and speak of Kings; or physiognomies which promise Presidents. Peace be with them. I have a strong desire to know also whether this name of G. Forest be a fiction; and whether the oaks and beeches, leaves and vines, with which I have richly decorated your dwelling, do or do not cover your daily walks? I make no doubt you have culled all the beauties of murder, ghost, and battle, which the tradition of the neighbourhood affords, to add to the North Country stories you used to tell me. I have wanted once or twice a story you told me about Tyngsboro'.[42] [V]Think you[V] there is any limit to human invention? Or [VI]that our Scottish Enchanter is not *one,* but *many*? Peveril of the Peeke long since announced has halted on his journey. As to the " Fortunes " I think it rather shews hurry than exhausted strength. There is a great deal of merit in supporting the interest of the book so long by nothing but conversation; and I think every body who has been to College recognizes Lord Dalgarno.[VI] Since Scott has failed to equal

41. Scott represented that the schoolmaster and parish clerk of Gandercleugh was the editor of *Tales of my Landlord.*

42. Hill was from Mason, N. H., not far from Tyngsboro, Mass. I suppose it possible that Emerson, remembering some of the Tyngsboro lore he had from Hill, prompted Thoreau to write certain passages in *A Week.*

himself in his two last works our young novelist has grown the greater; I suppose you know that the Spy, translated into French, is popular at Paris; but of the " Sources of the Susquehannah," [43] his second birth, I have heard nothing. What is the reason? Have you never yet sanctioned it with a " bon! "

[VII]One good book I advise you to read, if you have not, with all convenient celerity — Stewart's last Dissertation [44] — one of the most useful octavos extant. It saves you the toil of turning over a hundred tomes in which the philosophy of the Mind, since the Revival of Letters, is locked up. There is a class of beings which I very often wish existed on earth — Immortal Professors, who should read all that is written, and at the end of each century, should publicly burn all the superfluous pages in the world.[VII] Or if they thought that such a merciless law would go far to set the world on fire, they should publish an Index Expurg. (as the Catholics do, proscribing heretic books,) at convenient periods, which, if books multiplied as they do now, would be as often as once a month. [VIII]Now such a book as Stewart's, answers this purpose admirably under the head — Philosophy. — if our Immortal Professors were appointed today,[VIII] and a *carte blanche* given them for a lease of life, — what sublime rummaging we should have among the forgotten folios! [IX]We should rapidly find that the literary world was but a Don Quixote's library,[IX] and our Monthly Index would verify Montesquieus account of Spanish books — " le seul de leurs livres qui soit bon, est celui qui a fait voir le ridicule de tous les autres." [45]

Please to consider it as a proof of my vast affection that I have written so long and thick a letter. I have denied you all the pleasure of knowing what fine books I have upon my table, and have written you just such a letter as you write me; for you pay no sort of regard to my repeated admonitions to write me a serious lett[er,][46] that is, either philosophical, learned, or at least pedantic. [Such] a letter as milord Withington writes me. For, (will after-ages believe it?) — Mr H. corresponded with a poor unlettered man, without instructing him a whit.

43. *The Pioneers* was not actually published till 1823.

44. Emerson apparently was thinking of the second part, or perhaps even both parts, of Dugald Stewart's *A General View of the Progress of Metaphysical, Ethical, and Political Philosophy, since the Revival of Letters in Europe,* an edition of which appeared at Boston in 1822.

45. This version of Montesquieu's clever gibe is from the seventy-eighth of his Persian letters (*Œuvres,* Paris, 1817, II, 229).

46. The manuscript is mutilated; a portion of this word and at least one word of the following line are lacking.

After this salutary severity I shall leave you to your supper; I hope this comes at supper, for I hold that to be the best hour in the day to recieve a letter from a voluminous correspondent. What altered your plans of staying so suddenly? [47]

To William Withington, Boston, November 21, 1822

[MS owned by the Library of Congress; ph. in CUL. Printed completely in *The Century,* XXVI, 456–457 (July, 1883).]

47. The absence of the signature is explained by the following notation on this sheet of the original letter: "Nov. 25 1883 I cut off the name subscribed to this & sent it in a letter to Samuel A Christie Waltham Mass who wrote to me a letter requesting a sample of the signature." The MS copy owned by RWEMA was probably made before this date, as it has the ending "Your friend & Classmate
R Waldo Emerson."

1823

To John Boynton Hill, Boston, January 3, 1823 [1]

Boston, I January 3, 1823. I —

A happy new year to my Southern correspondent; if a Southern old year is no better than ours, if time be as dismal, & hope as bright at ten degrees lower latitude, why, you will be glad to be rid of 1822. This shadowy personage has borne a character as little decisive, & with as few memorable passages, as any of his elder brethren, since the time when they were marked by Napoleon's name. Of course, its *private*, will be very different from its *public* history; and its months may be most memorable to individuals. Your's, perhaps, have been crowded with study; mine have not. II My sole answer & apology to those who inquire about my studies is — I keep school. — I study neither law, medicine, or divinity, and write neither poetry nor prose; II nor, as you curiously imagined, have I the most vague intention of inditing Romances. I admire to hear, and aim to tell good stories, & therefore want the Tyngsboro' tale; [2] but that is all. So I shall expect it, at full length, in your next sheet. III I am happy to contradict III my own account of IV the rumours about Bancroft; IV and to overthrow your triumphant complacency in the supposed success of your predictions. V I heard him preach at New South, a few Sabbaths since, and was much delighted with his eloquence. So were all. He needs a great deal of cutting & pruning, but we think him an infant Hercules. All who know him, agree in this, that, he has improved his time thoroughly in Gottingen. He has become a perfect Greek scholar, and knows well, all that he pretends to know; as to Divinity, he has never studied it, but was approbated abroad. Our theological sky blackens a little, or else the eyes of our old men are growing dim. But certain it is, that, with the flood

1. MS owned by the Johns Hopkins University Library; ph. in CUL. Excerpts I–IX were printed in Cabot, I, 93–95, apparently from the MS copy now owned by RWEMA (ph. in CUL).

2. See Nov. 12, 1822.

of knowledge & genius poured out upon our pulpits, the light of Christianity seems to be somewhat lost. The young imagine they have rescued & purified the Christian creed; the old, that the boundless liberality of the day has swept away the essence with the corruptions of the gospel, and has arrived at too sceptical refinements. An exemplary Christian of today, and even a Minister, is content to be just such a man as was a good Roman in the days of Cicero or of the imperial Antonines. Contentment with the moderate standard of pagan virtue, implies that there was no very urgent necessity for Heaven's last revelation; for, the laws of morality were written distinctly enough before, and philosophy had pretty lively dreams of the immortality of the soul.[V] After Plato's dialogue & Cicero's declamations [3] upon the subject, it must have been no uncommon matter of belief; And indeed it is very hard to concieve how sensible men should have passed their lives without it, whilst life itself was an abstruse enigma as long as it wanted this ready & simple explanation. [VI]Presbyterianism & Calvinism at the South, at least make Christianity a more real & tangible system and give it some novelties which were worth unfolding to the ignorance of men. And this, I think, is the most which can be said of orthodoxy. When I have been to Cambridge & studied Divinity, I will tell you whether I can make out for myself any better system than Luther or Calvin, or the *liberal besoms* of modern days.[VI] I have spoken thus because [VII]I am tired & disgusted with preaching which I have been accustomed to hear. I know that there are in my vicinity clergymen who are not merely literary or philosophical.

I have been attending Prof Everett's Lectures, which he has begun to deliver in this city, upon Antiquities.[4] I am as much enamoured as ever, with the incomparable manner of my old idol, though much of his matter is easily acquired from common books. We think strong good sense to be his most distinguishing feature; he never commits himself, never makes a mistake.[VII] Rumour saith he is digging upon Law. His brother John has returned from the Hague,[5] & is at Cambridge.

3. For evidence of special interest in the famous passage of Cicero's *De Senectute,* XXIII, 84, see below, VI, 333. As for Plato, the reference may be to the *Republic* or to the *Phaedrus,* but is more probably to the *Phaedo,* whose dramatic setting makes it particularly memorable. When Emerson later compares Plutarch's teachings on immortality to Plato's, he mentions only the *Phaedo* among Plato's writings (*Plutarch's Morals,* Boston, 1871, I, xix).

4. Announced in the *Boston Daily Advertiser,* Dec. 17, 1822.

5. Alexander Everett, brother of Edward and John, was *chargé d'affaires* at the Hague, 1818–1824.

Item. Lord Withington wrote me a fine classical Latin epistle the other day.

To this day, you have never mentioned the name of a book since the Forest hath held you. And why? Are you crowding, in secrecy & silence, your time with treasures, to dazzle the world the more, because they were unnoted before. There is something portentous in mystery, and undoubtedly you have a motive. Seriously, it would please me much to know the pursuits of a living thing, besides myself. If the Garrison is really gone, & the forest is cut down, why then, you have society, manners, & libraries, instead of elms & Whortleberries, and a bookworm will profit by the change. I believe, you propose to be a lawyer; if I remember right, you have forsworn the pulpit; and perhaps the comparative ease of acquiring the professional qualifications, will tempt you to remain at the South. If you have ever dreamed of such things exorcise the fiend indolence, & come to the North, where Webster fought his way up.

[VIII]Barnwell, I am told, is about finishing, or has actually finished his studies. If you know any thing about him, or poor Motte,[VIII] (I have heard a terrible story about his sickness) [IX]or Robert Gourdin, communicate, communicate. You have other correspondents here, or I would subjoin a list of the Acts & Lives of your classmates in my vicinity. I fervently hope, unsocial being as *I* am, that the warm fraternal feelin[gs][6] which burn so brightly at the first separation of a Class, are no[t] wholly quenched as we grow older;[IX] we do not grow wiser, [if we suffer] them to go out. But the connection of a Class consists in the friendship of the individuals, and it is idle to sit & blame the class without making one personal effort to form kindly connexions with its members. If you see Lyon, remember me particularly to him. And excuse the tediousness of your friend & classmate —

R. Waldo Emerson.

To William Withington, Boston, January 29, 1823

[MS owned by the Library of Congress; ph. in CUL. Printed in *The Century,* XXVI, 457–458 (July, 1883).]

6. This and the two pairs of brackets following indicate fragments of the text that have been torn away completely or badly mutilated. Parts of a few letters in the phrase " if we suffer " are still legible and make that reading highly probable. Here the MS copy made by Cabot and owned by RWEMA supplies " in allowing," in square brackets, but this is certainly an error.

To John Boynton Hill, Boston, February 28, and April ? c. 8? 1823 [7]

Boston, [I]28th Feb. 1823[I] —

An uncle of mine [8] proposes to pass through Baltimore, and will leave this letter in the Post Office; therefore, although, if I remember right, my friend is in my debt, upon the epistolary score, I deem it incumbent to ask after his welfare. How are my little urchins of the Académe? How doth their great moral & intellectual 'Ipse'? Have the frosts departed from your roof to open the spring? Have the garrison decided who shall be President? (which I take to be an equivalent question to that ancient one, 'Have the Praetorians decided who shall be Emperor?') Has Mr Tudor's new book [9] found its way to your rustic abodes, (should I not say) palaces? What school of philosophy holds in domination your southern souls? How far, how high has human perfectibility got? &c?

But if you are not, as I dream, a nation of Emperors, a mob of unutterable scholars, philosophers, astrologers, — and are really, as you profess to be, only common men & women, — why then, I say unto thee, [II]come out thence, & pluck out thy lot of life from the abundance of the North. Every thing will pass, in this land of Notions.[II] Summon the children of the soil to a Gymnasium, as our German friends Bancroft & Cogswell propose,[10] and I warrant they will come. Open a College, a School, a Menagerie, a puppet shew, & still they will come. Deliver lectures, shew pictures, or stand on your head, & still they will come. Why, man, if I found myself galloping to Starvation, I should advertise a Soliloquy upon the Square Root, to be held in the Old South Meeting House; or an Invisible Ox to be *seen* in Faneuil Hall; or any other shining unintelligible matter of fact that should shower down wealth into my lap. 'Is this a world to hide Virtues in?' [11] [III]Courage & confidence will

7. MS owned by Vassar College Library; ph. in CUL. Excerpts I–VII are printed in Cabot, I, 95–96, apparently from the MS copy now owned by RWEMA (ph. in CUL). Though Feb. 28 is the only date given, the last sentence of the letter could hardly have been written earlier than Apr. 8 and certainly not more than a few days later. The election was held on Apr. 7, and, after a brief period of uncertainty, it was found that William Eustis, and not Harrison Gray Otis, had been chosen governor (*New-England Palladium,* Apr. 8 and 11, 1823).

8. William Farnham, as the superscription shows.

9. William Tudor's *The Life of James Otis* had been published on Feb. 1 (*Columbian Centinel,* Boston, Feb. 1, 1823).

10. See June 19 and July 2, 1823.

11. Not quite accurately quoted from Shakespeare's *Twelfth Night,* I, iii.

match the world, will take human affections & gold by storm;[III] Why, who get Fortune's favours? None but your moral highwaymen; resolute but reputable decievers of Society; madcaps, with a character to gain, & none to hazard. Notable examples of this species, I know your experience will furnish in abundance. As to that matter, however, [IV]the complaint is as old as the world, that merit is neglected. The humble, the bashful, the poor, the whole uncounted host of all the unlucky take up this cry[IV] from one side of the globe to the other, [V]and repeat it, till they believe it, themselves. For my part, I was always one of the loudest, holding it to be a sound & profound remark.[V]

Did you ever read Sully's Memoirs? [12] I suppose I might as well ask — did you ever see a whale? the book is so little read. I got deep in the volumes by accident and as I abhor the leaving of a book half-read, am forced to finish it. On some accounts & in some places it is prodigiously interesting; but the bulk is every where disproportionate to the consequence of the affairs. Thus, the Prime Minister very frequently crowds the public transactions of a year into a paragraph while he expands a private quarrel of his own over many pages. The history is moreover exceedingly confused & sometimes inaccurate. Hume,[13] in a single page, will often give a more distinct & perfect account of an [14] course of events, than Sully will, of the same, in a whole voluminous chapter. So much to give vent to my wrath against the Duke.

[VI]The Pioneers,[15] I like very much; I hope they have found their way to the Garrison. The last N. A. Review[VI] (Do you see them?) [VII]is full of wit & literature of which the *Idol* [16] wrote *six* articles.[VII] His wife has been very sick & remains so; but hopes are now entertained of her recovery. He has this winter delivered a noble course of Lectures on Antiquities — Roman, Etruscan, Greek, Celtic, &c. including a beauti-

12. Probably Emerson used Charlotte Lennox's translation.

13. Emerson must have had some acquaintance with Hume years earlier. According to a MS charge-book at HCL, he withdrew, between Feb. 20 and July 31, 1818, five volumes of the history of England.

14. The word " event " followed but was canceled.

15. According to Thomas R. Lounsbury, *James Fenimore Cooper,* n.d. (c. 1882), p. 41, *The Pioneers* was published Feb. 1, 1823. It had been advertised for sale in the *Columbian Centinel* on Feb. 19.

16. Emerson was, as usual, well informed regarding the authorship of unsigned articles in the periodicals. According to William Cushing's *Index,* 1878, p. 128, Edward Everett wrote six of the articles in *The North American Review* for Jan., 1823. The letter is also characteristic in its praise of Everett, of whose lectures in Boston Hill had already been informed on Jan. 3.

ful [lec]ture [17] on Sculpture, all which I have heard — on[ly] desire to hear more. (" Tut! " says Mr Hill —) I heard Upham preach at Cambridge lately before the Divin. Stud. his first sermon and likewise Mr Nortons eulogy & critique upon the same. And these are all the items I can think of, except that Mr Otis is our Governor elect, to eke out my letter which brings many good wishes from

Your friend & classmate
R Waldo Emerson

To John Boynton Hill, Roxbury, Massachusetts, June 19 and July 2, 1823 [18]

ILight Lane, Lower Canterbury
Roxbury, Massachusetts, June 19
1823I

Of what earthly use, a letter, which is a mere letter, can be (billets-doux, of course, being exceptions) I am at a loss to concieve. Under these impressions I formerly bade Mr Hill write me *Treatises* — imagining that in his forest solitudes it would be easy & amusing to him to write golden lines of instruction to his younger brethren of the city. But Mr Hill, as the review said of Mr Stewart, ' consults his ease rather than his ability ' [19] — in perversely persisting to omit all account whatsoever of his studies, of his readings, of his writings, of his thoughts & is fallen into a vein of scribbling, as good humoured & commonplace as his humble correspondent's. Here I sit in the barren-minded North, hungering & thirsting for something to think about & open my letters with greedy impatience for a morsel that shall last me a month — to chew the cud of thought — &, ye stars! my friends have sent milk for babes & kept their meat for strong men. True, I have heard indeed of another purpose besides instruction which letters propose to answer. You yourself, in your vale of tears, your Babylonish captivity, assure me that a letter is a source of consolation. If it be so, I will multiply my trash upon you tenfold. But remember I am in the pleasant land of my fathers, & of my

17. The fragments of the text inclosed in this and the following pair of brackets were mutilated by the seal. The word " only " may have been followed by " I," but probably was not.

18. MS copy, in Cabot's hand, owned by RWEMA; ph. in CUL. Excerpts I–IX are in Cabot, I, 96–98.

19. Freely quoted from the article on Dugald Stewart's second dissertation, *The Quarterly Review,* XXVI, 475 (Jan., 1822). The Babylonian Captivity, alluded to below, is a recurrent theme in the *Old Testament.*

sons & sons sons peradventure; lounging out my life after such a sort, that I need to be goaded to action, rather than comforted in my repose. So if my friends put the 'Cui Bono' as strictly as my better judgment does, they would rather task me with a Hebrew Epistle or Egyptian Hieroglyphics than give me an ordinary human letter. I am ten times as selfish as any of my neighbours, & in consequence shall fret until I see clearly the selfish advantage of my correspondence.

I have spit my venom, & am sour no more. And [II]I commend to your especial notice the date of this epistle which will shew you that I am living in the country. Here my only ejaculation is — 'O fortunati nimium'! [20] As of yore,[II] my brother, [III]& I teach, aye teach teach in town,[III] in the morning, [IV]& then scamper out as fast as our cosset horse will bring us to snuff the winds & cross the wild blossoms & branches — of the green fields. I am seeking to put myself on a footing of old acquaintance with Nature, as a poet should, — but the fair divinity is somewhat shy of my advances, & I confess I cannot find myself quite as perfectly at home on the rock & in the wood, as my ancient, & I may say, infant aspirations led me to expect. My aunt, (of whom I think you have heard before & who is alone among women,) has spent a great part of her life in the country, is an idolater of Nature, & counts but a small number who merit the privilege of dwelling among the mountains. The coarse thrifty cit profanes the grove by his presence — & she was anxious that her nephew might hold high & reverential notions regarding it (as) [21] the temple where God & the Mind are to be studied & adored & where the fiery soul can begin a premature communication with other worlds. When I took my book therefore to the woods — I found Nature not half poetical, not half visionary enough. There was nothing which the most froward imagination could construe for a moment into Satyr or Dryad. No Greek or Roman or even English phantasy could decieve me one instant into the belief of more than met the eye. In short I found that I had only transported into the new place my entire personal identity, & was grievously disappointed. Since I was cured of my air-castles, I have fared somewhat better; & a pair of moonlight evenings have screwed up my esteem several pegs higher by supplying my brain with several bright fragments of thought, & making me dream that mind as well as body respired more freely here. And there is an excellence in Nature which familiarity never blunts the sense

20. Vergil's "O fortunatos nimium" (*Georgics,* II, 458).

21. The parentheses in the MS copy probably indicate a conjectural reading.

of — a serene superiority to man & his art in the thought of which man dwindles to pigmy proportions.[IV] In short, parti-coloured Nature makes a man love his eyes. I thought tonight when I watched in the West " Parting day die like a dolphin " [22] what a mutilated mind & existence belongs to the blind. The history of poetry, however, seems to say, — Pluck out his eyes before he meddles with the harp & so fared poor old Maeonides, blind Thamyris, Ossian, & the equal to them in fate & equal in renown who sang Man's disobedience [23] &c. (July 2') I had almost dropped my purpose of sending you this ancient scrawl in the long interval which has elapsed since I left it last. [V] In writing as in all things else, I follow my caprice & my pen has played me merry tricks lately in taking a holiday somewhat longer than his wont & sore against my will, for if my scribbling humour fails to come upon me I am as uneasy as a cow unmilked — pardon the rusticity of the image — & in the end must yield my brain's yesty burden or die.[V] But as I discern already the close of my epistle I hasten to tell you that [VI] Bancroft & Cogswell have recently issued their prospectus[VI] giving an account of their intentions in forming a Gymnasium.[24] [VII] They have obtained a house at Northampton & propose to begin with 15 scholars only in October. Board & tuition[VII] of each pupil [VIII] $300 per annum. I mourn — because good schoolmasters are plenty as whortleberries but good ministers assuredly are not — & Bancroft might be one of the best.[VIII] Qentin Durward [25] is a very respectable novel, & in point of historical correctness I am informed by a reader of Philip de Comines — a very near & faithful copy of the times. The last Edin. Review (75) is very fine & was the subject of my last meditations. Its latter numbers you know are enhanced in value by Sir J. Mackintosh's contributions, as e. g. the noble article on Partitions in (74) [26] This gentleman is of the puissant of

22. Slightly altered from Byron, *Childe Harold's Pilgrimage,* IV, 258–259.

23. Emerson had in mind *Paradise Lost,* I, 1, and III, 33–35; and possibly *Night Thoughts,* I, 450 ff.

24. According to the *Prospectus of a School to be Established at Round Hill, Northampton, Massachusetts, by Joseph G. Cogswell and George Bancroft,* dated June 20, 1823, p. 5, the new institution was for those years which, in France, were spent at a collège, and in Germany, at a Gymnasium.

25. The *Boston Daily Advertiser,* June 18, 1823, shows that *Quentin Durward* was placed on sale in Boston that day.

26. The unsigned article in *The Edinburgh Review,* for Nov., 1822, on books about the partitions of Poland. In the MS copy of this letter " 74 " is followed by two doubtful symbols, perhaps " &c &c." For Sir James Mackintosh's defeat of Scott as candidate for the Lord Rectorship at Glasgow, see David Murray, *Memories of the Old College of Glasgow,* 1927, p. 330. Mackintosh's *History of the Revolution in England* was not published till after his death.

Scotland, & gained recently some literary election against Sir Walter Scott. He has been busy for several years upon English History, proposing to publish a continuation of Hume. If the Sequel shall equal the original I would go on a pious pilgrimage (like the neighbour of Hercules' Pillars to Livy) [27] to do the historian homage, for I am an idolater of David Hume save when he meddles with law & prophets — I think you said you propose to return into the bosom of the Yankees in a few months. You shall be welcome. It may be long ere my pen will let me send a letter as long as this, & therefore [IX] I am going to tell you where I live. The Dedham Turnpike wh. is only a continuation of the Main St. in Boston leads you after about 2 miles, to a *lane* (the first left-hand turning upon the Turnpike. Go to the head of said lane & turn to the right & you will straightway be in the neighbourhood of Mr Stedman Williams, a farmer of 30 yrs standing, in whose vicinity we live & whose tenants we are. Ask him.[IX] Having exceeded all decent limits I subscribe myself with esteem Yr obedt servt —

R Waldo Emerson.

To William Emerson, Roxbury, Massachusetts, October 8, 1823 [28]

Roxbury, Evg of 8th Oct

Dear William,

I have recieved today through a most meandering channel 4 letters of introduction for you to Göttingen, from Prof Everett. They are enveloped in a note to you which, I need not say, has been faithfully read. The Professor brought them to Stephen Perkins,[29] the same day, the Havre vessel sailed, thinking you were embarking in *that*. They have been all this time finding their way to me. He has of course recieved no account of them; and, since such marked politeness deserves its proper return, I thought fit to write to you.

27. Pliny the Younger, *Epist.*, II, 3, tells the story, which Emerson probably read in Melmoth's translation (*cf.* Mar. 12, 1817).

28. MS owned by RWEMA; ph. in CUL. An endorsement, not by William Emerson, suggests 1821 and 1823 as possible years. But the correct date is 1823. Emerson was then living at Roxbury, and William actually sailed for Europe on the 5th of the following December (*cf.* May 20, 1824). The superscription is to William, at Dr. Ripley's, in Concord.

29. Possibly the young Perkins who had gone to Europe with Everett in 1815 (*cf. Edward Everett,* p. 36). Everett's and Ticknor's examples doubtless had something to do with William Emerson's going to Göttingen.

Secondly, Uncle Thomas says Mr Thaxter [30] will put up a vessel for Bremen, in a few days.

In my poor judgement, if the comparison be not irreverent to your excellent quarters, you are like Achilles staying from Troy; — and as to substituting your Patroclus why I believe Hector will kill him. These, bills, & this business, will prove too big for his shoulders. Why, man, creditors [31] double a bill if they know I am to pay it. As to Nichols I can make nothing of the rude Thread-the-Needle. I shall deliver him over to Uncle Ralph. Jacob Gragg, king of trucks, charges you 90 cents a day for ten days use of his chaise; Alack, alack! Did you count Jepson in your Pr Contra list? He presented his grim visage at the School room, & his due-bill at the Stable & I paid the rogue. Notary Blagge will not be at his office, but his next door neighbour Whitmarsh opened his purse wide as his shears, to recieve my contributions amounting to $51. As to Mr Ticknor,[32] I have not yet been, counting upon some future day to possess my senses & cravat in more composedness than amid this vulgar din of affairs. Many Albums wait your return, also, messages of love & honour. Your mother says, Come, Pegas [33] & I say Come; so come. To the adamantine Maj.y of Tartary.

With obeisance & affection

R. Waldo E.

Mother, & all send their love to Grandfather & Grandmother & Aunt & are expecting Aunt Sarah & you daily, for the World is on wheels.

P. S. Mrs Emerson says, Shout to the Kidderminster lady, A Carpet! a Carpet! Where's my Carpet? I gave you patchwork & you send me no carpet. Give her filthy lucre, if she lack — like the horse-leech.[34]

30. The uncle was Thomas Haskins, and the "ship and merchandize broker" (so styled in *The Boston Directory*, 1823) must have been Thomas Thaxter.

31. *The Boston Directory*, 1823, duly lists a Charles C. Nichols, woolen-draper and clothier; Jacob Gragg, truckman; two Jepsons, of whom Benjamin was a house painter and Samuel a hairdresser; Samuel Blagge, notary public; and Thomas and Samuel Whitmarsh, owners of a clothes warehouse next door to Blagge.

32. George Ticknor to William Emerson, Dec. 1, 1823 (owned by Dr. Haven Emerson), inclosed letters of introduction for use in Germany. Probably Emerson's intended call on Ticknor was for the purpose of asking advice or introductions for his brother.

33. Charles Emerson wrote from New York, May 24 (1829), that "the tinkling gig, & nervous Pegas" were still fresh in his recollection. The only other clue to the identity of Pegas which I have found is in the letter of May 20, 1824.

34. Possibly Emerson was thinking of *Henry V*, II, iii; but more probably he meant *Proverbs*, 30:15.

To Mary Moody Emerson, Roxbury, Massachusetts, October 16, 1823[35]

IRoxbury, Oct. 16th 1823.I

The satirist of women claimed the love of being sought as a prerogative of the sex, & the design of being followed as the reason of retiring.[36] I will not insinuate that my dear Aunt is liable to these frailties or that aught but motives which I respect restored her to her mountains. But the consequence follows as a thing of course, & IIII have a catalogue of curious questions that have been long accumulating to ask you.II You have been no indifferent spectator of the connexions existing between this world & the next & of all the marvellous moral phenomena which are daily exhibiting. Every day (that is, every day of the few & seldom visitations of my coy & coquettish muse,) IIII ramble among doubts to which my reason offers no solution. Books are old & dull & unsatisfactory the pen of a living witness & faithful lover of these mysteries of Providence is worth all the volumes of all the centuries. Now what is the good end answered in making these mysteries to puzzle all analysis? What is the ordinary effect of an inexplicable enigma? Is it not to create opposition, ridicule, & bigoted scepticism? Does the Universe great & glorious in its operation aim at the slight of a mountebank who produces a wonder among the ignorant by concealing the causes of unexpected effects. All my questions are usually started in the infancy of inquiry; but are also I fear the longest stumblingblocks in philosophy's Way. So please tell me what reply your active meditations have forged in metaphysical armoury to What is the Origin of Evil? And what becomes of the poor Slave born in chains living in stripes & toil, who has never heard of Virtue & never practised it & dies cursing God & man?III It cannot be but that in the frightful variety of human misery the counterpart of this picture is often found. IVMust he die in Eternal Darkness because it has been his lot to *live* in the Shadow of death?[37] — A majority of the living generation, & of every past genera-

35. MS owned by RWEMA; ph. in CUL. Excerpts I–VII are in Cabot, I, 103–105.

36. A somewhat similar comment on women occurs in Ovid, *Ars Amatoria*, I, 41–44. Vergil, *Eclogues*, III, 65, illustrates the point exactly; and Montaigne, II, xv, repeats this. But possibly some passage in Martial, Juvenal, or Horace which I have not found is meant.

37. Mary Moody Emerson, Oct. 24 (1823), admits that the questions about slavery are hard, but counters with the opinion that the state of the Negro slave is not so despicable as that of the slave of court favor.

tion known in history, is worldly & impure. or, at best, do not come up to the Strictness of the Rule enjoined upon human virtue. These then cannot expect to find favour in the Spiritual region whither they travel. How is it, then, that a Benevolent Spirit persists in introducing onto the Stage of existence millions of new beings, in incessant series, to pursue the same wrong road, & consummate the same tremendous fate? And yet if you waver towards the clement side here, you incur a perilous responsibility of preaching *smooth* things. And, as to the old knot of human liberty, our Alexanders must still *cut* its Gordian twines. Next comes the Scotch Goliath, David Hume; [38] but where is the accomplished stripling who can cut off his most metaphysical head? Who is he that can stand up before him & prove the existence of the Universe, & of its Founder? He hath an adroiter wit than all his forefathers in philosophy if he will confound this Uncircumcised. The long & dull procession of Reasoners that have followed since, have challenged the awful shade to duel, & struck the air with their puissant arguments. But as each new comer blazons ' Mr Hume's objections ' on his pages, it is plain they are not satisfied the victory is gained. Now though every one is daily referred to his own feelings as a triumphant confutation of the glozed lies of this Deciever, yet, it assuredly would make us feel safer[IV] & prouder, [V]to have our victorious answer set down in impregnable propositions.[V] You will readily find a reason for my putting down this old A, B, C, of moral studies, to wit, to get a letter upon these threadbare enigmas. [VI]You have not thought precisely as others think & you have heretofore celebrated the benevolence of De Stael who thought for her son.[39] Some revelation of nature you may not be loath to impart & a hint which solves one of my problems, would satisfy me more, with my human lot. Dr Channing is preaching sublime sermons every Sunday morning in Federal St. one of which I heard last Sunday, & which infinitely surpassed Everett's eloquence. It was a full view of the subject of the light of Revelation compared with Nature & to shew the insufficiency of the latter alone.[40] Revelation was as much a part of the order

38. In letters to Hill earlier in 1823 Emerson tells of his admiration for Hume; but his aunt, who was then reading Hume's essays, wrote him, Jan. 20 (1824), that she was never more disappointed and was irritated by the mist of sophistry she encountered.

39. Mary Moody Emerson, in her MS diaries for 1821, notes that Mme de Staël treasured up sentiments and ideas for a son.

40. *Cf.* "Evidences of Christianity" in *The Works of William E. Channing*, Boston, 1875, pp. 188 ff., especially pp. 193, 212, and 213.

of things as any other event in the Universe.[VI] Give my love & respect where they are due. [VII]Your affectionate & obliged nephew

R. Waldo E[VII]

To Mary Moody Emerson, Roxbury, Massachusetts, November 11, 1823

[Parts of this letter are printed in *Journals,* I, 324–327. The following passages, omitted there, are from the typescript *Journals:* " Do they more or less realize the vulgar adages that life is a smoke a dream a bubble &c? . . . A diligent devotion to earth & its pleasures, the surrounding ones self with wife & children wh. are hostages to faith as well as fortune, with houses & lands banquets beds & wine-cups; this comfortable acquaintance with matter will keep a man in tolerable confidence of the reality of existence. Next . . ."]

1824

To Mary Moody Emerson, Roxbury? Massachusetts, February 1, 1824

[According to Mary Moody Emerson, Apr. 13, 1824, this letter was stately in subjects and in style, probably assumed " *Humism* " merely for the sake of amusing, commented ingeniously on her diaries, and contained welcome news of William Emerson. An unpublished entry in the journals for about this time (the date " Apr. 6, 1824," at the end may belong to it or to the following entry) is labeled " Letters " and may be merely material for epistolary filler or may be from a letter or letters actually written by Emerson to his Aunt Mary – or, much less probably, by her to him. There is the bare possibility that it was part of this letter of Feb. 1. It begins: " Letters. Does a bold eye never grow impatient of the ill-starred monotony of history nor ask *to what end* (cui bono) this everlasting recurrence of the same sin & the same sorrow? Why does the same dull current of ignoble blood creep through a thousand generations in China without any provision for its own purification . . ." The entry continues with a pessimistic estimate of Chinese and other Asiatic contributions to civilization and raises the question of how such results can be consistent with the wisdom of Providence. " Calvinism is one hypothesis to solve the prob but as bad itself." (Typescript *Journals*.)]

To Mary Moody Emerson, Roxbury? Massachusetts, March 21, 1824

[Partly printed in *Journals*, I, 356–359.]

To Mary Moody Emerson, Roxbury? Massachusetts, April 30, 1824

[Partly printed in *Journals*, I, 374–377. So far as I know, this letter might have contained the passage on the choice of the ministry quoted in *Cent. Ed.*, VII, 365, and described as written, at the age of twenty, to Mary Moody Emerson. At any rate the passage there quoted seems to consist of excerpts from an entry of Apr. 18, 1824, in *Journals* (I, 363–364). The same entry is apparently the source of the epithet " the Dupe of Hope," set down in *Memoirs of Members of the Social Circle* (2d series, 2d part, p. 31; same page in *Emerson in Concord*) as from a letter Emerson writes to his Aunt Mary " before he enters the study for the ministry " but described in *Cent. Ed.*, I, 432, as from a letter he sends her " when a Divinity student." There may, of course, have been a letter of Apr. *c.* 18, 1824, which was approximately identical with the *Journals* entry.]

To William Emerson, Roxbury? Massachusetts, May 20, 1824 [1]

Boston, N. America,
Canterbury, May 20, 1824.

My dear brother,

I have the pleasure to inform you by Mr Gustorf [2] that we are all well; that I have not recieved [3] any letter from you, but Mother & Edward have; that your trunk has come back by the Ocean, but I can only guess wherefore; [4] that Mr Gannett is to be settled with Dr Channing & Mr Greenwood at New South; [5] that Dr Eustis comes in invincible Governor.[6] that Jane Sigourney is engaged to Fred[k] Farley; that Geo. Emerson's wedding will be attended by me this ev[g]; that I

1. MS owned by Dr. Haven Emerson; ph. in CUL. This letter is followed at the bottom of the last page, in the margin of the superscription, by a brief note from Charles; and a line in the margin of the first page is, I think, also by him. William Emerson's MS journals of his European voyage and travels (owned by Dr. Haven Emerson) contain pretty full information of his movements. According to entries of Jan. and Feb., 1824, he embarked on the brig "Ocean" at Boston on the morning of Dec. 5, 1823, bound for Cork; spent some time in Ireland, sailing from Dublin on Jan. 29; landed at Havre on Feb. 12 from the "Ocean"; and, two days later, reached Paris, where he remained more than a week. His letter to his mother dated March 20 (owned by Dr. Haven Emerson) shows that he arrived at Göttingen, to begin his residence as a student at the University, on Mar. 5, 1824. For his account of the stormy passage of the Atlantic, during which the little boat more than once threatened to go down, see a note on Dec. 14, 1832. The whole story of William Emerson's European travels and studies is of much interest to the student of American and European cultural history; and the example of the older brother, prying into the mysteries of the new German school of theologians and historians, could not have been without influence on the future author of the Divinity School address.

2. Presumably the Frederick I. Gustorf who had appeared in the Harvard catalogue of Oct., 1820, as a private teacher of German. This letter was apparently carried to Cassel by some traveler and thence sent by another hand to Göttingen, where it arrived on Sept. 2, more than three months after it was written (William Emerson to his mother, Sept. 13, 1824; owned by Dr. Haven Emerson).

3. This was an old error, but most of the unusually large number of mistakes in spelling here and in the letter of Nov. 1? 1824, are apparently due to haste or carelessness rather than to habit.

4. William Emerson, Göttingen, Apr. 1, 1824 (MS owned by Dr. Haven Emerson), explained that he found baggage an extra expense in European travel and so purchased a much smaller trunk in Dublin, sending back the larger one by the "Ocean," with as much of his clothing — "the imperial purple" of the present letter — as he could spare.

5. Ezra Stiles Gannett was ordained as colleague pastor of Dr. Channing on June 30 (*Christian Register,* July 2, 1824). F. W. P. Greenwood declined the invitation to return to the New South, and was installed as colleague pastor of King's Chapel on Aug. 29 of this year (*ibid.,* June 25 and Sept. 10, 1824).

6. Dr. William Eustis, first elected in 1823, was reëlected the following year.

attended Supply Thwing's, Tuesday Evg last, & Isabella Stevenson was married last week; [7] that E. Everett is the Orator, & Percival (probably) the poet of the ensuing Φ B K anniversary.[8] that E. E. publishes in July the first No. of his Annual Register of U. S.[9] for which I drop the N. American. that L. S. Pegas [10] like Troy is fallen; unlike Troy's horse [11] his bowells fell not in short his leg was lamed. Time & Chance to all. I am sorry to hear or to conjecture pains in Dublin, inconveniences in Paris, or expenses anywhere. Thro' E. Everett, heard you dined with his brother.[12] Edward has as of yore equal chances, I suppose for Oration; [13] Everett has noticed him a good deal. Io Paean for the first Page! [14] Io triumphe! too for the Grand Mogul in Germany; son of Japhet among the children of Japhet; [15] How like you the old Teutonics? (wh. is 2 questions,) & will not the very Semester himself flag his Dutch wings & come *later* to soothe the alarmed majesty of Tartary? Why send the imperial purple back? — fear peradventure the turbulence of royal life when the people of Clovis shall lift you on their shields [16] or the phegmatic blue eyed Germans hale you to Vienna to the seat of Maximiliens & Chas V. True, but pity they shd lose the royalty of that glance & gesture yea of the Napoleon [17] itself wh. I

7. Farley, William Emerson's classmate at college, reappears, with his wife, in a letter of Mar. 28, 1840. George Barrell Emerson married Olivia Buckminster on May 20, 1824, according to the *Columbian Centinel* of the 22nd; the same issue of the *Centinel* reports the wedding of Supply C. Thwing and Elsey F. Davis at Roxbury on the preceding Tuesday; and the *Centinel* of May 15 had reported the marriage of Isabella Stevenson to James Freeman Curtis on the 13th.

8. The *Christian Register,* Aug. 27, 1824, notes that Dr. Percival, who had been expected to read a poem, was not present and that Henry Ware took his place. But Everett's oration on "The Circumstances Favorable to the Progress of Literature in America" was doubtless one of his great efforts, as he knew beforehand that La Fayette would be in his audience. A full account of the occasion appears in *Edward Everett,* pp. 82–86. Whether or not Emerson was present, the subject must have helped to direct his thought toward the theme of his own Phi Beta Kappa address of thirteen years later.

9. This was, I believe, an error.

10. *Cf.* a note on Oct. 8, 1823.

11. *Aeneid,* II.

12. Alexander Everett had been *chargé d'affaires* at the Hague since 1818. William Emerson wrote to his mother on Mar. 20, 1824 (MS owned by Dr. Haven Emerson), that he had an invitation to dine with Everett at Brussels on his way to Göttingen.

13. See the letter of July 8, 9, and 10, 1824.

14. The first page of the MS ends here.

15. *Cf. Genesis,* 10:1–5.

16. For Emerson's earlier mention of what he says was the Frankish custom, see below, VI, 335.

17. William Emerson, writing to his brother Edward from Paris, Feb. 23, 1824

gathered from the letter to Ed. to be gane bock agen to the emerald isle. Pray keep copious journals. Such a letter as the last is sufficiently captivating in these parts. Can't you send information of a sort relating to Colleges, politics, institutions, &c of which creditable use may be made by the Neady writers at home? I have made some embryo motions in my divinity studies & shall be glad of any useful hints from the Paradise of Dictionaries & Critics. How much study is practicable in a day? Are the fables of literary romance about 13, 14, 15 hours turned into sober earnest? Present prospects forebode that good preaching will be in high demand for many a long year to come. Howbeit nobody dreams that You, Caesar, could fall on evil days. When you shew yourself with a sickle in your hand, ma foi, a harvest will spring up to your hand ready to be reaped. So go on in your career of goodnesses & greatnesses, eagle plumed!

As you see, I have nothing very particular to say & am writing because the good bearer can take a letter & passes through the town of sweet Matilda Pottingen.[18] When you send me a line do you tell me if every you borrowed a Map of Massachusetts of Mrs Thos Haskins & where the same may please to be. Tell me if I ought to study German. & any thing else which you think worth sending into the land of Egypt. Pray remember in the quantity of your Communication — that no good seed can be lost on that Cormorant tribe the Schoolmasters; they can glut on all things, yea on garbage, for they devour to give again digested or digested not to their young. Every little while the men of that vocation need to have these dry bones of theirs shaken & revivified to have the impulse of a new start; else old blood & proud flesh will mortify & issue in sore & sour feeling[s or][19] dull unprofitable apathy, in lean indolence, or sound sleep. I tremble to count my unfruitful hours, sometimes. I blame myself for lounging away from school preparation to amuse myself with this dull scrawl. — School [20] is not full &

(MS owned by Dr. Haven Emerson), told how his surtout had been carried off by mistake to La Rochelle in the "Ocean." Possibly this loss is referred to here.

18. Doubtless Emerson refers to the witty "Song, by Rogero" (probably George Canning), which is to be found in *Poetry of the Anti-Jacobin*, 4th ed., London, 1801, pp. 190–192. In these stanzas "sweet Matilda Pottingen" appears as the daughter of a professor at "Gottingen."

19. Conjectural. The MS has been mutilated by the seal.

20. The school William had left. In a letter dated June 24, July 23, and Aug. 1, 1824, their mother wrote to William that "Waldo with unrelaxing industry, & perseverance, pursues the labours of the school, & the cares & studies at home." She added that the number of scholars had not changed much, but that those he had seemed

I wait in vain for it to be fuller. Fowle runs afoul of me a little in that particular, with his Bell & Lancaster.[21] I have as yet recieved no order for money from Mr Searle.[22] Good bye.

Your affectionate brother.

R W E

Very particular love &c from the friends present at this moment in the room to wit, Mother, Aunt Betsey & bauld Buccleugh.[23]

To William Emerson, Roxbury, Massachusetts, July 8, 9, and 10, 1824 [24]

Roxbury, July 8, 1824.

Tis several days, I believe, since my dear brother heard anything from home, notwithstanding all his long letters. But do not, I pray you, murmur. It is just as it shd. be. What mummery it were, to send letters to you from this barren land; what mirth to send coals to Newcastle! But, in truth, it is rather your misfortune than our fault that has hitherto deprived you of our precious autographs, as it is now nearly two months since I sent a letter to Gustorf, who was to set out on a fine Monday morning for Hamburgh & to pass thro' Gottingen but whatsoever gods or goddesses he encountered certain it is I saw him parading the Maine Street (now to be called Washington St. from end to end!!)

---

much pleased with the "good new room back of Trinity church" which he provided for them at a rental of $150 a year. (MS owned by Dr. Haven Emerson.)

21. *The Boston Directory* of 1825 lists William B. Fowle as keeper of a "monitorial school" in Washington Court. This was, no doubt, the William Bentley Fowle who, like Emerson, attended the Latin School and later became a teacher (Jenks, p. 148).

22. William's letters home show that a certain Searle served as his financial agent, honoring his drafts from abroad. George & Thomas Searle appear in *The Boston Directory* of 1823 as dealers in European goods, and a T. Searle, perhaps Thomas, is mentioned as an agent in a letter from George Bancroft to William Emerson, Jan. 1, 1825 (owned by Dr. Haven Emerson). William's expenses abroad are the subject of many passages in his letters at this time, and he writes to Emerson on May 29, 1824 (MS owned by Dr. Haven Emerson), that he still thinks $400 a year, without books, is a reasonable estimate of his needs.

23. Apparently Charles Emerson. The name was doubtless from Scott's "Kinmont Willie," which Emerson could have read in *Minstrelsy of the Scottish Border*.

24. MS owned by CUL; ph. in CUL. William Emerson wrote, Göttingen, Aug. 27, 1824 (MS owned by Dr. Haven Emerson): "I had the pleasure today to receive my first letter from home, purporting to be written by you on the 8th July." It had reached Göttingen before the letter of May 20, which was sent by a different route — the superscription shows that Gustorf was expected to carry it.

some three or four days agone. Therefore, Wondrous Sir, be not offended at the seeming neglect of yr. mightiness.

The second momentous head of this treatise is to express the public sentiment in this country concerning that lost Napoleon of yours.[25] Why, pray, sir, who could be so one eyed of understanding nay so wall blind as not see that the French nation would conspire en masse to possess themselves of that royal array, or at the least to prevent its perilous exhibition on the Mogul's person in the susceptible city of Paris? Why, if old Machiavel had been the tailor, & wanted to forge faster the chains of the people he could devise in a thousand years no more enthralling imperial shape.

Today is Thursday; by Saturday next, before which day I shall not seal this letter, I can inform you whether your brother Edw. has a conference or not at Commencement & shall so grace the stage by standing in his elder brother's shoes. For a conference, if I decieve not myself, is a sort of hereditary honour in his family, an ancient sinecure enfeoffed in the house, & if old tales be true, by whatever private wrongs, feuds, or revenges it came, actually descended to the sons from the sire.[26] The young satrap wears a crown of thorns for a few days trusting doubtless to change them for laurels. And now what more have I to say or ought you to hear? If you ache for news and have a vulgar appetite for " shocking casualties " &c I would tell you that yesterday 15 brick houses were burnt out in Boston on Charles St. & Beacon St. causing no small distress & great alarm.[27] Harrington Carter occupied one of them, & within a fortnight his type foundry was burnt down. A little while since, Morton's house & stable were burnt & his loss of 4000 dollars wholly made up to him by contribution. If your thirst for intelligence be literary & is not sated in Germany — I would add that Judge Marshall is issuing subscriptions for a History of the U. S. of America [28] — that Everett &

25. *Cf.* May 20, 1824.

26. The conferences in which Emerson and his brother William had participated at their graduations are mentioned in the letters of July 20 and 21, 1818, and Aug. 22, 1821. Their father had had a similar part in his commencement program (*Independent Chronicle and the Universal Advertiser,* Boston, July 23, 1789). For Edward's oration — he was to achieve that honor in spite of the family tradition — see a note on Aug. 1, 1824. C. W. Upham's part in the same program is recorded in the source cited in that note.

27. The serious fire of July 7 is described in detail in the *Columbian Centinel* of July 10, 1824. The burning of T. H. Carter's type and stereotype foundry and printing establishment is recorded *ibid.,* June 26; and the destruction of Andrew Morton's property and his relief by public subscription are narrated *ibid.,* June 23.

28. *A History of the Colonies,* 1824, was a reissue of the introduction to the life

Percival are orator & poet for Φ B K, that Upham is orator for our class at Commencement I would add that Gannett is ordained Colleague of Dr Channing & the Dr's Ordination Sermon is expected from the press with unmeasured applause. If you still hunger to know somewhat about us, we are well; or still more insignificantly about *me,* why have at you. Your school this summer quarter contains 23 or 4 having lost 3 or 4 at its commencement. It is profitable enow to promise to support you & me a year longer. As mig[ht] be expected, it does not probably lose in character with those whose children make it up, but does not gain abroad, being encountered & vanquished by the better reputation of your friend's. George B. E. is well & has a noble wife, & increases in good works, in love & in honour. Edward will probably take a private school for boys here in this renowned metropolis of Roxbury with $6 or 7[oo per][29] annum. I take a hebdomadal walk to Mr [Cunn]ingham or Dr. C. for the sake of saying I am studying divinity, & not to have 3 years of poortith when school deserts me. as it may, nay, will. for they wax old. Catharine Tilden & Ann Carter cry aloud for their letters. Charles got the first prize for Latin Poem, Saturday. Bulkeley is boarded out in this town. Grandfather & Grandmother Ripley send their love to you, so does Aunt Sarah. Geo. Ripley & Geo. Emerson would be remembered to the Majesty of Tartary. So of Mother, & Chas. & divers more.

Yr affectionate brother

Waldo

Books, for Mr Dewey havenot yet come, I guess. Directions for study &c would be acceptable you know to me from the land of literary toil. Your trunk arrived a good while ago. Tell me if Mrs T. Haskins lent you a map, & where. Thursday ev.[g]

---

of Washington. For the Phi Beta Kappa program, for Gannett's ordination, for the school which William Emerson had left in his brother's care, and for George B. Emerson and his new wife, see May 20, 1824, and notes. The third edition of Channing's *A Sermon, Delivered at the Ordination of the Rev. Ezra Stiles Gannett . . . June 30, 1824,* bearing the imprint date of this year, is evidence that Emerson's prediction was well warranted.

29. The MS is slightly mutilated, and I have taken the bracketed portions of the text from an incomplete copy of this letter in Cabot's hand, possibly made before the mutilation occurred (owned by RWEMA; ph. in CUL). For Edward's school, *cf.* a note on the letter of Nov. 18 and 19, 1824. Emerson's relations at this time with William Ellery Channing, the Unitarian leader and forerunner of Transcendentalism, are mentioned in Cabot, I, 102. Cunningham may have been the Francis Cunningham of Feb. 24, 1847. For the Misses Tilden and Carter and for Dewey's books, see notes on Nov. 18 and 19, 1824.

Friday ev.g. Edward has just been home to say he has got a first prize for a Dissertation on China.[30] *Sat ev.g.* Edward brought home Newell to dine today & also a card with something written on it, in which the words 'oration,' & "commemorating the benefactors of the University," & "Emerson" could be distinguished. On Tuesday, when the class leave, Newell is orator, & Lunt, poet.

Now, venerande Vir, you & I'll go sleep.

Neither of the boys who eat custards & strawberries with us today have determined on their profession. Edward thinks he is too good for a lawyer & too bad for a divine. Did you ever read a Roman tale about Paulus Emilius & Perseus?[31] My modern Perseus has the heart of a gentleman for the chains of a captive.

To Daniel Bliss Ripley, Roxbury? Massachusetts, July? *c.* 25? 1824

[Mentioned in Aug. 1, 1824. For Daniel Ripley, Emerson's half uncle, *cf.* Sept. *c.* 6, 1818. Fitts (p. 73) is apparently wrong in giving 1823 as the date of Ripley's death. According to *The Ipswich Emersons,* p. 126, he died on Apr. 20, 1825.]

To Mary Moody Emerson, Roxbury? Massachusetts, July 26, 1824

[Partly printed in *Journals,* II, 4–5. It seems probable that Emerson wrote another letter to his aunt about the 1st of the following September, as she seems to praise some writing of his in her letter of Sept. 15 (1824?).]

To Sarah Ripley, Roxbury, Massachusetts, August 1, 1824[32]

Canterbury, 1 August. 1824

My dear Aunt

I have found in my Geometry a certain problem that I never read there before, couched in words of great kindness, & containing gold, & demonstrating certain *moral* truths with the force of mathematical. Every body loves to be the object of kind & partial feelings,

30. He received a first Bowdoin prize for his dissertation on the "Antiquity, Extent, Cultivation, and Present State of the Empire of China" (*Columbian Centinel,* July 10, 1824).

31. The story of the defeat and captivity of Perseus the Macedonian is told in Plutarch's life of Aemilius Paulus and in other classical works.

32. MS owned by RWEMA; ph. in CUL. For Sarah Ripley, *cf.* Aug. 22, 1821.

& I more than any. But nevertheless I wish my Aunt were less openhanded; for, in the first place, there was nothing to reward, the debt being on our side; &, in the next, if there had been, you thereby strip us of our poor merit of goodwill; for goodwill that is to be recompensed in this world, it seems to me, has got, among the moralists, an ignoble name. Besides, you & your house have already laid us under so many obligations that you put it out of our power to pay our just debts; which an honest man always counts a calamity. I shall keep this pledge of your kindness which it were churlish to reject, but I shall keep it as a pledge, which I ought to restore. If you wish to know about us, — the whole Archbishopric of them are well. Edward broods over the Oration; [33] Charles over the School Dissertation; Mother keeps them in order; and Old Mortality in his cell smiles, admires, & moralizes.[34] Time & Chance hold on their old way & we shape ourselves to them as well as we can. Young men & old soon find that these ancient principles, whether they shall call them fates or providences are the lords of life, to whose ordinations they must conform themselves & despite all the big looks of ambition & all the declamations of poets concerning the majesty of man, must yield up their plans & their pride. The seed may be the best that ever was planted, but if it fall on stony ground [35] it will not grow. The man & his project, the most plausible in the world, but out of tune with his times, & cannot prosper. Like all the rest, we at home strut in a straight line to the end of our string & then, must needs, like all the rest, turn or stop. Proud & poor spirits are not very far divided in this world, and with all the difference of their pretensions may end in a like event. Men cheat each other & themselves with ostentatious distinctions of Master & disciple, of Monarch & Slave but in those hours of each mans life when the truth comes out he finds (excepting moral distinctions) not the choice of a hair's breadth among the multitude of his fellows; they are all the disciples & slaves, & your only true Masters & Emperors are Time & Chance.

After this long homily I have only to add that I have sent my letter to Uncle Daniel [36] & Mother has sent your ribbon to Concord by Stage. Mother & Edward send their love & respects [to] Grandfather, & Grandmother & much love to yourself. How does your cough? As soon as it troubles you, you must try Canterbury again Edward begs you &

33. *Cf.* the letter of July 8, 9, and 10, 1824.
34. Like Scott's Old Mortality, Emerson was only narrating the doings of others.
35. *Mark,* 4:5.
36. July? *c.* 25? 1824.

Grandfather to rememb[er] how much he depends on your Company at Holworthy, No 4, by 9 o'clock A. M. Commencement Morng.[37]

Your affectionate nephew
Waldo

To William Emerson, Boston, September 12, 1824 [38]

Boston [I]Sept 12' 1824[I]

x be sure when you come back you be licensed to preach since for dear poverty's sake we must be frugal of time. Edward smitten to the bowels with ambition will speedily count if he does not already count the tedious hours of his own captivity & others w'd probably be impatient for him if he were not. For his own professional education he is ready to plunge knee-ear-deep nay overhead in debt. Of course I must not be left in the lurch, nor will my dilapidated academy [39] let me if I would So I trust by basket or store by begging or borrowing to be studying regularly in a year at least. Thus far I have not been at all incommoded by your demands wh have not entrenched unexpectedly on their means. You shall have all the overplus of family expenditure only the less you have the longer it will last you. x Everett has relinquished the Review for $11,000 to Sparks.[40] Bulkeley is now boarded out & at a charge of $100 pr. ann. x x Geo Ripley looks towards Concord which looks towards you if you be wise or me if you be ambitious Two years & G R will preach [41] x x [II]Why talk you not of my studies how & what I do.[II] German advice must needs be weighty. [III]As to the voyage you mention for me, alas! I shall come to fairy-land as soon. Unless I c'd take the wings of the morning [42] for a packet & feed on

37. According to Dr. Pierce, who duly attended the commencement of Aug. 25, 1824, Edward Emerson " did himself great honour " in spite of " an oppressive cold "; the subject of the oration was " The Advancement of the Age " (*Proc. Mass. Hist. Soc.*, 2d series, V, 191–192). I have supplied the bracketed portions of this paragraph where the MS is slightly mutilated.

38. MS owned by RWEMA; ph. in CUL. This is an incomplete copy in Cabot's hand. Excerpts I–III are in Cabot, I, 109–110.

39. The school left by William Emerson to his brother's care is mentioned in earlier letters.

40. Sparks now took charge of *The North American Review* for the second time. Everett, it seems, was only one of the shareholders who owned the *Review*, and from whom Sparks purchased it at a price, including the value of the share he already held, of a little short of $11,000 (George E. Ellis, *Memoir of Jared Sparks*, 1869, p. 38).

41. But he was to preach in Boston, not in Concord (see Sept. 29, 1826).

42. Emerson probably knew *Psalms*, 139:9, better than Bryant's " Thanatopsis."

wishes instead of dollars & be clothed with imagination for raiment I must not expect to go. I sh'd be glad to try the new scene but it might not do me any good[III] x x

To William Emerson, Roxbury? Massachusetts, November 1? 1824[43]

Be not jealous if we tread on your kibes in our projects but we are not so much impatient of school as of delay; and convinced tis better to be losers of money than of years. for there comes the blind fury with the abhorred shears & slits the thinspun life – praise & all, in the teeth of Phoebus.[44] If my Lycaeum shd. suddenly flourish I wd. keep it till April, else, I pull up its groves root & branch in January. I can never go to Germany, twould be foolish therefore to keep longer and die daily like Rev H. Colman.[45] I have not taken up any money on your notes.

Yrs between sleeping & waking but affectionately

W

In yr next please mention what you did with letters the Irish woman Eliza[46] intrusted to your care. She has never heard of the reciept of the money she sent before you & of which you carried an account.

We have recd I believe 10 letters from you and have sent you 5. the vessel that bore the last 3 put back on account of a leak. I am filling up the vast margins of Ned's letter I know not how, for Ive been asleep about an hour but insanity is better than inanity. If you could in a letter designate in what particulars consist the superior advantages of Gottingen you would convey much desired information into your poor dear country who wants booklearning. Sibyl Farnham[47] is engaged to

43. MS owned by Dr. Haven Emerson; ph. in CUL. This letter is entirely written in the margins of a much longer one from Edward to William. The date "Nov. 1, 1824," at the top of the first page, is, I think, in Edward's hand; but internal evidence seems to indicate that what is here printed was written on the same day. The order in which the paragraphs were written is somewhat uncertain. The unusually careless spelling may have been partly due to the sleepiness which Emerson mentions more than once.

44. Adapted from Milton's "Lycidas," ll. 75–77.

45. Ruth Haskins Emerson wrote to Edward, Apr. 9, 1820, that the Rev. Mr. Colman, from Hingham, had lately opened a school in Boston in rivalry with William. According to the *New-England Palladium,* Nov. 16, 1824, the Rev. Henry Colman was soon to become pastor of a new Unitarian church.

46. William replied Jan. 17, 1825 (MS owned by Dr. Haven Emerson), that he had delivered the letters "of Irish Eliza" to the post officers in Dublin.

47. For Sibyll Ainger Farnham, Emerson's cousin, see *Vital Records of Newburyport,* 1911, I, 135. In a letter to Emerson dated Augusta, Sept. 21, 1875, her name

a Mr Lambert a merchant & man of merit I am told. She has been keeping school in Hollowell & there found her captive

Put your learning in forwardness for use. Forget not that here the practice surpasses the theory. that ready money is better than real estate (even on Carver [48] or Orange Sts) & therefore be not dependent on amenable to any professors here for any priveleges or approbation

TO WILLIAM EMERSON, ROXBURY, MASSACHUSETTS, NOVEMBER 18 AND 19, 1824 [49]

Roxbury, Nov. 18, 1824.

Dear William,

We have recieved every letter of yours up to the date of Aug 27 [50] according to your list of the same & the last came this day to the great joy of all Canterbury. While their contents are fresh in my seive like memory I shall propound to you all the replies & intelligence I can command. You shd have rested in peace as long as you heard nothing from home & congratulated yourself that the famous breeder of news — revolution — kept aloof from its quiet seats. But the ambition of change crept in upon the sleep of its inhabitants & then, & not till then portfolios began to give up their paper & letters began to be written. The innocent ciphers which the Arab invented were tortured into representations of annual expenditure & made to exhibit a long array of the pros & cons concerning a change. Young men made odious comparisons between the present & the possible, between the advancement of their coevals & themselves & ever & anon felt themselves twinged by the rheums & burdens of Maturity who trod on their kibes. At last since an election was to be made between keeping Penury before us, as now, or behind us as in case *rerum novarum,*[51] it was thot best to *go by* the rogue, & see if we could not distance him in the long

appears as Sibyl A. Lambard; and the spelling "Lambard," apparently correct, occurs in the letter of May 24, 1831. According to letters from Ruth Haskins Emerson to William dated June–Oct., 1824 (owned by Dr. Haven Emerson), the school, or academy, was at Augusta, which is, however, close to Hallowell.

48. The family property on Carver St. is mentioned in Jan. 18, 1825.

49. MS owned by Dr. Haven Emerson; ph. in CUL.

50. William's letter of Göttingen, Aug. 27, 1824, and several earlier ones from abroad are owned by Dr. Haven Emerson.

51. The phrase gives a mock heroic touch to this account of the "revolution" occurring at home. This subject is continued in the same jesting manner in the letter of Jan. 18, 1825.

run. In conformity with these views it was deemed wisest to give up teaching & make haste to be taught and in the very poverty of this course to forswear Germany & go to the cheapest stall where education can be bought. Therefore in a few months I shall probably be at Cambridge & attempt to enter the *middle* Class,[52] which if practicable will be an economy of time not to be despised by a hard handed American who reckons acquisitions by dollars & cents not by learning & skill. I tell you your German towns are Castles in the air to me.[53] But as to yourself. All I have paid Mr Searle inclusive of Mr D's & Mrs L's accounts [54] is $493.43. Of this $112 00 was taken up in Paris. Mr Dewey pays me about and Mrs L's was already paid I suppose in $15- So that the year on this side the water has not cost more than was expected. For I have yet rec[d] no bill of money taken up in Sept. as you propose. But I have taken up no note. But if I go to Cambridge Edwards coppers [55] will not cover your demands and if he supply $200 (as perhaps he can) your notes must begin to bring you in debt. Therefore altho' for me to say *Stay* is like saying Be ye warmed [56] & be ye clothed &c yet I certainly would, in your circumstances, — & bring home foreign travel enough in your budget for three. In fine you see you remain more at your own peril than ours, as we shall make no scruple to throw the expense on you as soon as it chafes our precious selves. Unless travelling expenses be enormous you will not certainly be within 5 or 600 miles of Venice & Florence aye & Rome, without risking something for the sake of bringing home the anecdotes & associations that shall exhilarate the ears that hear even in the cold unclassical but intelligent country to which you return. If you hesitate as I know you will not, I wish I were in your place as I shall not be. The diploma [57] I shall try to get & send immediately. We do not know

52. *Cf.* Jan. 18, 1825.

53. In a number of letters William urged the advisability of coming to Germany for further study. On Aug. 27, 1824, he wrote: "Learn German as fast as you can, for you must come here, even if I take to school-keeping again."

54. William Emerson's MS journal (owned by Dr. Haven Emerson) contains drafts of letters to Orville Dewey and a Mrs. Lee, explaining the delay in sending books purchased for them.

55. In his part of the letter of Nov. 1, 1824, Edward says, "My school brings about 700, & we shall get along by hook & crook & by taking up $1,000 on the estate . . ."

56. *James,* 2:16.

57. William wrote to Edward on June 27, 1824 (MS owned by Dr. Haven Emerson): "I leave it entirely to you and Waldo to determine whether you will send me a diploma of A. M. or not, to enable me to become Dr. here. The Germans are so title-mad that it would much increase their respect for me, but I am personally, I

when that semester ends which you say ends your stay. Edward studies law & as he that wd know the origin of Saxon laws is told to seek them in the woods of Germany he bids you peep into every forest you shall chance to pass.[58] For *us,* as bulletins always pass concerning the parishes between hapless candidates — Upham has accepted a call at Salem to settle Colleague with Dr Prince.[59] Young is preaching popularly at N. South. I have rec^{d} & despatched letters to C. B. T. & A.-C. & the monumental J F.[60] Charles well in college chums with Loring under Otis [61] — rank not sure. Edw. wants an English translation of Herder's phil. of history.[62] You had better get us some Theol Interpretation books, for if we do not want them others will. More people than I can name bid me remember them to you & ask all the questions; & among the relatives particularly Grandfather & Grandmother Aunt & Uncle Ripley of Waterford (for they are of that ilk,) & thither we may send Bulkeley who is now at home & pretty well but as anxious as ever to be remembered. Very grateful & very glad are we all of these precious budgets from Gottingen & none more than your affectionate brother Waldo.[63] Buy says Edward 10 dollars worth of something for me whether books or soap or cambric or curiosities 10 dollars worth of European Commodities.

You shall not lack letters if you will keep us in the knowledge of an

---

believe, wholly indifferent about it." Apparently the Harvard degree, which in those days required only a period of waiting after the A.B. was granted, appearance at commencement, and a small fee, was sent. But in his letter dated Rome, June 14, and Genoa, June 24, 1825, William writes this unexpected conclusion: "I might have had the Doctorate of Philosophy at Göttingen, but it would have cost me 60 dollars, which I thought too much for the whistle" (MS owned by Dr. Haven Emerson).

58. William, Jan. 10, 1825, replies, describing the German law courts (MS owned by Dr. Haven Emerson).

59. The *New-England Palladium,* Nov. 16, 1824, reports that Charles Wentworth Upham is to become colleague pastor with Dr. Prince at Salem. For Young, see Jan. 18, 1825.

60. C. B. T. was probably Catherine Tilden; A.-C., probably Ann Carter, who appears in a letter of May 4, 1860, as one of the former pupils of the Emersons' school in Boston at the reunion that year; and J. F., almost certainly William's college classmate John Fessenden. William's MS journal for the summer of 1824 (owned by Dr. Haven Emerson) contains drafts of letters to all three of these persons.

61. Charles Emerson to William, Sept. 11, endorsed 1824 (owned by Dr. Haven Emerson): "I chum with Loring, & room under Mr. Otis, in no 1. Holworthy."

62. William Emerson wrote, Aug. 27, 1824 (MS owned by Dr. Haven Emerson): "Read all of Herder you can get . . ." Herder's *Outlines of a Philosophy of the History of Man,* tr. T. Churchill, had been published at London in 1800.

63. The rest of the letter was obviously an afterthought.

address & conveyance as now thro' Calvert.[64] Here I am chatting on till I can touch the End of my Sheet but as this is to be sent tomorrow I must close it So Heaven keep you guide you bless you & restore you. Friday Night Nov 19

Mr Everett goes to 19th Congress from Middlesex by a large majority. D. Webster from Suffolk *unanimously*. Rufus G. Amory probably from Norfolk. Mr Adams is not sure. Presidential election will come before Representatives doubtless. Clay Crawford Jackson. – & Calhoun for V. P. A. Everett is in Washington with present leave of absence from Hague.

To William Emerson, Roxbury, Massachusetts, November 20, 1824 [65]

x x x [I]If you think it every way advisable, indisputably, absolutely important that I shd do as you have done & go to G – & you can easily decide – why say it distinctly & I will make the sacrifice of time & take the risk of expense, immediately. So of studying German[I] x x We are all subject to whiffs of melancholy & ill humour but for the most part I have much confidence in my own success, when I shall preach. If I hope, of course I am an Aeneas in a cloud & impatient to break it.[66] If I sh'd obtain in the School such standing as to be prepared *with* you, it wouldnt be good sense for two to come out together & peradventure I might bridle the rage of teaching, six months or so in my bosom. [II]Say particularly if German & Hebrew be worth reading for tho' I hate

64. George Henry Calvert, a great-grandson of the fifth Lord Baltimore, had been a sophomore at Harvard during Emerson's senior year. William, Göttingen, Apr. 1, 1824 (MS owned by Dr. Haven Emerson), says, "But I can't possibly describe the pleasure I felt in finding Calvert here. We were of course immediately well acquainted. He is very much of a gentleman in his manners, and studies with great diligence." In his letter of June 27, 1824, to Edward (owned by Dr. Haven Emerson), William gave the name of Calvert's agent in London who would forward letters to an uncle of Calvert's in Antwerp, who, in his turn, would send them on to Göttingen. Calvert, who appears in later letters, came to be known, not only for his translations from the German, but for numerous original works.

65. MS owned by RWEMA; ph. in CUL. This is another incomplete copy in Cabot's hand; and excerpts I–II are printed without place or date in Cabot, I, 109. William wrote, Mar. 2, 1825 (MS owned by Dr. Haven Emerson): "I have received Charles' 2 letters of 20 Nov. and 27 Dec. with no little pleasure, eked out by scraps from you (not to forget the diploma). . . . You ask me to be distinct in regard to studying German and Hebrew, and coming to Europe. . . ." William had already acknowledged Emerson's long letter of Nov. 18 and 19 on Jan. 17, 1825 (MS owned by Dr. Haven Emerson).

66. *Aeneid,* I, 579–581.

to study them cordially I yet will the moment I can count my gains. Had I not better put on my hat & take ship for the Elbe[II] x x ? If the account of Eichhorn had come in a letter to me instead of Fessenden[67] (   ) I sh'd have printed it in the "Literary Register" which Theophilus Parsons conducts & may yet[68] x x

To Mary Moody Emerson? Roxbury? Massachusetts, December 17, 1824

[A fragment printed in Cabot, I, 105–106, without date, and in *Journals,* II, 32–33, under date of Dec. 17, 1824. There may be some doubt, I think, whether this is from a letter or from a scrap of Emerson's journals, perhaps sent to Mary Moody Emerson in a letter.]

To Mary Moody Emerson, Roxbury? Massachusetts, December 24, 1824

[Mentioned in Mary Moody Emerson, Sept. 24? and Dec. 13, 1825.]

To William Emerson, Roxbury? Massachusetts, December? *c.* 27? 1824?

[Described in a note on Nov. 20, 1824, as a scrap which eked out a letter from Charles dated Dec. 27.]

To Hannah Haskins Ladd, Roxbury? Massachusetts? *c.* 1824[69]

There are 24 hours in every day; And if you sh'd sleep & dream thro 8 of them, there will 16 left. Now since mortals must eat & drink &

67. For the study of German and for Fessenden, see the letter of Nov. 18 and 19, 1824, and notes. A phrase inclosed in parentheses following Fessenden's name is illegible.

68. Notes on the letters of Sept. 13 and 29, 1826, relate to the question of William Emerson's contributions to *The United States Literary Gazette,* probably the magazine referred to here, and to Theophilus Parsons as an editor.

69. MS owned by Dr. James I. Wyer; ph. in CUL. There is no date; but the writing is Emerson's of approximately 1824, and the letter is described, by an unknown hand, as "Written about 1824 or 1825." The name of the person addressed is nowhere given, but the late Mary Elizabeth Wyer wrote me on Feb. 13, 1929, that this letter was written by Emerson to her mother "after her graduation from his brother's school for girls in Boston, and was advice as to her reading." This information fits 1824 or 1825 and accords with what internal evidence I have noted. Hannah Haskins Ladd (1810–1890), who married James Ingersoll Wyer in 1839, was the daughter of William Ladd and Mary Haskins, sister of Emerson's mother. The "sister E" of the present letter must have been Elizabeth, b. 1807. (See Warren Ladd, p. 291.)

since moreover cares abound in the world & must needs encroach on hours, I will set apart to these evils ten, & leave but six to devotion, study, & thought. A small allowance for our best & chief employments —

One of these six hours every day I would give to history So go get Hume, (not the Vol. I) but the reign of Elizabeth & if your sister E will begin it with you, so much the better for both. It is always best to note how many pages you read in an hour & accustom yourself to talk over what you have read, & think (& if possible write too upon it. After finishing Hume from that reign you will find yourself sufficiently interested in English Story to go back to Henry VIII. Read at the same time Shakspears fine play of that name & then you will be ready to take up Robertson's Charles V, who was contemporary with Harry. This last is a book in 3 Volumes The first contains a sketch of the general State Europe, which though very good, yet may be read as well at another Time —

As for French, read some more of the chefs 'd oeuvres; — and Telemachus & La Bruyere[70] if you can find them, are entertaining and instructive —

Then for English, get the old sterling sense of the Rambler and Spectator & you know not what pleasant companions your mornings & evenings will find — If you love poetry make acquaintance with Milton Pope and Cowper, & if you love romance you may read Scott's Novels without sin or scandal. —

For books of science, besides Paley,[71] which you will not discontinue, the Conversations on Chemistry,[72] they contain a great deal of curious & beautiful knowledge much more than many who have read it are aware. Joyce's dialogues [73] will perhaps tell you a fact or two you did not know before —

70. Fénelon's *Les Aventures de Télémaque* had been for a century a favorite book for the young, often translated. La Bruyère's *Les Caractères* was equally old and famous. Emerson's French phrase probably exhibits carelessness rather than ignorance of the language.

71. Doubtless William Paley's *Natural Theology,* an American edition of which had appeared at Philadelphia in 1802.

72. Jane Marcet's *Conversations on Chemistry,* which was intended especially for women and of which there were a number of editions by this time, is almost certainly meant.

73. In the MS the spelling is doubtful and looks more like "Joyle's" than "Joyce's," but it seems altogether probable that the book Emerson means is the popular *Scientific Dialogues,* by the Unitarian minister Jeremiah Joyce, of which new editions were published at Philadelphia in 1815 and in 1825.

But among other books be sure you dont forget the one you covered with my name. The others must all lose much of their interest after a few years; this will affect the utmost bounds of your existence —

When you go home make my respects to your father & mother & believe me

Your sincere frd.

R Waldo Emerson

1825

To William Emerson, Roxbury, Massachusetts, January 18, 1825[1]

[I]Roxbury, Jan 18, 1825.[I]

A happy new year to my dear brother. You are I doubt not suitably shocked at the innovations & rumors of innovations which by this time have thunderstruck you.[2] The Radicals have not only concerted their measures, but have begun to execute them; & that with a stoutness of heart quite beyond calculation 18 or 20 months ago. [II]I have cast my bread on the waters, locked up my school,[3] and affect the scholar at home. The truth is we think we have got to the Candlemas day of our winter, & that we may be bold to borrow the second half of our wood & hay, assuming that the spring & summer of lucrative exertion is nigh.[II] Fear not but due allowance is made for the sweat & merit of Atlas who bore the burden of all; and a pennyworth of consideration is affected for poor Hercules who stood in the stead of the giant.[4] But [III]ambitious hopes have been engendered by the real or supposed increase of value of the old property on Maine Street. A great hotel has been builded thereon[5] whose cost it is hoped the Carver St land will pay — and

1. MS owned by Dr. Haven Emerson; ph. in CUL. Excerpts I–IV are printed in Cabot, I, 110. The letter ends on the upper half of the third page of the MS, without signature. Probably Emerson had intended to continue it later, but the remainder of the sheet is occupied by Edward, who mentions the foregoing paragraphs by "my theolog. brother."

2. William Emerson had already recorded his consternation (Jan. 10, 1825; MS owned by Dr. Haven Emerson), upon receipt of the letter of Nov. 1? 1824, which deals with this same subject of the "revolution" in family plans. It was, he said, "a rather bold plan which looks forward 2 or 3 years without any certain means of bread. . . . And I rejoice that you are rushing to jail in such good spirits. Had I dreamed of such a revolution when at home, I should as soon have gone to Greenland as to Göttingen."

3. In the MS *Autobiography* Emerson says he closed his Boston school on Dec. 31, 1824.

4. Earlier letters refer to William's years of teaching to support the family and keep his brothers in school. Emerson himself had now taken his turn.

5. Edward had written on the same sheet with Nov. 1? 1824: "Advertisements. The La Fayette hotel, having 35 rooms &c. built opposite the Boylston market-house

thereafter $200 pr. annum shd. come to every thirteenth, with a reasonable prospect of more.[III] In hour of need this can be easily mortgaged for $1000. [IV]Moreover if I go to Cambridge at the end of the present vacation,[6] as I shall, the learned & reverend have consented to admit me to the Middle Class[IV] of which measure whatever may be the moral & general expediency, the pecuniary is apparent. Next I possess in fee simple $518 at interest. Lastly Edward retains his private school of 7, or $800, though the uneasy child whispers pretty loudly of slipping his neck from the ancient noose in August. When I have added that in April we shall probably migrate in a flock to Cambridge & occupy Mr Mellen's old house for $100 or 200, you will have all the data whereon our calculations proceed.

I think the last payment I made for you was in September or the beginning of October. and you have mentioned in your letters money taken up or to be taken about that time, but Mr Searle has not recieved advices of it. That will subtract from my dollars, as I have anticipated. After that, your travelling expenses (which ought not be forborne) must draw on your own notes (yet inviolate), on Edward's purse, or on the projected mortgage. This may make your economy yet more vigilant, but cannot deprive you of the sight of Rome, Naples, & London. It would indeed be a sorry sight, much as your return is reckoned on at home, to behold eyes that had not looked on Italy, albeit they had saluted the sun of Germany & France. So beware of my wrath. I think it will be of small importance to us ultimately, to be approbated at the same time. If any objections should be, I shall be glad to see London & Paris until you choose a diocess wherein to scatter thunder, light, and good.

Your classmate Barrett is a fine preacher & to be ordained at Twelfth Congregation in February.[7] He promises to write you. Young is to be

---

to let. Apply to R. or T. Haskins." This was, as the present letter makes clear, a promising means of investing the inheritance of Emerson's mother and of her brothers and sisters. The name was a timely choice in the year of La Fayette's visit to Boston. The *Boston Courier* of Jan. 5, 1825, reported that this tavern had been rented; and the writer described, with some enthusiasm, the newly-painted sign showing the beloved general, in uniform on one side of the board, in citizen's clothes on the other.

6. He probably registered as a student in divinity on Feb. 11 (*cf.* Feb. 10, 1825), though he gives the date as Feb. 9 in the MS *Autobiography*. I have been unable to find full official records of Emerson's residences at the Divinity School.

7. His ordination is announced for Feb. 9, 1825, in the *Boston Courier* of that date. The ordinations of A. Young, Jr., John Flagg, and Sewall (at Amherst, N. H.) are noted in the *Christian Register* for Jan. 22 and Feb. 5, 1825.

ordained Wednesday at New South. Flagg — the following week at Mr Bradford's in Roxbury. Edmund Sewall in Amherst Dr Lowell wants a colleague; it may be, Hall will go there. Nine weeks after Mrs Bradford deceased, her daughter Katherine died also.[8] I have perhaps told you, Lucy will be provided for. Mrs Clark is thankful for the great kindness she says you have manifested to her son.[9] I forgot to say I gave 10 of my scholars on New Years day to Thomas Bradford and the girls made me at parting a present of beautiful books. Whereat I answered & said — There is no emblem of a fine woman so well chosen as a good book in beautiful covers, & that I should always (as the rest of mankind) love fine sense the better for fine binding. — Could the Mogul have outprettied that? But the gift was kind & unexpected and there were more pangs than I tho't at parting. I have Ariosto Dante and Milton, &c. Charles who is a high scholar, perhaps third, has gone on a pilgrimage to our lady at Waterford — who has written me a prodigiously fine letter 'from Plato.' [10]

To William Emerson, Roxbury, Massachusetts, February 10, 1825 [11]

Roxbury, Feb. 10, 1825.

My dear brother, Three months have elapsed since we have had any word from you which makes mother contract her brows, & even your philosophic brothers expect letters eagerly. Mrs Clark told me as I have since told you that Noel was delighted with & grateful for your attentions, & she wonders we hear not of him thro' you. We have had no letter since you told us you were departing on a fortnight's jaunt [12] & shd. write when you returned. So drive your quill incontinent.

8. The death of Ann, widow of the elder Samuel Bradford mentioned in earlier letters, is recorded in the *Christian Register* of Oct. 22, 1824. The daughter's death is noted *ibid.*, Dec. 31, 1824.

9. See the letter of Feb. 10, 1825.

10. Mary Moody Emerson, Aug. 10 and probably earlier (1824), contains a remarkable imaginary letter from Plato in answer to one Emerson wrote into his diary (*Journals,* I, 380–388) and sent to his aunt.

11. MS owned by HCL; ph. in CUL. Emerson's letter is followed, at the bottom of the first page, by a brief note from Edward; and the second and third pages contain a letter from their mother, dated Feb. 11.

12. Three manuscripts owned by Dr. Haven Emerson tell the story of the walking tour of Sept. 16–Oct. 8, 1824. William wrote to his mother from Göttingen, on Sept. 15, "Yesterday Eichhorn finished his lectures, and tomorrow evening, with knapsack on back, I set off on a fortnight's excursion — possibly as far as the capital

Tomorrow morn[g] I enter my name Student in divinity at Cambridge, and shall expect mother there in April. Your friend Barrett was ordained yesterday at Twelfth Ch. Yesterday the President of U. S. was elected by the House of R. but we must wait till Sunday to know if Adams or Jackson is he; Probably the former. Gov. Eustis is dead, & is

---

of Saxony." An interesting account of the journey itself is preserved in William's MS *Journal of a Tour from Gottingen to Dresden. 1824.* The young American student was a keen observer of the men and manners and of the country through which he passed, but the event of the fortnight was his meeting with Goethe: "We soon left Erfurt for Weimar," he writes, "and I must forget all the scenery, to hurry forward to that, which rendered this an ever memorable day to me. As I felt much at a loss for time, in arranging my journey from Göttingen, nothing but the hope of seeing Göthe would have induced me to take this circular route. I knew that he was very seldom visible to strangers, but resolved to hazard the attempt. We arrived in the pleasant town of Weimar at noon, and I immediately repaired to his house, and sent up my card, on which I had previously added 'Boston, N. America' to my name. He sent me word that he was then surrounded with company, but if I would call at 4, he would see me. It may be supposed, that I did not forget the appointment. I was shown into a room, that was filled with works of art. A huge bust of Minerva was placed over one of the doors. A large case with books, which from their great size, must have been drawings, stood in one corner. Göthe, the gentle and venerable poet, entered almost immediately. I was so struck with the difference between him who came into the room, and the formidable portrait that is commonly to be seen of this great man, that I almost expected to see another person behind him. His address and manner were perfectly simple and unconstrained. After finding out my profession, he led the conversation immediately upon the state of religion in the U. S. and afterwards upon the state and hopes of our country in general. His tone became gradually that of an instructer, and yet it ceased not to be unassuming, but all was uttered quietly, as a mere private opinion. He said he thought we had nothing to do with the different systems of philosophy, but that the highest aim of life should be for each one to accommodate himself as perfectly as possible to the station in which he was placed. He asked many questions, and talked willingly, yet seemed not loath to be interrupted. The only thing that was American in my possession, a number of the Palladium, I ventured to offer him, as our papers are a great curiosity in Germany. He accepted the trifle very graciously, and said it was 2 years since he had seen one. He shook me kindly by the hand when I took leave. I left Weimar immediately, but I shall not hastily forget this exceedingly interesting visit. He was of the common size, with pleasing but not striking features; his dress was a blue surtout, over a white vest. I should not have judged him to be more than 65, yet he is said to be about 10 years older. ——— Between 2 and 4 I had amused myself with looking at the city that has been so much honoured by the residence of Wieland and Schiller and Herder and Goethe. I thought it much prettier than Gotha or Erfurt. It is true, many of the streets were old and narrow throughout; but there were many handsome dwelling-houses, and many indications of a prevalent good taste. The Grecian Chapel is admirable for its simplicity in architecture and ornament. The new castle bears much resemblance to the style in which the Louvre is built, though it wants the beautiful colonnade of the latter. The public walks or gardens in its neighborhood are in better taste than those of Gotha, and extremely pleasant. A pleasure-to be paraded into the dust tomorrow.[13] Everett made a great speech in the Senate Chamber before Overseers of H. Univ. a week since. Twas without notes — three hours & a half long — logical — commanding — ; but the Vote against it was unanimous. Twas defence of Immed. Gov. who ask to be admitted into ye Corporation.[14] I have had no Order for money since September tho' you were to take up some in that month. I have crowded these black words together merely that Mr Gray may tell you we are well Your affectionate brother.[15] Come back as soon as you can seeing what is worth sight for our ears are open for your tidings — & eke our hearts.

R. W. Emerson.

This comes to you I suppose thro' the kind offices of Mr John Henry Gray Edward's friend & classmate travelling with Mr Peabody.

To Mary Moody Emerson, Cambridge? March, 1825

[Partly printed in *Journals,* II, 63–66. The passage omitted on p. 64 is as follows: "The accumulating witness of history I know was less then than now. Thotful men cd not so distinctly detect those moral results wh. ye progress of Society ye rise greatness & decline of communities, ye policy of war & of peace ye pursuit of arts & of agric. (when bro't in comparison) thro many ages disclose. But . . ." (Typescript *Journals.*)]

To Edward Bliss Emerson, Cambridge, August, 1825

[Mentioned in Edward Emerson, Jan. 27, 1827, as containing philosophic consolation and as not having been received until "the other day," when Edward was expecting a letter from Charleston instead of this old one.]

---

saloon of the grandduke's, which stands in these grounds, I took for a Gothic church; the architecture is fine. — 20 Sept. — Gera. From Weimar I hastened to Jena."

Finally, a letter written home on Oct. 10, 1824, soon after the return to Göttingen, adds detail to the story of the meeting with Goethe: "He was all I could wish to see in a great man and a beautiful poet. He is 75 years old, yet his form is erect, his manner in the highest degree kind and friendly. . . . He hardly ever admits a stranger, since he is so often plagued with requests of that kind; but the words — 'of Boston, N. America' — which I wrote on my card, served as a passport. I was half an hour with him, and it was an half hour I shall not soon forget." Goethe recorded in his diary, with his usual brevity, under date of Sept. 19, 1824: "Will. Emerson aus Boston, Nordamerika, in Göttingen studirend, protestantischer Theolog. Blieb für mich." (*Goethes Werke,* Weimar, 1887 ff., Part III, IX, 271.)

A much later comment on William Emerson and Goethe is mentioned in a note on Sept. 13, 1868.

13. An account of the funeral, on the 11th, is given in the *Boston Daily Advertiser,* Feb. 12, 1825.

14. For Everett's speech of Feb. 3 and the unanimous negative vote, see the *Boston Daily Advertiser,* Feb. 4 and 5, 1825.

15. Here Emerson signed the name "Waldo" but canceled it.

To Mary Moody Emerson, Chelmsford? Massachusetts, September? *c.* 20? 1825

[Acknowledged as just received in Mary Moody Emerson, Sept. 24? and Dec. 13, 1825 (in the part written Sept. 24?). She comments upon her nephew's ill health.]

To ———, Chelmsford? Massachusetts, December? *c.* 18? 1825

[Mentioned in Dec. *c.* 20? 1825.]

To William Emerson, Chelmsford, Massachusetts, December *c.* 20? 1825 [16]

Dear Wm,

In obedience to your letter I am about to close my school here & to migrate to your latitudes. One thing is unlucky — that same lame hip of mine which I have been magnifying into a scarecrow, maugre Dr Dalton's opinions who nicknames it rheumatism. But for safety's sake I insist on its being dandled and hunted as the worst

16. MS owned by HCL; ph. in CUL. The endorsement, which contains the only date, is equivocal as to the year but gives the month definitely as December. It is clear, however, that the letter was written some time in December, 1825; and apparently it precedes that of Dec. *c.* 28? of this year. In the MS *Autobiography* Emerson states that he opened the academy in Chelmsford on Sept. 12, 1825, and remained there till the end of the year; and this exactly agrees with the evidence of the bill copied below. But according to Wilson Waters, *History of Chelmsford Massachusetts*, 1917, p. 818, the Classical School in that town was opened Sept. 1, 1825, "by Mr. Ralph Waldo Emerson, who left Dec. 30." Emerson, according to the same account, was a popular instructor, but was lured to Roxbury by some person there who led him to expect a profit of $2000 a year. Dr. John C. Dalton is mentioned *ibid.*, pp. 561 and 563, as a member of the Chelmsford committee to examine the schools in 1825 and as a trustee of the Classical School in that year. Josiah Gardiner Abbott's vague recollections of Emerson as a teacher at Chelmsford are recorded in Holmes's memoir of Emerson (*The Works of Oliver Wendell Holmes*, Boston and New York, n. d. [c. 1892], XI, 38). Mr. Owen D. Young owns a bill made out in Emerson's hand as follows:

" Mr Saml. C. Hunt to R. W. Emerson, Dr
" To the instruction of his brother.
" from Sept. 12, 14 w. at 40. cts
" 5.60
" Chelmsford, Dec. 31, 1825 "

At the bottom of this scrap of paper Emerson acknowledged the receipt of the amount stated. An endorsement shows that this bill was for the instruction of Benjamin P. Hunt. Emerson later proved himself a good friend to this early pupil, and several letters printed in the present volumes were written to him. For Emerson's memories of Chelmsford, many years later, see *Journals*, IX, 235–237.

form of hip complaint, whereat he laugheth. Obsta principiis.[17] I make much of the matter because said malady hath crippled its hundreds & slain its tens.[18] Please tell Uncle Ralph I will God willing keep school here till 1st of January & hope then or 2 or 3 days after to drive & clinch the nails of instruction into at least 30 brains of the State's good town of Roxburgh.[19] For 20 is not enow. I shall probably bring boarding scholars 3 or four if room cd. be readily found. But don't take a house till I come Better begin moderately by boarding teacher & taught with some resident family. They are pleased to say in Chelmsford that they are in the gall of bitterness.[20] If you send me a letter again put it into that old odd Vol of Montaigne [21] & send it bundlewise by stage. If you can find an old Liber Primus [22] to spare put it in also. The first I must have before I leave C. I use my eyes to write. Bulkeley is perfectly deranged & has been ever since I have been here. I shall try to leave him here.

I enclose a letter [23] writ without great expense of eye at 3 sittings which transmit if you please.

Love to mother & tell her not to look grave at the beginning of my letter for I wrote such a horrible story to shew how careful an old lady I am

R. W. E.

Geo is very well

17. The exact sense is in Ovid's *Remedia Amoris,* 91; but it is possible that this and some other Latin phrases used in the letters may have been familiar to Emerson as proverbial sayings wholly detached from their classical sources.

18. Probably an allusion to *I Samuel,* 18:7.

19. On account of failing health, Edward had to give up his private school for boys at Roxbury; and it was this school which Emerson reopened early in Jan., 1826, and continued till Mar. 28 following in the second story of Octagon Hall in that town (D. G. Haskins, pp. 87 ff. and 109–111). Haskins gives the date of the reopening as Jan. 3, but the MS *Autobiography* says Jan. 1.

20. *The Acts,* 8:23.

21. Within a few years Emerson was an enthusiastic admirer of Montaigne's robustness, generosity, and downright truth (see the letter of Dec. 25, 1831, to Mary Moody Emerson), and it cannot be doubted that a reading of the worldly-wise Frenchman, long before the time of the famous lecture in *Representative Men,* influenced the American writer toward greater directness of style and bolder observation of life.

22. Book I of the *Aeneid,* probably.

23. Dec.? *c.* 18? 1825.

To William Emerson, Chelmsford? Massachusetts? December c. 28? 1825 [24]

Dec. 1825
Dear W^m^

The word has at last come forth tho' with the travail of an oracle wh- sanctions my departure but they that speak it can almost hear in its echo the crash & ruin of their school. So I have promised to write to you & ask you whether in consideration of the fragility of yr brother's resolution & of the egregious disappointment of the patrons of the new institution here you are not willing to take it in trust for a few weeks & make good the appearances of a quarter that so the mocker & the scorner who are as plentiful as in the days of Solomon need not shake the head & say [25] You've starved one schoolmaster & tis vain to try to maintain your school. There are serious apprehensions here in the expectation of getting another master, & particularly when tis remembered they are anxious to fix *the School* here in spite of the rich & growing Corporation. Besides the disappointment of the parents who tho't their children well provided for the term. There are only 18 with my family but that number w'd soon be made good no doubt in the event of your coming Tis a grand place to study & I will guarantee you (& strange to tell I risque something in so doing) your board, room & fire & 5.00 pr week

I shall keep school Sat. A. M.[26] & shall expect Chas. & Chas. Wain to transport me & Geo. & Chas. Andrews all & severally with budgets & bags [27] x x

24. MS owned by RWEMA; ph. in CUL. This is an incomplete copy in Cabot's hand. As the time for leaving Chelmsford is more definitely set than in Dec. *c.* 20? the present letter is presumably the later one.

25. *Psalms,* 22:7.

26. Presumably Saturday, Dec. 31 (*cf.* a note on Dec. *c.* 20? 1825); and this makes it very probable that the present letter was written during the last week at Chelmsford.

27. Charles Emerson was, it seems, expected to bring a vehicle of some sort and carry away his brother and the "boarding scholars" mentioned in Dec. *c.* 20? 1825.

1826

To Mary Moody Emerson, Cambridge? January 8, 1826

[Partly printed in *Journals,* II, 77–79, where it is dated simply Jan., 1826. The exact date is fixed by Mary Moody Emerson, Apr. 27, and, again, June 13 (1826). The place is shown pretty conclusively by the letter of Feb.? *c.* 10? 1826. Emerson may have been at Cambridge on a week-end visit, as he had begun his teaching at Roxbury only a few days before.]

To Mary Moody Emerson, Roxbury? Massachusetts, February? *c.* 10? 1826

[Incompletely printed in *Journals,* II, 83–85. Apparently the letter mentioned in Mary Moody Emerson, Feb. 26 and Mar. 22 (1826), as received on Feb. 16.]

To Charles Folsom, Cambridge, March? 30? 1826? [1]

Cambridge, Thursday.

Mr Folsom

Dear Sir,

A twelvemonth since I obtained from the President the privelege [2] of the library as a resident graduate. If it may be permitted, I shall be glad to resume the privelege without the trouble of a new ap-

1. MS owned by the Public Library, Boston; ph. in CUL. The date is not later than the academic year 1825–1826, the last for which Charles Folsom is listed as librarian at Harvard. It is probable, on the other hand, that when Emerson returned to college in Feb., 1825 (see the letter of Feb. 10, 1825), he obtained the usual library privileges. If so, that date might well be the " twelvemonth since " of the present letter. He kept his school at Roxbury till Mar. 28, 1826 (*cf.* a note on Dec. *c.* 20? 1825). A MS charge-book for 1825–1826 (HCL) shows that some books were drawn in his name by his brother Charles on Mar. 30, 1826. This fact would fit well the statement that " I am confined by a lameness to my chamber," and apparently the same ailment is alluded to in Apr. 6, 1826. Finally, it happens that Mar. 30 of this year fell on Thursday. In the catalogue for Sept., 1826, Emerson appears among the " Resident Graduates," with the information that he lives at Mrs. Emerson's.

2. This spelling is the usual one in other letters of this period.

plication, as I am confined by a lameness to my chamber. I return one or two books which were charged to my name. Respectfully yr. obed. serv.

R. W. Emerson.

To Mary Moody Emerson, Cambridge, April 6, 1826 [3]

[I]Cambridge, April 6, 1826.

My dear Aunt,

Epicurus said to his fellow men ' We are a sufficient spectacle to each other '; [4] and he said truly; for it is the business & pleasure of life to make the best acquaintance we can with the individuals of the enormous crowd of the living & the dead. They so press on each other in the innumerable procession that tis little we can learn distinctly of each [I] yet we can distinguish here & there a man clad with the purple of empire, & another with the motley of prejudice, a third disfigured with the dust of libraries & a fourth with the blood of his brethren. [II]But altho we are by the distance necessarily made strangers to infinite numbers the same distance helps us to group them together and to trace the general direction & many windings of the march. And who are the guides & where the encampments whither the progress & when the period of this tragic journey of humanity thro' the champaign of the world? [II] Nation travels after nation some in chains, & some in mail, of diverse complexions of diverse tongues, some in weeds of peace singing paeans to every muse in accents of noble harmony and some stumbling onward with heavy step & downcast eyes, the ensigns of former honor dragging — in the dust whilst now and then bursts of bitter lamentation answer to each other from space to space in this funeral Congregation of mourners.

[III]Let us draw nearer & make the most of our vantage-ground to satisfy our curiosity respecting the intents & condition of those we are favourably situated to observe. They are banded into companies in the outset of their array for better defence against the wolf & the lion, against famine & storm. They are organized under governments for the convenience & protection of the individuals But who leads the leaders & instructs the instructor? I behold along the line men of reverend pre-

3. MS owned by RWEMA; ph. in CUL. Excerpts I–VI are in Cabot, I, 112–115.

4. I have not found this in the extant fragments. Perhaps Emerson's source was an indirect one. Later he knew something of Epicurus through Landor's conversations (*Journals,* II, 517: Oct. 9, 1832), but he does not seem to have borrowed here from them. It is barely possible that he remembered vaguely a saying attributed to Epicurus by Cicero, *De Finibus,* I, xx, 65.

tension who have waited on mountains or slept in caverns to receive from unseen Intelligence a chart of the unexplored country a register of what is to come. But, wo is me! as they proceeded the gods of the nations became no gods, the facts belied the prophecies, & the advancing journey betrayed the falsehood of their guides. Goodness was not found with the servants of the Supremely Good, nor Wisdom with those who had seen the all Wise. — But still, on they went — the stately procession by tribes & kindreds & nations, substituting experience of the past for knowledge of the future, advancing with courageous heart into the unexplored wilderness, tho' with many delays & many retrograde wanderings,[III] thro' sunshine & storm [IV]whilst many a day of beauty lighted their march, & many a halcyon sign of hope & knowledge illuminated the future.

At the last an obscure man in an obscure crowd bro't forward a new Scripture of promise & instruction. But the rich & the great leaned to their ancient holdings & the wise distrusted this teacher for they had been often misled before. But the banner inscribed with his Cross has been erected and it has been to some a cloud & to some a pillar of fire.

We too have taken our places in the immeasurable train & must choose our standard & our guide. Is there no venerable tradition whose genuineness & authority we can establish, or must we too hurry onward inglorious in ignorance & misery we know not whence, we know not whither. Perhaps you are tired of my metaphors but I write to get answers not to please myself — and cannot tell how much I was disappointed to find my long expected letter nothing but an envelope.

My eyes are well comparatively, my limbs are diseased with rheumatism.[IV]

I beseech you again to write. Samuel Gilman of Charleston, S. Carolina writes the Brown Reviews.[5] Norton wrote the last review of Byron, & Alex. Everett the one before. [V]Edward writes that he mends daily.[6] Your affectionate nephew

R. Waldo E.[V]

5. Articles on the works of Dr. Thomas Brown were printed in *The North American Review* for July, 1824, and for July, 1825. Samuel Gilman reappears, as a correspondent, during Emerson's winter in the South. The reviews of books on or by Byron were also in *The North American,* Alexander Everett's in Jan., 1825, and Andrews Norton's in October of the same year. William Cushing's *Index* confirms Emerson's statement regarding the authorship of all these contributions.

6. Edward had sailed for Marseilles the preceding October to pass the winter in Europe in search of health (William Emerson to Mary Moody Emerson, Oct. 27, 1825; owned by Dr. Haven Emerson).

Mother hopes a favourable opportunity will occur by which Hannah [7] can come.

VI Why so anxious about C. — He stands we suppose first in his class; he loves letters, he loves goodness; But goodness is an abstraction & we cannot always be goodhumoured even tho' we love to madness. He will be eloquent, & will *write* but comes not up to the force & nobleness of the transatlantic boy — certainly not to my cherished image of the same.VI

TO MARY MOODY EMERSON, CAMBRIDGE? APRIL 10, 1826

[Printed incompletely in *Journals,* II, 90–92, where the following paragraph at the end of the entry is omitted:

"The aphorism of Bacon shd. never be forgotten, which is hardly truer in the corrupt govts. of the old world than in the corrupting govt. of the New, 'All greatness &c." (typescript *Journals*).]

TO RICHARD HENRY DANA, SR., CAMBRIDGE? MAY 13, 1826

[MS listed in American Art Association Anderson Galleries, May 17, 1934. I conjecture that this letter may have related to the school which Emerson kept in Cambridge this year and which was attended by Richard Henry Dana, Jr. (*cf.* a note on Oct. 23 and 24, 1826).]

TO MARY MOODY EMERSON, CAMBRIDGE, JUNE 15, 1826

[Apparently incomplete in *Journals,* II, 99–105.]

TO MARY MOODY EMERSON? CAMBRIDGE, JUNE 30, 1826

[Apparently incomplete in *Journals,* II, 105–110.]

TO MARY MOODY EMERSON, CAMBRIDGE, AUGUST 1, 1826 [8]

I Cambridge, 1 August, 1826.

My dear Aunt,

Neither my silence nor my volubility succeeds in extorting the old fashioned long letters I am writing after; I One who is equal to the production of the letter from Plato [9] & Charles's Lafayette

7. Hannah Haskins (later Parsons). For her dedication, "since her childhood," to the care of her aunt, see *Journals,* IX, 508; and *cf.* the letters of May 5 and June 1 (to William Emerson), 1863.

8. MS owned by RWEMA; ph. in CUL. Excerpts I, II, IV, and VI–VIII are in Cabot, I, 116–118; excerpts III and V are in *Journals,* II, 111 and 112, and parts of excerpts II, IV, and VI are printed *ibid.,* 111–113.

9. See Jan. 18, 1825. I have not found her letter to Charles Emerson about La Fayette.

letter shd. be kinder to the starving souls that besiege her than to put them off with such bald ridicule as " diffidence." IITis said the weaker party is ever the recommender of moderation, in like manner the poor in spirit will be strenuous to enforce the duty of imparting out of their affluence on their patrons. None feels his poverty so sordidly as he who contemplates prodigious expenses, and I am already turning my little pennyworths to account in the preparation of Sermons. In the fall, I propose to be *approbated,*[10] to have the privelege, tho' not at present the purpose, of preaching but at intervals. I do not now find in me any objections to this step. — Tis a queer life, and the only humour proper to it seems quiet astonishment. Others laugh, weep, sell, or proselyte. I admire. There are, I take it, in each man's history insignificant passages which he feels to be to him not insignificant; little coincidences in little things, which touch all the springs of wonder, and startle the sleeper conscience in the deepest cellII IIIof his repose; III IVthe Mind standing forth in alarm with all her faculties, suspicious of a Presence which it behoves her deeply to respect — touched not more with awe than with curiosity, if perhaps some secret revelation is not about to be vouchsafed or doubtful if some moral epoch is not just now fulfilled in its history, and the tocsin just now struck that severs & tolls out an irreparable Past. These are not the State Reasons by which we can enforce the burdensome doctrine of a Deity on the world, but make often, I apprehend, the body of evidence on which private conviction is built.IV VIn solitude & in silence, memory visits her inmost chambers to produce these treasured tokens of Connexion & immortality. Much of what is subtle & mysterious in our intervals of mentality is more flattering & more favoured than the ordinary acquisitions in the general progress of the soul, and — but what congratulation ought to be heard in the earth from theist & patriot, when God in these eminent instances of these our latter days departs from the ancient inviolable sternness of an unrespecting providence to harmonize the order of nature with the moral exigences of humanity. Arise from the dust, put on thy beautiful clothing oh thou that wast despised for depravity, for want, & for presumption! V VIHuman nature will go daft in our times like the Grecian father who embraced two Olympian Victors in one day.[11] Tomorrow Everett

10. According to the MS *Autobiography,* Emerson was approbated to preach by the Middlesex Association Oct. 10, 1826, and preached his first sermons five days later, at Waltham, for his half uncle Samuel Ripley.

11. Probably a reference to the story of Diagoras of Rhodes. *Cf.* Hans Licht, *Sexual Life in Ancient Greece,* London, 1932, p. 106. But Diagoras died as he greeted his victorious sons.

is to open his lips on this signal topic[VI] to give & to get immortality; [VII]and Webster the next [12] day.[VII] — I have received your letter of July 18 since I began this letter and had already written you a sheet which touched this sole Event but it disgusted me. As for your letter I rejoiced thro' the first page at this windfall of intellections but grew sour to be bereft by the dire *business* of half my prize. I am whole Cormorant. I mea[nt][13] above to put a contrast between private & p[ublic] coincidence in reference to Jeffe & Adams. — [VIII]In the wind of these great events I am to assume my office, the meek ambassador of the Highest. Can you not suggest the secret oracles which such a commission needs; the lofty truths that are keys & indexes to all other truth, and to all action on society? Can you not awaken a sympathetic activity in torpid faculties? Whatever heaven has given me or withheld, my feelings or the expression of them is very cold, my understanding & my tongue slow & unaffecting. It may be each excitement administered from within may impel a swifter circulation in the outer channels of manner & power. The letters I get from the Vale prove this purpose better than any other compositions,[14] so I beseech you to forgive the importunity of your nephew.

Waldo.[VIII]

To Edward Bliss Emerson, Cambridge? August 12, 1826

[Printed in *Journals,* II, 113–114, where it is apparently incomplete.]

To William Emerson, Cambridge, September 3, 1826 [15]

Cambridge Sept 3d 1826

Dear William

I have sent Balestier's letter (found on window seat) with Judge Parkers by mail enclosed to you. Whitney has bro't this

12. Edward Everett's eulogy on Adams and Jefferson at Charlestown and Webster's oration on the same theme in Faneuil Hall are reported in the *Christian Register* of Aug. 5, 1826. Emerson was present at Faneuil Hall (*Journals,* II, 113).

13. The " nt " of " meant " was carried away with the seal and now stands next to the opposite margin directly over the illegible part of the word " public " in the same sentence.

14. On the back of this letter Mary Moody Emerson wrote the characteristic note: " Flattery I love it." The Vale, more properly Elm Vale, was the farm on which she lived at Waterford, Me.

15. MS owned by Mr. Edward Waldo Forbes; ph. in CUL. The Judge was doubtless Isaac Parker, of the Supreme Judicial Court of Massachusetts. *The Boston Directory* for 1826 lists Hezekiah and Levi Whitney as truckmen and also gives Capt.

Certificate wh. I enclose for you to get your trunk by — He found no such Smith as you described & seemed very stupid. I hope the Certificate is not slow & late. Have you Aunt Mary's note wh. shd. be shown Mr T. H? She is in want of the money to send to Waterford and does not know if you made any application for it. Shall enquire duly at office for letters from you let them not fail.

Abundant love from all & from
Yr afft brother
Waldo.

To William Emerson, Cambridge, September 13, 1826 [16]

Cambridge Thursday Sept 13

Dear William,

The wagoner Whitney carried your goods to Capt. Nickerson of a N. Y. packet who was to sail on that following Wednesday (for want of finding Smith.) and I enclosed to you in a letter by mail containing also Balestier's & Judge Parkers letters, Nickersons certificate by presenting wh. you are entitled to your baggage.[17] I grieve at your griefs. I go to Boston today to look after Smith, Nickerson, and other pedlars concerned & to put this with Farleys Germ. Dict. in a way to you. Dr Bradford sd. t'other day that Wigglesworth wd settle here the old debt from Lit. Gaz. as the New work is not responsible for the old one's debts, and W. will call on me.[18] Charles got a first

---

John Smith, probably the same mentioned in the letters of Sept. 13 and Oct. 23 and 24, 1826. "T. H." was doubtless Emerson's uncle Thomas Haskins. William had gone to New York, apparently only a few days before, to begin his apprenticeship as a lawyer; and either that city or Staten Island was to be his home nearly all the remainder of his life. The letter of Sept. 13 is addressed to him in care of Stephen Griggs at 9 Front St., but street addresses on succeeding letters vary. William first appeared in the New York directory in 1827–1828, when his address was given as 60 Wall St. It is possible, I think, that the following advertisement, printed in *The New-York Evening Post,* Sept. 29 and later, 1826, was his:

"A GENTLEMAN (a graduate of a New England College) proposes to instruct a few young ladies or gentlemen in Latin, Greek, the Mathematicks, or Belles Lettres . . . References for character and abilities R. Sedgwick, Esq. and Geo. Sullivan Esq. . . ."

16. MS owned by Mr. Edward Waldo Forbes; ph. in CUL. Emerson's letter is followed by a brief note from his mother to William, written on the same sheet. The year 1826 is given in William's endorsement and is obviously correct.

17. *Cf.* Sept. 3, 1826. *The Boston Directory* for this year lists a Captain David Nickerson.

18. Apparently William Emerson had contributed to *The United States Literary*

prize [19] G. Ripley spoke as well as he ought. G. H. also.[20] Sampson Reed has published a pamphlet of 44 pp. on the Growth of ye Mind wh. I think one of the best books I ever saw.[21] We have a letter from Edward dated July 17, mentions Lagrange but the letter describing it [22] he says he wont send. Was parting next day via Waterloo Brussels Rotterdam for England. Had been to Versailles, but the Catacombs of Paris closed on strangers. God speed you beyond your best hopes —

Your affectionate brother

Waldo.

Gazette before it changed ownership and name about the time of the present letter. Possibly the "Letter from an American in Europe," addressed to "Dear W—," and headed "*Göttingen*" without date (IV, 290–293; for July, 1826) is William's. This seems very doubtful, but *cf.* Nov. 20, 1824. *The Boston Directory* for 1826 lists Edward Wigglesworth as an attorney; and this person, who had graduated from Harvard in 1822, a year after Emerson, may have acted for the magazine. According to *Coll. Mass. Hist. Soc.*, 3d series, IX, 79, Dr. Gamaliel Bradford was a contributor to the *Literary Gazette,* and so was perhaps well informed regarding the prospect of the payment of its debts. Later letters mention William's contributions to the press in New York.

19. *The Evening Gazette,* Boston, Sept. 2, 1826, which reports the commencement of Aug. 30 of that year, notes that Charles Chauncy Emerson, junior sophister, received one of the two first Boylston prizes in elocution, of $15 each, or a gold medal of that value.

20. Dr. John Pierce (*Proc. Mass. Hist. Soc.*, 2d series, V, 195) says that "The palm of the day was assigned to Ripley, English orator of the Masters, on 'The Claims of the Age on the Young Men of America.' He was 27 minutes long, but highly interesting." G. H. was probably George Foxcroft Haskins, whose name duly appears in the official *Order of Exercises.*

21. *Observations on the Growth of the Mind,* Boston, 1826, continued to impress Emerson for many years, and his acquaintance with its author led to an interest in Swedenborgian readings. He lost no time, it seems, in sending a copy to Mary Moody Emerson, who revealed in her letter of Sept. 25 (1826) that she found triteness, obscurity, and "swedenishness" in it, and thought its rare parts culled from Wordsworth, who was no Swedenborg. *The Boston Directory* for 1826 lists Sampson Reed & Adonis Howard as druggists, and Reed appeared in the directories for many years to come as in the same business, though with various partners. The Henry E. Huntington Library owns an order for drugs, written by Emerson and directed to Reed & Cutler, undated as to year but falling somewhere in the period 1846–1869, I believe, and probably before 1860.

In later years, but long before he drew the by no means wholly flattering portrait of Swedenborg that was finally placed in the gallery of *Representative Men,* Emerson discovered that Reed had become a slave to dogma. "I should like to get at S. R. very well," he wrote in an unpublished paragraph of his diary, "but entrenched as he is *in another man's mind,* it is not easy. You feel as if you conversed with a spy. . . . And you have not the satisfaction of a good deliverance yourself because of the malign influences of this immense arrogancy & subtle bigotry of his church." (Typescript *Journals,* June 22, 1838.)

22. An eighteen-page typed copy of Edward's letter dated Paris, July 14, contains the enthusiastic story of his visit to La Fayette at La Grange.

To Mary Moody Emerson, Cambridge, September 23, 1826 [23]

Cambridge, [I]Sept 23d 1826

My dear Aunt,[I]

I need small persuasion to send you pretty long letters [24] of which fact you have already had some sad experience. But I am so pleased to get rid of my mean cares a little & sculk into the lobbies that lead into the heaven of philosophy and listen when the door is open if perchance some fragment some word of power from the colloquy sublime may fall on mine ear – Such words purify poor humanity. They clear my perceptions for my duties.

[II]Is it not true that modern philosophy by a stout reaction has got to be very conversant with feelings? Bare reason, cold as cucumber, was all that was tolerated[II] in aforetime, [III]till men grew disgusted at the skeleton & have now given him in ward into the hands of his sister, blushing shining changing Sentiment.[III] And under this guardian of public opinion, it is respectfully submitted that public opinion will be apt to run to & fro, a little. [IV]Be that as it may, it is one of the *feelings* of modern philosophy, that it is wrong to regard ourselves so much in a *historical* light as we do, putting Time between God & us; [25] and that it were fitter to account every moment of the existence of the Universe as a new Creation, and *all* as a revelation proceeding each moment from the Divinity to the mind of the observer.[IV] If this position have a foundation as it would seem in genuine Sentiment, another remark of a parallel tendency may hold also. [V]It is certain that the moral world as it exists to the man within the breast is illustrated, interpreted, defined by the positive institutions that exist in the world; that in the aspect that is disclosed to a mind at this hour opening in these parts of the earth, Christianity appears the Priest, the expounder of God's moral law. It is plainly a fit representative of the Lawgiver. It speaks the voice God might speak. We ought not therefore to have this mighty regard to the long antiquity of its growth, and to the genuineness or fallacy of pretensions on which the dust of 16 or 18 centuries has gathered, but to consider its present condition as a thing entirely independent of the

23. MS owned by RWEMA; ph. in CUL. Excerpts I–V are in Cabot, I, 159–160.

24. In her letter of Sept. 11 she had alluded to a recent meeting with him at which their conversation was unsatisfactory and, concluding that they could really commune only with the pen, had asked for a long letter.

25. This is noteworthy as early evidence of Emerson's interest in an idea which was to come to full fruition in the Divinity School address a dozen years later.

ways & means whereby it came into that condition & neither seeing what it was nor hearing what it said to past generations, examine what it is & hear what saith to *us*.

This is probably the most plausible statement of the doctrine of relative and absolute truth. That it *is absolutely* true is perhaps capable of evidence. That it is relatively true is certain, and thus it may procure for us all the eternal good it ever pretended to offer[v] Such reasoning we know is admitted in law. The subject is never required to know whether the prince on the throne (de facto) is the prince of right (de jure) and cannot afterward be challenged for his allegiance at any time to a successful usurper.

There is a sort of truth in all this but it will never bear a statement. The understanding recoils as insulted from an attempt to disguise a sophistry and is less pliant in the lesson, than she is in the world. This is called sophistry. but it is precisely this reasoning which under one or another colour men use, when they unite Mysticism to the profession of Christianity. It has always the apology that we hold truth by a tenure so subtle that the most grave speculation carried many steps from our first principles, loses itself in irrecoverable cloud. ' Despise nothing was the old saw. and this ambiguous light in wh. we live is authority for the rule. To grow wise is to grow doubtful; and it ill becomes that man to pronounce an opinion absurd who feels in the consciousness of the changes his mind has already undergone, that before another sun the truth of that exploded dogma may be dearest to his mind. How does Aunt Sarah? Mother sends with mine her best love. And respects to Grandfather & to Mrs R. I depend on the letter for wh. I have waited by G. R.[26]

Yr affectionate nephew

Waldo.

To Mary Moody Emerson, Cambridge? September 28, 1826

[Partly printed in *Journals*, II, 121–123.]

26. Sarah Ripley, daughter of Dr. Ezra Ripley, died Nov. 2, 1826 (*The Ipswich Emersons*, p. 126) . Mrs. R. was no doubt Sarah Bradford Ripley. G. R. may have been George Ripley, who had attended the Ripley school at Waltham in 1819 (O. B. Frothingham, *George Ripley*, 1886, pp. 6–7) , and who is certainly the G. Ripley of the letter of Sept. 29.

To William Emerson, Cambridge, September 29, 1826 [27]

Cambridge Sept. 29 1826

My dear Brother,

What is the reason we hear nothing from you? I trust you are well. But we are all curious to hear the ups & downs that make the beginning of a young mans history who goes forth expressly to make his fortune. In all the approved fairy tales, if I remember right he meets many dragons many ferocious giants pretty soon after "Once there was"; and the sing-song groves & the palaces & the princesses dont come till some pages after. But the first part of the story is ever most romantic, & most instructive. So please send us a few sheets. Pray let us know if the letters & budgets have arrived for we have got but a single letter from you. Edward has written from London, Aug. 13, nothing particular excepting a little higher estimate of expense. Still hopes to be at home in October. G. Ripley has rec^d^ a call at Purchase St.[28] Mr Editor Carter [29] goes to Europe to prepare himself to teach a school for schoolmasters to be a sort of captain of the "soul of the soldiery." Folsom takes his place I believe. Sampson Reed has printed here & perhaps at N. York a noble pamphlet after my own heart called Observations on Growth of the Mind. in my poor judgment the best thing since Plato of Plato's kind, for novelty & wealth of truth. It ought to give him Frisbies chair.[30] Tis droll, but it was all writ in the shop.

Among my other scarecrows to fill the gaps of conversation, are my lung complaints. You must know in my vehement desire to preach I have recently taken into my bosom certain terrors not for my hip which does valiantly, nor for my eyes which deserve all commendation, but for my lungs without whose aid I cannot speak, and which scare me & thro me scare out poor mother's sympathies with strictures & jene-

27. MS owned by HCL; ph. in CUL. The lower half of the second leaf is missing; but probably there was no postscript, and only a part of the superscription has been torn away.

28. For his pastorate there, see *George Ripley*, pp. 36 ff.

29. *Cf.* Sept. 13, 1826, for William's interest in *The United States Literary Gazette*. According to MS notes on the copies of Vols. I and IV of this magazine owned by HCL, those volumes were edited by Theophilus Parsons and James Gordon Carter. F. L. Mott, *A History of American Magazines 1741–1850*, 1930, p. 331, names Carter as an editor only for 1824 and Parsons only for 1825–1826, but, on p. 333, gives Charles Folsom as the Boston editor after the magazine was merged with *The New-York Review, and Atheneum Magazine* in Oct., 1826.

30. Levi Frisbie's service as professor of natural religion, moral philosophy, and civil polity had ended four years earlier.

saisquosities. But we must not cry before we are hurt, and any sufferings of this sort are so few & small that tho' they may fill a paragraph of my letter such has got to be my desire to call out sympathy they may not give you or me any farther distress.

Mother is very desirous you shd send us your address. We have lost the card you left us and we know not where G. Ripley or other future travellers shall seek you. Mother also bids you beware of the noxious diseases of the season in a dirty city.

It is plain I took up my pen in wrong time from the texture of my narrative. But you must let a schoolmaster fresh from his cave of Trophonius [31] be garrulous and silly. He will be the better for it afterward.

Charles very well & sends love Heaven bless & keep & prosper you prays

Your most affectionate brother

R. Waldo E.

To William Emerson, Cambridge, October 23 and 24, 1826 [32]

Cambridge, Oct. 23. 1826

My dear William,

Will you please to eat some dinner tomorrow. Edward [33] has struck us all with sincere alarm by his account of your excessive abstemiousness. It cannot be prudent. It cannot be prudent. We look to you for the stock, whatever winds may wither or brush away the branches. You will please to conform your theories to the practice recommended by the average wisdom of all the Yankees. It cannot be doubted you & I and all shd. be in a very wretched plight, on the failure

31. The cave is commonly enough mentioned in classical literature and the effect of a visit to it is proverbial. Emerson, in the postscript to his lecture on Plato, credited that author with the "fable," but in doing so, apparently confused two very different caves.

32. MS owned by HCL; ph. in CUL. A brief note from Mary Moody Emerson follows this letter on the same sheet.

33. According to the MS *Autobiography,* Edward came home from Liverpool on Oct. 19, 1826. In an unpublished entry of a diary for 1841 (typescript *Journals*) Emerson wrote:

"I copy from a fragment of Edward's 'Certificate of Departure' from Liverpool these fugitive shadows —

"1826 Aug 31 Edward B Emerson native of Boston aged 21 years, height 5 feet, 10;. light hair, blue eyes, sharp nose; *from* London; Going *to* New York, in the ship Cincinnatus."

of an experiment; and your regimen is an experiment. Aunt Mary denounces it as unsafe & worse. Edward denounces it. Mother & Charles & I denounce it. So please, pray, do overcome the Stoic to be an Animal.

For me, I have resigned my understanding into the hands of my doctors Moody & Bliss. & Warren [34] I give up my school this week.[35] I journey next I know not where. I am not sick nor very well.

I did receive and tho't had acknowledged $15.00 by post. Did last night receive from Dr Bodé your letters. The trunk I enquired a week ago after, at John G Smith in vain. He sent me to India Wharf somewhere but in vain too. Please send the name of the packet in which it came. I sent to N. York by mail two weeks ago a letter to you from E. B. E. (at Liverpool) on which I had altered the direction from Camb. to N. Y. It shd. have told you that E. was bound to N. Y. & you shd. keep a lookout. We are rejoiced to see him. He expects a tutorship.

Oct. 24. He does not. He has sent to you a letter, covering a draft for 107 [36] dollars. yesterday. G. R. wont go south for he is to be ordained 2d week of November.[37] Your gazette [38] came but was a duplicate; for it had already come on the old rêgime,[39] now to be altered by my request. Give us any private opportunity and I will send Sampson Reed and anything else. Dont infer that my maladies have affected my brain from the shallowness & coarseness of these bed-quilts of letters that I write between school & dinner &c &c —

But believe me your afft brother
R Waldo E.

To Mary Moody Emerson, Cambridge? October, 1826

[Printed, apparently in incomplete form, in *Journals,* II, 124–125.]

34. That is, doubtless, Mary Moody Emerson, Edward Bliss Emerson, and Dr. John C. Warren of Boston. *Cf.* the letters of Oct. *c.* 23, 1816, and Mar. 7, 1817.

35. The Cambridge school here referred to was the last Emerson was to teach. Charles Francis Adams, *Richard Henry Dana,* 1890, I, 5, gives the year, incorrectly, as 1825. When *Two Years before the Mast* appeared, Emerson wrote of Dana, "He was my scholar once, but he never learned this of me: more's the pity" (letter of Oct. 19, 1840). Oliver Wendell Holmes, *The Works,* XI, 39, quotes his brother's recollection of this school, but is vague as to the date. *Cf.* also Cabot, I, 115–116. According to the MS *Autobiography,* the end came in October, but no day is mentioned.

36. Apparently the "7" is written over an "8" or possibly a "0."

37. See a note on Sept. 29, 1826.

38. Apparently a second copy of *The United States Literary Gazette* for Sept., 1826, had arrived instead of the October number of its successor, *The United States Review and Literary Gazette. Cf.* letters of Sept. 13 and 29, 1826.

39. For Emerson's French, *cf.* a note on *c.* 1824.

To Ruth Haskins Emerson, Charleston, South Carolina, December *c.* 7, 1826

[Ruth Haskins Emerson, Jan. 14 and 30, 1827, thanks Emerson for the early information his letter gave of his arrival in Charleston.]

To Edward Bliss Emerson, Charleston? South Carolina? December *c.* 10? 1826

[Described in Edward Bliss Emerson, Dec. 27, 1826, as a letter just received.]

To Samuel Ripley, Charleston, South Carolina, December? *c.* 10? 1826?

[Samuel Ripley, Feb. 14, 1827: " I am your debtor for two letters . . . Your first letter did not give us a very flattering idea of Charleston . . ." As Ripley advanced the money for the Southern trip, it is probable that Emerson wrote him soon after arriving at Charleston on Dec. 7.]

To William Emerson, Charleston, South Carolina, December 20, 1826 [40]

Charleston, S. C. Dec 20, 1826

Dear William

It is really the most extraordinary event I remember to have happened to me — the entire separation for good & evil which a few hundred miles of one & the same country have effected between us. If you were in the moon or in Symmzonia [41] there might be a reason But now it ' puzzles all analysis.' I am determined out of a spirit of ro-

40. MS owned by HCL; ph. in CUL. Excerpt I is in *Memoirs of Members of the Social Circle in Concord,* 3d series, 1907, p. 18. In the letter of Oct. 23 and 24 Emerson had written of his plan to travel " I know not where " in search of health. The " Clematis " " cleared " at Boston on Nov. 24 and arrived at Charleston on Dec. 7 (*Boston Daily Advertiser,* Nov. 25 and Dec. 19, 1826) . In the MS *Autobiography* the date of sailing is given as Nov. 25. According to the *Advertiser* for the 19th, the voyage took eleven days, but William Emerson, Dec. 23, 1826, mentioned the newspaper report of the arrival of the " Clematis " at Charleston and added that it must have been a twelve days' passage. Charles Emerson, Nov. 25–Dec. 2 (1826) , remarks that it is early for him to write, as it has been only a short time since he saw his brother sail away on a noble ship that brought all of Lord Byron to mind.

41. An allusion to the then famous geographical theories of Captain John Cleves Symmes and very probably to *Symzonia,* a humorous extravaganza by " Captain Adam Seaborn " (*cf.* R. L. Rusk, *The Literature of the Middle Western Frontier,* 1925, I, 258–260) . The Biblical " man does not live by bread alone," toward the end of this paragraph, seems to echo verbal peculiarities of both *Matthew,* 4:4, and the ultimate source in *Deuteronomy,* 8:3.

mantic adventure to attack this dragon uncertainty, & sally out to the post office forthwith. I am informed moreover that every week, once or twice, opportunities occur by ship between this place & New York, so that you can receive or send a letter anytime for a tonnage & poundage of 6 cents. These important preliminaries being settled – How do you do? & what? for man, I remember me, lives by bread; and your studies? for man does not live by bread alone. I am coming in May to see with my own eyes your manner of life & get you to go back like a good person to your own land; for " happy is he who hath never seen the smoke of the stranger's fire." Meantime I am desirous of having circumstantial & speedy accounts of these particulars.

[I]For me, Mr S. Ripley [42] lent me seventy dollars and supplied me with letters of credit for more & sent me to Charleston to get health & strength in its milder climate.[I] I came by sea in the good ship Clematis, Capt Low. I board in the family of Mrs Fisher East Bay St. at 6.00 pr week. I have been here a fortnight nearly and made some acquaintance with the city & citizens. The main purpose of my coming is not however fully answered. My chest is a prey to certain oppressions & pangs, chiefly by night, which are very tolerable in themselves, but not very agreeable in their auspices to such an alarmist as I. My friend Motte [43] is in the city; has lately become an Unitarian & resigned his parish; he has shewed me much kindness, & by introducing me to the C. Library Society has furnished me with occupation for my reading hours.

I propose as soon as the spring opens to set out for home, to spend some time in Alexandria and make the whole journey by land. If I am well enough as I trust in Heaven I shall be I shall probably have an opportunity to give you some sound doctrine from your Unitarian pulpit in passing. As soon as you have read this please to inquire for a packet sailing for Charleston. Vessels of some sort constantly sailing. – And put a letter on board to your most affectionate

brother

Waldo –

42. Samuel Ripley, of Waltham, a friendly figure in both earlier and later letters. When Emerson received in England the news of Ripley's death, he wrote of him to the widow (Dec. 26, 1847), " I may well say benefactor, for in will & in act he was both early & late one of mine, – & never otherwise."

43. Mellish Irving Motte, Emerson's classmate at Harvard. The Charleston Library Society informs me that a search for records of Emerson's admission and of his reading has proved fruitless.

To Charles Chauncy Emerson and Edward Bliss Emerson, Charleston, South Carolina, December 30, 1826 [44]

Dec 30, 1826.
Charleston, S. C.

Dear Charles

I am very glad to get a letter from you.[45] Its fault was that it came alone. It shd. have been 'e pluribus unum.' It comes however at a convenient time to get answered, and I am glad to have that work to do. It cannot be a new matter of speculation to you, — the effect of science on the bulk of mankind. That the effect of successful abstruse inquiries is minute &, for long periods, inappreciable is the burthen of many a sigh. But that in the event Jack & Gill are the better for the painful speculations of Leibnitz & Kant is equally undeniable. The search after truth is always by approximation. The wise man begins a train of tho't whose farthest results he does not live to see, nor perhaps do his children's children. We have an instinctive perception of the value of certain ideas, which are the seeds of great conclusions, which all our efforts often are unable to unfold. The clown sees these beginnings, these first gropings of the intellect after something which he does not see and which he is satisfied are very far removed from any vulgar interest & scoffs of course at "studies which end in new studies, & do not tend to lessen the price of bread." [46] Whenever a new truth results, it is readily made known to many more minds than were acquainted with the inquiry; for truth is attractive; and it enlightens many more subjects than the one in whose discussion it was ascertained; for all truth is correlated. Whatever therefore be the indifference with which the majority of men regard the ordinary *studies* of the philosopher, the moment he arrives at any signal discovery, the good contagion of truth is propagated from the higher circles of society to the lower and all men are in some manner affected by it. Conspicuously in our day has science become practical when the seas are navigated by Bowditch's book & by the Nautical Ephemeris annually issued by the philosophers of the

44. MS owned by RWEMA; ph. in CUL.

45. Charles Emerson, Nov. 25 and later (1826), is largely a philosophical discussion; and the present letter attempts to answer the skepticism expressed there regarding the value to mankind which philosophers attribute to truth. The last paragraph preceding the postscript criticizes Charles's style in the same letter. Leibnitz and Kant do not seem to appear in the *Journals* until many years later.

46. From the 118th number of *The Rambler*.

Royal Soc. at Greenwich,[47] and when the government of England, France, America takes lessons from the Political Economist. But tis shame to write so dully about what mt. be triumphantly represented with a little labour. Besides the subject has another face, to wit, That the distinctions of society were intended, and there is a fine saying of Voltaire's which is something like this, " le triomphe de la raison, c'est de bien vivre avec ceux qui n'en ont pas." [48] Amid all the distinctions, there is a wonderful equality, & however distinctly a man of genius, may perceive his advantage when he walks in a crowd, he can hardly encounter any one individual of the crowd in a casual conversation, without a disposition to doubt his own pretensions. As to what you say respecting universal genius I am not satisfied that your latest opinion was the truest. There have been unquestionably men whose genius was equally excellent in grand & minute performances. And Cato you know seemed born only for that one thing he was at any moment doing.[49] Nevertheless, it cannot be denied, there are trifles, & they are to be valued as trifles. But much I doubt if the blood & temperament you were born to will let you spurn names manners & compliments in your way to great distinctions which I know they will not deny.

This letter I see is open to great exceptions, but I shd. be ashamed to withhold it after having written so far, so let it lie as quietly on the shelf as may be. By the way, it is strange you shd. be so incorrect a writer, when so scholarly, — " landlegs " for sea legs — ' day of a port ' for *in*, &c. besides unfinished sentences. It raised the gall of Holofernes [50] in me tho' I cd. almost cry for joy at the letter. Tell them all I love them & am a little better. As to Aunt Marys advice, & your question, I add my solemn Yea.

Y. a. brother Waldo

Edward Edward why dont you write.[51] Why one wd. think I was in the same country with you & not as I am beyond the farthest islands moun-

47. Nathaniel Bowditch was author of *The New American Practical Navigator*, Newburyport, 1802. *The Nautical Almanac and Astronomical Ephemeris* was already appearing annually in London, published by order of the Commissioners of Longitude.

48. Also in *Journals*, II, 125; the source is Voltaire's *Socrate*, I, vii.

49. Livy, XXXIX, 40, on the elder M. Porcius Cato.

50. Though the name was the common one for the pompous schoolmaster, Emerson probably had in mind Shakespeare's use of it in *Love's Labour's Lost*.

51. Edward's letter of Dec. 27, 1826, was probably already on its way.

tains swamps in these offscourings of the world. I think of going to the W. Indies, for greater heat. If I do, I shall first write to Waltham.[52]

52. That is, to Samuel Ripley, who would have to advance funds for the voyage. Emerson did not go, but the letters of a few years later contain many references to the residence of both Edward and Charles in the West Indies.

1827

To William Emerson, Charleston, South Carolina, January 6 and 9, 1827 [1]

[I]Charleston S. C. 6 Jan. 1827.

Dear William,[I]

I received with great joy a letter from you [2] a few days since & suppose that before this time you have received mine, written a fortnight ago [3] & sent by I know not what ship. I believe I recounted in that letter the plagues which had fallen upon me & which appear to have excited your kind curiosity. [II]The cold has been so considerable here as to prevent me[II] from deriving [III]any signal benefit from the change of climate. Indeed I am scared out & tis more than probable that I shall take passage for St. Augustine,[III] where I am promised the most balmy air in the world, [IV]in the sloop William next Tuesday or Wednesday.[IV] I beseech you however not to be in any particular alarm on my account. [V]I am not sick;[V] I am not well; [VI]but luke-sick[VI] — and as in my other complaints, so in this, have no symptom that any physician extant can recognize or understand. I have my maladies all to myself. [VII]I have but a single complaint, — a certain stricture on the right side of the chest, which always makes itself felt when the air is cold or damp, & the attempt to preach or the like exertion of the lungs is followed by an aching. The worst part of it is the deferring of hopes — & who can help being heart sick? Moreover it makes me dependant inasmuch as my excellent friend in Waltham undertakes to supply me with funds without appointing the pay day.[VII] I have books & pens enough here to keep me from being desperately homesick [VIII]but have not succeeded in overcoming certain physical & metaphysical difficulties sufficiently to accomplish any thing in the way of grave composition, as I

1. MS owned by HCL; ph. in CUL. Excerpts I–VIII are in Cabot, I, 120.
2. Dated Dec. 23, 1826.
3. Dec. 20, 1826.

had hoped.[VIII] There are here scarce any materials for "Letters from S. Carolina," if I were ambitious.

But I wish you the happiest of years and do rejoice you have got something to eat,[4] & do particularly hope & pray that you eat it. We are not cameleons we are not anchorets but being born to the roast beef of New England must eat it or smart for it. You say nothing of *law*. What is your expectation with regard to the term of study prescribed to you? Have you any definite prospects of any kind which I do not know? Do you really mean to abide by the City of N. Y. As to what you say about 2d Unit. Ch. I am very glad. Shd. be glad if H. Ware wd go. they can better spare him in Boston than there. For myself, I had rather be a doorkeeper at home than bishop to aliens.[5] tho' I confess it mends the matter that there is such a huge fraction of Yankee blood.

I have always intended to return by land & if possible to preach for Furness in Phil.[6] & to you in N. Y. but do not expect to get out till April. I want to make a visit at Alexandria.[7] Your room is better than your company O January February & March! Am sincerely obliged for your good will in the money matter but shall be your debtor fast enough, if my ails last. I scribble on in my bluebooks & remind Edward that Müller left his MSS. to public auction [8] to pay his debts.

Tuesday 9 Jan. I have been compelled to leave my letter till this time unfinished, & have now to say that I have engaged my passage to St Augustine, for very cold, & shall sa[il][9] probably tomorrow in the sloop William.[10] There I intend to pass 7 or 8 weeks on air & oranges said to be all that the city affords except fish. Any vessel bound thither from

4. In his letter of Dec. 23, William wrote that he was released from all fear of immediate starvation, as he now had an income as "private instructor to a family of 'She's' as you call them," in addition to his three dollars a week for his services in the law office of Ketchum & Fessenden.

5. On Dec. 23 William wrote that he had wanted his brother to preach, on his return northward, at the Second Unitarian Church in New York and offer himself as a candidate, but that Henry Ware had now been invited, though his decision was doubtful. John Ware, *Memoir of the Life of Henry Ware, Jr.*, 1854, I, 218–224, shows that Ware never gave the invitation much consideration. The Biblical allusion (*Psalms*, 84:10) is characteristic of the letters of this period.

6. William Henry Furness, Unitarian minister in Philadelphia, was Emerson's friend from boyhood; many later letters were written to him.

7. That is, to the Haskins family there. *Cf.* the letters of May 3 and 15, 1827.

8. *Cf.* Bernhard Seuffert, *Maler Müller*, Berlin, 1877, pp. 56–57.

9. Apparently torn away with the seal.

10. *The Charleston Courier* of Jan. 10, 1827, announced that the sloop "William," with Swasey as master, had cleared for St. Augustine (transcript of the newspaper report supplied by Professor Alfred J. Hanna).

N. York must bring me letters. Otherwise send by water to Charleston to the Care of S. Davenport & Co [11] & they will send them by water to me, as I have requested. I am pretty well, tho not as you see particularly brilliant. Yr affectionate brother

Waldo —

I saw Wm Geo Reed the other day who was first scholar in class before mine, & who is recently become a flaming Roman Catholic. He is a lawyer settled in Baltimore, & did once run away with the daughter of a wealthy Mr Howard of that city.[12]

To Samuel Ripley, Charleston, South Carolina, January? *c.* 6? 1827

[Described in Samuel Ripley, Feb. 14, 1827, as "Your last letter, which I received ten days since" and apparently written about the time Emerson decided to leave Charleston for St. Augustine. *Cf.* also the note on Dec.? *c.* 10? 1826? Probably there were letters to Ripley from St. Augustine also which are now lost.]

To Ruth Haskins Emerson, Charleston, South Carolina, January 9, 1827

[Ruth Haskins Emerson, Jan. 14 and 30, 1827, sends her thanks (under date of Jan. 30) for "your welcome letter of the 9th inst" and mentions her disappointment because the traveler has not found a warmer climate.]

To S. Davenport, St. Augustine, January 17, 1827

[S. Davenport, Charleston, S. C., Jan. 31, 1827: "Your esteemed letter of 17 came to hand 27th inst. I am truly glad you find St Augustine pleasant and trust your visit there will prove beneficial."]

11. The *Directory . . . of the City of Charleston* for 1829 lists Davenport & Co., merchants. S. Davenport, Charleston, Jan. 31, 1827, forwards mail to St. Augustine. A letter to Emerson from Davenport dated Feb. 16 of the same year is also extant. Samuel Ripley wrote from Waltham, Feb. 14, that he would at once repay the sum advanced by Davenport and that Emerson should continue to draw, as he found it necessary, on the same agent.

12. There is a notice of Read's marriage to the daughter of John Eager Howard, former governor of Maryland, in J. D. Warfield, *The Founders of Anne Arundel and Howard Counties, Maryland,* 1905, pp. 240–243. Read was in the class above Emerson in college and was from Charleston.

To Charles Chauncy Emerson, St. Augustine, January 27, 1827[13]

St Augustine, E. Florida —
[I]27 Jan. 1827.

Dear Charles,

In these remote outskirts of civilization the idea of home grows vivid, & grave men like me are sometimes pestered with a curiosity, very unbecoming doubtless, & very keen, to know what is done & said by certain beardless aspirants who are giving their days to philosophy & virtue. Whosoever is in St Augustine resembles what may be also seen in St A. the barnacles on a ledge of rocks which the tide has deserted; move they cannot; very uncomfortable they surely are, — but they can hear from afar the roaring of the waters & imagine the joy of the barnacles that are bathed thereby. The entertainments of the place are two, — billiards & the sea beach; but those whose cloth abhors the billiards — why, theirs is the sea beach. Here therefore day by day do I parade, and think of my brother barnacles at a distance[I] as aforesaid. I place before my eye a youth well born & well bred moving in colleges with the assured step of one at home in learned societies, commencing a pure noviciate not to vain superstitions, or transitory sciences but to Truth, serene, immutable, divine Truth. I see him conscious of the dignity of the vows that are on him, measuring with impatient eye the sin & ignorance of the world and hailing the tokens that glimmer in the horizon, of a better era to come. I behold him with industry, with vigils, & with prayers, arming himself in the cause of humanity reconciling a lowly mind with the high ambition to be fellow worker with God in the regeneration of man. May good angels accomplish him in his preparation, & send him out conquering & to conquer.[14] Let him disdain the fading echoes of vulgar renown whilst he remembers that praise is the reflection of virtue. Let him blush to rest satisfied with partial attainments, adjusting a petty balance of venial faults with compensating merits but hew out to himself a great & perfect character which the world present & to come may behold & take pleasure in — the spectacle. —

[II]Thus you see the poorest of us hath his ideal; a small greycoated gnat is wagoner to the Queen of Fairies,[15] and we who walk on the

13. MS owned by RWEMA; ph. in CUL. Excerpts I–II are in Cabot, I, 122–123.
14. *The Revelation,* 6:2.
15. *Romeo and Juliet,* I, iv.

beach are seers of prodigious events & prophets of noble natures. Let us make the ordinary claims of our class — [16] 'It is not us, it is not us; we are but pipes on which *another finger* plays what stop it pleases.' [II]

It is not to be denied that the agency of an individual may be immense. The nature of man or the face of society is wonderfully plastic, and tho' it be conceded that it requires certain rare combinations of events to create the greatness of Washington, yet every hour that passes may contribute to open the genius of Milton, of Newton, of Rousseau, engines of forces that can never be computed for the production of good & of evil. I do not therefore, exaggerate, I use no unauthorised language when I figure to myself the youthful glory of such an one whose vein of genius leads him to literature and whose taste has received its bias from Everlasting beauty. You will pardon therefore the preceding page & not imagine that your exhorting brothers use you as the whetstone on which to sharpen their wits, but believe me to be in very truth your fond & loving brother

Waldo

If the vessel stays another day, I shall write to Waltham.

To William Emerson, St. Augustine, January 29 and 31, 1827 [17]

[I]St Augustine, E. Florida
29 Jan. 1827.

Dear William,[I]

I learn that a little sloop in our little harbour is bound for New York and am determined it shall not go thither without some token to you. I wrote to you twice from Charleston & received from you one letter. Others I doubt not are on their way home, in that city. [II]In about a week the sloop William will arrive here which is to us what the Spanish galleon is to Manilla[II] or what, if I better remembered my 'Cummings,' [18] many more vessels doubtless are to many more places. In short it is our all. [III]It brings at every trip to St Augustine inhabitants, victuals, newspapers, & letters. It is one of two sloops which make all the *shipping* of this port, & its regular arrival & departure are the only events that agitate our provincial circles.[III] Of course over our antiquated newsprints we are looking grave at events that were long

16. This bears some resemblance to two passages in *Hamlet,* III, ii, of which Emerson may have had a vague memory.

17. MS in HCL; ph. in CUL. Excerpts I–IX are in Cabot, I, 121–122. In the margin of the superscription is written a laundry list, apparently in Emerson's hand.

18. *Cf.* the letter of Jan. 13 and 15, 1816.

since discussed & forgotten in your vulgar thoroughfares of Washington & N. York; and [IV]if a cross wind detain Capt. Swasey [19] not only our news gets old but our barrel of meal gets empty, & the lean kine begin to cast most significant glances on the fat.[IV] But what I meant to say when the merits of my city of refuge forced out of me this honest eulogy was that I expect in said sloop letters from you in return for mine, neither of which you had received when you wrote before. [V]I beleive myself to be a great deal better than I was when I came. The air & sky of this ancient fortified dilapidated sandbank of a town are really delicious. I am therefore very decidedly relieved from my stricture which seemed to hold its tenure from Boreas[V] — and this makes me uncertain whether if Boreas were come again, his tenant would not be fully reinstated. Nevertheless I flatter myself that I gain ground daily, through God's blessing. For many days back our thermometer has ranged between 65 & 75° night & day.

[VI]It is a queer place,[VI] this City of St Augustine. [VII]There are eleven or twelve hundred people & these are invalids, public officers and Spaniards or rather Minorcans. What is done here? nothing. It was reported one morning that a man was at work in the public square & all our family turned out to see him. What is grown here? Oranges — on which no cultivation seems to be bestowed beyond the sluggish attentions of one or two negroes to each grove of 5 or 6 hundred trees. The Americans live on their offices. The Spaniards keep billiard tables, or, if not, they send their negroes to the mud to bring oysters, or to the shore to bring fish, & the rest of the time fiddle, masque, & dance. The Catholic clergyman lately represented at a masquerade the character of a drunken sailor with[VII] the most laudable fidelity.

Here then in Turkey I enact turkey too. [VIII]I stroll on the sea beach, & drive a green orange over the sand with a stick. Sometimes I sail in a boat, sometimes I sit in a chair. I read & write a little, moulding sermons[VIII] & sentences [IX]for an hour which may never arrive. For tho' there may be much preaching in the world to come yet as it will hardly be after the written fashion of this pragmatic world, if I go to the grave without finding vent for my gift, the universe I fear will afford it no scope beside.[IX] So pray for the perfect health of your loving brother

Waldo —

I ought to have said that St A. produces 1200,000 oranges per ann.

19. The superscriptions of Davenport's letters to Emerson, already cited, show that Swasey was captain of the "William." The Biblical allusions which follow are to *I Kings*, 17:12–16, and *Genesis*, 41:20.

Jan 31

I live very comfortably & shall stay here perhaps till the middle of March. Mr Davenport in Charleston receives & forwards my letters from home at least that is the theory but not a solitary line have I yet seen. It is more than two months since I left home & I have rec[d] but one letter — from Charles. But the sloop is coming that shall make amends. If you write home, tell them I am better for they have not heard from me lately, but do not say more; for I sometimes distrust the improvement.

To S. Davenport, St. Augustine, February 9, 1827

[S. Davenport, Charleston, S. C., Feb. 16, 1827, acknowledged " yours of 9th inst.," which stated " that your health is improved and that you find the climate of St Augustine beneficial & pleasant," and added: " The letter for M[r] E B Emerson I sent by mail, as no vessel was immediately to sail for Boston, and the one enclosed in your former letter not having been forwarded for want of opportunity . . . it is now on board the Brig William enclosed with the other you sent, and she will probably sail tomorrow."]

To Edward Bliss Emerson, St. Augustine, February *c.* 9, 1827

[See the note on Feb. 9, 1827; and *cf.* note on Feb.? *c.* 9? 1827.]

To Ezra Ripley, St. Augustine, February? *c.* 9? 1827

[Mentioned, with " another to Edward," in the first part of Ruth Haskins Emerson, Mar. 2, 11, and 12, 1827; acknowledged in Ezra Ripley, Mar. 24 and 25, 1827, which apologizes " for my neglect to answer sooner your entertaining & respectful letter. . . . I am highly gratified by your account of St. Augustine & the fortress." *Cf.* the note on Feb. 9, 1827.]

To Charles Chauncy Emerson, St. Augustine, February 23, 1827 [20]

St Augustine, E. F. [I]23 Feb. 1827.[I]

Dear Charles,

[II]How is it with the ambitious youth? he of the sometime melancholy temperament, he that was called the ardent, eloquent, irresistible scholar, he who loved[II] great men [III]& defied fair women, he who adored virtue on a great scale, but was squeamish at viewing it on a small one, he who had enthusiasm from nature, but it was almost all

20. MS owned by RWEMA; ph. in CUL. Excerpts I–VI are in *Journals*, II, 170–172, where a few slight changes of individual words occur and where there are a few additional words.

evaporated in the kneading, he whose taste would be correct were it more manly, & whose form would be good, if it were more stout — thyself. I am prone to mercy[III] or I [IV]would draw your character to the life, so that your own eye shd acknowledge the fidelity of the portraiture. The memory is sharp when home is distant and the dim congregation which my fancy nightly & daily visits, always appear in costume, — each in his virtues & vices.[IV] So beware, & bid Edward beware of provoking me or I will use my vantage ground to set him down in black & white putting him in sore peril if he remember the story of Archilochus.[21]

I have not yet recd your letters of which I heard in Edw.'s letter Write half a dozen. The world is before you for topics & when sense is not to be had, nonsense is a thousandfold better than nothing. [V]You are in the heyday of youth when time is marked not by numbering days but by the intervals of mentality the flux & reflux of the soul. One day has a solemn complexion the next is cheerful, the south wind makes a third poetic, and another is ' sicklied oer with a pale cast of thought,' [22] but all are redolent of knowledge & joy. The river of life with you is yet in its mountain sources bounding & shouting on its way & has not settled down into the monotony of the deep & silent stream. Vouchsafe then to give to your poor[V] patriarchal exhorting [VI]brother some of these sweet waters. Write. write. I have heard men say (heaven help their poor wits,) they had rather have ten words viva voce from a man than volumes of letters for getting at his opinion. — I had rather converse with them by the interpreter. Politeness ruins conversation. You get nothing but the scum & surface of opinions when men are afraid of being unintelligible in their metaphysical distinctions, or that the subtlety & gravity of what they want to say will draw too largely on the extemporaneous attention of their company. Men's spoken notions are thus nothing but outlines & generally uninviting outlines of a subject, & so general, as to have no traits appropriate & peculiar to the individual. But when a man writes, he divests himself of his manners & all physical imperfections & it is the pure intellect that speaks. There can be no deception here. You get the measure of his soul. Instead of the old verse, " Speak that I may know thee," [23] I write ' Speak, that I may suspect thee; write, that I may *know* thee.' Brandish your pen therefore, & give me the secret history of that sanctuary you call *yourself;* what new lights illuminate, what fragrant affections perfume it; what litanies are sung,

21. For Emerson's own version of this story, see below, VI, 335.

22. *Hamlet,* III, i.

23. Possibly Emerson vaguely remembered *Exodus,* 33:11–13.

what work is daily done in its mysterious recesse[s][24] and to what god it is consecrated. A[nd] if you have any inclination to re[tort] & play the La Bruyere on me, I defy you. It will give me extreme pleasure to see you miss your mark, & more if y[ou] hit it.[VI] Any thing sent as late as 1st April I suppose will reach me in Charleston; Afterward tis doubtful. I am going to write to Alexandria to advertise them of my purpose of spending a few weeks there if no objection exist — & expect to get home about Election. They say here I am fatter than when I came, I know not. I weigh 141½ pounds. Possibly Edward may remember what I weighed in Cambridge. I forget. My love & honour to Mother & she is welcome to see all my letters when she comes to town, but it is scarce worth while to send much trash so far. And love to all from your affectionate brother Waldo.

I have just recd a letter from Edward without date out of some diplomacy I suppose & one from Aunt Mary both which were abundantly grateful. Say to E. that I know nothing about Barrow or Dante.[25] Edward speaks of your oration at Hasty pudding.[26] Take in time a just resolution Be proud & honest, & let it be *original* to the word & to the letter.

To Edward Bliss Emerson, St. Augustine, February? *c.* 23? 1827

[Partly printed, under date of Feb., 1827, in *Journals,* II, 170; probably one of the " two excellent letters recd this week " acknowledged in Edward Emerson, Mar. 28, 1827, and perhaps sent inclosed in the letter of Feb. 26 as far as Charleston. Edward wonders that Emerson talks of school-keeping again, doubting whether that occupation would be better for his brother's health than preaching.]

To Mary Moody Emerson, St. Augustine, February *c.* 23? 1827

[Partly printed under date of Feb., 1827, in *Journals,* II, 173–175. Possibly the letter to Mary Moody Emerson admired in Edward Emerson, Mar. 22, 1827.]

24. This and the three pairs of brackets which follow inclose portions of words that must have been torn away with the seal.

25. Edward, undated (Jan.? 1827?), asks whether Emerson took " Dante & Barrow." Numerous Barrows produced more numerous books, but it seems probable that the reference here is to the famous Dr. Isaac Barrow some of whose sentences Emerson had tried to improve in *Journals,* I, 24–25.

26. The *Records of the Hasty Pudding Club,* VIII, 63 (MS in HCL), mentions the " eloquent and animated oration " pronounced by " Br. Emerson " at the meeting of Feb. 22, 1827. *The Thirteenth Catalogue & a History of the Hasty Pudding Club,* 1907, pp. 64–68, shows that Charles was the only undergraduate named Emerson who belonged to the Club at this time.

To S. Davenport, St. Augustine, February 26, 1827

[Acknowledged in S. Davenport, Mar. 7, 1827.]

To William Emerson, St. Augustine, March 15, and Charleston, South Carolina, April 7, 1827 [27]

St Augustine, E.F. 15 March, 1827

My dear brother,

Have you lost your eyes or hand or cunning that one who was so exemplary a correspondent shd. become utterly dumb? I wrote two letters in swift succession to N. Y.[28] between which came one from you & in one of mine bid you if you tho't of costs to find any one of the packets that every week sail for Charleston & put on board some intelligence of your health hopes pursuits thots – and ever since have been waiting to hear. Indeed I put a third letter by a sloop which sailed to N. Y. from this place. Meantime I have recd a letter from Mother who charges me if I write to Wm to ask " why he does not let her hear from him, if he remembers where she lives – that it is 6 months since she had a letter from him " and adds " It will take much longer time to wean me from my children than it will take probably to wean them from me." What is the reason you are so naughty? press of business? or have the letters miscarried?

I am just getting ready to leave this place by water for Charleston – much better I think than when I came, but, as I think because the weather is much better, & if it were colder again I shd. be worse, so pray for south winds.

[I]Charleston Apr. 7. I arrived here yesterday after a direful passage of 9 days from Augustine; – the ordinary one is one or two days. We were becalmed tempest tossed and at last well nigh starved.[I] The barrel of meal & the cruse of oil [29] were nearly exhausted in a calm; but ' Caesarem vehis ' [30] thot we, the wind blew, & we put into St Mary's for supplies All this did vex the vulgar mind, for we had five & twenty passengers on board [II]but your beloved brother bore it not only with equanimity but pleasure for my kind genius had sent for my shipmate,

27. MS owned by HCL; ph. in CUL. Excerpts I–VII are in Cabot, I, 126–127; I–III reappear in *Journals,* II, 182, where the date is wrongly given as Apr. 23.

28. Probably the letters of Dec. 20, 1826, and Jan. 6 and 9, 1827. The third letter, mentioned below, was probably that of Jan. 29 and 31, 1827.

29. *I Kings,* 17:14.

30. The story is in Plutarch's life of Caesar.

Achilles Murat,[31] the eldest son of the old king Joachim, who is now a planter at Tallahassee and is at this time on his way to visit his uncle at Bordentown.[II] We boarded together in St Augustine but I did not become much acquainted with him till we went to sea.[32] [III]He is a philosopher, a scholar, a man of the world very sceptical but very candid & an ardent lover of truth. I blessed my stars for my fine companion & we talked incessantly. Much more of him when I shall see you.[III] In Charleston, I have found 5 letters, one from yourself which I was very glad to see. I rejoice in the triumphs of truth. I am glad when God touches with fire such minds as Channing I feel the swift contagion that issues from such as he & stimulates the young to purposes of great & awful effort. &c.

I am going to stay here not long; perhaps a fortnight. I design as I told you to go to Alexandria & perhaps preach in Baltimore. [IV]As to health, I gain courage.[IV] I feel well today. [V]I feel that my success depends upon it, mine more than many others' and am therefore[V] naturally very [VI]sensitive on the subject. I weigh 152 lb. To increase the weight I study very little; or as Wamba [33] might say I study very much to increase my weight by studying very little. And journeying with this intent I have not written a sermon since I left home.[VI] Wo is me, the way to make a little wit go a great way is to travel with it, as Wamba might also say, but in my intention it means I am getting as much celebrity in the Union as I may with only two sermons in the world. Tell it not in Gath! for I am coming to Gath to preach them.

I have " sixty six " things to tell you and am feeding the fires of affection with the hope of seeing you shortly & hope the world has ceased to go hard with you. I hope " the world *is* your friend, & the world's *law*." [34] I have seen a woman who has seen Edward & says he is much

31. I am indebted to Professor Alfred J. Hanna for an excerpt from *The Charleston Courier,* Apr. 7, 1827, reporting the arrival of the sloop " William," 9 days from St. Augustine, with Emerson and Murat and his wife among the passengers. The MS *Autobiography* gives Mar. 28 as the day of sailing " with Murat " and notes that the boat put into St. Mary's, Ga., on the way. Later letters, including that dated Apr. 10, 1827, contain some references to the remarkable young Frenchman, a nephew of Napoleon and son of Marshal Murat, his colorful cavalry leader. See also, especially, *Journals,* II, 185–191, and Régis Michaud, " A French Friend and Inspirer of Emerson," *University of California Chronicle,* Apr., 1921.

32. This makes it seem very improbable that Emerson visited Murat at Tallahassee, as some have believed.

33. The jester in Scott's *Ivanhoe.* Gath, at the end of this paragraph, is from *II Samuel,* 1:20.

34. Slightly altered from *Romeo and Juliet,* V, i.

courted. I wish he cd. come honestly by some money for I am afraid he will get sick in the pursuit. Charles wrote me once confidently of his prospects of success, but since, with qualification. An unlucky bird has made T. W. Haskins call his boy after me — " Me, me, in me convertite telum." [35] [VII]As to your wishes for my settlement, Avaunt New York! I am a bigo*t*ed Yankee (one t or two?) and your affectionate brother, Waldo Emerson [VII] —

To Mary Moody Emerson, St. Augustine, March *c.* 25? 1827

[Partly printed in *Journals,* II, 179–181, where it follows an entry dated Mar. 25. It could not have been written more than a few days later than the 25th, as Emerson says in the letter of Mar. 15 and Apr. 7, 1827, that he arrived at Charleston on Apr. 6 " after a direful passage of 9 days from Augustine."

The two passages omitted on p. 181 of the printed version are these: " It is certainly very easy to conceive of cases wh require more than the exaltation of the martyr's virtue who triumphs at the stake. I mean . . . and who nourishes in silence far from fame the secret virtue the gift of which was accompanied with a consciousness of its worth — than it is for such a youth meekly to surrender his hopes in the outset of his career to forego all these fairy visions & say with uncompromising self devotion Thy will be done. Many a man has died with firmness who yet had never broke his spirit or rather sublimed his spirit to such resignation. Resolution was on his face but regret sat on his heart. Yet we can conceive of one so united to God in his affections that he surveys from the vantage ground of his own virtues the two worlds with equal eye & knowing the true value of the love & praise of men challenges rather the suffrages of immortal souls. And what we can conceive of virtue, it may be we can exhibit." (Typescript *Journals.*) The words from the " Lord's Prayer " are as given in both *Matthew,* 6:10, and *Luke,* 11:2.]

To Mary Moody Emerson, Charleston, South Carolina, April 10, 1827

[Partly printed in Cabot, I, 127–128, and, at greater length but not completely, in *Journals,* II, 183–185. The passage omitted on p. 184 is as follows: " It is the peculiar excellence of our condition that however the account of happiness may stand the account of knowledge is always improving; every event fortunate or unfortunate contributes to the wealth of my intellect; that is to say, every moment makes me a more powerful being." Following the paragraph ending on p. 185 this has been omitted without any indication of omission:

" I write little; one cannot live much in two ways, & nowadays I utter my soul in talk This must account for the meagreness of my letter."

Both the passages I quote are from the typescript *Journals.*]

35. Not quite exactly quoted from the *Aeneid,* IX, 427.

To Samuel Gilman, Charleston, South Carolina, April 14, 1827

[On Apr. 14, 1827, Samuel Gilman wrote Emerson two letters: the first was a request that he preach on the following day; the second was an acknowledgment of his compliance, with a suggestion that he preach in the morning instead of in the afternoon, as at first arranged. Probably Emerson wrote a second note in reply, of which, however, there is no further evidence.]

To Samuel Ripley, Alexandria, District of Columbia, May 3, 1827 [36]

Alexandria May 3d 1827

My dear Sir,

I received before I left St Augustine your very welcome letter [37] & but for my journeyings in the meantime it had been answered before. I think I had scolded in an earlier letter [38] to you about the wretched aspect of Charleston I liked the town no better at our second interview. But I began to doubt whether I was not deceived by the juvenile error of thinking all that was unaccustomed to be precisely in that degree *wrong;* & I so bigoted a Yankee as not to be honest to the beauty of Southern municipal architecture. But when I got to Baltimore,[39] my judgment sat firm in his seat again, for I found fine houses streets churches abounding in a place where I am yet more a stranger than in Charleston. It is a fine city & in general & in particular looks like Boston. The interior of the Unitarian Church is noble.

I found in Baltimore Rev Mr Barrett of Boston who had preached four out of six·Sundays of his engagement, & Mr Greenwood [40] is to succeed him for six more. Of course I shall not preach in the city; the dii majores are sufficient to their work. I arrived here last Sat. night and have been housed most of the time since, to keep out of harm's way, for it is here as every where else, where your illstarred servant has gone this winter, colder than was ever known since the Deluge, I be-

36. MS owned by HCL; ph. in CUL. Only half the original sheet remains; but, though the letter as here printed is unsigned, it may well be all that was written, as it does not fill the second page. The remaining space there contains the endorsement "Waldo to Mr Ripley May 3/27" and the name "George Washington" or "Washington" repeated a number of times, in what seems to be the same hand.

37. Of Feb. 14, 1827.

38. Probably the letter of Dec.? *c.* 10? 1826?

39. In the MS *Autobiography* Emerson notes simply that he sailed for Baltimore in Apr., 1827 — from Charleston, no doubt.

40. *The Boston Directory,* 1827, lists both Samuel Barrett and F. W. P. Greenwood.

lieve; and I expect at every turn to be taken up & burnt alive as the genius of Winter travelling in disguise; for as soon as I come, so do the snow storms. You had better advise the farmers of Middlesex of these " signs that mark me extraordinary " as Glendower says [41] as it may be worth their while to make up a purse to keep me at a safe distance from their cornfields. –

But when the South wind shall blow, I shall present in Washington two or three letters which I have, & if I get rid of a cold, may preach for Mr Little.[42] I have also procured a letter to Mr Sparks who is keeping or rather ransacking house at Mt Vernon in the absence of Judge Washington at Philadelphia.[43]

To Edward Bliss Emerson, Alexandria? District of Columbia, May 8, 1827

[Partly printed in *Journals,* II, 202.]

To Mary Moody Emerson, Alexandria, District of Columbia, May 15, 1827 [44]

[I]Alexandria, D. C. 15 May – 1827

My dear Aunt,[I]

It is harder to get words from you than from those weird women who say " now my weary lips I close, leave me leave me to repose." [45] Wont you please to break silence. Wont you abandon your favourite game of Father Mum to those in whom it is most becoming. [II]I am waiting here in pleasant durance until the sun will let me go home. For I am too delicate a body to brave the north & east winds with

41. From *I Henry IV,* III, i; as usual, the quotation is slightly altered.

42. The *Washington Directory,* 1822, lists Robert Little, pastor of the Unitarian church.

43. Herbert B. Adams, *The Life and Writings of Jared Sparks,* 1893, II, 11–13, tells the story of Sparks's exploration, during Bushrod Washington's absence, of the remarkably rich collection of manuscripts then at Mount Vernon.

44. MS owned by RWEMA; ph. in CUL. Excerpts I–IV and VII–VIII are in Cabot, I, 128–130; V–VI are in *Journals,* II, 204–205, and parts of what Cabot prints are also given *ibid.,* pp. 203–204. The *Journals* draft shows a number of slight differences from the MS and contains a few additional words.

45. Thomas Gray, " The Descent of Odin." Mary Moody Emerson was a correspondent of very uncertain temper. Sometimes she demanded more letters than her nephews could write; at other times she refused to answer them. Charles Emerson wrote to William on Feb. 24, 1828 (MS owned by Dr. Haven Emerson), " Aunt Mary is in Andover Me. & wrote to me the other day what she ordered me to receive as a long farewell letter, because she hates to write & will not write any more."

impunity. If I told you that I had got well I believe I deceived you & myself. For I am not sure that I am a jot better or worse than when I left home in November. Only in this, that I preached Sunday morning in Washington without any pain or inconvenience. I am still saddled with the villain stricture & perhaps he will ride me to death.[II]

Enough & more than enough of this. [III]I have not lost my courage nor the possession of my tho'ts. It occurs to me lately that we have a great many capacities which we lack time & occasion to improve. If I read the Bride of Lammermoor a thousand imperfect suggestions arise in my mind to which if I cd. give heed, I shd. be a novelist. When I chance to light upon a verse[III] or two [IV]of genuine poetry, it may be in a corner of a newspaper, a forcible sympathy awakens a legion of little goblins in the recesses of the soul and if I had leisure to attend to the fine tiny rabble I should straightway be a poet. In my day-dreams I do often hunger & thirst to be a painter. beside all the spasmodic attachments I indulge to each of the Sciences & each province of letters. They all in turn play the coquette with my imagination & it may be I shall die at the last a forlorn bachelor jilted of them all.

But all which makes these reveries noticeable is the indirect testimony they seem to bear to the most desireable attributes of human nature. If it has so many *conatus*[46] (seekings after) as the philosophic term is, they are not in vain but point to a duration ample enough for the entire satisfaction of them all.[IV] [V]They suggest a just idea of the world to come which has always been made repulsive to men's eyes from the inadequate representations of systems of religion which looked at it only in one aspect, and that, (I am forced to use a word in a limited sense it ought not to bear) a *religious* one. But regarding the future world not so much as the place of final moral reward but as the *after state* of man [& probably a moment of that infinity holds no more relation of reward to the past than doth a moment of the present life for every moment of this life involves a relation of reward][47] it is assuredly more consistent with our most elevated & therefore truest notions of God that the education of man should there be carried on by furnishing space & excitement to the development of every faculty that can add accomplishment to the noble being. And though our poor tools of art the colours, the pallet, the chisel, rhyme, & the pipes & strings of sound must yield to

46. Perhaps remembered from Paley's *Natural Theology,* a book which Emerson recommended to his cousin in the letter of *c.* 1824.

47. In a number of other letters Emerson makes similar use of square brackets.

finer & more efficient means, yet it would be[V] unjust to the exhibitions [VI]of intended intellectual progress disclosed in our nature to doubt that scope wd. be afforded to the compassing of the great ideal results, of wh. these tools are now the poor inadequate instruments[VI] But the muse is not now propitious. I grieve to find myself clouding a gleam of truth with heaps of words.

Have you read Mrs Hemans' poetry? There are some fine verses about the Lost Pleiad.[48] — You know we can't count but six of the Seven Stars. Mr Norton wrote a fine article in the Chr. Examiner in review of Mrs H. But it is idle to theorize respecting poetry. I suppose all inquirers must at last acquiesce in the opinion that its charm is inscrutable, & whatever circumstances may heighten the effect there is in all souls an original affinity to the elements of that complex creation. The Theist the Christian can not speak of it but with reverence for it links itself to whatever is brightest & most permanent in his nature. Whatever associations lose their freshness, to this there is an immortal health, an unabated glory. [VII]On a sick bed, the name of Shakspeare will induce a feeling of vigour, and I may say, of longevity, which is all independent of the decay of the body.[VII] Far be it from me however to defy the speculator [VIII]I know there are some intelligences that see far into the structure of these our mortal entertainments and hazard shrewd guesses at the principle of the arts, of manners, — and can shew the cause why now the barm works, & why now no Spirit broods upon the face of the darkling waters.[49] — Will you not please to disclose some of these lights to your poor blinded but very affectionate nephew

Waldo —

I have been staying some time in the very hospitable house of Mr Ladd [50] & design to set out this week for Philadelphia & after some delay there & at New York [51] for home. William has been delivering some lectures on Germ. literature [52] with honour to himself at N. Y.[VIII] Edward

48. Emerson probably read the poem in *The League of the Alps . . . and Other Poems,* of which there was a Boston edition in 1826. The review mentioned is in *The Christian Examiner,* Sept. and Oct., 1826.

49. *Cf. Genesis,* 1:2, and *Paradise Lost,* VII, 233 ff.

50. See the letter of May 24, 1827.

51. For Philadelphia, *cf.* May 24 following. The MS *Autobiography* dates the New York visit simply June 1, 1827.

52. I have not found the account which, according to Edward Emerson, Apr. 5, 1827, appeared in a New York paper. This notice, says the letter, praised the lectures as happily illustrating the importance of the study of German.

Edward Emerson, Apr. 9, 1827, says that on the 8th he heard Dr. Channing preach to a crowd as great as Everett or Webster ever drew.

hath a spark of grace for he writes me with enthusiasm almost about sundry sermons of Dr Channing. I shd. be glad you cd. see Charles's correspondence such queer letters for a youth of such sense & spirit no lack of tho't or choice of language and yet mighty *simple,* and he so much a dandy in his ways! If this morning shall get rid of his clouds I visit Mt.Vernon – 9 miles off, so good bye. R. W. E.

Please to write to me at Cambridge

To Charles Chauncy Emerson, Alexandria? District of Columbia? May 19? 1827 [53]

Give yourself to study with boundless ambition. despising as much as you please the primary & vulgar landmarks of success in the consciousness y[t] you aim to raise your rank not among your compeers alone but in that great scale of moral beings which embraces the invisible & the visible. There is one drop in the number of its drops wh makes the ocean greater than any sea. & by every discovery of a thot or a relation wh. your diligence accumulates perchance you overtop another & another individual in those enormous congregations of aspirants which in the body & out of the body environ you.

To John Haskins Ladd, Philadelphia, May 24, 1827 [54]

Philadelphia, 24 May, 1827.

My dear Sir,

I am here at the appointed time without having recieved any interruption from the importunate civilities you apprehended and having found my friend Mr Furness in the city & glad of such aid as I can offer, I design waiting till Tuesday morning when I hope to see yourself & wife. My journeyings have been very easy & pleasant altho I was disappointed here as every where in finding it colder than I desire. You see winter is chained to my chariot wheels &c &c. – My friend waits & therefore I must close my note with love & duty to yourself & family. I

53. MS, owned by RWEMA, part of Emerson's diaries. This is an incomplete copy or draft, which I print from the typescript *Journals.* It is undated but follows immediately an entry dated Alexandria, May 19, 1827. The next date following is May 21. The heading, "To C C E," shows that Charles is the person addressed.

54. MS owned by Dr. James I. Wyer; ph. in CUL. The superscription is to John H. Ladd, of Alexandria, D. C., the cousin mentioned in Jan. 31, 1820. For William Henry Furness, see the letter of Jan. 6 and 9, 1827.

shall meet you at the Steamboat, or U. S. Hotel — Your obliged & affectionate

R Waldo Emerson.

To William Emerson, Boston, June 24, 1827 [55]

[I]Boston, 24 June, 1827.[I]

Dear William

With shame & confusion of face I take this opportunity, &c. How dost, dumb man? [II]I am all clay, no iron. Meditate now & then total abdication of the profession on the score of ill health. It is now the ev^{g} of the Second Sunday y^{t} I have officiated all day at Chauncy Place.[56] Told them this day I wont preach next Sunday — on that acc^{t} Very sorry — for how to get my bread? Shall I commence author? of prose or of verse. Alack of both the unwilling muse! Yet am I no whit the worse in appearance I believe than when in N. Y. but the lungs in their spiteful lobes sing Sexton & Sorrow whenever I only ask them to shout a sermon for me.[II] I have spent all the time since my return, Sabbaths excepted, at Concord. where is your mother who is well & your Grandfather the old man who is yet alive he is well.[57] Edward B is not so stout as once but insists most petulantly y^{t} he is, to all who will believe & some more. Charles is swimming on his easy tides. Seems to be the pink of the fair state, chums next year with Winthrop [58] — a fact that has always been told me with significant looks as if I ought to be thunderstruck with the Communication. I have read his Oration [59] which is bursting into birth. a rainbow rhapsody with perhaps a scruple or two more of sense than belongs to that profound department of literature the College Orat. Edward is magnanimously slow & indifferent in his work. Not yet begun. Designs to accept an offer of Websters to

55. MS owned by HCL; ph. in CUL. Excerpts I–III are in Cabot, I, 131–132.

56. Edward Emerson, Apr. 27, 1827, stated that Frothingham (the pastor of the First Church, in Chauncy Place) was in Paris when last heard from and that a Cambridge candidate was supplying the pulpit. On May 7 following, Edward wrote that a letter had come from the First Church, asking that Emerson make no engagement on his return home before conferring with the officials there, who would be glad to have his services for a while. This was the church of which Emerson's father had been pastor, and Frothingham was an old friend of the family.

57. *Cf. Genesis,* 43:27–28.

58. This agrees with the information given in R. C. Winthrop, Jr., *A Memoir of Robert C. Winthrop,* Boston, 1897, p. 6.

59. In the letter of Aug. 16, 1827, Emerson dictates his comments on the delivery of this oration.

attend him to Washington in November & instruct his children. But Charles is a pleasing stripling, & locuplete of friends.

I am writing alone in G. B. Emerson's parlor. I spend the night here. He has a little daughter 4 days old. He left your Lectures [60] with Barkeeper & promised to write to him & to you. Whether he has so done I will inquire when he returns from a call. [III]I have taken a room in Divinity Hall & perhaps shall live there a little.[III] I call my address — Cambridge — & now I have run out, — having nothing more to tell & being afflicted with a wonderful cavity in my contemplations. I remember however that Mother insists that the expense of your ingress into the fatherland cannot be an obstacle to the shrewd calculator who recollects that his living here the while will not cost him a groat & will save him a guinea pr week. Think of that Master Brook What d'ye say to that Zerah Colburn.[61] No more talk of Newton Hook or Archimedes in the teeth of these our logarithms. Webster was tremendously sick off Pt. Judith in our steam boat passage, & almost no one else of the men folks. He spouted like a whale & roared like a leviathan yea outroared the steam engine & vomited as he wd. address the House. Poor Bulkeley has been rambling 14 days but is housed again & quite well. In a town in N. Hampshire he carried about a paper proposing to teach a singing school & succeeded in getting 15 or 16 subscribers, ere the wise men of Gotham found him out. T'was at Mt. Vernon. I have promulgated as I might your legal connexions & good men seem to take it as a thing of course that you [62]

To Mary Moody Emerson, Concord? June, 1827

[Partly printed in Cabot, I, 130, and more fully, but apparently incompletely, in *Journals,* II, 210–212.]

To Achille Murat, Boston? July? *c.* 28? 1827

[Murat, Point Breeze, N. J., Sept. 3, 1827 (addressed to Boston): "I have received nearly one month ago, your very polite letter . . ." In all probability Emerson wrote a second letter soon after receiving this reply, but I have no further evidence. Prince Charles Murat has searched the Murat papers for letters from Emerson, but in vain.]

60. *Cf.* May 15, 1827.

61. Probably Master Brook is the great spender of money in *The Merry Wives of Windsor,* II, ii. Zerah Colburn was celebrated in Emerson's boyhood as a youthful arithmetical prodigy. "Hook" is doubtless Robert Hooke, the seventeenth-century philosopher and mathematician.

62. The second half of the sheet is wanting.

To Ezra Stiles Gannett, Concord? July 29, 1827 [63]

Sunday Evg 29 July

Dear Sir,

I received last evening the note containing the vote of the Association, & have to express my obligations to the society for the kindness manifested in the appointment. But I believe I better consult my health by remaining in the country, & preaching only half days in Boston. I shall not therefore accept the appointment. I designed to have called upon you tomorrow, not knowing of your absence & promise myself that pleasure the next time I am in town.

With great regard Your friend & servt
R. Waldo Emerson.

To Mary Moody Emerson, Concord? August? *c.* 10? 1827

[Described in the second part of Mary Moody Emerson, July 23 and Aug. 15 (1827), as " the last meagre letter," which calls " for answers."]

To William Emerson, Concord, August 16, 1827 [64]

Concord August 16.

My dear brother:

Waldo 'stretched at his length the lubber fiend ' [65] is waiting the moment of inspiration to dictate a beginning worthy of this epistle the joint heir of our meagre stock of wit. " I hope you are sitting pleasantly at the feet of Gamaliel. I hope that Gamaliel, singular or plural, has more sense than to hide you in an Attic. Lex de

63. MS owned by the American Unitarian Association; ph. in CUL. On July 25, 1827, Emerson was appointed to serve for three months as a missionary in western Massachusetts, under the direction of the Franklin Association, at an expense not exceeding $10 a week; on Aug. 9 following, a letter from him (presumably the present letter) was read in which he declined the appointment; and on Sept. 10 of the same year his departure for Northampton, to supply the place of Hall while the latter should be absent on a missionary tour, was reported by the secretary (MS *Records of the Executive Committee,* owned by the American Unitarian Association). *Cf.* Aug. 31, 1827, and letters of the two months following.

64. MS owned by Dr. Haven Emerson; ph. in CUL. Emerson wrote only the last two paragraphs, but he dictated some of the passages that are in Charles's hand. Charles describes the letter, with partial accuracy, as " the joint heir of our meagre stock of wit "; and the contributions of the two authors, though distinguishable, must not be separated.

65. Considerably changed from Milton's line, *Paradise Lost,* I, 209.

altissimis minime curat.[66] Edward proves with the utmost vehemence, Waldo vehementer contradicente, how fast William will rake together the coin of his country, by the coming harvest of his practice — It will be all Thanksgiving day with you." So far so well — he pauses for a new tide to repair the exhaustion occasioned by such an outpouring of &c. &c. Hark! he speaks once more — " I speak, Waldo I attended the Exhibition [67] & in deference to the hand that writes, I shall thus describe the performance. It was not the indignant Demosthenes thundering to the Greeks; It was not Tully bending in elegant persuasion to every listening Roman; It was a sculptured form (elegant leg) in classic costume, from whose lips the muses poured their inspiration, (the very hand blushes scarlet) the form itself passive to the influence. It was Memnon's marble harp renowned of old by fabled Nilus (what a smile as we college boys say) uttering its beautiful strains to move all but the utterer. The nations counted it a triumph, the Romans a defeat. (Waldo disclaims the above maimed conclusion to his eloquent critique; maimed under the hands of his bungling scribe.) The listening crowd admired the song of the minstrel,[68] but the soul of Pindar sunk within him, that the dream of his earlier days (Pindar that's I) was not fulfilled." The oracle has ceased — Apollo has given out — partly from want of breath, & partly perhaps chiefly from want of matter. Quite a flight our Longinus hath flown in his audacious criticism on Homer. He is growling out his indignation, at my sad marring of his sweet English by certain vile parentheses, which he hears of but sees not, & which I assure you are inserted merely to afford some break, some relief in the midst of his ' brilliant conflagration. Hark! again — " Waldo says he will not be abused for dozing out his remarks, lolling on the sofa (tis in fact a poor rag calico couch) because you are to remember the saying of (nobody knows less who, than he) upon the dreams of Homer. ει ονειροι εισι εισιν ονειροι διοσ." [69] Well here I am once more on my own bottom floundering in the very centre of the sea, my high-blown brother

66. Probably Emerson intended a humorous adaptation of the legal saw " De minimis non curat lex " to fit better the beginner at the law lodged in his garret. Gamaliel is from *The Acts,* 22:3.

67. The official *University in Cambridge. Order of Performances for Exhibition, Monday, July 16, 1827* announces " An Oration in English. ' The Value of Letters,' " by Charles Emerson.

68. Adapted from Dryden, " Alexander's Feast," l. 34.

69. *Cf. Iliad,* I, 62–63. There was, perhaps, no more definite source. Here I am indebted to Professor Clinton W. Keyes, who has more than once reinforced my little Latin and much less Greek.

having broke under me. I must sink or swim, for there's no land in sight quite yet. President Kirkland you know is just at present on Debateable land — Hymen & Death are fighting for his body, Hope & Fear contending in his soul. Miss Cabot & a brace of sharp Paralytics have seized on him at one & the same hour.[70] But it is wrong to speak jestingly of so serious a misfortune to him & to the community. Were it anybody else, it would remind one of the marriage of Uncle & Aunt Wait, after both were bedridden.[71] Mother tells me to cross out the above, although she laughs, because tis naughty; & in respect to her opinion & my own I beg you to consider it as annulled.[72] Edward is slaying himself with the exertions made in the condensation of his copious pages.[73] He has written a great deal of great stuff, but he worries himself vainly in reducing it to form. He will be up to the high water mark. Poor Sturgis' fate [74] you have heard & lamented. His loss is irreparable to his friends, his class, & perchance to his country. An eulogy will probably be delivered next term by Storrow his rival & friend.

I hope sir you dont find the sentences lag & halt by the way, now that I am bereft of the aid of that ' Roman Hand.' I am exceeding anxious that you should not perceive any lamentable falling off; so to't again. Whenever you have a moment to spare from the quillets of the law, to the advices of friendship or the topics of literary discussion, you will please to enlighten with your discourses the camera obscura of my confused understanding. Confused with the irreconcileabilia of the moral world. I am, & shall be I hope a great many years, of the sect of Seekers. And all that I see, & all that my brothers & friends see for me, is a help in my inquiries. So pray keep a sharp look out for things new & old that shall swell the little inventory of my knowledge; you command a broader prospect from your loophole in the citadel, than the scholar in the tufted seclusion of his Academy. — Mother beseeches you, William, not to catch a fever while you catch at clients & coppers — she is sorry not to have you here at commencement, & she makes my letter

70. See the letters of Aug. 17 and 22 and Aug. 31, 1827.

71. Emerson's grandaunt Ruth Emerson was about sixty when she married her second husband, Samuel Waite (*cf.* George Tolman, pp. 3 and 5).

72. The whole passage about Kirkland and the Waites is accordingly crossed out, but very ineffectively, so that it is emphasized rather than deleted.

73. For an account of Edward's oration at the commencement this year, see Aug. 31, 1827.

74. William Watson Sturgis, a young Harvard student, was accidentally injured on a packet boat and died on Aug. 2 (*Boston Patriot,* Aug. 8, 1827). Charles Storer Storrow belonged to the same class.

the channel of a large stream of love. Tis a terrible cold rainy day & the chill of the atmosphere creeps over my thoughts. You must therefore be content with a shorter letter & the assurance of my being

Your ever affectionate brother

Charles.

P. S.

Miss Buckminster's marriage to Mr Lee [75] you may not have heard of – they were married by the Prest. a week or two since. The Praeses was very happy & fluent in his exhortation to the couple & Mr Webster there present observed that 'if you were to put a corn-cob in the president's mouth, eloquence would stream from it.'

I cant think of decorating this ragged scrap letter & so am to write maudlin on the edges. I have to give you the information that I am whortleberrying in Concord and am stouter in health than when I wrote a letter to you some weeks back. I have continued to preach at Chauncey [76] Place one half of every Sabbath since that time Mr Frothingham is daily expected. On his return I have the phantoms of two strings to my bow. Auspicious babes be born!

Edward is the uncomfortable victim of a splendid ambition To read DeVere [77] or to see him, how crooked & uneasy, were enough to cure a dozen poor aspirants. I wish the inspection of my brother Williams study might not also serve to the intelligent as a medicine for vaulting political ambition which Heaven condemned your poor brother Waldo to want all his life.

To Mary Moody Emerson, Concord, August 17 and 22, 1827 [78]

[I]Concord, 17 August. 1827 –

My dear Aunt,

I sent Hume's Essays to Boston to go by Robert [79] but they were neglected & not sent. I can lend them for 3 months from the

75. The marriage of Thomas Lee and Eliza Buckminster by President Kirkland is reported in the *Christian Register* of Aug. 4, 1827.

76. Emerson uses both the standard forms of this name at different times.

77. *Cf.* Feb. 1, 1832, where Emerson recommends this anonymous novel by Robert Plumer Ward as reading for a young lady. In 1827 it was a new book. In the third edition, also published in 1827, I, iii, the author remarks that " the following work treats much of independence of mind, and of the effects which ambition produces upon the heart and character of man . . ."

78. MS owned by RWEMA; ph. in CUL. Excerpts I–IV are in Cabot, I, 132–134.

79. Possibly Robert Foxcroft. *Cf.* Oct. 8 and 10, 1827.

time you get them, & will send them when an opportunity occurs. Baillie's plays not easily procured. What do you want them for? Only as I do in my slovenly way of thinking? for a kind of better word hunting that a phrase which catches the eye may be tortured in the mind till it chances to suggest a new thought or an old one with a new face. I cannot, be sure, bring you down to my level without great ignorance & discourtesy. but I wondered what you want Miss B. for. The instructer in a school is pleased to see the children play tricks with figures on a slate & is glad if they are learning arithmetic by puzzles & in sport; & our Governor consents that the apparent object of our intellectual existence on earth the learning of Language should be accomplished by calculation or by fancy. Anyhow, there is a person of very insignificant pretensions assuredly, but who believes he has sometimes owed the best of his poor tho'ts to this unhonourable expedient of bringing verses & phrases to the rack. The profit is much as the hangman's who doing his office skilfully, sometimes stands legatee to the very respectable sufferer. I would not trouble you with what I know you consider degrading particulars, but that they may go farther than more showy facts to teach what stuff we are made of.[I] I begun a letter which yet lies by me on subjects more to the tune of your taste but I am played on by another finger[80] & cannot finish that letter till the hour comes. [II]I preach half of every Sunday. When I attended church on the other half of a Sunday & the image in the pulpit was all of clay & not of tuneable metal I said to myself, that if men would avoid that general language & general manner in which they strive to hide all that is peculiar and would say only what was uppermost in their own minds after their own individual manner, every man would be interesting. Every man is a new creation; can do something best; has some intellectual modes & forms or a character the general result of all, such as no other agent in the universe has; if he would exhibit that it must needs be engaging must be a curious study to every inquisitive mind. But whatever properties a man of narrowed intellect feels to be peculiar, he studiously hides; he is ashamed or afraid of himself; and all his communications to men are unskilful plagiarisms from the common stock of tho't & knowledge & he is, of course, flat & tiresome.[II] We shall become wiser with age, that is, with ages.[81]

80. *Cf.* Jan. 27, 1827. The unfinished letter mentioned here may have been rewritten under a later date; but I cannot identify it, and probably it has vanished completely.

81. The preceding passage suggests slightly the essay "Self-reliance."

All your letters are valuable to me; those most so I think which you esteem the least. I grow more avaricious of this kind of property like other misers with age, and like expecting heirs would be glad to put my fingers into the chest of "old almanacks"[82] before they are a legacy.

22 Aug. I have received your letters and very glad of them the commentary upon my letter of 'love of life'[83] is the greatest gift. I confess it sounds like divine philosophy only I believe it is one degree too refined. If any sentiment is universal tis that which holds on to this existence And Burke said "Never was there a discord between genuine sentiment & sound philosophy."[84] I know very well the 'poetic letter' if it means the one that speaks of days when "the sun takes no note of earth no shadow on dial &c & wish it were longer. but it does not exhaust the perhaps inexhaustible question. & it may be I shall ask it again & again. III To *ask* questions, is what this life is for, – to answer them the next. & those intermediate people who, like my correspondent, seem to partake of both. My eyes are not so strong as to let me be learned. I am curious to know what the Scriptures do in very deed say about that exalted person who died on Calvary, but I do think it at this distance of time & in the confusion of langu[ages][85] to be a work of weighing of phrases & hunting in dictiona[ries.] A portion of truth bright & sublime lives in every moment to every min[d.] It is enough for safety tho' not for education: III I see this to be at variance with what you intimate about the immortality at risk of a fallen world. A mole's eye can discern when the beam is of pure light & when it is of coloured. As to the other position about the constant progress of a mind in knowledge I see it with the force of intuition. The meanest degraded thing that grows old under the human shape has a respectable experience (tho' he is in that wretched estate to put his knowledge to no use) he is without doubt a more formidable worm than he was ye[ars][86] before, is more sly, more competent to the care of his

I take a wretched case to show the truth reaches b

82. That is, Mary Moody Emerson's diaries.

83. Possibly the letter of May 15, 1827, or one now lost.

84. *The Works of the Right Honourable Edmund Burke,* Boston, 1826, IV, 431, slightly altered.

85. The parts of words bracketed in this sentence and the following were presumably torn away with the seal.

86. The lower corner of the second leaf has been cut or torn away, so that several sentences here and at the end of the letter are left incomplete.

Burke said there is no knowledge that is not valu[able][87] President K. has had a bad paralytic shock which griev[es] community & the more because not one candidate has been named at all qualified to fill his place. Until the unruly populace have kicked Everett in his turn, or until Mr Adams shall have retreated from civil broils, it is pity for the country that the Prest shd vacate the academic chair — I have burned one of yours in obedience to your instructions & because I like to have requests of that kind observed, & when I have good eyes to write off the papers may return them as you say but you had better unsay it. You will not need them. I will send back the letter of mine

I dont know that you will find this letter to be anyway dis[tin-g]uished for flatness. I hope you will. Some glorious weather we [have] had. How do men's seasons of thinking answer to the divisions us. One day is a ballad, another day is an epic, with many to high or soft recollections — a third is dull commentary st. & so we weave our patchwork & the sceptics say [that the g]ods sit in the clouds & mock us. Truth says, I distinguish.

IV Yours affectionately Waldo IV —

To William Emerson, Cambridge, August 31, 1827 [88]

I Aug 31. 1827.
Cambridge. I

Dear William,

The channels of intercourse are obstructed a little but I have heard by casual travellers of your health, & I hope the announcement of an article in the Am. Qu. Rev on Germ. literature [89] means yours. — I heard Charles's oration & day before yesterday, Edward's.[90] Of the first, I gave you, thro another hand, some account.[91] Of the last, voici. The matter was excellent & illuminated all along with fine & in one passage sublime ornaments of the imagination. It was

87. *The Works,* Boston, 1826, I, 459.

88. MS owned by HCL; ph. in CUL. Excerpts I–VI are in Cabot, I, 134.

89. *Cf.* Oct. 31, 1827.

90. At the Harvard commencement of Aug. 29, 1827. The *Boston Daily Advertiser* for that date announces Edward's subject as "The Importance of Efforts and Institutions for the Diffusion of Knowledge." Dr. John Pierce commented: "The English oration for the Masters, by Emerson, was a fine specimen of composition and elocution, at the uncommon length of 36 minutes. . . . it was received with a good degree of *éclat*" (*Proc. Mass. Hist. Soc.,* 2d series, V, 196).

91. See Aug. 16, 1827.

spoken in a manly graceful significant manner & with a fine voice. But it was spoken with so much deliberation, that in my poor tho't, very much of the effect was lost. I anticipated a flaming excitement in mine & in the popular mind, and if the oration which occupied 30 minutes had been delivered in 15, I think it would have answered this purpose. As it was, people were pleased & called it the finest of orations &c &c — no lack of praise — but I meant they should be electrified. *and too* much astounded to be complimentary. [II]I am going to preach at Northampton,[II] in the service of the Unitarian Assoc., [III]for Mr Hall, a few weeks,[III] whilst he goes into the adjoining towns to missionize [IV]His church is a small one, & I shall be able to preach all day I suppose without inconvenience.[IV] Afterward I am at liberty to do the same for Mr Willard of Deerfield & send him on the same errand.[92] But that shall be as health & circumstances may be. Meantime be pleased to rejoice, that I have in my trunk eleven entire sermons all which I have preached at First Ch. Mr Frothingham has come home in excellent health & spirits & would not exchange his recollections of the Capitoline hill for any possessions. The President's illness cast a sadness over Commencement day, & every body is sincerely sorry for him. & the more because it is tho't the chair which he will probably resign, will not be easily worthily filled. Yet Mr Eben. Francis told Furness a few days ago, that he had not any doubt that if Everett were elected he would accept the place. And Mr F. is one of the corporation in virtue of being treasurer, & no gossip. Mr Walker did decently but disappointed any one that expected much, at Φ. B. K. Dr Bradford delivered a poem [93] abounding in jokes good & evil. Greenwood was elected into the Society, & Charles Sprague black balled. The new class that has entered contains about 70, which has much refreshed the courage of the friends of the college. And the President is to be married on Sunday night.[94] And now I have finished the gossip floating in Cambridge that may interest you. I have no news of home Mother returned to Concord, Wednesday evg. Charles begins now his term. Edw. continues with Webster. George Ripley was married a week since, & Stetson of Medford the same day.

92. See letters of Oct. 7–31, 1827, for Emerson's preaching at Northampton, Deerfield, etc.; and *cf.* the note on July 29 of this year.

93. The *Christian Register,* Sept. 1, 1827, tells of the Phi Beta Kappa poem by Dr. Gamaliel Bradford and of the oration by James Walker.

94. President Kirkland was married, on Sept. 2, to Miss Elizabeth Cabot (*Boston Daily Advertiser,* Sept. 5, 1827). The *Christian Register,* Aug. 25, 1827, reports the marriages of Ripley and Caleb Stetson, both on Aug. 22.

Prithee, dear William send me some topics for sermons or if it please you better the whole model 'wrought to the nail.' For much of my time is lost in choosing a subject & much more in wishing to write. Everett in his early discourses used great plainness & simplicity. I have by me seven of them in MSS. [V]I aspire always to the production of present effect thinking that if I succeed in that, I succeed wholly. For a strong present effect is a permanent impression.[V] Perhaps sooner than I wish I may come & repeat my sermons to you in N. Y. My health has mended with the weather, heat being my best medicine. [VI]I am not so well but that the cold may make another Southern winter expedient.[VI] I hope not. What of Scott's Napoleon? [95] A real Gazetteer in appearance. I have not read it. But I like Everett's America [96] very well, & eagerly expect the Quarterly Review & am your

Affectionate brother Waldo

I preach in Northampton the 2d Sunday in Sept. & shall stay 4 weeks I believe.

You will say to Edward if you say anything that you have heard from Waldo of his success for, I have heard today that "it was the perfection of speaking" & he looks sad under the suspicion that it was not. I send you with the Orders a ridiculous jeu d'esprit that was stuck up one morning about College. A previous one had promised the tragedy of Job. Job — Mr Noyes [97] — &c

I shall try send this by my friend Rev Mr Motte who is to preach in N. Y. & afterwards in Washington.

To Charles Chauncy Emerson, Greenfield, Massachusetts, September? 30? 1827

[Charles Emerson, Oct. 20 (1827), says he has begun two or three letters since he received Emerson's favor of Greenfield. The letters of Oct. 7 and 9, 1827, seem to show that Emerson preached at Greenfield on Sept. 16 and 30.]

To Mary Moody Emerson, Northampton? Massachusetts, October? *c.* 3? 1827

[Described in the letter of Oct. 8 and 10, 1827, as "a character of you" sent to "your Aunt Mary . . . last week."]

95. The American edition of *The Life of Napoleon* was published in Philadelphia on Aug. 18 (*Commercial Advertiser,* New York, Aug. 18 and 21, 1827).

96. The *Boston Daily Advertiser,* Apr. 17, 1827, announced that *America* had just been published. Alexander Everett was the author.

97. George Rapall Noyes, Harvard tutor, gained some fame by his revised version of *Job.*

To Ezra Ripley, Deerfield, Massachusetts, October 7, 1827 [98]

Deerfield 7 Oct. 1827

My dear Sir,

I have led such a roving life since I left your hospitable roof, that it has not always been easy for me to write when I have been disposed, or I should sooner have consulted my inclination as well as my duty in sending you some account of my motions It was, you know, my expectation in coming here, to spend four successive weeks at Northampton, and then I was to be at liberty to do the same at Deerfield or perhaps at Greenfield, whilst the clergyman whose pulpit I supplied, should preach in the waste places. This plan I acceded to very readily, when proposed by Mr Gannett, in obedience, as he said, to the wishes of the Franklin Association.[99] It promised me retirement, leisure for increasing my stock of sermons, and such advantage to my health as this inland mountain air might bring me. But wo to him that trusts to the frailty of human plans. . broken reeds. The second Sunday it was found convenient to send me to Greenfield; the third to Deerfield; on the Tuesday following, the association met at Northampton,[100] & could not make their mutual plans tally without Mr Emerson would go to Greenfield again for the following Sabbath, & to Deerfield on the next after. Now, Sir, as it would not do for a missionary to set up his Ebenezer [101] & be stiffnecked I must needs comply with what grace I

98. MS owned by Professor James B. Thayer; ph. in CUL. The superscription is to Dr. Ripley at Concord. A small portion of the MS following the complimentary close, on p. 3, has been cut away. It doubtless contained only the signature.

99. MS *By-laws and Records of the Franklin Evangelical Association* (owned by American Unitarian Association), I, 36 (Aug. 14, 1827): "Received by Mr. Hall a communication from the American Unitarian Association, relative to a Missionary to be sent to the three Counties on Connecticut River, and Berkshire County. Agreed to encourage such a mission. Voted, that brothers Willard, Hall, and Bailey be a Committee to designate the missionary . . ." Edward B. Hall and Samuel Willard, who are mentioned by Emerson in these letters, were both graduates of Harvard.

100. Emerson himself was the preacher on this occasion. MS *By-laws and Records of the Franklin Evangelical Association,* I, 37 (Northampton, Sept. 25, 1827): "F. E. Association met according to agreement . . . Mr. R. W. Emerson preached from I Thess. V: 17. Pray without ceasing. . . . Sept. 26. Met according to adjournment; and attended to the dissertation of Brother Hall on the question, What is the design of prayer? Offered remarks on the same. Question for the next meeting: — What is to be understood by praying in the name of Christ?" Apparently Emerson, at Northampton, fell back on the theme, if not the substance, of his first sermon (*cf.* Cabot, I, 112), and he was already thinking much, and making others think, on a subject that was to come to the surface during the crisis of his ministry in 1832.

101. *I Samuel,* 7:12.

could. So I carried my scrip & my doctrines to the courthouse at Greenfield last Sunday & am to give my testimony here tomorrow. Then, as I told the association I was not engaged until November, I shall probably supply Mr Hall's pulpit for three Sabbaths, — unless new emergencies shall again turn out of doors the wayfaring divine. All this, Sir, as you will readily perceive, is not a little unfavourable to my purposes of study. One of the plots of the reverend gentlemen against my peace was to send me into Conway hoping that my name & consanguinity to the last minister might peradventure take captive the confidence of some of his parishioners in that stronghold of Calvinism. But owing to some unforeseen circumstances this project miscarried. Mr Henry Ware wrote to me lately to engage me to supply Mr Deweys pulpit during the three first weeks of November, which I consented to do,[102] much against my will, for I wanted to go to Concord for a little time. On my journey thither I promise myself the pleasure of a day or two at your house.

I do not find orthodoxy so strongly rooted as I had imagined. At elections in this County Unitarians almost always get majorities. Intelligent men are of opinion that the majority of this County is unitarian. I had supposed it must be so, from my acquaintance with the human mind, but feared to be contradicted by acquaintance with the County.

Please to give my affectionate respects to my mother. I trust this will find you, Sir, in as vigorous health as you enjoyed in the summer That God may long preserve it to you, & enrich it with blessings is the prayer of

Dear Sir, Your affectionate Grandson

To Charles Chauncy Emerson, Deerfield, Massachusetts, October 8, and Northampton, Massachusetts, October 10, 1827[103]

Deerfield, Oct. 8.

I am sometimes kind, when I am uncomfortable because to retreat on our own affections is the best way to put a rampart between us & fortune. Being now a little cold, & the prospect of the two or three next

102. See later letters for Emerson's repeated visits, as minister, to New Bedford. Orville Dewey to E. S. Gannett, Oct. 16 (1827), states that his pulpit is to be supplied by Emerson (MS owned by the American Unitarian Association). Presumably Emerson's consent to Ware's proposal was given in a letter, of which, however, I have no further evidence.

103. MS owned by RWEMA; ph. in CUL. The year of the letter is clearly 1827. The superscription is to Charles at Cambridge.

days of my pilgrimage somewhat cheerless, I will test the force of my love for you, O plaything, & see if it can make of myself what true love should, a little heaven below. For please to distinguish – distinguish. As you exist to yourself & as you exist to me, you are two persons, darling. I, as may be proved, have no knowledge, &, of course, no care of thy real existence, thy consciousness. I know not what thou art. You may be full of pains or hypocrisies or daemons. You may be conscious to worlds of thought & being, whose doors are shut on me. You may be a wandered angel. Of all these little anecdotes of your autobiography, my ignorance is profound. (There was a *lastly* which I forgot in its place, that, peradventure, you have no consciousness, are not, phantom.) With all this I have no manner of concern It may be your nature & your interest that you should suffer deeply, drag through uncomfortable years. You may be marked for vice, for selfishness, & to pay back the bitter usury of remorse. But to me, you exist only for my use & behoof. I am to make of you an instrument of pleasure as much as I can; a mere barber's block, whereon I am to hang my affections as a wig, and get the greatest amount of delight from the contemplation, I may. Of course, youth, (now for a precious bit of the philosophy) I write to thee not as thou art but as I am able to make thee appear. I am not affectionate to thee but to my image of thee. When I praise or admire or love thee, in terms, be perfectly assured it is not thine but mine which I applaud. And be as sure that this tractate is no rag of Pyrrho [104] nor yet of Berkley but a sweet tissue of my own, of which the warp was taken from the one, & the woof from the other Having thus achieved my apology for the kind words into which I may be sometimes surprised, for I despise to be affectionate, I give you leave to demolish my cobweb in your next letter provided your logic be neat & unexceptionable.

10th Oct. And now I am come to Northampton and will finish my letter. I received yesterday your Wells' [105] letter, & thank you. A magnanimous resolution no doubt you have taken concerning that poor freshman it puzzles me to know whether you got the hint from Socrates or Tom Coolidge. It augurs well to the country which you are to enlighten & carry forward. When you go to Boston, I want $10.00 of Cole's money pd. to my acct at Whitmarsh's & a receipt taken; the remaining 1.94 may go towards liquidating your own monumental claim. which I have some vague idea has already been minished of a dollar? not by

104. Pyrrho of Elis, the skeptic philosopher.

105. According to the Harvard catalogue for 1827–1828, Benjamin Pratt Welles was a sophomore. I do not know to what other person Emerson could refer.

literary contributions. If the day is as wet with you as with me, I fear you will lose the oration at Concord,[106] and your chum will lose a pleasure which I covet of visiting the manse. — The next article in my head is to bid you call at Cummings & Hilliard in Boston & demand for W. Emerson the 11th & 12th nos. of Sparks Tracts; [107] they are charged to me on my bill and I pay for them, but they were not sent, & in Cambridge they referred me to Boston. I fear the edition is exhausted so insist strenuously. They are the two best numbers, very much, that have issued. Wilkins [108] perhaps is ignorant that my debt there is in rapid progress of liquidation. Tell him. But especially do you read all of Locke that is in those numbers. He never I think wrote any thing so good. deep & serene sense. Tenthly I want Humes Essays sent to Aunt Mary. I rolled them up & left them at Mrs Foxcrofts but Robert left them, and aunt grows clamorous. I tell her she may keep them 3 months. I live now at Judge Lymans who has a monopoly of the hospitality of the town. A fine family,[109] & your friend comes honestly by his attractions. Lastly, I have read the essay on Conversation [110] with great satisfaction. Tis better than the oration [111] and I shall be most happy to communicate the author's name to inquirers. One of my favourite entertainments is to draw moral likenesses and I sent your Aunt Mary at her request a *character* of you last week [112] which it would have pleased & stung you to see. It displeases me today that with all this writing I have not a floating idea in my mind — am not strung for the discussions for which you threw out a ragged glove. But a person offered to carry a

106. The *Columbian Centinel,* Boston, Oct. 17, 1827, notices Edward Everett's oration delivered at Concord, Oct. 10, during the Middlesex County Cattle Show. Charles Emerson, Oct. 20, says he went to Concord in spite of the rain and that Everett pleased the yeomen but not the scholars, being plain and straightforward, and lacking oratorical flights.

107. Jared Sparks had published *A Collection of Essays and Tracts in Theology.* The parts here meant are probably those in Vol. VI, one of which is a selection from John Locke.

108. *The Boston Directory* for 1827 lists a J. H. Wilkins as member of the firm of Hilliard, Gray & Co., booksellers; but the firm name given in the directory for 1826 was Cummings, Hilliard & Co. (Emerson's Cummings & Hilliard).

109. Emerson's friendship with the Lymans lasted many years. Lyman Coleman, *Genealogy of the Lyman Family,* 1872, p. 394, shows that Joseph Lyman (b. 1767), the "Judge," married, as his second wife, Anne Jean Robbins — to whom Emerson addressed a number of letters — and that their first child was Joseph (1812–1871), Charles's friend mentioned in the present letter.

110. Charles Emerson's "Conversation" appears over the signature "E" in *The Harvard Register,* pp. 236–240 (Oct., 1827).

111. See Aug. 16, 1827.

112. See Oct.? *c.* 3? 1827.

letter to you, so I hurry through the mud of messages. If anybody would know why I go to New Bedford, — because there I shall be at home & the weather will be so cold, I need to be in a chimney corner. And if you will write such a letter as shall wake me I will roar you an answer of my best. Your affectionate brother

Waldo —

To Ezra Stiles Gannett, Northampton, Massachusetts, October 9, 1827

[MS owned by the American Unitarian Association; ph. in CUL. George Willis Cooke, *Unitarianism in America,* 1902, p. 151, prints the body of this letter, but with considerable changes: he alters a few unimportant words and condenses the fourth sentence — the original has: ". . . and I went there; the third Sunday, Mr Hall could not leave home, & I preached at Deerfield, and Dr Willard went to Colrain." Finally, he omits the following postscript:

"Mr Hall has formed several associations but none at Enfield. The tracts were received. I went to Bowles & Dearborn on the morng of my departure to hasten them, but they were at your house & I had no time."

According to *The Boston Directory,* 1827, Bowles & Dearborn were booksellers.]

To William Emerson, Concord, October 31, 1827 [113]

Concord, 31 Oct. 1827.

Dear William,

I have just got home here from Northampton and sit with my mother in the old sittingroom and having read all the learned & versatile speculations of the Journal [114] with great pleasure have to congratulate you thereupon & upon the breaking up I hope of the old starvation system the system of retrenchment — retrenchment to the bone. Since your pen is so fluent & grave & sensible I wonder you do not write for the Quarterly [115] which seems not very richly supplied and

113. MS owned by RWEMA; ph. in CUL.

114. William Emerson, Dec. 30, 1827 (MS owned by Dr. Haven Emerson), says that his articles in the *New York Journal of Commerce* have been copied, number after number, into other papers. In a letter to his mother dated Jan. 12, 1828, William says he translates the news from French and Spanish papers, reports the proceedings of the New York common council, and writes editorials, chiefly on foreign politics and on local and state institutions. Many articles that fit this description appear in the *Journal* for the fall of 1827 and the following winter. For William's life at this time, see also a note on Feb. 8, 1828.

115. As late as Feb. 24 (1828), Charles Emerson wrote to William (MS owned by

which pays better I shd think than any newspaper can. What do you receive from the J. of C? I am going to New Bedford 3 weeks. Afterwards I shall have time to put my papers in order & settle my accounts. I believe I owe you about $6.00 which were pd to my account from yours at Hilliard's in Cambridge for I never paid it, & it is paid. I will inquire. Then you gave or loaned me money when I was in N. York [116] and I have wholly forgotten what amount & on what conditions Will you please to say exactly what is what on that score. For as my sermons are worth several dollars apiece I am growing honest & beginning to pay my debts & advise you to take the early tide of my power & disposition. As to ms.s. for your Journal, I have none — some are too bad; some too good — not for your paper but for me to afford — some wholly inapt.

At N. I have spent some pleasant weeks. Four last weeks I lived in Judge Lyman's family most agreeably. Ashmun sends particular remembrances to you; wd. be glad if you wd. write him, &c. He is already reckoned a learned lawyer will succeed to perhaps most of Mr Mills' business, who dies, & assists Judge Howe in the Law School.[117] Judge Howe is a fine man, a great lawyer, & a kind friend of mine. I was going with him on his circuit to Berkshire last week but bad weather prevented. I went however on Thursday in his chaise to bring him back & spent a day at Mr Chas. Sedgwicks in Lenox Went over to Stockbridge & bro't Miss Sedgwick to Lenox.[118] preached there in evg. & returned by stage to N. on Saturday — the Judge being detained by a silly cause till noon. Miss S. spoke with great approbation of your speaking & writing. It is a grand region — that Berkshire — a Scotland having granite mountains & very thunderous little rivers jumping down therefrom & taking their first lessons in roaring before they reach the ocean & take up the business in earnest. Here tis a jest.

Glad am I that Sir J. McIntosh is to publish his history shortly & as

Dr. Haven Emerson), asking why his lectures on German literature had not appeared in the *Quarterly Review*. Whether William Emerson contributed any such articles, I am not sure; but *The American Quarterly Review* has, within the next two years, several anonymous reviews of books on Germany or German literature: "German Literature" (Mar., 1828); the same title again (Sept., 1828); and a review of Henry E. Dwight's *Travels in the North of Germany* (Sept., 1829).

116. See a note on May 15, 1827.

117. John Hooker Ashmun, William Emerson's college classmate, had become, about 1820, a junior partner in the law school which had been founded by Elijah Hunt Mills and Samuel Howe. Mills did not die until May 5, 1829, though he was too ill to begin his second term as United States senator in 1827 and was succeeded by Daniel Webster.

118. Doubtless Catharine Maria Sedgwick, already known as a writer.

announced in the Art. on Scientific instruction in last Ed. Rev.[119] is to publish a discourse on Uses of History. Whether we know or do not know history we always revere it. That muse seems to be premiere in the Cabinet and that often in the face of the fact that we have just closed a voluminous history without the certainty of augmented wisdom. It is perhaps a just deference to the theoretical character which is never the practical character of history namely that it is the whole truth & nothing but the truth. Now it is at best but an imperfect disclosure partial gleam & does not at all answer the purpose wh. we feel wd. be answered to our understandings if this supposed omniscience cd. be attained.[120]

. . . . .

I go to New Bedford tomorrow. Charles has writ an article on Conversation in ye Harvard Register, of which I suppose you know, which is very creditable. He is quite a progressive & loveable young man. Four educated young men, tho' each may shine with but moderate lustre, have an aggregate of good name that accumulates in the geometrical ratio of their numbers: 3 stars have 9 times the effect of 1. Edward follows Jackson's [121] rules & is perhaps a little better; that he should be no worse is quite encouraging for if his complaints have been so long compatible with general health they may be with longevity. Am always delighted to hear from you & am

Your very affectionate brother Waldo.

Please to look in last Edin. Rev. XCI p. 185 It is an account of Richter's wh. exactly describes Aunt Mary's style.[122] I have a letter from

119. *The Edinburgh Review,* XLVI, 225 (June, 1827).

120. A section of the second leaf has been cut away at this point, with probably some six or more lines of writing.

121. Dr. James Jackson, Harvard professor and Boston physician, whose son of the same name was a close friend of Charles Emerson, is mentioned in a number of letters.

122. Any reader of Mary Moody Emerson's letters would probably agree with this observation. Jean Paul, according to the review cited, is not ignorant of grammar or spelling or parsing, but uses them "in a certain latitudinarian spirit; deals with astonishing liberality in parentheses, dashes, and subsidiary clauses; invents hundreds of new words, alters old ones, or, by hyphen, chains, pairs, and packs them together into most jarring combination . . . indeed the whole is one tissue of metaphors, and similes, and allusions to all the provinces of Earth, Sea, and Air; interlaced with epigrammatic breaks, vehement bursts, or sardonic turns, interjections, quips, puns, and even oaths! A perfect Indian jungle it seems; a boundless, unparalleled imbroglio; nothing on all sides but darkness, dissonance, confusion worse confounded! . . . the most erratic digressions . . . Ever and anon . . . some 'Extra-leaf' . . . no mortal can foresee on what. . . ." Emerson's notice of this anonymous review is particularly striking in view of the fact — which he could hardly have known, and which would

Murat.[123] He wrote the Florida article in Q. Rev.[124] Edward is requested by Everett who take [125] the N. A. R. whilst Sparks goes to England to send him his oration as an essay.[126] But perhaps I am telling a secret, so, mum. I gave Noel Clark who studies at N. your address (wh. by the way I dont know) [127]

To Edward Bliss Emerson, New Bedford? Massachusetts, November *c.* 15, 1827

[Edward Emerson, Nov. 17, 1827, regrets " not having rec^{d} yrs till this moment " and says Emerson has been expected home " these three days."]

To Mary Moody Emerson, Concord? November 20, 1827

[Printed, apparently incompletely, in *Journals,* II, 220–223.]

To Edward Bliss Emerson, Concord, *c.* November? 1827? [128]

Concord Tuesday Evg

Dear Edward,

Why hesitate? The way is clear to the Temple of fame thro' the Mechanics Institutes.[129] or the converse. Carve your way

---

then probably have meant nothing to him if he had known it – that Thomas Carlyle was the reviewer.

123. This letter from Murat is still preserved, and a printed version is to be found in *Journals,* II, 187–191.

124. " Florida," in *The American Quarterly Review,* II, 214–237 (Sept., 1827), is a review of seven books on Florida published 1765–1827. The editors, though they altered the article in such a way as to annoy Murat, did not clear his manuscript entirely of awkward idioms.

125. The omission of an inflectional ending is an unusual fault in Emerson's MSS.

126. For Edward Everett's editing of *The North American* in Sparks's place, see Herbert B. Adams, I, 357. If Cushing's *Index* is complete, Edward Emerson was not a contributor.

127. The tops of a few characters, which are all that now remain of what originally followed, make it seem probable that Emerson repeated here his complimentary close and signature. If so, the mutilation of this second leaf, already described, would be explained. In any case, there could not have been more than six or seven lines written here in the margin of the superscription, part of which is also missing.

128. MS owned by RWEMA; ph. in CUL. This letter was broken off abruptly and left without signature or superscription, though it may have been sent under another cover. The handwriting, particularly the form of the pronoun " I," indicates pretty clearly a date not later than the early months of 1828. The reference to the failure of New Harmony seems to show, on the other hand, that 1825 is the earliest possible year, that 1826 is more probable, and 1827, most probable. The Concord heading puts out of the question late 1826 and the following winter and spring, when Emerson was traveling in the South and to Philadelphia and New York.

129. Later Edward Emerson did appear as a lecturer.

thro' the objections which you will first magnify & then demolish It would on any arena of Controversy be gravely urged y^t the scheme of universal education was fanciful inasmuch as neither laws nor customs but sovran Nature alone distributes the lights of the mind. There is no entail of Genius. No court probate to secure to the heir of Pindar the inheritance of Song. The son of Cicero may be a prolix talker; the Child of Chesterfield a wrong-headed clown. Now the same power that expands at the birth the native force of a few individuals in a generation far, beyond the common mark, fired the desires of those individuals to reach their proper ends. It was not then the education of Pericles that gave him the controul of the Peloponnesian War but the inward craving of a great intellect that drove him on from height to height of knowledge till his education was the institution of a perfect hero. The same fiery soul & not peculiar fortunes enlisted him in the service of the state & in the sequel made his opinion the preponderant opinion of Attica & Greece — In like manner the lowest of men, the drudges that worm along thro' the mud & bottom of society — it is not for want of cultivation of their powers but the want of powers themselves. Hence tis vain to attempt to regenerate mankind by a patent education whilst the evil we would cure is out of the reach of education viz. the original inequality of intellect.

Now this reasoning would be wonderfully conclusive if applied to the brute creation; would serve in a world of lions; in a prairie of buffaloes. Would serve wherever instinct supplied the place of reason. But in the world of forecasting reasoning men, of men advancing on themselves, drawing daily accessions of light from the innumerable objects about them & depending for their character on the series of circumst^s into which they are thrown, — it will not do. I am no fanatic disciple of Mr Owen; [130] I nourish no predilection for the exploded experiments of New Harmony — I do not adopt the cant of the *pupilage* of *circumstances* Yet I must venture on the repetition of an ancient truism that every man's character depends in great part upon the scope & occasions that have been afforded him for its development. That the Mind is something to be unfolded & will disclose some faculties more & some less just in proportion to the room & excitements for action that are furnished it. Is it not known to you on the great scale of nations as well as in the history of individuals. Is it not remembered hath it not been told you how in past times the exigences of the state have evoked

130. Robert Owen, the philanthropist and founder of New Harmony.

as with a clarion voice men of war & men of council, armed & wise equal to her need altho' till that moment their existence had not been surmised. Is the age of the Revolution forgotten so soon when the volley of a rustic militia line at Concord was a signal note whose thundering echoes were heard in every glen of the Alleganies calling out the farmer from the tillage of his few paternal acres to take his post in the loading platoon; reading backward the mighty prophecy of peace [131] to turn his scythe into a sword & his pruning hook into a spear; & Liberty sat on the mountain tops astonished at the multitude of her armed sons, who flocked by scores of thousands to her holy side.[132]

To William Emerson, Cambridge? December 14, 1827

[A fragment is printed in Cabot, I, 134.]

To Mary Moody Emerson, Cambridge, December 17? 1827

[Mary Moody Emerson, Dec. 28 and 29 (1827), mentions his "excelling letter" and remarks, with surprise, upon his being at Cambridge again as a student. Her comment upon his letter makes it seem likely that he had included the substance of the paragraph printed in *Journals,* II, 223–224, under date of Dec. 17, 1827.]

To Ezra Ripley, Concord, New Hampshire, December 31, 1827 [133]

Concord, N. H. 31 December, 1827.

My dear Sir,

Before the old year is wholly dead & gone, I hasten to anticipate the Compliments of the new; to hope that it finds you well & will keep you well; that it may bring with it many enjoyments, and, since it cannot restore what the past has taken, strength & faith to bear its evils, & the purest & steadiest hope to console them. —

I preached a sermon last evening upon the close of the year. Mr Farr [134] spent the Sabbath in town & preached in the afternoon. The people were anxious to have an evening service which always attracts the members of the other societies, so I adapted one of my sermons to

131. *Isaiah,* 2:4; and *Micah,* 4:3; reversed in *Joel,* 3:10.

132. The remainder of the third page of the MS and all of the fourth are blank.

133. MS owned by RWEMA; ph. in CUL. The superscription is to Ripley.

134. Probably the Jonathan Farr listed in the Harvard catalogues of 1826 and 1827 as a candidate for the ministry.

the occasion as well as I could. On Christmas day I preached a new sermon which I wrote on Monday & Tuesday; so you see, sir, I am in a fair way of increasing my slender stock of pulpit ware. To put Mother at ease I must mention that I am comfortably lodged & provided for. but New Concord is a bitter cold place & cannot in any respect, in my judgment compare with the Old. The village is large the street I suppose is a mile long, and the population perhaps 3500. The Unitarian Society is small & meets for public worship in the Court House, but have already purchased land, & design to build a meeting house in the Spring. The Kent family, which is large & respectable are the most forward in the establishment of the new church.[135]

I believe I told you, Sir, that when I found myself comfortably seated in my arm chair at Divinity Hall [136] I was disturbed with an apprehension that my prosperity was too genuine & complete to last. But Mr Gannett's representations were such that I could not properly refuse to come hither. It happened however that two days after I had given my consent a gentleman came to me from Brighton to engage me to go there. I was sadly sorry he had not come before as it was precisely such an engagement as I desired, since it would permit me to reside wholly at Cambridge. I have only come however for 3 sabbaths & hope to return to Cambridge next Monday & try my good fortune again trusting that

135. The Kent family, prominent in the church, is important in later letters, after Emerson's marriage to Ellen Tucker, step-daughter of Col. William Austin Kent. According to the *History of Concord New Hampshire,* ed. James O. Lyford, 1903, II, 741–743, Col. Kent gave the ground for the new Unitarian church dedicated in 1829, in Emerson's presence, but it was a William Kent (probably the Colonel's son by his first wife; *cf.* L. Vernon Briggs, *Genealogies of the Different Families Bearing the Name of Kent,* 1898, p. 76) who was one of the organizers of the society and who arranged for preachers from Boston and vicinity. On July 7, 1828, this William Kent wrote to Ezra S. Gannett of the Association headquarters in Boston (MS owned by the American Unitarian Association): ". . . we want a man of force & popular address, as our society is at this moment in a situation the most critical & important . . . Such a man was Mr Emerson, the society was constantly increasing while he was here, & our meetings fully attended, his leaving will operate to our disadvantage unless he can be prevailed upon to return or his place supplied by some one possessing qualities somewhat resembling; would Mr E consent to return, the society would be very well satisfied with one sermon a week of his own & read another from some author, making the duties as light as possible, cannot he be induced to return by persuasion and remain with us a few months?" The Kent family must have known of Emerson for years from Edward (apparently Col. Kent's fourth son, who bore that name), a member of the class of 1821 at Harvard. According to the MS *Autobiography,* Emerson saw Ellen Tucker, presumably for the first time, on Dec. 25, 1827.

136. In the MS *Autobiography* Emerson says he moved to 14 Divinity Hall in Dec., 1827. He seems to have engaged a room there some months earlier (*cf.* June 24, 1827).

Providence will not say me Nay. Mother mentioned in a note which I received just before I left Cambridge that Dr Hurd [137] had made me a very handsome present. I regretted that I could not receive his note & return it a suitable answer. When you shall see him, Sir, I hope you will tell him I have heard of his kindness, & shall have, I hope, an opportunity to acknowledge it. As I shall probably find on my arrival in Cambridge Mr Norton's exercises in full operation, it may be, I shall not very soon come to Concord; nevertheless, habits are strong; the eyes & the thoughts will turn up the Lexington road, & I doubt the feet will be swift to follow.

I find my fortnight to be a pretty long one. I get no letters, though I plague the Postmaster, from either of my busy brothers. Fortunately I stocked my trunk with books & the company of the dead I find, as I always found, to be both wholesome & pleasant. Still, I am always glad to hear a little from the living, especially from those twelve or twenty of my contemporaries that make up the best part of my world. Next to hearing from them, the best way to occupy my thoughts with them, is to write to them, which has set me upon this business of troubling you Sir, with a letter which will answer its purpose if it serve to convey to my Mother & to yourself with how much affection & respect I am Yours.

Waldo Emerson.

137. Probably Dr. Isaac Hurd of Concord, who, says his biographer, was at one time reputed to be the wealthiest man in that town (*The Centennial of the Social Circle in Concord,* 1882, p. 166).

1828

To Charles Chauncy Emerson, Concord, New Hampshire, January 1, 1828 [1]

Concord, N. H. 1 Jan. 1828

A happy new year to my dear brother & many blessings may it bring vigour to the intellect & charity to the soul golden dispositions & happiness their fatal fruit. May it bring the desert of honours & under its wing may it find a snug corner wherein to tuck a particular honour a mere appendix to your merits but a balm to the fretted expectations of one of your ancients. I am in no hurry I wait the leisure of the Year — Lay it up in the later constellations; near Lyra, for example, which ascends in August. And how did the new comer from eternity find you employed Did it ever come to your sharpened ear — that rumor once rife among the immortals, that Saturn & Nemesis were at league together [2] — the wary witness & the implacable retributor and according to the work of the mortal when Saturn came in, should Nemesis deal with you as Saturn went out? It is an idle fashion of your College to let the new year commence in vacation. But I will generously trust that ardent virtue shall be guard for itself.

I would give more than I now own to find a convenient acquaintance such as I have read of & heard of & thought of times without number that would answer anyhow to the fabulous descriptions of a friend — yours for instance in the Register.[3] I would not be difficult; he should rub & go.

The creature must have at least as much sense as God has given me, which, malice might say, was an easy condition of the advertisement, &

1. MS owned by RWEMA; ph. in CUL. Though without salutation or signature, the letter was mailed: the superscription is to Charles C. Emerson at Cambridge, and the Concord, N. H., postmark is dated Jan. 2.

2. Perhaps Emerson's own mythology.

3. "Friendship," in *The Harvard Register,* pp. 333–336 (Jan., 1828), is unsigned, but a MS note in a copy owned by HCL attributes the article to Charles. The difficulty of finding a fit friend is a theme that reappears in many of the letters as well as in Emerson's famous essay.

then his condition must be cleanly; that is, not a vile mechanical person, but having education & manners, a decent slovenly gentleman who believes in the resurrection of the dead. Now these are not hard terms; there are many such in the community looking, doubtless, after just such a person (I contemn your mirth) as I myself. And yet no tongue can tell how much inconvenience & loss of time I suffer for the want of this useful person. Here in the snows, and at Cambridge in the chambers, I want him. A thousand smart things I have to say which born in silence die in silence for lack of his ear. A thousand goodly plans of thoughts or things to be farther unfolded that perish untimely; & hours of idleness & pain that might by his help be crowded with action & virtue. Brothers, even if I had decent ones, can never in any manner answer this purpose. Their education is so uniform & their habits of tho't so similar that they make insipid society; & furthermore my stars! they take such liberties, that literally a man can hardly say his soul is his own; if the soul is not very quiet if she say any thing above her breath it will be cabbaged & leave the poor soul nothing but her wrath. If you could see me as I uncomfortably draw my pen thro this sheet bent over my knee with a stranger by my side you would guess how great must be the inconveniences which send me for refuge to such idle employment how sincere is the want I have exposed.

My quarrel is with my race which will not give me what I want, either in the shape of man or woman. I look out impatient for the next stage of my existence that is the bodiless & expect there to ride my ray (you have read Tucker's vision) [4] in this quest with more diligence than Diogenes bare his lanthorn Behold my resentment was kindled & my wrath said unto men ye are an insect race. But the historian Gibbon said I, remarks — The historian Gibbon, interrupted anger, is a learned pismire. Newton was a calculating pismire Voltaire an unbelieving pismire and your poor idol Everett is — a delightful pismire, added I. Nay said relenting wrath there is ichor in *his* veins. It is worth all the blood of all the pismires.

I am going if the day be fair tomorrow to the Shaker Society, at Canterbury [5] with a sleighing party, & perhaps I will put on the drab cowl.

4. Abraham Tucker ("Edward Search"), *The Light of Nature Pursued,* London, 1768, especially II, 170–174. President Kirkland of Harvard had recommended the book (John W. Francis, *Old New York,* 1866, p. 156).

5. *Cf.* Hawthorne's story "The Canterbury Pilgrims." Emerson revisited the Canterbury Shakers the following year (see Aug. 7, 1829); and in 1842 he and Hawthorne walked together to Harvard, Mass., to observe the Shaker colony there (*Journals,* VI, 258–263).

Among the earliest institutions to be invented, if I read the stars right, is a protestant monastery, a place of elegant seclusion where melancholy gentlemen & ladies may go to spend the advanced season of single life in drinking milk, walking the woods & reading the Bible & the poets. I have a treatise on this subject in preparation. How is my brother Edward? I am impatient to hear him at the bar. When you next declaim you shall find a noble passage or selection from the last article in the XCI number of Ed. Review [6] & I hope soon to see you & am yours.

To Mellish Irving Motte, Cambridge? January? 1828?

[Mentioned in Feb. 8, 1828.]

To William Emerson, Cambridge, February 8, 1828 [7]

Cambridge, [I]8 Feb. 1828[I]

Dear William,

Motte has been absent at New London & did not get a letter that I sent him [8] or I cd. have written before. He has just returned. When I talked with him he said the question was hardly a fair one. &c. that in the Episcopal Church it was considered duty to go without regard to inclination wherever one was called & that he had there accepted the first offer yt. was made him that was feasible. &c. that he should never accept a call against the wishes of a respectable minority, because so much evil grew out of such a connexion, & instanced Young's unpopularity in Boston. There were some desireable circumstances about the Ch. in N. Y. but his determination in y[e] case of a call must of course entirely depend on the contingent circumstances of the invitation.

All this seemed to me very right & diplomatical. And I did not know that you were entitled to any more direct answer. A fine pulpit orator will come out in August — Lunt; [9] is fine, & when ripened by age & oc-

6. The article, beginning with the pretense of a review, is in reality a defense of the ministry then in power.

7. MS in HCL; ph. in CUL. Excerpts I–VI are in Cabot, I, 135.

8. Jan.? 1828?

9. The *Christian Register,* May 10 and June 28, 1828, reports the unanimous invitation William Parsons Lunt was said to have received from the Second Unitarian Church in New York and his ordination there, on which occasion an original hymn by William Cullen Bryant was sung.

casions will be superfine. I dont write because with all my leisure I've none. [II]I am writing sermons. I am living cautiously yea treading on eggs to strengthen my constitution. It is a long battle this of mine betwixt life & death & tis wholly uncertain to whom the game belongs. So I never write when I can walk or especially when I can laugh. But my companions are few; so, sometimes I must read[II] Vivian Grey pt. II. [III]Have you read that contemptuous chapter of Rousseau's [10] Emile upon the Slavery of the Sick?[III] My friend Burton is just going to be settled by acclamation at Lechmere's Point [11] on a thousand a year. [IV]Charles comes down to see me occasionally; he is still the same honey catcher of pleasure, favor, & honour that he hath been & without paying for it like Edward with life & limb. He reads Plato & Aristophanes in Greek & writes, as Pres^{t} sd. of the brood, like hoary hairs.[IV] He must bring you the Harvard Registers when he comes, in which one of his peices is much admired. [V]Edward lasts so well[V] maugre these [VI]unutterable murderous diseases of which he talks that I think his chance is good to last long; quite as good as mine.[VI] The salvation of him is his perfect living He does not transgress by a crumb. His rules are Medes.[12] Charles thinks Doctor Spittergen in Vivian means him.[13]

But scamper scamper; this fine day (the finest I can think of) is dying away & I have not walked to the end of the rope of my rheumatism so have little more time for brotherly love. for tho it is strong as death yet wd I not have death prove the stronger & so I must fight inches with him. How is Sam.[14] My love to him & hope he likes New York better than I do. Of late as I go not to Concord I see no Journals & know little of you more than to suspect you are sunk into the vulgarest man of business who has no correspondence for any but the Jews with whom you have dealings — as ye aforesaid Edward. Do you know we have lost a great man in Judge Howe,[15] & myself a new & valuable friend. Mrs

10. There is a passage of some pages in the first book of *Émile* in which Rousseau ridicules doctors and the common run of patients.

11. Warren Burton, Emerson's college classmate, was ordained at Lechmere Point on Mar. 5 (*Christian Register,* Mar. 8, 1828).

12. The allusion is to *Daniel,* 6:12.

13. Dr. von Spittergen, in Disraeli's *Vivian Grey,* 1826 and 1827, is much given to expounding his views on diet and hygiene.

14. Samuel Bradford, according to *Some Incidents,* pp. 62–63, went to New York as a clerk in Oct., 1827, and found William Emerson studying law in the office of Ketchum & Fessenden. William, he says, hired two garret rooms over the office in Wall St. and shared them with him.

15. For Judge Samuel Howe, see Oct. 31, 1827. He died on Jan. 20 (*Boston Daily Advertiser,* Jan. 21, 1828).

Lyman of Northampton has just written me a sorrowing letter about it wh. it highly behooves me to answer [16] & so I am in all affection

Your faithful brother
Waldo

To Anne Robbins Lyman, Cambridge, February 11, 1828

[In Susan Lyman Lesley, *Memoir of the Life of Mrs. Anne Jean Lyman,* privately printed, Cambridge, Mass., 1876, pp. 247–248; reprinted in the various editions of the same author's *Recollections of my Mother.*]

To ———, Cambridge, March 17, 1828 [17]

Divinity Hall
17 March 1828.

My dear Sir — I am very much obliged to you for your kind remembrance. I see & hear a great deal of your pen but very much too little of yourself. — As to your inquiry touching translations the standard translation of Plato is Taylor [18] a huge book of [19] quartos very expensive & in my humble judgment not good. It contains however seven of the dialogues translated by Floyer Sydenham which Mr Norton once quoted as models of good version. I am profoundly ignorant of the original but Taylor seems to me very faulty inasmuch as it is very Greek indeed. I had some years ago out of the Boston Library a Plato which was Englished from Mme. Dacier's French [20] it was any thing but classical, being full of colloquial vulgarisms but as far as I recollect it, was very much more intelligible than this Taylor Besides it was a commodious duodecimo.* Beloe's Herodotus [21] is an excellent translation in four octavo volumes.

* I believe it was only a selection of the Dialogues in 2 vols.

16. See Feb. 11, 1828.

17. MS owned by RWEMA; ph. in CUL. This is obviously a rough draft. I have not found the letter sent or learned to whom it was addressed.

18. *The Works of Plato . . . Nine of the Dialogues by the Late Floyer Sydenham, and the Remainder by Thomas Taylor,* 5 vols., London, 1804. The complete copy of this work now in the Emerson library at the Antiquarian House was evidently acquired later, for in it the inscription "Charles Lane 1842" precedes Emerson's own signature. Presumably the same copy is alluded to in the note on June 20, 1844. The importance of this translation to Emerson is well known. *Cf.* John S. Harrison, *The Teachers of Emerson,* 1910, pp. 3–8 *et passim.*

19. Emerson left room for the number but failed to supply it.

20. There were various eighteenth-century editions of *The Works of Plato Abridged,* translated by several hands from the French version by André Dacier — not by his wife, Anne Lefèvre, who happened also to be a classical scholar of note.

21. *The History of Herodotus,* tr. William Beloe, 4 vols., London, 1791. Accord-

Smith's is the only version of Thucydides they have in the college library [22] & I never heard of another.

Xenophon has no continuous English version Spelman rendered the Anabasis & Ashley the Cyropaedia [23] but there is no popular translation of the rest.

I am very sorry to send you so imperfect an account but Dr Popkin whom I consulted knew nothing about the matter & the Greek tutor quite as little. Mr Norton who could tell me all about it, I am sorry to say is quite sick & it is feared will be confined some time with dyspeptical complaints.

To Mary Moody Emerson, Concord? April? *c.* 1? 1828?

[Mary Moody Emerson, Apr. 6 (1828?), says she did not receive her nephew's letter " till 4," *i.e.*, probably, Apr. 4. She comments on the illness of Edward, which Emerson had reported.]

To William Emerson, Concord, April 3, 1828 [24]

Concord, ^I^April 3^d^ 1828^I^

Dear William,

I cannot persuade myself but that I have a brother of this name, and that I am wide awake in this my present purpose to address him, notwithstanding all the presumptive evidence to the contrary that stares me in the face from the past twelvemonth. To get some more glimpses of your being & attributes I mean to provoke you to garrulity by my own. ^II^I am just returned^II^ hither this evening ^III^from preaching all (Fast) day at Lexington, where I fill the pulpit till the return of Mr Briggs^III^ from the South where he has wintered.[25] ^IV^Perhaps Edward told you I was agreeably disappointed (for so it was) in escaping all engagements at the New Church in Boston. I am embarrassed at present whenever any application is made to me that may lead

---

ing to the MS charge-book for 1827–1828 at HCL, Emerson had borrowed the second volume a short time before he wrote this letter.

22. *A Catalogue of the Library of Harvard University,* 1830, II, 779, lists two editions of William Smith's translation of Thucydides.

23. There was an edition of *The Expedition of Cyrus,* tr. Edward Spelman, London, 1740; and of the *Cyropædia,* tr. Maurice Ashley, London, 1728.

24. MS owned by HCL; ph. in CUL. Excerpts I–IV are in Cabot, I, 135–136.

25. *Cf. Christian Register,* Jan. 19, 1828. In the MS *Autobiography* Emerson notes that he supplied the Lexington church in March and April of this year.

to permanent engagements. For I fancy myself dependent for my degree of health upon my lounging capricious unfettered mode of life & I keep myself & I slowly multiply my sermons for a day I hope of firmer health & solid power.[IV] Tis vacation at Divinity Hall, & so I am here. Do you know Grandfather is going to Baltimore with Burnap? [26] I am to live & preach here the while. 4 weeks. He proposes to leave Boston the 15th of this Month. I trust you will receive him in N. Y. — not be out of town, I mean. President Kirkland you will have learned has resigned — compelled to that step by some slights if not insults put upon him by the Salem junta in the Corporation. Charles wrote a letter to him [27] in behalf of his Class which was quite eloquent — respect gratitude indignation. Some of it was a little Irish. The College has got into a hand gallop on a wrong road. tis queer that little men should show Everett & Bigelow & Judge Parker the door, & now spill the President out of the window. Our friend the Treasurer is in as bad odour within the walls as a pot of onions. And Bowditch is sincere assafoetida. Of course all conversation swarms with candidates for the vacant seat. & they are of all conditions from the mean to the mighty.

But how do the Lectures [28] come on? One who is no better than echo reported very favorably to me of one of them which he heard. I trust all these extempore occupations will not knock the law in the head; yet I hardly know how it should be otherwise, but have always hoped that the Mogul's best bower anchor lay fast in the depths of jurisprudence — say boldly — the mud of jurisp. whereinto so few have bone & pluck & wind enow to meddle. I've ruined my figure, so do not your your [29] prospects.

Mother & Edward are hatching some conspiracy against the old fur-

26. See Apr. 18, 1828.

27. This letter, dated Apr. 2, 1828, is printed in the *Boston Courier* of Apr. 5, over the names of Charles C. Emerson, Robert C. Winthrop, and George S. Hillard, "Committee of the Senior Class." It is a warm defense of Kirkland. The official record of proceedings relating to the acceptance of Kirkland's resignation on Apr. 2 appeared in the *Boston Daily Advertiser*, Apr. 8. Edward Everett had been compelled, against his will and expectation, to vacate his professorship when he was elected to Congress (*Edward Everett*, pp. 89–90). Jacob Bigelow vacated the Rumford professorship in 1827 but remained on the faculty for many years. Isaac Parker's connection with the law faculty had ended in 1827. "Our friend the Treasurer" was Ebenezer Francis. Nathaniel Bowditch was a member of the Corporation.

28. On March 6, 13, and 27, William Emerson lectured on "English Literature," under the auspices of the New York Athenæum, in the Chapel of Columbia College (*New York Journal of Commerce*, Mar. 6 ff., 1828).

29. Probably intended for "you your," but the "y" of the second "your" is blurred, possibly intentionally.

niture dismissing it to the hammer — so Mother asks if there are articles which you want? [30] Mother also would know how long she may promise herself will your visit be? No dodging. But bring your knitting & come a fortnight or two. And then the lady sends her usual measure of love. And Mr Charles who sits across the table sends his love also & so doth & so shall

to the end your affectionate brother —
Waldo.

To John Haskins Ladd, Concord, April 18, 1828 [31]

Concord, 18 April. 1828.

My dear Sir,

My Grandfather Dr Ripley left Boston last Monday on his way to Baltimore where he is to take part on the 25th instant in the ordination of Mr Burnap.[32] I did not mean to let him go without a letter to you, but being much engaged the evening he was in Boston I neglected it. He has yielded to very strong solicitations of his son [33] & many other clergymen to undertake this journey which appears formidable to a home keeping man of nearly fourscore. Besides the younger clergymen who are engaged on this occasion it was desired that there should be two or three venerable men who should answer for the antiquity of what are sometimes called new opinions. So I wish with all my heart it was 37 miles nearer to my cousin Hannah [34] of Washington —

Dr Ripley, who never was out of New England before, means to visit Washington & Alexandria & Mount Vernon. I cannot wish him a better fortune than when he comes into your parts, to fall into your hands. He is already an admirer of your wife, & has very kind recollections of little

30. William wrote to his mother "& brother Waldo" on May 13, 1828 (MS owned by Dr. Haven Emerson), not to keep anything from the hammer on his account, as nothing would be worth shipping to New York.

31. MS owned by Dr. James I. Wyer; ph. in CUL.

32. The *Christian Register,* May 3 and 10, 1828, tells the story of George W. Burnap's ordination at the First Independent Church in Baltimore on Apr. 23, and reprints a long and favorable account of Dr. Ezra Ripley's part in the proceedings.

33. Samuel Ripley.

34. Hannah Haskins Ladd, sister of the John Haskins Ladd to whom this letter was written. Ladd's wife — "Cousin Eliza" — was Eliza Smith Wyer before her marriage to Ladd in 1819; "little John" was their son John Gardiner Ladd; and "cousin Joseph" was Joseph Brown Ladd, cousin of John Haskins Ladd. (Warren Ladd, pp. 291 ff.)

John. John, I have no doubt, would show him the way to Spa spring [35] with all his heart, if Uncle Waldo's grandfather could walk half as fast and as far as uncle Waldo.

I trust yourself & Cousin Eliza are well, tho' tis long since I have seen any one who could tell me. Wont you please to tell my fair cousin that what interests us, & especially the ladies, the most at this time is the great fret which has not yet spent itself concerning the resignation of President Kirkland. If I rightly remember, this great man was not half so much a favourite with her, as he has always been with her sex generally. But now they, and all good men are in a whirlwind of rage because Mr Bowditch, one of the Corporation, spoke to him so coarsely at a meeting of that body as to induce him to resign instantly. Now that the President is assured of the public sympathy the only good that can be expected to flow from all this indignation is that the the Corporation may be scared into a respect for the public opinion & elect Edward Everett to the vacant seat instead of some meaner men whom they are tho't to have in their eye.

I hope to hear by Grandfather the best possible accounts of John. Pray tell him that if he is not the best boy in all America I shall be disappointed.

My mother sends particularly her love to yourself & to Mrs Ladd. She remembers with great pleasure her short visit last year & if she will contrive to come on with the ministers will depend upon more of her time, & assures John that his [sw]ing [36] shall be ready on the willow tree

Pray give my love to cousin Joseph before whom I am guilty of a heinous sin of omission which I shall try to repair.

With great regard
Your affectionate kinsman
R Waldo Emerson

To Ezra Ripley, Concord? April *c.* 20? 1828

[Mentioned in Apr. 30, 1828, as sent in care of William Emerson.]

To Mary Moody Emerson, Concord? April? *c.* 20? 1828?

[Mary Moody Emerson, (Apr.) 27 and May 2 (1828?), answers a letter which was apparently recent.]

35. *Cf.* Mary G. Powell, *The History of Old Alexandria,* n.d. (1928), p. 52.

36. The "s" and part of the "w" were carried away with the seal and now stand in the opposite margin.

To William Emerson, Concord, April 30, 1828 [37]

Concord, [I]30 April. 1828.[I]

My dear brother,

I am very much disturbed, & so is my mother, at the idea of your Sickness, and the more, because we have no confidence that you have recovered. Since you did not tell us when you were seriously sick, it may be that you are so now. You naughty boy how dare [II]you work so hard? Have you forgotten that all the Emersons overdo themselves? Dont you die of the leprosy of your race – ill weaved ambition.[II] Pah how it smells, I'll none of it. [III]Why here am I lounging on a system for these many months writing something less than a sermon a month[III] for my main business, – all the rest of the time being devoted to needful recreation after such unparallelled exertions. And [IV]the consequence is – I begin to mend, and am said to look less like a monument & more like a man. I cant persuade that wilful brother Edward of mine to use the same sovereign nostrum.[IV] If I have written but five lines & find a silly uneasiness in my chest or in my narvous system to use the genuine anile word (& the old women are almost always right – I take them to be the antipodes of the Garmans) [38] [V]I escape from the writing desk as from a snake & go straight to quarter myself on the first person I can think of in Divinity Hall[V] who can afford to entertain me, i. e. on the person whose time is worth the least. [VI]Especially do I court laughing persons; and after a merry or only a gossipping hour where the talk has been mere soap bubbles I have lost all sense of the mouse in my chest, am at ease, & can take my pen or book. I always take as much exercise as my hip can bear and always at intervals & not in a mass.[VI] Norton says tis certain this climate will not admit of the sedentary habits that scholars in Europe have always indulged. Clear I am that he who would *act* must *lounge*. And please to be assured that all contrary theories or convictions are crockery ware & must be shivered before the irresistible weight of this truth. Therefore it is expected that you will on the receipt of this, labour after the acquaintance of all the trumpery people you can find & give each of them an hour every day or two of your ' do nae good ' time. How do you like Lunt? I heard him say some eloquent things one evening & I think you will not do better by waiting longer for a min-

37. MS owned by HCL; ph. in CUL. Excerpts I–VIII are in Cabot, I, 136.
38. Perhaps Germans, but the meaning is not clear.

ister. Do you know Motte is to be ordained presently at South End? [39] I am glad. I suppose you think I am carrying my theory of the lounge into my epistolary labors. Exactly so; rem acu tetigisti.[40] I was at Exhibition yesterday & saw Mr Gould [41] there who told me he had sent in his resignation of his office — but I understood him yt he was to remain a month or more yet. I saw others who were boiling with the hope that begins to to be spoken louder (n.b. the splendid Pindaric confusion of images) that Edw. Everett shall be nominated to the chair of the College. Such enthusiasm shall be felt in that event as has not been equalled since Petrarch's Coronation, nor then either, in that frigid scholastic nonsense. I am going to Concord N. H. to preach for some time.[42] 6 weeks perhaps. [VII]I have just refused an invitation to preach as candidate at Brighton[VII] One should preach Bucolics there. [VIII]It is the third No to which I have treated the Church Applicant or Vacant.[VIII] Myself & some of mine advisers exhort me to wait a great while — 2 or 3 years — for sound head & wind & limb & sermonbarrelfull before I settle. I wait the advice of the Mogul — himself a divan. I wait I toss with impatience for his presence promise[d in][43] August. I desire to know something about the $29 on your debt to Whitmarsh. You probably know if I made myself responsible for it. The only testimony I have to the contrary is that I have never paid & was astonished at its existence a few weeks ago — which it seems to me wd. have hung as a millstone strung on wire to my collar, if I had ever felt myself the debtor. Please to look up if you have any your family memoranda & examine what the engagements were on my part. I made to you some time since a foolish menace of paying my debts but it was a momentary toss of the head. I am now very slowly getting even with the world — but my great debt to Mr S Ripley $275.00 must wait the lapse of some Egyptian years.

Most affectionately yours
Waldo

39. This college classmate, who had welcomed Emerson in Charleston, in the winter of 1826–1827, was ordained as minister of the South Congregational Society in Boston on May 21 (*Christian Register,* May 24, 1828).

40. The figure is in Plautus, *Rudens,* V, ii, in slightly different form; but Emerson may have remembered it from an American edition of Alexander Adam's *The Rudiments of Latin and English Grammar,* the classic text of his boyhood days.

41. See a note on Jan. 13 and 15, 1816.

42. The MS *Autobiography* gives May to Concord, Mass., and June to Concord, N. H.

43. A fragment has been torn away with the seal.

Dr Ripley will come directly: I hope you have got the letter I sent to your care for him.[44] To him belong my best regards and my mother sits by my side & saith that she approves of all I have written & hopes you will mind it & further gravely saith something about spring complaints & the best physician to be consulted & no neglect and if she knew Latin wd undoubtedly have said Obsta principiis[45] And I have written 18 sermons & Charles is a little scared about rivalry and I am yours.

Also your mother indefatigably adds that she has received your letter & was much obliged to you for it. And it is a great labour for a lounger to write a letter. Concord air which has enriched me whole ounces will give you pounds & they live here on custard & cream and they lounge when they eat & they lounge when they write letters — —

To William Emerson, Concord, June 2, 1828[46]

[I]Concord, 2 June, 1828[I]

My dear brother,

Edward is a great deal better.[47] [II]We were all thoroughly scared, & I was hastened hither from New Concord. He had fainting fits, & delirium, & had been affected strangely in his mind for a fortnight.[II] He is now restored to his former habits of thinking which I cannot help saying were always perverse enough. Dr Jackson however said to me what I think is true that he will never be cured of a notion that he had that he was suddenly & totally recovered from his old disease a fortnight before he came here. Dr J. recommends that he should not touch a book for a year but as the imperious patient is up & dressed this

44. See Apr. *c.* 20? 1828.

45. See Dec. *c.* 20? 1825.

46. MS owned by HCL; ph. in CUL. Excerpts I–II are in Cabot, I, 140.

47. Edward's health, though apparently better for brief periods, was fast approaching a crisis after years of overstudy and nervous strain during a brilliant college career. Correspondence owned by Dr. Haven Emerson adds something to what the letters here published contain. Edward wrote to William Emerson, May 19 (1828), "I read no law — almost no letters. . . . and the consequence is that from the moment of surrender I have been gaining & tho feeble from the struggle of so many years, yet I am wiser, & *healthier* & happier than ever in my life." But Charles Emerson told William, May 29, that Edward had been seized with fainting fits the preceding Sunday and had been almost stupefied since. On June 6 Edward was, however, able to write to William, stating that he had quit Boston and his legal affairs for a rest in Concord. Later letters in these volumes record his collapse in the following July and his subsequent recovery but continued struggle against tuberculosis till the time of his death, in 1834.

morning, the doctor's dominion will shrink back into an advisory council, & come in, I doubt not, for a due share of contempt.

Tho' tis but yesterday he was very weak on his bed & tho' mother perhaps expects to keep him here a month, yet I believe he will be in Boston before a great while & attend to your business, if business you have, with usual precision.

I confess I watch him with painful interest. I fear that any future disorder may again affect his nerves. Still he reasons on business & affairs with force & rapidity & for aught I know his health may be really recovering. I shall presently I know not how soon go to N. Concord for a few weeks. Write to Charles at Cambridge.

Yours entirely

Waldo

by mail of course if you write concerning Edward.

To William Emerson, Cambridge, June 30, 1828 [48]

[I]Divinity Hall, 30 June[I] —
1828 —

Dear William,

[II]We are born to trouble. I have just received a letter from Concord to say that Edward is ill again — worse than before — in a state of violent derangement, so as to require great restraint. Mother[II] writes, as you may well suppose, in great affliction. & [III]speaks of the Hospital, as perhaps a dismal necessity.[III] I go up tomorrow morning. It will do no manner of good that I know for you to come — so do not think of it.

I do not know but if it continues it will become necessary to send him to *Charlestown*. For besides the state of feeling produced by watching him being unutterably wretched & ruinous to infirm health — it removes me from employment the profits of which are only more necessary to me on account of this calamity.

I have nothing else to say — no spirits to say any thing else You know Henry Ware is very ill & I fear from the last accounts no good ground of hope exists for a real restoration. However, his friends do not think so yet. — I have engaged to supply his pulpit [49] but shall probably relinquish it. —

Charles has just been down to see me — full of manuscripts and prepa-

48. MS owned by HCL; ph. in CUL. Excerpts I–III are in Cabot, I, 140.

49. This was the beginning of a connection which was to result in Emerson's brief service as a regular minister. The archives of the Second Church, at present de-

ration — and all unprovided for my mowing tales of wo. He delivers an oration to his class a fortnight from today.[50] Strange how all our prosperous days have been overcast! As in case of both Edward's orations — & before — & since — & now again to be.

You will determine what course to take upon your own business. You won't fail to come at Commencement, I hope. — Mother leans on that hope as a staff.

Write to me at Concord, or to Charles here.

Your affectionate brother
Waldo —

To William Emerson, Cambridge, July 3, 1828

[MS owned by HCL. One excerpt is printed in Cabot, I, 140–141. After describing Edward's collapse and giving some details regarding Edward's financial affairs, Emerson closes his letter thus: " But you will be here in August to advise. Charles's debts end now & if God is merciful to him, he will be in a condition to help us. On Bulkeley's notes, my name stands as principal tho' I have paid nothing hitherto except by lending Edw. a small sum. Write to me here at Cambridge, I will call at Munroe & Francis for letters. Yours affectionately Waldo

" Charles, as if in a kind of mockery, has a first prize for dissertation — "

The award of a first Bowdoin prize to Charles Emerson for an English dissertation is reported in the *Boston Daily Advertiser,* July 4, 1828.]

To William Emerson, Cambridge, July 14, 1828 [51]

Divinity Hall — Cambridge.
14 July 1828

My dear brother,

I have great pleasure in introducing to your acquaintance Mr Barry a member of the Middle Class in the Theological School

posited in the library of the Massachusetts Historical Society, contain the records of Emerson's connection, which are cited also in notes on later letters. MS *Second Church & Society — Standing Committee Records January 1825 to April 1845,* p. 39 (meeting of July 30, 1828, at the home of Emerson's future friend Abel Adams): " The Committee on supply of the Pulpit verbally reported that they had engaged Mr. R. W. Emerson to supply the Pulpit for the present, and that he would continue to supply untill he should give notice to the contrary." And the MS records of the treasurer of the Second Church contain Emerson's signed receipt, dated Aug. 7, 1828, for " Sixty dollars being for the supply of Revd Mr Ware's pulpit four Sabbaths including & ending July 20th."

50. See July 15 following.

51. MS owned by Mr. Edward Waldo Forbes; ph. in CUL. An undated note signed by William Barry, Jr., written on the same sheet of paper, shows that he failed to find William Emerson in and was forced to leave town without seeing him.

— which he is now quitting with the design of spending a year or two in Germany. As you have been over the ground already — perhaps it will be in your power to give him some letters or information that will be useful to him.

Yours affectionately —
Waldo —

To William Emerson, Cambridge, July 14, 1828[52]

14 July

Dear William,

I have received the letter inclosed in Charles's and shall be here doubtless thro' the whole of August as I supply for an indefinite term Mr Ware's pulpit. Then as sorrows come in pairs C has got the second oration[53] with loud clamours on his part, & that of his friends, of injustice He has a good harangue ready for next Tuesday.[54] I saw Edward on Thursday & walked out with him. He was calm & in a mood he has sometimes had before of unlimited acquiescence to all you would or said. But I defer all communication on that painful subject till we meet. I do not know your address in New York & so use the old one.

Waldo —

To Charles Chauncy Emerson, Cambridge? July 15, 1828[55]

15 July, 1828.

This day I heard Mr C. C. Emerson deliver a valedictory oration to his Class.[56] This young man's performance deserves particular notice. He is a beautiful orator but never eloquent. His advantages for speaking both natural & acquired are very great. His voice his person & his action are (to that end) excellent. But the vice of his oratory lies here — he is a *spectacle* instead of being an *engine;* a fine show at which we look, in-

52. MS owned by HCL; ph. in CUL. The superscription shows that this was sent by the William Barry, Jr., of the preceding letter.

53. For Charles's commencement oration, see Aug., 1828.

54. See July 15, 1828, for this class-day oration.

55. MS owned by RWEMA; ph. in CUL. This letter, though unsigned, was folded and superscribed " Charles C. Emerson." It is possible that Emerson himself delivered it to Charles; and, if so, the lack of a signature would be easy to understand.

56. The *Boston Courier* of July 17, 1828, reported that the oration on Tuesday by Charles Emerson, was " highly meritorious."

stead of an agent that moves us. There is very good management of the voice, fine tones, varied & delicate sounds — some that are music to hear; there is very elegant and very nervous gesture; and these are used to convey beautiful & forcible periods indeed a very finished oration — to all who have a mind to hear it. Theres the rub [57] — you may hear it or not as you choose. The orator leaves you to your option. He does not address you. He has chalked around him a circle on the floor & within that he exhibits these various excellences to all the curious. I happened to see the Manuscript before it was pronounced, & noticed a particular passage which was a sudden & touching appeal to the audience with the remark that Mr E. would not speak it well. It was even so. Though he uttered the words, *he did not appeal* to the audience. And so that moving passage passed with no more effect than if the same elegant speaker had said Butterfly, butterfly butterfly. — In short during this very pleasing performance I was many times reminded of Mr Everett's remark upon the ancients that they made the greatest advances in arts & commerce & politics & yet in each, thro' some strange mischance fell short of the last advance. So Mr E. with noble elements for eloquence, was all but eloquent. I felt that that voice should have thrilled me as a trumpet. I only heard it with pleasure. I felt that he should have made me laugh & cry at his will. He never touched me.

The cause of this peculiarity in this gentleman's harangue appeared to me to be that he came with a wrong feeling to the rostrum. His rank in College is very high. He has long enjoyed a considerable reputation for talents & acquirements & particularly as a speaker. The whole audience were known to him & were drawn together by the expectation of witnessing his powers. Mr E. was fully aware of all this, and aware, that, whatever he said would be eagerly & favorably listened to. Instead, therefore, of feeling that the audience was an object of attention from him, he felt that he was an object of attention to the audience. This of course is the reverse of what should be. Instead of finding his audience — like other orators — an angry master who is to be pacified, or a sturdy master who is to be cajoled, — &, in any case, one whose difficult regard is to be won, — he takes it for granted that he has the command. He makes a *King's Speech;* condescendingly drops very fine things, which, if you listen with all your might, will pay you.

As Revolutions take place in Colleges as well as monarchies, it appears that Mr E's situation is changed. He has been removed with some

57. *Hamlet,* III, i.

violence from the first to the second place. I suppose this event will do more than all masters or instructions, to mend the great error I have remarked — to push him out of his enchanted circle. He no longer claims deference by an unbroken prescription. His best title has been formally denied. At his next public appearance, he is to struggle uphill; he is to vindicate a right which has been set aside. Let him feel his situation. Let him remember that the true orator must not wrap himself in himself, but must wholly abandon himself to the sentiment he utters, & to the multitude he addresses; — must become their property, to the end that *they may become his*. Like Pericles, let him " thunder & lighten." [58] Let him for a moment forget himself, & then, assuredly, he will not be forgotten. —

To Sarah Foxcroft Haskins, Cambridge, July 23, 1828? [59]

Divinity Hall —
23 July —

Dear Sarah,

I received yesterday your kind invitation for this ev[g]; but besides that I am hardly in spirits at this time to venture out of my cloister, I am particularly occupied this week with some writing, so that I shall not be able to come. Charles is at Concord but talked of coming down today if he should I will tell him to come. You must remember me kindly to my old friends (for they will let me call them so) & to your parents. Yr. aff[t] cousin

Waldo E.

58. This goes back to Aristophanes, *The Acharnians*, ll. 528–531; but Emerson probably got it from Plutarch's life of Pericles.

59. MS owned by RWEMA; ph. in CUL. The date " 1826? " has been supplied in an unknown hand but is probably incorrect. Emerson would hardly have occupied a room at Divinity Hall while he was conducting his school in the house his mother had taken in Cambridge (*cf.* Cabot, I, 115, and notes on Oct. 23 and 24, 1826). On the other hand, the form of the pronoun " I " in this letter is one that Emerson seems to have adopted early in 1828; he wrote letters from Divinity Hall during July and August of this year; and the statement " I am hardly in spirits at this time " would be perfectly clear in the light of other letters of July, 1828. The superscription is to Thomas Haskins " for Miss S. F. Haskins," Carver St., Boston. Carver St. is the address given in the directories for Emerson's maternal uncle for many years before and after 1828. The death of Sarah Foxcroft Haskins is mentioned in Mar. 4, 1850.

TO WILLIAM EMERSON, CAMBRIDGE, JULY 26, 1828 [60]

Divinity Hall, 26 July –

Dear William

I have the pleasure of introducing the bearer, Mr Sibley, to your acquaintance. Mr S. has just left the School, & is on his way to Philadelphia, to supply Mr Furness' pulpit a few weeks. As Mr Sibley is desirous to pass thro' your great Babylon, & stop & look at it without scathe or detriment I have told him that perhaps you can entertain him at your bachelor's hall with better economy than he can practise elsewhere. If you have not the same advantages now as formerly, you can give him information where he will be best housed for we men of peace & of paper do not enter your huge & roaring town without apprehension of what may befal us there. That Mr S. may have a good deliverance therefrom, & that this may find you well is the hope of your affectionate brother

Waldo

Both those sums $15 & $20 were received. The first was paid 13.50 to M. M. E. The second remains with me. Edward was quite calm when I saw him last: has been to *meeting* with Dr W. but unsettled. I have carried Bulkeley to Chelmsford. Mother is pretty well. Chas. at Northampton.

TO SARAH BRADFORD RIPLEY, CAMBRIDGE, JULY? 31? 1828? [61]

Divinity Hall, Thursday.

I send the letter & scrap so characteristic which came to me from Aunt. The letters patent of course I read. They have the usual amount

60. MS owned by HCL; ph. in CUL. The year 1828, given in the endorsement, is obviously correct. John Langdon Sibley, described as having "just left the School," is listed as a senior theological student in the Harvard catalogue for 1827–1828. The sums of money acknowledged are mentioned in various letters which William Emerson wrote home from June 3 to July 5, 1828 (MSS owned by Dr. Haven Emerson). "Dr W." was doubtless Dr. Rufus Wyman, superintendent of the McLean Asylum, in Charlestown (*The Boston Directory,* 1828).

61. MS owned by RWEMA; ph. in CUL. The superscription is to "Mrs Ripley" at Waltham. The date "? Oct 1828" has been supplied in another hand, but there is some reason for conjecturing that the actual date was July 31, 1828. It seems likely that the letter is earlier than that of Aug. 4, 1828, which shows that Emerson preached at Waltham on Aug. 3; and it is fairly probable that the last paragraph of the present letter refers to that date. Emerson was at this time supplying the pulpit of the Second Church but was no doubt expecting to "enter into captivity" as a regular

of ludicrous profoundness. Aunt Mary is a she-Isaiah but alive to the comedy of her pretensions & costume. She quotes as wildly as she talks, and as I happen to be behind the curtain of one of her allusions, perhaps I shall help you to the sense of her riddles by putting it down as tis in Ben Jonson —

" Wait occasions & obey them,
Sail in an egg shell, make a straw your mast,
A cobweb all your cloth, & pass unseen,
Till you have scaped the rocks that are about you." [62]

I meant to come & give Mr Ripley a labour of love before I enter into captivity & if I cd. do it in such a way as to give the supply of my pulpit where I wish to, would come next Sunday. But probably not, as I do not know his engagements on that day. Perhaps he will be at Thursday Lecture this morng. Yours affectionately

Waldo E.

To John Farmer, Cambridge, August 1, 1828 [63]

Divinity Hall, Cambridge
1 August 1828

My dear Sir

I take the opportunity of Mr Wiswall's visit to Concord to send you the extract which I made several weeks since from Mr Emerson's letter.[64] I am not sure that it will furnish you with any one desired fact. It is however satisfactory to me as showing me precisely the distance between me & that primitive Joseph whom I tried to make John. Nor have I seen the copy of the Septuagint [65] again to read the

---

preacher in the near future. There is, however, some ground for supposing that this letter belongs to the period between Emerson's election as colleague pastor at Second Church, on Jan. 11, 1829, and his ordination exactly two months later. *Cf.* the reference to " the execution day " in the letter of Feb. 20, 1829.

62. *The Sad Shepherd,* III, ii. Emerson later had the same passage in mind in *Journals,* II, 476.

63. MS owned by the Henry E. Huntington Library; ph. in CUL. Farmer was an authority on local history and genealogy, and his work here referred to as a biographical sketch was published in 1829 under the title *A Genealogical Register of the First Settlers of New-England.* An account of the Emerson family appears on pp. 96–97.

64. When the present letter was offered for sale in Goodspeed's Book Shop, May, 1904, it was described as accompanied by two pages of MS in Emerson's hand headed " Extract from a letter from Rev. Reuben Emerson, dated South Reading, Mass., March, 1828."

65. William Emerson had written to his mother and brother on May 13, 1828

name there. I am now so deep in the matter that I will just trouble you with what troubles me. I want the name of my second ancestor from Joseph & of his wife, if Mr Coffin's notes will give them. Mr Coffin I believe named him & gave you some note. It is that son of Joseph who is stated in the letter to have settled in Newbury & is the father of Joseph of Malden, my great grandfather. Do not give yourself any trouble however about it for doubtless I could learn the fact somewhere in my own family. With great regard, your friend & servant,

R Waldo Emerson

My cousin Mr Geo B. Emerson of Boston wishes to have his name set down as subscriber for a copy of your Biographical Sketch. Please make my remembrances to Mr & Mrs Breed & to Mr Hough.[66] I hope to come to Concord again — [67]

To Charles Chauncy Emerson, Waltham, Massachusetts, August 4, 1828 [68]

Waltham, 4 August, 1828.

Dear Charles,

Whilst I sit here whither I came to preach yesterday [69] I can better acknowledge your letter than look at my fingers till breakfast time. I am glad you are in such good spirits, but you are a wicked lad to sharpen your pen against your kind cousins at Amherst.[70] You would be worth your weight in gold if you wd. fulfil the law of love as well as they. But tis good ground for the depravity men, that simple goodness, merum vinum, without the alcohol of wit, is apt to disgust the young madcaps of the world. But the wheel goes round — the black hours come to them as to others; they become the greybeards in their turn; virtue loses its vulgarity in their eye & they learn to feel that one plain

---

(MS owned by Dr. Haven Emerson), that he had intended to send "Waldo's Septuagint" but was waiting for an opportunity.

66. Farmer seems to have been living in the home of Stephen P. Breed, in Concord, N. H. (John Le Bosquet, *A Memorial . . . of John Farmer,* 1884, p. 96). Emerson was doubtless well acquainted there through his pastoral visits. Hough may have been George Hough, the pioneer printer of the town (*cf.* James O. Lyford, I, 435).

67. A fragment of Emerson genealogy follows, written in another hand, presumably Farmer's.

68. MS owned by RWEMA; ph. in CUL.

69. *Cf.* July? 31? 1828?

70. Children of Emerson's aunt Deborah Haskins and the Rev. Mase Shepard, who appear in other letters.

look or act of honest benevolence is worth all the frolic, fashion, & pride.

But there's no use of preaching You must like all your race eat your own pill of experience — so I'll save my sermon for another occasion

I hope you are not so sinful in what you very well understand as to leave your work unattempted till you return. When I told some of your friends that you had not written your oration,[71] but were loitering in the temptations of the best company in the world, they said, yes, but the boy's trick was to work under the show of idleness; so, I hope you will have the grace to be guilty of thus much hypocrisy.

I am going to Concord today if it don't rain, & to Cambridge tomorrow. From what I heard of your chance for scholars in Boston I judge it would be best to go forward by all means.[72] But I only heard my particulars thro' a byway.

You must present my particular respects to Mrs Lyman. It would give me the greatest pleasure to see Northampton [73] again but have no reason to promise myself that gratification at present.

Edward is altered again, though hardly for the better. I saw him Saturday & Friday. His present idea is that he is suffering punishment for great offences. It was consoling however that for the first time he exhibits great interest in my visits & great affection for me, & begs me to stay with him all the time. I shall see him tomorrow probably. Right or wrong, I got more hope of him from my last visit than ever before. He stands in need of nothing but God's aid.

Your affectionate brother,
Waldo.

To William Emerson, Boston, August 7, 1828 [74]

Boston 7 Aug

Dear W^m^

I take a moment to say I am well & Edward in a somewhat more hopeful state. I have not given you from time to time particulars because I expect you so soon & Edward changes very much & very fast

71. For Emerson's own suggestion of the theme actually used, see Aug., 1828.

72. For the progress of the school which Charles soon opened, see Oct. 17, 1828.

73. This letter was addressed to Charles, in care of Judge Lyman, at Northampton, Mass.

74. MS owned by HCL; ph. in CUL. The endorsement and the references to Edward and to the sums of money, which were mentioned in the letter of July 26, 1828, fix the year.

in his moods. I hope his present composure & self acquaintance will remain till your arrival which he expects fondly & mother eagerly. I sent you word I believe that I had rec^d^ the $20 & the $15 which you sent in several letters & I am always

Yours Waldo.

Shall be at Cambridge at No 14 D. H.[75] doubtless when you come

To Charles Chauncy Emerson, Cambridge, August, 1828 [76]

Divinity Hall

Dear C

Suppose you should try your pen upon the subject of *Public Opinion* [77] — a topic on which we have been a good deal dinged lately & which therefore must have some real foundation in present interests. What makes the value of any one man as precise & as well known as the stamp on a coin? Public opinion. What is a throne? What is a legislature? What is a Congress? What is a Constitution? Mere pipes, mere mouth-pieces for the expression of public opinion. The moment they cease to give it vent, the moment they resist & set up for original powers that moment they shrivel to cinders as cords in a flame. In fact there can be no resistance & there is no exception. For observe this is not a local doctrine — a limitary Genius dwelling only in the unfenced soil of a republic — with an ear too noble & hands too restless to bear the sound or to wear the shackles of monopolies, of priveleges, of birthrights; No; for these also are founded upon *it*. And the czar of Russia sits on his iron throne over fifty millions of human souls in the old continent by precisely the same power that would crush him in attempting the same supremacy in the New.

Of course this part of the subject the general view will admit of very varied & splendid illustration.

Nations furnish sublime spectacles sometimes of horror sometimes of

75. In the Harvard catalogue for 1828–1829, Emerson is listed, among the candidates for the ministry, as living in 14 Divinity Hall.

76. MS owned by RWEMA; ph. in CUL. Though without signature, the letter was folded and superscribed simply "Charles C. Emerson," and Charles endorsed it "R W Emerson August 1828." This date is confirmed by the suggestion of the subject Charles actually used in his oration, which he had not written by Aug. 4, as the letter of that date would seem to show.

77. Dr. John Pierce (*Proc. Mass. Hist. Soc.*, 2d series, V, 198) notes that Charles Emerson's commencement oration of Aug. 27, 1828, was on "Publick Opinion" and was "very acceptable. 20 min."

happiness when public opinion changes. When it quits its ancient bed & bursts thro' the mounds & levées that dammed it up, & strikes terror into ancient societies & institutions, that lie peacefully over the land, by the roar of the inundation. The outbreak of the French Revolution; the second expulsion of the Bourbons by Bonaparte; the triumphal progress of Lafayette thro' the States; The Restoration of the English Stuarts in 1688; [78] are all fine commonplaces, & a thousand more.

In the next place where is the origin of Public Opinion? — In individual character & opinion. Each great national feeling, wave after wave, has been first the opinion of a few, the opinion of one. And is it not a better inquiry than hunting new minerals or dissecting spiders or counting lobes & petals of flowers to explore observe the obscure birth of a sentiment at the frugal board perhaps of a poor wise man & see how slowly it struggles into fame — to mark the earliest inadequate efforts that are made to propagate it; to note when it bands its friends into a sect — small misrepresented despised — till it waxes formidable enough to be persecuted — count its martyrs & see how truth makes men brave; then observe the reaction the impulse it derives from oppression — it scatters like wildfire it beats down resistance it annihilates prejudice & attains at last to omnipotent force, — Sometimes this *opinion* has been wrong sometimes it has been right but will not the history of the world be my warrant when I say it has been always strong? What were the Crusades those renowned emigrations that turned back the old current of population from Europe the colony to Asia the parent — What were those extravagant enterprizes but proofs that the opinion of of one had become the opinion of many that a fanatic voice saying 'It is the voice of God' [79] — was able to bring an echo, a tremendous echo of a million voices to that shrill & evil sound? What was the Reformation but as you yourself said did you not? the opinion of one become the opinion of many — the feeling of a lonely monk become the sentiment of armed & angry nations? &c &c &c

What of all this? Cui Bono? Why — infinite good to be sure. An invaluable fact. What! is *public opinion* so strong that it will do its merry will, how grand or hideous soever, & never fail a hair? And then is *private opinion* so much stronger, that tho' it wont face this hippopotamus, it will yet get on its grand elephant back, & lead it with a word

78. Emerson may have meant to cite either the Restoration of the Stuarts or the Revolution of 1688.

79. Emerson was no doubt familiar with Hallam's account of Peter the Hermit, where, however, the famous slogan of the crusaders is given as "It is the will of God!"

or a goose quill over land & sea? As Peter Hermit & Dean Swift & Mirabeau, & Burke can attest? Why, then, what a clean Damascus blade of an inference can you not draw, about the value of a brave lad in the world, that knoweth how to keep his hands clean & heart pure & then write a tract or speak a speech?

To Samuel Emerson, Cambridge? October? *c.* 10? 1828

[See Oct. 10, 1828.]

To John Farmer, Cambridge, October 10, 1828 [80]

Divinity Hall, Cambridge
10 October, 1828

My dear Sir,

I am very much obliged to you for the several kind favours I have received from you which I am ashamed to have left so long unanswered. But I have had nothing to communicate on the subject on which you were kind enough to interest yourself. I went to Mr Bigelow's office [81] to look up the births of the family of the Mendon man, but the Number marked *3* did not reach so far down as [82] & contained only 3 short pages of Mendon records in which my name did not occur. The next volume which carried on the registry of the same events for the County did not contain the town of Mendham. I found nothing to catch my eye except the record of the marriage of Rev. Joseph E. to Elizabeth Bulkley [83] which you had already given me; & the marriage of Peter Bulkley (who I suppose is the son of Peter) two years after to Rebecca Wheeler, & the birth of a son Edward.

I have written to Mr Samuel Emerson of Newburyport, who is a cousin of a few removes, to me, to ask him what he knows of that Newbury John, & if he cannot identify him as Joseph of Malden's father: for that is a point about which I think I cannot be far mistaken, since unless he be I do not see what I have to do with the Bulkeleys whose blood, I have always understood was in me for good or for evil. But that it was a better or farther descended drop than another, I never heard till Mr Reuben E. dignified it with a baron's coat of arms. As soon as I get in-

80. MS owned by the Public Library, Boston; ph. in CUL.

81. Abijah Bigelow was clerk of the courts at Worcester (*The Massachusetts Register* for 1829, p. 66).

82. Emerson probably intended to fill in the blank but did not.

83. Perhaps the variant spellings of the name in this letter reflect recent readings in the old records.

formation from Newburyport or elsewhere that shall make that ancient born where he ought to be, I shall send you word.

I received from you a little memoir of your own house which you kindly sent & read it with much interest. I hope it will not be a great while before I shall have an opportunity of visiting Concord again. I do not learn from Mr Thomas that the new Society have got any farther with their House [84] than when I was there. If I had been at liberty I think I should have accepted Mr Thomas' offer, & have gone thither for a few weeks now. But I shall probably be expected to supply Mr Wares pulpit, till December,[85] – an engagement which suits my present convenience better than any other.

Please to remember me particularly to Mr & Mrs Breed. With great regard

Your friend & servant
R Waldo Emerson.

[I h][86]ope Mr Fessenden will be the bear[er] of this. He is an old & kind friend of mine & tho' he has suffered much from ill health he was the first scholar in the largest class that was ever graduated at the University.[87]

To William Emerson, Cambridge, October 17, 1828 [88]

Divinity Hall 17 Oct.
1828

Dear William

I begun my letter, as might be expected from the ardour of my fraternal impatience, upside down,[89] & was saying that it is

84. For the completion and dedication of the new church, with Moses G. Thomas as minister, see Nov. 13, 1829. According to the *History of Concord New Hampshire*, 1903, II, 742, Thomas formally accepted the pastorate in Dec., 1828.

85. The MS records of the treasurer of the Second Church show that Emerson supplied the pulpit pretty regularly till about the end of November. The reason for his refusal to continue during December is given in the letter of Dec. 4 following.

86. As in several other cases, the first letters in the line have been carried away by the seal and now stand directly over the final letters of the same line, completely obscuring them. Thus the " I h " is plainly legible where " er " ought to be.

87. John Fessenden was the ranking scholar of the class of 1818 and graduated from the Divinity School in 1821.

88. MS owned by HCL; ph. in CUL. Excerpt I is in Cabot, I, 144–145.

89. Before he discovered his mistake he had written at the bottom:

" Divinity Hall

" Dear William,

" Tis as well if one has a brother now "

as well if one has brothers now & then just for form's sake to say so that the fact may not be forgotten by ourselves or others which wouldn't be reputable you know, so here's to you. I set the bureau on his way last Friday morng. It had had two fore legs amputated but one was put in the drawer & the other tied up in a corner of the carpet wh. covered it. You will find a little glue will make the fracture as though it had not been, for the loss is an ancient one & yet the bureau writes as Francis from Pavia We ve lost all but our honour.[90] I have now in charge two shirts for you from mother. What shall I do with them. I will consult David Francis upon this question. Tis a bit queer you have never written to me especially as tis probable you were in debt one or two letters. Your mother is amazed when I tell her we never correspond.

Edward continues to be & to grow better. He is now better than I dared expect two months ago. His bodily health is much mended & his discourse in general very sane. But he has some word or expression in a conversation which betrays an unsoundness. Lately he has written one or two letters & very well. He showed me a draught of one which he was writing to you requesting some information about the present condition of the Newell business.[91] I told him that it was highly improper in present state of his health that he shd. meddle with it & that you did not wish it. He told me he shd. like to have that wish under your own hand. I told him I wd. send you word – And as he remembers all things you had better send him a few lines about health & weather, & that fact, with the advice not to write much or any – & enclose it to me or Charles.

[I]Mr Ware is ill again, & all good men are sorry. You see what lies before your brother for his mortal lot. To be a good minister & healthy is not given. This event will probably confine me where I am for the winter. It has some obvious advantages over any other service but involves more labor.[I]

Could you not inform me by a line or two what are your performances & projects in the way of getting bread, just to save us any apprehensions with regard to your taking the highway. What of the lectures? What of the law? Do you want any books that can be borrowed here?

I never knew whether you called on Mrs Cook or whether you advised Mr Francis of my intention to call upon him in the business way.

90. In the letter of Francis I to his mother after the defeat of Feb. 25, 1525.

91. Edward Emerson to William, June 6, 1828 (MS owned by Dr. Haven Emerson), said he had had to turn over the affairs of Newell & Niles to others, as his health would not permit him to go on with legal business.

I called on Brown at the Bookstore [92] respecting your books. He told me that he had long ago sold all he could sell & given the proceeds to Edward with the deduction of his commission, & he was anxious to get rid of the remainder. So I bid him send them here & here they are & wait the decree of Tartary. Two books of Eichorn's; Walch 9 vols. Augustus. Plutarch, Aristophanes, & some more. —

I went horseback into the country lately for air & exercise lately, & enjoyed it much. My day & night companion am I bereft of. For the school committee & Lewis Stackpole & the youth's own fears & follies did kidnap him & left me alone. Cuique Philomelae sua sufficit spina. Who *him* is, I see I have forgot to mention but it is confidently asserted in the public prints that Mr G. P. Bradford is appointed usher of the Latin School. He means to preach in one year.[93] And I am now going to Dover N. H. for two Sundays by an exchange & am always your affectionate brother,

Waldo —

I believe Charles gets along as fast as is good — [94]

To John Farmer, Cambridge, October 29, 1828 [95]

Divinity Hall, Cambridge. —
29 Oct. 1828.

My dear Sir,

I have received yesterday a letter from Mr Samuel Emerson of Newburyport (who by the way is son of Bulkley who was son of

92. Hilliard & Brown advertised themselves as booksellers to Harvard in the *Boston Daily Advertiser,* Oct. 17, 1828. The books were probably some of those William Emerson had bought in Germany a few years earlier. Johann Gottfried Eichhorn, author of introductions to both *Old* and *New Testaments,* had been William Emerson's teacher at Göttingen. Copies of *Einleitung ins alte Testament,* 1780, and *Die hebräischen Propheten,* 1816 ff., both bearing the signature "R. W. Emerson," were included in the Wakeman sale (Nos. 257–258 in American Art Association, Apr. 28 and 29, 1924). There were several noted scholars of the family of Walch. Christian Wilhelm Franz Walch, the church historian, had been a professor at Göttingen but had died long before William Emerson went there.

93. George Partridge Bradford, already mentioned as Emerson's friend, is listed with him as a candidate for the ministry in the Harvard catalogue for 1828–1829. Jenks, p. 24, shows that Bradford remained as usher at the Latin School only during 1828–1829.

94. That is, apparently, with his school. He wrote to William, Oct. 10 (MS owned by Dr. Haven Emerson), that he expected soon to have six or seven scholars and that he found teaching not so dreadful — a sober, straightforward, dull occupation.

95. MS in the possession of the Chicago Book & Art Auctions; ph. in CUL. This

Joseph E. of Malden) in answer to my request for information about Rev. Joseph E's parentage. He has accordingly inspected the records of Newbury, & sends me this minute from thence. " Joseph Emerson the son of Lt. John Emerson & Judith his wife, born 2^d^ March 1696." He adds — " Saml Emerson, son of Lt. John Emerson & Judith his wife born Nov 2, 1699." Now you say in your letter that Rev. J. E. shd. be born in 1699. This difference is not very considerable, & must not deprive my ancestor of the lieutenant for a father, unless we can find him a better. Then one of J. E's sons is named Bulkeley, (& I have a brother bearing the same name) and this makes it probable, he came of that line. So pray, my dear sir, do not let a few refractory impossibilities, if any such should appear, lose me the lieutenant. It sets all my pedigree adrift.

I have the happiness to inform you that my brother, concerning whose health you kindly expressed your interest, is very much better — both in body & mind, & we begin to indulge the strongest hopes of his entire recovery. — I hope to have the pleasure of renewing my acquaintance with my friends in Concord, in some of the revolutions of our ecclesiastical system, though candidates are comets, & describe very eccentric orbits. Meantime have the goodness to remember me to Mr & Mrs Breed, & family. Pray save me the Lieutenant also, & believe me your friend & servant

R. Waldo Emerson

To William Emerson, Cambridge, November 10, 1828 [96]

ID. H. Camb. Nov. 10 1828I

Dear W^m^

Have only time to say I received your letters & gladly. Sorry you do not know how to get bread. Shall possibly be able to send you monies. An unknown friend sent me thro' G. B. E. for Edward's use sixty dollars. I suppose, with scarce any data, it is Jona. Phillips.[97] But God is good & a portion of the Deity lives in men. Was the seed of the righteous ever forsaken? IIEdward is a great deal betterII We are devising how he shall leave Charlestown. IIII propose getting an engagement

continues, with fuller recognition of the comedy of ancestor-hunting, the subjects of Oct. 10, 1828. Joseph Emerson of Malden was actually the son of Edward Emerson of Newbury.

96. MS owned by HCL; ph. in CUL. Excerpts I–III are in Cabot, I, 142.

97. See Orville Dewey, *Autobiography*, 1884, pp. 50–52. G. B. E. was George Barrell Emerson. The second sentence following alludes to *Psalms*, 37:25.

to preach in y[e] country & taking him with me.[III] Perhaps not before last of November. I will speer y[t] question of y[rs] to Mr R. of Waltham.[98] Send me word of yr necessities. For I am going to spend upon Edw.'s debts & can instead upon yrs. R. W. E

To William Emerson, Cambridge, December 4, 1828 [99]

Cambridge, [I]4 Dec[I] 1828.

Dear William,

All that I hear of you is good but it has all the value that rarity can bestow. My mother lately bade me tell you that she had looked (I think) three months, with impatience for a letter from you, but had received none. I received & transmitted the letters containing cards which you sent. Had you not better send me half a dozen cards, without direction, to exercise my worldly wisdom in distribution? I am a great professor of that art, within these few months past, that I have meddled with Edward's matters. Did I not tell you that Peter C. Brooks [100] sent me $100.00 for him? I paid thereof $50. to Mrs Cook on E.'s note of $150. The other $50, I paid to Mr Francis, on his note of $100. & he gave me the note therefor. A generous gentleman. [II]Edward is quite well — it seems. He is going with me day after tomorrow [101] to Concord. N. H. to spend three Sundays & then returns to Concord Ms.[II] But to finish my detail of business for tis better since I act without counsel I should at least have a confidante & the better that he is learned in the law — I found that it was Mr Frothingham who had intercepted Bulkeleys bill at the Asylum & told them it shd. be paid otherwise. On receiving therefore this donation to Edw[d], I told Dr Wyman, they had done what they intended & I paid the debt which was $47.57. — something more than one quarter. I have since been to Chelmsford & saw Bulkeley in beautiful health & frame of mind. Mr Putnam [102] said he had earned his board for some time back, &, that for the first 6 weeks of his residence there, he shd charge him 6 dollars. There were some other matters making a dollar or two, &, I gladly gave him $10.00. You understand this is all the charge from the middle of

98. Samuel Ripley.

99. MS owned by HCL; ph. in CUL. Excerpts I–II are in Cabot, I, 142; III is *ibid.*, I, 145.

100. Peter Chadron Brooks, merchant and philanthropist, was father-in-law of two friends of the Emersons — Edward Everett and Nathaniel L. Frothingham.

101. The MS *Autobiography* gives the date as Dec. 6.

102. Israel Putnam, mentioned frequently in later years; *cf.* especially two letters of Sept. 8, 1842.

July till the first of December, at least for board: something for clothes. I have furthermore settled fully with Charlotte Farnham [103] on Edw[ds] a/c & paid his interest to Mrs Cook; to Φ B K; [104] & settled Marshalls a/c — a note travelling with comp. int. Did I tell you one of those beautiful angels the ' unknown benefactors,' which are in the universe the correlative terms of the ' silent poor ' had given G. B. E. $50. to give me for E B E's behoof? This has enabled me to do as I have said. Edward will find himself on 1st Jan. '29 in much better fiscal state than in '28. — I also find it in my ledger (for I keep accounts) that in July & August I received from Mrs R. E. 21.50 pd. by you to her for R. B. E's use. I am myself meantime not the ower of any considerable debts excepting about $300 to Mr S. Ripley something of which, I hope to discharge in Feb. when its anniversary comes, not a penny to C. & H.[105] once dire initials! not a penny to Whitmarsh, & little to Hall — Now for my professional affairs. I have preached a good while at Mr Ware's. I was on no definite agreement as to time. It is well understood Mr Ware wd. shortly resign & go to Cambridge. I did not think it very delicate to hang on longer; if the parish was to be regarded as open for candidates I was monopolizing. So having spoken with Dr Ripley I told them I wd. come away at the end of November.[106] They made a fuss & sent me word that if they heard candidates there wd. be a division & therefore the best people in the society wanted me by all means to stay [107] I told them if there was a chance they wd like any body better than I, t'was a reason why I should leave them forthwith, for [III]if I am settled, I choose it should be on my own merits & not because I have kept a better man from being heard.[III] So I have left them. All this in confidence, about the committee coming to me, & Mr Ware's leaving. Why I should come away is in plain daylight. Now I have told you my whole story & my body is very well & I love you.

Waldo Emerson.[108]

103. Emerson's cousin, daughter of William Farnham and of Emerson's paternal aunt Hannah Bliss Emerson (see *Vital Records of Newburyport,* 1911, I, 135).

104. For Emerson's own recent election as an honorary member of Phi Beta Kappa — on Aug. 28, 1828 — see the *Boston Daily Advertiser,* Sept. 4, 1828.

105. Perhaps the Cummings & Hilliard of the letter of Oct. 8 and 10, 1827, where a Whitmarsh also appears.

106. Nov. 27, 1828, is the date given in the MS *Autobiography.*

107. Part of the letter " y " has been torn away with the seal, and there may have been a period.

108. In the space below the signature are some jottings of names, mostly abbreviated, and, apparently, sums of money. I am not certain that these are in Emerson's own hand.

To Charles Chauncy Emerson, Concord, New Hampshire, December 10, 1828 [109]

Concord N. H. Dec. 10 1828 ne la montrez vous pas.[110]

I have in my pocket, you varlet, an unopened letter for Edward, waiting his return from his walk. Dare you expect a gratuitous epistle from me? As I have a patch of time now between my promenade & my prandium, I will bountifully give you a little piece of one of the finest days that ever made a part of the felon December. Nothing but light & oxygen allowed in New Hampshire today. Wherefore my outward man is much refreshed & my inward man doth sympathize comfortably. We are living along with great decorum & ease — The legislature of this State are in session & we have the satisfaction of observing, as Edward says, quam parva sapientia regitur mundus. Edward has called on Mr Ezekiel Webster [111] who was not at home, but, as we are told, threatens him with a descent. I have made a most commendable collection of pithy sentiments within two days past upon one of the virtues which is now up for a speedy public examination and to this cause as usual I have subpoenaed a good deal of private history, & dragged 'the family' like so many Guatemozins [112] over the coals of my vituperations. The five brothers are my six militia men. I cook them up & shall cook in every form. I roast, broil, fry, & mince. I salt and I pepper them well. I make sugar candy of their virtues & if they have said a word against me, I cut them into sausages. So you had best walk with circumspection.

Much obliged to you for the Plutarch tis fine reading though I have seen most of this volume before in French.[113] I have not read a line yet in the German volume wh. I brought with me.[114] How goes on the

109. MS owned by RWEMA; ph. in CUL.

110. Why this admonition was added is difficult to conjecture unless Emerson, within a week of his engagement to Ellen Tucker, suspected that his letter, which is written in an unusually hilarious mood, betrayed too much enthusiasm.

111. Daniel Webster's brother.

112. That is, I suppose, as Guatemozin was tortured by the Spaniards.

113. Later letters, like the *Journals* and the essays, show that Plutarch's biographical and moral writings were prime favorites with Emerson.

114. Probably the Vol. III of *Goethe's Werke* which Emerson drew from the college library on Dec. 5 of this year (MS charge-book, HCL). Earlier letters give evidence of William Emerson's active interest in German writings, and doubtless the example of Edward Everett and others who had returned from German universities, as well as the considerable number of articles on German literature in the reviews of the day, helped to awaken in Emerson himself an interest that became much more active a decade later.

school? The whole object is attained when you have learned to make all your reading tell. When the youths come to regard you as an encyclopedia of all beautiful & valuable knowledge — & strike what key they will the instrument shall return music — &c &c & I should think you would read Beloes Herodotus unless you like the Greek better. The account of the fall of Croesus — the intercourse betwixt him & Cyrus in the Clio [115] is fine narrative for boys. Have you looked at Marcellus' life [116] that we talked of? I fancy when our school keeping epoch (which answers to the age of brass in univ. hist.) comes to an end we could make up "a Schoolmaster" among us that should beat Ascham's to consist of plans of government, cunning fetches of dignity & discipline, bon mots, stories, & so forth.

I have no abounding confidence in your discretion & trust more to your kind Daemon than to you when I hope you will keep or be kept in the golden mean neither going too much into company nor too little neither studying like a scholiast nor like a fop. But you may sit down & write me a letter & tell me what is new or pleasant or grave. What are those unhappy persons at Washington doing? for I read no papers, but you need not tell me, for I do not wish to know. I understood Mr Ripley to say he should be happy to see you at Waltham, Christmas day. But if you can dine with Winthrop [117] I should think you had better. I have nothing very surpassing in the pulpit way, and all your expectations are young falcons, sky high.

I have given you a longer letter than you deserve & must stop short. Give my respects [to y]our [118] kind host & hostess. Edward does not [th]ink it worth while to show me your letter for what cause I know not. But write away to your brother

Waldo.

115. *Herodotus,* tr. William Beloe, 2d American ed., 1828, I, 40–45.

116. Doubtless Plutarch's life of M. Claudius Marcellus.

117. For Robert C. Winthrop as Charles Emerson's college chum, see June 24, 1827. For the falcons of the following sentence, *cf.* Shakespeare, *II Henry VI,* II, i, and Matthew Prior, "To the Honourable Charles Montague," l. 21.

118. The bracketed letters here and in the following sentence were torn away from the context with the seal but remain intact and easily legible in the opposite margin.

To William Emerson, Cambridge, December 24, 1828 [119]

[I]Divinity Hall, Cambridge –
Dec. 24, 1828

My dear brother,

I have the happiness to inform you that I have been now for one week engaged to Ellen Louisa Tucker [120] a young lady who if you will trust[I] my account [II]is the fairest & best of her kind.[II] Not to drive you to skepticism by any extravagances, I will tell you a simple story. [III]She is the youngest daughter of the late Beza Tucker [121] a merchant of Boston[III] of whose children you may remember William Sewall was guardian. When we were at Roxbury they lived in the Sumner house on the Dedham turnpike. [IV]The mother has been now three or four years the wife of Col W. A. Kent of Concord, N. H. It is now just a year since I became acquainted with Ellen at that house – but I thought I had got over my blushes & wishes when now I determined to go into that dangerous neighborhood again on Edward's account. But the presumptuous man was overthrown by the eye & the ear & surrendered at discretion. He is now as happy as it is safe in life to be[IV] in the affection of the lady & the approbation of the friends. [V]She is 17 years old, & very beautiful by universal consent.[V] Her feelings are exceedingly delicate & noble – and I only want you to see her. Edward is very highly gratified.

I shall have time soon to say much more upon this matter and am [VI]your affectionate

Waldo [VI]E.

I am preparing today to go to Waltham & preach a Christmas sermon tomorrow Mother Grandfather & all will be there. I hope I am the first teller of my news & would have written it earlier if I had tho't it possible you cd. have known it indirectly –

119. MS owned by HCL; ph. in CUL. Excerpts I–VI are in Cabot, I, 143.

120. *Cf. Journals,* II, 255. Her picture is reproduced opposite p. 256. For the beginning of her acquaintance with Emerson, *cf.* a note on Dec. 31, 1827.

121. According to *Vital Records of Roxbury,* 1926, II, 652, he died May 16, 1820, aged 48 years. Other members of the family are named in the letter of July 12, 1871, to Thayer.

To Henry Ware, Jr., Cambridge, December 30, 1828 [122]

Rev. Henry Ware jr.
Brookline

Divinity Hall 30 Dec. 1828

Rev. & dear Sir

I am very grateful to you for your kind note which I received yesterday, & for the suggestions it contains. I have affected generally a mode of illustration rather bolder than the usage of our preaching warrants, on the principle that our religion is nothing limited or partial, but of universal application, & is interested in all that interests man. I can readily suppose I have erred in the way you mention, of failing to add to my positions the authority of scripture quotation — & am very much obliged to you for the particular improvement you have suggested, which I shall not fail to avail myself of, when I shall have occasion to repeat that sermon.

I shall always esteem it, Sir, the greatest kindness when you will be good enough to remark upon my performances, — as it is an object of serious ambition with me to make preaching as effectual an engine as I can —

The connexion which all good men hope to see formed between yourself & our School will give me room to expect this advantage.

I trust, Sir, your health will allow this connexion to take place, that your character & exertions will be spared to your country for many years, that this compensation in the course of Providence will be made to the community for the loss it suffers in the interruption of your services in the Church

With great respect & affection, Dear Sir, your friend & servt

R Waldo Emerson

122. MS owned by RWEMA; ph. in CUL. This is a copy in the hand of Cabot. His marginal note refers to a letter from Ware dated Apr. 15, 1829, which I have not seen, but which apparently shows that Ware had given warning against using irreverent or profane illustrations in sermons. It is clear from the present letter, at any rate, that Emerson had already shown in the pulpit some signs of the departure from orthodoxy which was to result ten years later in his address to the Divinity School and Ware's open censure. For Ware's prospective migration from the Second Church to the Harvard faculty and for the possibility that Emerson might succeed him as pastor, see Dec. 4, 1828.

1829

To George Adams Sampson, Cambridge, January 2, 1829[1]

Divinity Hall 2nd Jan.
1829

My dear Sir,

I have just received your kind note & the elegant & valuable volumes accompanying it. I am deeply obliged to you for the particular kindness you have shown me since I have had the happiness of your acquaintance, & now, for this new instance of it. I shall always set the highest value upon this mark of your goodwill to me, as I am grateful for your friendship & anxious to cultivate it.

Yours truly
R Waldo Emerson.

To Mary Moody Emerson, Boston, January 6, 1829

[Partly printed in Cabot, I, 147–148, and more fully, but not completely, in *Journals,* II, 258–260. Instead of the four lines of verse printed on p. 259 of the latter work Emerson actually wrote, " 'In every joy &c my heart shall find delight in praise or seek relief in prayer' " (typescript *Journals*). Mary Moody Emerson, Jan. 28 (1829), possibly refers to this letter, but more probably to another of some six days later, when she tells of her desire to hear of " this call " and of her pleasure in learning of it in his " speedy communication." Yet it is, of course, possible that Emerson had written her in advance of the official invitation, which was not voted till Jan. 11.]

1. MS owned by RWEMA; ph. in CUL. This is a copy in Cabot's hand. A note by the copyist describes the original (probably in 1883) as " in possession of Mr J. L. Bates, Bromfield St." Joseph L. Bates's address, according to *The Boston Directory* for 1883–1884, was on that street. Sampson, an active member of the Second Church during Emerson's years there and one of his closest friends, appears in several later letters.

To William Emerson, Boston, January 28, 1829 [2]

[I]Boston, 28 January, 1829

Dear William,[I]

I received a letter from you yesterday for which I am much obliged to you But [II]since I wrote before my beautiful friend has made me very sorry by being very ill & with that dangerous complaint which so often attacks the fairest in our stern climate.[3] She has raised blood a week ago[II] & I have been one of her nurses most unskilful but most interested & am writing my letter in her chamber. [III]Beauty has got better & so I am better[III] & now though in such a place I fear you will put no credit in my account, yet am I sorely tempted to give you her character. Well then she is perfectly simple though very elegant in her manners; then she has common sense; then she has imagination & knows the difference between good poetry & bad; then she makes fine verses herself, then she is good, — & has character enough to be religious. then she is beautiful, & finally I love her. If my story is short, it is true. [IV]I have abstained in much[IV] hesitation & [V]perplexity from giving any answer to the call at the Old North. thinking that perhaps the doctors might tell Ellen she ought to go away; & then —

But now that I have talked with Dr Jackson & talked with the committee men I believe next Sunday I shall say Yes.[V] As to going to New York in the Spring, I believe not. I shall probably be ordained the second or third week in March & until that time I must find supply for the pulpit which I do by exchanges.

I do not know that there is any chance of rescuing Edward from the Law nor do I know that it were desireable. If his talents look any way, it is that way. And his health certainly appears more firmly established than any one cd. have believed possible a year ago. It is strange. [VI]I wish you could see Ellen. Why can't you come to my ordination (if such thing shall be) & see the queen of Sheba & of me.[VI] You shall say as she said. —

2. MS owned by HCL; ph. in CUL. Excerpts I–IX are in Cabot, I, 144 and 145.

3. Many later letters tell of the vain struggle against tuberculosis through the two remaining years of her life. A letter of Jan. 22 (1829) from Charles Emerson to William (owned by Dr. Haven Emerson) seems to show that before he married her, Emerson knew she was doomed — that she was "too lovely to live long" — but believed that even if she died "tomorrow" it would be a blessing to have loved her. The epithet "queen of Sheba," applied to her in a later paragraph, is from *I Kings*, 10.

Charles is very well. In these times of tribulation I am living at house of T. W. Haskins Sumner St. Charles is very well & doing finely. Mother is very well & I am your affectionate brother

Waldo

I told Charles to enclose to you $5.00. It was because Hilliard & Brown paid themselves some time ago by transferring the balance of my debt to your account, & it was I believe a little more than that sum. When I can think of it I will find the exact account.

The vote at 2^d Church was ^VII 74 ^VII for me ^VIII out of 79 ^VIII total. 4 for Dr Follen; 1 for John Lothrop – that means S. K. L. ^IX Three given for Dr F were by one person holding 3 pews who declares himself no wise unfriendly to Mr E but wants to wait a little.[4] Every thing in reference to this call is in ye highest degree gratifying as far as a decided & strong good will can be so.^IX

To the Second Church and Society in Boston, Cambridge, January 30, 1829 [5]

To the Second Church & Society in Boston.

Cambridge, 30 January, 1829.

Christian brethren & friends,

I have received the communication transmitted to me by your committee inviting me to the office of junior pastor in your church & society. I accept the invitation.

4. The MS *Proprietors Records* for the meeting of Jan. 11, 1829 (owned by the Second Church), records exactly the same total vote for each candidate, but notes that there were four additional votes "given in blank." At the same meeting it was "*Voted* That the salary of the colleague Pastor be fixed at the sum of twelve hundred dollars per annum," payable quarter-yearly. But it was also provided that whenever the connection with Henry Ware, the senior pastor, should be dissolved, Emerson should be sole pastor at the full salary paid to Ware – $1,800. The same MS has, in the proceedings for the meeting of Feb. 1, 1829, an undated copy of the letter to Emerson inviting him to become colleague pastor. Abel Adams, John Ware, and George B. Emerson were among the members of the committee who signed this letter.

5. MS, now on deposit in the library of the Massachusetts Historical Society, owned by the Second Church, Boston; ph. in CUL. On Oct. 15, 1883, the *Boston Evening Transcript* printed what was announced as the text of the original letter, said to be in the possession of the Indianapolis Public Library. Neither the *Transcript* nor the *New-York Tribune* of the same day, which printed substantially the same version except the first part of the heading, gave a date line; but both furnished the er-

If my own feelings could have been consulted, I should have desired to postpone, at least, for several months, my entrance into this solemn office. I do not now approach it with any sanguine confidence in my abilities, or in my prospects. I come to you in weakness, and not in strength. In a short life, I have yet had abundant experience of the uncertainty of human hopes. I have learned the lesson of my utter dependency; and it is in a devout reliance upon other strength than my own, in a humble trust on God to sustain me, that I put forth my hand to his great work.

But, brethren, whilst I distrust my powers, I must speak firmly of my purposes. I well know what are the claims, on your part, to my best exertions, and I shall meet them, as far as in me lies, by a faithful performance of duty. I shun no labour. I shall do all that I can.

In approaching these duties, I am encouraged by the strong expression of confidence & goodwill, I have received from you. I am encouraged by the hope of enjoying the counsel and aid of the distinguished servant of God who has so long laboured among you. I look to the example of our Lord, in all my hopes of advancing the influence of his holy religion, and I implore the blessing of God upon this connexion to be formed between you and myself.

I am your affectionate friend & servant,

Ralph Waldo Emerson.

roneous information (perhaps responsible for the later misdating of this letter) that Emerson was chosen in Mar., 1829. In the *Boston Daily Advertiser* of Nov. 10, 1883, Dr. Francis H. Brown revealed the fact that the supposed original at Indianapolis was spurious and unreliable, and he printed the text of the last three sentences in the second paragraph from the original, which was then, as now, actually in the possession of the Second Church. The debate over the authenticity was widely heralded by the press, but the very corrupt Indianapolis version was the one which actually survived. The letter as printed under the erroneous date of March in *Uncollected Writings . . . by Ralph Waldo Emerson*, n.d. (c. 1912), pp. 200–201, is, with a few exceptions, the same as the *Transcript* version of Oct. 15, 1883, and is widely different from the text here printed in complete form for, I believe, the first time. In the text of *Uncollected Writings* there are eighteen important errors in single words or in whole phrases or sentences. For example, the " solemn office " of the original text appears as " solemn affair "; " In a short life, I have yet had abundant experience " is transformed into " In short, I have not yet had an abundant experience "; " I shun no labour " is omitted entirely; " servant of God " becomes " servant of the Lord "; and " your affectionate friend " is simply " your friend."

To William Emerson, Cambridge, February 2, 1829[6]

Cambridge. 3 Feb. 1829

Dear William,

I received a few days ago your letter to me & &[7] Edward — & now I remember — have already acknowledged them. Ellen is mending slowly & I am very much encouraged about her. Yesterday my answer of acceptance was read to Mr Ware's society & already we are plotting the things that concern an ordination. Edward is quite well & is in Boston this day. I have nothing earthly to say — not a feather stirs within my memory of matter to interest you. Mr Quincy is gone to Charlottesville & other colleges & will be inaugurated perhaps not before May. The vote was 66 of wh. 40 were for, 26 against him.[8] He came out to Camb. ye same afternoon to see ye Pres^{t}s house. People in Cam. glad on the whole since they could not hope for an Everett & good men generally quite satisfied — danger from Mr Q s irregular impetuosity — answered, that theres an immense vis inertiae in Drs Hedge Ware & Popkin & Mr Willard[9] who will not fail to be ballast when he shall begin to soar & scheme. Tis feared he will rout Mr Dabney & all the den & college house folk to build a marble Hall; that the Genius of the Mayoralty will expend itself in a reform of the whole system of goodies, & that Gammers Morse & Currier may have to sweat for it. & theres much more speculation I suppose if I had ear or you time. Mr Dane has given the college the profits of his Digest to found a law lectureship &

6. MS owned by HCL; ph. in CUL. Emerson started, apparently, to write Feb. 2, the correct date, but decided on 3 instead. That the letter was actually written on Feb. 2 is, however, satisfactorily proved by the statement that "Yesterday my answer of acceptance was read to Mr Ware's society . . ." Emerson could hardly have been mistaken in his recollection that the day his letter was read was "Yesterday." It happens that Sunday, the day when the reading before the society would naturally have occurred, was Feb. 1; and the MS *Proprietors Records* (already referred to), p. 107, under date of Sunday, Feb. 1, 1829, shows that "the answer of Mr. Ralph Waldo Emerson" was "read to the Society this afternoon, from the Pulpit, by Mr. Hedge."

7. Emerson first wrote "your letter & Edwards." Then he inserted "to me & to"; then he struck out the "to" but failed to cancel the "&" preceding it. The acknowledgment referred to is doubtless that in the letter of Jan. 28, 1829.

8. The vote for Quincy, earlier "the Genius of the Mayoralty," was reported as given here in the *Boston Daily Advertiser,* Jan. 30, 1829. The *Boston Courier,* Feb. 4, says he left a day or two before to visit the "University of Charlotteville, Vir." and other principal colleges. He was inaugurated on June 2 (*ibid.,* June 3, 1829).

9. All the persons named here were officers of Harvard and are listed in the catalogues. But I have not identified the Morse and Currier mentioned below.

himself nominated Judge Story for the first lecturer. The Christian Examiner is forthwith to be changed into a Quarterly book as Mr Norton says 'to be of a very high character.' Dr Channing, Dr Follen, Mr Norton, Mr Nathan Hale, Dr John Ware Mr Palfrey & others to give their gratuitous aid. Dr C. is preparing an article on Fenelon. Dr F. on Ecclesiastical history, I believe.[10] This last has just commenced a course of lectures on history to y[e] undergraduates. You understand he is teacher of hist. now & has to all men's view the reversion of y[e] McLean Professorship when it cometh. Young men put up their lips & talk of native genius [11] I hope I have told you some news. Mr Ware is not expected to remain senior pastor more y[n] a few months — so I am to look for no efficient aid from him. Mr S. Higginson y[e] bearer is son of S. H. of Cambridge. In all love & honour yours.

Waldo —

To William Emerson, Cambridge, February 2? 1829 [12]

Cambridge 3 Feb. 1829 —

Dear William,

I am happy to introduce to your acquaintance, Mr Stephen Higginson, jr. of Boston, who comes to New York to establish himself in business as a merchant. His name & his family are well known to you — and I shall begin to have some hopes of your poor town of N. York, when so many of our good men go there.

Yours affectionately

Waldo Emerson.

10. *The Christian Examiner* did not become a quarterly at this time, but it did commence a new series in Mar., 1829. According to Cushing, Charles Follen's first contribution was "On the Future State of Man," not published till Jan., 1830. For Channing's article on Fénelon, see Apr. 25, 1829.

11. Follen was a native of Germany and had lived in several European countries.

12. MS owned by Mr. Edward Waldo Forbes; ph. in CUL. The subject matter seems to indicate that this letter was written on the same day as the letter just preceding, wrongly dated Feb. 3. *Longworth's American Almanac* for 1829–1830 shows that Stephen Higginson, Jr., had become by that time a member of the New York firm of George & Stephen Higginson, merchants.

To William Emerson, Cambridge? February 20, 1829 [13]

[I]20 Feb. 1829[I]

Dear William

Very well but casting many a lingering look at my chamber as the execution day approaches. — [II]Ellen is mending day by day[II] therefor I thank Heaven. She rides out every day. [III]Twould take more time than I can spare to tell how excellent a piece of work [14] she is.[III] Mr Ripley of W. preaches my sermon, Dr R. the Charge Mr Frothingham y[e] right hand Mr Parkman y[e] Ord[g] Prayer, Upham & Palfrey perhaps the etc. 11th of March [15] Mr Samson a very good man & good friend of mine in y[t] society is going to take a house some where in the Hyperborean End of y[e] city in order to take me to board. Shall be happy to see you, sir. Come & take a bed & stay a twelvemonth Did you ever read Byron's Island? A beautiful poem when you have not a better. But I dearly love Geo. Herbert's Poems.[16]

Edw[d] well & Charles & all

Goodbye I am yours,

Waldo E.

To Edward Bliss Emerson, Cambridge? February? *c.* 25? 1829

[Edward Emerson, Feb. 27, 1829, acknowledges this letter and sends a message from Ezra Ripley which seems to be a reply to a passage in it.]

To Edward Bliss Emerson? Cambridge? March 3, 1829

[Edward Emerson, Mar. 4, 1829, mentions "yours of yesterday." It is possible that this was to some other member of the family.]

13. MS owned by HCL; ph. in CUL. Excerpts I–III are in Cabot, I, 144; the last sentence printed there is not in the original.

14. Perhaps Emerson vaguely recalled the similar phrase in *Hamlet,* II, ii; or *The Taming of the Shrew,* I, i.

15. The minutes of the council which ordained Emerson on Mar. 11, 1829 (MS owned by the Second Church), show the program as approved by the council included all parts mentioned in the present letter except Palfrey's. The printed copy of *Order of Services at the Ordination of Mr Ralph Waldo Emerson* owned by the Second Church does not name the speakers.

16. Apparently the first definitely dated mention by Emerson of poems which remained favorites long enough to occupy a prominent place in *Parnassus.* But W. H. Furness, Feb. 15, 1844 (*Records of a Lifelong Friendship,* ed. Horace Howard Furness, 1910), tells of finding "in an old commonplace book" some lines from George Herbert "in your handwriting."

To William Emerson, Cambridge, March 6, 1829 [17]

Divinity Hall 6 March 1829

Dear William,

Tis very strange you should never write me. I have written I shd. think three letters to you since I had one. The last I sent was by Stephen Higginson [18] which I hope you received.

Why can't you come to my ordination next Wednesday There shd. you see ye Lady mother, & Edward [19] comes Grandfathers *alligator,* as the phrase is, & Charles comes on his own account & you shd. be right welcome Hast no curiosity to see the Beauty of the world? [20] the diamond idea that illuminates my retirements & rejoices my intercourse or if that is poor English — makes my society. Now the sentence is straight. Alas for your indifferency. Ye had better come, Khan, to know what there is in the world & that ye may not look low your nain sell. But then my dear brother the time is really nigh when I am to leave forever the delicious sloth of an accustomed life & go work. I cast many a lingering look around the walls of my chamber. Very pleasant have they been

17. MS owned by HCL; ph. in CUL.

18. See the letters of Feb. 2 and Feb. 2? 1829.

19. Edward Emerson to William (owned by Dr. Haven Emerson):

"11 March. — 1829.

"Dear Wm.

"I am again at leisure in the evening after the interesting solemnity of Waldo's ordination. I have seldom if ever been more moved by any services of any sort. — The candidate or pastor elect was so near & dear, his appearance so elegant & dignified, his senior brethren around him so successful in their performances, & 3 or 4 so well known to us all — Dr & Mr R. — Mr F. & Mr Upham, — & indeed Dr Pierce & Mr Parkman not strangers & Mr Gannet frequently heard & seen — the allusions so honourable & so touching to our lamented father, — & the very nature itself of the occasion one of the most truly important & holy in the universe of events on our little ball, all conspired alternately to elevate or to humble the mind. — After the ordination, we dined very pleasantly, together at four long tables in the Hancock-School-house hall. — Grandfather appears yet nobler in old age, like an oak that gathers in venerableness what it loses in luxuriance. His charge, which you will, doubtless, soon see printed, must have attracted general commendation. He presided also in the Council with great propriety & prayed with eloquence. — Mother has just returned from taking tea with her daughter intended, whose recovery seems progressive — She sends again her love, saying that she has enjoyed a great deal to day, & mentions particularly the fervor of the prayers. Waldo also considered Mr Parkman's ordaining prayer as remarkably excellent. — And now, Good-bye,

"says your brother

"Edward. — "

20. Apparently Emerson was thinking again of *Hamlet,* II, ii.

unto me. I do not know certainly where I am to live. I have been disappointed by an unexpected difficulty in my plans of boarding with Mr Samson of the Second Church & shall probably spend my first month at his house in North Allen St & afterwards board with Mr Abel Adams,[21] a good man, a merchant belonging to the society.

I have not yet written the first of my two occasional introductory discourses in which I am to unfold my views of a Christian ministers duty & of the duties (few certainly & susceptible of very brief statement) of the people to their pastor. I am only taking breath in this horrible scrawl & shall go back to my work again. Mr Ware is not so well & designs directly after my settlement to sail for Charleston S. C. & avoid the Boston spring winds.[22]

It wd. be very gratifying to many of your friends in N. England & mainly to me to know very explicitly what you are doing & how you live. Whether you are rolling in riches or whether like Dr Johnson you have ceased to sleep in a bed finding the nocturnal patrole of the street more economical. I shd. be glad then to learn what you read & what you write -- whether you, like the black peaceful people of Divinity Hall, are intoxicated with "The Disowned" or have changed your politics & your manners & are drinking brandy to the health of the President Ginral.[23] Please to r[e]member[24] that all the particulars that respect the day & night of the great Cham wd. be read with eager interest by his affectionate brother,

Waldo E.

Another letter that I sent — I believe it was another — contained a letter to you from Aunt Mary. Have you got that. Goodbye

21. *The Boston Directory* of 1829 states that Emerson "boards at Adams's, Chardon," and describes Abel Adams as a merchant at Central Wharf. The letter of Sept. 22, 1867, recalls the first meeting with this friend, in 1828, and his long series of kindnesses in later years. The MS *Treasurers Receipt Book* for 1805–1842 (owned by the Second Church) shows that Adams became treasurer of the Second Church in 1829. But for many years after Emerson's connection with the Second Church ceased, he remained a staunch friend, tireless in giving advice on financial matters and taking responsibility for petty business transactions off the shoulders of his former pastor. A considerable number of letters to Adams are printed in these volumes.

22. Ware went to Europe instead. *Cf.* Mar. 22 and 23 following.

23. Jackson had just succeeded John Quincy Adams in office.

24. The word is partly covered by the wax seal.

To Ezra Ripley, Boston, March 22 and 23, 1829[25]

Boston, Sunday Evg.
22 March, 1829

My dear Grandfather,

I have to acknowledge the receipt of two letters in the past week, from you & to thank you for both. The letter which Phebe carried to you from the Committee, was not to be presented until Uncle Ripley had given his answer. Mother, to whom I gave it was to tell you this, but as she did not go, she sent it without its proviso. Now Mr Ripley has refused to print his sermon, for which I am sorry, & so are a good many, & the more so, that it will deprive us of the Charge. Mr Frothingham says Mr R. does not consult his laurels in refusing to publish. — I shall state to the Committee when they receive your answer, the account of the slight mistake.

I have been exceedingly busy the last week in making my introductory visits in the parish. It is a new labour & I feel it in every bone of my body. I have made somewhat more than fifty pastoral visits and am yet but in the ends & frontiers of my society.

This day I have preached at home all day & married a couple & baptized a child & assisted in the administration of the supper. I fear nothing now except the preparation of sermons. The prospect of one each week, for an indefinite time to come is almost terrifick.

Mr Ware has been regularly appointed Professor by the Corporation[26] & his salary voted to begin from last Saturday. [The][27] new income added to his present one, will enable him to comply with the wishes of his friends & go to England instead of Charleston, during the summer. he has to spare. His connexion with the Church will not probably, last beyond July.[28] In every house which I enter I find the same voice of love & commendation of the virtues of this excellent man.

25. MS owned by Professor James B. Thayer; ph. in CUL. Samuel Ripley (the " Uncle Ripley " of this letter) had preached the ordination sermon on the 11th of March, and Dr. Ripley had given " the Charge " (*cf.* Feb. 20, 1829). Phebe was, perhaps, Phebe Ripley Haskins, Emerson's cousin, who had married John Chamberlain in 1824 (*The Ipswich Emersons,* pp. 180 and 446).

26. Of Harvard.

27. Mutilated by the seal. Parts of some letters still show, but the reading is conjectural. The word may have been " His " or " This."

28. Ware's salary as pastor actually continued till July 1, 1829, when Emerson's was increased to $1800; and Ware's resignation was formally accepted on Sept. 26, 1830 (MS *Proprietors Records,* owned by the Second Church).

I hope you do not find yourself at all injured by your visit to the city. It was a welcome one I believe to all who saw you.

Very affectionately & respectfully
Your grandson
Waldo Emerson.

Monday

Mother & Edward whom I have seen this morning are still waiting & do not know how many days longer [29]

To William Emerson, Boston, April 10, 1829 [30]

Boston 10 April 1829

My dear brother,

I have received this morng. your letter containing one to Mother one to R. H & one Rev W. G.[31] and it occurs to me that you may not have been informed of Uncle Ralphs disasters. He stopped payment about a fortnight ago & will not I am told easily get out of his trouble, tho' his conduct I believe is honourable.

Now perhaps you know this & perhaps not. I should not have troubled you with this letter but that I tho't from the look of your letters you were begging off from R. H. & paying Greenough which in this present seemed so unfit that I tho't I wd. keep them in my hands a day or two for further orders. I am sorry I am no richer at this time having abundant use for two or three hundred dollars more than I have got. My income is 300 pr. quarter but before I was settled I gave away so many Sundays that my debts grew large & old & bold & undeniable. Still I would rather pay $12 to R. H. than have it withheld from him. I count among my debts to be pd. as soon as I can, the books. — After July 1 I shall have $1800 for $1200 & hope to grow easier in my worldly condition. but Charles is looking to me for support when he gives up his School, as he may possibly after 6 months. —

I was very sorry to learn from Chas that Mrs N.[32] had left town when he called on Friday or Saturday as I was meditating an immediate call but supposed she wd. be in town some time. My parish visits — they

29. The remainder of p. 3 is filled by a brief letter from Edward Emerson to Dr. Ripley.

30. MS owned by HCL; ph. in CUL.

31. Apparently his uncles Ralph Haskins and William Greenough, both mentioned below. For Greenough, *cf.* a note on Mar. 14, 1838.

32. Charles Emerson wrote to William on Apr. 12 following (MS owned by Dr. Haven Emerson) of this call upon " Mrs. Newell."

cannot be numbered or ended. I am, as Charles says, a pelican in the wilderness.

Please present my respects to Mrs Newell & tell her I am sorry to have lost the opportunity of renewing my acquaintance with her & thanking her for her ancient hospitality when I was in N. Y.

Yours affectionately

Waldo E.

Ellen is pretty well. Miss Goodridge [33] visited her today for the last time to finish her miniature wherewith I shall shortly be enriched Mother is well Edw recovering his voice George B & Charles C & all the Es a[re][34] well as need be. Goodbye – I say I will keep both letters till I hear from you.

To Edward Bliss Emerson? Boston? April *c.* 18, 1829

[Edward Emerson to William, Apr. 19, 1829 (owned by Dr. Haven Emerson): "Letters came today from Waldo & Charles, saying that Miss E. was doing well . . ."]

To William Emerson, Boston, April 25, 1829 [35]

Boston, 25 April, 1829.

Dear William

I have received a good many envelopes from you & one or two letters (among enclosed letters I have rec^{d} & forwarded the money letter to R. H. & have one for Aunt Mary) I hear today from Derby [36] that you are going into a connexion with Mr Sullivan.[37] You say nothing of it. I hope you are gratified with it & Derby seemed to think it might be very desireable. I suppose I must not say timeo Danaos et dona ferentes [38] If it is pleasant I give you joy. If it is not, why still

33. *The Boston Directory* of 1829 lists Sarah Goodridge, "miniature painter." The miniature of Ellen here referred to may be the same which is reproduced in *Journals,* II, opposite p. 256, and described, *ibid.,* II, xvii, as "*From a miniature, painted in 1829; artist unknown.*" It was apparently the same Miss Goodridge who painted the miniature of Emerson himself described by F. B. Sanborn, "The Portraits of Emerson," *New England Magazine,* n.s., XV, 453.

34. Torn away with the seal; possibly the word was "as" instead of "are."

35. MS owned by HCL; ph. in CUL.

36. Possibly Elias Hasket Derby, listed as a lawyer in *The Boston Directory* of 1829. There was, however, an Ezekiel Hersey Derby who was William Emerson's classmate at college.

37. According to *Longworth's American Almanac* for 1829–1830, a George Sullivan was a lawyer at the same address with William Emerson; but they were not listed as partners.

38. *Aeneid,* II, 49.

light is sown for the righteous,[39] & I give you joy – of yourself; as a stoic might, & a Christian shall, – let fortune (which does not exist & yet is a fitter word than Providence which does) ordain what it may. I am coming to the end of my epigrams presently. I am labouring abundantly in my vocation [40] so have little time for study of books less for writing of letters Two or three hours of the morng. I spend in writing all the afternoons, saving contingences, in visiting. I hardly expect to preach at home more than half the time for a long while to come. But tis Saturday afternoon & my duties are dogging my kibe you know & so goodbye. Yours affectionately

Waldo.

Ellen is getting well I hope. Next week herself & mother & sisters go a journey – & afterwards home to Concord N. H. leaving me a forlorn bachelor. Oh she is fairest, virtuousest, discreetest best.[41] Can you not find her a sister?

If you have seen the New Series Examiner – Mr Channing you know wrote the Fenelon Article in the Examiner Norton the Pollok & the Hemans – Dewey the diffusion of knowledge Greenwood the Mont blanc & Walker the Controversy [42]

39. *Psalms,* 97:11.

40. There are several accounts of Emerson as preacher written about this time by his brothers (MSS owned by Dr. Haven Emerson). Charles wrote to William on Apr. 12 (1829): "Waldo grows more & more eloquent, every Sunday. He visits his people without any other guide or introduction, than his own knowledge of the street wherein they live. And thus he has sometimes made long calls, kindly & affectionate on families who had no other claim to his attentions, than that of bearing the same name with his parishioners." And Edward wrote to William on May 3 of the same year: "If God wills that I should be well, I hope by industry to live in Boston, & hear the sermons which if they 'freeze to ice' the preacher have I think no such congealing effect on his audience; & which perhaps demand the time & labor of Waldo to such an extent as may make him less frequently your correspondent & less apparently fraternal or ardent in his affection than when unordained & unengaged." In a letter dated May 10 and 15 following, Edward wrote again to William, telling of the young preacher's part in an ordination on the 14th, "where R. Waldo gave a good right hand of fellowship which Grand father thought perfect." William H. Sanger and Frank E. Bridgman, *A Manual for the Use of the General Court,* Boston, 1931, pp. 262 and 265, show that Emerson also served as chaplain of the state senate in 1829 and of the house in 1832. The date of his election as chaplain of the senate is given in the MS *Autobiography* as June, 1829. *Cf.* a note on May 27, 1830.

41. *Paradise Lost,* VIII, 550.

42. William Ellery Channing, Andrews Norton, Orville Dewey, Francis W. P. Greenwood, and James Walker were the anonymous authors of these articles in *The Christian Examiner* for Mar., 1829 (*cf.* Cushing's *Index*). This paragraph stands alone on the manuscript quite separate from the earlier part of the letter.

To William Emerson, Boston, May 20, 1829 [43]

Boston 20 May

Dear William

I wont let Charles go [44] without saying my Salam to you in the wilderness especially as my nearest dearest engrossing relation has fled fled like the Phenix bird. I shd like to have you see her & if I have sufficient self denial will let Charles have her miniature for you to see; & the rather may I miss it for a week, because tis a very imperfect copy of her face, & is so judged by those who know her much less nearly than I, & yet have seen her much — Still tis a copy, & so wd. be better to you than none at all —

I cannot promise myself the pleasure of seeing you very soon unless you ride on some ray of business to Boston as Tuckers ghosts did ride on rays.[45] Still the steamboat may be more convenient & glad shd. I be to house you here, & my bed is wide, & our board is good, & my keepers kindest. & I shd like to preach some sermons to you & to be instructed in your entire manner of life & I

am yours faithfully

Waldo.

To Charles Chauncy Emerson, Concord, New Hampshire, June 19, 1829 [46]

Concord N. H 19 June

Dear Charles,

Yesterday Ellen was taken sick in the old way, — very suddenly, & suffered in the night great distress, but the quantity of blood raised has not been much & some symptoms her mother says are much

43. MS owned by HCL; ph. in CUL. The year is clearly 1829.

44. Charles Emerson, New York, May 24 (1829), tells of his journey from Boston, and in his letter to William, June 3 following (owned by Dr. Haven Emerson), recalls his visit in New York and tells of his return home by way of the Hudson.

45. *Cf.* Jan. 1, 1828.

46. MS owned by RWEMA; ph. in CUL. The year is obviously 1829. The visit to Concord, N. H., at this time is mentioned in two letters (owned by Dr. Haven Emerson). Charles Emerson wrote to William, June 15 (1829): " Waldo goes to Concord N. H. tomorrow to see the seasons, he says; (he preached yesterday a sermon about the beauty of the seasons & the lessons to be learned of them) but we know there are fairer flowers than those of the field." Edward wrote to William on July 2 of the same year that " Waldo returned from Conc[d] N. H. last Monday eve[g] leaving E. L. T. on recovery."

less unfavorable than at former times – but tis bad enough at the best & has wonderfully changed my visit. I was perfectly happy now I am watching & fearing & pitied. – We have no physicians here in whom any kind of confidence can be reposed & so I write today to Dr Jackson a letter which will come in the same mail with this & if he is not in town please ask James J. to forward it to him at once.

I may write to Mr Adams [47] tomorrow or next day but please go there & tell him I am disappointed once more but rejoiced that since this was ordained I am here at the time. It wd have been unspeakable trouble to me if I had been in Boston. Ellen has an angel's soul & tho very skeptical about the length of her own life hath a faith as clear & strong as those do that have Gods kingdom within them.

The moment the queen of me gets relief from one of her ill turns her spirits return also & she is playful & social as ever tho' her sociability is imprisoned in whispers. And now I write in her room & she sends you her love & I am yours affectionately

Waldo E.

Is Edward in town Tell him to be in no hurry to return for Mr Thomas [48] will not probably go down till Thursday of next week. & tell him human happiness is very unstable & I am sorry I have no better letter to send you.

To James Jackson, Concord, New Hampshire, June 19, 1829

[Mentioned in the letter of the same date to Charles Emerson. Edward Emerson, June 22, 1829, says he called on Dr. Jackson that day and found him about to answer this letter.]

To Abel Adams, Concord, New Hampshire, June *c.* 21, 1829

[Mentioned in advance in June 19, 1829, to Charles Emerson. Edward, June 22, 1829, speaks of it as a letter of that morning. Probably it had been sent from New Hampshire the day before it was received in Boston.]

To Henry Ware, Jr., Boston? June? 30? 1829 [49]

. . . I have succeeded in finding out most of my family . . . I have baptized two children privately after some remonstrances . . . I board with Mr Adams . . .

47. See June *c.* 21, 1829.
48. Probably the Moses Thomas mentioned in the letter of Oct. 10, 1828.
49. MS owned by RWEMA; ph. in CUL. This is a fragmentary copy in the hand

To Henry Ware, Jr., Boston? July 1, 1829[50]

1 July, 1829. . . . . I was very grateful for your kind letter & its suggestions. One thing is suggested that never occurred to me & would give me great uneasiness if it is well-founded. I mean that the idea sh'd be given to my audience that I did not look to the Scriptures with the same respect as others. I shall certainly take great pains to remove any such impression. I consider them as the true record of the Revelation which established what was almost all we wanted to know, namely the Immortality of the Soul – & then, what was of infinite importance after that was settled, the being & character of God. With the revelation, we have very strong evidence of this immortality in Nat. Religion but without it very insufficient. I look at this book as of divine authority & sh'd lose a great deal more that I [ ] spare, if I lost this faith. All I meant [ ] sermon was to say that my views of a preacher's duties were very high & he sh'd be ashamed of so shabby a discharge of them as who has not witnessed in numberless written & printed sermons that are nothing but a patch-work of unchosen texts. . . .

To Mary Moody Emerson, Boston? July? *c.* 15? 1829

[Mary Moody Emerson, endorsed July, 1829, says she has just read her nephew's letter and that her craving for Kantism is satisfied for the day. She goes on to discuss philosophical questions which must have been raised in his letter.]

To William Emerson, Boston? July 18? 1829[51]

Dear William I have great pleasure in asserting my rights of connexion to the lawyer albeit late, far between. I am going to Concord N H next week if I can steal away, for Ellen says I mt. leave my ninety &

of Cabot, who records that the postmark was dated July 1, 1829, but gives no place. For Emerson's pastoral activities, *cf.* Apr. 25, 1829, and for Abel Adams, Mar. 6 of the same year. A bracketed interpolation by Cabot indicates that the second passage omitted was a chronicle of "deaths &c." in the Second Church.

50. MS owned by RWEMA; ph. in CUL. This is an incomplete copy in Cabot's hand. The brackets presumably indicate imperfections or, less probably, illegible passages in the original MS. Like Dec. 30, 1828, this letter shows Ware's anxiety about Emerson's heretical tendencies but also shows that the young pastor still had a long way to go before he could write *Nature*.

51. MS owned by HCL; ph. in CUL. This undated note follows, on the same sheet, a letter from Charles Emerson to William dated "Saturday Morng." The endorsed date, July 18, 1829, is in all probability correct for at least Charles's letter, as July 18 fell on Saturday in 1829.

nine & come & h[unt][52] my stray sheep in ye wilderness.[53] Wo is me my [bro]ther that sickness & sorrow steal into the fold of this world & prey on what is preciousest. I hope you will come & see you [54] I will promise you bed & board in Chardon St. as long as you will stay with Yrs affectionately

Waldo E.

To Mary Moody Emerson, Boston? July 24, 1829

[Mary Moody Emerson, Oct. 7 (1829), says she received the trunk containing "yours of July 24," which was, apparently, a sketch of his intellectual development.]

To William Emerson, Boston? July 25? and 27? 1829 [55]

Charles is very well and is rejoicing like a strong man to run the race [56] of distinction y^t he opens upon or y^t opens upon him next Sept in your land of barren glories — ye Law. Much good may it do you & the country. But we are fallen on evil days.[57] That word Country must make us blush or lament.[58] Up heart [59] however the word now is to hope against hope. And every man has some influence & mothers four sons may lift off some ounce of opprobrium or sow a good seed. And always I am you[r][60]

Affectionate brother

Waldo.

Have just got a letter for mother & glad to hear that you mean to come in August [61] Do not fail. Tis Monday Morng. Last Saturday Chas & I went to Canterbury — tied our horse at ye old barn & played gipsy in

52. Or possibly "help." The brackets here and in the following sentence inclose portions of words mutilated by the seal.

53. *Luke,* 15:4, but considerably altered.

54. Both this unusual error and the brevity of the note are perhaps evidences of the writer's haste.

55. MS owned by HCL; ph. in CUL. These paragraphs, written on a half sheet, with the address to William Emerson and the endorsement "R. Waldo Emerson July 25/29," were probably the last part of a letter of which the earlier section has been torn away and lost. If the first part was dated July 25, as the endorsement suggests, the final paragraph written on "Monday Morng." belongs to July 27.

56. *Psalms,* 19:5.

57. *Paradise Lost,* VII, 25.

58. Emerson more than once records his dislike for Jackson.

59. Probably from the "sursum corda" of the mass.

60. The word was mutilated by the opening of the seal.

61. *Cf.* the letter of July 31, 1829.

all the old pastures identified y[e] old localities & eat up y[e] sons or great grandsons of y[e] old berries. I hope to live there again yet.

To Mary Moody Emerson, Boston, July 31, 1829

[MS owned by RWEMA; ph. in CUL. Printed in F. B. Sanborn, "A Concord Note-book Sixth Paper The Women of Concord – I," *The Critic,* XLVIII, 159 (Feb., 1906); reprinted in Sanborn, *Recollections,* II, 373–374. No year was given by Emerson; but 1829, the date supplied by another hand, is clearly correct. The statement that "Ellen writes me every other day" is one of many evidences that Emerson must have written many letters to her, though, as I am informed by his heirs, none is known to be extant. There still exist a number of her letters to him, but they are not available to me and seem not to contain definite proof of the dates of his own. Mrs. Ward I. Gregg has kindly supplied extracts from the extant letters, belonging, apparently, to the period May 1 to Sept. 25, 1829, which seem to indicate letters written by Emerson about Apr. 28; May 1, 5, 11, 27; June 1, 7, 15; July 4, 22; Aug. 6, 22, 24, 29; and Sept. 24, together with a few more that may belong to the same period. In addition to these letters to Ellen Tucker, one of about July 4 to her mother, Margaret Tucker Kent, and one of about June 9 to a Mr. Thomas – probably Moses Thomas, the Unitarian minister – are mentioned in the extracts. All the dates are uncertain; and doubtless the record is incomplete even for this brief period, though Emerson spent parts of it at Concord, N. H.]

To Charles Chauncy Emerson, Canterbury, New Hampshire, August 7, 1829 [62]

Canterbury N. H. 7 Aug. 1829

My dear brother,

Here am I quietly seated at Deacon Winkleys [63] table among brothers & sisters of Shaking faith, and Ellinelli & her mother are upstairs writing also. – Ellen & I came hither in a chaise this morng. an easy ride of 12 miles from Concord. Her mother followed us an hour or two later in coach with our fair & reverend baggage. Ellen bore the ride beautifully & if tomorrow shd. prove fair & she continues as well we mean to go on to Meredith bridge – (or even possibly to Centre Harbor = Red Hill. Mother Winkley or Sister Winkley hath given

62. MS owned by RWEMA; ph. in CUL.

63. According to James O. Lyford, *History of the Town of Canterbury New Hampshire,* 1912, I, 355–356, Francis and Sarah Winkley were among the first signers of the Shaker covenant in that community (in 1796); and *Some Account of the Proceedings of the Legislature of New Hampshire in Relation to the People Called Shakers, in 1828,* p. 16, cites a Winkley as "one of the elders of the Society" at Canterbury.

Ellen & I a long & earnest sermon on the " beauty of virginity " & striven to dissuade us from our sinful purpose of " living after the way of manhood & of womanhood in the earth " but I parried her persuasion & her denunciation as best I might & insisted we were yoked together by Heaven to provoke each other to good works so long as we lived — This society is divided into three families & own about 2000 acres of land, and excepting a shrewd handful of male & female oligarchs are a set of clean, well disposed, dull, & incapable animals. One man I have talked with was very well read in the bible & talked very logically from the Scriptures literally taken, but was strangely ignorant for a Yankee about every thing beyond his daily & weekly errands in the country round. —

We shall govern ourselves in this present excursion wholly by Ellen's health & dispositions & return or proceed as very slight things may dictate. I shall write you presently again, & tell you where to send me tidings of yourself & my friends. Please carry my affectionate regards to Mr Adams & the family & tell them to be glad with me for so much health as Ellen has & I will tell them when she has more, which God grant may be very speedily. I do not expect now to be absent beyond next Sunday from the pulpit & yet I may.

Love to Mother & Edward when you see or write & pray keep Aunt Mary here till William comes and I am yours affectionately

Waldo E.

To Charles Chauncy Emerson, Centre Harbor, New Hampshire, August 10, 1829[64]

Centre Harbour 10 Aug. 1829
Monday Morng.

Dear Charles,

I cannot tell you until the ladies appear, precisely what are our plans for this day which must depend on Ellen's health. But on Saturday morning at 7 o'clock we left the Shakers & came thro' noble scenery 20 miles in 4 hours & dined & rested at Meredith Village. Late in the afternoon we we went up & down 5 miles more of perpendicular (almost) hills & and so reached this part of the Winnepisiogee lake (W. lake 25 miles long a spiderlegged thing only 6 miles wide where broadest) Red Hill is a fine mountain before our eyes so called from colour of ground & its ascent is 3 miles off. —

64. MS owned by RWEMA; ph. in CUL.

8 o'clk.

Ellen hath come down & is so well that we trot off toward Conway today, perhaps only to Tamworth. (Yesterday we went to Church at Meredith & heard Mr Porter [65] preach who knowing there was a heretic in the village wd not come near him & so kept the orthodoxy & the hospitality or charity of his pulpit both unimpeached. The morning sermon a very good one mais je crois que M. le pretre ne l'écrivit after noon not good & je crois que M. P. l'ecrivit. Oh Calumny. Ellen is sometimes smart, sometimes feeble, & hates to say, I am sick, almost as much as Edward. I doubt much, now that I am just 100 miles from home, whether I shall return next Sunday so hope you will retain a good man, & one that like Aaron " can speak well " [66] and if it is necessary as may be it will be retain him unconditionally but if he have no other field for his work on the provision that may be I shall be at home myself. And so with kindest remembrances to Mr & Mrs Adams & Miss Charlotte & Abbynabby [67] & to Edward if in town I am your affectionate brother

Waldo E

Please write to Conway, N. H. that all is well or what may not be. as quick as you can & I will take order to find the letter there or transmit it to my whereabout. We are going off immediately. — I shall write Mr Adams next.[68] —

To Abel Adams, Conway, New Hampshire, August 11, 1829 [69]

Conway N. H. 11 Aug. 1829
Tuesday Mor^ng^.

My dear Sir,

Here we are 30 miles from the Notch of the White Hills [70] having been soundly jounced over 30 miles of pine plain & gridiron

65. For the Rev. Reuben Porter, who had been installed as preacher in the Congregational church of Centre Harbor and Meredith on Jan. 1, 1829, see Robert F. Lawrence, *The New Hampshire Churches,* 1856, pp. 501–502.

66. *Exodus,* 4:14.

67. Abby Larkin Adams and her adoptive parents, Abel and Abby Adams, whom she called her uncle and aunt, appear frequently in later letters. See especially a note on Dec. 2, 1833.

68. See Aug. 11, 1829.

69. MS owned by RWEMA; ph. in CUL. The superscription is to Adams, at Boston.

70. That is, Crawford Notch.

bridge & steep & stony hill thro much wind & some shower — yesterday. Yet Ellen bore it all very well & really looks better this morning though I trembled many a time yesterday lest she shd. suffer serious injury from the roughness of the road. A pretty chill air these mountains have. A good fire would be no bad thing this August morning. Mt. Washington has not taken off his morning cap of clouds & I am afraid will not show us his bald head this day. We are sitting in Mr Abbot's very comfortable hotel [71] in council upon the question whether t'were best to make one more stage toward the hills & go to Mrs Hall's in Bartlett 14 mls. hence — or turn & go east to Fryeburgh 8 mls. off, but one of those points will probably be the limit of our outward journey. At any rate I see no chance of my being at home next Sunday & wish Charles mt. be able to secure Mr Furness's services. The journey is excellent for Ellen & so much better than her nurse & little hot chamber at home that I feel it to be very important to use such favorable circumstances as now we have — and I extend my absence with the less hesitation, that I do not expect to be absent in the fall for any island expedition.

I hope nothing adverse has happened in your family or among our friends but have had no opportunity of hearing from you.

Will you have the goodness to enclose me twenty dollars in a newspaper or book & give it to *Huntington,* who goes up to Concord on Tuesday Thursday & Saturday & tell him to leave it carefully at Col Kents house to wait my coming. —

10' o'clock — And now we propose to set off for the aforesaid Mrs Halls in the hope of getting a little nearer view of these solemn looking highlands & tiring Ellen into another good night's rest. & so with kind remembrances to all the house I am your friend

Waldo E. —

To William Emerson, Hanover, New Hampshire, August 16, 1829 [72]

Hanover N. H. 16 Aug. 1829

Dear William,

It is the most serious regret I have on this pleasant & prospered ride that I am absent from home when you propose to be there. I promise myself to be in Boston on Wednesday night if we are

71. Apparently Capt. Nathaniel Abbott's Conway House (*cf. The Granite Monthly,* XXXIX, 221: July, 1907).

72. MS owned by HCL; ph. in CUL.

not stopped in our homeward journey on Monday & Tuesday by rain or other accident. We have been to Bartlett N. H. thence I ran over to the Notch & spent a night in the throat of the Mountain at Crawfords; from Bartlett we returned to Centre Harbor thence came to Plymouth, a fine town; thence to Orford on the Connecticutt, & so to Dartmouth College, where we shall spend Sabbath & then to Concord. By all this riding Ellen has been very much benefitted so that we had no heart to go home sooner — (the very best thing that she cd. do wd. be to ride about in the self same way as long as the season wd let her.) I cannot well be absent from my duties so long as this but this absence was a duty of impossible omission. I hope you have been lodged in mine own chamber else shd I mourn much. It was wholly uncertain when we set out how far we shd go, & whether the first stage of 12 miles to Shakers village wd. not be the end of the journey so very delicate was Ellen's health. It did not occur to me therefore to look so far ahead as to August 15th, & leave it in charge to my kind friend Mr Adams to receive you as me, which however I trust he has done

Well, in the second place, I am very sorry you have not seen & are not likely to see the queen of me — if you can spare 3 days to go to Concord N. H. she promises you full leave to look at her — a sight I wd go much farther to see strange if you will not leap at the privelege.

Hanover is a very pretty village lying round a common Why do not all peoples build towns in the same way. The single-street villages are always dusty & the area form begets almost of necessity a greater attention to architecture. And in New Hampshire generally is a most Catonic desire that houses should be houses & not *seem* such.[73]

Hitherto I find no occasion upon the road to exercise my gift-public & shall not probably here, but dont dont go away till I see you for I cannot come to N. Y.

Yours affectionately

Waldo E.[74]

73. Possibly Emerson vaguely remembered a passage in Plutarch's life of Cato the Censor, where Cato's liking for simple country life is recorded; but I think it probable that the idea came from the opening passage of Bacon's essay " Of Building " and not from any account of Cato.

74. At the end of the letter appears the following, all of which is in Emerson's hand except Ellen Tucker's own signature:

" I cannot come & see you but you are heartily welcome to come & see me & I desire to learn from you how you used to live with Waldo E.

" Your affectionate sister

" Ellen L Tucker "

To Anne Robbins Lyman, Boston, August 26, 1829 [75]

[I]Boston 25 Aug. 1829

My dear Madam,

My friend Mr Geo. P. Bradford has promised to give Mr Hall a labour of love next Sunday on his return thro Northampton from N York whither he has gone with his sisters a victim of the travelling passion & as Mr B. is a man of mark among his friends I want him to have the happiness which I shall grudge him too of spending half an hour at your house. But who is Mr Bradford? He is Mrs Ripleys brother & a fine classical & biblical scholar & a botanist & a lover of truth & an Israelite in whom is no guile [76] & a kind of Cowper & a great admirer of all admirable things & so I want him to go to your house where his eyes & his ears shall be enriched with what he loves.

I went yesterday to Cambridge & saw your friend Professor Ashmun inaugurated[I] & a good many people wd. rather have heard what he had to say for himself than to hear Judge Story. but Mr A. contented himself with promising to behave well. [II]As far as I can guess the appointment of him is a very judicious one. It was a fine assembly free of all crowd & fatigue, & contained some of the finest people in America. I sat (as tis always expedient to do on public occasions) next to Mr Upham of Salem [77] & got him to point me out the lions, for he is a man having the organ of society in very large development & knows all men in United States & one could not desire a more eloquent expounder of their various merits.

I hope yourself & Judge Lyman are well. I am truly sorry that the distresses of the times should have come so near your friends. God seems to make some of his children for prosperity, they bear it so gracefully &

75. MS owned by Professor James B. Thayer; ph. in CUL. Excerpts I–IV are in *Memoir of the Life of Mrs. Anne Jean Lyman,* pp. 256–257. As the inauguration of John Hooker Ashmun and Joseph Story occurred on Tuesday, Aug. 25 (*Boston Daily Advertiser,* Aug. 27, 1829), and as Emerson would almost certainly not have confused "yesterday" with "today," the letter was in all probability written on the 26th, which happens also to be the date of the postmark. The history of the ownership of the manuscript is recorded in this marginal note by the James Bradley Thayer of Emerson's day: "Given me by Mrs Lesley Dec. 7, 1875. J B T." For the Lymans, see the letter of Oct. 8 and 10, 1827. Edward B. Hall is mentioned in Oct. 7, 1827.

76. *John,* 1:47.

77. Charles Wentworth Upham appears earlier as Emerson's classmate at college. He had become colleague pastor at the First Church in Salem in 1824. He was later to gain some fame by his account of Salem witchcraft.

with such good will of society & tis always painful when such suffer. But I suppose it is always dangerous & especially to the very young — In college I used to echo a frequent ejaculation of my wise aunt's — 'oh blessed blessed poverty! ' when I saw young men of fine capabilities whose only & fatal disadvantage was wealth. Tis sad to see it taken from those who know how to use it but children whose prospects are changed may hereafter rejoice at the event.

We get no good news from Mr Ware except that he is no worse, but he now writes that he is really no better than when he left home. We had so many flattering rumours that this sounds worse. It is really good ground to hope that he has no seated consumption I think if after so long an interval he remains as well, and a winter in Italy may do much.

Charles has just been in to see me much rejoicing in having turned the key for the last time in [II] the door of [III]his school house. & in the prospect of living again with Joseph L. at Cambridge.[III] You will not forgive me if I shd. omit to tell you that Miss Ellen Tucker is a good deal better for being jounced over two hundred miles of hard ground in N. Hampshire lately. We went in a chaise to the Notch of the White Hills. Mrs Kent went in a carriage as a safe resort in case of showers or sickness but Ellen did not once enter it; and [IV]I am with respectful remembrances of Judge Lyman, & to the family,

Dear Madam, yours affectionately
R. Waldo Emerson.[IV]

To William Emerson, Boston, August 28, 1829 [78]

28 Aug. 1829

Dear William

Welcome home but Boston is your home make haste & let Charles & me look at you. I am in the roots & seeds of a sermon this A. M. & cant write another word more than to say that I shall preach in town doubtless all day tho' probably at home only in y[e] morn[g] & that Mr & Mrs Adams are impatient to see you at home here as well as yr aff[t] brother

Waldo —

78. MS owned by Mr. Edward Waldo Forbes; ph. in CUL. For William Emerson's homecoming, *cf.* Aug. 16, 1829. The present letter is addressed to William in Dr. Ripley's care at Concord.

To Mary Moody Emerson, Boston? September 6, 1829

[Mary Moody Emerson, Oct. 7 (1829), says she has just received the letter of this date, apparently by way of Andover, Me.]

To Abel Adams, Springfield? Massachusetts, September 12, 1829

[See the postscript of Sept. 15, 1829.]

To Charles Chauncy Emerson, Springfield, Massachusetts, September 12, 1829 [79]

Springfield, Mass. 12 Sept

My dear Charles

Here sit the Queen & I over a table & the result of our meditations is that you shall have a letter. Said queen is in tolerably good health & in excellent spirits. Her strength has been increased by her journey, & tomorrow we shall spend in this fine town & Mr Peabody [80] shall get what good he can from our poor professional aid. — Our journeys if you care to know them have been 1st day to Merrimack second day to Worcester, 3d day to Springfield, & we mean Monday, if the weather serve, to go to Hartford, & thence back to Worcester, & so home. Therefore I think I shall get home to Boston next Friday or Saturday night tho peradventure (wh. being interpreted is — in all probability) sermonless. But we have had very good times & very little physical harms tho' the weather has been so funerally cold. And how is the law & how holds the prized vacation Have the colours faded out of the bow! is it as fresh as when &c. Or does the old age of a few weeks tarnish its holiday brightness. Woes me for you my poor neophyte of the world — untried in ye deceptions of time — laetus venire solet tristis abire But may be the guilding has not worn off the gawds yet, well well —

And how is the Aunt who gives me no syllable sybilline I am desirous she should see my radiant muse here. Bid her for dear love's sake, stay a few weeks & see me & mine *at home.* Prithee visit that town clerk & get his certificate whenever tis due. & return my books to the library if

79. MS owned by RWEMA; ph. in CUL.

80. William B. O. Peabody was pastor of the Third Congregational Society of Springfield from 1820 to 1847 (*A Sketch of . . . the Third Congregational Society of Springfield, Mass.,* 1869, pp. 35–42).

you have a chance & tell Mr Adams to make Mrs Keating [81] easy as to our intentions of coming thither wh. we certainly hold, & shall, if Providence will let us.

And be not wise for thyself alone but see with greedy eyes & hear with generous ears for thy brother in his wanderings. Especially shd. I be glad of all documents ecclesiastical or as our technics have it I believe — paraenetical. Elia is a very good book on a journey but I believe you have read it we have 6 vols of new novels &c beside & a couple of octavos. And we botanize & criticise & poetize & memorize & prize & grow wise we hope & I am your loving brother Waldo — Ellen says give my love to him.

I tho't it possible we might meet Edward on this river side. I hope he has set out on his journey but know nothing.

My love to mother & Ellens likewise.

To Abel Adams, Worcester, Massachusetts, September 15, 1829 [82]

Worcester, 15 Sept. 1829
9 o'clock P. M.

My dear Sir,

My friends & myself have just got our supper here after riding 48 miles for it from Vernon in Connecticutt and we are all very well. The ladies have gone to bed & left me at leisure to tell you how they do & when I am coming home. Here we are about 70 miles from Concord which space we must traverse in the course of tomorrow & the next day if the weather permit & on Friday morng I hope to set out for Boston. Tis high time I was there. — The weather has been extremely favourable for our ride & " the winds of heaven have been tempered to the shorn lamb " [83] — Ellen has borne all extremely well, & appears much stronger; & except a damp morning & one or two piecings out of our journey after dark — has ridden always in the chaise. Margaret & Mrs Kent in the carriage. At Springfield I preached all day for Mr Pea-

81. Charles Emerson wrote to William, Oct. 4 following (MS owned by Dr. Haven Emerson), " Waldo & his bride will be at their home at Mrs. Keatings, tomorrow before the sacred hour of dinner." *The Boston Directory,* 1829, lists two widows named Keating, one of whom, Hannah, lived " rear Chardon." *Cf.* Oct. 25, 1829. For the wedding, see a note on Oct. 21.

82. MS owned by RWEMA; ph. in CUL. The superscription is to Abel Adams, at Boston.

83. This is not quite the form of the proverb given in Laurence Sterne, *A Sentimental Journey,* London, 1768, pp. 175–176.

body — & the next day had one of the most agreeable rides that ever was or ever can be ridden in this imperfect world from S. to Hartford on the west bank of the river. At Hartford I saw the new & yet unfinished Episcopal Church [84] — a Gothic model, & am clearly of opinion that tis a much finer exterior than the new one in Summer St.[85] Tell Charles that in the Hotel at Hartford I saw Mrs Kast & Mr & Mrs Shepard [86] & introduced them to E. L. T. This day we stopped at Stafford Springs a few minutes & other than these I cannot recollect a single object or incident that we have met on our route. The fewer the better. We travel for air & jolting & these we have gotten & our own company was sufficiently good. Books we carry, & at the taverns we read & scribble — but not sermons. Where there is so little to relate I may mention that all the way I am nursing a lame knee which I got before I left Chardon St. but it grew worse in N. Hampshire & much camphor & much advice have not yet done much good. If I were at home I shd. have to sit still in my chamber & so I may as well (almost) be riding.

I have heard no word from home since I left Boston — nor cd. I expect it. I rejoice not to see in the obituaries in the papers any new names. Nor need I ask any questions, since I cannot expect to have them answered. I will hope that you are all well if you are all at home & that my little pet lamb that repeats Nathan's parable [87] has not wandered into the mountains of N. H. I promise myself the pleasure of seeing you on Friday & of preaching at home a part, at least, of Sunday. & so with particular remembrance to Mrs Adams & Miss Charlotte — I am yours affectionately

R. W. Emerson

I wrote by Mr Dwight on Sat. Morng last & to Charles same day. — Ellen desires to be remembered to you.

84. Christ Church, consecrated Dec. 23, 1829, was said to be far in advance, architecturally, of other churches of that time (J. H. Trumbull, *The Memorial History of Hartford County*, 1886, I, 406).

85. New Trinity Church, dedicated some weeks later (*Columbian Centinel*, Boston, Nov. 11, 1829).

86. Probably Emerson's aunt Hannah Haskins Kast and her daughter and son-in-law Sally Kast Shepard and George Shepard.

87. *II Samuel*, 12:1–9.

To William Emerson, Boston? October 21, 1829 [88]

Oct 21

Dear Wm,

Cannot a married man write & say that tis excellent to double his being? [89] Ellen & I will be very glad to see you at our house in Chardon St. whenever you can first come. Ellen has been very well ever since she has been in town. I am very lame not being able to walk a step without a cane — & Sundays I preach, *sitting*. So we ride every day when the sun & wind will let us to keep life & soundness in what is yet whole [90] grandpa & grandma. Our family consists now of six. I am sorry to hear from New Bedford that Mr Dewey has lost his fine little boy Wm. nearly 6 years old.[91] — Mrs G. B. E. has another son.[92]

To Henry Ware, Jr., Boston, October 25, 1829 [93]

Boston Oct 25 — 1829. . . . We are very pleasantly situated at board at Mrs Keating's in Chardon St — with Mr & Mrs Kent & the two Misses Tucker.[94] Meantime I am laid up in my chair a cripple by an un-

88. MS owned by HCL; ph. in CUL. The first two pages of this MS are occupied entirely by a letter dated Concord, Oct. 21, 1829, from Edward Emerson, in which he tells William of his admission to the bar on Oct. 20 and of Samuel Hoar's consent " to my taking a chair in his office for the winter & spring, more or less." "I go to Boston to-day," he wrote; and Emerson's own letter, on the third page of the same sheet, was probably written at Chardon Street.

89. The wedding had occurred at Concord, N. H., on Sept. 30, 1829 (*Journals*, II, 266; *Christian Register*, Oct. 10, 1829). According to the *History of Concord New Hampshire*, 1903, p. 1079, the old mansion belonging to Col. William A. Kent, where the wedding occurred, had been honored by La Fayette's presence as a guest in 1825, and Daniel Webster was a frequent visitor there. Charles Emerson wrote to William, Oct. 4 (1829), his impressions of the occasion — " 3 whole days in that big house full of women, sat I, putting all the time a sober face on the fool's errand I went to do, while W. & the fair Ellen were whispering honied words above stairs, & I was turned over to the compulsory attentions of the stranger folk. These lovers are blind — purblind these lovers be — I forgive them freely." (MS owned by Dr. Haven Emerson.)

90. The MS was mutilated by the removal of the seal, and only illegible fragments of the word or two that followed remain.

91. The death of William O. Dewey, son of Orville Dewey, is reported in the *Christian Register*, Oct. 24, 1829.

92. For Francis Buckminster Emerson, son of George Barrell Emerson and Olivia Buckminster, see Robert C. Waterston, *Memoir of George Barrell Emerson*, 1884, p. 34, and Harvard catalogues.

93. MS owned by RWEMA; ph. in CUL. This is a fragmentary copy in Cabot's hand. The copyist names Ware as the person addressed.

94. *Cf.* Sept. 12, 1829, to Charles Emerson. This was shortly after Emerson's mar-

lucky sprain of my knee wh happened 6 weeks ago [95] & has resulted in a chronic inflammation . . .

To William Emerson, Boston, November 13, 1829 [96]

Boston, 13 Nov. 1829 —

My dear brother,

I returned last ev.g — from Concord, N. H. whither I went (wifeless) to attend a Dedication [97] & a Wedding, & on my return found your letter & Edwards from Montreal [98] for which I was glad. — They were much disappointed not to see him in N. H. at y[e] nuptial occasion. Ellen is pretty well & is now gone out. The knee — ne melius quidem — I write now merely to assure you of my love & enclose my mammy's letter & to say please send me that account & appraisal of your-my-books- which I gave you. You know — the thing you drew up years ago. Men call me richer — I hope it will prove so — but shall be glad if the equipage of the king & the queen for each hath their own doth not eat up master Mammon on his quarter day. — Woe is me my knee weak are we.

I have a letter from Aunt Mary at Greenfield.[99] Has your friend failed? Mr A.[100] says it will not interrupt his business I hope it will not interrupt yours. Love to Edward,[101] I suppose I shall see him shortly. Your affectionate brother

Waldo

Mr Dewey delivers the Φ Β Κ oration & Mellen the poem.[102]

---

riage to Ellen Tucker (see a note on Oct. 21, 1829). Her sisters Margaret and Paulina are mentioned in a number of letters.

95. *Cf.* Sept. 15, 1829.

96. MS owned by Mr. Edward Waldo Forbes; ph. in CUL. The superscription is to William Emerson, in New York.

97. At the dedication of the new Unitarian (Second Congregational) church in Concord, N. H., on Nov. 11, Emerson began the exercises with a reading from the Scriptures and a prayer (*Boston Recorder and Religious Telegraph,* Nov. 18, 1829; and *Christian Register,* Nov. 14, 1829).

98. Edward Emerson, Montreal, Nov. 2, 1829, tells of his journey.

99. She wrote to Emerson from Greenfield on Oct. 28, 1829, about Plato, Shakespeare, and Coleridge; on Nov. 10 following she wrote him again from the same town. Emerson had borrowed *Biographia Literaria* as early as Nov. 16, 1826 (MS charge-book for 1826–1827 in HCL).

100. Abel Adams, no doubt.

101. Edward was now apparently visiting William in New York.

102. The *Columbian Centinel,* Nov. 18, 1829, announced the appointment of Orville Dewey and Grenville Mellen.

To Mary Moody Emerson, Boston? November 15, 1829?

[Printed incompletely in *Journals,* II, 272–274. Following the first complete sentence printed on p. 273 Emerson wrote: " Among ye capabilities of our nature no lover of truth can overlook *one,* that of *piety,* — a disposition so peculiar so decided & so progressive yt it were silly to call it accidental; ye disposition yt is gratified by a psalm of David or an ejaculation of exalted devotion " (typescript *Journals*). Probably Emerson had written his aunt another letter about two weeks earlier which she answered in hers of Nov. 10 (1829). She comments upon his lame knee, his offer to send her *The Edinburgh Review,* and his views of the rationalists.]

To William Emerson, Boston, December 1, 1829 [103]

Boston, 1 Dec. 1829

My dear brother,

I am a good deal surprized that you think Edward had better stay at New York. I tho't Mr Hoar's a singular good offer [104] for any young man in the profession, & in its local advantages to Edward indisputably the best. I find I am not alone in my opinion — All the household, & Mr Webster, & M. *On,* (as the French hath it) all tho't so too. Well now for no one reason that I have heard hinted, except *climate* alone, you concur with him in preferring the uncertainties of New York. Grandfather is amazed, Uncle Ripley vociferates, & Mother looks very sad. So pray change your mind, or send us the reasons that weigh with you. I have got last night Edward's letters to me & Charles. If he is not pretty soon on his way back I hope he will write to Mr Hoar, for Mother says that he comes to the manse & not one word is said touching Edwards altered views.

My old knee is about the same. I am still prisoner of chairs & chaises. Tonight I have received the visit of the quack doctor Hewitt,[105] having quitted Drs Warren & Ware.

Alexander Everett is to edit the Mass. Journal. & I hear is in treaty for the N. A. Review also [106] — buying out Sparks. but uncertain. Mr

103. MS owned by HCL; ph. in CUL. The superscription is to William Emerson, in New York.

104. See a note on Oct. 21, 1829.

105. Simon C. Hewett is listed as " surgeon bone setter " in *The Boston Directory,* 1829, where Drs. John Ware and John C. Warren also appear.

106. According to the *Boston Daily Advertiser,* July 3, 1830, No. 68 of *The North American Review,* published two days earlier, was the first under the superintendence of the new editor, Alexander Everett. I have found nothing about his connection with a " Mass. Journal."

E. E. told Mr Ripley that his brother meant to practise law in Boston. He is to lecture Friday Ev[g] before the Soc. for Diffus. Knowledge.[107] So the Haskins cause declines. How can you betray your household gods by loitering in N. Y.? – I hear that the Holyokes gained the verdict of the jury last week – having claimed this time one eighth of the estate – & mean in successive causes to get the remaining seven. Aunt Betsey is my sad authority & I am sorry.

Dr Channing is preparing an article on Inspiration in answer I suppose to Mr Norton on Hebrews.[108] Ellen is very well & I am your affectionate brother

Waldo.

Charles said Yes W[m] will be respo[n]sible [109] for Edw's additional dollars but cannot at all afford it.

And then you are going on presumption that Edw can earn money & he ought only to earn as an amateur, & not with that deadly pinch called *for bread.*

To William Emerson, Boston, December 8, 1829 [110]

Boston, 8 December.
1829.

My dear brother,

I am walking about with great firmness, thanks to Dr Hewett [111] – who cured me in two hours. Mother is in town inquiring after blanket & bag. Charles raving about some pilot who is roving peradventure in Narragansett Bay when he should be doing his best to sign his name in Court Square. As I hear nothing of repentance much less of reformation from you N. Y reprobates, I am to learn like mother to call evil good – to make advantages for myself in Edwards plan since you wont for me. I enclose in this or some neighbour letter his key

107. Apparently an error. Dr. Walter Channing was announced to lecture before the Society for the Diffusion of Useful Knowledge on that day (*Boston Daily Advertiser,* Dec. 3, 1829).

108. Andrews Norton's review referred to is in *The Christian Examiner,* for May and July, 1829. According to the index of the same journal, the articles dealing with inspiration (in May and July, 1830) were not by Channing but by F. W. P. Greenwood and Orville Dewey.

109. Mutilated by the seal.

110. MS owned by HCL; ph. in CUL. The superscription is to William Emerson, in New York.

111. See the letter of Dec. 1, 1829.

Dont let him work but with lounging moderation; run slowly. & any other saws you can think of. Inspire him with that unaccountable Economy which some people have from fairies I think (Edward never had it from anywhere) to live luxuriously comfortable & spend nothing & owe nothing. & any other honest witchcrafts. And when the latest day of a windy purse comes send me word & I will summon my forces. I doubt such are my sinful habits I shall not send till I am summoned & rated. But if it will be necessary to send 3.00 pr week I will furnish that. I have a fancy that if you shd examine my income & outlay since my marriage you wd say I was poorer not richer, therefor. But richer I surely am by all Ellen, if she bro't no penny.

Ellen sends her love to both of you & Mother as I said is exploring the advantages of Edwards present plan — Give him my love which includes all good wishes & I am your affectionate brother

Waldo —

But here comes Dr Hewett my nightly visitor who has done me knights service [112]

To Mary Moody Emerson, Boston, December 10 and 13, 1829

[Partly printed in Cabot, I, 161–162 and 163, and wholly in *Journals,* II, 276–279, with the text rearranged.]

To Ezra Ripley, Boston, December? 12? 1829? [113]

Boston, Saturday Morng.

My dear Sir,

I received your letter yesterday morning & its contents. I am much obliged to you for your kind sympathy in my recovery. My foot from long disuse complains a good deal of being put back to its old duties of carrying half the body & really seems more diseased than the knee. But I walk miles per day. —

112. A brief note by Charles Emerson follows on the same sheet.

113. MS owned by RWEMA; ph. in CUL. The outside address is to "Rev. E. Ripley D.D." at Concord. Dec., 1829, is the date pretty clearly indicated by the references to recovery from lameness, and it fits also the mention of Ellen and the Kents. The account of the progress of recovery here given seems to indicate that this follows closely the letters of Dec. 1 and 8. In Dec. 8 it is stated that "Mother is in town . . ." The present letter, in which it is reported that she is to remain in town till Monday, was written on a Saturday, and so probably on Saturday, Dec. 12, 1829. On the other hand, it is barely possible that the time is early 1830.

Mother sends her regards, but her friends mean to keep her in town till Monday. We hope that your brother has arrived before this to relieve your solitude.

Ellen is very well, & sends her affectionate respects. Col. & Mrs Kent promise themselves a visit to Concord to pay their respects to you. But my sermon waits & will only permit me to say how truly I am

Dear Sir Your affectionate grandson

R. Waldo Emerson

1830

To William and Edward Emerson, Boston, January 4, 1830[1]

Boston, 4 Jan. 1830 –

Excellent men, I hope you will not be afflicted with Charles's caricature of a New York letter – He says he is determined to give as good as he gets. If you scold, I send herewith the antidote, oil for the sore from a sisters flagon. Did not somebody ask me what books I read? I heard it in my sleep or waking. Coleridge's Friend[2] – with great interest; Coleridges " Aids to reflection " with yet deeper; Degerando Hist. Comparée des Systemes de Philosophie,[3] I am beginning on the best recommendation. & one more book – the best Sermon I have read for some time, to wit, Combe's Constitution of Man.[4] You see the present is too mighty for me, I cannot get away to do homage to the mighty past. Yet what commands me in the present is its relation to the future. & so with sincere wishes that the New Year may be your best year & yet only seed of good to come I remain your affectionate brother

Waldo –[5]

1. MS owned by HCL; ph. in CUL.

2. All three volumes of the 1818 edition of *The Friend* are in Emerson's library at the Antiquarian House in Concord. The influence of this work and of *Aids to Reflection* is obvious.

3. Marie Joseph de Gérando's *Histoire comparée des systèmes de philosophie,* important in Emerson's reading, seems to appear in the *Journals* for the first time (II, 283) three days after this letter was written. The four volumes of the Paris edition of 1822–1823 are still in Emerson's house, at Concord, and bear his signature.

4. A Boston edition had appeared in 1829. George Combe was partly responsible, no doubt, for such interest as Emerson took in phrenology, one of the popular enthusiasms of the day.

5. In the margins of the superscription appear, in a doubtful hand, two lists of names, which have no connection with the letter, and the following notes, certainly by Emerson, on current periodicals:

In N. A. Review –
1 art. Mr Sparks
2 Mr Cushing

To Anne Robbins Lyman, Boston, January 6, 1830

[Printed in *Memoir of the Life of Mrs. Anne Jean Lyman,* pp. 263–264; reprinted in various editions of *Recollections of my Mother.*]

To Anne Robbins Lyman, Boston, January 21, 1830

[Printed in *Memoir of the Life of Mrs. Anne Jean Lyman,* p. 264; reprinted in *Recollections of my Mother.*]

To William Emerson, Boston, January 25, 1830 [6]

Boston, 25 Jan. 1830 –

Dear William,

I received directions the other day from Aunt Mary what to do with money from you, & so I sent her $14.00 by Mr Franklin Ripley,[7] which you will please to charge to my account of the books. T. W. Haskins has failed, as all his fathers do. Oh sorrow sorrow: he appears as much mortified & sad as you wd expect. Tis a cheerless thing. but his religious faith comforts him. The news from Bulkeley are more favorable. Take a moment of leisure if there is so respectable a thing in N. York, & write him a letter. He will take it very kindly. Charles delivers his lecture at Concord a week from tonight.[8] Ellen is very well. & sends her love to you & Edward. & I am truly yours,

R. Waldo E.

Nova Scotia – C. W. Upham
Indians. Gov. Cass
Lafayette. E. Everett
Tariff. A. H. Everett
Hoffman. Cruise
Dana. Greenwood
In Examiner Dr Channing has written I learn upon Inspiration –

The information about *The North American Review* for Jan., 1830, agrees with that given by Cushing in his *Index*. For the article in *The Christian Examiner,* see the letter of Dec. 1, 1829.

6. MS owned by Mr. Edward Waldo Forbes; ph. in CUL.

7. Apparently George Ripley's brother, who lived at Greenfield, Mass. (*cf. George Ripley,* pp. 1–2). For Mary Moody Emerson at Greenfield, see Nov. 13, 1829.

8. Charles's lecture must have been inspired by George Combe's book (*cf.* Jan. 4, 1830). The entry for Feb. 3, 1830, in the MS record book of the Concord Lyceum for 1828–1859 (owned by the Concord Free Public Library) gives the subject: "*The Constitution of Man as affected by outward circumstances.*"

To Edward Bliss Emerson, Boston? February? *c.* 18? 1830

[According to Feb. 20, 1830, Emerson had sent Edward $30 "by mail." This money may have been sent in the same letter from Emerson and Ellen Tucker Emerson which is mentioned in Edward, Mar. 4, 1830, as still to be answered.]

To William Emerson, Boston, February 20, 1830 [9]

Boston, 20 Feb. 1830.

Dear Wm, I Received yesterday your packet for Messrs T. & R. Haskins & I hasten to deliver two messages that sorely harass my memory for not having vent given them sooner. 1° Mr S. Ripley said tell W^m^ to send home again the note of Kendall's for K. is hereabouts. 2° Mr T. Haskins says that the Holyokes offer by way of compromise to sell their claims for one fourth of the Estate.[10] & Mr Hubbard had tho't if they wd. offer $\frac{1}{8}$ it mt be well to compromise But Charles C. E. says not one stiver & Madam Emerson echoed back, not one. & as far as I cd. see the mind of Mr T. H. he was averse to compromise. & I am yours & Edwards brother in a great hurry but true love

Waldo.

Has E. B. E. rec^d^ the $30 I sent him by mail. over.[11]

I send this by my friend Mr Geo. Merrill, who to my great regret is leaving the Second Church & the First Town to settle in Philadelphia. Any attention to him will be gratefully acknowledged as paid to Yrs Waldo E.

To Abel Adams, New Haven, Connecticut, March 16, 1830 [12]

New Haven, 16 March, 1830.

My dear Sir,

I cannot help devoting to you a few minutes now that I have got away from the College & fine things of this pleasant city. I preached in Hartford three times on Sunday to a small but attentive congregation. My wife was not so well on that day as before but on Monday we got to New Haven by 6 o'clock P. M. (that is 34 miles in 8 hours) in very comfortable health. We expected here to find a boat which would carry us *fast asleep* to New York but were told on our ar-

9. MS owned by Mr. Edward Waldo Forbes; ph. in CUL.
10. *Cf.* Dec. 1, 1829.
11. What follows is written on the opposite side of the leaf.
12. MS owned by RWEMA; ph. in CUL. The address is to Adams, at Boston.

rival that we must wait for boat passage till Wednesday mor[ng]. — summer arrangements not beginning till next week. When we had made up our minds to this loss of a day, what was our chagrin to learn at 10 minutes before 8 o'c. that a boat wd. sail at 8' in the ev[g] & we all unpacked both in our baggage & purposes. The stages go so irregularly & so slowly that we it [13] seemed best not to meddle with them & now we are ready to set out tomorrow morn[g] at 7 o'clock.

We have been amusing ourselves as we easily could in this academical town. There is I shd. think no town in New England of its size that can compare with it for beauty. so many & so fine public buildings — great square — fine avenues of trees — & spacious & ornamented graveyard — I have a Cousin who is an Assistant Professor here Mr Shepard [14] — & he carried me to Mr Augur's sculpture room [15] — a native artist, who exhibited some of his workmanship in Boston no long time since — There I saw besides his marble people — the real Dr Percival the poet — a proper sloven. I attended prayers in the College Chapel & supped in the Commons Hall but had no opportunity of making acquaintance with any of the professors — which I regretted. I regret also losing a fine day for sailing to N. Y. as I fear I may not have as much time as I wish for settling the best part of me in Philadelphia since I should be very loth to be absent more than one more Sunday. One thing more I regret. I got last Sunday at Hartford a very sore throat which threatens to spoil my poor powers next Sunday & truly would it grieve me to go to Mr Furness without ability to pay him for his labour of love last summer.

How are you & yours & mine? I expect to learn all in a letter from you in N. Y. By the time we get there I hope to write the best bulletins of Ellens health. She is pretty well today & has walked abroad 3 times — yet not so well as we could wish. Marga[r]et [16] is very well. Please to carry my love & duty into Lyman Place & leave a large portion thereof in Chardon St.

Yours truly
R. W. Emerson.

13. The break in the structure of the sentence occurs at the beginning of a new page.

14. The Yale *Catalogue* of 1830–1831 lists Charles U. Shepard as assistant to the professor of chemistry and as lecturer on botany.

15. Hezekiah Augur gained some contemporary fame as a sculptor. His two best-known statues are still to be seen in the art museum at Yale.

16. Margaret Tucker, Emerson's sister-in-law. The MS is slightly mutilated.

To Charles Chauncy Emerson and Margaret Tucker Kent, New York, March 19, 1830[17]

New York, 19 March, 1830.

Dear Charles,

We had a very stormy passage through the Sound from New Haven. We got on board the boat at 6 A. M. & expected to be at N. Y. at 4 P. M. But a gale came up from the Southwest which we cd. not weather & so at 12 o'clock we made into Norwalk roads as well as we could & came to anchor. There we lay pouting & snuffing the insufferable mephitis of the cabin, & hearing the rain patter & looking at each other grimly, forty stout passengers, (though fortunately only two beside E. & M.[18] in the ladies cabin) & lastly sleeping or trying to sleep in an air that wd doubtless have put out a lamp on the floor. But morning came, the wind abated, & the steam chimney began once more to puff. The clouds broke, & we were repaid for our troubles by a noble passage up the Sound — fine sun mild air, swift vessels, beautiful shores, noble seats — & through all — got to this long London town — to the American Hotel at 2 o'clock yesterday. You may imagine I bit my lips with mortification to find I had got the queen into this bad navigable box. She bore it very well — all but the impossibility of sleep. Glad we were to get to this house & shall stay here today, & tomorrow take the Phila. boat — another sort of thing & on other sort of waters viz inland instead of outland.

Friday P. M. Ellen is quite weak today, & though she insists upon our going tomorrow — as we shall probably try — yet I fear that she will not be so well at Philad. as to suffer me to leave her for a few days. I therefore think it probable I shall not be able to get home to preach as soon as the third Sunday. Of course I shall compass it if possible but you must engage somebody to supply the desk that day positively, & then if I get home I will preach half the day. If you can, engage a young man from C.[19] with the request from me that he will be so good as to exchange with Mr Ripley of Waltham (who promised to gratify me on such an occasion recently) or with Dr Ware or any of the Boston ministers half or the whole day, he will gratify our people's love for old preachg. This you can forbear doing or saying if you judge expedient in the par-

17. MS owned by RWEMA; ph. in CUL.

18. Ellen and Margaret. *Cf.* Mar. 16, 1830.

19. Cambridge.

ticular case. But see that good word is dispensed on that day from Sec Ch pulpit on the 28th instant. as you love your loving brother

Waldo.

To Mrs Kent [20] —

My dear Mother,

Ellen is troubled today as yesterday with her " red wheezers " as we call them & considerable fulness in the head. Still she has walked out twice, tho' weak. On the whole, we think it prudent to hasten southward and are in every particular so cautious that you must rely on Margaret & me as yourself. I shall write again speedily. —

To Abel Adams, Philadelphia? March 20? 1830

[Mentioned in Mar. 20, 1830, as " inclosed." As the letter of Mar. 16, 1830, was postmarked New Haven, this is obviously a later letter and was probably written from Philadelphia.]

To William Emerson, Philadelphia, March 21, 1830[21]

Philadelphia, 20 March.
Sunday Evg
U. S. Hotel
10 3/4 o'c.

Dear William

I have only time to say we are here in safety. Mrs Vaughan [22] Merrill [23] Furness & Frost called on us last evg & promise active assistance tomorrow in getting a house. Will you have the goodness to put the inclosed into ye shortest way of getting to Boston. Ellen is pretty well — but I shall not like to leave her until the evil symptoms go by. & so perhaps shall stay here a week. I will write again when I have longer time

& am yours affectionately

Waldo

On second tho'ts, I will leave Mr A's letter open, — please seal it.

20. Above the superscription, to Charles, Emerson wrote: " To be opened by Mrs Kent. in Mr E.'s absence. — "

21. MS owned by Mr. Edward Waldo Forbes, ph. in CUL. Emerson has misdated the letter; Sunday fell on the 21st.

22. See Mar. 26, 1830.

23. See Feb. 20, 1830.

To Charles Chauncy Emerson, Philadelphia, March 25, 1830 [24]

Philadelphia 25 March 1830
Thursday

Dear Charles,

I staid here boldly Monday & Tuesday in the expectation that Mr Furness would decide to exchange with me as he had partly proposed, for two or three Sundays. That hope is gone. And now I stay because I cd. not properly leave Philad. soon enough to get home next Sunday, & so shall stay till the latest opportunities offer for returning at next weeks end. I am as anxious to be at home as any one can be to have me but it would not do to leave Ellen here among strangers too suddenly. I shd. have no confidence in the comfortableness of her abode. We have very good accommodations at Miss McElroy's — Corner of Chesnut & Eleventh Streets.[25] — good in rooms & in board — but it has this unsuitableness that there are no females in the family except the hostess & she does not sit at her dinner table. There are three gentlemen — respectable people — & Madam promises that when I go away she will sit at the table: I mention these circumstances because in writing to you I write to Mrs Kent also & that you may partly understand why I must stay — As to Ellen, she is pretty well but I would rather see her a grain more robust before I go away.[26] . . . Ellinelli has finished my letter with her royal hand whilst I visited with Wm's partner Dana the Waterworks & Pagoda &c & really I am very glad to be relieved from the responsibility of filling all my sheet. For whatever I may acquire in Philad. the love of letter writing is certainly not a part. of my learning. I write suddenly because Mr Merrill offers me an unexpected opportunity to assure you how affectionately I remain your brother

Waldo

What a fine book Jefferson is [27]

24. MS owned by RWEMA; ph. in CUL.

25. *Desilver's Philadelphia Directory,* 1830, gives this address for Sarah M'Elroy's boarding house.

26. The part omitted is entirely in Ellen's hand and is signed by her. It begins: "Really! — I have given him leave yea have urged his going away *now* — for he is every whit as much out of his element as at *Concord N H* — and (oh tell it not) not a text has he expounded not a skeleton of a sarmint has he formed not a sonnet has he perpetrated since he turned his back *B ward* — . . ."

27. For more critical comment on Jefferson, see the letter of Mar. 26 and Apr. 1, 1830.

To Mary Moody Emerson, Philadelphia, March 26, and New York, April 1, 1830[28]

Philadelphia 26 March 1830.

I enjoyed highly the company of my dear Aunt & the pleasure of making her acquainted with my faery queen who wrote verses about you which perhaps she will send you some day. And since we arrived here we have been delighted with a letter.[29] I am getting to be sadly impatient of my life here, which has petty engagements which tear time into slivers, and are singularly unfavorable to any thing like intellectual progress. Oh fie that we – no – that I should be so enthralled to small accidents, that the first derangement of my domestic routine should put a chain on the wheels of the spirit – & the old trains of thot are broken up – the landmarks are gone – the favorite speculations grow faint & dim, and when I come back to my arm chair, I shall be recreated not enriched. Some indirect advantage roaming certainly furnishes, some side glances at other minds some comparative observations that if they do not lead to new conclusions keep you from making premature conclusions on human nature as all of us are prone to do. What stone walls of incommunicability do exist between mind & mind. I converse with a man whose faculties are active & healthy enough yet I find his horizon is limited in some place where mine is extended; yet can I not, (with the clearest perception that he does not see far enow) for the life of me tell him what is the difference between us. Linnaeus classified plants by their stamens Another botanist by their fruit. What feature or fact shall be assumed to classify the immortal plant – man? Each of the professions underrates the other, each science, each art, each habit of life. Dr Channing thinks the *Reformer* the first mind; the great mob think the *Conqueror,* the smaller mob the *poet.* I think respectfully enough of Statesmen, – yet I have been reading Jefferson & can't but think that he & his great mates look little already, from this short distance where we stand, & he would be sorry to know my feelings about their ambition. – Not by their objects then can they be measured – for the naturalists are ridiculous when they so often forget their end in their means & learn nothing but the anatomy of a leaf or a fly – & not

28. MS owned by RWEMA; ph. in CUL.

29. Mary Moody Emerson to Ellen Tucker Emerson and her husband, postmarked Mar. 18 (1830).

less ridiculous though far worse are the polemic theologians when they are only polemics. But *virtue* is always venerable, & the *attention* which seems proper to the condition of humanity set in this world to learn whatever lesson God chuses to teach — surprized at nothing — greedy of all knowledge & arranging all upon the vast conception of God's being. The seeker the seeker is your only philosopher after all. Christianity teaches him to seek better but there is no absolute finder in this world. The first moment of consciousness after we have shot the great Gulf we shall cry Found with an infinit[e][30]
again. I shall

Do write to Ellen again here, & write to the care of Mr George Merrill, Philadelphia.

New York. 1 April. I have boldly left Ellen in Philad. ramparted round with troops of friends. She seems better, & there is a good physician, and *there is a good Physician*. I shall be in Boston tomorrow & will see W. H.[31] presently. Write me very soon.

To William and Edward Emerson, Philadelphia, March 26, 1830 [32]

Philadelphia, 26 March
1830

Dear William & Dear Edward,

Mr Dana [33] tells me he goes in the morn^{g}. and so I seize the last moment & also the last bit of paper that is left me to tell you how much I love & how soon I shall see you. Having established Ellen & Margaret in good lodgings in Chesnut St. I shd have come back ere this but I wanted to see Ellen look a little firmer, or at least more acquainted with her housemates. I shall set out for home probably next Wednesday. Thank you for sending the bundle, it arrived safely. Thank you much more for Mr Dana's acquaintance. I like him very much.

30. The bottom of the second leaf has been torn away. Only fragments of two lines remain, while probably two or three lines are entirely wanting. It is possible that there was a signature or other writing on the opposite side of the missing portion of this leaf.

31. Possibly Emerson's cousin William Haskins.

32. MS in HCL; ph. in CUL.

33. Probably Alexander H. Dana, New York attorney, listed in *Longworth's American Almanac*, 1830.

I have been reading Jefferson's last volume [34] with great pleasure. Mr Furness has been showing & telling his old & new things. & his wife has shown much attention & hospitality. And Lucy B.[35] likewise has been kind. And Mr John Vaughan [36] the tutelar genius of Phila. &c &c.

Your affectionate brother

Waldo

I have taken one of Ellinellis ms.s. as you see [37]

To William Emerson, Boston, April 16, 1830 [38]

Boston Apr 16 1830

Dear W.

The powers of Mass. are very eagerly engaged I believe in a compromise [39] wh. Charles if he wd. mt. tell you all about, you poor folk in the provinces who have yr estate sold over y^{r} head or under feet & know nothing about it. I shall be glad if you can send this packet to Phila. It contains no very *official* letter or I doubt if it wd. tarry in New Amsterdam,[40] famed for speed of transmission of intell[igence.] I am going to Concord tomorrow for Sunday. I hear good news from time to time of the Queen & am yours affectionately.

Waldo.

34. Presumably the fourth of Jefferson's *Memoir, Correspondence, and Miscellanies,* published at Charlottesville in 1829 and at Boston and New York in 1830. Vol. IV consisted mainly of letters.

35. *Cf.* Jan. 18, 1825.

36. *Desilver's,* 1830, shows John Vaughan was a merchant and vice-consul for Sweden, Norway, and Brazil.

37. In the margin of the first page Ellen had written their names and " Boston Mass "; and a face drawn there, but scratched over, was probably her work. The upper fourth of the first leaf has been mostly torn away, but it apparently contained nothing belonging to this letter.

38. MS owned by Mr. Edward Waldo Forbes; ph. in CUL. The superscription is to William Emerson.

39. *Cf.* Feb. 20, 1830.

40. A word immediately following has been almost completely torn away with the seal, and what remains is illegible. A part of the last word in this sentence is missing for the same reason.

To Ezra Ripley, Boston, April 22? 1830 [41]

Thursday P. M.

My dear Sir

Mrs Kent & her daughter Paulina [42] arrived in town this P. M. with very good accounts from Ellen. Col Kent & his wife are very unwilling to go to N. Hampshire, (wh. they propose doing next Monday or Tuesday,) without seeing you. They have therefore been planning to go up to Concord next Saturday — day after tomorrow: & I tell them you will expect them to dine, for they were arranging to dine at the Hotel. I trust this arrangement will not find you particularly busy on that day.

With my best love to mother & my respectful remembrance to Mr Ripley — & to Mr Goodwin

I am your affectionate grandson
R. Waldo Emerson

To Mary Moody Emerson, Boston? May 1, 1830

[Described in Mary Moody Emerson, June 7 (endorsed 1830 in her nephew's hand), as of May 1 and containing some poetry by Ellen. Apparently Emerson had commented on theological questions and had asked for some of his aunt's diaries.]

To William Emerson, Boston, May 11, 1830 [43]

Boston 11 May 1830

Dear William,

I received your letter & Edw^ds^ tonight, & thanks therefor. Aunt Mary is at Springfield & I neglected to send you the message which she bid me a fortnight ago. viz that she was there & wd. there

41. MS owned by RWEMA; ph. in CUL. The date clearly falls between Dec., 1828, when Ellen Tucker became engaged to Emerson, and Feb. 8, 1831, when she died; and the postmark of Apr. 23 makes both 1828 and 1831 impossible. As the marriage had not occurred by Apr., 1829, the year 1830 seems much more probable; and this fits the apparent reference in the letter to Ellen's absence from home, for she was in Philadelphia at this time in 1830. Finally, the mention of "Mr Goodwin" is almost conclusive proof of 1830, for he had been settled at Concord only in February of that year and Emerson himself had on that occasion delivered the "Right Hand of Fellowship" (*cf.* James Kendall, *A Sermon Delivered at the Ordination of Hersey Bradford Goodwin, as Colleague Pastor with Ezra Ripley, D. D. . . . Feb. 17, 1830,* Concord, 1830).

42. Paulina Tucker, who appears in later letters as Mrs. Nash.

43. MS in HCL; ph. in CUL.

receive your $18. " or, said she, tell him if it is not convenient to pay me, I will come there & see him " — or words to that effect — a proposition whose tone or import — whether minatory or whether affectionate — I did not & cannot determine. She is at Rev. Dr Howards,[44] boarding. I also found lately the lost book-account, all my disclaimers notwithstanding, & I shall probably inclose it.

Next Monday I mean to go to Philadelphia and the disagreeing hours of the boats *threaten* me with a day in your city which my fraternal affection would more covet on the return than on the outward journey. Forgive me — but I have been sonneteering now ever since March opened — and — when you are married —

I expect mother in town Thursday or Friday & she will go to Brookline & take possession of our lodgings at Mrs Perrys — (in old Aspinwall house where Uncle Ralph lived one summer long ago) where we have a parlor & 3 chambers one for Mother one for wife & one for you when you will come & welcome.[45] Perhaps I have told you all this before. Family cares — old age. — In the fall Ellen & I & Madame Mere mean to keep house. I shall immediately on Mothers arrival send Edwards chattels which Mother shall select on board a packet & will send or bring him notice of the same.

I have no more facts but much love to him & to yourself from Yours

Waldo

To William Emerson, Brookline, Massachusetts, May 27, 1830[46]

Brookline, 29 May, 1830 —

Dear William,

Here are we all safe Mother, Ellen, & I, though submitted ever since we set foot heredoon to the impiger atrox inexorabilis[47] chafing of an east wind. We got here you know by the shortest

44. Doubtless the Rev. Bezaliel Howard. Mason A. Green, *Springfield*, 1888, p. 377: " Men still talk of Parson Howard, and honor his memory."

45. According to the MS *Autobiography* Emerson lived at Brookline from May 20 to Oct. 15 of this year.

46. MS in HCL; ph. in CUL. According to the *Christian Register* of May 29, 1830, Channing preached the election sermon, before the governor and both houses of the legislature, on Wednesday, the 26th, not the 28th. It is, then, practically certain that the correct date of the letter is May 27. Charles Emerson wrote to William on May 28 (MS owned by Dr. Haven Emerson) : " Waldo was chaplain on Election day. I envied him his comfortable seat in the Pulpit." *Cf.* a note on Apr. 25, 1829.

47. Apparently a free quotation of Horace, *Ars Poetica*, 121.

passage ever made through the Sound 14,h. 53′ to Providence. And now we have got through nearly the burdensome bustle of this week.[48] Dr Channing entertained us one hour thirty five minutes yesterday with a noble discourse.

One of the things however that moved in my brain to make me write this moment is what I hope you will excuse me for saying. viz that you err in killing all your visitors with talking about New York.[49] Go any where else and after the first casual compliments you hear nothing particular of the *where.* it is left to speak for itself. But Ellinelli asks with utmost simplicity — ' What is the reason Waldo y[t] William & Edward keep talking to you about N. Y.?" And Eliz. Salisbury & Anna Jones [50] each separately wondered to me how Mr Em. had got such an *enthusiasm* for N. Y. And Charles wonders at home; & in the midst of the Seven Wonders here comes a letter tonight to Mother of wh. the subject is the indifference of ——— divers to N. York!! Now I take three quarters of the blame fully & fairly for my share knowing that I always set myself to mock at the town & of course you shd. magnify it. But after all it is nothing but a town & there are much greater & better things than streets or men considered *numerically.* e. g. y[e] same things considered morally, intellectually, historically, & so on. But I will hold my tongue about it if you will let us go free of its praise for time to come. Chip chop chain.

Mother sends her love. When Ellen comes down stairs she will send hers. Charles has spent a night or two of this holid. week in our cottage & the inconveniences of splendour have already made themselves very sensible to me in one weeks travelling four miles out & home daily — which english & proposition I hope you can understand.

Dr Ripley made a very good address to Berry St Conference,[51] agree-

48. Aside from the Election Day ceremonies, there were numerous church and society meetings (the *Christian Register,* May 22, 1830, gives the program for the week). The annual meetings continued long after Election Day was a thing of the past, and as late as 1849 a writer in the *Boston Daily Advertiser* (May 29) told of the throngs of persons passing from one meeting to another, following a round of religious, philanthropic, and intellectual studies and enjoyment from sunrise till night, and of the many unfamiliar faces which, as an old citizen could tell at a glance, belonged to guests from other cities and towns of New England.

49. In the letter of June 27, 1830, there is an apology for this paragraph.

50. Both, probably, former pupils of William Emerson in Boston (*cf.* May 4, 1860, to him).

51. This and the addresses of Joseph Story, James Walker, and Charles Lowell (father of the poet) were delivered at the anniversary meetings already mentioned and are all noticed in the *Christian Register,* May 29, 1830. Lowell's is reported there

ably to an appointment. Judge Story a good speech to Unit. Assoc. Mr Walker — a history of the Sects in this country — to the Evang. Miss. Soc. last ev^{g}. Dr Lowell addressed ye convention touchingly indeed on ye subject of ye diminished contrib. from year to year because of y^{r} own unchrist. differences & persistence in exclusive system in appointment of preacher for 5 years past. He spoke for the widow so y^{t} ye blood flew to my cheek & I saw that many a face beside was flushed. I guess I can repeat a sentence. "Sir, I thank God that the sighs & groans of these widows will never disturb *my* slumbers. And if they they are to perish I thank God that their blood shall not sprinkle the skirts of my garments." He is a natural orator

Love to Edward & I am yours affectionately

Waldo —

To William Emerson, Brookline, Massachusetts, June 27, 1830 [52]

Brookline, 27 June, 1830.

My dear William,

I blame myself for neglecting so long to write. We think & talk much of our N. York brothers. And two or three days ago at tea-table Mother & Ellinelli & I did hold in honouring remembrance the filial piety that I think is not often equalled in these times. I mean the beautiful Kennebunk year when the Stoic son received 420 dollars, & bro't 400 to his mother's lap; [53] &, as mother relates with glistening eye, *did not go to Portland,* that he might do this. Ellen loved him well when she heard it, & I tho't what right had I to tax such a person with talking about New York — for some particle of unkindness must have *seemed* in my letter I suppose, though none was really there.

What gave it peculiar value a value that reaches to me now was the critical time. For if you had been as other young men are it would have embarrassed the lone mother & hindered doubtless most effectually the education of her sons. So that Charles talking of it said, What holy madness was it!

But truly I rejoice to hear from Dr Emerson [54] that you are coming

at some length. According to H. E. Scudder, *James Russell Lowell,* 1901, I, 8, Emerson thought Dr. Lowell the most eloquent extemporaneous speaker he had ever heard.

52. MS owned by HCL; ph. in CUL.

53. See the letter of Apr. 1 and 10, 1819.

54. Possibly B. H. B. Emerson, listed as a physician in *The Boston Directory,* 1829.

presently to B. And the Doctor returns delighted with the attentions "of his sons" at N. Y & talks of your success. Heartily glad will you make us if you will fill the spare chamber a fortnight. & we live beautifully here. Tell Edward the same message for him in August, since he tells mother he can come then. He knows, does he not? that I never send a dollar of his Exhibition till I receive an order for the same. For I have not yet arrived at the Thule of having a superfluous dollar at the end of a quarter.

Edward Everett speaks tomorrow at the II Century of Charlestown.[55] & 4 July at Lowell [56] & A. H. E. at Boston.[57] I have got a copy of Dr Channings Works [58] waiting here for you if I can get a chance to send them. So I hope you have not bought them. Mother is very well Charles also flourisheth in pristine favour & is much a comforter to the old follks to wit Ellen & I.

I have a letter from you touching Faust. I read Gower's translation [59] & Shelleys [60] & liked the last far the best & tho't I had got some just [no][61]tion of the original, very bold varied grotesque creation, but out of nature & wide of Shakspeare. I am content with Chatham's language. Yours affectionately

Waldo

Your sister saith she will write you

To Edward Bliss Emerson, Brookline? Massachusetts, July 26, 1830

[Acknowledged in Edward Bliss Emerson, Aug. 4 (endorsed 1830 in Emerson's hand).]

55. His oration of June 28 is reported in the *Boston Courier,* June 29, 1830.

56. This oration is printed in Edward Everett, *Orations and Speeches,* 2d ed., Boston, 1853, II, 47–68. It was actually delivered on Monday, the 5th.

57. Reported in the *Boston Daily Advertiser,* July 7, 1830.

58. A collection of Channing's miscellaneous discourses and reviews was published in Boston on May 20, 1830, according to the *Boston Courier* of that date.

59. *Faust,* tr. Francis Leveson Gower, London, 1823. It is an interesting fact that Emerson had borrowed a volume of Goethe in German — Vol. III of *Goethe's Werke,* perhaps of the Stuttgart and Tübingen edition — as early as Dec. 5, 1828 (MS chargebook at HCL).

60. According to Harry Buxton Forman (*The Works of Percy Bysshe Shelley,* London, 1880, IV, 284), "Scenes from the Faust of Goethe" first appeared in Shelley's *Posthumous Poems,* 1824.

61. Mutilated by the opening of the seal.

To William and Edward Emerson, Brookline, Massachusetts, July 30? 1830[62]

How shall I dare come in the rear of — but it will not do for husband & wifey to compliment each other at their poor brothers' expense hungering for news.

Have you read the Edinb.[63] Beautiful article on Astronomy; better on Thos Munro. Witty on poor Bob. Montgomery which pray recommend to Edwards critical consideration, who was unlucky enough, if I remember rightly, to mistake him, the mongrel, for the amiable James of Sheffield. What new books can you tell me of who tread yet my college round[64] of Wordsworth Sampson Reed & Montaigne. Nothing newer on my table than Stewarts Mor. Phil.[65] & Degerando. Mrs Ripley[66] said to me How seldom is a book any book better than one's own tho'ts! a sentiment I questioned then & still deny but am wholly Yours

Waldo

Mothers love.

62. MS owned by HCL; ph. in CUL. Pp. 1–2 and a part of p. 3 contain a letter written by Ellen Tucker Emerson to " W. & E.," with some lines from Bryant's poem " The Old Man's Funeral," which she admired. At the top of p. 1 Emerson himself wrote " 30 July Brookline," and on p. 3 is his own letter, printed here.

63. All the articles mentioned are in *The Edinburgh* for Apr., 1830. Macaulay's fierce attack on Robert Montgomery is famous.

64. In an unpublished entry in his diary — one of the earliest extant entries, apparently made in Mar., 1819, or soon afterwards — Emerson wrote:

" I have thirsted to abuse the poetical character of Mr. Wordsworth whose poems have lately been read to me. . . . At once then his poetry is the poetry of pigmies. It belittles the mind that is accustomed to the manly march of other muses. I am pleased with the prettiness . . . but I am soon conscious of a disagreeable sensation wh. soon becomes intolerable . . ." (typescript *Journals*) .

Emerson's interest in Sampson Reed's writings has already been noted, and there is evidence that his brothers were also readers of the Swedenborgian philosopher and druggist. Charles wrote to William and Edward on Sept. 24, 1830 (MS owned by Dr. Haven Emerson) , asking to borrow William's MS of Reed's Master's oration.

65. Dugald Stewart, *The Philosophy of the Active and Moral Powers,* 1828.

66. Sarah Bradford Ripley.

To Edward Bliss Emerson, Boston? September 4, 1830 [67]

Saturday, 4 Septr.

Dear Edward,

I tho't I shd. see you by coming & may yet, if not goodbye & every blessing go with you to the strange city.[68] Carry the book to William & much love.

Tell him I feel rich today (o rare day) & so want to pay him ten of ever so many dollars that I in behalf of the *Concern* owe him. which I enclose.

Yrs

Waldo.

To William Emerson, Boston, September 6, 1830 [69]

Boston 6 Sept. 1830

Dear William,

Edw. sailed Sat. night. in packet.[70] I enclose a letter just rec^{d} for him. Ellen has just sent me word of her arrival in Concord N H last Saturday morn. I carried her to Lexington Thursday on her way. She mends fast. We ponder many plans,[71] but she inclines after all to stay at home this winter. Dr Jackson leans to that opinion. I was very sorry not to see your splendid friend Mr McCrackan [72] Please to present

67. MS owned by HCL; ph. in CUL. Sept. 4 fell on Saturday in 1830, and the date " Sept. 4/30 " is endorsed.

68. Edward was returning to New York after a visit in Boston and Brookline. On Aug. 23 he wrote to William from Boston (MS owned by Dr. Haven Emerson), telling of his safe arrival on that day.

69. MS owned by HCL; ph. in CUL.

70. On Saturday, Sept. 4, Edward wrote to William (MS owned by Dr. Haven Emerson) that he expected to sail that night on the packet " Gen. Stark " and arrive in New York perhaps the middle of the following week.

71. The history of Emerson's many anxieties and changing plans because of his wife's illness is best told in several letters from Charles to William owned by Dr. Haven Emerson. On Aug. 11, 1830, Charles reported a new attack " by her old & deadly enemy the bleeding. . . . It casts trouble & anxiety over her husband's prospects. They will probably go off this Fall to Southern latitudes." On Aug. 14 he wrote: " Poor Waldo feels the disappointment strongly, & seems now to make up his mind that he must break or untie all bonds that fasten him here, & go off in search of kinder elements. For my part, I doubt whether there is any climate that will save Ellen . . ." On Oct. 1, Charles thought it good news that, by the doctor's advice, Ellen was not to travel but that she and her husband were to spend the following winter " quietly keeping house."

72. *Longworth's American Almanac,* 1830, lists H. and John M'Crackan, both New York merchants.

my compliments to him & tell him, that the next time he is in the city I hope he will give me the pleasure of seeing him at my house. We were just on the wing from the sick chamber at Brookline to Concord, when I found his card at my study! — Edward appears very well & content with N. Y. Shaw [73] is approved & sworn. Dr Channing, I learn goes to Cuba this winter for his *wifes* health!! [74] Mr Ware is getting quite well. Dr Gardiner is dead in London. What a tremendous responsibility for Lafayette's old age.[75] If he gets well thro' it he may have the first fame in history.

Your loving brother
Waldo.

To Benjamin Peter Hunt, Boston, September 6, 1830 [76]

Boston, 6 Sept. 1830 —

My dear Sir,

When I was lately at Chelmsford [77] Dr Dalton showed me a letter he had received from you, which interested me very much. It contained expressions of great kindness toward me, which except that they overestimated a very little kindness were very grateful to me. Then it contained an account of yourself which looked very much like an old acquaintance for some time past lost to me in a cloud. It has been one of the puzzles that outran the skill of my philosophy how any one of that small class of persons who love goodness & truth for their beauty simply should choose an oblique course instead of a straight one. I never learned any particulars but knew you had not made your residence in

73. Lemuel Shaw — later Herman Melville's father-in-law — as chief justice of the Supreme Judicial Court of Massachusetts.

74. Channing spent the winter of 1830–1831 in St. Croix instead, and for his own health (*Memoir of William Ellery Channing,* 2d ed., Boston, 1848, III, 135 ff.) . Both Edward and Charles Emerson were soon to follow his example in seeking a milder climate in the West Indies. The letter of June 17, 1831, seems to show that Channing saw Edward Emerson in St. Croix. The *Christian Register* reported, on Dec. 4, Channing's sailing from Boston; on Sept. 4, the return from Europe of Henry Ware, Jr., in health; and, on Sept. 11, the death, in England, of J. S. J. Gardiner, rector of Trinity Church, Boston.

75. On Sept. 4 the *Daily Evening Transcript* had the old news of La Fayette's appointment as commander of the National Guard and of Louis Philippe's prominent part in affairs; and repeated the rumor, soon verified, that Charles X had abdicated.

76. MS owned by Mr. Owen D. Young; ph. in CUL.

77. For Hunt as one of Emerson's pupils at Chelmsford five years earlier, see a note on Dec. *c.* 20? 1825. Dalton is mentioned in the same letter.

College pleasant & had gone suddenly [78] without leaving that respect for your powers & feelings which I had felt, & tho't all good people wd. feel. I am quite sorry I did not borrow the letter & bring it home. But certainly your account of yourself was interesting & relieved me as it put a better than reputable face on the matter by suggesting the principles on which you acted. They are good & I honour them. I see far less independence of character, & scorn of patronage than I could wish in the world, & your *Soul* cannot have better friends. But, my dear Sir, I cannot bring myself to believe that the times are so out of joint that these virtues are proscribed & must damn the possessor's worldly interests. Johnson was as proud, yet strode shod or barefoot through Oxford & took his degrees.[79] It seems to me that a generous mind goes naturally to the highest places in society & not to obscure resorts & has that nobleness to assert its own title to all such advantages in spite of poverty or opposition. Go to Cambridge & eat bread & water & live to *think. Think* your way up to your true place among men, — no doubt it will be accorded. I believe the world is far more just than is often said & that every man will have in it every inch of his merits allowed him, & that not by its pleasure or displeasure but by God's order.

I was glad to see you mean to go to Yale. If you do not return to Cambridge, do not fail to go there. But do try to work — intellectually I mean. F[orce][80] yourself to something regular & methodical if only for the experiment & for vir   humdrum maxims about industry & order are apt to prove stronger than we, when we are wayward.

But I had almost forgot to say what first set me on writing now, & that is, that I never pretended to have done anything for you that shd. give me a right to feel angry or cold on your going away, as your letter seemed to charge me. My recommendation to the College Gov't [81] was

78. The Harvard catalogue for 1828–1829, published in 1828, listed Benjamin Peter Hunt of Chelmsford as a freshman, but the MS *Records of the College Faculty* (in HCL) has an entry of July 13, 1829, which names him with others who "cannot be matriculated and their connexion with the College ceases of course." Hunt wrote Emerson on Sept. 28, 1830, that he had been misunderstood and misinterpreted in some degree and was glad to leave. He seems not to have entered Yale.

79. Emerson had doubtless read the story about the shoes as told by Boswell, who, however, did not make the mistake of stating that Johnson stayed at Oxford long enough for a degree.

80. Page 3 of the MS is somewhat mutilated, and several words are partially obscured. Part of this word (presumably "Force") and a portion of the second line following are entirely lacking.

81. This makes it seem probable that Emerson wrote to the Harvard authorities

what I wd. have done for a stranger, & I only *promised* more. So you are free of me. — I will not plague you with offers of service now (yet you may command me) but I will say that if you have the valour to borrow money I can procure you probably one or two hundred dollars at the usual interest to be paid when your convenience serves. You will deeply gratify me if you will write me any news of your inner self what you purpose, what you think, what you doubt, what you know; what progress you make in developing the great Idea which Time develops the idea of God. May his blessing guard & direct you. Your friend

R. Waldo Emerson.

To William Emerson, Boston, October 4, 1830 [82]

Boston 4 Oct

Dear William,

Ellen is pretty well & we hope in a fortnight to begin our housekeeping & are busy buying carpets & the like. Mother is very well & Charles. Bulkeley has not been so well lately & is now at Charlestown with Dr Wyman. I have nothing to add but the needless assurances of my love to you & Edward

Your aff[t] brother
Waldo.

To William Emerson, Boston, November 29, 1830 [83]

Boston, 29 Nov. 1830.

Dear William,

We are all anxious & grieved to hear such ill news of Edward. If the vessel has not sailed & there is any prospect of his being really sick, would it not be better to bundle him up warm, & send him here immediately — for Mother & Ellen to nurse him. He can here be effectually taken care of. If it is advised to keep him out of doors I should

on Hunt's behalf in July, 1829, or some time between that date and Sept., 1830; but I have found no other evidence.

82. MS owned by HCL; ph. in CUL. The endorsement, "Oct. 4/30," is clearly correct. For Emerson's earlier uncertainty whether he must leave Boston and travel with his wife, for the decision to spend the winter "keeping house," and for Edward's departure for New York, see Sept. 6, 1830, to William Emerson, and notes. Charles wrote to William, Saturday, Sept. 25 (endorsed 1830; MS owned by Dr. Haven Emerson) that Bulkeley was at Charlestown.

83. MS owned by HCL; ph. in CUL.

think the Magnolia [84] plan a very favorable one, especially in the circumstance of Mr & Mrs Haskins [85] company. Mother looks at it with a little more alarm – the idea of a severe cold & his going so far from friends than I yet do. but we are utterly unable to judge at this distance & must depend on your extremest prudence for us as well as for you. What money will he need? I will send you a letter to Mr Delafield. Whatever *seems expedient must be done, cost what it will,* & that first settled, we must then use the rigidest economy in accomplishing it. I hope he will board with W. E. H. If he goes do be careful to multiply his *clothes* for shipboard.

And pray write again forthwith about him. and do be careful of yourself.

Yours affectionately

Waldo E.

If he goes there I will write to Murat who may be useful to him.

To William Emerson, Boston, December 3, 1830 [86]

Boston 3 Dec. 1830

Dear William,

Grieved are we to hear no better news of Edw. than your letter brings today. But why not go to Magnolia. Mr Nuttall [87] says there is no better climate & there he has the great advantage – which I suppose you must have some particular reason for forgoing – of W. L. H. & his wifes care. –

Santa Cruz has the very serious objection of great expense. Mrs Clapp [88] tells me that it cost her $14. pr week apiece to be boarded & that a single gentleman may be accommodated for $10.00 & further that

84. Magnolia, one of several mushroom towns near Tallahassee, was founded in 1828, flourished for a time, but soon declined. Eventually, nothing was left but some oak trees and a cemetery. (James Owen Knauss, *Territorial Florida Journalism,* 1926, p. 5.) The letter of Dec. 3, 1830, shows that Emerson was interested in the place particularly because it was near Murat's plantation.

85. Later in this letter Emerson refers to " W. E. H.," but in Dec. 3, 1830, he writes clearly " W. L. H." It seems probable, however, that he refers to William Emerson Haskins – a cousin – and his wife, Frances Hodges (*cf.* Almon D. Hodges, *Genealogical Record of the Hodges Family,* 1896, p. 412).

86. MS owned by HCL; ph. in CUL.

87. For Nuttall in Florida, see *Proceedings of the American Philosophical Society,* VII, 301. Emerson may well have had some acquaintance with the naturalist, who was curator of the botanical garden at Harvard.

88. Possibly Mary Paine Clapp. *Cf.* Mar. 26, 1842.

expenses of physicians nurses &c are extremely large. It would be a pity to send him alone & friendless to a place where he shall be continually embarrassed by what he will think unreasonable charges. If he goes to Florida he will not be confined to a strip of island 15 by 25 miles but will have the continent where to choose & the chance of agreeable hospitality on plantations. For myself I would pay a hundred dollars to live a little while with Murat. Do think seriously before he goes to Santa Cruz, which is said indeed to be very warm but is somewhat humid. Pray enquire diligently concerning Florida. Give my love to Edward & tell him our hopes & prayers are warm & strong for him & Ellen mourns that he shd. be sick again and Mr & Mrs Adams are much interested.

We had a pleasant Thanksgiving feast here yesterday & faces met that had not before in our anniversaries. And much we missed the usual good tidings from N. Y.

Yours affectionately
Waldo

To William Emerson, Boston, December 5, 1830 [89]

Boston Sunday night 5 Dec

Dear William,

I have just rec[d] your letter of yesterday. Mother would go to N. Y. if a boat went tomorrow, but now she fears lest Edw[d] sail on Tuesday & she mt. miss of him. We have talked over the matter a good deal & are all pretty strongly of one mind — that he ought to come here rather than go alone to sea. It was his very decided conviction when he came home from Europe [90] that it was a great mistake to send him as he was sent for his health. He suffered every thing at sea & much on shore. I am afraid his chance cannot be much better now. It wd. be adviseable if anybody could go with him; but as no one can it seems best he should not undergo so much certain exposure for uncertain advantage. Better far it seems to me roll him up in hot blankets & send him here to hybernate in a chamber by a coal fire & the first of March when the east winds blow we will send him to Carolina if need be. Charles & Mother & Mr Adams all concur strongly in this view of the matter. Had he not better let Capt Lotman go alone & wait for Mothers careful counsel. Perhaps she will set out Tuesday morng. We

89. MS owned by HCL; ph. in CUL. The year 1830 in the endorsement agrees with conclusive internal evidence.

90. *Cf.* a note on the letter of Oct. 23 and 24, 1826.

all feel for your embarrassments which must be very great. Much love to Edward & tell him we have seen six troubles & shall be carried thro' the seventh by the same hand which will yet lead us when we quit this sickening planet.

Yours affectionately
Waldo.

Please write immediately on rec^{g} this mother says what your conclusion is. but I think mother will go Tuesday.

To Ezra Ripley, Boston, December 15, 1830 [91]

Boston 15 Dec. 1830

My dear Grandfather,

We did not get any letter until last night; & that bro't us no very good news. Mother had arrived in New York, but had been detained two days at Newport by weather so that Edward sailed out of New York [92] about half an hour before she arrived, on Sunday morning. William states that Edward was well cared for & had a fine wind to set out with. But the disappointment was necessarily a sad one to mother & a privation to Edward. We expect mother home with the first fair weather.

I saw Mr Barrett yesterday, & he promised to inspect the Record of the Conference [93] & send you a copy of the vote you desire.

I hope you do not find yourself the worse for your kind visit. Grandfather is such a favourite with my wife as well as her husband that we hope he will always make our house one of his homes.

Charles has not been in town. Ellen sends her love & respects. With remembrances to Dea. Ripley [94] & Miss R.

I am your affectionate Grandson

R. Waldo Emerson.

91. MS owned by RWEMA; ph. in CUL.

92. For Santa Cruz (St. Croix) — *cf.* Dec. 16, 1830, and later letters.

93. *Cf.* May 27, 1830, which mentions Dr. Ripley's address at the Berry Street Conference. According to the *Christian Register,* May 29, a Mr. Barrett was chosen scribe of the Berry Street Conference. It is not clear whether he was the Rev. Samuel Barrett mentioned in the same issue of that paper as having been elected a director of the American Unitarian Association.

94. Probably Ezra Ripley's brother Noah, "the good deacon" of *Journals,* II, 296 (Apr. 24, 1830). *Cf.* also Dec.? 12? 1829? Noah's daughter Sarah, who succeeded her sister Lucy as the wife of John Jewett (H. W. Ripley, *Genealogy of a Part of the Ripley Family,* 1867, p. 33), appears in later letters and may be the "Miss R." mentioned here.

To Ezra Ripley, Boston, December 16, 1830 [95]

Boston Dec 16 1830

My dear Sir,

I have been to Waltham this afternoon & find Uncle Ripley quite lame with the gout which attacked him last Monday night. It is in one foot & very painful. He wishes me to write this line to ask you if it will be possible for you to come & preach for him next Sunday as he is wholly unprovided & will not be able to preach himself.

Ellen & I went to Waltham to find Aunt Mary, & bro't her with us to Boston. She means to spend a week with us. Mother returned this day very safely & tho disappointed yet in some degree comforted by seeing William & Dr Perkins [96] & learning that Edward improved for a few days previous to embarking for St Cruz.

Very affectionately yours
R. Waldo Emerson

To Edward Bliss Emerson, Boston? December c. 20? 1830

[An unfinished letter described in Dec. 24? 1830.]

To Edward Bliss Emerson, Boston, December 24? 1830 [97]

I find wifeys letter [98] here unfinished & so to prevent her destroying it which is always a strong probability until it has got into the postmasters fingers I will put thus much insurance hereon. I have mislaid a letter I had half written,[99] & wonder what shd come of it. The only fact there stated of importance was that G B E has pd. the remaining $50. due to you & $10 interest.

95. MS owned by RWEMA; ph. in CUL.

96. Dr. Cyrus Perkins of New York appears in *Longworth's American Almanac,* 1830. *Cf.* also May 3, 1836.

97. MS owned by RWEMA; ph. in CUL. A date line, "Boston, 24 Dec. 1830," is in Emerson's hand; the remainder of p. 1 and three lines at the top of p. 2 are Ellen's letter to Edward, here omitted; then follows, on pp. 2 and 3, Emerson's own letter, which I print. The superscription is to Edward at "Santa Croix" — Emerson, still unfamiliar with this new geography, had confused the Spanish and French names of the island. Dec. 16, 1830, has another version of the name, equally impartial.

98. Ellen, in her part of the letter, here omitted, congratulates Edward on his escape from the northern winter and tells of a recent visit from Mary Moody Emerson, who seemed to her "not of the earthy nor altogether of the heavenly — to be wondered at and in some sort admired."

99. Dec. *c.* 20? 1830. "G B E" was, no doubt, George Barrell Emerson.

How are you. We all sympathize with & pray for you. Follow Ellens advice about inquisitiveness. Pray make *written minutes* of places & prices & persons & climate [100] that may be of use to any of us hereafter.

Carried you any books? If not, stick to the stout principle of both the wise & the ignorant ' the fewer the better.' No other man's thot's can be comparable in value to my own whenever my experience or reason will deign to utter a conclusion of theirs. But the long & often intervals, — question comes how to use them, whether in hoeing the proper ownty spot or getting a graft from a better soil. But perhaps sickness & home-sickness may lead your tho'ts more directly to the Source of Being & the hope of living with him & owing to him directly & to no second source your knowledge & your morals. I saw a man yesterday to wit, Sampson Reed, who told me that it was now ten years since he had known the fear of death: His new faith teaches him not to regard it as a *punishment,* he says. I trust in Heavens care of you & that we shall yet pass pleasant days of health together but let us rejoice in the New Testament which makes sickness & distance safe to us.[101] Yours dear Edward with all my heart.

Waldo. —

Be sure not deny yourself any necessary or comfortable accommodation. —

100. In his letters from the West Indies, Edward furnished lengthy descriptions of landscapes, climate, and people.

101. It is noteworthy that during his years as pastor of the Second Church, Emerson's letters are most likely to contain conventional theology, especially those letters relating to sickness and death. Yet in the present letter there are also the germs of the Divinity School address, " Self-reliance," and " The Over-soul."

1831

To Edward Bliss Emerson, Boston, January 24, 26, and 29, 1831[1]

Boston, 24 Jan. 1831.

Dear Edward,

Blessings from the Father of all blessing, upon my dear brother. I trust this sheet warm from home finds you with salved lungs & stouter frame than before. We have heard nothing from or of you yet since you left N. Y. And mother expects this week or next to receive tidings Of William we hear from week to week.

Ellen sends her love. Poor girl, she is more sick & has been probably than you & I wish with all my heart we were both of us with you As soon as the snows melt so as to give us passage and as soon as she recovers her diminished strength so as to ride & walk we shall set out for Philad. or Baltimore, God helping us. Meantime she sends a sisters love & I a brothers. Mother is very well. Charles also — at Cambridge & all alive upon this nefarious Indian Subject. U. S. versus Cherokees.[2]

26. I stopped writing because the opp^{y} was deferred. Ellen has been more weak & sick since, but gets out to ride a little way yesterday & day before. If she can only continue to do this with impunity I shall hope the reestablishment of her health but we have come to the prefixing of *if* to all our plans.

You can not write too frequently after once we get a letter. Say what you want & we will try to serve you. J. T. Austin is the Φ B K Orator; Pierpont, the Poet; Edson chaplain.[3]

Aunt Mary is at Concord. Your affectionate brother

Waldo —

Forgive this little letter but the poor nurse & husband on Sat mor^{n} has no thots to utter.

1. MS owned by RWEMA; ph. in CUL.

2. See Jan. 31, 1831.

3. For the parts of James T. Austin and Theodore Edson, see *Boston Commercial Gazette,* Sept. 1 and 5, 1831. John Pierpont was unable to appear. His place was

To William Emerson, Boston, January 31, 1831 [4]

Boston 31 Jan

Dear William

'A brother that is far off' [5] is pleasant to the soul though seldom talked with by tongue or pen. My poor Ellen has been sadly sick [6] &, we flatter ourselves, is a little better. Nurse is rubbing her cold hands this moment to quicken her circulations. (I write in her chamber) Soon, please God, we hope to pass by your house in our jou[rney][7] southwards. Yet perhaps February & its snow must melt away first before we can have strength or roads. I wish you would tell me what you know of Murat whom you have twice mentioned. I hope no harm has befallen him. Has he forsaken this country? I look forward to opportunities of conversing with him again in the body or in the spirit. Nelly sends her love & says you may see her in more sorry plight this year than last year when we come.

No news from Edward yet? Charles has stirred up an Indian indignation in Cambridge & the meeting is tonight.[8] Ashmun [9] & the Danas, &c to speak perhaps the young Tully himself. His health is not so robust as his mind. Yours affectionately

Waldo

---

offered to Emerson, but he refused and suggested Benjamin Kent, who actually read the poem (see the letters of June 28 and June 29, 1831).

4. MS owned by HCL; ph. in CUL. The year 1831, in William Emerson's endorsement, is obviously correct.

5. From *Proverbs*, 27:10.

6. This was written eight days before her death.

7. Torn away with the seal.

8. Charles Emerson wrote to William on Jan. 6, 1831 (MS owned by Dr. Haven Emerson): "I have just heard a report of certain resolutions of the Legislature of Georgia, which I pray God may not prove true— . . . I wish if matters must be driven to a crisis, that it might result in a peaceable secession, of Georgia—tho' I see not how this could be—since we are bound by every solemn obligation, to assert the claims, & protect the rights of the poor Indians, whom Georgia assails—" On Jan. 30 Charles again wrote to William on the same subject (MS owned by Dr. Haven Emerson) and informed him that the citizens of Cambridge were to meet the next day for protest. No communication from such a meeting at Cambridge seems to have been printed in the sessional papers of Congress, though there are a number of protests on the same subject from other towns in various states. Emerson's own famous protest to Van Buren (see Apr. 23, 1838) could not have been uninfluenced by Charles's earlier example.

9. Ashmun was probably the lawyer and, later, professor mentioned in the letters of Oct. 31, 1827, and Aug. 26, 1829.

To Mary Moody Emerson, Boston, February 8, 1831 [10]

Tuesday 11 o'clock Feb. 8th

Dear Aunt

My angel is gone to heaven this morning & I am alone in the world & strangely happy. Her lungs shall no more be torn nor her head scalded by her blood nor her whole life suffer from the warfare between the force & delicacy of her soul & the weakness of her frame. I said this morn & I do not know but it is true that I have never known a person in the world in whose separate existence as a soul I could so readily & fully believe & she is present with me now beaming joyfully upon me, in her deliverance & the entireness of her love for your poor nephew. I see it plainly that things & duties will look coarse & vulgar enough to me when I find the romance of her presence (& romance is a beggarly word) withdrawn from them all. But now the fulness of joy occasioned by things said by her in the last week & by this eternal deliverance is in my heart. She has a great deal to say always about Aunt Mary & would gladly have seen you when Grandfather came, & said then she should like now a letter from you.

But the past days the most eventful of my life are all a dim confusion & now the pall is drawn over them, yet do they shine brilliantly in my spiritual world. Say, dear Aunt, if I am not rich in her memory?

Respectful love to Grandfather & tell him Ellen blessed him for his prayer — of which her lips repeated every word.

Your nephew

Waldo E

10. MS owned by RWEMA; ph. in CUL. On p. 3 is a brief note from Charles, stating that Ellen died at nine o'clock. Other letters from Charles to William (owned by Dr. Haven Emerson) add some detail not given in the present letter. On Feb. 6 he wrote that Ellen was near death — ". . . when I saw her yesterday, I was convinced . . . Waldo is as you may believe a one over whom the waters have gone." And in a letter of Feb. 6, 7, and 8, he completed the story: "Saturday morng. I . . . found her sadly altered & her husband & mother without any hope of her recovery — . . . Waldo . . . is bowed down under his affliction, but he says 'it is like nothing, but an angel taking her flight to Heaven.' . . . Monday . . . 4 P. M. Grandfather has been here — He prayed with Ellen — . . . She looks saint like — . . . Tuesday — 10 A. M. . . . She died about an hour ago — Waldo is well & bears well his incalculable loss — " Emerson himself wrote, a few months later, a fitting epitaph (*Journals*, II, 384):

". . . Ellen is dead,
She who outshone all beauty, yet knew not
That she was beautiful . . ."

To William Emerson, Boston, March 7, 1831 [11]

Boston, 7 March, 1831

Dear William,

I have not written you since I was left alone—but shall never forget the kindness of your first letter. I did not feel my solitude when all spoke & tho't of nothing else as now I feel it when I come home and all have forgotten it—& the common things go on and she is not here. But her memory is blessed & every tho't of her is happy & the grave is pleasanter to me than the house. She longed to be acquainted with her brothers whom she loved beforehand—

But the reason of my writing now is to introduce to you my friend Mr George A. Sampson who is to spend a few days in N. York on his business & was not sure that you knew him. He is one of the ten righteous men that save a city,[12] & it is a happiness to know him, & Ellen esteemed him very highly. I have been to Concord to see Aunt Mary & try to persuade her to come & live with Mother & me, but no reasons can reach her & you must wait her mood. I think she will come shortly for Concord is never long agreeable to her.

Good news from Edward I think. I wish he cd. find reason to stop there. It will all be to be done over next winter if he comes home & to disadvantage. Set it before his eyes plainly if you write & bid him find any employment that can be tolerable & feasible.

And the first time you can come to Boston, it will make glad mother &

Yours affectionately

Waldo

To William Emerson, Boston, March 30, 1831 [13]

Boston, 30 March, 1831

Dear William,

I send you my Mother & sister on their way southward—but two of the intended party dont go with them—one is in heaven, & the other walking in his little mill path—

But both Mrs Kent & Margaret need the journey very much & I trust it will prove beneficial. They have been faithful faithful to Ellen, & if life is desireable *here* to them I pray they may find all of good & sweet it has. Margaret has been sick a week in her chamber & may not set out

11. MS owned by HCL; ph. in CUL.

12. *Genesis,* 18:32.

13. MS owned by HCL; ph. in CUL.

for days yet, especially if this rain lasts. They talk of going to Richmond. Va.

We received this morng your letter inclosing one from Edw. to Aunt Mary. who is here. Edward writes always sadly. His faith is not strong & he clings to life. I can readily believe that such debilitating disease shd. have this effect but in health the prospect of death is far less gloomy.

I enclose Aunt Mary's fine scrap to him because you probably will send it sooner than I, & it is worth your reading.

Yours affectionately

Waldo –

To William Emerson, Boston, April 14, 1831 [14]

Boston 14 April – 1831

Dear William,

I am quite anxious about my travellers whom I commended to you a fortnight since.[15] Have they come to N. Y? Have they gone to Phil? I have not had one word from them since their parting, & they promised to write me soon. I enclose this letter to them & you must direct it according to your information of their goings. I trust they have no more sickness to fight with on the way. –

Mother & Aunt Mary & Charles are well. Charles is spending Vacation here, but is gone today to Concord with Mrs Barnard.[16] We had a letter yesterday from Edward in the usual tone of sluggish convalescence. He speaks with uncertainty of the manner of returning but not at all of any employment there. I suppose he has neither the power nor the opportunity.

You never speak of coming here. When will your visit be. Mother is sure you will come this summer. In June Charles & I mean to journey a little, when my Vestry lectures are done [17] so give us warning beforehand when to expect you and we will not fail to be at home.

Yours affectionately

Waldo.

14. MS owned by HCL; ph. in CUL.

15. See Mar. 30, 1831.

16. Perhaps the wife of George M. Barnard, partner of Abel Adams (*cf. Stimpson's Boston Directory*, 1831).

17. The *Christian Register,* Apr. 30, 1831, gives notice " that the Course of Sunday Evening Lectures, at Messrs Emerson's and Motte's churches, for the present season, is concluded."

Bulkeley does not appear to get any better & is still at Charlestown. A longer illness than any for years. I went to hear Dr Taylor of N. Haven [18] preach last ev^{g}. in ye Revival meetings. He wisely identified his cause with the conscience & so made us subscribe to almost all he said.

TO EDWARD BLISS EMERSON, BOSTON, APRIL 20 AND 23, 1831 [19]

Boston 20 April 1831

Dear Edward,

I do not know whether I have written to you since Ellen left me. Her loss is a universal loss to me. It makes all life little worth & I go backward to her beautiful character for a charm that I might seek in vain thro the world.[20] But faith is strong — her faith stronger than death & the hope of heaven is more distinct to me by the aid of affection such as hers. A little while before she died — (a few days —) she said, ' she should like to live to hear of Edward's safe arrival in S. C.' [21] — & always loved her brother. And now — the whole happiness & the whole sorrow is told in the text — I shall go to her but she shall not return to me.[22] — But why shd. I sadden you with my sorrows who have your own. I trust they are ending or ended. I hope your aches & pains have all gone. Have you formed any definite plans for coming months? Have you corresponded with Dr Morell in Cuba respecting the instruction of his family, or are you not strong enough? Young Norwood [23] says he shall write to Dr Morell for himself, if you do not go there. Mother depends upon your company to help her take care of your poor lonely brother this summer in Chardon St. & I suppose if you do, it were better to sail for Boston, & not for N. Y. & we will send you out again if neces-

18. The Yale catalogue of 1830–1831 names the Rev. Nathaniel W. Taylor, S. T. D., as professor of didactic theology. He is attacked in the *Christian Register* of July 16, 1831.

19. MS owned by RWEMA; ph. in CUL.

20. Perhaps an echo of Payne's famous song. *Clari* was first performed some eight years earlier. But *cf.* also *Paradise Lost,* IV, 272.

21. St. Croix; see earlier letters.

22. Adapted from *II Samuel,* 12:23.

23. Probably John Greene Norwood, college classmate of Charles Emerson. Dr. Morrell — not Morell — was the master of a Cuban plantation. Sophia and Mary Peabody lived for some time in his home; and the correspondence between them and their sister, Elizabeth, and their mother has much to say about the education of the children there, mainly, it seems, under Mary's direction. (MSS, mostly of 1833 and 1834, owned by Mr. Horace Mann.)

sary in the fall. But you must think on all things for all of us who know nothing of your health or particular advices & only are sure of a boundless good hope & good will towards yourself —

Ralph Emerson [24] has been here this evg He has suffered from fraud, & from sickness in Porto Rico, & now has a good prospect of work in Europe at Paris, & sails next week. Aunt Mary is here & in very good spirits & Charles in his vacation

Apr. 23 Before I close my letter I will tell you a pleasant circumstance because a rare of ye Haskins Estate Uncle Ralph called to tell mother that the property was improving & yt he had $300. for her ye result of ye compromise due to her from ye family. And so it was put to ye acct of Insurance Office, & makes her debt $1200. only. Dear love from all & from

Your affectionate brother
Waldo.

To William Emerson, Boston, May 24, 1831 [25]

Boston 24 May 1831

Dear William,

I know not when I have written to you before & gladly take a few moments now. I am sorry to find now & then a passage of your kind letters written as in low spirits. Let there be peace & good fortune to the good. Yet seems nothing more natural than that sometimes you shd. feel lonely. With more of my own blood around me I am lonely enough at some hours myself. And just so much gloom as it gives to life just so much does this feeling take off from death. 'The sublime attractions' — I wish they may never be less.

I have been reading 7 or 8 lectures of Cousin — in the first of three vols. of his Philosophy.[26] A master of history, an epic he makes of man

24. A second cousin, the brother of George Barrell Emerson; he lived in Porto Rico and later in France and in California (see Mar. 1, 1861). William Emerson wrote to his mother and Charles on Sept. 2, 1831 (MS owned by Dr. Haven Emerson), that he had just received word from Ralph Emerson in Paris. *Cf.* also June 29 and July 5, 1833, and letters of later years.

25. MS owned by HCL; ph. in CUL.

26. This reading of Victor Cousin's first volume, *Cours de philosophie,* 1828, was particularly significant because it was this book which gave Emerson his first taste for the *Bhagavadgita* (see Aug. 4, 1873). Meantime, Charles had written to William, Mar. 3, 1830 (MS owned by Dr. Haven Emerson): "Do you read the Edinburgh? The new article on Cousin's Philosophy, is said to be great — a key to the

& of the world — & excels all men in giving effect, yea, *eclat* to a metaphysical theory. Have you not read it? tis good reading — well worth the time — clients or no clients.

I am going a little journey,[27] as I believe Charles has told you, & mean to set out next Monday morn. & go to Burlington. The second Sunday I expect to preach in Northampton. & the third at home. I expect to leave Aunt Mary & Mrs Lambard [28] & son (whom we expected tonight from N. Bedford,) in the house to pass the time with mother, & if they desert her perhaps she will. go to Concord.

It is Election week & Grandfather will come down tomorrow It is the last probably of its race,[29] for the people have agreed by their Nays to have no more spring sessions of legislature.

Bulkeley is a little better, but still at Charlestown. You asked of his expenses — they are 3.00 pr week & some new clothes & new shoes. If Edward should get employment & have no bills, I suppose I can pay for B. without difficulty. especially as it seems that Ellen is to continue to benefit her husband whenever hereafter the estate shall be settled. but at this present time I am going fast in arrears, I believe. I please myself that Ellen's work of mercy is not done on earth, but she shall continue to help Edward & B. & Charles.

Mother is very well & not unmindful of you. Oh no Glencairn.[30] And Aunt Mary is as heavenly & unreasonable as ever. I believe I never acknowledged the receipt of her interest money which was received & paid.

How soon shall we see you. Tell them you shall stay a good while with

Your affectionate brother
Waldo.

We have a letter in excellent spirits from Edward at St Johns Porto Rico.

---

whole German system. I cant understand it at all — " A copy of the *Cours* of 1828 is still in Emerson's house, at Concord, and bears his signature.

27. See June 19, 1831.

28. Emerson's cousin, who was Sibyl Farnham before her marriage. *Cf.* Nov. 1? 1824, where the apparently incorrect spelling "Lambert" is used. I am uncertain whether her husband was the Orville D. Lambard of July 16 and of July 17, 1862.

29. The *Christian Register* of May 21, 1831, had commented on this occasion as "perhaps the last as a civil anniversary, that we shall celebrate." According to the same paper for May 28, Dr. Ripley was chosen moderator of the meeting of Liberal Ministers held in the Berry Street vestry on Election Day.

30. Probably Burns's "Lament for James Earl of Glencairn," with its characteristically extravagant promise to remember Glencairn, was a recitation piece in the family or at least familiar to Emerson and his brothers.

TO EDWARD BLISS EMERSON, BOSTON, JUNE 17, 1831 [31]

Boston 17 June 1831

My dear brother, I enclose to you two letters which came back to me from St Croix last night forwarded by Mr Hill who mt. have sent them I shd. think to P. R.[32]

I rejoice to hear of yr mending health. Please God it mend more & faster. Dr Channing gave mother in ye street a good account of you [33] & has promised to come & tell the rest. I have just returned with Charles from a fortnight's absence in the country, but travelling is a sad recreation to one who finds Ellen nowhere yet everywhere.

Aunt Mary has gone to Waterford, & Sibyl [34] whom I left here has also gone home. Mother is very well. Things go kindly with us, yet is it hard to be happy. Who is? not one. God is the only unfailing resource – the only good which the first ages described in wh the last ages have not exposed any falsehood And the evidence augments with time – Yet who has found him? – Who seeks him?

Mrs Kent & Margaret T. are here in town returned from journeying southwards yet not much strengthened. Margaret looks least well. They will journey I hope all summer.

I hope you find your new engagements pleasant & profitable or promising. I hear well of Mr Mason [35] from every body who knows him But you need care & I shd. think something of generous living – yet I know nothing. Keep your tranquil temper as the apple of your eye & if it

31. MS owned by RWEMA; ph. in CUL.

32. Edward had established himself at San Juan, Porto Rico, instead of staying in the island of Santa Cruz (St. Croix). *Cf.* May 24, 1831. The present letter is addressed to Porto Rico. Of the two letters sent back to Emerson, one was doubtless that of Apr. 20 and 23, 1831, which bears the endorsement: "R.W.E. April 20 Rec^d^ July 14/31 Sent by St Croix – Boston, & St Thos. to Porto Rico – . . ." I conjecture that the other letter returned was that of Jan. 24, 26, and 29, 1831, which is now without address and so was probably sent under the same cover with a letter from some other member of the family or with a package. The statement in Apr. 20 and 23, 1831, that "I do not know whether I have written to you since Ellen left me" – Ellen died Feb. 8 – would account for the long gap in the correspondence.

33. For Channing at St. Croix, see a note on the letter to William Emerson, Sept. 6, 1830.

34. See a note on May 24, 1831.

35. The superscription is to Edward Emerson in care of "Sidney Mason, Esq. St Johns Porto Rico." Mason appears in a number of later letters. For the employment he gave Edward, see Dec. 14, 1831.

comes, as I hope, from a spirit of boundless *trust,* come life, come death, come eternity, this shall be armour & preparation.

Your affectionate brother

Waldo

All friends inquire warmly — & particularly Mrs Standfast Smith [36] desired I wd. not fail to send her regards to you.

To William Emerson, Boston, June 19, 1831 [37]

Boston 19 June 1831

Dear William,

It occurs to me that I have sent you no word of our return from Vt.[38] If I had not been so unhappily good-natured as to promise sermons to Northampton people, I should have gone down the river to N. Y. which would have pleased me far better than to come back as I did. My journey was a strange one so pleasant & cheering & yet so sad. My memory was far more busy than if I had staid at home & my memory is a bitter sweet.

I hoped to write on the road but I wrote nothing. And now I hope you are preparing to come hither. June is melting into July & we expect your speedy & welcome visit. Mother is very well & Charles. Dr Channing gives a pretty favorable account of Edward,[39] but we must never be sanguine again.

Do you know Mr W. C. Bryant? At Northampton I saw a brother of his — a farmer & botanized with him a little for the sake of learning about his brother & family. A remarkable race sons of the soil yet chemists botanists poets. — Why had not Cullen the grace to go back to corn & potatoes & spit at " dirty & dependent bread

From pools & ditches of ye Commonwealth " [40]

I talked much to his brother Cyrus about your man's folly in leaving poetry, in the hope y^t^ it mt reach him that his Verses have ardent and all unprejudiced admirers.[41] He should know at least of Ellen's

36. Standfast Smith, merchant, and, later, his widow appear in Boston directories of the 1820's and 1830's.

37. MS owned by HCL; ph. in CUL.

38. *Cf.* May 24, 1831.

39. *Cf.* June 17, 1831.

40. Cowper, *The Task,* III, 808–809.

41. Bryant was to give much of the remainder of his long life to his newspaper,

suffrage. The 'death of the Flowers' was meat & drink to my noble flower.

But tis after eleven o clock & so good night. Your affectionate brother

Waldo.

To Charles Folsom, Boston, June 28, 1831 [42]

Boston, 28 June, 1831.

My dear Sir,

I am much obliged to the Committee of Appointment for the honor they have offered me. A few months since I should have received it with sincere pleasure, but I have not at present any spirit for a work of that kind, which must not be a dirge. And so I must decline it. [I]May I take the liberty to ask whether Mr Kent of Duxbury [43] has ever been requested to write a poem for the Society — He was much the most successful Poet who appeared on the College stage for many years.[I]

With great regard.

Mr C. Folsom
Cor. Sec. Φ. B. K. Soc.

Your friend & servt
R. W. Emerson

To William Emerson, Boston, June 29, 1831 [44]

Boston 29 June 1831

My dear brother

It is sad to hear you talk so gravely about your own business. I hope you wont edit,[45] or at any rate will not make any thing but the law the *main business*. Think how little time the experiment has been making — three years — & nobody but the halcyons & butterflies of birth & fortune ever get on in less than five. Every body who knows any thing about you has a good impression about your capabilities & your doings. And how uncertain must be a new newspaper in the

in New York. For Ellen Tucker Emerson's admiration of his verse, see a note on July 30? 1830.

42. MS owned by the Public Library, Boston; ph. in CUL. Excerpt I is in Walter Eliot Thwing, *History of the First Church in Roxbury Massachusetts,* 1908, pp. 247–248. For the appointment and its rejection, see also June 29, 1831.

43. *Cf.* a note on the letter of Jan. 24, 26, and 29 preceding.

44. MS owned by HCL; ph. in CUL.

45. William Emerson wrote to his mother on Aug. 21, 1831, that the men interested in establishing the paper would probably abandon the project (MS owned by Dr. Haven Emerson).

fluctuation of our politics — today a great party, tomorrow all moonshine. What advantage hath not the Law (tho' tardy) of this drudgery in comfort & respectability.

As to Mr Brown,[46] I know him hardly by sight, He is never at home when I go there but I will go & see him & talk with him, but I hope you will have nothing to do with these Danaos dona ferentes [47] tho' you did before with Alexander.

Do you not die of the Jews to whom you pay usance? What is your debt? I dare not yet promise you any help, because I do not know what I am worth. Ellen's estate remains wholly unsettled but as much as I understood of a long legal opinion sent me by Mr Cutler [48] the other day was favorable to my claims. I do not know what authority is to determine the questions, but I suppose the discretion of the Judge of Probate. If he should adopt the opinions of Mr Ashmun & Mr Washburn I think I shall be rich enough to help you. But some circumstances, to my mind make this quite uncertain. I may have legal rights which I shall not choose to enforce. Besides there are I am told many questions to be settled of serious difficulty, & they are very slow to take them up.

Ellen's mother & Margaret have gone to Bristol R. I. they will return presently. They comfort me with kindness. Yesterday I was asked to make the poem for Φ B K society.[49] I told them it wd. have been welcome a few months ago, but I had no spirit for such a work now, & recommended Kent. Pierpont who had been appointed is to be absent somewhere. Charles is very well & mother, & they hope you will not leave the office. Better come & set up in Concord We depend upon you in August.

Yours affectionately

Waldo.

46. Possibly William Brown, a Boston editor (*cf. Stimpson's Boston Directory,* 1831).

47. The same passage from the *Aeneid,* II, 49, is quoted, somewhat more accurately, in the letter of Apr. 25, 1829, where it likewise serves as a warning against entering into a business agreement.

48. Pliny Cutler was the executor of the estate of Beza Tucker, father of Ellen Tucker Emerson (see July 12, 1871, to Thayer). Washburn may have been W. T. Washburn, probably a relative of Ellen's (*ibid.,* and Jan. 19, 1834).

49. See June 28, 1831.

To Mary Moody Emerson, Cambridge, June? 30? and Boston? July 5, 1831 [50]

Cambridge June 31, 1831.

My Dear Aunt —

I was glad to hear from you from Newbury Port; Fox spoke with great pleasure of having seen & conversed with you. — July 5. The sultry suns go over my head almost undistinguished, so uniform is the colour of each day's toil — all *facts*, all human convention — no redeeming hours given to the study of the ' form of forms ' — Yet my conscience does not accuse me; I pray to be guided right — for in every moment of reflection I feel how incompetent to guide myself, I shall ever be —

Last Saturday I dined with Edw. Everett by invitation, at his own house — The other company were people of no interest to you or to me — Well you say, what cheer? What tidings did star eyed science fetch? If not the tidings of dispair, at least of dullness & polite insipidity. Why hide your light under a bushel? Why should a son of learning, of genius, of sprightly parts, prefer to sink the scholar & the wit in the trig landlord or the dry man of affairs? Let the world how can we but mourn. beholding thy lapse into vulgar places —

Yesterday I heard the late President of the U. S. John Quincy Adams, deliver an oration at Quincy.[51] He looked all that was fine — the Roman Senator, the classic statue, the ' face & gesture of command ' [52] — His voice is cracked & consumed with age — but his action was more majestic, I think, than that of any other orator I have heard or seen. The matter of his speech was good — occasionally eloquent, but sometimes in bad taste — a sin I believe which always cleaves to his public discourses. The church is a beautiful stone building, & one side of the pulpit is a marble slab against the wall, supporting a bust of old John Adams, with an inscription composed by his son, engraved beneath it — There were some great associations suggested by the scene, & on these I feasted —

50. MS owned by RWEMA; ph. in CUL. The date in the heading is inaccurate. The signature has been cut away leaving a hiatus in the second paragraph.

51. *An Oration Addressed to the Citizens of the Town of Quincy, on the Fourth of July, 1831*, Boston, 1831.

52. Possibly an echo of Milton's description of Satan, *Paradise Lost*, I, 589–604, but probably from some source I have not found. The " light under a bushel " in the preceding paragraph is from *Matthew*, 5:15.

Certainly the day was full of matter. Fifty five years ago a people hardly known to the history even of their own age, declared themselves free & independent, & put all at risk for the sake of a pri [53]

To David Hatch Barlow, Boston? August? *c.* 10? 1831

[Mentioned in Aug. 15, 1831.]

To Edward Bliss Emerson, Boston, August 15, 1831 [54]

Boston, 15 Aug. 1831 —.

Dear Edward,

I read with great pleasure two or three letters which Charles bro't home from N. Y. from you last night dated (one of them) 18 July. Glad am I at your stronger hand & more cheerful tone. The favor of the spiritual world fill your inner man & heal the outer. I carried your letter to R C D to Mrs Derby & talked with her. I enclose to you Barlows letter which pleased mother & me very much [55] & which I answered forthwith favorably.[56] William has spent 10 days here & returned. I am sorry he should have no better prospect of business. I told him he had better come here where he can live without expense & have just as good prospect in his profession. And I think he will come. It is but a little while & we may as well live together. Geo. M Barnard arrived at N. Y. sick with fever. C. C E went there with Mrs B. George recovered & they all arrived safely here last evg. Mr Adams is to speak an eulogy of Jas. Munroe 25 Aug.[57] I heard him speak a good deal at two special meetings of Φ B K lately.[58] He is antimason & the Φ B K have been convened to consider whether they will not alter their constitution & abolish secrets & obligations &c & fine meeting we had the speakers being A H & E Everett Judges Story & Jackson & Davis — J Q Adams,

53. The remainder of the letter is wanting.

54. MS owned by RWEMA; ph. in CUL.

55. For David Hatch Barlow, see Dec. 14, 1831.

56. Aug.? *c.* 10? 1831.

57. Emerson wrote in *Journals* on Aug. 26 that John Quincy Adams on this occasion held his notes so close to his mouth that he could hardly be heard; and the reporter for the *Boston Commercial Gazette* (Aug. 29, 1831) gave up his attempt to hear and came away.

58. *Cf. Journals,* II, 404–406. Judges Jackson and Davis were, no doubt, Charles Jackson and John Davis, who, like all the others named, were members of Phi Beta Kappa. The action regarding secrecy and veto is reported in the *Boston Commercial Gazette* of Sept. 1, 1831.

C. G. Loring, Dr Lowell Theoph Parsons & many more. and in conclusion we accepted report wh. made the changes & takes away the *veto,* & makes $\frac{3}{4}$ of the votes a sufficient majority – & takes off the injunction of secrecy. Kent of Duxbury is poet for the Anniv. J. T. Austin, orator. Sad political disclosures every day brings. Wo is me my dishonored country that such poor wretches should sit in the chairs of Washington Franklin & Adams. How doth the air now thunder with that once despised whisper ' You cant make a whistle out of &c I am trying to learn to find my own latitude but there is no horizon in C. St. If I was richer I wd. have an observatory. I am trying to learn the ethical truths that always allure me from my cradle till now & yet how slowly disclosed! That word *Compensations* [59] is one of the watchwords of my spiritual world – & time & chance & sorrow & hope do not by their revelations abate my curiosity. My poor sister Margaret Tucker is now suffering in her turn from the deadly malady of her family but she is pretty well. I tell her & her mother that if they want to go to St Croix this winter they must make a bargain with you to come to a Southern port, say Baltimore & escort them out, for Col. Kent will not risque himself upon the waters. & perhaps they must go. – Sad sad it will be to me to lose my highminded sister & yet every star that sinks on this rises in the other firmament & makes the vision of that more full of glory & delight – awful & sweet to me. Mother is very well. & our friends generally. Take care of yourself within & without

Your affectionate brother

Waldo.

To Mary Moody Emerson, Boston? August 30, 1831

[Mentioned in Mary Moody Emerson, Sept. 23, 1831, as " your of 30 of Au.," which she has been reading over and over, apparently because it is more orthodox in tone than most of his commentaries on religion. It is barely possible, however, that his aunt refers to another and more recent letter as pleasing because of its religious sentiments.]

59. Emerson's concern at this time with the theme of his famous essay of many years later was, I believe, partly due to his wife's death and his brother's serious illness. The theme had already appeared in the *Journals* (*cf.* II, 389 ff.: June 29, 1831).

To Edward Bliss Emerson, Boston, September 16, 1831 [60]

Boston, 16 Sept. 1831.

Dear Edward

How do you since the hurricanes of which we hear Porto Rico has had some part? [61] Winds & diseases & wars shake the old earth sadly & threaten the peace of the race she keeps on her rind. High over all calamities, high over all fears, let the constant soul linked by philosophy & faith to the First Cause, calmly pursue her own appointed & glorious path careless of the moment when she passes the confines of matter to keep that identical path in other states. Friends warm & true there are to beckon & welcome us there, — & perhaps you & I shall not meet till we meet there; & yet I suppose we have many years of earthworm fellowship yet to wear out side by side. I hope your body grows stronger & with the the strength of that servant the whole house — the house not built by hands [62] — grows great & prosperous.

We are all well. Mrs Kent & Margaret are settled in town & will not probably come to your islands. Mr Winslow [63] (son in law of Mr Cutler) minister of Dover N. H. will probably go to St Croix for health. If in any way you meet & can show him kindness, do for the love of orthodoxy.

Wm spoke in late letters of coming here. We have not heard from you for a long time. but love you very much

Yours affectionately

Waldo

To William Emerson, Boston, September 25, 1831 [64]

Boston, 25 Sept. 1831

My dear brother,

We hear nothing lately of your packing up & coming away. Yet your chamber is all ready & your welcome is chiding the tardy

60. MS owned by RWEMA; ph. in CUL.

61. The *New-York Spectator,* Sept. 16, 1831, mentions the hurricane that swept only a small part of Porto Rico on July 12.

62. From *II Corinthians,* 5:1; but Emerson was probably thinking, too, of Coleridge's "Youth and Age," the opening lines of which had already been printed several times.

63. Hubbard Winslow (*The First Parish in Dover, New Hampshire,* 1884, p. 100).

64. MS owned by HCL; ph. in CUL.

gaited steamer. Certainly I would not with your self subsistent habits leave a profitable business or one that promised speedily to become so; but I would not stay one uncomfortable day after I had made up my mind that I must wait a lustrum to get by fair means my hat & shoes. Moreover I would not stay there one second for the looks of the thing. A man may change his place & still be a man, I hope. Yea & his change accuse not him but the town, or not to be petulant, may denote him of too fine a clay for a common success. But I wont refine upon Thursdays & Fridays. Tis very likely some plain old world reason that has kept you still. But glad we shall be to see you & life is not very long & perhaps short for all of us. My friends in Central Court [65] are no firmer than before, nor have they heart enough unsupported as they are to venture to the South this winter. I fear a hard winter may bereave me of them both. Whilst they live I keep a living monument of Ellen. She will be farther from my mortal sight when they are gone, & I love them for themselves.

Mother is very well & Charles is not half so robust as I wish So pack up incontinent. Your affectionately

R. Waldo.

To Edward Bliss Emerson, Boston? September 27, 1831 [66]

Dear Edward

I have written to you I believe within a fortnight [67] (may be not) & what can I have to add? We are well — I wish Charles was stouter — he is in body like a wilted apple but as fresh of spirit & as disdainful of all the rest of poor human nature — all except his own platoon — as ever. " He that shows contempt &c hath faculties that he hath never used " — You know the saw. We got a very good letter from you touching Wm the Editor [68] a few day's since & it had one happy & happy making line about an improvement in your own health. Please God it continue. We cannot spare you. and want you here. Ellen is not — & you must stay. I have got a few days since a packet of Ellen's letters in years past to her mother & sister M. & pleasant pleasant it is to me to

65. Mrs. Kent and her daughter. *Stimpson's Boston Directory,* 1832, gives Margaret Tucker's address as 7 Central Court.

66. MS owned by RWEMA; ph. in CUL.

67. Letter of Sept. 16, 1831.

68. *Cf.* the letters of June 29 and Oct. 23, 1831.

fill up link by link the diamond chain of so lovely a history. When you come here I will tell you what I had & trust in God to repossess.

Yours affectionately

Waldo E—

Tuesday, 27 Sept. 1831.

To William Emerson, Boston, October 2, 1831 [69]

Boston Sunday Evg. 2 Oct. 1831.

Dear William

I have just rec^{d} your letter & hasten to reply because it seems things hang on the decision of an hour. We have no 800 $ to offer you, no moderate certainties even, nothing to grow rich on, nothing to marry on, nothing, in short, as you know, beyond a good bed & board & the warm ties & conveniences of a Mother's house. Whether all the rest may not follow in timely succession here as well as in N. Y. your knowledge of this town & that, must tell you. The strong side of our cause is not shown in one year but in the sum of advantages that may arise in twenty years from three well meaning brothers dwelling together; & this is an account in which money will rank low — but what money is for — ease, well-being, fellowship, rank high.

Moreover Charles was born with a tongue [70] you & I with a pen. And I did not know but you & he would make a partnership of your opposite excellences that would turn the whole Suffolk bar out of doors. However I grow timid about advising since I opened my eyes to the incredible fact that you had actually made $400 out of that phantom

69. MS owned by HCL; ph. in CUL.

70. Charles's triumphs as an orator during his college years are recorded in earlier letters. Of his own notion of oratory, he wrote to William on Nov. 16, 1831 (MS owned by Dr. Haven Emerson): "I asked how should a man become eloquent, & the answer was — Declaim every day. As if the poor exploded practice of ancient Rhetoricians, & Sophists, the quack prescription of modern "Teachers of Elocution" could be pressed upon philosophers & men of sense — upon those who would *be* not *seem* who have in their eye as examples of the orator, no artificial ——— but the Ameses & Chathams Burkes & Websters — I am after not the body, but the soul of eloquence — I do not inquire how he who has the spirit, shall give it vent, but what is this spirit, & how it shall be breathed into human souls. If your Gazetteers & Lexicons could describe and define this rare faculty — tell where it is born, what is its essence, the secret of its power, & the mode of its action, — why I would speak a good word for Gazetteers & Lexicons." Emerson's own final opinion of Charles was that he was a great speaker but not an able penman. "I mourn that in losing him I have lost all, for he was born an orator, not a writer. His written pages do him no justice . . ." (*Journals,* IV, 40.)

office of yours which had never stood before me as a reality, but always loomed up as an appendix to the Sullivan story or the preface to something unknown. But entities like 400 received & 800 offered deter me from assuming any responsibility of advice touching them. I would not stay there but perhaps you should. And so I leave you in your thicket & shall be truly glad to see you emerge on the eastern end of long island Sound. Yours affectionately

Waldo.

. . . . .[71]

In lieu of adding her opinion Mother sends with her love the letter from Edward. So lest the well poised scale shd. incline the other side, I have a mind to tell you how many faces smile when the Imam[72] is promised. Mother *lends* the letter wh. must be returned —

To William Emerson, Boston? October? *c.* 10? 1831

[Mentioned in Oct. 19, 1831, to William Emerson.]

To Edward Bliss Emerson, Boston, October 19, 1831[73]

Boston, October 19, 1831.

My dear Edward,

I learn just now that a vessel is sailing for St Johns. I am sorry to have no better news from home to give you than that Charles is quite unwell. He has been laboring for some time under a bad cold & cough which now is continual tho' pretty loose, & attended with a great stupor & indisposition to any exertion even so much as to speak. He is pale & weak — all sad signs in a frame so slender. Dr Ware attends him & Dr Jackson will come tomorrow. I told Dr Ware he must send him away the first moment he thinks proper to find you in P. R. He thinks it may be highly proper to do so, but not until the inflammation (catarrhal inflam.) subsides. His friend Lyman[74] sits all day with him & reads & cares for him. & Motherer nurses with faithful love. He rode in chaise today & yesterday, the weather being unusually fine. He desponds

71. The part of the MS here omitted is a letter from Charles, covering p. 3 and the top of p. 4. At the bottom of p. 4, in the margin of the superscription, is the paragraph in Emerson's own hand printed below.

72. This seems to be a return to Emerson's old habit of applying humorously such epithets as " Khan " and " Grand Mogul " to his older brother.

73. MS owned by RWEMA; ph. in CUL.

74. For Joseph Lyman, see Aug. 26, 1829. The repeated syllable of " Mother " begins a new page.

of his health but talks as Christian & philosopher, of the future, & has been reading Greek I believe today.

I trust in God his life is to be preserved & yet I have some serious apprehensions about him & so I thot it necessary to inform you accurately of his condition. If he shd. presently get better I think he will come to you, or to S. Croix.

There is nothing else that occurs to me that can much interest you. We have lately got some welcome letters from you; one particularly which gives us details of your present condition & prospects with Mr Mason. I hope you will not be dismissed for a Protestant until the spring, & then if you be well enough to come home it is not so much matter. Mr & Mrs Nash arrived in town today. Paulina [75] is on the eve of being confined. Mrs Kent is better & Margaret much better of late & some earthly health I hope yet remains for them. Mother is very well. William has not yet determined to come here & pray God my dear brother that Charles may live for our sakes & for the sake of his country

Your affectionate brother

Waldo.

Charles committed Col Flinter's [76] enquiries to Mr Joseph Lyman who has made one or two fruitless attempts to see the printers but will answer them soon.

To William Emerson, Boston, October 19, 1831 [77]

Boston 19 October 1831
Wednesday Eve.

Dear William,

Charles gets no better than he has been; is not so well as when I wrote of him on an envelope.[78] He has a continual though pretty

75. Paulina Tucker, Emerson's sister-in-law, mentioned in numerous letters, was the wife of Joshua Nash, of Boston (Thomas W. Baldwin, *Vital Records of Cambridge Massachusetts, to the Year 1850,* 1914, I, 510).

76. Joseph Lyman, n.d. (endorsed as received Nov. 26, 1831), says he has taken over the work from Charles, and mentions samples of paper, lithography, and engraving that have been obtained. There is also extant a letter from Col. George D. Flinter, Dec. 10, 1831, about his attempt to get permission for a friend of Emerson's to visit "the Morro." Finally, Edward wrote to William from San Juan on May 15, 1832 (MS owned by Dr. Haven Emerson), that he had given Col. Flinter a letter of introduction.

77. MS owned by HCL; ph. in CUL.

78. Oct.? *c.* 10? 1831; perhaps on the back of a letter from his mother, or from Charles himself, to William.

loose cough & a great stupor & much weakness — pretty sad signs in his slender frame. He desponds of himself though perfectly calm & wise. Lyman reads to him almost all day — law — travels — or he reads Homer himself — but he speaks almost never. He rode out in chaise yesterday & today. Dr Ware thinks his illness shd. give no uneasiness in a person of common constitution, but with his frame & habit is more dangerous, & thinks him a little better these two days tho' not materially.

I slept little last night with sad tho'ts & now write this that you may be prepared to hear he is better or worse which I shall regularly tell you. Dr Jackson will see him tomorrow. Who would have thot that Edward & Charles on whom we put so much fond pride shd. be the first to fail whilst Ellen, my rose, is gone

I have yet some hope, that with God's blessing the climate which helped Edwd so much may do much for him. But Dr W. says this is not yet the stage of ye disease to be benefitted thereby. Wait till ye inflammation subsides. Mother nurses with faithful love

Yours affectionately
Waldo

To Mary Moody Emerson, Boston? October 19? 1831

[Mary Moody Emerson, Oct. 23 (1831), bitterly laments the news of Charles's serious illness and says she has "torn" Emerson's last letter lest any one of earthly mold should pity her half so much as she does herself. For the probable date, *cf.* the letters of Oct. 19, 1831, to Edward and William.]

To William Emerson, Boston, October 23, 1831 [79]

Boston Sunday Eve 23

Dear William

Charles we think is much better. Blisters & leeches & bleeding have been the means of relieving his pleurisy & his pleurisy seems to have been the means of relieving his lungs. And so we rejoice before God that the boy promises to get well soon. & if we can we will keep him in New England. But perhaps he is to mend very slowly & this relief may not yet be at the root of the matter. But Dr Jackson tho't very favorably of his case from the first sight. Lyman scared me by drawing a parallel between all his symptoms & those of young Mills who died at

79. MS owned by HCL; ph. in CUL. The letter is postmarked New York, Oct. 25, and the endorsement gives the date as "Oct. 23/31." Oct. 23 fell on Sunday in 1831, and the contents of the letter confirm that year.

Charleston a year ago [80] & C. desponded of himself & said he shd. never get rid of his cough which yet seems better.

Mr Frothingham pleased Mother with his joy that you shd. stay in N. Y. where he said you were just rising up into consideration. &c.[81] Every account favorable & it wd. not do for you to think of coming away. And I am glad you stay since you refuse the paper.

Your brother Waldo.

To Joseph Lyman, Boston? November 30, 1831

[Recorded in Emerson's endorsement on Joseph Lyman (undated but marked received Nov. 26) as an answer to Lyman's letter. Lyman was a close friend of Charles Emerson.]

To Charles Chauncy Emerson and Edward Bliss Emerson, Boston, December 10, 1831 [82]

Boston 10 Dec. 1831

My dear brothers,

I greet you both & congratulate you on your meeting. The mule bearing Jasper sails tomorrow, so I write to say we are well; that Paulina Nash has a fine son; that Mr Lyman will probably be chosen mayor; [83] that I fear I shall not be turned out of my office in the School Committee, for this morng's paper publishes me as candidate upon the new nominations,[84] vae mihi! that the President's message is

80. According to Solomon Clark, *Antiquities . . . of Northampton,* 1882, p. 332, Elijah Hunt Mills, Jr., died at Charleston, S. C., in Nov., 1830. *Cf.* Oct. 31, 1827, for Emerson's knowledge of Mills's father and other persons at Northampton.

81. Charles wrote to William on Oct. 28, 1831, his congratulations on William's new title of "Counsellor of the Supreme Court of N. Y." (MS owned by Dr. Haven Emerson).

82. MS owned by RWEMA; ph. in CUL. Following Emerson's letter, on p. 3, is a letter from his mother. The superscription, in Emerson's hand, is to "Edward B. Emerson, Esq. or Mr C. C. Emerson – Care of Sidney Mason, Esq. St John's Porto Rico." Charles had sailed from Boston on Dec. 7 (see Dec. 25, 1831, to William Emerson), and he arrived in the harbor of San Juan on Dec. 22 (Charles Emerson, Dec. 23 and 24, 1831).

83. The prophecy was wrong. *Cf.* Dec. 25, 1831, to Edward Emerson.

84. Emerson was nominated by the National Republicans at a meeting of Ward 4 on Dec. 9 (*Columbian Centinel,* Dec. 10, 1831). The letter of Dec. 14 following reports his defeat in the election. According to the MS *Autobiography,* his service on this committee had begun in 1830. Other notices are in *Journals,* II, 431, and in Charles Emerson to William, Nov. 16, 1831 (MS owned by Dr. Haven Emerson): "Waldo is at School-Committee meeting, defending a poor Master against whom the deep voiced mob have opened their calumnious throats – " A few years later he ap-

published [85] which I suppose I shall pack with this sheet; that Mr Stevenson is chosen speaker; [86] that Uncle Robert is staying here in Chardon St; that W. Burton the Manichee [87] is coming here to spend a week; that Joseph Lyman will come & live with me if I will tell him when I am tired of him. that Mrs Ripley came into town the next evg after Charles' departure to see him & staid the ev^g^.; and that is the last item in my budget. We are shrinking & being braced & being blued by the cold. You I hope are expanded & heated & exhilarated by calorie the great anti-consolidator. The great misfortune of travellers is that the expectation & the eye gradually form themselves to the new scene — in the West Indies they become West Indians in a few days — so that they cannot if they would tell the New Englander of this moment what he wants to know. You shd. keep one eye a patriot & the other an emigrant at the same time as the seaman keeps home-time with one watch & *apparent* with the other. So put on paper, Charles, instanter your early impressions,[88] the first contrasts & surprises however slight & shortlived. Champion am I of first impressions & hug the saying that first & third thots coincide. But it is Saturday & that day is an Issachar.[89] So good bye. Your affectionate brother

Waldo.

I shd. be glad if each of you would write me a letter about the other & not show your communications before they are sent. So shall I gather the very truth.

To Edward Bliss Emerson, Boston, December 14, 1831 [90]

Boston, 14 Dec. 1831.

Dear Edward,

We have rec^d^ this evg. your letters to mother & to me of 16 & 31 Oct. I am glad to hear so good news & though it is well nigh bed-

---

peared, though in no official capacity, as a defender of another schoolmaster, Amos Bronson Alcott.

85. Andrew Jackson's message to Congress appears in the *Columbian Centinel* of Dec. 10.

86. Andrew Stevenson, of Virginia, was Speaker of the House, 1827–1834.

87. For Emerson's classmate Warren Burton, see *Journals,* IV, 124. *Cf.* also Jan. 19, 1832.

88. Some of Charles Emerson's observations were not made in vain. For the publication of his account of the voyage to Porto Rico, see Apr. 3, 1843.

89. Probably the reference is to *Genesis,* 49:14–15; and, if so, Emerson simply meant that Saturday was a day of hard labor for him.

90. MS owned by RWEMA; ph. in CUL.

time as perhaps you discover from this heedless writing yet I must say a word. Mr Mason's offer you will probably have accepted before this comes to your eye. & why, shd. you not? If it is not too hard work,[91] I suppose you ought to reckon yourself fortunate in being able to support yourself so well in a strange land. To be sure we mt expect that the ripe service of Edward Emerson shd. be bo't with bags of sequins — sacs of rupees; but the incapable world can't tell prince from peasant, never could. Only get health spirit constitution self subsistence, — & then bread & salt by the way. But be sure get this sound body fit to bear a Boston snowstorm and as soon as it is secured, crowd all sail & come home.

But we have writ our joint epistle on the end of Charles's tongue & why should I say more.

You say nothing of Mr Barlows [92] baby. And every time I see him he asks about you & I have never a word of acknowledgment. Yet have we writ in several letters to you that he has baptized his baby with your name.

You say you have not rec^d^ my sermons Have a care Monkbarns [93] I sent you two & must have them safe back.

I told Charles in a letter among other tidings that I shd probably serve on School Committee but they have turned me out by unquestionable authority.[94] Phebe Farnham is to be married speedily. Make

91. *A Register of Officers . . . of the United States* for Sept., 1829, lists Sidney Mason as commercial agent at "St Johns, Cuba." In 1831 the *Register* describes him as "consul" at the same city. So far as his service for the government was concerned, his only compensation was derived from fees; but it is clear from the letters of Charles and Edward Emerson that he was also engaged in the merchant trade, and the offer to Edward concerned this business. Several letters to William owned by Dr. Haven Emerson throw light on the kind of offer Edward accepted and on Charles's life at San Juan. On Jan. 4, 1832, Charles wrote: "Edward is in his counting room from 6 A. M. till 4 P. M. & in that space I put all my little study, which does not indeed deserve the name. After dinner we stroll in company over the beach or the ramparts, battening (would I might say fattening) on the fresh & fragrant air." On Mar. 16 of the same year, Edward described himself as "the clerk of the Consul here, to wit y^r^ humble servant," and told of questioning a captain "according to the invariable usage with all masters of Am. vessels entg this port." On May 29 following, Charles, then back in Boston, wrote of hearing that Edward was "turning merchant in earnest — sending hogsheads of sugar — &c — "

92. David Hatch Barlow later wrote verses on Edward Emerson's death (see the letters of Oct. 24, 1834, and Dec. 16 and 18, 1834).

93. Jonathan Oldenbuck, Laird of Monkbarns, in Scott's *The Antiquary*. Emerson alludes to a passage in the second chapter of that novel.

94. Emerson was one of the few ward candidates of the National Republicans who failed of election (*Columbian Centinel*, Dec. 14 and 31, 1831).

Charles say to you when you want a sermon what he can remember of Wordsworths sonnets & of Dion.[95]

Yours affectionately

Waldo.

Pray never write me a *duplicate*. I hate the sight. of these wraiths of letters.

To ———, Boston, December 14, 1831?[96]

Dec 14

Dear Sir

I have read over this sermon this morng & do not find it so long as I had imagined. I think it may be printed as it is, & be very useful.

Yours respectfully

R. W. Emerson.

I shall be glad of half a dozen copies of it R W E

To Edward Bliss Emerson, Boston, December 25, 1831[97]

Boston 25 Dec. 1831

My dear Edward,

Thank you for a large pacquet of letters most welcome received this ev^{g} by Mr Cunningham who arrived in N. Y. he says after a hard passage of 29 days. Glad of the letter to Barlow & of so much good news respecting your health. Sorry for the vexation the loss of your clothes will have cost you. But they are clothing persons who but for this rough charity you might never have benefitted. Before this you have got Charles into your company and you will be rare society for each other for a fortnight. What shall I tell you. Mr Wells is made

95. " Dion " is praised in *Journals,* II, 429; and when Emerson visited Sicily a couple of years later he regretted that he could find nothing associated with Wordsworth's hero (see Feb. 26 and Mar. 5, 1833, to William Emerson).

96. MS owned by the Massachusetts Historical Society; ph. in CUL. The year " /31 " has been added in pencil. The handwriting of the letter proper proves no definite date but may well be Emerson's of 1831. I have been unable to discover the name of the person addressed or the sermon referred to, which, if it was printed, and was Emerson's own, would now be of much interest because of its early date. It may be noted that Emerson seems to have visited the House of Industry in Boston on Tuesday, Dec. 13, 1831 (see *Journals,* II, 437); but I know of no evidence that he preached there at that time. A number of sermons by other preachers are advertised or reviewed in the Boston papers for Jan. and Feb., 1832.

97. MS owned by RWEMA; ph. in CUL.

Mayor by a majority over Mr Lyman of 700 votes.[98] Miss Hannah Adams & Mrs Codman are dead last week.[99] What a beautiful life the last has led. We are sure the store of human nature is infinite or we shd say what an irreparable loss — I went last Sunday to Lynn to exchange with Barlow the mercury being at zero here & below zero there — for the sake of seeing him & his wife & letting the Second Church see him. His wife is one of the most sensible & best young women I have met with. & her baby really a beautiful child.

This A. M. I preached a Christmas sermon the fourth I have written; this P. M. exchanged with Mr Frothingham, who tell Charles dont like Tennyson which I lent him as a gem to a virtuoso.[100] I have however extended to him the long suffering at his desire to send him two Vols of Wordsworth — Dion & the sonnets & mark for him what he shd. read.

The cold of the season here is wonderful. It has never abated but increased steadily since C. C. E. sailed, & the waters being shut up all along the coast, east & south a month earlier than usual, the fuel of the winter was not got in; so that coal & wood are very scarce & costly. Yesterday it kindly thawed & thermometer rose to 40° It has ranged from 6 to 20 before. Today has been fine. God save the poor. The Sunday Evg lectures begin this Evg Dr Channing was to have preached y[e] first at my church. When I told Mr Parkman y[t] he wd. not, he broke out " With all my respect for genius that man is a plague to Christendom." That's for Charles. Phebe Farnham is to be married on Wednesday.[101] Laura Dewey the bridemaid will come here tomorrow to spend a few days with lonely mamma. Mr Henry, tell C. has left his people & is living in Cambridge with Felton [102] who has fallen in love with him. I expect daily when he will visit me. I will attend punctually your commands touching Mr Cunningham. Mother sends her love. Mr Mason's offer appears very good to my ignorance. Love to Charles. Your affectionate brother

Waldo.

98. Charles Wells was chosen, in the second balloting, by a majority of 704 votes over all other candidates, according to the *Columbian Centinel,* Dec. 24, 1831. Theodore Lyman later became mayor of Boston and was reëlected for a second term.

99. The deaths of Hannah Adams, a writer of some contemporary repute, and Mrs. Catherine Codman are mentioned in the *Independent Chronicle,* Boston, Dec. 21 and 24, 1831.

100. A copy of *Poems, chiefly Lyrical,* London, 1830, is still in Emerson's house, at Concord, and bears his signature.

101. The marriage of this cousin of Emerson's to Matthew Cobb is reported in the *American Traveller,* Boston, Dec. 30, 1831.

102. Probably Cornelius Conway Felton, who had become tutor at Harvard in 1829.

To Mary Moody Emerson, Boston? December 25, 1831

[Incompletely printed in Cabot, I, 167–168. The same excerpt, with another passage not printed in Cabot, is in *Journals,* II, 440–441. This letter, the original of which now seems to be lost, was mentioned in Mary Moody Emerson, Feb. 22? and 23 (1832).]

To William Emerson, Boston, December 25, 1831 [103]

Boston, 25 Dec. 1831 –

Dear William,

We were very glad to get your budget of W. Indian news this evg by Mr Cunningham.[104] Mother wrote you some time ago that Charles had sailed on 7 Dec. Have you not recd the letter. He caught cold whenever he went out, & we were discouraged concerning him. but now doubt not he will do well. We sympathize with your city in the scarcity of fuel, but the price here is not so enormous. God save the poor. But pleasant is this Christmas thaw. I think I ought to have a Nott stove by your description of its beneficence.[105] When will you come & see me.

I will advertize Aunt Mary of so much money in my hands, but Charles uses to keep it till her occasions. I wrote Edward [106] some time since that to my ignorance Mr Mason's seemed a good offer. Poor fellow to be stripped of his new azul casada [107] with botones metallurgic Little thot Mother sowing so unweariedly in Chardon St that she wrought for the Spanish soldadoes. She is not flattered at all by the new destination of her needlework.

What can I tell you? I have just read Herchels Discourse (part of

103. MS owned by HCL; ph. in CUL.

104. Probably Charles Cunningham, dealer in West Indian goods (*Stimpson's Boston Directory,* 1831).

105. William Emerson to his mother, Dec. 18, 1831, reported fuel scarce and high-priced, so that suffering among the poor was in prospect, and described his Nott stove, "the greatest comfort ever devised in the matter of warming rooms. . . . The Revd Prest [of Union College] is said to be growing rich very fast by the sale of these patent stoves." (MS owned by Dr. Haven Emerson.)

106. Dec. 14, 1831, is doubtless meant, though the phrase used in the present letter is almost exactly repeated in the letter of the same date to Edward.

107. For "casaca," no doubt; and "soldadoes," in the following sentence, must be for "soldados." Edward wrote many later letters in Spanish. Emerson himself seems to have made no effort to master the language thus brought to the attention of the family; but his brother William, already made familiar with it, probably, by his work as a translator for a New York newspaper, used it in some of his letters to Porto Rico.

which is printed in ye Am. Lib. Useful Knowledge)[108] a noble work enough to tempt a man to leave all duties to find out natural science. When I am a man I will have an observatory & a telescope & a laboratory & a battery But we are just such persons as Bottom the weaver whose fancy is hit by every part in the piece & wd play all himself.[109] For if I read poetry it is just as contagious & I versify. If I hear boys recite Colburn,[110] I wd leave all & follow a + b, & there is almost no walk of the muse & more almost no way of life but at some time or other, I have caught the romance of it. farmer, stageman, merchant, editor, but far far above all the herb & berry woman.

These news are good from Edward. Much love from mother & from your affectionate brother Waldo.

108. J. F. W. Herschel's "The General Nature and Advantages of the Study of the Physical Sciences" is in *The American Library of Useful Knowledge*, Boston, 1831, I, 267–320.

109. In *A Midsummer Night's Dream*, I, ii.

110. Zerah Colburn.

1832

To Charles Chauncy Emerson, Boston, January 19, 1832 [1]

Boston, 19 January, 1832.

Dear Charles,

I sit talking with my present companion [2] & yet wd. the while take care that the packet which sails Sunday shall not go without a word to the absentees Political municipal news I will not tell, for I send you newspapers. Sorry am I not to have been at home yesterday when Mr Longfellow the poet called upon me [3] I know not with what letter or with what business but we hungerers for sympathy never mind the occasion. Are we not like the poor girls who sing so feelingly nobody coming to marry me. Burton is gone out who sat with me. He is spending a fortnight here & hammering the old truths never the worse for wear people think upon my patient tympanum. How many plans what glorious philanthropies what associations what developments is not the poor age to ache under before this tutoring generation is fairly unhorsed & laid under foot of men. This is my new paper what of a little blotting — it costs me a dollar less in the ream. & so to my story again. The race tis a very good race & a patient if it do not tire of its teachers But the discussion of its genius so oft may make it say with my thunderer, He is oft the wisest man, who is not wise at all.[4] Friend Taylor [5] of Zebulon of ships made his plea in behalf of ye Sailors last Monday Evg to a crowded congregation at Dr Channing's with most impressive elo-

1. MS owned by RWEMA; ph. in CUL.

2. Apparently Warren Burton. *Cf.* Dec. 10, 1831.

3. This seems to be the earliest reference in the letters to Longfellow, who was still a professor at Bowdoin College. The reason for his unsuccessful attempt to see Emerson is not clear.

4. Wordsworth, " The Oak and the Broom," ll. 63–64. This was for Emerson a time of high admiration of Wordsworth. In general, favorable and unfavorable comments, scattered through the *Journals* and other writings, are about equally balanced.

5. " Father " Edward Taylor, ex-seaman, preacher at Sailors' Bethel, at Boston's North End — " that living Methodist, the Poet of the church " (*Journals,* III, 421). He reappears in later letters. In alluding to Sailors' Bethel as " Zebulon of ships," Emerson was doubtless thinking of *Genesis,* 49:13.

quence. Dr C. heard ye whole. Glad was I to have ye Dr hear somebody as good as himself do what he could not. Fifteen thousand dollars will be subscribed, tis thot, to the Port Soc.[6]

Everetts Sequel to his Reform Article is as good as the Primal & another piece upon Greece by him is valuable too.[7] Nothing very lately from Aunt M. Margaret Tucker is better lately & Mrs K. well.[8] They & every body glad y^t you have got safely out, though you were so cowardly glad to get ashore as to have no wit left to certify the same under your hand & seal.

Mr Ashmun is about to take out letters of adm. for me but in ye tho't of ye parties ye day of final settlement is far off. Mr Cutler — says — as long as I live — Well we will try to adhere to ye right remembering y^t there are worse things yⁿ being defrauded to wit, defrauding, though there is no occasion for using either of these words.

But what I write to you steals from my people whose spiritual interests this Friday night I ought to begin to consult. So fare you well, my brother my brothers & he that keeps the journeying bird keep you wanderers & bring you safe home to your native nest & to your affectionate brother

Waldo.

To William Emerson, Boston, January 23, 1832

[WmE List.]

To Elizabeth Tucker, Boston, February 1, 1832

[MS owned by RWEMA; ph. in CUL. This is a copy in an unknown hand. Printed in *Cent. Ed.*, VII, 400–403, and in *Journals*, II, 458–462.]

To Charles Chauncy Emerson, Boston, March 5, 1832[9]

Boston, 5 March, 1832.

Dear Charles, I have just read your letter dated Feb 2 concerning Man Spanish, American, & Heavenly, concerning Mme de Stael & the pro-

6. *Memoir of William Ellery Channing*, ed. William Henry Channing, 2d ed., 1848, III, 61–62. *Cf.* also Robert Collyer, *Father Taylor*, 1906, pp. 21–25.

7. Edward Everett, in *The North American Review*, July, 1831, and Jan., 1832.

8. Charles Emerson to William, Nov. 27 (1832), tells of the burial of Margaret Tucker that day (MS owned by Dr. Haven Emerson); *Journals*, III, 110 (May 8, 1833), mentions the recent death of Mrs. Kent.

9. MS owned by RWEMA; ph. in CUL.

priety of sitting still &c. & other such philosophies which doubtless in due time I shall examine & set upon their true foundations. I am glad meantime you have the grace to be homesick which Joseph Lyman tells me from his letter which by the way he wd not show me and I am pleased in your pleasure at Mme's Germany [10] but I do not know how you have contrived to read nothing but a piece of y^{t} volume What are you doing – Indian contemplations – a gymnosophist broaching manicheism in the undoing climate of P. R. Do you study Spanish? Do you marry immortal verses? or stir the ancint mud of Coke?

Tell Edward that ever since you went I have been sternly deprived of all my waste paper to keep regular files forsooth of newspapers for the donogoods of P. R. & they have been duly sealed & sent. And this week we mean to send what are now on hand a goodly bundle probably in two pacquets by the Only Son & the America which will both sail before Sunday 11th. [11] I say this that he may see if he gets his own. I do not remember any gossip – do I? Mr S. P. Miles, is to marry Sarah Appleton who was the medalbearing Minerva of our school Linberg whom Edward knew probably at S Cruz a Swedenborgian Anglo German has translated & published 1 Vol Cousin.[12] Your friends the Cherokees are in town Mr Walker-on-the-Mountains addressed a great meeting the other evg at Federal St Ch. & put to shame our orators A H Everett & Mr Hoar & Dr Beecher who spoke on same occasion.[13] A stately gifted person is Mr W O T M. He is called Ridge. Lyman [14] thinks they shd call him Mr Walker. He said he wd. speak like an Indian, plain, right on, & fine Indian eloquence it was. What is most strange he fully understood the oratorical advantages of his situation – the romance – & availed himself to the full thereof. Everett spoke as ill as usual, & sitting down as if one wd say the mind of man can scarce steadily contemplate the grandeur of my effort – Boudinot followed & Dr Beecher spoke extremely well bating the *o's* & *ahs.*

10. Mme de Staël's *Germany* was already a classic.

11. According to the *American Traveller,* Boston, Mar. 13, 1832, the brig "America" and the schooner "Only Son" both cleared for St. Thomas on Mar. 9.

12. This volume, *Introduction to the History of Philosophy,* by Victor Cousin, tr. Henning Gotfried Linberg, Boston, 1832, is still in the Emerson library at the Antiquarian House. Emerson was already acquainted with the French original (see May 24, 1831).

13. The *American Traveller,* Mar. 2, 1832, reports the meeting of Feb. 29, at which Samuel Hoar and the other persons mentioned in the letter spoke. The newspaper praises the Cherokee orators Elias Boudinot and John Ridge. Ridge appears in H. R. Doc. 219, 20th Cong., 1st Sess.

14. Probably Joseph Lyman.

The Washington Statue Society had a small balance say $800. left in their hands They have made it $1250.00 & bo't of the Stuart family the Unfinished heads of Washington. & Lady W., framed them suitably & given y^m^ to y^e^ Atheneum.[15] They make a good instance of prudence. $8000. were subscribed: this sum was put into y^e^ hands of P. C. Brooks; he made it 16,000. y^e^ cost of y^e^ statue. Bunker Hill Soc. by a different course have come it is said to mortgage y^e^ monument. But what care you f[or][16] stones? John A. Washington what a splendid churl. Time & chance have given him an opportunity of fame like Erostratus.

Mother is very well. I read & moan & admire as usual. Yesterdays sermon counts 146. How many & not one! Make haste & come home as soon as spring to woods & wastes around brings bloom. Yours affectionately

Waldo —

To William Emerson, Boston, March 15, 1832 [17]

Boston, March 15. 1832

My dear brother

Are you alive & well? Please signify the same as speedily as possible to me under your own hand. There was a bugbear of an advertisement in the obituary of ye death of W. Emerson aged 26,[18] which has made all your acquaintances start. A man came here yesterday saying he had written to you on business & wished to know if you were alive. And Mr Ripley came here today to relieve Mrs Joy's [19] fears at Waltham. Had you not better direct me to put into the Advertiser your old advertisement for a day or two to set strangers right — that W. E. continues to offer his services as counsellor &c or what you please.

There is a lady of my society a very serious sensible worthy girl named Lucy Richards (at the house of her sister Mrs Tarbell in your city) whom I heard you have seen. Her sister Mrs Kendall is one of the excellent of the Second Church intellectually & morally. This young lady I know less but I commend her to you as a stranger in your town.

15. See Josiah Quincy, *The History of the Boston Athenæum,* 1851, p. 128. It was the Washington centenary, and statues and pictures were the order of the day in Boston as elsewhere. Peter Chadron Brooks, the philanthropist, was treasurer of the Washington Monument Association, which had unveiled the Chantrey statue in 1827.

16. Mutilated by the seal.

17. MS owned by HCL; ph. in CUL.

18. *Boston Daily Advertiser,* Mar. 13, 1832: "DIED. . . . In New York, Mr William Emerson, 26."

19. For Mrs. Hannah Joy, see Apr. 2, 1842.

You asked me if I liked Mackintosh's Ethics. Assuredly. It is the most important work on the most important science. It not only traces the history of ethics but on a historical basis proposes a new theory. & certainly deserves a careful study as being an attempt by a master, with great advantages too, to reconcile the great repugnant theories that have appeared & reappeared for so many ages & have hitherto seemed irreconcileable. The book has a great deal of incidental value as it contains a great many opinions about men & books uttered by this Oracle.[20] But perhaps you have read it & know all.

Yours affectionately
Waldo

To William Emerson, Boston? March 26, 1832 [21]

26 March

Dear William

I send you by Mr Lyman [22] 2 vols of ye Polyanthos. I find no more. One I procured from Dr Wyman who says y^t^ Bulkeley lent another to Dr Haskins [23] & he destroyed it. Shall I apply to Buckingham for more? [24] Possibly Bulkeley has a vol. at Chelmsford but we have no means of communication therewith.

We have new letters from Charles & Edw dated 5 March. Mr Frank Loring is Mr Lyman's companion. I cannot tell whether I shd. rather go to Washington City or to Mt Washington but ye latter monster sublimes it in my memory & these spring days warm my heart to the wilderness. Mr Frothingham enquires after you often & has spoken once or twice of a purpose to write to you, if I rightly understood him because he wanted a correspondent in N. Y.

His sister Abby is to be married to Mr T. B. Wales [25] who has 7 children. The connexion I believe is very agreeable to all.

20. A Philadelphia edition of this work was entitled *A General View of the Progress of Ethical Philosophy* and bore the date 1832. For a less favorable opinion, see *Journals,* II, 470 (Mar. 30, 1832) ; *cf.* also the letter of Aug. 19, 1832.

21. MS owned by HCL; ph. in CUL. The year 1832, given in the endorsement, is correct, as is shown by evidence cited below.

22. The superscription shows the letter was carried by "Mr J. Lyman jr" — Joseph Lyman.

23. A Dr. Haskins is mentioned in July 3, 1828.

24. J. T. Buckingham published both *The Polyanthos* (1805–1807) and *The Polyanthos Enlarged* (1812–1814).

25. The marriage is recorded in the *Boston Daily Advertiser* of June 30, 1832.

Mr Walker & Mr Parkman go in May to Cincinnati to ordain Mr Peabody.[26] Probably Dr Nichols also who in y[t] month marries Miss Martha Higginson [27] I cannot think of another item. – Greenoughs bust of Pres[t] Kirkland has come out & is in y[e] Atheneum. The likeness I suppose will not satisfy. Did I tell you already or y[e] W. Indians, yt Stewarts sketches of Washington & Lady have been bo't for $1250.00 & given to Atheneum [28] But blessed be Swift who said it was a vice to know too much news if I have to repeat my own. Will not the summer bring you here. Do do come, & tell me y[e] month & I will not take my vacation in y[e] same. Come & hear our bad spelling Creole's story of his long nap for he seems to have laid stone still.[29]

Pestered was I sadly one day lately by a quoted conversation y[t] came to my ear yt Mr E. had refused all compromise with his wifes friends & was gone to law with them." For y[e] first time I saw to my sorrow yt y[e] thing admitted of y[t] face. The facts are y[t] by a mutual advised consent we get y[e] Supreme Court to distribute y[e] estate, & I take no step without advising with Mr & Mrs Kent & Margaret Tucker; and if ever such a story shd. be quoted to you refer to those persons or to Mr Cutler. Capt. Nash very possibly takes another view of it but if he do, has certainly had opportunity to know better. Sometime next summer we hope to know whether y[e] Court will confirm our legal opinions.

Yours affectionately

Waldo.

To Ezra Ripley, Boston, April 1, 1832 [30]

Boston, 1 April, 1832

My dear Grandfather,

It has been my intention for several days past to answer your kind note received week before last, but an unusual press of little engagements has prevented me. I gladly take a few moments this evening to express my thanks for your attention, & to send mothers love & mine to you & your family. We had heard by repeated oppor-

26. The *Christian Register,* June 2, 1832, mentions these persons in its account of the ordination of Ephraim Peabody at Cincinnati, on May 20.

27. *Ibid.,* May 12, 1832.

28. See Mar. 5, 1832, for the Stuart pictures.

29. Perhaps one of the Cherokees mentioned in Mar. 5, 1832.

30. MS owned by Professor James B. Thayer; ph. in CUL.

tunities of your gradual amendment in health after your return, & had hoped you were quite well ere the date of your letter. And I trust you read these lines in boots.

You mention your letters from Edward & Charles. They have been exemplary correspondents all winter. Charles writes us that he has left the country, & will probably stay in the city of St John's until he leaves the island. He seems to be quite satiated with his Southern excursion & proposes to set his face homeward about the first of May.[31] Edward seems inclined to settle in the West Indies where at last he has found a climate agreeable to his constitution.

You have seen, no doubt, an account of the late special meetings of the Am. Unitarian Association.[32] I attended one of them. Mr Henry Ware in behalf of the Executive Committee accused him & them of supineness & in these stirring times tho't that something more was due from a population of (I think) 170,000 Unitarians than the circulation of a few Tracts; & so proposed 1. the appointment of an Agent who shd. be supported by the Assoc. & whose business it shd. be to procure the formation of more auxiliaries & give the whole institution a more efficient character. & 2. the appointment of missionaries. These propositions are well received & they mean no doubt to have a man of standing & energy as Agent. Mr Gannett I suppose they would be glad to get if he could be spared.

The West is the leading topic [33] at all such meetings. I am glad to find that Mr Walker & Mr Parkman are going to Cincinnati & Louisville in May & possibly Dr Nichols who is to be married about that time.

I suppose before this Deacon Ripley [34] must have returned. Please to present my respects to him. Mother wishes me to say that she depends upon holding Miss Sarah to her promise of spending a week or fortnight with us in the course of the spring, whenever she can most conveniently come from home. And you must remember, Sir, that it is not always as cold in Boston as on the 22[d] February, & not let the gout persuade you to forsake us. I hope it will not be long before I shall have an oppor-

31. On Mar. 28, 1832, Charles wrote that he expected to be on his way home before his letter reached Boston; and he probably arrived toward the end of April. He wrote to William on May 14 that he was sitting once more at his table in a law office. (Both MSS are owned by Dr. Haven Emerson.)

32. The *Christian Register,* Mar. 31, 1832, reports the A. U. A. meetings of Mar. 18 and 23.

33. The remarkable effort made by the Unitarians in the Middle West within the next decade is recorded in the files of *The Western Messenger,* 1835–1841.

34. See Dec. 15, 1830, for the deacon and his daughter Sarah.

tunity of [pa]ying[35] you a visit. These relenting winds that sometimes blow, set me hankering after hills & woods & the well beloved river.

With great respect & affection,
Your grandson,
Waldo Emerson.

To William Emerson, Boston, April 25, 1832[36]

Boston, 25 April, 1832.

My dear brother,

My friend & classmate Mr Henry Bulfinch you will probably remember as an old school mate. Mr B. is seeking employment & has some hope of finding a school or other good occupation in your great town. I told him that possibly you might know of some situation that he would like to fill. Mr B. you remember graduated at H. U. in 1821 with high honours from the Govt & the great respect of his class.

We are all very well, & heard from Edw & C C E as late as 28 March.

Yours affectionately
R. Waldo E

To the Second Church and Society, Boston? June? c. 2? 1832

[In the archives of the Second Church, Boston, is a MS report, dated June 16, 1832, from " The Committee to whom was referred the communication of the Pastor of this Church, stating a change in his opinions concerning the ordinance of the Lord's Supper, and recommending some change in the mode of administering it . . ." The entry of June 2, 1832, in *Journals* (II, 491) makes it seem probable that this letter to the church was written about that time.]

To Edward Bliss Emerson, Boston? July 24, 1832

[Mentioned in Charles Emerson to William, July 24 (owned by Dr. Haven Emerson), as being written at that time.]

To Charles Timothy Brooks, Boston? August 8, 1832

[MS listed and partly quoted in American Art Association, Apr. 28 and 29, 1924. Emerson said he could not at once answer Brooks's proposal for an exchange of pulpits on the last Sunday of August. He was still sick, but, if he could preach the following Sunday, he meant to inform his people of his intention to give them, a week later, a full account of his views respecting the Lord's Supper. In that case it might be necessary for them to take some action on the

35. The MS has been slightly mutilated.
36. MS owned by HCL; ph. in CUL.

subject, and in the meantime he would not wish to administer the ordinance. But as his communion was on the last Sunday of the month, he might after all be very glad to have Brooks take his place at that time. Brooks, who was from 1832 to 1835 a theological student, preaching irregularly, appears as minister at Newport, R. I., in the first letter of Mar. 30, 1840, and in later letters.]

To Charles Timothy Brooks, Boston? August 14, 1832

[MS listed and partly quoted *ibid.;* shows that Emerson had not preached on the last Sunday and that, though he expected to be in his pulpit the following week, he would have to delay his sermon on the Lord's Supper till September. Meantime, he agreed to the proposed exchange of pulpits on the last Sunday in August.]

To Mary Moody Emerson, Boston, August 19, 1832 [37]

Boston, 19 August, 1832

My dear Aunt,

I have been shut up almost ever since I returned home with the meanest complaint & though I came home stronger & fatter

37. MS owned by RWEMA; ph. in CUL. From the days of his preparation for the ministry, Emerson had been wont to question frankly and boldly the teachings of orthodox and unorthodox religionists, and he clearly entered upon his profession with no complete devotion to it. The question of what he would do if the requirements of his office should sometime conflict with his private view of the truth he had certainly confronted before he was ordained, and perhaps decided. His brother William, then a theological student in Germany, where liberalism was already advanced, had put this question to him in plain words in a letter of Jan. 17–22, 1825 (MS owned by Dr. Haven Emerson) : ". . . every candid theologian after careful study will find himself wide from the traditionary opinions of the bulk of his parishioners. Have you yet settled the question, whether he shall sacrifice his influence or his conscience? "

The Second Church had pretty definitely committed itself against Emerson's views of the sacrament some months earlier, when the disagreement had first become acute. His letter of June? *c.* 2? 1832, had been turned over to a committee, two members of which, George A. Sampson and George B. Emerson, were among the young pastor's best friends then and later. This committee, on June 16, 1832, reported that they held Emerson in " undiminished respect " and, moreover, recognized the right of private judgment in matters of religious belief — " But they cannot regard it as the duty of the Church to consent to any change in the mode of administering the ordinance . . ."; and on June 21, a meeting of the Second Church confirmed the committee's decision and the moderator, the same day, wrote a letter to Emerson, informing him of this action (MSS owned by the Second Church) . Meantime Emerson was all but ready to quit the ministry, no matter whether the Church accepted his view or not, and he confided to his diary on June 2: " I have sometimes thought that, in order to be a good minister, it was necessary to leave the ministry. The profession is antiquated."

than for years it has stripped me to bones. The air is poisoned here to every person who is only slightly imprudent. It is high time I was well but I have been put back several times But what cares your sphered

---

Several letters from Charles and Edward to William, owned by Dr. Haven Emerson, throw further new light on this period of crisis. On June 18 Charles wrote that " Waldo proposes setting out for Waterford on Friday next to be absent 4 weeks or so while his ch. is repairing " and while people at home were " engaged in discussing his lately declared views of the Lord's Supper." Charles decided to go along on the northern trip, but had returned alone by July 6, writing on that day of the " comfortable little house of a private family " " in the pleasant town of Conway under the brow & shaggy lid of the White Mts.," where he had left his brother, " health . . . improved — . . . spirits pretty good — He preached last Sabbath, & will preach next Sabbath at Fryeburg — Aunt Mary means to journey with him to the Notch — She went with us from Waterford (where we staid a week) last Saturday to Fryeburg, & there she is at present.

" Our journey was full of creature comforts of sweet air, green earth, rustic diet &c — . . .

" Waldo's affairs ecclesiastical I suppose you had an account of from Mother – I think enough has now been done, (perhaps too much) for the expression of individual opinion, & I hope his own mind will be brought to the persuasion that it is his duty to stay where he is & preach & pray as he has done & administer the ordinance as nearly as he conscientiously can, in accordance with the faith & wishes of his pious parishioners — "

And on July 24, Charles wrote again: " Waldo has got home — is for this last day or two troubled with a diarrhœa which he is nursing lest a worse thing come upon him. As to telling you what his views are, I have not wished to enter on so considerable a subject in a letter — better wait for word of mouth or at least for W's own manuscript which waits your reading when you come, or which can be sent to you. Partly I agree with him — that the Institution was not intended to be *enjoined* as a perpetual observance — but much farther I cannot go — He will preach to his *Society* (to them he has not hitherto mentioned the matter publickly, — only to the *Church*) his opinions the 2d Sabbath in August, — & will probably afterward ask a dismission — this will bring things to a legal *issue* This however is not yet said to any but a few friends — Thus we are still rocking — motion & progress you know is the law of man — I had hoped Waldo was to be fixed for some years longer exactly where he is — The prospect seemed brightening & enlarging before him — But he must follow conscience wheresoever it leads — & I acquiesce & sometimes think I am not sorry." In his letter of Sept. 7, Edward, back for a few weeks from the West Indies, added the bulletin that " Waldo is gradually recovering his strength, having now preached two Sabbaths & intending to preach on the coming, for which agreeably to his promise he is now preparing the Sermon relative to the sacrament of the Supper."

Meantime, Mary Moody Emerson was making, not her last effort, but the last that had any chance of success, to halt her nephew's advance toward a new liberalism. In a letter posted on Feb. 24, 1832, when Emerson was already pondering a decisive step, she had pleaded with him to remain in the ministry as his ancestors had done and so leave a name to be " enrolled with the Mathers & Sewalls of that venerable City " of Boston. Her influence was still strong enough to draw him straight to Waterford when the decision had to be made, but he was presently off to himself " under the brow & shaggy lid of the White Mts.," where he made up his mind in his own way.

spirit for stomach aches If I had others, I would tell you; but I have not yet come to any point with my people, my explanation being postponed by my ails, and have not come to any new point with myself. I remain of the same mind not prepared to eat or drink religiously, tho' it seem a small thing, & seeing no middle way, I apprehend a separation. This, tho' good nature & prudence condemn & possibly something else better than both, yet promises me much contentment & not the less opportunity of usefulness in the very partial & peculiar channel by which I must be useful if at all. — The farthing candle was not made for nothing — the least leaf must ope & grow after the fashion of *its own* lobes & veins & not after that of the oak or the rose, and I can only do my work well by abjuring the opinions & customs of all others & adhering strictly to the divine plan a few dim inches of whose outline I faintly discern in my breast. Is that not German enow? It is true. How gay & glorious the prospect looks. In the darkest event the human fancy can portend is nothing very black, for if we hasted to nothing, what signifies whether the clean swept cobwebs were well or ill spun? And if we are to be what the constitution of the mind predicts, every change is instruction & every misfortune is a trifle & it is the being we are to build up, & not situation & influence that import. So I will sing the hymn of hope in light or gloom for a time or forever as pleases Heaven. Ellen is beyond misfortune, & I will not invite any others to penury & disappointment if I am doomed. I am entering into acquaintance with Goethe who has just died.[38] The Germans think there have been but three men of genius — Homer, Shakspear, & Goethe. If I go into the country to books, I shall know him well, & you will come & board with Mother & me, & we will try him whether he deserves his niche. S. A. R. grieved he shd. die because he & Mme de Stael were suited to this world. The Germans regard him as the restorer of Faith & Love after the desolations of Hume & the French. that he married Faith & Reason, for the world. In the Wilhelm Meister he leads a child of Nature up from the period of ' Apprenticeship ' to that of ' Self production ' & leaves him, Schiller says, assured on the way to infinite perfection. But the *form* of the book is for us so foreign that it long repels, — full of theatricals, green room, &c

---

On July 15 she wrote to him at South Conway her hope that in time he would return to the truth of dogmatic theology, bade him " Farewell, if for aye," and seemed to declare, in her usual cryptic manner, her conviction that he had suffered a decisive defeat and that his career was ruined.

38. This active interest in Goethe is of special interest as beginning before Emerson met Carlyle, though not before he read some of Carlyle's writings.

How is my friend Stone?[39] Quicken him to write me what he promised, an account of Mackintosh's Ethics. William & Edward are both here. William has just come from Portsmouth where he has engaged himself to Susan W. Haven[40] daughter of John H. & his mother & his brothers are mightily pleased. Edward has come to spend a month & then returns to P. R.[41] He is very well & in fine spiri[ts.][42] Charles is disposed to go to Concord when he opens his office in October. Much better on som[e] accounts – health, reason, & comfort. but he has not decided. I have suggested so many topics that I ardently hope to have a letter on some one. Do Write Give my respects & love to both families. Your affectionate nephew

Waldo.

To the Proprietors of the Second Church, Boston, September 11, 1832[43]

To the Proprietors of the Second Church.

Boston, 11 September, 1832.

Christian Friends,

In the discourse delivered from the pulpit last Sabbath,[44] I explained the circumstances which have seemed to me to make it my duty to resign my office as your minister. I now request a

39. Thomas Treadwell Stone appears in later letters, especially during the period of *The Dial;* and Emerson seems to have had a high opinion of his ability.

40. For their marriage, see Nov. 18, 1833, to William Emerson.

41. The *New-York Commercial Advertiser* of Aug. 13, 1832, listed "E. B. Emerson" among the passengers arriving in the brig "Chariot" from Porto Rico. He sailed again for that island on Oct. 6, 1832 (Charles to William, Oct. 9, 1832; owned by Dr. Haven Emerson).

42. This and a word in the second sentence following were mutilated by the opening of the seal. Possibly Emerson wrote "several" instead of "some."

43. MS owned by the Second Church; ph. in CUL.

44. Printed in *Cent. Ed.,* XI, 3–25. Charles Emerson to William, Sept. 18 (MS owned by Dr. Haven Emerson): "A week ago Sunday Waldo preached his 'opinions' to his people – It was a crowded house – a noble sermon – If the Parish were to be polled probably $\frac{3}{4}$ would be for keeping their minister on his own terms – but this will not be done – because certain of the most influential men in the Church & Society adhere to the ordinance, & would be thereby grieved & sent away – So they have chosen a committee which is to confer with Waldo & which will probably after some talk & expressions of unfeigned regret, let him go & bid him God speed. What he will do is uncertain – I think he will gather a parish of his own by & by – He behaves magnanimously to the bone – & will not print his sermon which would justify & make proselytes for him, because he does not wish to do anything in hostility to the ordinance or shocking to good but weak vessels."

dismission from the pastoral charge.[45] On this occasion, I cannot help adding a few words.

I am very far from regarding my relation to you with indifference. I am bound to you, as a society, by the experience of uninterrupted kindness; by the feelings of respect & love I entertain for you all, as my tried friends; by ties of personal attachment to many individuals among you, which I account the happiness of my life; by the hope I had entertained of living always with you, and of contributing, if possible, in some small degree, to your welfare.

Nor do I think less of the office of a Christian minister. I am pained at the situation in which I find myself, that compels me to make a difference of opinion of no greater importance, the occasion of surrendering so many & so valuable functions as belong to that office. I have the same respect for the great objects of the Christian ministry, & the same

45. Charles's letters to William (owned by Dr. Haven Emerson) again throw some light on the progress of his brother's affairs. On Sept. 26 he wrote: "Waldo is very feeble — His people dont like to let him go away from them — At present the disposition is to make arrangements so as to keep him — He will probably stay where he is this winter — His friends are many & kind — " Then in an undated letter, endorsed Oct. 5, 1832: "Waldo's parish committee are still in session, & considering ways & means of keeping their minister, if that may be, without dismembering their church." On Oct. 29 Charles added this final chapter of his history: "Last evening the connexion between Waldo & the Second Ch. & Society was dissolved by a vote of the Proprietors, 34 to 25 — many stayed at home rather than vote to lose their minister — Mr. Adams & Capt. King & others. Geo. Emerson & Dr. Ware urged the people to this dissolution. They part from their pastor, whom many of them tenderly love, & all respect, with heavy hearts. And Waldo looks very sad. He would have been glad to have been well these few last months & done more for those to whom his attachment seems the stronger when the bonds of it are just snapped. What the immediate arrangements of the household will be, I know not. Waldo is for the present to supply the pulpit with ministers & receive the salary."

The official story of the separation, told less personally, is preserved in the MS *Proprietors Records* for 1804–1845, pp. 135–140 (owned by the Second Church). Emerson's letter of Sept. 11 was opened and read at a meeting of the proprietors on Sept. 16 and referred to a committee of twelve. This committee reported on Oct. 21, merely stating the question whether it was expedient that the connection with the pastor be dissolved and advising a vote on it. This report was accepted, but the vote was deferred till the meeting of Oct. 28, when the proprietors cast sixty-one ballots, thirty-four yeas, twenty-five nays and two blank. Immediately afterwards it was voted thirty to twenty, with four blank ballots cast, that the pastor's dismission be granted. A motion that the pastor's salary should be continued for the present was then carried. The MS *Treasurers Receipt Book* (owned by the Second Church) shows that the salary was continued to the end of the year, and that on Dec. 21 Emerson received the instalment due on the first of January following. He was thus better provided for his voyage to Europe, though he was obliged to supply the pulpit with ministers.

faith in their gradual accomplishment through the use of human means, which, at first, led me to enter it. I should be unfaithful to myself, if any change of circumstances could diminish my devotion to the cause of divine truth.

And so, friends, let me hope, that whilst I resign my official relation to you I shall not lose your kindness, & that a difference of opinion as to the value of an ordinance, will be overlooked by us in our common devotion to what is real & eternal.

Ralph Waldo Emerson.

To William Emerson, Boston, November 19, 1832 [46]

[I]Boston, November 19, 1832.[I]

My dear brother,

How long it is since I have written this same superscript. We hammer our own nails & walk in our worn paths & who can break a habit & drive an extra nail even to rivet the fraternal bond. If my sentence hath Egyptian darkness, why I write at mother's tea table & there are eaters & talkers around & I apologize for my incivility in writing by throwing in a word occasionally into the miscellaneous clamour. Thank you for your kind remembrance & letter. I flatter myself I am getting better at last [47] in good earnest. I have wiredrawn to an infinitesimal ductility all the sympathies of men women & children. for there is a limit beyond which peoples interest in other peoples bowels cannot go. Meantime [II]the severing of our strained cord that bound me to the church is a mutual relief. It is sorrowful to me & to them in a measure for we were both suited & hoped to be mutually useful. But though it will occasion me perhaps some, (possibly, much) temporary embarrassment yet I walk firmly toward a peace & a freedom

46. MS owned by HCL; ph. in CUL. Excerpts I–IV are in Cabot, I, 171–172.

47. Nine letters from Charles to William now owned by Dr. Haven Emerson supply so many bulletins on Emerson's health from Sept. 24 to Dec. 3, 1832. On Sept. 24 Emerson was recovering from a relapse and was going out of town for a few days of rest; on Sept. 26 he was at Hopkinton to stay until Saturday and was " very feeble "; on Oct. 9 he was " a little better "; on the 14th, " mending "; on the 19th, " better "; on the 29th he was recovering from a new attack " of his tedious complaint, & looks very thin & is very weak "; on Nov. 13 he was continuing to grow better. Presently there was another relapse, however, and, then, talk of a voyage. On Nov. 27 Charles wrote: " Waldo is sick again — very much dispirited — & talking of the South, the West Indies & other projects — We may break up & disperse at any moment." And on Dec. 3 he added: " Waldo is mending a little perhaps — He will probably go away this winter & by sea, but where he knows not nor any of us — as yet — "

which I plainly see before me albeit afar. Shall I pester you with half the projects that sprout & bloom in my head, of action, literature, philosophy? Am I not to have a magazine — my ownty downty — scorning co-operation & taking success by storm. The vice of these undertakings in general is that they depend on many contributors who all speak an average sense & no one of them utters his own individuality. Yet that the soul of a man should speak out, & not the soul general of the town or town pump is essential to all eloquence,[II] to originality. [III]The objection to a paper conducted by one man is the limits of human strength The Goethe or Schiller [48] that wd do it must have a constitution that does not belong to every lean lily-livered aspirant of these undigesting days. But give me time, give me strength & *cooperation, on my own terms, και την γην κινησω.*[49] Will we not sweep the tables of atheneums & the escritoires of the learned & the fair clean of all the American periodical paper, green yellow olive & gray?

What assistance too can I not command. Give me my household gods against the world. William & Edward & Charles. Why the plot is the best plot that ever was laid. Wait & see what a few months shall do — to hatch this fair egg.[III]

Meantime how do you & when do you come hither. Does not the silken string draw yet? In the old time its contractions were spasmodic & at short periods. But stoicism & prudence in our time do violence to the royal law of love & make it sing its edicts as softly & graduatedly as a music box. Meantime we should be very glad to hear some stray word of our sister that shall be & when she will be here. Remember me to her with best & most affectionate wishes. Mother is very well & Charles also. [IV]Yours affectionately,

Waldo[IV]

G. B. E. has lost his little babe [50] who has gone to his mother.

To George Adams Sampson, Boston? November 29? 1832

[Printed incompletely in *Journals,* II, 537–538. It seems probable that the text there given is partly a paraphrase of the text actually sent.]

48. The names are significant in a letter which reveals Emerson as rapidly reorienting himself in the direction of a literary career.

49. Probably Emerson was thinking of the famous story of how Archimedes offered to move the world if given a place to stand. One version of this story he may well have known from Plutarch's life of Marcellus, which, it seems, he had recommended to Charles in the letter of Dec. 10, 1828.

50. The *Christian Register* of Nov. 24, 1832, records the death, on the 6th, of Joseph Buckminster Emerson, aged five months.

TO WILLIAM EMERSON, BOSTON, DECEMBER 10, 1832 [51]

Boston, 10 December, 1832.

[I] My dear brother,

My malady has proved so obstinate & comes back as often as it goes away, that I am now bent on taking Dr Ware's advice & seeing if I cannot prevent these ruinous relapses by a sea voyage. I proposed to make a modest trip to the West Indies & spend the winter with Edward but in a few hours the dream changed into a purpureal vision of Naples & Italy [52] & that is the rage of yesterday & today in Chardon St. A vessel sails this week for Sicily & at this moment it seems quite probable I shall embark in it [I] — the brig Jasper. — [II] Mr Adams & mother are smoothing the way.[II] Now as my departure involves the breaking up of our little household why can you not anticipate your Christmas visit by a fortnight & throw your wisdom & affection into the breach & chaos-come-again of our domestic counsels. Why can you not come & bring your mattresses & itineraries, & Italian dictionaries, & Addison's Italies,[53] & any other word or thing or person that will help fit out an extempore adventurer. The vessel I suppose will not sail before Saturday. And even if it should & I be gone yet you will much aid & comfort mother, who will be, very likely a solitary boarder at Aunt Ladd's [54] in Newton before Christmas. Charles will probably live with George B. Emerson. So come whilst we have house & hearth to offer you.

Yours affectionately

Waldo

Mother says that you must bring a mattress with you for me.

TO WILLIAM EMERSON, BOSTON, DECEMBER 14, 1832 [55]

Boston, 14 Dec 1832

Dear William,

I wrote you the other day [56] of instant departures & urgent haste, but our bark is worse than our bite like the worlds. Here

51. MS owned by HCL; ph. in CUL. Excerpts I–II are in Cabot, I, 175.

52. Edward Emerson, Porto Rico, Aug. 16, 1833, said he was glad his brother had not come to the tropical island — "this daubed & miniature caricature of life," which was nothing to "the mighty Spectacle" of Europe. For, said he, "I have already read your letters from Syracuse & am to see those from Rome."

53. If Emerson carried with him Addison's *Remarks on Several Parts of Italy,* he allowed it to influence his letters from Italy very little.

54. Mary Haskins, wife of William Ladd, lived in Newton, Mass.

55. MS owned by HCL; ph. in CUL.

56. Dec. 10, 1832.

sit I yet, here fret I still, here sigh I unceasingly for that shop of horrors the sea, & that bed of mephitis & discomfort a stateroom, & am not yet punished with gratification nor like to be for a week. Truth is I am a-weary of my helpless hopeless arm chair I gain nothing, I rot ever, & have a keen appetite for the stimulus of Gods charitable air, which all the forms of bad weather in turn deny me but which is freely dispensed to such as sail upon the sea. Brig Jasper is expected to sail, say next Thursday.[57] I trust it will not go before you can get hither with your

57. There were further unexpected delays before (as the *Boston Daily Advertiser* of Dec. 24, 1832, records) the brig "Jasper," commanded by Capt. Cornelius Ellis, cleared from Boston for Malta on Saturday, Dec. 22, with this passenger list: "S. P. Holbrook, Mrs Holbrook, Miss E. E. Holbrook, Samuel Kettell, and Mr. Emerson." In the letter of July 9, 1833, Emerson says he has had the honor of traveling with Peter Parley, and it is certain that the S. P. Holbrook and Samuel Kettell of the passenger list were the persons of those names who were about this time collaborators with Samuel Griswold Goodrich in some of his "Peter Parley" books; and one of these fellow passengers of Emerson's already had to his credit the three-volume *Specimens of American Poetry,* published by Goodrich in 1829. The collector of this storehouse of early American verse may well have engaged in some discussion of native writers with the young minister who was now dreaming of a literary career.

As for the long voyage, however, it did not begin on the day of clearance. *Journals,* III, 3, shows that Emerson sailed from Boston on Christmas Day, and Charles Emerson wrote to William in his letter of Dec. 27 and 29 (owned by Dr. Haven Emerson): "Waldo went away Tuesday morng. about ½ past ten — I hope he got a good offing before the cross old North Easter gan to blow." The same letter shows that William had come from New York for the occasion but, apparently, had to return before the boat actually sailed.

At least one Boston paper published a friendly notice of Emerson's departure. The paragraph in the *Evening Gazette,* Dec. 29, 1832, though anonymous, was said by Charles (Jan. 11, 1833) to have been written by Miss Eliza Townsend: The traveler was followed by the prayers of the people to whom he had been a beloved and admired pastor, and "by the best wishes of all who were privileged with knowing such a signal example of devoted integrity, eloquence and disinterestedness."

Some account of the passage to Malta is given in *Journals,* III, 3–25. The voyage began with the storm which Charles had feared, and in the little ship of 236 tons the passengers were miserable. An excellent idea of what a transatlantic voyage could be in the small sailing ship of the early nineteenth century is to be had from William Emerson's record of his own experience in a letter to his mother dated Dec. 31, 1823 (MS owned by Dr. Haven Emerson): "I hardly knew any thing that occurred on deck for more than a week, I was so seasick . . . during which time I subsisted upon air and peppermint-water. . . . we had many head winds and rough seas, which washed our deck, and even penetrated into the cabin, the floor of which has not been dry since the day we left Boston, as the water would every now and then come in by gallons through the dead lights. . . . 3 or 4 times the sea broke over the deck so much, that they were able to cook but one meal in the day, and a third part of the time but 2 meals." But the voyage of Dec., 1832 — Jan., 1833, was on the whole a prosperous one for the young minister.

benediction & counsel. I said that mother wished you to send a mattress. I think there will still be time for it to come round Cape Cod. I told you I believe that my first destination is Malta then thro tribulation of quarantines menaced Messina or Palermo then Naples, that worlds wonder — If I get well & do well after the way of flesh, that is, I shall come back I suppose either via Leghorn or Havre next June July or August. Meantime I believe I did not tell you that we are to disperse our chattels to the four winds by that domestic crack of doom & type of all forlornness, an auction, & if you would ruin yourself by some excellent bargains why you may come & bid on us. I thank you for the letter you sent me the other day. The answer is, No. I am sorry Mr Lunt is in trouble.[58] We have a big gossip here about Trinity Church as being about to adopt the Reformed Liturgy of Stone Chapel. But I fear we shall not have the happiness of that handsome tower in our wiser Zion. If the story were true that only 3 men set themselves strongly against such a project in that parish it were a striking example enough of the preference of forms to things in our planet. & I am your affectionate brother

Waldo.

To the Second Church and Society, Boston, December 22, 1832

[Printed in *Letter from the Rev. R. W. Emerson, to the Second Church and Society,* Boston, n. d., a leaflet of eight pages, and on an elaborately ornamented silk broadside with the heading *Rev. Mr Emerson's Letter to the Second Church and Society.* Both leaflet and broadside bear the name of the printer, I. R. Butts. Isaac R. Butts, printer, duly appears in *Stimpson's Boston Directory,* 1832, but he is also in the directories of the same city for many years thereafter. That the date was, however, about the end of Dec., 1832, or early Jan., 1833, seems probable. An official record of Dec. 23, 1832, tells of the reading of the letter " this forenoon from the Pulpit by the Rev Mr Greenwood " and of the vote of the Standing Committee " that Three Hundred copies of this Letter be printed & distributed to the Proprietors, & Worshipers " (MS owned by the Second Church). Charles Emerson wrote to William, Dec. 27 and 29 (1832; MS owned by Dr. Haven Emerson): " The farewell letter which Mr. Greenwood read is to be printed (not published) & every member of the Society is to have it — I will send you one — " A copy of the broadside is owned by RWEMA (ph. in CUL), and a copy of the leaflet is in the library of the Boston Athenæum (ph. in CUL). The text has been reprinted in O. B. Frothingham, *Transcendentalism in New England,* 1876, pp. 232–236; in Cabot, II, 685–688; and elsewhere.]

58. William Emerson to his mother, Dec. 3 and 5 (1832), had told of the probability that the New York church would drop Lunt because of his failure to arouse interest (MS owned by Dr. Haven Emerson).

1833

To Ruth Haskins Emerson? on board the "Jasper," February 2, and Malta, February 11, 1833

[Charles Emerson, Apr. 9 and 13, 1833: "Joyfully dined Mother & I at Mr. Adams' yesterday, for we had your letter of the 2d & 11th February — . . ." It is possible that this letter was addressed to Charles or to both him and his mother. It must have been at least partly the basis of the notice printed in the *Christian Register,* Apr. 20, 1833: "We understand that letters have been received from the Rev. Ralph Waldo Emerson . . . stating that he arrived in Malta, the beginning of February, and was in good health.]

To Ruth Haskins Emerson and Charles Chauncy Emerson? Malta? February 21, 1833

[Charles Emerson, Apr. 26 and 27, 1833: "Apr. 27 — We this moment have received per Jasper a letter dated 21 Feb. & another 7 March — brief — & seemingly written merely to tell us of others — but they say you are well . . . I shall receive & keep safely the vases & candlesticks — "]

To William Emerson, Syracuse, February 26, and Messina, March 5, 1833[1]

ISyracuse, 26 Feb. 1833

Dear William, As you so strongly urged my visit to Sicily I cannot help taking a spare moment to date a letter to you from this oldest of towns. Here have I been dwelling, now four days, in the little peninsula of Ortygia, with Mt. Etna visible from one window, the pillars of the temple of Capitoline Jove from another, & the tomb of Archimedes & the Ear of Dionysius from the house top. I have drunk the [2] waters of the Fountain Arethusa; I have plucked the Papyrus on the banks of the Anapus; I have visited the same Catacombs which Cicero admired [3] for

1. MS owned by HCL; ph. in CUL. Excerpts I–VI are in Cabot, I, 179–181.

2. The slight mutilation of the MS at this point probably occurred before the letter was written. Apparently no part of the text is missing.

3. *In Verrem,* II, v, 27.

the prodigious depth & extent of the excavations[I] – the quarry of an enormous city. – [II]I have heard mass said in the ancient temple of Minerva now converted into a cathedral. For my breakfast they give me most fragrant Hyblaean honey; & quails (in Ortygia) [4] for dinner. Yet is it a poor grey shabby place, the ruin of ruins. The Earthquakes have shaken down its temples & there is scarce any thing that speaks of Hiero or Timoleon or Dion.[5] Yet I am glad to be where they have been & to hear the bees & pick [II] up dozens of [III]beautiful wild flowers only three or four miles from the fountain Cyane[III] where Proserpine went down with 'gloomy Dis.' [6] [IV]But my ignorance, as I supposed, is my perpetual tormentor. I want my Virgil & Ovid. I want my history & my Plutarch. I want maps & gazetteers.[7] Were I 14 days earlier here I would sit down in the Capuchin Convent here & take my chance of begging or buying the right books. It is more Roman than Rome. It is the playground of the gods & goddesses who went to Italy only in the progress of war & commerce.

5 March. Since I began my letter, I have come by mule from Syracuse to Catania & now by coach between Etna & the shore hither. From Taormina to Messina, 30 miles, is the most picturesque country, I judge, that for the same extent is anywhere to be found. The towns are as the towns of goats – every one on a precipice, rich soil. stone villages. sunny sea beach lined with fishermen drawing their nets – steep mountains of marble abruptly rising on the other side;[IV] & very pleasant four Sicilians a tailor a priest & his two nephews my companions in the coach But how can one describe so tediously line by line what the swift eye & ear receive so fast or how could you bear to read the long detail? [V]Here

4. An allusion, no doubt, to the meaning of the name "Ortygia."

5. It is obvious from *Journals*, III, 41, that Cicero, who seems to have been much in Emerson's mind during the Sicilian visit, had something to do with the interest shown here in the three ancient worthies (*cf. In Verrem, passim*). Timoleon and Dion Emerson knew, no doubt, from Plutarch, where he probably also read the brief passages on Hiero II. For his admiration of Wordsworth's "Dion," see Dec. 14, 1831.

6. *Paradise Lost*, IV, 270.

7. Of what guidebooks Emerson was making any use, it is not clear; but he might have got much help, and perhaps did get some, from Mariana Starke's *Travels in Europe between the Years 1824 and 1828 . . . Comprising an Historical Account of Sicily with Particular Information for Strangers in that Island*, 1828. This attractive work has much of the information that Emerson put into this and the following letter. But his mention of the papyrus along the Anapus seems to indicate that he was unaware of the distinction made between the true and false varieties by Mariana Starke. And in general I conclude, after examining a number of guidebooks, that Emerson's travel letters have few verbal echoes from such works.

am I in Messina famous from Sparta downward yet having now no antiquities to show as Syracuse & Catania have. & no modern wonders of art; only Nature has been very kind to it.[V] Here between Scylla & Charybdis one a little north on this shore the other a little south on the other, are from 40 to 50000 people very busy & noisy. Mr Payson the American Consul [8] & his lady recd me very kindly. I drank tea with them last eve. & he will take this letter to America next week. I have just engaged my passage in the steamboat to Palermo & Naples & am to sail tomorrow at 12 o'clock [VI]But I suppose you would know how these out courts of the old world impress the poor hermit who with saucer eyes has strayed from his study. Why, non so, c'e la medesima cosa, same faces under new caps & jackets, another turn of the old kaleidoscope. Every place you enter is a new lottery; chance may make you acquainted with an honest & kind man therein then will that place disclose its best things & you may know nobody then will go out of it ignorant & with disagreeable impressions.[VI] The fault of travellers is like that of American farmers, both lay out too much ground & so slur, one the insight the other the cultivation of every part. Ætna I have not ascended. The winter will not let the traveller go higher than Mount Rosso & that crater is long extinguished.

What a comedy is all one's tuition in a new language. I much overestimated my knowledge of Italian & the ease of speaking it. These Sicilians have not only an accent but a dialect of their own & printed books in it. The worse for me. I might as well meet Arabs for conversation. In Italy, I expect better speed in this particular.

How are you, my dear brother? I long for some tidings from the cold west. At Naples I shall rejoice to fulfil my promise to my sister not *in law* but in hope.[9] I must bid you good bye for the present & finish a letter to Mother & Charles. I tell no stories to such a veteran traveller but will bring you home a full journal perhaps. Your affectionate

Waldo —

8. John L. Payson was American consul at Messina (*The National Calendar, and Annals of the United States,* 1833, p. 151).

9. See Mar. 22, 1833, to Susan Haven.

To Ruth Haskins Emerson and Charles Chauncy Emerson, Syracuse, February 26, and Messina, March 5, 1833 [10]

Syracuse, 26. Feb. 1833

My Dear Mother & brother C.

I have just broken off a bit of stone from the tomb of Timoleon, whose "successes were like Homer's verses, they were so smooth & natural." [11] As our little party were sitting at dinner this P. M. the servant announced Un Frate dei Padri Capuccini, & in came the barefooted & bearded man with a dish of lemons in one hand & a small plate of olives & salad in the other, as his present, & would know if we did not mean to visit his convent. Now 'do ut des' is the motto of all this world & especially of Capuchins who live by alms, yet we took the monk's compliment in good part & were glad to set out with him forthwith to the Chiesa di San Giovanni & its Latomié which we had not seen. A pleasant walk of a mile from the gates of the city brot us to the old sanctuary, not large, but old; walls, posts, antique masonry, tell the same story as one of its inscriptions, 'nullum antiquius in Siciliâ.' The granite or granite-like stone was honey-combed with length of time & doubtless the house was built in the first ages of Christianity. Through the low old door we entered a small & unfurnished chapel & thence with torches descended into another below, of a more solid & bold architecture, its walls graved with most deep & durable sculptures — probably built before the Christian era & converted long thereafter into a church. It is good to see the strong handwriting of that masterly Greek generation who wrote in granite, in æternitatem, with more ease & elegance than others in wax, & who could not hew a stone, or mould an utensil that did not forthwith become a model of grace to the human eye.

A short distance from this church we descended into a cavern cut into the living rock & with torches explored long passages to which no end appeared — say boldly streets — having on either side chambers larger or less the repositories once of the dead; but for a thousand years "the very sepulchres lie tenantless —" [12] How far do these reach,' asked I — "Non So, Mal aria, Signore," was the reply whenever we turned back.

But I will not pester you with long stories of buildings & ruins &

10. MS copy, in Charles Emerson's hand, owned by RWEMA; ph. in CUL.

11. Plutarch's *Lives,* "Timoleon," XXXVI, 2. Emerson recalled the passage in his "Milton," published some five years later.

12. Byron, *Childe Harold's Pilgrimage,* IV, lxxix, 6.

landscapes seen — twere long to tell, & you shall have it in my journal. How smell the streets — pah! how narrow they are, how full of beggars. Every hand almost is outstretched in the street — The boys beg piteously, pointing with their fingers to their open mouths, ho molto fame mio caro signore ' Indeed they speculate on their infirmities, farm them out, & go snacks in misery. One old woman in this street, Strada Amalfitana having begged several times in her own right, besets me now with an old blind wretch whom she leads up pointing at her eyeballs which she rolls dreadfully " Ella e cieca, Signore, vedova miserabile " Then the artists & mechanics & antiquity venders with bags of broken lamps & old coppers & cameos all come to the Locanda to pay their respects to the traveller & you can scarce look at a man in the street but he will step up with " che vuol il signor " & expect to be paid if he tells you the name of the Street.

5 March — Messina —

By mules I came to Catania & after spending 3 days there came here in coach —

x x x x — — — — —[13]

It seems to me now that I shall be ready to come home in September or October —

And so with much love & much thanksgiving, & ardent prayers for your continued happiness I am wholly your

Affectionate Waldo. E.

To Charles Chauncy Emerson, Messina, March 6, 1833

[Mentioned in Charles Emerson to William, May 14 and 15 (1833; owned by Dr. Haven Emerson), as " another brief line fr. Waldo dated March 6, Messina."]

To Ruth Haskins Emerson and Charles Chauncy Emerson? Palermo? March 7, 1833

[See the note on Feb. 21, 1833.]

To Ruth Haskins Emerson? and Charles Chauncy Emerson, Naples, March 22, 1833

[Acknowledged in Charles Emerson, June 1, 1833; and summarized in Charles to William, May 31, 1833 (owned by Dr. Haven Emerson) : ". . . a letter from Waldo, date 22 March Naples, — written in entire health & good spirits, &

13. Charles Emerson so indicates the omission of a passage which may, I conjecture, have repeated parts of the letter to William written on the same day.

speaking very decidedly about visiting France & especially England where he means to stay some time — He wants his letter of credit enlarged — says he shall be in Paris in July or early in August — . . ." That Charles and his mother received other letters from Naples seems to be indicated by his letter of June 27 following: "We have got all your letters from Naples . . ." But it is possible that this account includes letters sent to William Emerson at New York and to George Sampson at Boston.]

To Susan Woodward Haven, Naples, March 22, 1833 [14]

Naples, 22 March, 1833.

I promised my brother William to write a letter from this city to my dear sister that shall be. I regretted my sickness last summer the more because it prevented me from seeing you. But Time, they say, brings roses, & makes acquaintances, & so, I trust, we shall be good friends yet. But what can I tell you of this famous town now that I am here? It takes some time for a peaceable person who for the first time has strayed away some thousand miles from his armchair & inkstand into this monstrous hurlyburly — to recover himself & walk with his eyes straight before him. However having had my pockets picked twice in the course of the same day, I have learned to behave on the Toledo with tolerable composure. Naples is set down in all the books for a Paradise, & I suppose with reason, but it rains every day & my first impressions are that it is a very large boisterous disagreeable city. Now do not think the fault is mine. I am very easy to please. Since I landed at Malta I hardly pass a monastery but I ask them on what terms they will receive me for life; and in Sicily when I saw them taking cicinelli [15] in their sunny bays I had half a mind to be a fisherman & draw my net at Taormina the rest of my days. The hymn says "Man wants but little." [16] — Calm civil people, warm weather, a fine prospect, a few books & a little coffee will content my philosophy but here in Naples I am lonely & a-'cold & my chamber is dark, & who can go to Vesuvius or Paestum or the Villa of Cicero when the rain pours? However, to be just, when the sun shines, it does seem a decent place, yea, its Chiaia (as they call the range of palaces on the margin of the bay,) its islands, & surrounding mountain country,

14. MS owned by Dr. Haven Emerson; ph. in CUL.

15. I am informed that the word "cicirelli," here misspelled, is used locally for a kind of fish.

16. Emerson might have remembered Goldsmith's line in "The Hermit," viii (which was probably borrowed from Young's fourth night, 118); but "The Hermit" is not a hymn.

marvellously beautiful. I crawled out the other day between the drops to Baiae, & since, have been to Pompeii & Herculaneum, & I could not help thinking I was paid for my pains. Baiae was 2000 years ago a sort of Nahant — a pleasure ground where the Roman senators & Emperors built beautiful villas on the edge of the bay. Time & earthquake & volcano have made sad work with the palaces. The whole soil is made of broken brick & marble, & dig where they will, they open chambers & cellars & baths. But the natural beauties of the spot which recommended it to the taste of the Romans still remained to charm my poor eyes the day before yesterday. But I am not going to pester you with descriptions of this unrivalled landscape. I leave it to the painters. One day, tis likely, you will come hither yourself. And though a hermit such as I, may find his profit now & then in going alone to these old places, yet the true way for profit & delight doubtless is, to come & see them with those whose society is our daily food. So one of these days as I said, when the courts of New York are closed in the summer heats — I wish you a very pleasant excursion.

In a few days I go to Rome, where I hope I may find your brother George,[17] who I am glad to know is in these parts. Every body is crowding to Rome just now, for the Holy Week begins on the 1st April[18] & that is the season of the great annual pomp of the Catholic Church. I follow the multitude & yet without much curiosity. I go to see old Rome, not new, & if I were not satisfied with seeing Naples, I would remain here till the Show was over. Perhaps I shall think differently when I see the purple & gold, & hear the Pope & his monks chaunt the "Miserere" in St Peters.

And so I greet you well, my fair sister, till I have the pleasure of seeing you, which I hope I shall have some time in the next autumn. I do not feel as if I was writing in the dark in addressing a letter to a lady I have not seen, for an earnest good will unites people more than neighborhood, and with sincere desires for your present & future happiness, I am your affectionate servant, R. Waldo Emerson.

17. *Cf.* Mar. 23, 1833, to William Emerson.
18. Easter fell on Apr. 7 in 1833.

To William Emerson, Naples, March 23, 1833 [19]

Naples, 23 March, 1833.

Dear William

I am much obliged to you for a letter recd here accompanying a passport & letter to Mr Haven. With Mr Hammatt's [20] advice I have dropt the old passport & shall use the new. Today I am going to Vesuvius & Monday or Tuesday I depart for Rome. I might stay here longer & see many things; but trifles determine the movements of so humoursome a traveller. Every town is a lottery & not its real merits but his petty chances of lodging, acquaintances, & weather make it agreeable or otherwise. Naples at this moment is crowded with an unusual concourse of foreigners & I have not had a pleasant room, tho' I have changed once; & it has rained I believe every one of the ten days that I have been here. Then San Carlo's famous Theatre is closed on account of Lent. However I have seen all the best of the wonders, but have not visited Paestum as I would. I keep a pretty precise journal, that must atone for few letters, if I write few. Mr McCrackan,[21] Senr of your city is here but I have not seen him. Mr Rogers,[22] my banker, tells me he is in very delicate health. At Rome I may stay 5 or 6 weeks & at Florence probably the whole of May. Now I am fairly in I shall probably fulfil the whole orbit & tamely walk in the steps of the whole travelling public thro Switzerland, France, & England. As to Vienna, I doubt. Venice I would see. But the time & the course of my wayfaring will depend on what news I get from Charles. I believe there is nothing known to me here of special interest to you. His majesty, I have not chanced to see though he rides much in the streets. His hobby is his troops who are ever parading the streets both horse & foot with all kinds of music. The Museum is truly rich Beautiful remains of ancient sculpture. It is more than meat & drink to see so many princely old Greek heads Apollos, Dianas, Aristides, Demosthenes, Seneca and emperors & heroes without end. The picture gallery too. Five genuine Raffaelles & Guido & Titian & Spagnoletto each of which you may safely admire without risk of its being a *copy*. But the churches everywhere impress me most. Strange that the Americans should not build one temple in this magnificent

19. MS owned by HCL; ph. in CUL.

20. Peter Force, *The National Calendar,* 1833, p. 151, lists Alexander Hammett as consul at Naples.

21. *Cf.* Sept. 6, 1830, to William Emerson.

22. *Cf. Journals,* III, 69.

manner. It is hard to charge the Orientals with immoveableness. Every people is just as much padlocked to its own customs whether of eating or architecture or worship or what not, & we, no doubt, shall continue in America, fancy free though we be, to build mean churches with pews for a thousand years to come, instead of these sublime old temples so lofty & many-chapelled, covered with the marble & gold of ages & every wall & nook alive with picture, statue, or inscription. But I hate travelling. Happy they that sit still! How glad I shall be to get home again. I dread especially the entrance of each new city — the fearful Dogana, the boatmen the porters, the uncertainties of the Locanda, — & hug myself when this gauntlet is fairly run thro. If once I should get quietly lodged to my mind & fixed too in good company, tis a chance if you see me again till I have spent all in the far country But to every man is his castle in the air which never alights on the firm earth.

I enclose a letter [23] to — when will she be my sister? If it wont do, you need not send it, for I very much desire her good will. I enquired for Mr Haven here, but he has not been here. It is in vain to bid you write me at Rome or Florence tho' I hope you have but be sure that Mr Welles & Co., *Paris* shall. have letters for me. In that expectation & in much love I remain your affectionate brother

Waldo —

To George Adams Sampson, Naples, March 23, 1833 [24]

ᴵNaples, 23 March, 1833.

My dear friend,ᴵ

What is the reason I have not written to you all this time? I cannot tell but shall please myself with writing now. ᴵᴵHow go the days & the months with you & yours? How fares the soul under the wear & tear of vulgar events? What new thoughts? What brighter hope? I long to have a good talk with you which the rolling moons may soon grant. I am so much indebted to your manly friendship, specially in the last year, that I miss my counsellor much in this vast Babel too where there is so much argument for conversation always occurring. Time which brings roses, will bring us topics, I trust, less sombre than the old ones.[25] I have regretted the vexation they gave you. It looks now to me

23. Of Mar. 22, 1833. The Biblical allusion near the end of the preceding paragraph is to *Luke,* 15: 13–14. Babel, in the following letter, is from *Genesis,* 11:1–9.

24. MS owned by RWEMA; ph. in CUL. This is a copy in Cabot's hand. Excerpts I–IX are in Cabot, I, 183–185.

25. Emerson refers especially, no doubt, to the dispute over the Lord's Supper in the Second Church.

as it always did,[II] — only Dr Kirklands opinion a more just bon mot. — [III]I am moving about here in much noise & myriads of people & see much grandeur & much poverty, but am not very sure that I grow much wiser or any better for my travels. We put very different matters into the scales but the balance never varies much. An hour in Boston or an hour in Naples have about equal value to the same person[III]; the pains of travelling are as real and about as vivid as the pleasures. Besides a thousand petty annoyances that are always fretting an inexperienced traveller, he is perpetually disappointed — his plans of study his hopes of good society, above all, his covenants with himself — the heroism, the wisdom, he is to make his own — are always flying before him — never realized. [IV]Still, though travelling is a poor profession — bad food, it may be good medicine. It is good, like seasickness, to break up a morbid habit, & I sometimes fancy it is a very wholesome shaking for me.[IV] One thing however I rejoice at. It furnishes the student with a perpetual answer to the little people that are always hinting that your faith & hope belong to your village or your country, & that a knowledge of the world would open your eyes. He who thinks for himself knows better, & yet is glad to have his most retired & unuttered thought confirmed & echoed back to him by his observation of new men & strange institutions. [V]I am glad to recognize the same man under a thousand different masks & hear the same commandment spoken to me in Italian, I was wont to hear in English.[V] But the new discipline is only begun, & I can give you a maturer opinion by & bye. [VI]My greatest want is the very one I apprehended when at home, that I never meet with men that are great or interesting. There are such everywhere, & here no doubt, a just proportion; but a traveller, for the most part, never learns even their names,[VI] whilst he sees in every city a good deal of its very worst population. [VII]That is why we ought not to travel too young. If you know the language your chance of acquaintance is very much increased; if you are yourself great & good, why I think your chance would be best of all.[VII]

I have been now to Vesuvius & was almost suffocated with the hot vapors of the Crater.[26] Tis a fearful place. I have been also to Pompeii & Herculaneum & seen the handiwork of the volcano. This whole country is an unrivalled picture The Bay is a beauty look from whatever side

26. Some weeks later, it seems, the activity of the volcano attracted throngs of sightseers. The *Boston Daily Advertiser* reported on Aug. 14, 1833: " Mount Vesuvius has been in a state of eruption since the 28th of May, and is daily thronged with thousands, many of whom pass the night at the brink of the crater . . . At about fifty paces from the burning bed of lava, booths are erected for supplying refreshments."

you will. But I will not pester you with descriptions which you may find better in all the books.

VIII Where shall I find a letter from you? VIII At Rome or Florence? And surely another at Paris. IX I have some letters from home, but they say not a word of the Second Church. Tell me of it – particularly. But chiefly tell me of youself. I hope this finds your wife in health, & the little household of my nephews.[27] Remember me with much kindness to Mrs S. & so to all your friends & mine. Monday I am going to Rome, & there & everywhere am your affectionately [28]

Waldo Emerson IX

To Charles Chauncy Emerson, Rome, April 16 and 21, 1833 [29]

Rome April 16, 1833

My Dear Charles,

I suppose you would gladly know the experiences of the traveller in Rome. Very good & pleasant & instructive it is to be here. We grow wiser by the day, & by the hour. Here are the manifest footprints of the nations & the ages. Here is the town of centuries, the capital of the ancient & of the modern world. All is large, magnificent, secular, & the treasury of the arts is evidently the contribution of the whole civilized world. I have been here three weeks & my eyes are now familiar with the objects whose forms in pictures & models & casts are familiar to all Christendom. I see almost daily the Coliseum, the Forum, the Pantheon, the Apollo, the Laocoon, the Gladiator, besides St. Peters, & the Transfiguration & the last Judgment. By degrees the topography of the old City arranges itself in my head & I learn to find not only a Church or a picture, but even a shop or a trattoria, by refer-

27. The title was, of course, only one of convenience.

28. The error may be the copyist's. So, presumably, is the spelling " youself," a few lines above.

29. MS copy, by Charles Emerson, owned by RWEMA; ph. in CUL. Charles, who wrote on June 27 (1833), " I have your sun-bright letter from Rome," said that it made him wish, more than ever before, to cross the ocean. Apparently the present letter lacks something more than the signature or else there was one from Rome that is now lost, for the following unpublished passage occurs in an undated notebook: " I wrote home from Rome, in 1833, to the disgust of Charles, ' I collect nothing that can be touched, or tasted, or smelled. I collect neither cameo, nor painting, nor medallion, but I value much the growing picture which the ages have painted, & which I reverently survey. Tis wonderful how much we see in 5 months, or, in how short time we learn what it has taken so many ages to teach.' " (MS *S Salvage*, p. 228.)

ring it to the Column of Trajan or the Arch of Constantine. It is a grand town, & works mightily upon the senses & upon the soul. It fashions my dreams even, & all night I visit Vaticans. I am in better health than ever since I was a boy. Would you know how I spend the days? Today I crossed the Tiber in a ferry & ascended the Monte Janiculo[30] to find the Church of St. Onofrio. It is a far away church & nobody goes there. But here was the tomb of Tasso. After reading the epitaph, we went into the adjoining convent, & the courteous fathers showed us the poet's bust. It was taken in wax from his body directly after his death. He died in this convent after being sick a month. Few things in Rome are better worth seeing than this head. What an air of independence & genius it hath! I think there is no such face now upon this planet. My companions in this visit were three painters & they were all so much charmed with this noble head that they betook themselves to their pencils & each sketched a likeness of the bard. Here also we were shown a Madonna by Leonardo da Vinci,[31] whose pictures, they say, always make you contemplative. — Then yesterday I went to see Michael Angelo's statue of Christ, & tomorrow, maybe, I will go see his Moses, reputed one of the grandest of sculptures. Goethe says in a letter from Rome that a man's existence is enlarged is doubled by having seen the head of Medusa, an antique marble in the Rondanini Palace.[32] I am sorry that I must remain only half myself, for I am told I cannot see that work, but he truly speaks of the sights of Rome. I lie down at night enriched by the contemplation of great objects. But I do not tell you what I see, for you know already — The Vatican Museum is an endless collection of all precious remains of ancient art; a quarter of a mile of statues, with branching galleries. And here too are Canova's works. Upstairs one story are the chambers of Raffaelle containing his world renowned frescoes; go up another story, & you enter the picture gallery where is the Transfiguration & its rainbow companions. All this unrivalled show is thrown open twice in every week, & our due feet never fail. At the other end of the town is the Capitoline Museum & Gallery also open twice in the

30. Gianicolo, or, in English, Janiculum.

31. Or rather, doubtless, of the school of Leonardo.

32. Goethe wrote on July 29, 1787: ". . . in dem Palast Rondanini. Ihr werdet euch aus meinen ersten Römischen Briefen einer Meduse erinnern . . . Nur einen Begriff zu haben dass so etwas in der Welt ist . . . macht einen zum doppelten Menschen." Emerson, already awakening to the charm of the German poet, might have read this in *Goethe's Werke,* Stuttgart and Tübingen, 1829, XXIX, 40.

week. Then on common days, we may go to Thorwalsdens' [33] Studio, or to Gibson's or to Wyatt's [34] (English sculptors) or to the Quirinal Hill, & see the reputed statues of Phidias & Praxiteles,[35] or to any of a dozen palaces, each a picture gallery, or to some church, where as in the chiesa d'Araceli (once the temple of Jupiter [36] Capitolinus) the ground has been a place of worship, three thousand years; or to the Ponte Sublicio, & see the vestiges of Cocles' bridge; or to the Mamertine Prison, & see the undoubted jaĩl of St Peter, & earlier still, of Cethegus & Lentulus; & so on & so forth, to the end of the Guide book,[37] & the end of the year. Ah great great Rome! it is a majestic city, & satisfies this craving imagination. And yet I would give all Rome for one man such as were fit to walk here, & could feel & impart the sentiment of the place. That wise man whom everywhere I seek, here I hunger & thirst after. Yet I have found several pleasant & one valuable companion, Mr. Cranch.[38] I have found here too a friend of Carlyle in Edinburgh,[39] who has given me a letter of introduction to him. 21. Next Tuesday I depart for Florence, in company with Mr Wall of New Bedford, a painter, Mr Walsh of Phila. son of the Reviewer, & Mr Mayer of Baltimore.[40] It takes 5½ days

33. Again the double fault is probably the copyist's.

34. Both John Gibson and Richard James Wyatt lived much in Rome.

35. The contemporary A. Nibby, *Itinéraire de Rome,* Rome, 1830, I, 231–232, described the so-called " Castor " and " Pollux " as doubtfully ascribed to Pheidias and Praxiteles. For a modern opinion more favorable to the ascription, see Adolf Furtwängler, *Masterpieces of Greek Sculpture,* London, 1895, pp. 95 ff.

36. Emerson might have come by this bit of misinformation in such a guidebook as Nibby, 1830, where it appears on pp. 84–85 of Vol. I.

37. Possibly Nibby, 1830, again, where the story of Cethegus and Lentulus appears, I, 113, and the tradition about St. Paul, on the following page.

38. Doubtless John Cranch, brother of C. P. Cranch. He was then in Italy studying art. (Leonora Cranch Scott, *The Life and Letters of Christopher Pearse Cranch,* 1917, p. 19.)

39. Eichthal. In an unpublished passage of the diaries for 1848, Emerson wrote: " Memo. In 1833, I met Gustave D'Eichthal at an evening party at Mr Horace Gray's, in Rome. He was what was then called a Saint Simonian. He was well acquainted with Carlyle, & offered to give me a letter of introduction to him. The next day he called on me & gave me a letter to John Stuart Mill in London, requesting him to introduce me to Carlyle. In London, I found Mr Mill at the India House, & he wrote to Carlyle, & advised my visit." (Typescript *Journals.*) *Cf.* also Mar. 11, 1835.

40. William Allen Wall, the artist, is mentioned in Daniel Ricketson, *New Bedford of the Past,* 1903, pp. 42–43 and 159; and he reappears in later letters. For Emerson's appreciation, in old age, of the copy Wall had made for him of " The Three Fates," see the letter of Mar.? 1880? Robert Walsh was well known as an editor. His son Robert M. Walsh lived much in Europe. For Brantz Mayer, see Jan. 8 and 9, 1843.

to go to Florence. We stop at Terni to see the famed cataract of Velino. I shall probably spend May in the Etrurian Athens.

To Mary Moody Emerson, Rome, April 18, and Florence, May? c. 17? 1833 [41]

IRome, 18 April, 1833.

My dear Aunt

The sights & names of this wonderful town remind me much of my gifted correspondent, for the spiritual affinities transcend the limits of space and a soul so Roman should have its honor here. How glad should I be of a letter to make the image livelier.I I trust I shall find one at Florence where I hope to receive a large pacquet. IIDid they tell you that I went away from home a wasted peevish invalid. Well I have been mending ever since & am now in better health than I remember to have enjoyed since I was in college. How should one be sick at Rome?II It is a wonderful town. Yet I strive to possess my soul in patience, &, escaping both giddiness & pedantry, to feel truly & think wisely. III'Here is matter for all feeling,' said Byron [42] and yet how evanescent & superficial is most of that emotion which names & places, which Art or magnificence can awaken. It yields in me to the interest the most ordinary companion inspires. I never get used to men. They always awaken expectations in me which they always disappoint, and I am a poor asteroid in the great system subject to disturbances in my orbit not only from all the planets but from all their moons. The wise man — the true friend — the finished character — we seek everywhere & only find in fragments Yet I cannot persuade myself that all the beautiful souls are fled out of the planet or that always I shall be excluded from good company & yoked with green dull pitiful persons. After being cabined up by sea & by land since I left home with various little people, all better to be sure & much wiser than me but still such as did not help me — I cannot tell you how refreshing it was to fall in with two or three sensible persons with whom I could eat my bread & take my walk & feel

41. MS owned by RWEMA; ph. in CUL. Excerpts I–IV are in Cabot, I, 185–187. The date of the paragraph written from Florence could not be earlier than Apr. 28, when Emerson arrived there, nor later than May 28, when he left (*Journals,* III, 104 and 125). The mention of the tombs of the famous Italians makes it reasonable to conjecture that May 17, when the similar passage in the letter of May 16 and 17, 1833, was written, is approximately correct; but there is no other evidence.

42. *Childe Harold's Pilgrimage,* IV, cix, 1–2, slightly condensed.

myself a freeman once more of Gods Universe. Yet were these last not instructers & I want instructers. God's greatest gift is a Teacher & when will he send me one, full of truth & of boundless benevolence & heroic sentiments. I can describe the man, & have already in prose & verse. I know the idea well, but where is its real blood warm counterpart. I know whilst I write thus that the creature is never to dawn upon me like a sun-burst I know too well how slowly we edge along sideways to every thing good & brilliant in our lives & how casually & unobservedly we make all our most valued acquaintances. And yet I saw Ellen at once in all her beauty & she never disappointed me except in her death. And why may not the Master which the soul anticipates, so appear. You are so far off that I shall scarce get your answers very soon, so I may as well set down what our stern experience replies with the tongue of all its days. Son of man, it saith, all giving & receiving is reciprocal; you entertain angels unawares [43] but they cannot impart more or higher things than you are in a state to receive But every step of your progress affects the intercourse you hold with all others; elevates its tone, deepens its meaning, sanctifies its spirit, and when time & suffering & selfdenial shall have transfigured & glorified this spotted self you shall find your fellows also transformed & their faces shall shine upon you with the light of wisdom & the beauty of holiness. — You who cling with both hands to the literal Word & to venerable traditions will find in my complaints a confession & a self accusation no doubt. You will say I do not receive what Heaven gives. But you must not say any such thing. For I am, you see, speaking truly as to my Maker. That excellent Teacher whom He sent who has done so much to raise & comfort human life & who prized sincerity more than sacrifice, cannot exist to me as he did to John. My brothers my mother my companions must be much more to me in all respects of friendship than he can be.[III]

I began this letter at Rome, I am finishing it at Florence close by the tombs of Galileo, of Michel Angelo, of Machiavel, & the empty urn of Dante.[44] My letter sheet has got sadly soiled & so I give the history of its places. — I get no letters from home here as I hoped & have heard very little from any one there since I came hither. [IV]Let me dear Aunt find a letter from you in Paris & believe me most affectionately your nephew

Waldo[IV]

43. *Hebrews,* 13:2. Other Biblical phrases, which Emerson probably hardly thought of as quoted, are scattered through this letter.

44. *Cf.* May 16 and 17, 1833.

To George Adams Sampson, Rome, April 20, and Florence, May 20, 1833 [45]

Rome, 20 April, 1833

My dear friend,

A few days ago I was rejoiced by your letter of 20 February. I was glad of its news, glad of its speculations, but most glad of its kindness. The more people I see, the fewer men I find there are, & I learn to prize my three or four, the more. It is like yourself to have adhered to the old Church, & I hope you will a long time yet. There is always a reward preparing for every sacrifice, & an apostle perhaps will sit in the seat of the Mathers.[46] At any rate, you who need to depend so little upon the pulpit for your edification, will not go away until you have found certainly a wiser teacher & lips that are touched.[47] When you find *the* man, go in the name of the Lord, & send me word also, & I will come & go with you.[48]

I live here with artists & very young travellers — how hard it is to be pleased — Now & then I have a good hour, & sometimes (but how seldom!) good conversation.

20 May, Florence. It will be a little ridiculous to a merchant to find such dates on his letter but forgive a traveller whose situation none but a traveller conceives. All that hasting race know well that they have no time to write. It is necessary in order to see what is worth seeing & especially *who* is worth seeing in each city, to go a little into society. Now no man can have society upon his own terms. If he seek it he must serve it too. He immediately & inevitably contracts debts to it which he must pay at a great expense often of inclination & of time. Then so inveterate is my habit of depending upon my books that I do not feel as if my day had substance in it, if I have read nothing. So I labor at German & Italian a little. Then this climate is & has been for a fortnight so hot

45. MS owned by RWEMA; ph. in CUL. This is a copy in Cabot's hand. At the top of the first page appears what Emerson must have written in the superscription: "Mr George A. Sampson, Boston United States of America via Havre." Charles Emerson, June 27 (1833), says, "Mr. Sampson has your letter & is writing & you will hear from him by the next packet." But this may refer either to a letter of Mar. 23 or to the present one. The spelling "frindship" is presumably the copyist's error.

46. Both Increase and Cotton Mather were pastors of the Second Church.

47. *Isaiah,* 6:7.

48. The style is Biblical enough, but perhaps Emerson had no definite passage in mind.

that only a few hours can be energetically applied. Lastly when I come home, I hope to tell you by word of mouth what I have seen & what I have thought

I tell you again I love real men & therefore I meet continual rebuffs & disappointments in seeing so many & yet none. Sincerity, in the highest sense, is very rare. Men of talents want simplicity & sincerity as much as others. They have the vulgar ambition of keeping fashionable company & are more afraid of intrusion than they are desirous of truth & sympathy. Even Mr Landor dared to tell me the other day that " Socrates was a vulgar sophist, & that he could not pardon vulgarity even in a man of genius." [49] Out upon his assurance! I should think their souls would starve. I should think they would sometimes be pinched with curiosity to know what a fellow-traveller in the same regions of speculation had found or thought. So obstinate indeed is my own conviction that in minds of the first class this hunger for truth from others must exist that I rather deny that I have met any wise man than admit that any such can be indifferent to the topics which interest me. Do you say I ought not to have wandered from my place: I found sincere people at home — why did I not stay there? Well I rue my fault & will hasten back & grow old, if God please, in my chimney corner amidst my own friends. But never do I despair that by truth we shall merit truth; by resolute searching for truth ourselves we shall deserve & obtain wisdom from others. If not now, yet in God's time & the souls, which is ages & ages. There is a worthy man here from New Bedford, Mr Wall an artist, with whom I walk in the afternoons. His hostess, a Catholic, of course, understands that I am a priest in my own country, & inquired of him yesterday, if he *confesses* to me. I told him he must tell her, yes. All frindship is confession, is it not, my dear friend? It is not only so, but possesses in some sort the power of absolution also — I have spent my time very pleasantly here but have anxiously expected letters which do not come. I hoped for many & two came creeping with dates as old as this will have when it reaches you. I am going to Venice next Tuesday, where I shall stop but two or 3 days & thence go to Milan, Geneva,

49. In *Journals,* III, 117–118, Emerson is not quite sure that the remark was about Socrates. Walter Savage Landor, the first great literary figure with whom Emerson became acquainted in Europe, appears in a number of later letters, but especially in May 16 and 17, 1833, and in the letter to Landor himself dated May 28, 1833. Many years later, comments upon the temperamental Englishman in *English Traits* (where, however, there was only the most inoffensive allusion to his judgment of Socrates) provoked Landor's famous open letter.

Paris. There surely I shall hear from you all & again in London if I am rich enough to go thither. Remember me affectionately to Mrs Sampson & to the boys & to Mr Adams & to Albert & to all

Yours truly
R. W. Emerson.

I have seen nothing in the way of art which has tempted me much to buy it for you. I think I shall bring my money safe home.

To William Emerson, Rome, April 21, 1833 [50]

Rome, 21 April, 1833

Dear William,

I must not deny myself the rare pleasure of addressing you a letter from this venerable old egg shell of nations, institutions, arts, religions. It justifies its fame. I am glad I came. So splendid a spectacle which grows ever upon the eye & upon the mind ought not to be hid. The idea of Rome nothing else but Rome can supply & though it be my stubborn faith that the elements of man's intellectual & moral life abound everywhere for all, and a man may be trained in a barnyard who shall measure with Scipio, yet this particular picture has so much beauty & greatness that I am well pleased that it forms a part of my education to have seen it. You bid me in your letter mark well all the Raffaelles I shd see, & so I have, & I love the Transfiguration [51] with all my heart. Yesterday afternoon I went to the Church of S. Pietro in Vinculo to see Michel Angelo's statue of Moses. What a wonder it is! It is as great as the Greeks without reminding you of them. It is the Jewish Law embodied in a man. I could wish the horns away. So violent a type suits not us western Puritans, but it surpasses even the Laocoon & the Apollo in expression. The story is that the sculptor struck the statue with his hammer & said ' Alzate, parla.' [52] whence the crack in the knee. I have seen his Pietà in St Peters, his Christ in the Minerva which are both memorable but this is his masterpiece in stone as the Last Judgment in painting. Yet few things have pleased me more than the beautiful face of the figure of Justice on the monument of Pope Paul III in St Peters. I know not if you remember it, but it was designed by Michel Angelo, executed by William de la Porta & is on the left side of the Tribuna. I shall remember it all my life. When I see these fine objects

50. MS owned by HCL; ph. in CUL.

51. *Cf.* Apr. 16 and 21, 1833.

52. I have not found a printed source which Emerson could have used.

I think of Plato's doctrine of the original forms that are in the Divine mind. These things take a place that seems to have waited for them in our own minds. They are almost *recognized,* as Fontenelle said of new truth. But you have seen all these things & felt all the emotions of this place. There is nothing new here – all that is of any importance is the old. Camuccini is thought a respectable painter, but no genius. Thorwaldsen has executed an admirable statue of Byron [53] which goes to England shortly. He sits on a broken column with an owl behind his feet. The Christ of this Sculptor is much admired but I was not impressed by it. Then I saw the studios of Gibson & of Wyatt two English sculptors and a good model of Huskisson,[54] in clay, at the first, & a pretty nymph stepping in to the bath,[55] at the second. Greenough at Florence has more genius, his friends here say, than all the other artists in Italy put together. He is besides a high minded man & a warm patriot withal. He has finished a statue of Medora (the heroine of the Corsair) which is to be sent to America in a few weeks, & which is much admired. I hope to be in Florence in time to see it. Willis is here [56] & Alexander [57] & Cranch,[58] American artists. The last is son of Judge C. of Washington, & is a most agreeable & sensible companion, & a great comfort to me all the time I have been here. I have found here also two Miss Bridgens of Albany N Y Miss Anna B. is a friend of Miss Sedgwick [59] & a very intelligent & worthy lady. Her society was very refreshing to me whilst she staid, for you may see many people & find no conversation, & I hope to rejoin them at Florence. Then I found Mr Halsey & his family from N. Y. here, very pleasant people. & Mr & Mrs Horace Gray. Next Tuesday morn. I depart for Florence with young Walsh son of Mr W. of Phil. & Mayer [60] of Baltimore & Wall an artist from New Bedford. Let me

53. For this statue, later placed in Trinity College, Cambridge, and for the "Christ" of the same sculptor, see Eugène Plon, *Thorwaldsen,* Boston, 1873, pp. 125–126 and 219–220.

54. Gibson had begun the clay model of his first statue of Huskisson in 1831 and finished it in five months (T. Matthews, *The Biography of John Gibson, R. A.,* London, 1911, p. 79).

55. R. J. Wyatt's "Girl at the Bath."

56. He spent the winter of 1832–1833 and the following spring at Florence, Rome, and Naples (Henry A. Beers, *Nathaniel Parker Willis,* n. d. [c. 1913], p. 123).

57. Francis Alexander's own account of his life at this time is given in William Dunlap, *History of the Rise and Progress of the Arts of Design in the United States,* 1834, II, 432–433. *Cf.* also the letter of July 31, 1833.

58. See Apr. 16 and 21, 1833.

59. Probably Catharine Maria Sedgwick.

60. For Walsh and Mayer, see Apr. 16 and 21.

not forget to name among the Americans Lewis Stackpole[61] whom it was charming to see & who is gone to Naples & to Constantinople nor the Livingstons of N. Y. very well bred fine young men. One day I counted 15 persons here from Boston.

I have seen the Pope Gregory XVI many times during the Holy Week. He is reputed a good scholar & a worthy man. There is a learned man here, Mezzofante (I believe I spell right,) who is just appointed or being appointed librarian of the Vatican.[62] He understands thirty languages. Stackpole had a letter to him but did not succeed in seeing him. But I hate to be in Rome & know nothing of present Rome which much excites my curiosity. If I knew I might, I would sit down here for months & take measures to win my way into Italian society which is always accessible to those who really wish to enter it. Here are American students in the Propaganda & English & Irish priests in some religious houses who could & would tell me all I wish to know of the theory & order & politics of the Church. But the unhappy traveller revolves ever in a little eddy of an orbit through Museums & caffés & the society of his countrymen & the inner Italy he never sees. And yet so little enterprize is in the Artists who reside here that it is commonly said that he who stays in Rome a fortnight, usually sees more than he who stays for months. I think I shall stay in Florence a month, possibly go to Venice, probably to Switzerland & trust to find letters from you both at F. & at Paris. Your affectionate brother, Waldo.

To Charles Chauncy Emerson, Florence, May 16 and 17, 1833[63]

Florence May 16 1833

Dear Charles –

x x x – Yesterday I went to San Domenico di Fiesole[64] & dined with Mr. Walter Savage Landor. He is about 60 years old & a very good looking gentleman, talks very well, but quite decidedly, as if used to command the opinions of his friends; but has no

61. Joseph Lewis Stackpole graduated at Harvard in 1824.

62. Giuseppe Mezzofanti, reputed master of fifty-eight languages, was appointed chief keeper of the Vatican library in 1833 and became a cardinal in 1838.

63. MS copy, in the hand of Charles Emerson, owned by RWEMA; ph. in CUL. I have tried to reproduce the copyist's peculiar method of indicating omissions. Excerpt I is in Cabot, I, 190.

64. For the Villa Landore, a little way from San Domenico di Fiesole, half-way up the hillside toward Fiesole, see Augustus J. C. Hare, *Florence,* London, n. d., pp. 206 ff.

conversational display; is quite a connoisseur in art, has himself fine pictures, lives in a finely situated villa on (not ' the top,' [65] but) the side of Fiesole; has a very pleasing family — a wife & four children. He was very courteous, & I catechised him as freely as was decent upon all his opinions. I am going to breakfast with him tomorrow & shall ask him all that was omitted yesterday.

Greenough [66] has at last got a letter from Mr. Livingston [67] confirming the Statue commission, & he goes to work in good earnest. When I arrived here I found him a little anxious lest in the hot politics of the time the statue should be forgotten & the necessary steps not taken by the Congress.[68] It happens fortunately for him that the Baptistery, here, the same whose Gates of bronze Michel Angelo thought " degne chiudere il Paradiso," [69] is a building very nearly of the same dimensions in every way as the Rotunda at Washington, & as it contains several statues of saints, he is very well able to determine what size he must give his work to fill the eye. He thinks about 12 ft. but it may need more. He is reputed here by a few, for he is not much known, to have the most genius of any sculptor in Italy. Thorwaldsden has made a fine Byron but nothing else I think, & the Italians are tame enough in sculpture & painting & poetry. I saw at G's studio today an Achilles in clay which he is moulding; it is colossal & is good, though it is a poor subject.

17th Last eveg. I went to the Cascina as the noble planted grounds along the Arno are called from a Dairy & villa of the Duke's — a great festival it was, & all Florence went out thither to dance under the trees — all brilliantly illuminated. The Grand Duke took a turn in his coach around the Cascina & bowed gracefully to the uncovered multitude. I believe they danced all night. This morning I went with Greenough &

65. Doubtless Emerson is thinking of the famous passage in Milton's *Paradise Lost,* I, 289.

66. According to John Forster, *Walter Savage Landor,* London, 1869, II, 261, it was the American sculptor through whom Emerson received his invitation to the home of the British author. For Emerson's recollection, in later years, of his conversation with Greenough in Florence, see Jan. 7, 1852, to him.

67. Edward Livingston was Secretary of State, 1831–1833.

68. For Congressional action regarding the employment of Greenough to execute a statue of Washington for the rotunda of the Capitol, see *Register of Debates in Congress,* VIII, *passim.* Years later Emerson saw the sculptor's unsuccessful experiments in lighting the colossal figure (letters of Jan. 12 and 13, 1843). Its subsequent fortunes and locations varied with the whims of legislators, until more sophisticated critics definitely consigned it to obscurity.

69. Vasari's life of Ghiberti (*Vite,* Milan, 1808, IV, 139) is an early source, but the phrasing is different from that quoted here.

breakfasted with Mr Landor. He [I]does not quite show the same calibre in conversation as in his books. — It is a mean thing that literary men, philosophers, cannot work themselves clear of this ambition to appear men of the world. As if every dandy did nt understand his business better than they. I hope better things of Carlyle who has lashed [70] the same folly.[I] I saw Mr Hare there, again, the author of Guesses at Truth.[71]

A fine town this Florence, full of pictures & sculpture & picturesque houses, & bridges across the Arno, & in the bosom of mountains sprinkled with villas far & wide around. It is a cheap place to live in, as you get all you want for little money — but it is now very hot & I must soon go away.

x x x

Here is Santa Croce where are the tombs of Michel Angelo, Galileo, Machiavelli, Alfieri, Giotto, & many more who are less known — I honor them all, & the empty tomb of Dante.[72] But when I write to you I undervalue them all, struck by the desire of Home.

x x ————

To Edward Bliss Emerson, Florence, May 25, 1833

[Mentioned in Edward Emerson, Porto Rico, Nov. 13, 1833.]

To Abel Adams, Florence, May 28, 1833 [73]

Florence, 28 May, 1833.

My dear Sir,

I cannot deny myself the pleasure of stealing a few moments of this last day of my stay in Florence to address a line or two to my kind & honored friend. I trust the last five months have brought nothing but peace & continued prosperity *real* as well as temporal, inward & outward to yourself & your family. I had no promise to be sure but still I hoped either at Rome or here, to have found one word from

70. Perhaps Emerson is thinking of a passage in the review of Jean Paul Friedrich Richter in *The Foreign Review*, V, 27, but I am uncertain.

71. The two brothers Julius Charles and Augustus William Hare seem to have been the joint authors.

72. Emerson doubtless remembered Byron's *Childe Harold's Pilgrimage*, IV, liv, where Santa Croce's tombs are described, but not those of Dante or Giotto. Dante, as Byron says (lvii), "sleeps afar"; and he has only a monument in Santa Croce. Giotto, according to Vasari, was buried in Santa Maria del Fiore (the Duomo).

73. MS owned by RWEMA; ph. in CUL. The superscription is to Abel Adams at Boston.

your own hand. I go away from Florence without any letters from home later, than one from my mother of 15 March. At Paris I ought to be richly compensated for this long drought of news. Mr Henry Miles an American merchant here, to whom Miss Welch [74] gave me a letter, has been very kind to me in many ways, & among others in furnishing me with some Boston Newspapers as late as of 6 April. Here I have met again with Mr S. P. Holbrook & family [75] with whom I came to Malta, & tomorrow morning in company with them & Mr Wall of New Bedford & Mr Stuardson [76] of Philadelphia, I set out for Venice – a journey of 5 days. In Venice I shall stay only a few days & then go to Milan Geneva & Paris, where I expect to spend probably the whole month of July. If my letters which I have sent through the post office here to Havre for New York, should not have arrived, (one to Charles,[77] one to Wm,[78] one to Mr Sampson,[79]) tell mother I am perfectly well & am glad to be here & shall be glad to come home.

Of the Second Church I know nothing & think much, & hope the best. God has provided it with so many good hearts who pray for & seek its prosperity that I cannot think it will fail of wise counsel or of a good minister. I was sorry however to learn, sorry on all accounts, of Mr Ware's ill health & ceasing to preach.

The way to learn to value America its churches its government its manners & all is to come hither. They say here that no nullifier holds to his nullification one month after he arrives in Europe, & surely the

74. Possibly the Eliza H. Welch of *Stimpson's Boston Directory,* 1833, where Sarah Welch, keeper of a boarding house, also appears.

75. See a note on Dec. 14, 1832.

76. *Desilver's Philadelphia Directory* for 1833 gives Thomas Stewardson, gentleman; and W. S. W. Ruschenberger, Philadelphia, Sept. 10, 1878, wrote asking for Emerson's recollections of Thomas Stewardson, who, he said, had met Emerson on the Continent about forty years earlier. On p. 4 of that letter Emerson wrote a brief note, apparently a first draft of a reply: " In 1833 I met Mr Stewardson in Italy & we traveled for some time with him . . ." In *A Sketch of the Life of Thomas Stewardson,* Philadelphia, 1883, p. 8, Ruschenberger tells of the conversations Emerson and Stewardson had in Europe, and how Stewardson afterwards recalled that he was greatly startled at pantheistic utterances, which long reverberated through his memory.

77. Probably May 16 and 17, 1833.

78. If " here " means Italy rather than Florence, the letter of Apr. 21, 1833, mailed from Rome to New York by way of Havre, may be meant; if not, there must have been a letter of May? *c.* 18? 1833, which I have not found. In the letter of June 29 and July 5, however, Emerson tells William: " I am not sure I have written you more than three times " – and the three letters are extant.

79. Apr. 20 and May 20, 1833.

liberal Christian will value his light & hope the more for all the *idolatry,* the *idolatry* of Italy, producing as it does of course the other extreme of unbelief & loosest morals. Two days ago I saw in the Duomo or Cathedral a priest carrying a silver bust of Saint Zenobio which he put on the head of each person in turn of the kneeling crowd around the altar. This ceremony is esteemed a preservative against the head-ache for a year, till Saint Zenobio's day comes round again.[80] Remember me affectionately to Mrs Adams & to your sisters & to Abby. And if I should send my love to all to whom it is due, it would need a new sheet. I hope to see you in the autumn & to give a good account of the doings & seeings of your affectionate friend

R. Waldo Emerson.

I bid Charles [81] ask you some time ago to fortify me with new credit at Paris or London. Probably I shall not need to use it yet shall be glad to have it.

To Walter Savage Landor, Florence, May 28, 1833 [82]

Florence, 28 May, 1833.

Dear Sir,

I regret very much that the sudden departure of some friends whom I wish to accompany to Venice, deprives me of the pleasure of paying my respects to you once more, in person. Permit me, Sir, to thank you for your ready hospitality to a stranger, &, [I]at the same time, to acknowledge a very deep debt of pleasure & instruction to the author of the Imaginary Conversations.[I] I pray to be remembered respectfully to Mrs Landor.

With great respect,
Your obedient servant,
R. Waldo Emerson.

80. According to F. G. Holweck, *A Biographical Dictionary of the Saints,* 1924, p. 1049, Zenobius, Bishop of Florence in the fifth century, was famous for his miracles, and his day is May 25.

81. In a letter of Mar. 22 preceding.

82. MS owned by the Victoria and Albert Museum; ph. in CUL. Excerpt I is in John Forster, *Walter Savage Landor,* II, 264. Emerson's visits to Landor are mentioned in Apr. 20 and May 20, and in May 16 and 17, 1833. His enthusiasm for Landor's writings is shown by a number of letters written in later years. The three volumes of the second edition of *Imaginary Conversations,* London, 1826 and 1828, are still in Emerson's house, at Concord; and Vol. I bears his signature.

TO RUTH HASKINS EMERSON? AND CHARLES CHAUNCY EMERSON? MILAN, JUNE c. 10, 1833

[Charles Emerson to William, Sept. 6 (1833; owned by Dr. Haven Emerson): "I mean to inclose in this envelope a letter or two of Waldo's – Have you recd. the Paris & Milan twain?" Emerson was in Milan June 8–11 (*Journals*, III, 142–147).]

TO CHARLES CHAUNCY EMERSON, PARIS, JUNE 25 AND 26, 1833[83]

Paris, 25 June 1833.

Dear Charles

I have been here 5 or 6 days[84] & am very little enamoured of the gay city x x x x In my opinion it is very vulgar to make such a fuss in praising it as men do. It is because it abounds in all conveniencies for leading an easy, fat, amused life. You may have always fragrant coffee, polished shoes, the Newspaper, a coach a theatre, superb shops, the daintiest pastry cooks, & even without walking out of your way; & then over all there is what young persons admire, far too large a population for anybody to concern himself with what you please to do. x x x x x x x. Yet young men must live, & the present generation as well as Trajan & his cotemporaries & far be it from me to repine at the symptoms of prosperity & comfort. x x x x x x. x x

P. S. 26th. My habits of perpetual docility are perfectly suitable to my faith, that I am in the world to be taught, but with anybody else's they would be pitiful or rediculous enough. Do the men of this world crow? Nothing is a match for pride but humility & thus I outcrow them. How I shall dogmatise when I get home! How I shall dogmatise – for do you know that my European experience has only confirmed & clinched the old laws wherewith I was wont to begin & end my parables.
x x I spent a few days in Geneva[85] & saw Gibbon's house & Calvin's & fell in with worthy orthodox people who gave me arguments & good advice both in French & English.

x Paris, all modern, cannot compare with Rome or with Florence, whose glory is departed or departing. Viewed after those famous towns

83. MS owned by RWEMA; ph. in CUL. This is an incomplete copy, partly in Cabot's hand, but mostly in another hand, which was presumably responsible for an unorthodox spelling in the second paragraph.

84. According to *Journals*, III, 155, Emerson had arrived in Paris on June 20. The two letters immediately following have much more to say about his visit there.

85. See *Journals*, III, 151–154.

it is like a Liverpool or New York all alive with an Exchange & new gloves & broadcloths.

To William Emerson, Paris, June 29 and July 5, 1833 [86]

IParis, 29 June, 1833.

Dear William,I

I hoped to find letters here from you but Messrs Wells', Lane, Draper, Storrow,[87] — all answer no. Charles had prepared me one solitary sheet — & therein tells me that you are not married till the fall of the leaf. Well tis the man makes the time, & the wise man does every thing in the right time, do it when he will. I promise myself the happiness to be a witness of yours. Did you ever receive the letter I wrote from Naples to Susan? [88] Give my love to her. Her brother I have not seen. He is now in England & I may meet him. Ralph Emerson [89] tells me he is a very accomplished scholar. They went from Paris to Venice together. Well, what of Paris? Why it leads me twice to brag of Italy, for once that I see any thing to admire here. I go to the Sorbonne & hear lectures.[90] I walk in the Jardin des Plantes. I stare & stare at the thousand thousand shop windows. I go to the Louvre, the Kings Library, the

86. MS owned by HCL; ph. in CUL. Excerpts I–III are in Cabot, I, 192.

87. The firm of Welles & Williams, bankers, appears as early as 1822 in *Galignani's Paris Guide*. In 1841 *Galignani's New Paris Guide* gave the firm name as Welles and Co. The other names do not appear in any guide or directory examined; but a Simeon Draper, apparently connected with the Drapers of Paris, is mentioned in the letter of Mar. 1, 1861, and a Mr. Storrow wrote a note on a blank page of William Emerson's journal (owned by Dr. Haven Emerson) in Paris on Feb. 16 or 17, 1824.

88. Mar. 22, 1833.

89. See Apr. 20 and 23, 1831.

90. Among the Emerson papers there is still a copy of the *Programme des cours de l'Academie de Paris, a la Sorbonne. Facultés des Lettres, des Sciences et de Droit* for the second semester, 1833, which lists courses by such professors as Villemain (or J. J. Ampère), on French literature; Cousin (or Poret), on ancient philosophy; and Fauriel, on Dante. And with the outline of lectures at the Sorbonne, there is also a copy of *Programme du Collège Royal de France,* which lists, among other notables, Jouffroy, on the Greek language and philosophy; Eugène Burnouf, on the Sanskrit language and literature; Biot (apparently alternating with another professor), in physics; Thénard (also with an alternate) and Gay-Lussac (at the Jardin des Plantes), in chemistry; and Élie de Beaumont, on natural history. The passages in *Journals* for the Paris days show Emerson's particular enthusiasm for scientific lectures and for the Jardin des Plantes, an enthusiasm not without importance in view of his continuing development in the direction of liberalism.

Theatre & I admire the liberality with which every door is opened to me; but in the arts Paris is poor compared with any Italian city. I suppose I am walking only on the crust. There are numberless institutions here which I ought to acquaint myself with, & many great men. I shall stay here, perhaps, three weeks more & will try to keep my eyes & ears open. I am at 'pension' in a family where unfortunately there are several Americans, & so the language thrives less.

5 July. I learn Aunt Marys habits of letter writing & contempt of posts & dates. you see. I dined yesterday with 98 Americans at Lointier's.[91] There was the grand Lafayette, but not much else. Unluckily there was nobody here who could make speeches & toasts & therefore nothing was said worth remembering, except his own speech which like all of his was idiomatic simple & happy. He had been for 50 years, he said, endeavouring to import liberty into Europe. &c His son made a speech. & the grandson also being toasted — gave "Independence of character." "If my grandfather had been a *courtisan,* he would not have been a citizen of the United States."

I was surprized to find many acquaintances there John Gray, William Pratt, & others. Most of the Bostonians here, & there are many, I had already met. But you may live in Paris long & never meet your countryman, which is impossible in any city of Italy. I wish I had not taken my place here for a month I am quite satiated & ready to part for London tomorrow & certainly without being insensible to the advantages of living here. It would be desireable to many. It is not to me. [II]For libraries & lectures — my own library has hitherto always been too large & a lecture at the Sorbonne is far less useful to me than a lecture I write myself; then for literary society & all that, — true it would be inestimable if I cd. get at it,[II] but no man can dive into literary society even in Paris & I cannot wait the long initiation — no nor the doubtful result. [III]Probably in years, it would really avail *me* nothing. My own study is the best place for me, & there was always more fine society in my own little town than I could command. So, si le roi m'avoit donné Paris sa grande ville,[92] Je dirois au roi Louis, je prefère my inkstand.[III] I spend much

91. *Cf.* John T. Morse, *Life and Letters of Oliver Wendell Holmes* (n. d., c. 1896), I, 105, cited by the editors of *Journals.* Morse, I, 103–104, prints Holmes's letter of June 29, 1833, the writing of which was interrupted by a call from Emerson.

92. These lines are adapted from the old song which Alceste repeats and praises in Molière's *Le Misanthrope* (Act I, scene ii). Emerson copied the whole of it on the cover of a notebook of 1824 (typescript *Journals*), but the date of this irregular entry is uncertain.

time at the reading rooms — Galignanis [93] & another. Tis wonderful the variety of interests & purposes consulted in the 217 Parisian papers. Every mountain & every mouse finds a tongue. Then Paris is the centre of Christendom or civildom & therefore here thunders or squeaks every portion of the human race to whomsoever will hear. At Bennis's reading room they receive 400 journals.

But how strange it is that you should not have written me but a single letter that to Naples — you! I suppose you have received my sheets & sheets — or sheets & *sheet,* for I am not sure I have written you more than three times. I see I must hasten home to ensure my existence being remembered. So expect me by the first of October & believe me

Yours affectionately

Waldo —

To Samuel Ripley and Sarah Bradford Ripley, Paris, July 9, 1833 [94]

Paris, 9 July, 1833.

To Mr & Mrs Ripley

My dear friends,

I have been looking round me to see if I could not pick up some facts in the great town that would interest you but it is such a vulgar superficial unspiritual marketing community or I so bad or so ill conditioned an observer that I am much at a loss. To be sure if the splendid soirées where Fontenelle or Madame de Stael might talk, existed, the traveller in his fortnight would not find them but he might hear the fame of them & some effect would go out from them into this immense extemporaneous literature, so called, with which the press groans here from day to day. But Politicks have spoiled conversation & men in France. Cousin has quit Plato & M. Arago his magnet & galvanic battery since those unlucky 3 days.[95] And to such paltry purpose. The press to be sure is free & says the sauciest things every day but otherwise the government has very much the character of the old government & exiles shoots or imprisons whom it pleases.

93. John A. and William Galignani of Paris had long been well known for their activity as publishers. The spelling "Bennis's" is somewhat doubtful, and I have not found that name in Paris guides of this period.

94. MS owned by Professor James B. Thayer; ph. in CUL.

95. The Three Glorious Days — "les Trois Glorieuses" — of July, 1830, had brought Louis Philippe into power.

The charm of Paris to so many people seems to consist in the boundless domestic liberty which releases each man from the fear of the eyes & ears of all his neighbors, opens a public parlour for him to take his coffee & read his newspaper, in every street; go where his business may lead him he can always find an ice, a bath, a dinner, & good company, at the next corner; and next in the ample provision for what the newspapers call ' nos besoins recreatifs.' From 15 to 20 theatres open their doors to him at a small price every evening — the best of them splendid beyond a Yankee's belief. I saw at Malta a masqued ball given by the English Governor in the ancient Palace of the Grand Masters. Yet it did not compare for good taste & imposing effect with a masqued ball introduced by way of ballet into the Opera of Gustave [96] on the stage of the French Opera. Yet the Englishman had half a dozen grand saloons each of which seemed half as big as Fanueil hall Ah they understand here the powers of the lookingglass; and all Paris is a perpetual puzzle to the eye to know what is object & what is reflection. By this expedient reading rooms & cafés have all a bewildering extent & the wealth of the shops is multiplied. Even on the dessert service at the dinner table they set mirrors into the fruit-stands to multiply whips cherries & sugar plums, so that when I took one, I found two were gone. Then the poorest Frenchman may walk in the kings garden every day; he may go read if he chuse, in the kings library — wide open — the largest in the world, or in the Mazarine library, or in several more. He may go hear lectures on every branch of science literature at the Sorbonne, or the College of France, or the College of Law, or the Garden of Plants. If he love botany he may go to this last place & find not-quite-all plants growing up together in their scientifick classes; then by a public placard, Jussieu gives notice that next Sunday he goes out on a botanical excursion & invites all & sundry to go with him naming the village of the rendezvous. But if the Frenchman prefer natural history of animals he has only to turn down a green lane of this garden of Eden, & he shall find all manner of lions bisons elephants & hyenas the giraffe 17 feet high and all other things that are in the dictionary but he did not know were in the world — large & small ostriches white peacocks golden pheasants & the like — not to mention the museums & cabinets which in this garden & elsewhere on certain days of every week are thrown open. So [is][97] the

96. Probably *Gustave III, ou le bal masqué,* Auber's opera, which had been first performed on Feb. 27 of this year (*Grove's Dictionary of Music,* 3d ed.).

97. This word, carried away with the seal from the left side of the page, now stands in the right-hand margin.

Louvre,[98] so is the Luxembourg. What strikes a stranger most of all is the splendour of the shops – such endless profusion of costly goods of every sort that it is a constant wonder where they find purchasers. This is accounted for by the idolatrous love which Frenchmen all over the earth have for Paris. The merchant in Montreal & the planter in Louisiana are toiling patiently, they say, in the expectation of coming to Paris to spend their gains. Mr Horace Gray told me of an acquaintance of his in Florence who as often as he earns a hundred louis goes to Paris to spend them. He is a French teacher & now 76 years old. " He did not think that this year he should be quite able to make the sum complete, but next winter he should." Yesterday I went to the Institute & saw Biot, Arago, Gay Lussac, Jussieu, Thenard –

But whilst I see the advantages of Paris they are not very great to me. Now that I have been here fifteen days I find I spend most of my time in the reading room & that I can do at home. So I promise myself soon the pleasure of seeing you & earnestly hope to find you both in the best health. I send my love to all my little grandchildren & flatter myself that I shall have an iliad of stories for them that will rival Peter Parley. At least I have had the honor of travelling with this last gentleman.[99] – I saw Lewis Stackpole at Rome. Very respectfully & affectionately yours, Waldo E.

To ———, London, July *c.* 30, 1833

[In the letter of July 31, 1833, to William, Emerson said he had just written up all he had for Boston and added: " You shall open the letters on their way if you wish . . ." This would indicate at least two letters about this time.]

To Charles Chauncy Emerson? London, July, *c.* 31, 1833

[See the note on July *c.* 30, 1833. One of the letters for Boston was most probably to Charles Emerson or, if not to him, to his mother.]

98. There is a mark over the last letter which may have been meant for an acute accent.

99. Apparently the allusion is not to Goodrich but to Samuel Kettell or, possibly, S. P. Holbrook. *Cf.* a note on Dec. 14, 1832.

To William Emerson, London, July 31, 1833[100]

[I]London, 31 July, 1833

Dear William[I]

Mr Alexander[101] who has been studying his art for two years in Italy, came with me from Paris to this place & has been boarding in the same house with me. I seize the occasion of his return to thank you for your letter of 16[102] June & 1 July which I received day before yesterday & which bro't me the first news of the favorable termination of my suit.[103] I forgot until just now that Mr A. was sailing for New York & so had written up all I had to say, for Boston. You shall open the letters on their way if you wish, though there is little news in them. I met I remember at an evening party a Mr & Mrs Bell of whom you speak but I never spoke to them twice. If they knew you, why did they not tell me so. You say perhaps you will not be married in September; then in October I will attend myself. [II]I am sorry I did not write a good letter to Susan[104] I am afraid I tried too hard. Tell her to have patience with me, for when I was young I thot I wrote excellently & hope to have occasion to write to her many & many a time

Noon. I have been to see Dr Bowring who was very courteous. He carried me to Benthams house & showed me with great veneration the garden walk the sitting room & the bed chamber of the philosopher. He gave me also a lock of his grey hair & an autograph[105] of the Utilitarian.[II] He is anxious that Bentham should be admired & loved in America. He tells me that this morning he sent to the press the first volume of Benthams Code, with the publication of which he is charged.

[III]I walked in the garden, on one side of which is the house[III] in which [IV]Milton lived when he was Cromwell's Secretary.[IV] Hazlitt occupied it a little while, & placed a stone upon it, with the inscription *John Milton*

100. MS owned by HCL; ph. in CUL. Excerpts I–IV are in Cabot, I, 194.

101. See Apr. 21, 1833.

102. Written over 26. In his endorsement on the letter of Feb. 26 and Mar. 5, 1833, to him, William notes that he wrote on June 16 and July 1.

103. *Cf.* Mar. 26, 1832, and earlier letters.

104. Mar. 22, 1833.

105. Sir John Bowring was literary executor of his friend Jeremy Bentham. The autograph later passed into the hands of Margaret Fuller, who describes it in her letter of Apr. 11, 1837, to Emerson as "that first most appropriate token of your regard, with which you honored me during my first visit to Concord, to wit the autograph of Jeremy Bentham."

— *the Prince of Poets.*[106] I promised to dine with Dr B. this evening and am to meet Dr Lant Carpenter. I am just come from the British Museum where I had an introduction to the Librarian Mr Carey [107] the translator of Dante. As to the Museum it does not appear so rich as one would expect from its fame. Its library is great. Your affectionate brother,

Waldo.

To Charles Chauncy Emerson, London, August 4 and *c.* 5? 1833

[Charles Emerson to William, Sept. 6 (owned by Dr. Haven Emerson): "I have a letter from Waldo dated Aug. 4. He has seen Coleridge, Miss Martineau heard Fox & Irving, attended Wilberforce's funeral — i. e. among the lookers on — " This letter dated Aug. 4 was doubtless continued on Aug. 5 or later (*cf.* the note on Aug. 5, 1833).]

To Samuel Taylor Coleridge, Highgate, August 5, 1833

[In *English Traits* (*Cent. Ed.*, V, 10), Emerson wrote: "From London, on the 5th August, I went to Highgate, and wrote a note to Mr. Coleridge, requesting leave to pay my respects to him." The account of the meeting given in *English Traits* is well known.]

To ———, Glasgow, August 23, 1833

[*Journals,* III, 176–180. The text here printed is pretty obviously a copy of a letter now lost.]

To Alexander Ireland, Liverpool, August 30, 1833 [108]

ILiverpool, 30 August, 1833.

My dear Sir,

A shower of rain which hinders my visiting gives me an opportunity of fulfilling my promise to send you an account of

106. The house into which Milton moved in 1651 remained standing till late in the nineteenth century and was occupied at one time by James Mill and then by William Hazlitt.

107. Henry Francis Cary (not Carey) had become assistant keeper of printed books at the British Museum in 1826.

108. MS owned by Mrs. Ward I. Gregg; ph. in CUL. Excerpts I, III, and IV are printed, with several changes, in Moncure D. Conway, *Thomas Carlyle,* New York, 1881, pp. 220–223; II is in Alexander Ireland, *In Memoriam,* 1882, pp. 53–55, where there are also some passages which are included in Conway's text. The superscription is to Ireland, at Edinburgh.

The calendar of Emerson's travels between London and Liverpool is given partly

my visits to Mr Carlyle & to Mr Wordsworth. I was fortunate enough to find both of them at home. Mr C. lives among some desolate hills in the parish of Dunscore 15 or 16 miles from Dumfries. He had heard of my purpose from his friend who gave me my letter [109] & insisted on dismissing my gig which went back to Dumfries to return for me the next day in time to secure my seat in the evening coach for the south. So I spent near 24 hours with him.[110] He lives with his wife, a most agreeable accomplished woman, in perfect solitude There is not a person to speak to within 7 miles. He is the most simple frank amiable person — I became acquainted with him at once, we walked over several miles of hills & talked upon all the great questions that interest us most. The comfort of meeting a man of genius is that he speaks sincerely that he feels himself to be so rich that he is above the meanness of pretending to knowledge which he h[as][111] not & Carlyle does not pretend to have solved the great problems but rather to be an observer of their solution as it goes forward in the world. I asked him at what religious development the concluding passage in his piece in the Edin. Review upon German Literature (say 5 years ago) & some passages in the piece called Characteristics, pointed? [112] he replied, that he was not competent to state it even to himself — he waited rather to see. — My own feeling was that I had met with men of far less power who had yet greater insight into religious truth. — He is as you might guess from his papers the most catholic of philosophers — he forgives & loves everybody & wishes each

in the MS memorandum book for this year and partly in an unpublished passage of the diaries (see typescript *Journals*) : London to Oxford, Aug. 9; Birmingham, 10–11; Kenilworth and Warwick, 12; Matlock, 13; Haddon Hall, Bakewell, and Sheffield, 14; York, 15; Newcastle, Berwick, and Edinburgh, 16 (the Edinburgh visit apparently continued till 21) ; Leith, Stirling, Doune, and Callander, 21; Loch Katrine, Inversnaid, Loch Lomond, 22; Glasgow, 22–23; Mossgiel, Nithsdale, Buccleuch, and Dumfries, 24 (the time between Dumfries and Carlisle is mostly accounted for in the present letter) ; Carlisle, 26; Penrith, Keswick, and Ambleside, 27; Kendal, 28; Lancaster, Burton, Manchester, and Liverpool, 29 (the Liverpool visit apparently continued till Sept. 4) ; sailed for New York, 4. In the unpublished passage in the diaries August is called July. The account printed in *Journals,* III, 174–193, has much additional detail.

109. *Cf.* the letter of Apr. 16 and 21, 1833.

110. For the visits to Carlyle and Wordsworth, *cf. Journals,* III, 180–183, and *English Traits* (*Cent. Ed.*, V, 14–24) .

111. The MS is slightly mutilated; this and later bracketed portions of the text are conjectural.

112. The "State of German Literature" appeared in *The Edinburgh Review,* Oct., 1827; and "Characteristics," *ibid.*, Dec., 1831.

to struggle on in his own place & arrive at his own ends, but his respect for eminent men or rather his scale of eminence is almost the reverse of the popular scale; Scott, Mackintosh, — Jeffrey; — Gibbon; — even Bacon are no heroes of his; stranger yet he hardly admires Socrates, the glory of the Greek world — but Burns & Samuel Johnson; Mirabeau he said, interested him, & I suppose whoever [els]e has given himself with all his heart to a leading instinct & has not *calculated* too much. But I cannot think of sketching even his opinions or repeating his conversation here. I will cheerfully do it when you visit me in America. He talks finely, seems to love the broad Scotch, & I loved him very much, at once. I am afraid he finds his entire solitude tedious, but I could not help congratulating him upon his treasure in his wife & I hope they will not leave the moors. tis so much better for a man of letters to nurse himself in seclusion than to be filed down to the common level by the compliances & imitations of city society.[I] — [II]And you have found out the virtues of solitude I remember with much pleasure.[II]

[III]The third day afterwards, I called upon Mr Wordsworth at Rydal Mount. He received me with much kindness & remembered up all his American acquaintance. He had very much to say about the evils of superficial education both in this country & in mine. he thinks the intellectual tuition of society is going on out of all proportion faster than its moral training, which last is essential to all *education* He don't wish to hear of schools, of tuition, — it is the education of circumstances which he value[s] & much more to this point. He says that he is not in haste to publish more poetry, for many reasons but that what he has written will be at some time given to the world. He led me out into a walk in his grounds where he said many thousands of his lines were composed, & re[peated to m]e three beautiful sonnets which he has [just fin]ished, upon the occasion of his recent vi[sit to] Fingal's Cave at Staffa.[113] I hope he will print them speedily — the third is a gem. He was so benevolently anxious to impress upon me my social duties as an American citizen that he accompanied me near a mile from his house talking vehemently & ever & anon stopping short to imprint his words. I noted down some of his words when I got home & you may see them in Boston, Massachusetts, when you will. I enjoyed both my visits highly & shall always esteem your Britain very highly in love for its wise & good mens' sake.

113. The four sonnets inspired by the visit to Staffa were all written in 1833.

I remember with much pleasure my visit to Edinburgh [114] & my short acquaintance with yourself It will give me very great pleasure to hear from you, to know your thoughts. Every man that ever was born has some that are peculiar.[III] Address to me " Care of Barnard, Adams, & Co., Boston." I left the letter at Stirling & the other here. [IV]Present my respects to your father & family

Your friend & servant

R. Waldo Emerson.[IV]

To James Fraser, Liverpool, August? c. 31? 1833

[Mentioned in May 14, 1834.]

To Edward Bliss Emerson? on board the " New-York," September? 25? and October? 2? 1833

[*Journals,* III, 215–216, contains verses addressed " Dear Brother " which describe him as

" Sitting under a gold September sun."

As the four lines beginning

" Going alway "

appear in Emerson's MS memorandum book for 1833 under date of Oct. 2, it seems probable that at least some of the verses belong to that date. There is no formal heading or close, but the whole poem seems to have been intended as a letter, whether sent or not.]

To William Emerson, Boston, October 11, 1833 [115]

Boston, 11 October, 1833

Dear William

A thousand thanks for your ready & efficient benevolence in helping me home [116] We had a fine passage & ride & I got me to the Tremont House in 22 hours. I went out with Charles the same afternoon to Newtown & brought Mother into town the next day. I have spent a most pleasant day in the most pleasant of cities. — so many

114. See *In Memoriam,* pp. 49 ff., for Emerson's visit to Edinburgh in Aug., 1833. On Sunday the 18th, says Ireland, Emerson delivered a memorable discourse in the Unitarian Chapel there.

115. MS owned by HCL; ph. in CUL.

116. Emerson had sailed from Liverpool Sept. 4 on the " New-York," Capt. Hoxie, with J. H. Henley and the Rev. P. R. Kenrick, both of Dublin, as fellow passengers; and he had arrived in New York on Oct. 7 (*New-York Commercial Advertiser* and the *Morning Courier,* Oct. 8, 1833) .

friends, — so much tidings — so many hopes — on such ground & under such a sky. May I tax your kindness again to enquire of the Steward on board the New York whether he has found the number of Fraser's Magazine which he promised to look for. It contains a capital print of Coleridge[117] which I should regret losing. Say too to Capt. Hoxie that I fully expected to have staid another day in N. Y. thinking it impracticable to *escape* so soon, under which impression I promised to call upon him.

As to Mr Henley I hope you found him though I knew no more of his whereabout than that he left me with the purpose of going to the City Hotel. I hope also that Kenrick found him for I charged him to return him some shillings that H. had overpaid me for coach fare & also with my address in Boston which I especially desire Mr H. to possess. If you see him do say so much. Give him Charles's address.

I go to Mr Sampson's this P. M. to spend a few days. Then perhaps to Newton for a pro tempore study. I have engaged to deliver the introductory Lecture to the Natural History Society in November.[118]

Live & be happy & love your affectionate brother

Waldo

I have not paid C. C. E. but will as quick as I can find a banker or a Jew that will trust me. —

To Edward Bliss Emerson, Newton? Massachusetts, October 21, 1833

[Acknowledged in Edward Emerson, Porto Rico, Nov. 13, 1833.]

To Charles Chauncy Emerson, New Bedford? Massachusetts, November 18, 1833

[Mentioned, and apparently summarized, in *Journals,* III, 228.]

117. *Fraser's Magazine,* VIII, opposite 64 (July, 1833).

118. The *Boston Daily Advertiser,* Nov. 5, 1833, announces that Emerson will deliver the introductory lecture before the Boston Society of Natural History at the Masonic Temple this evening. Charles Emerson wrote to William, in a letter dated Nov. 6 and 14 (1833): "Last Evening Waldo lectured before the Nat. Hist. Soc. to a charm. The young & the old opened their eyes & their ears — I was glad to have some of the stump lecturers see what was what & bow to the rising sun — T'was on the advantages of Study of Nat. Hist. Mrs Hoar happened to be in town & went & was delighted, & said to me coming out 'I suppose we are to thank your mother for all these good things, tho' she looks so quiet & says nothing about it.'" (MS owned by Dr. Haven Emerson.)

To William Emerson, New Bedford, Massachusetts, November 18, 1833 [119]

New Bedford, 18 November, 1833.

My dear brother,

Every pleasant & happy power rain its influences [120] on you & yours. I am heartily glad that your lonely days are about to be ended and anticipate for you the real happiness of a home.[121] Your constitutional & cultivated virtues alike entitle you to expect the full amount of its good. I should have been glad to have accepted your invitation & accompanied you to Portsmouth but could not easily avoid or shorten this engagement of mine in this town. Besides I am no hero at festivals & provided the knot is tied, & I see & enjoy the happiness of the parties, it is of little importance that I am absent from the ceremony. And I am glad Mother is not going, as the ride could give her no pleasure at this season & the seeing the form, amidst an assembly of total strangers, seems scarcely worth the journey for her. Charles is the best representative of the family and we will all endorse his commission. But he will not derive more pleasure from his visit & duties (for I take it for granted he is a groomsman) than will Edward & I in our several corners from the knowledge that they are performed, So carry my best wishes & kind affection to my sister Susan & tell her if I cannot meet her somewhere on my way pretty soon I shall go out of my way to that poor place called New York, since she pleases to adorn it with her presence, to assure her how truly I am your & her affectionate brother

Waldo.

119. MS owned by HCL; ph. in CUL.

120. Probably reminiscent of *Paradise Lost,* VIII, 512–513.

121. Earlier letters contain several references to William Emerson's engagement to Susan Woodward Haven, who henceforth appears frequently in the extensive correspondence between Emerson and her husband. The wedding, at Portsmouth, N. H., is reported, without date, in the *New-York Commercial Advertiser,* Dec. 12, 1833. Ruth Haskins Emerson, Staten Island, Feb. 11, 1839, sends, among other dates she wants recorded in her family *Bible,* that of William's marriage, Dec. 3, 1833.

To Horace Scudder, New Bedford, Massachusetts, November 18, 1833 [122]

New Bedford, 18 November, 1833

My dear Sir,

I send you on the other page some verses I wrote the other evening for the Ordination. If you & Mr Robbins like them, they are at your service & if they are too long or if you have already procured others, I am very willing they should lie still.

With great regard,
Your friend & servant,
R. W. Emerson.

To Mary Moody Emerson, New Bedford? Massachusetts, November? c. 18? 1833

[Charles Emerson to William, Nov. 21 (1833; owned by Dr. Haven Emerson), states that he has written to Mary Moody Emerson (apparently about a projected arrangement for her annuity) and adds: "& so has Waldo to reassure her – "]

122. MS owned by RWEMA; ph. in CUL. The superscription is to Horace Scudder, Boston. On p. 3 Emerson has written the seven stanzas of the hymn which is now printed in *Cent. Ed.*, IX, 223–224, as "Hymn Sung at the Second Church, at the Ordination of Rev. Chandler Robbins." The version given in the present letter shows a few differences from the printed form, chiefly in the first and last stanzas:

"We love the venerable house
Our fathers built to God; –
In heaven are heard their grateful vows,
Their bones are in the sod.

. . . .

"On him who by the altar stands,
On him, thy spirit send,
Speak through his lips thy pure commands,
Our Father and our Friend!"

The year 1831, given as the date of the occasion in *Cent. Ed.*, IX, 478, is, of course, a typographical error. An account of the ordination, on Dec. 4, 1833, is printed in the *Christian Register* for Dec. 7 of that year.

To Abby Larkin Adams, New Bedford, Massachusetts, December 2, 1833[123]

New Bedford, 2 December, 1833

My dear Abby,

Am I to stay here till I get a letter from you. Write soon, for I cannot stay much longer. And yet I live very pleasantly among kind people. The lady with whom I board, is a Quaker, and I suppose you know the Quakers use what they call 'plain speech.' When she helps me at the table, she says "Waldo, shall I give thee bread?" and she never calls the days of the week by their common names, but 'first day,' 'second day,' & so on, to 'seventh day.' This is because the old Saxons, whose descendants we are, called the days from the names of their gods, as the Sun's day, the Moons day, Thor's day, Woden's day, Saturn's day, & the Quakers disapprove of pagan names. But many of them are excellent people, and I have a long story to tell you of the goodness of this old lady on a particular occasion; & whenever she comes to Boston I want to introduce you to Mrs Deborah Brayton.

I hope the French comes on beautifully. I attended a French examination here, the other day, of a class of girls who spoke in French throughout the whole recitation; & then presented themes in French as candidates for a prize. I was one of the judges, and there were so many good ones that there was much difficulty in deciding on the best. Do you know where New Bedford lies on the map? It is worth knowing, for though it is a small town it has more ships than any other town in the United States except New York & Boston. At least they say so here. All these vessels are employed in chasing the poor whale[124] wherever he swims all round the globe, that they may tear off his warm jacket of

123. MS owned by RWEMA; ph. in CUL. The superscription is to Miss Abby L. Adams, care of Abel Adams, her adoptive father, whom she called her uncle. She was about ten years old in 1833, and Emerson must have known her only a few years (*cf.* Aug. 10, 1829, and Aug. 19? 1870). Aug. 11, 1842, gives some account of her, and there are numerous later letters to her in these volumes. The present letter again suggests the pretty obvious influence of the Quakers on Emerson's religious views, an influence stressed by Moncure D. Conway (*Emerson at Home and Abroad,* 1882, pp. 83–87). A significant avowal made by Emerson himself is recorded in D. G. Haskins, p. 118.

124. Students of Melville have not noticed, so far as I am aware, the entry in *Journals,* III, 261 (Feb. 19, 1834), in which Emerson records a story he heard from a seaman in the coach, apparently on the way from New Bedford to Boston — the story of "a white whale . . . who rushed upon the boats which attacked him, and crushed the boats to small chips in his jaws . . . A vessel was fitted out at New Bedford . . . to take him."

blubber & melt it down into oil for your lamp, & to steal from him his bone to make stays & parasols for ladies. If you get the volume of Harper's Family Library called 'Polar Seas & Regions'[125] which is a very interesting book you will find a good account of this fishery. Wait till I come home & I will lend it to you. Meantime give my love & respect to your Uncle & Aunt & to Aunt Mary also.

Your affectionate Uncle, —
R Waldo Emerson.

To Edward Bliss Emerson, Boston, December 22, 1833[126]

Boston, [I]22 December, 1833.

Dear Edward,[I]

Thank you heartily for your kind remembrances of me in two letters I have lately read. I rejoice to see a more cheerful tone in your recent letters than in those of the early summer. I hope I augur rightly therefrom your better health & greater ease of mind. You are in the same situation with hundreds of our enterprizing nation who eat the bitter bread of exile in their youth, that they may eat sweeter bread on their return. What has reconciled me to your expatriation is the belief that you had found a climate where you could live, when your own threatened to kill you & I have hoped & do hope that months & years are producing though slowly such a revolution in your constitution as will enable you to live in health through many Massachusetts Decembers. Meantime you are always dearly prized by those you have left & will find your place waiting for you whenever you seek it. But who are they that are at home? Mother has been living at Newton. I have just returned to this city from New Bedford where I have been for a month & am shortly to return thither. Charles sleeps in Washington St, boards with Geo. B. E., & spends the day in Court St.[127] So that in truth you are about as much at home as any of us. [II]One of these days if we may be-

125. No. 14 in *Harper's Family Library* was the *Narrative of Discovery and Adventure in the Polar Seas and Regions . . . By Professor Leslie, Professor Jameson, and Hugh Murray,* 1832.

126. MS owned by RWEMA; ph. in CUL. Excerpts I–III are in Cabot, I, 216–217. The superscription is to Edward in Porto Rico. There is a brief marginal comment in Latin and English by Charles. Some Greek words in another margin are probably by him or by Edward.

127. *Stimpson's Boston Directory,* 1833, gives George Barrell Emerson's address as Temple Place and lists C. C. Emerson, attorney, 17 Court St.

lieve the lawyers I am to be the richer for Ellen's estate [128] & whenever that day arrives I hope it will enable me to buy a hearth somewhere to which we pious Æneases may return with our household gods from all the quarters of our dispersion. If you wish to know what I do — I preach at New Bedford, sometimes in Boston; I have written a lecture upon Natural History [129] & am now preparing another for next Tuesday evg.[130] & have promised one to the Mechanics Institute.[131] I meditate something more seriously than ever before, the adventure of a periodical paper which shall speak truth without fear or favor to all who desire to hear it, with such persuasion as shall compel them to speak it also.[132] Henry Hedge is an unfolding man who has just now written the best pieces that have appeared in the Examiner [133] and one especially was a living leaping Logos, & he may help me.

Charles & I went to Concord a few days ago. He delivered a fine lecture upon Socrates; [134] But Charles looks often despondent & finds his

128. Pending the long-delayed settlement of his wife's estate, Emerson received, according to a letter from Charles Emerson to William, Jan. 25 (1834; owned by Dr. Haven Emerson), at least one small sum from the executor. For further details of the settlement of the estate, see especially May 31, 1834, and Apr. 12, 1837.

129. See Oct. 11, 1833.

130. I have found no notice of this lecture in the Boston papers. Cabot, II, 711, outlines a lecture "On the Relation of Man to the Globe" and dates it Dec., 1832 (pretty obviously an error for 1833).

131. The *Evening Mercantile Journal,* Jan. 17, 1834, announced that Emerson would lecture that evening on "Water" before the Boston Mechanic's Institution, at the Athenæum. Other lectures during the winter are mentioned, but without more definite dates, in *Journals,* III, 246, and in Cabot, II, 712. Though I have found no newspaper notices, I think it probable that these were delivered late in Dec., 1833, or early in Jan., 1834, for Charles Emerson wrote to William on Jan. 7 (MS owned by Dr. Haven Emerson): "Waldo is well & lectures well."

132. For more than a year Emerson had dreamed of a magazine or paper of his own (*cf.* Nov. 19, 1832), but no definite plan for such a venture appears in letters or diaries. His uncertainty regarding his future course is reflected in the correspondence of his brothers. Edward, Aug. 16, 1833, asked him whether he would preach on his return, since he had declared again and again that in some or other mode he would ever be a minister. On Sept. 9 following Charles Emerson wrote to William (MS owned by Dr. Haven Emerson): "I thought it possible Waldo might publish a Journal or somewhat of the kind — & I might get some pence by my contributions — Yet I hardly think he will."

133. Hedge had reviewed *Biographia Literaria* and other works of Coleridge in *The Christian Examiner,* XIV, 108–129 (Mar., 1833), and had written on Swedenborg, *ibid.,* XV, 193–218 (Nov., 1833).

134. The MS records of the Concord Lyceum (owned by the Concord Free Public Library) mention two lectures by Charles Emerson during 1833 — "One of the West India Islands," Jan. 9; "Life, Death & Character of Socrates," Dec. 18.

fate as hard as you yours. Indeed that property belongs to the race man rather than to any individual. How come on the adventures. I was sorry to hear of any disappointments. Pray rein in that sanguine genius of yours that risks & projects so magnificently & which I can well remember from Latin School & Andover upward, & make him trot tame & safe for a year or two, for nothing is so important as your health to which the anxieties of indebtedness will never contribute. We can get used to being poor for the first men & happiest men of the earth have been but we can't away with pain & disease[II] so easily. [III]& whatever loss you suffer by following this bad advice set down to my account & it shall be cheerfully & affectionately honoured by your brother Waldo.[III]

I regretted much not seeing Mr Mason.[135] I called at his house in Myrtle St the day after he left town. Before that I was at Newton, & did not know of his whereabout.

135. Sidney Mason, Edward's employer in Porto Rico, may have been temporarily at the home of Professor Lowell Mason in Myrtle St. *Cf. Stimpson's Boston Directory,* 1833.

1834

To William Emerson, Boston, January 18, 1834 [1]

[I]Boston, 18 Jan. 1834.[I]

My dear brother,

I seize the first vacation from this new drudgery of Lecturing [2] to thank you for your kind letter the other day & to inquire anew concerning my yet unseen but honoured sister. Can she reconcile herself to that obstreperous Babylon of yours? Portsmouth is a quiet civil place, but New York — And how have you decided these sad political questions? I am almost afraid to take up a newspaper I am so sure of being pained by what I shall read. Is it not a good symptom for society this decided & growing taste for natural science which has appeared though yet in its first gropings? What a refreshment from Anti-masonry & Jacksonism & Bankism is in the phenomena of the Polar Regions or in the habits of the Oak or the geographical problem of the Niger.[3]

Did you not ask me what I am doing. [II]I have been writing three lectures on Natural History & of course reading as much geology chemistry & physics as I could find.[II] A beautiful little essay is Playfairs on the Huttonian Theory [4] A very good book is Cuvier's on the Revolutions of the Globe.[5] He writes as if he had the planet on a table before him & turns it round & bores with his corkscrew wheresoever he listeth. And

1. MS owned by RWEMA; ph. in CUL. Excerpts I–IV are in Cabot, I, 214–215.

2. See Dec. 22, 1833.

3. For the book on Polar seas, see Dec. 2, 1833. Richard and John Lander's *Journal of an Expedition to Explore the Course and Termination of the Niger* had likewise appeared in *Harper's Family Library* in 1832. Emerson may have read of the habits of the oak in Gilbert White, *The Natural History of Selborne,* Edinburgh, 1833, pp. 321–322. These readings, useful, no doubt, as sources for the lectures, are among the many evidences of Emerson's recently quickened interest in science.

4. John Playfair's *Illustrations of the Huttonian Theory of the Earth,* Edinburgh, 1802, is a book of some size. I have not seen a separate " little essay " on that subject.

5. This book by Baron Georges Cuvier had been published in English translation at Philadelphia in 1831 as *A Discourse on the Revolutions of the Surface of the Globe.*

then Mrs Lees life of the old Mole [6] is a very pleasant book. And the Lardner books [7] & the Family Library [8] furnish some very good reading. [III]Meantime my ethics & theologics lie in abeyance, for you cannot preach to people unless they will hear. However some of the faithful remain upon this portion of the earth & by & by we may find a little chapel of the truth.[III] Pray do not ask me or cause me to be asked to come to New York for I have no disposition to go there, except to make you a visit. [IV]I am just on the edge of another journey to New Bedford where I may spend the month of February having been overpersuaded by their kindness & zeal. If nobody wants us in the world, are we not excused from action & may we not blameless use the philosophy which teaches that by all events the individual is made wiser & that this may be an ultimate object in the benevolence of the creator.[IV] He does not want hands. " Thousands at his bidding speed They also serve who only stand & wait " [9]

No late news from Edward. One day not very far off I hope he will come & live with me. And in the little Pilgrim city [10] we will keep a thanksgiving day & you & Sus[an] shall come & honor it. Will you not?

Your affectionate brother
Waldo

To Paulina Tucker Nash, Boston, January 19, 1834 [11]

Boston, Sunday Ev.g —
19 Jan. 1834.

Does Paulina remember an old friend who remembers nothing in his own life with such interest as his connexion with your sister. Today I have been reading verses & scraps of Ellen that only heighten my admiration & my sorrow every time I read them & I go to Aunt Washburn's [12] to find some living thing that is related to her & I desire to

6. Mrs. R. Lee, *Memoirs of Baron Cuvier,* 1833.

7. The Rev. Dionysius Lardner wrote a number of books on scientific subjects.

8. Harper's, no doubt.

9. For Emerson's opinion of Milton's minor poems, see Feb. 1, 1832.

10. For Emerson's engagements this winter in Plymouth, where he met Lydia Jackson, see *Journals,* III, 245–246 and 255; and the letter of Mar. 12, 1834.

11. MS owned by RWEMA; ph. in CUL. Paulina Nash, mentioned in a number of letters, was the sister of Ellen Tucker Emerson. As the last page of the sheet is without superscription or other writing, this may be a copy or draft.

12. Probably the wife of Abiel Washburn, Jr., whose daughter, Ellen, is mentioned in a letter of Feb. 23, 1838.

assure her sister & her sisters husband of my warm good will to them. . . .[13] I grieve to hear of your illness & that Captain Nash has himself been much an invalid. Now that you both have no anxieties no bonds but the care of your healths & of your child, I trust these infirmities will be removed.

I suppose you do wisely & avoid fatigue in taking the land journey & avoiding the sea but if you can gather strength enough for a voyage to Europe in one of those palace packets I should be glad to have you go to Italy & realize some of your ancient romances & teach that little George the Tuscan tongue in Florence which to me was a city of delights. Travelling is so systematized in Europe that you may be rolled all over England France & Italy almost without fatigue & with an uniform certainty of good accommodation. When you come northward in May or June I hope you will send for me to come & see you & tell you the story of my travels.

I say to you Sir & to you Madam that I wish you to put it down not in your tablets but in your hearts that the friends of such persons as Ellen & Margaret & your Mother ought to be good friends themselves as long as they live in this troublesome world & therefore if I can serve you in any possible way or amuse you by sending you an account of any thing doing here I shall be very glad to do it. And so let the one of you who is at this present the least occupied straightway send me an account of your joint health & say that it is improving every day. Tell me what particulars you can of your present situation & plans, that I may answer the many inquiries of your friends here. Yours affectionately,

R. Waldo Emerson.

To William Emerson, Boston, February 21, 1834

[WmE List.]

To James Freeman Clarke, Plymouth, Massachusetts, March 12, 1834

[MS owned by Mr. James F. Clarke; ph. in CUL. Printed in Oliver Wendell Holmes, *Ralph Waldo Emerson,* 1885, pp. 78–79.]

13. Five and one-half lines of the MS are here omitted.

To Samuel Ripley, New Bedford, Massachusetts, March 28, 1834 [14]

New Bedford, 28 March.

My dear Sir,

It will give me great pleasure to spend Fast day [15] with you & to lecture in the evening. I will bring sermons, and *that* we will talk about. I gladly infer from absence of all contrary tidings that Mrs Ripley & your family are well. I should more gladly hear something about them. Charles keeps a corpse like silence. I must come & see for myself — Mr Pierpont last night gave us a lecture on Phrenology [16] on his return from Nantucket. But I who know next to nothing of the matter knew all that he told me. — these eternal preliminaries, the same in every subject & this removing of objections which did not exist or are not removed. But it is innocent entertainment if one has the time. Your affectionate nephew,

Waldo Emerson

To George Adams Sampson, New Bedford, Massachusetts, March 28, 1834 [17]

New Bedford 28 March

My dear Sir

Why did you not come with Mr Robbins as delegate — you were appointed — bad times — you would have come, & I

14. MS owned by Professor James B. Thayer; ph. in CUL. The year, though not given on the MS, is clearly 1834. Numerous family letters refer to Emerson's preaching at New Bedford from late in January to the end of March of this year. Two letters from Charles to William (owned by Dr. Haven Emerson) bear especially upon the question of date. On Mar. 22, he wrote: "Waldo is still at New Bedford & stays thro' next week"; and on Mar. 31: "Waldo is to come back tonight."

15. The *Christian Register*, Mar. 22, 1834, prints the governor's proclamation appointing Apr. 3 as Fast Day. This day, mentioned in a number of later letters, long retained some official dignity. Arthur Hugh Clough wrote on Apr. 6, 1853:

"To-day is the annual Fast-day, so my little class in Ethics goes to church instead and come to me to-morrow. People all go to church to-day, and it is a sort of Sunday. Thanksgiving-day in November and Fast-day in March or April are the two state religious observances in Massachusetts." (*Letters and Remains*, London, 1865, p. 253.)

16. Mr. George H. Tripp informs me that the *New Bedford Daily Mercury*, Mar. 27, 1834, announces John Pierpont's lecture on phrenology to be given that day.

17. MS copy (made by Cabot in 1883 from the original then owned by J. L. Bates of Devonshire St., Boston) owned by RWEMA; ph. in CUL. As Chandler Robbins

would have gone with you to Nantucket. I designed to have written you but I have less time here than in Boston, so given are the kind Friends here to honouring the hireling priests. What should I have written about – some heresy of yours about education I had it in my head to lecture you concerning – as if some greek & latin, & living in Cambridge walls, made an education that is, qualified one to think & to write. or as if one might forget one moment that now & where he is & wherein he acts is his education, present, unending, always beginning. Certainly it is possible that one may utter himself in action or in speech. & another in writing. but then he shall plead preference or nature & not want of education which is wanting to none who exerts his faculties & his virtues. But the stage comes for Mr K.[18]

R Waldo Emerson.

To Edward Bliss Emerson, Boston, April 12, 1834 [19]

Boston, 12 April, 1834

My dear brother,

Rare is communication between us not the less sincere & welcome shall it be. I know not where the debt lies & will fain believe you owe me a letter. What have I to tell you What mouldy speculations to rummage up – Not one word – Only good will, only desires that God & you will keep & mend your health & send you brilliant success in affairs if such a thing were desireable. The use of action – what we gownmen covet of you round jackets – is the education of the will. The workman gets it the analyst misses it One is at home in all society The other ever a baby among the practical folk. One throws a dart like Priam the other is as effective as Hercules. Meantime Action no less than speculation imparts slowly the highest fruit of speculation, to wit, the knowledge of our own force & capacity & through this acquaints us with our destiny, what particular post in his Universe God meant I should fill.

Faith is always teaching us that no time is ever lost that is conscientiously employed The oyster fills a chink the diamond does no more

did not become pastor of the Second Church till Dec., 1833, and as George A. Sampson died in July, 1834 (see Sept. 1, 1834, to William Emerson), the present letter must have been written in 1834. That Emerson was at New Bedford on Mar. 28 of that year is shown by the letter of the same date to Samuel Ripley.

18. Probably the copyist's error for "R," *i.e.,* Robbins.

19. MS owned by RWEMA; ph. in CUL.

Each of us by Reverence or if you please by Reference makes the petty orbit of his daily works exceed in grandeur the Solar System, outshine all material lustre. But I have no call to speculate except you are well & strong. Do not stay where you are, ailing. The moment you have advice that you should not work or should voyage, come & stay with me. I flatter myself notwithstanding the sad account you gave of your sickness & of your cough that the tropical climate is yet working good changes in your system, & fitting you to live here. If it is not, do not stay there on any account of moneys to the disadvantage of your body. Not one week. Mother & I will speedily plant ourselves in the country [20] & I am poorest company for her — so whimsical & solitary my habits of composition make me — so here is your house & bed & book waiting for you.

Mother is now at Concord. We shall probably live at Newton at Mrs Allens. I carry out as you will suppose a head preposterously stuffed with projects of thoughts studies books philanthropies whereof may much good come to the petty sphere of our influence & no charge of waste to the projector.

William one would judge is a very successful young man in his profession. Charles does not despond & every one is successful so long as he does not despond. Unbroken courage is the highest success. The Romans cannot be defeated. Meantime God is around us & in us & the feeblest is yet divine. So commending you to Him I am nearer to you. Cease not to remember your affectionate brother

Waldo

Where is your Dissertation on China? Where that on Asia?

To William Emerson, Boston, April 18, 1834 [21]

Boston, 18 April, 1834.
Morning.

My dear brother,

I had the satisfaction of seeing Susan though but a very short time yesterday & the day before.[22] She arrived in safety on

20. In the MS *Autobiography* Emerson notes that he and his mother took board in Newton, in Apr., 1834, for the summer. *Cf.* Apr. 18, 1834, and later letters.

21. MS owned by RWEMA; ph. in CUL. This letter is followed, on the same sheet, by a note from Charles Emerson.

22. Emerson had not hitherto seen his sister-in-law. Charles wrote to William on Mar. 31 (MS owned by Dr. Haven Emerson): "So I hope Susan's visit will be in the wane of April. . . . & I hope this time she will meet Waldo."

Wednesday afternoon but found no lodgings at the Tremont which is being painted & thence went to Mrs Ladd's Tremont St but Mother & aunts had removed to Front St [23] & moreover Mother was at Concord. Mrs Ladd however received her & by accident (if the good gods & genii & lares did not oversee & direct such throws) Charles got a notice of her being in town as we were going from the Natural History Society to Newton so we put up the horse again & sallied out to find her a boarding house. Mrs Palmer in Franklin Place with whom I board agreed to accommodate her & so I went to Tremont St to find the lady. She had suffered sadly from headache & was quite sick but exerted herself to get into the coach & ride to Mrs Palmers, but arrived there quite faint & ill. They put her to bed & took care of her & she was soon much relieved though doubtful of ability to ride another day. But the next morning when I went to breakfast, I found her up & dressed to go to Portsmouth. She was evidently much better than the day before & said she was quite well. So I had fifteen minutes acquaintance with my sister before the stage came. The day was fine & though there was nobody in the coach bound for Portsmouth yet I commended her to the coachman who knew her & promised every attention. I was very sorry Mother happened to be at Concord & have related thus particularly the advent of Mrs W. Emerson that Mr W. Emerson may henceforward give me a hint *the day before,* when his lady is journeying hither, as it might chance to save her a good deal of discomfort. For if we had stepped into the chaise to go to Newton, I should have been vexed. Lastly I am very happy to have seen though but a glimpse of so pleasant & worthy a lady & must trust time for the ripening of our love. I ought to apologize for sending this letter so late that perhaps Susan's will arrive as soon. Then mine for candle-paper.

Thanks from all good men to the patriots of your city [24] & yet the times might make the sanguine despair. Let the sanguine despair the resolute the wise never despair In God is our aid. Your affectionate brother

Waldo.

23. *Stimpson's Boston Directory,* 1834, gives William G. Ladd's residence as 103 Tremont St. and Ann Haskins's as 13 Front St. Jerusha Palmer's boarding house is listed, *ibid.,* as at 18 Franklin Place.

24. For the story of the riotous election in New York, see the *New-York Commercial Advertiser,* Apr. 8, 9, and 11, 1834. Charles Emerson wrote to William, Apr. 12 (MS owned by Dr. Haven Emerson), that it was better to take clubs and muskets to the polls than to die the death of slaves to a crazy administration.

TO THOMAS CARLYLE, BOSTON, MAY 14, 1834

[MS owned by RWEMA; printed in *C–E Corr.,* 1883. Carlyle received this first letter of the long series on July 26, 1834, and recorded its coming as a comfortable circumstance in the midst of innumerable discouragements; it was, he said, sincere and not baseless but gave an exaggerated estimate of him (James Anthony Froude, *Thomas Carlyle,* New York, 1882, II, 358–359).]

TO WILLIAM EMERSON, NEWTON, MASSACHUSETTS, MAY 26, 1834 [25]

Newton, 26 May, 1834.

Dear William,

If we have not quite lost one another in the crowd, I pen this advertisement of my whereabout. It is quite possible that I shall go eastward & spend a few missionary weeks at Bangor in July; [26] so this comes to say that these Chaldaean plains of ours where nothing but the heavenly bodies is seen to move unless it be perhaps a few thrushes & the cows, offer to you all the fragrance of their pines during the pleasant month of June. Can you not shall you not fix the day of your departure northward so early as to bring Susan here to spend a week or a fortnight for the unquestionable benefit of both your healths, in that month.[27] For Mother means to visit Concord the first week in July whilst Miss Ripley [28] goes to N. Y. Tis of course a settled question that no man can possess his soul — his business only in that city of yours. To revisit yourself tis absolutely necessary you should be aired & insulated in the fields. So hither, hither, bend your way. Omnis chorus scriptorum amat nemus.[29] Better stop at Charles' room *and mine,* when you first come to Boston, 276 Washington st, & a stage coach at 4 P. M. will bring you out here to tea.

Mother is pretty well not perfectly & has not been much alone. what with aunts, cousins, & friends. Yours affectionately,

Waldo E —

25. MS owned by RWEMA; ph. in CUL.
26. *Cf.* letters of June 8 and Sept. 1, 1834.
27. The visit of William Emerson and his wife occurred about the time here suggested, as is shown in Charles to William, July 8 following (owned by Dr. Haven Emerson).
28. See a note on Dec. 15, 1830.
29. Slightly altered from Horace, *Epist.,* II, ii, 77.

To Edward Bliss Emerson, Newton, Massachusetts, May 31, 1834[30]

[I]Newton, 31 May, 1834.[I]

My dear brother,

Your last letter to mother postpones to a pretty distance our prospect of seeing you but as some of our feet were shod with quicksilver when we came into the world there is still an even chance that you may slip in upon us in some of these revolutions of Night & Morn. [II]Here sit Mother & I among the pine trees still almost as we shall lie by & by under them. Here we sit always learning & never coming to the knowledge of. — The greatest part of my virtue — that mustard seedlet that no man wots of — is Hope. I am ever of good cheer & if the heaven asks no service at my hands am reconciled to my insignificance yet keeping my eye open upon the brave & the beautiful. Philosophy affirms that the outward world is only phenomenal & the whole concern of dinners of tailors of gigs of balls whereof men make such account[II] is a quite relative & temporary one — [III]an intricate dream — the exhalation of the present state of the Soul — wherein the Understanding works incessantly as if it were real but the eternal Reason when now & then he is allowed to speak declares it is an accident a smoke nowise related to his permanent attributes. Now that I have used the words, let me ask you do you draw the distinction of Milton Coleridge & the Germans between Reason & Understanding.[31] I think it a philosophy itself. & like all truth very practical.[III] So now lay away the letter & take up the following dissertation on Sunday. [IV]Reason is the highest faculty of the soul — what we mean often by the soul itself; it never *reasons*, never

30. MS owned by RWEMA; ph. in CUL. Excerpts I–VI are in Cabot, I, 217–218. In his reply from Porto Rico, dated July 7, 1834, Edward Emerson welcomed the idea of a retreat into Berkshire and promised that, next year, when he returned home, he would talk over what might then remain "unvanished" of the project. As to "the transcendental lecture" about reason and understanding, he protested against the claim of either Coleridge or the Germans to the merit of the discovery of "this all important distinction."

31. The passage in Milton is *Paradise Lost,* V, 486–488. Coleridge had discussed reason and understanding in *The Friend* for Sept. 14, 1809, and in Chapter x of *Biographia Literaria;* but it seems probable, I think, that Emerson remembered both the Milton passage and Coleridge's discussion of the same theme from *Aids to Reflection,* ed. James Marsh, Burlington, Vt., 1829, pp. xxxix and 136 ff. For Coleridge's perversion of Kant's teachings on this subject, see *The Cambridge History of English Literature,* XI, 151–152.

proves, it simply perceives; it is vision. The Understanding toils all the time, compares, contrives, adds, argues, near sighted but strong-sighted, dwelling in the present the expedient the customary.[IV] Beasts have some understanding but no Reason. Reason is potentially perfect in every man — Understanding in very different degrees of strength. The thoughts of youth, & 'first thoughts,' are the revelations of Reason. the love of the beautiful & of Goodness as the highest beauty the belief in the absolute & universal superiority of the Right & the True But understanding that wrinkled calculator the steward of our house to whom is committed the support of our animal life contradicts evermore these affirmations of Reason & points at Custom & Interest & persuades one man that the declarations of Reason are false & another that they are at least impracticable. Yet by & by after having denied our Master we come back to see at the end of years or of life that he was the Truth. 'Tell him,' was the word sent by Posa to the Spanish prince 'when he is a man to reverence the dreams of his youth.' [32] And it is observed that 'our first & third thoughts usually coincide.' [33] Religion Poetry Honor belong to the Reason; to the real the absolute. These the Understanding sticks to it are chimaeras he can prove it. Can he, dear? The blind men in Rome said the streets were dark. Finally to end my quotations, Fen[elon] said, 'O Reason! Reason! art not thou He whom I seek.' — The manifold applications of the distinction to Literature to the Church to Life will show how good a key it is. So hallelujah to the Reason forevermore.

[V]But glad should I be to hold academical questions with you here at Newton.[V] Whenever you are tired of working at Porto Rico & want a vacation or whenever your strength or your weakness shall commend to you the high countenances of the Muses, come & live with me. [VI]The Tucker estate is so far settled that I am made sure of an income of about $1200.[34] wherewith the Reason of Mother & you & I might defy the Un-

32. Schiller, *Don Carlos,* IV, xxi.

33. *Cf. Journals,* III, 299 (May 21, 1834). The MS has been slightly mutilated by the opening of the seal, and the bracketed letters near the end of this paragraph are conjectural.

34. Charles wrote to William on May 13 of this year (MS owned by Dr. Haven Emerson), that Emerson had then received one half his inheritance from Pliny Cutler, the executor, by order of the court — 67 shares of City Bank stock, 19 of the Atlantic Bank, and 31 of the Boston and Roxbury Mill Dam, together with cash amounting to between $3000 and $4000, making altogether about $11,600. The second "half" paid in July, 1837, was $11,674.49, so that the total amount he received from Ellen Tucker's estate seems to have been $23,274.49, or approximately that (see

derstanding upon his own ground, for the rest of the few years in which we shall be subject to his insults. I need not say that what I speak in play I speak in earnest. If you will come we will retreat into Berkshire & make a little world of other stuff. Your brother

Waldo.[VI]

To George Adams Sampson, Newton, Massachusetts, June? 1? 1834[35]

Sunday ev'g

My dear Sir,

[I]Why have you not been out here to see the pines & the hermit.[I] Dont you come now until Wednesday when I shall see you in town & perhaps you will come out that evening with me. If I knew you would, I would come into town in a chaise. [II]It is calm as eternity,[II]

the letters of July 10 and July 28, 1837). Charles's letters to William dated May 13, May 20 and 21, and May 22 and 23 (all owned by Dr. Haven Emerson) show how the income was spent at that time. Their mother's income from the La Fayette Hotel was only $80 or $90 a year, so that her expenses of about $6 a week caused a deficit of perhaps $225 a year. Emerson's own expenses were about $6 a week, and he was now paying Bulkeley's. "Therefore for the present," said Charles, "we seem pretty nearly as poor as ever only Waldo does without a Profession." Yet, he adds later, Emerson was now troubled by "solicitations for money, which come thick at these times."

35. MS owned by RWEMA; ph. in CUL. This is a copy in Cabot's hand. Excerpts I–IV are in Cabot, I, 205–206. The copyist has written at the top of his sheet what was doubtless the superscription or part of it, "Mr Geo. A. Sampson. Boston," and has supplied the heading, also in square brackets, Newton, May 4, 1834, "from internal evidence." There can be no doubt about the place or the year, but I believe the day was more probably the first of June. It is true that the plan to go into town on Wednesday would fit Wednesday, May 7, when, according to the *Boston Daily Advertiser,* May 7, 1834, Emerson was to deliver an address at the annual meeting of the Boston Society of Natural History; and the description of the quiet of the Newton woods suggests the *Journals* entry of May 1 as well as the letters of May 26 and May 31. On the other hand, the only very positive evidence I have found is the entry in *Journals,* III, 302 (June 2, 1834): "Preached at Waltham yesterday"; *i.e.,* on Sunday, June 1. A letter from Charles Emerson addressed to Newton and dated simply "Wednesday" but endorsed June, 1834, says that he and Geo. A. Sampson mean to come out to take tea "tomorrow" afternoon and that George Bradford will come on the steam car to pass the night and return to his teaching Friday morning. The *Christian Register* of Apr. 12, 1834, told of the running of the first passenger train on the Boston and Worcester Rail Road and stated that within a few days regular trains would be running between Boston and Newton. In *Journals,* III, 305–306 (June 10, 1834), Emerson describes a ride on a railroad. Sampson's death, a few weeks later, is mentioned in the letter of Sept. 1, 1834, to William Emerson.

out here, [III]& will give you lively ideas of the same. These sleepy hollows full of savins & cinquefoils seem to utter a quiet satire at the ways & politics of men. I think the robin & finch the only philosophers. I listen attentively to all they say & account the whole spectacle of the Day a new speech of God to me, though he speaks not less from the wharf & the market. Few men are listeners; but there are more *there* than here. I went to Waltham today & preached to deaf or hearing, next Sunday I go to Watertown & the following to Fall River, so you must come out here in the week & 'tis deep Sunday in this woodcocks nest of ours from one end of the week to the other — times & seasons get lost here sun & stars make all the difference of night & day.[III] But to return to the precincts of vulgar humanity [IV]there is a walk through the woods of about two miles which I will show you on the first occasion from our house to the railroad,[IV] which will make us very accessible to you, whenever the hours of the cars will suit, & they promise shortly a morning trip; — then you can spend nights out here.

Yours
R. W. Emerson.

To Mary Moody Emerson, Newton? Massachusetts? June? *c.* 1? 1834?

[Charles Emerson to William, June 11, endorsed 1834 (owned by Dr. Haven Emerson), quotes this from a letter from Mary Moody Emerson probably written about June 5 of that year: " Could you see the brief letter of Waldo — the appointment to meet in some other world, — Philippi — you would say this is like the transient interests of life." The allusion might, I suppose, be to the story of the appointment with the evil genius told in Plutarch's life of Brutus.]

To Jason Whitman, Newton, Massachusetts, June 8, 1834 [36]

Newton 8 June 1834

Dear Sir,

Is it possible that you can tell me any thing about the church at Bangor? About two months ago I saw Col. Goss [37] from that place

36. MS owned by the American Unitarian Association; ph. in CUL. The superscription is to Rev. Jason Whitman, Boston. According to William B. Sprague, *Annals of the American Pulpit,* 1865, VIII, 553, Whitman had preached at Saco, Me., for several years but came to Boston in Apr., 1834, to be general secretary of the American Unitarian Association.

37. Cyrus Goss, Dec. 15, 1854, asks Emerson, when he comes to lecture in Bangor, to be his guest " to renew the acquaintance which was begun many years ago." Goss

& made him a contingent promise to go there in July.[38] Since when I have heard nothing from them. Your brother said you had some correspondence with them. If you know how they stand – specially if they have any expectation of a visit from me, I should be obliged to you to drop a line addressed to me in *Boston,* in the post office.

Yours with respect,
R. W. Emerson.

To Frederic Henry Hedge, Bangor, Maine, July 12, 1834[39]

x x They are very anxious to have a minister of ability settled here & have got beyond the period when a violent Unitarian is wanted. x x

ᴵI am almost persuaded to sit down on the banks of this pleasant stream & if I could only persuade a small number of persons to join my colony we would have a settlement 30 miles up the river, at once.ᴵ x x

To Charles Chauncy Emerson and Ruth Haskins Emerson? Bangor, Maine, July *c.* 15, 1834

[Charles Emerson to William, July 18, endorsed 1834 (owned by Dr. Haven Emerson): "We had letters from Waldo yesterday – He writes that Bangor is a sort of city of the woods . . ." This seems to show that there was more than one letter about this time. Charles, July 17 and 18 (1834), apparently answers a letter about Bangor.]

---

appears in *The Bangor Directory,* 1834, as a merchant and director of a bank. Mr. Elmar T. Boyd informs me that, according to *The Bangor Historical Magazine,* II, 234, a William Emerson lived with Cyrus Goss. *Journals,* VII, 232, refers to "My friend William Emerson, at Bangor."

38. In an unpublished diary kept during a part of July, 1834, Emerson notes that he left Boston in the mail coach on the 3d for Bangor by way of Portland (typescript *Journals*). Charles, July 24, shows that Emerson was expected home from Bangor the following Wednesday, July 30. In the letter of Sept. 1, 1834, to William, Emerson says he spent a month at Bangor.

39. MS owned by RWEMA; ph. in CUL. This is a fragmentary copy in the hand of Cabot, whose introductory note records the place and date and describes the letter as "asking him [Hedge] to come there & preach." Excerpt I is in Cabot, I, 228, and in *Journals,* III, 319. For Emerson's visit to Bangor at this time, see especially notes on June 8, 1834. Hedge was later settled as a regular pastor in that town (*cf.* Apr. 30, 1835), but whether through Emerson's influence I do not know.

To William Emerson, Newton, Massachusetts, September 1, 1834 [40]

Newton, Sept. 1, 1834.

Dear William,

It seems to me, but can hardly be, that I have not written to you since you left us after your hasty visit.[41] I have had time in the interim to spend a month at Bangor then to lose the best of friends [42] and lastly to toil in the composition of a poem [43] in which Sampson would have taken a livelier interest — such was the quick apprehension

40. MS owned by RWEMA; ph. in CUL.

41. See May 26, 1834.

42. George Adams Sampson, one of Emerson's closest friends, died July 23, 1834. On July 26 Charles Emerson wrote the news to William (MS owned by Dr. Haven Emerson). Sampson, he said, "went to Portland a week ago, in the Steam boat, meaning to travel by land thence to Bangor, & return with Waldo. He was very sick on his passage, grew worse afterward . . . & died in great pain on Wednesday P. M.

"The company of good & just men on earth is the smaller by his loss. And Waldo, Sampson loved him like a brother. . . ."

On Sunday, Aug. 3, Elizabeth Peabody went with Alcott to Hanover St. and heard Emerson preach the funeral sermon. On that day or the next, apparently, she wrote in her journal letter of many dates to her sister Mary: "But *words* would vainly essay to do justice to his apotheosis of Sampson. His expression — his tones — his prayers — his readings of Scripture — his sermon which was an elaborate exposition of the character — in a subdued & chastened manner of setting it forth — which cannot be described — will live in my soul forever & ever — And *I know that man* as well as I could have known him had I been his acquaintance on earth." (MS owned by Mr. Horace Mann.)

43. In the course of August, Emerson had commented upon this Phi Beta Kappa poem in *Journals,* and Charles wrote to William in his letter dated the 26th and 27th of that month (owned by Dr. Haven Emerson): "Wednesday 27. Commencement day . . . Waldo has read me parts of his poem, & I believe his audience may be trusted to find out that tis both good sense & good verses." The *Boston Daily Advertiser,* Aug. 29, 1834, reports the Phi Beta Kappa exercises of the 28th and says, "The poem was brief and interesting, relating to topics of a general nature connected with our country. One of its most striking passages, was a warm eulogium of the character of Lafayette." A holograph MS of the poem, 15 pp. in length, is now in HCL. Emerson himself supplied also the title page — "R. W. Emerson's Poem, spoken before the ΦBK Society Aug. 1834." There is no further title, and the poem begins:

"Is not this house a harp whose living chords,
Touched by a Poet with electric words,
Would vibrate with a harmony more true
Than Handel's married thunders ever knew?"

The brief passage printed by Cabot, *Standard Library Edition,* n. d. (c. 1883), IX, 312, and reprinted in *Cent. Ed.,* IX, 398–399, begins on p. 13 of the MS. *The Phi Beta Kappa Key,* I, 25–28 (Jan., 1913), printed a much longer excerpt, described as "somewhat less than half of the whole poem."

of his friendship — than any scholar there. I debated with myself the question whether I should put such outrage on my solemn nature as to manufacture amusing verses, but decided to attempt poetry instead though at the penalty of almost certain failure as a declamation — a penalty which I believe has been fully paid. I shall send my poem to Susan, the more willingly that her husband has always had the praise of reading poetry well.

You ask for your Maps & guides — I have not yet seen Motte [44] though I desired & desire it much. I wondered what you wanted of books I tho't you had no time to use & Charles said it was as fractions of a library which was counted & appraised in your ledger. If he is right I think you had better charge me with the price of them at once for I know not yet what part of them is yet on this side the moon, & I have a suspicion that the insurers would demand a great premium for a policy. But I speak in the dark & will make Ajax's prayer whenever I go to Boston " Grant light." [45] Besides I think I want the tempest tossed tomes & I think you do not. So sir there's cold comfort for you touching your loaned books. And I hope when you lend your books you are not usually abused on asking that they may be returned. Mother & I have talked of going to board this coming Winter at Concord with Grandfather — but I doubted the plan was too pleasant to hold. And now Mr Dewey has made to me some unpleasing communications. wherewith I will not now trouble you.

George B. E., do you know, is engaged to Mrs Fleming [46] daughter of Wm Rotch of New Bedford & a lady everyway estimable, her friends say. I know her slightly. She was in Boston when I was among her friends. Mother is very well & sends love & so do I to my sister Susan & to you.

Yours affectionately
Waldo.

44. Perhaps this was Andrew Motte's translation of Sir Isaac Newton's *Principia* under the title of *The Mathematical Principles of Natural Philosophy.* The 1819 edition of this, at least, included considerable comments on the *Principia* by William Emerson, the well-known English mathematician of the eighteenth century, whose name might have attracted the American Emersons.

45. *Iliad,* XVII, 645 ff.

46. The *Boston Daily Advertiser,* Nov. 26, 1834, reports the marriage, on Nov. 24, of George B. Emerson to Mary R. Fleeming, daughter of William Rotch.

To Ezra Ripley, Newton, Massachusetts, September 1, 1834[47]

Newton, 1 September, 1834.

My dear Sir,

Forgive my delay in answering your kind letter received more than a week since. It found me in the agonies of the muse, and before the poem quitted me another obstacle appeared. Your letter was very agreeable both to my mother & myself, & the terms certainly very reasonable & I pleased myself with the intention of writing to you & fixing a time when we should come. I have since received a letter from Mr Dewey at New Bedford containing bad news of his own health & requesting my aid in his parish.[48] His communication is in a measure confidential and at any rate is one I am sorry to receive. I have as yet no fixed conclusion scarce a fixed opinion concerning it but am to visit him & preach for him next Sunday when I shall converse with him at large. I had promised myself great pleasure in going to Concord; perhaps I shall still; I hope however that in any event Mother will go there, as it is to her so pleasant a residence. As soon as I have made up my mind with regard to New Bedford, I shall write to you again.

With regard to the history of Concord Fight, I have never given the *two* sides any examination. If you will do me the honor to send me your History,[49] which by some accident I have never possessed, & inform me where I shall find the other account,[50] I will read them & will tell you whether I arrive at any result which is worth making known in the N. A. Review.[51]

I was quite grieved to learn that Bulkeley had made you a visit. Your kindness should have been saved that unreasonable tax, if it could have been foreseen. I shall write immediately to Mr Putnam [52] & to Bulkeley to prevent its being repeated.

Today's Boston Daily Advertiser quotes from a St Johns paper of Aug. 23, a notice of the death of Hon. John Murray Bliss at the age of

47. MS owned by Professor James B. Thayer; ph. in CUL.

48. For the decision not to accept the pastorate at New Bedford but to live in Concord instead, see Sept. 20, 1834. *Cf.* also Sept. 1, 1834, to William Emerson.

49. See Sept. 27, 1835.

50. Probably Elias Phinney's — see Sept. 27, 1835.

51. Emerson did not publish such an article, but he made use of these sources in his historical address of the following year.

52. *Cf.* Dec. 4, 1828. Probably the letters to Robert Bulkeley Emerson and to Putnam were written, but I have no further evidence.

63 years, after an illness of four weeks. He is mentioned with terms of high praise.[53]

I am glad to hear of your ability for all active & distant duty but a little sorry that it should be so heavily taxed as it seems to have been recently. You must use your strength with temperance that it may last you & your friends the longer. My mother sends her love to you, Sir, & to Miss Sarah [54] to whom I also beg to be remembered.

With great respect & affection
Your grandson
R. Waldo Emerson

To Ezra Ripley, Newton, Massachusetts, September 20, 1834 [55]

Newton, Sept 20, 1834.

My dear Sir,

After much conversation with the New Bedford people & Mr Dewey I have declined going there for the coming winter [56] & therefore I return with pleasure to our former prospect of spending the winter at Concord. We are not confined in our present quarters by any fixed term, yet I think it will not be convenient to us to go to Concord until the second week in October, say on the 10th. I wish to carry my books which are in Boston & some pieces of furniture & baggage which are here & I think I had better engage Mr Buttrick or some other person in Concord to transport them as Mr Allen [57] has not horses. I sup-

53. The *Boston Daily Advertiser*, Sept. 1, 1834, quotes from a St. John, N. B., paper of Aug. 23 an account of the death of John Murray Bliss, senior judge of the supreme court of that province. Bliss had left Massachusetts at the beginning of the Revolution.

54. *Cf.* Dec. 15, 1830.

55. MS owned by Professor James B. Thayer; ph. in CUL.

56. Several letters from Charles Emerson to William (owned by Dr. Haven Emerson) afford a commentary on the progress of the negotiations about the call to New Bedford. A letter of Aug. 26 and 27 says, "Mr Dewey is sick with old complaints at New Bedford, & asks Waldo to come be his successor — Ah me! I dont relish the plan, but we will have no choice, & be

'Of spirit too capacious to require
That Destiny for us her course should change.'"

On Sept. 12 Charles writes: "Waldo has come back from New Bedford uncommitted . . ." On Sept. 22: "Waldo has answered Mr Dewey that he does not wish to go to New Bedford . . . He movés to Concord with Mother the second week in October." Probably there were letters to Dewey about this time, but I have found no proof.

57. *Cf.* Apr. 12, 1834.

pose a large horse cart would carry all we have here; — A bureau; a small table; 2 bookcases containing each 2 shelves; 2 armchairs; a trunk & 2 beds; — & some small articles. I think it would need two horses. Mother & I will go to Boston & go up in the stage from thence. My books from Boston can go afterwards. May I ask you to engage Mr Buttrick to come here with his wagon, & I will write to you again to name the day. Aunt Mary is here, & is desirous of boarding somewhere in Concord. Mother thought perhaps Mr Prescott's would be a good place, if they would accommodate her.

With kind regards to Miss Ripley, believe me, dear Sir, Your affectionate grandson

R. Waldo Emerson

To William Emerson, Newton, Massachusetts, October 8, 1834 [58]

Newton, 8 October, 1834.

Dear William

I will come & see you with all my heart. I am packing bookshelves & trunks today, to go to Concord tomorrow. Our packing done & baggage despatched, Mother & I depart for Boston; & before I establish my inkstand at Concord, the country mouse shall refresh his ears with the roar of a metropolis. As Mr Dewey is waited for & as you will doubtless make permanent arrangements with him [59] I who am no candidate can fitly fill the crevice of the time. It is plainly so, is it? I will not preach as a candidate. If not countermanded I shall set out Friday 17 instant, to arrive in N York Saturday.[60] Can I not board with you or is there some 'prophet's chamber' [61] two miles off appointed unto the Levites. I will bring with me the Itineraries, &c & cancel that column.[62] I doubted when I wrote whether I should ever see them again & I assent to your remark that worth much or worthless they are not to be replaced. I should value them much & should do as you have done. As to the poem [63] I rejoice if you like it, but if you cannot make a smooth pentameter out of "To [64] pleased God the redeemed wilder-

58. MS owned by RWEMA; ph. in CUL.

59. Orville Dewey presently became pastor of the Second Unitarian Church in New York, as Emerson expected.

60. The entry in *Journals*, III, 346, was written at New York, on Oct. 18, 1834.

61. Probably an allusion to *II Kings*, 4:10.

62. *Cf.* Sept. 1, 1834, to William Emerson.

63. *Ibid.*

64. The first letter is carelessly made but seems to be "T" rather than "S."

ness " I commend you to Chaucer. Tell my sister Susan I trust to her to be screen between my muse & the hypercritical counsellor. With kindest remembrance to her I am your affectionate brother

Waldo

Mother insists that I send her love to Susan & to you.

To David Hatch Barlow, New York, October 24, 1834 [65]

24 Oct
1834

My dear Sir,

Thanks thanks for your kind & elegant tribute to the memory of your friend & my brother.[66] Though he was unknown in this city, certainly the public have a right to the sentiments which the short life of a silent poet & silent orator could inspire, the rather that I believe had opportunity favored him none of its living members would have devoted, a warmer heart a loftier enthusiasm to the best interests of humanity.

I need not say that to his immediate friends both here & at home this new proof of your regard to him will be very gratifying. Am I right in understanding that you have another copy & that you will take order for its publication.[67] If so I shall carefully preserve this.

Yours affectionately
R W E

To Ezra Ripley, New York? October, 1834

[Described in F. B. Sanborn, *Henry D. Thoreau,* 1882, p. 48, as relating to a request for a lecture before the Concord Lyceum.]

65. MS owned by RWEMA; ph. in CUL. This is a rough draft and contains several variant phrases which Emerson canceled and which are here omitted. For Barlow and his admiration for Edward Emerson, *cf.* Dec. 14, 1831.

66. Edward died in Porto Rico on Oct. 1, 1834. Dr. Francis Armstrong, a companion of Edward on some of his trips into the country in Porto Rico, wrote to William Emerson on Feb. 5, 1835, an account of the fatal illness. In August, 1834, Edward got a wetting which increased his cough. On Sept. 27 he was suffering from pains in the chest, and a few days later there was pus on his lungs and Armstrong saw that the case was hopeless. Death was due to tuberculosis, the family scourge, and the New England scourge.

67. " Lines to the Memory of Edward Bliss Emerson, who Died at Porto Rico, October, 1834, Aged 29 " appeared in the *Christian Register,* Nov. 8, 1834, over the initials " D. H. B." For another poem by Barlow on the same subject, see Dec. 16 and 18, 1834.

To Ruth Haskins Emerson, New York, October? 31? 1834

[Mentioned in *Journals,* III, 353. Charles Emerson, Nov. 4 (endorsed 1834 by Emerson), acknowledges the receipt "Yesterday" of "yours for Mother."]

To Thomas Carlyle, Concord, November 20, 1834

[MS owned by RWEMA. Printed in *The Athenæum,* London, June 24, 1882, p. 796; reprinted in *C–E Corr.,* 1883. The 1883 version contains a few words not printed in 1882, and there are several minor differences.]

To William Emerson, Concord, November 23, 1834 [68]

Sunday Ev^g^
^I^Nov 24 Concord^I^

Dear William,

I grieve to hear from Charles that Susan continues ill. I trusted to hear before this that she was out upon her feet. And she must be temperate in her temperance & not starve. Mother is very sorry to hear of it. Do send us forthwith news of her & if possible better news.

I meant long before this to have informed you of my pleasant passage & safe arrival.[69] We traversed the 15 miles of railroad in 32 minutes. I found Dr Ripley recovering & he may probably enjoy tolerable health through the winter — is already talking of preaching a fortnight hence tho' he has not yet been out. Mother I found very sad but her health is good. ^II^Aunt Mary boards in the village & keeps a surprizingly good understanding with the people of this world considering her transcendental [70] way of living — Yesterday she came here in the shabbiest horse & chaise which she said she saw standing at the door where she was shopping & having found out who it belonged to she asked the man to let her go & ride whilst he was making purchases for she wanted to go up to

68. MS owned by RWEMA; ph. in CUL. Excerpts I–II were printed in *Memoirs of Members of the Social Circle,* 2d series, 2d part, pp. 52–53 (reprinted, with the same pagination, as *Emerson in Concord*). Evidence cited below makes it clear that the year is 1834, but Nov. 24 was Monday in that year, and Emerson could scarcely have been mistaken in naming Sunday as the day of the week. The letter was forwarded through Barnard, Adams & Co., with no Boston date, but has a New York postmark of Nov. 27.

69. A letter from Charles to William, Oct. 31 and Nov. 3, 1834 (owned by Dr. Haven Emerson), shows that Emerson had not returned home from New York by Nov. 3.

70. *Cf.* the use of the word in Scott's *Woodstock,* 1826, as cited in *A New English Dictionary.*

Dr Ripleys &c The man I suppose demurred; – so she told him 'that she was his own townswoman, born within a mile of him' & finally she says when she left him *in the gig,* he told her 'not to hurry.' [71] But so she lives from day to day.[II] Since I saw you I have a noble letter from Thomas Carlyle [72] now of Craigenputtock no more, but of London. I have also read Edw. Everetts Eulogy of Lafayette [73] & I beg you when you see Barlow to take back all my empty words concerning it. I told him on hearsay that it was a failure out of good taste &c all which I solemnly retract. I think it excellent.

I left in New York you remember the 'Wonder' sermon wh. Mr Sedgwick [74] was to have returned on Monday, also a MS with Mrs Barlow and the little pencil-scrawl of Edward which you was to have given me and my London memorandum book.[75] all which please send me. If you do not want Xenophon Minor Wks [76] send it me. Mr Higginson [77] said nothing to me of business so I suppose will deal with you. The fare in the stages was only 1.50 tho' there was expense for a hack on arriving I have delegated my message to Nancy [78] [to] Charles who doubtless will report to you Meantime tell Susan that I think of her with a great deal too much kindness to be content without much better news. Mother is downstairs or would send her messages. Your affectionate brother,

Waldo.

71. William Emerson, Dec. 21, 1834: "The anecdote of Aunt Mary in the borrowed gig is the best thing I have seen this long while."

72. The first letter from Carlyle, dated London, Aug. 12, 1834, was in answer to Emerson's letter of May 14, 1834.

73. *Eulogy on Lafayette, Delivered in Faneuil Hall . . . September 6, 1834,* Boston, 1834.

74. Probably Robert Sedgwick, who appears as a New York attorney in *Longworth's American Almanac,* 1834.

75. This may refer to passages in *Journals* written in 1833, especially those about London, but more probably to a small leather-bound MS memorandum book with a printed London title page – *Ruffy's Improved Series of Pocket Books. The Polite Pocket Repository for 1833.* This contains brief notes dated from July 21 to Oct. 2, and some undated entries. On the back flyleaf is a paragraph, unpublished, I believe, dated at Dumfries, Aug. 24, which tells Emerson's impression of the son and namesake of Robert Burns and records a conversation with a sexton's boy about the poet himself.

76. The edition may have been *The Minor Works of Xenophon,* tr. by "Several Hands," London, 1813. William Emerson, Dec. 21, 1834, mentions both the Xenophon and the memorandum book and says he must not delay to return them, with some of Emerson's MSS.

77. *Cf.* Feb. 2? 1829.

78. Perhaps the "Nancy" Colesworthy of later letters. The following word was mutilated by the seal.

To James Freeman Clarke, Concord, November 25, 1834

[MS owned by Mr. James F. Clarke; ph. in CUL. Printed in Holmes, *Ralph Waldo Emerson,* 1885, pp. 79–80, where it is practically complete except for the passage quoted from Carlyle's letter of Aug. 12, 1834 – a part of his apology for his style (to be found entire in *C–E Corr.*). The letter, not received until a month later, brought this response (MS owned by Mr. James F. Clarke):

" Louisville Jan 18th
" 1835

" Dear Sir –

" I am much obliged to you for remembering me in my distant workingplace – I rec. your letter on Christmas day and it was quite a Christmas gift. You speak of the article on Goethe and Carlyle, written but never published. I have felt sorry since, that I suppressed from prudential reasons or what I thought considerations of duty the result of a strong feeling. But my view was this. Here am I, a young man, just entering my profession, about to leave this town for a distant part, & my first act is to launch an arrow at a respectable senior, who has taught me much, & treated me well, on a topic wholly foreign from my immediate business, & which I shall be unable to follow up by anything more. So, reluctantly enough, I put back the shaft into the quiver, & pocketed Mr Norton's affront on my favourites. – If it were to do over again I should publish it – but you see, I have more self-confidence & self-respect now than then, all which to be sure does not affect the eternal fitness or unfitness of the things being published. ' Publish it now ' you say. I should willingly do that or any thing else for the good cause, as I think it. I still sympathize with Carlyle & still admire Goethe. But being at a distance, &c. I could not attend to the necessary alterations &c – It would be easier to write a a new article at once, & abuse Nortonism instead of Mr Norton. But why do not you write something of this kind – the review you speak of, of Carlyle's Diderot & Sartor Resartus? There is one in your neighbourhood (Groton) who has drank very deeply of the spirit of German Literature. I know not whether you are acquainted, though I think you must be somewhat at least with Miss Margaret Fuller. She has translated the Tasso beautifully into English blank verse. Do you see Henry Hedge often? I had a letter from him not long since in which he speaks of going to Bangor. – There is something I wish you to do & that is to write an article about Schleirmacher the German Platonic, Calvinistic, Spinoz*aic,* but wholly original theologian. De Wette says he is the greatest theologian since Calvin & Melancthon. Neander thinks he makes an epoch. At his death all Berlin was in tears as when the Queen of Prussia died. He was a faithful pastor ministering to the spiritual wants of high & low, rich & poor, one with another. Depth, Clearness, Freedom in thought united with Loftiness, Warmth, & Earnestness of Sentiment composed his peculiar character. He spurned equally the shallowness of rationalism & the cant of pietism – he had a soul above it all. His " lectures to the Educated " which first appeared in the last century made a great & salutary influence in the pool of theology. He sets forth in that the infinite intellectual dignity & moral of the religious principle. His religion was one of power, love & a sound mind if any one's. Now if you have read him, pray write something about him in the Examiner – if not read him, & then you will write. – Will you excuse the meagreness of this letter & write me again? Excuse also its being on a torn piece of paper & believe me

" Yours truly

" James F. Clarke "]

To Charles Chauncy Emerson, Concord, December 4 and 5, 1834 [79]

Concord, 4 December, 1834.

Dear Charles,

I hope the fog has blown off out of which you wrote today. New days will come The world – its Governor stand pledged that opportunity shall come home to each man. And opportunity commensurate with his qualification. Tis only near-sighted people that think any talents are to spare. Profuse as is the creation so strict is the economy, & doubt not the finer gifts are as indispensable on their occasions though those occasions seldomer come as are the necessaries meal & wool & hides. Blessed are the cold days in spring that keep the flower shut till it is strong enough to open without danger to the plant & blessed the cold years that make timber for flowers – Nothing nothing is lost. What a picture of man is that Watch-Watch at Waltham [80] of which you have heard which tells in the morning the doing & failing of every hour. So are the Socrates & Webster of the present hour not less faithful registers of all their past hours, & *now* they catch the sense of the disappointments & waitings at the door & find as much thunder & light in those recollections for their present use as in things whose drift was more obvious at first.

79. MS owned by Mr. Owen D. Young; ph. in CUL. The date " 4 " is written over a " 3." That the 4th and not the 3d is intended seems clear from the statement dated " 5th," " Thus . . . wrote I last eve. . . ." The superscription bears a Concord postmark dated Dec. 6. An incomplete copy of this letter in the hand of Margaret Fuller (owned by RWEMA; ph. in CUL) lacks, among other things, the name in the salutation; and when Emerson came upon it later – probably after Margaret Fuller's death – he was not sure to whom he had addressed it, for he wrote at the top of p. 1: " I think this to be the copy of a letter written by me to some friend. I cannot think who, perhaps my brother Charles.

" R. W. E."

80. It seems that Emerson had recently been preaching at Waltham and that there was even some possibility at the time that he would become pastor there. " Waldo," wrote Charles to William on Dec. 6 of this year, " is likely as the vanes now point to go to Waltham " (MS owned by Dr. Haven Emerson).

5th Thus homiletically wrote I last eve. on my return from a party. The fog you will say was in my brain. Scarcely had I any conversation with your worship during your late visit.[81] A few sincere & entire communications are all we can expect in a lifetime. They are they which make the earth memorable to the speakers and perhaps measure the spiritual years. For the rest we dodge one another on our diverse pursuits waste time in the ado of meeting & parting or usurp it with our pompous business. I like my books that you brought me well. A right royal soul is Luther [82] who stood upright with all his might let who would kneel shuffle or cringe He seems to have been impressed with a parallelism betwixt the historical position of St Paul & his own & the Epistle to the Galatians is a stalking horse to explain & defend himself. But in all points is he a Man angry joyful laborious witty affectionate considerate devout: in all his changes you can sympathize heartily with him.

But how are the Luther-hearted youths [o]f [83] this hour to discharge their office to society in the law or the state if the diseased world knows not its sickness & knows not its physicians? Only wait & outstare what is called Fortune with faith. How short too short will this inactive period presently look. Like Menander you can finish the poem all but the verses. The most important accomplishments are already within your reach. 'He that can speak well,' said Luther, 'is a man.'

I like what you tell me of George B. E.[84] Nature told no lie when she wrote gentleman on his manners.

I think I shall go down in the stage to Cambridge & B. Monday or Tuesday. Aunt signed the power of attorney & I will bring it.[85]

Waldo —

81. Charles wrote to William on Dec. 3 (MS owned by Dr. Haven Emerson), that he had spent the Thanksgiving holidays at Concord.

82. See Dec. 16 and 18, 1834, for the decision to write a lecture on Luther. The source of the saying quoted in the following paragraph is doubtful. Possibly Emerson remembered imperfectly some remarks attributed to the reformer in *Luther's Table Talk,* London, 1832, p. 244: "'. . . to speak much is no art, but to speak fine, significantly, and rightly, that gift is granted to few. No man ought to undertake any thing except it be given him from above.'"

83. Partly torn away with the seal.

84. George Barrell Emerson.

85. Charles had recently been arranging Mary Moody Emerson's affairs in such a way that she could depend upon an annuity, and he may now have been assuming further responsibility for her welfare (*cf.* Charles to William, Oct. 31 and Nov. 3, 1834; MS owned by Dr. Haven Emerson).

To Josiah Quincy, Cambridge, December 10, 1834

[MS listed in American Art Association, Mar. 3–4, 1925; described there as " requesting permission to borrow two volumes of Vasari's ' Lives of the Painters ' and the ' Rime di Michel Angelo ' in one volume, from the library." Also listed *ibid.*, Mar. 13–14, 1928. Quincy was president of Harvard. *Cf.* Sept. 9, 1839, for the edition of Vasari in the college library. A MS charge-book (HCL) shows that Emerson drew two volumes of the *Vite* as well as a " Buonnarot " on Dec. 10, 1834.]

To William Emerson, Concord, December 16 and 18, 1834 [86]

Concord December 16

Dear William,

Please to bear in mind that you are trustee of three Mss sermons of mine. One in the hands of Mr Higginson; one with Barlow; & one with Mr Sedgwick.[87] I need them all, as I am always liable to calls to preach. So please have a godfather's eye to them.

I rejoice to hear that Susan is so much better. She cannot be too careful of herself; for what is life without health? And it pleases me alway to remember her kind self.

Mother desires eagerly the Mirror which contains Mr Barlow's verses. Were they not published? [88]

For me I have got no farther in my selection of heads for my Lecture than to nominate four Luther Michel Angelo Milton George Fox [89] Many others gay dreadful or venerable uplift their brows out of the sea of generations but none yet have I dared to call mine.

18 Dec. In talking to you about Charles I did not say to you what I think important to be said for the sake of a right understanding between persons, this namely, that although the note of 500. in my keeping given by Charles to Edward ought to give the character of *solvency*

86. MS owned by RWEMA; ph. in CUL.

87. *Cf.* Nov. 23, 1834.

88. William Emerson replied on Jan. 4, 1835, that " the verses have never yet appeared in the Mirror, & now, I suppose, they will not "; and he added the information that " a part of them " had appeared in the *Christian Register*, Dec. 20, 1834. There, at any rate, is to be found a poem on the death of an unnamed friend which has only the heading " For the Christian Register " and is signed " D. H. B." Asterisks appear between stanzas 8 and 9, indicating that the poem is incompletely printed. It is entirely different from Barlow's poem on Edward mentioned in the letter of Oct. 24, 1834.

89. For Emerson's course beginning Jan. 29, 1835, and including lectures on all the subjects here mentioned, see a note on Feb. 1, 1835.

to Edwards estate, yet, as we all know had Edward lived & thriven, payment wd. never have been demanded, as he esteemed himself only the medium through which Mr Phillip's donation [90] flowed to Charles; and therefore Charles ought not in equity be bound by Edward's debts more than the rest of us. These I mean to assume & pay as fast as I can, since income & outgo considered I judge myself the richest today. If Mr Coil or Mr Leggett shd bring to No 60 Wall st a mountain of Spanish Claims [91] or the like you can help me hereafter. All I would say is, that I do not esteem this to be Charles's debt, yet it cripples my power of serving him. So send him — the thin philosopher — what business you can. E. B. E.'s debts as far as I know them are.[92]

Mrs Cook	100	R. Haskins' note is cancelled by an equal debt to mother on a/c. of compromise on Lafayette estate.[93]
Mrs Shepard	117.	
Barnard, A. & Co	50.	
E. Ripley	50.	
Whitmarsh	30	
Φ. B. K.	200	
Palfrey	50.	

Mr Hoar was undoubtedly elected last Monday to Congress. Perhaps he will want Chas to take his office here.[94] I hope C. will be able to stay where he is.

So with my love to Susan I am her & your affectionate brother

Waldo.

90. *Cf.* Nov. 10, 1828.

91. *Longworth's American Almanac,* for New York, 1834–1835, lists a Charles Coil, tailor, and a Patrick Coil, carter, and many Leggetts. The Spanish claims were doubtless bills due on account of Edward's residence in Porto Rico.

92. Some light is thrown on this list of debts by the letters of Apr. 30, 1828; July 3, 1828; Dec. 4, 1828; Oct. 16, 1836; and Oct. 23, 1836. It is clear from a letter written by George C. Shepard, Apr. 27, 1835, that the Mrs. Shepard mentioned here was his wife, Sally Kast. For both Shepard and his wife, see earlier letters.

93. *Cf.* Apr. 20 and 23, 1831.

94. When Samuel Hoar took his seat in Congress in 1835, Charles Emerson succeeded to his office and, if he had lived, might have taken over the practice of the man whose daughter Elizabeth he expected to marry. George Frisbie Hoar, Elizabeth's brother, rated Charles Emerson "the most brilliant intellect" Massachusetts ever produced, and quoted Webster's opinion that the young lawyer might settle anywhere, even in the backwoods of Maine, and clients would flock to him (*Autobiography of Seventy Years,* 1903, I, 62–69).

1835

To William Emerson, Concord, January 7, 1835 [1]

Concord, 7 January. 1835

Dear William,

I am unwilling to let Mr Prichard [2] go from us to you without token even if we have no news. We are all well here & were very glad to get better & better news of Susans health which we trust will go on unto perfection. I am ashamed to think I have never answered Mr Dewey's excellent letter to me & Charles in October.[3] If you see him tell him I hold myself much his debtor. Carlyle's letter [4] I shall send you but I think not today as a friend is coming who has some rights in it. I received by Mr P. your pacquet of books & sermon for which my thanks abound but I want the sermon on solitude &c which Mr Higginson has.

I was in Boston on Sunday at two live churches, to wit, the Swedenborgian [5] in the Morn & Taylor's Bethel [6] in the afternoon. I think when

1. MS owned by RWEMA; ph. in CUL.

2. The Concord vital records, the *Memoirs* of the Social Circle, and Shattuck's history all throw light on the Prichard family, various members of which appear with some frequency in later letters. Possibly the person here meant was Moses Prichard or, more probably, his son William Mackay Prichard, a Harvard graduate of 1833. Two letters from Charles Emerson to William (owned by Dr. Haven Emerson) may have some bearing on the question. On Aug. 26, 1834, Charles wrote that William Prichard would go to New York on the following Friday and would carry a letter or bundle. On the 5th of September following, Charles asked why his brother said nothing of William Prichard, " who, as I understood, would move under your eye & by your counsels in getting a school." William Prichard appears in letters of some years later as William Emerson's partner.

3. Probably about the death of Edward Emerson.

4. *Cf.* Nov. 23, 1834.

5. For further evidence of the growth of Emerson's interest in Swedenborgian thought at this time, *cf.* the letters of Jan. 23 and Feb. 1, 1835. William Emerson, Apr. 12, 1835, speaks of the " rumor of your Swedenborgianism." For an account of the visits to both the Swedenborgian church and Father Taylor's church, see *Journals,* III, 430–431.

6. For Edward Taylor, see Jan. 19, 1832. A letter to William Emerson from his mother dated Apr. 24, 1835 (on the same sheet with Emerson's own letter of Apr. 24? 1835), stated that Emerson was to preach for Taylor the following Sunday.

I have done with my lectures which begin shortly I shall write & print a discourse upon Spiritual & Traditional Religion, for Form seems to be bowing Substance out of the World & men doubt if there be any such thing as spiritual nature out of the carcass in which once it dwelt.[7]

Has Charles told you that Elizabeth Francis is engaged to young Bowditch & Olivia Emerson to Mr Norris.[8] I hope Susan will find us here in the Spring. The happiest year to you both.

Waldo –

To Benjamin Peter Hunt, Concord, January 23, 1835 [9]

Concord, Mass. 23 Jan. 1835.

My dear Sir,

I have just been reading an old letter from you dated Sept. 1830 [10] & which I believe was never answered. It was not because it was neglected for to my habits of intercourse a written page always comes more welcome than much conversation: the pen is a more faithful index than the tongue of those qualities in my fellow man that most excite my curiosity & whatever the proverbs may say of the untrustworthiness of words I know more of all my friends by them than by their acts. " Action is less near to vital truth than description " [11] And your letter interested me much by exhibiting the same consciousness of principles — the inward vision — which had attracted me before & which is the basis of all that is noble in the character. You have doubtless forgotten the letter but may remember its tenor. I write now to beg you to write me again & inform me of your manner of life, or better yet, your manner of thought. As we saunter along in the world we are soon apprized that the number of those in whose genius & faith we can take any strong interest is small, & we can ill afford to lose one.

7. This points pretty obviously toward the Divinity School address.

8. Olivia Maria Emerson, sister of George Barrell Emerson, married Sheppard Hains Norris on Mar. 5, 1835, according to *The Ipswich Emersons*, p. 154. *Stimpson's Boston Directory*, 1835, gives Shepherd (not Sheppard) H. Norris.

9. MS owned by Mr. Owen D. Young; ph. in CUL.

10. For Benjamin Peter Hunt and his letter to Emerson dated at Roxboro', near Philadelphia, Sept. 28, 1830, see Sept. 6, 1830, to Hunt, and notes.

11. Emerson was probably thinking of the passage in Book V of the *Republic* of Plato which the Sydenham and Taylor version of 1804 (I, 312) translates thus: " Is it possible for any thing to be executed so perfectly as it is described? or, is such the nature of practice, that it approaches not so near the truth as theory, though some may think otherwise? "

What are your books? Have you fallen in with the writings of Thomas Carlyle? In Scotland eighteen months ago I sought & made the acquaintance of this gentleman author of the pieces "Burns" "Characteristics" "Corn Law Rhymes — Review," &c. in the Edinburgh, & of many singular papers in the Foreign Review, & Frasers Magazine, — all alive — & all true. My friends think I exaggerate his merit but he seems to me one of the best, & since Coleridge is dead, I think, the best thinker of the age. His last Essay is a series of papers in Frasers Magazine called Sartor Resartus ending about Nov. 1834.[12] If you have not

12. "Sartor Resartus" actually appeared in *Fraser's Magazine,* VIII–IX (Nov., 1833 — June, 1834). That Emerson was not the only member of his circle who was an enthusiastic reader of Carlyle before *Sartor* was published as a book is attested by the following letter from George Ripley, which is also of interest because it contains a message for Emerson sent by Carlyle at a time when he was so busy with *The French Revolution* that he did not write to Concord for many months:

"Boston 5th Oct. 1835.

"My Dear Sir

"I presume that I have no reason to expect you in Boston at present, and I therefore take this opportunity to inform you, that I received a letter from Carlyle, a few days since, containing some special messages to you, which of course you will like to hear. I copy word for word the following passages, which are all that relate directly to yourself. The whole of the letter, which is in the true Teufelsdröck vein, is at your service, when you come in town.

"'On my side, as Emerson may have explained to you, I entertain always the project of looking on America one day, where now year after year I hear of new friends awaiting me. It is very "romantic" as they call it, and yet it is very just & true; brethren of the same blood, separated only by a piece of salt water (which they are learning to cross) and by parchment treaties, which to me are mainly pieces of sheepskin stained with copperas! Let us love one another, and forward one another as we can, as it is commanded us.' x x x — 'You are likely to see my worthy Emerson. Pray tell him that he has still no chance to be forgotten here. We hope he is wedded before this time & as happy as he ought to be. He & I had some correspondence about my coming to Boston this very winter. I have written him, (if I remember) two letters about it; the last full of mere uncertainty, but promising another so soon as there came any clearness. Will you tell him that it seems to be as good as settled, that I shall *not* get across this winter, and fully likelier than ever that I shall next winter. The medical brother of whom I wrote to him is still at Geneva only, all in uncertainty; I meanwhile had to make up my mind to recommence my poor *burnt manuscript* (of which E. knows enough;) you can add that before you read this to him the burnt ashes have again grown *leaves* after a sort; that the ugliest task ever set me is got done. Whereupon I determine that the Book of the French Revolution shall be written *out* before I leave it. Almost two volumes still to do; & no prospect whatever to be counted on but that of getting delivered from them! However, it may be long before the Upper Powers set one down with *tools* for another such task: having begun it, let us end it; and then — ?' —

"So much for the prospect of seeing your friend on this side the sea. Mr. A. Everett told me the other day, that he had sent him a copy of his Review of Sartor Resartus.

seen it pray make inquiry after it. Very early in your reading I remember you had discrimination enough to appreciate Sampson Reed. So does Carlyle,[13] to whom I sent Reed's Tract, & in very different costume they are of one faith. You used to talk of Self-Reverence [14] That word indeed contains the whole of Philosophy & the whole of Religion. I would gladly know how profoundly you have pierced it. Did you ever meet a *wise Quaker*? They are few, but a sublime class of speculators. They have been perhaps the most explicit teachers of the highest article to which human faith soars the strict union of the willing soul to God & so the souls access at all times to a verdict upon every question which the opinion of all mankind cannot shake & which the opinion of all mankind cannot confirm. Or I wonder if quitting this thin air & alpine ground you rather borne by the tide of the time that sets so strong to natural Science amaze yourself with those laws of terrible beauty which took the soul of Newton & Laplace & Humboldt Yet is to me far the best charm of Natural laws their correspondence with Spiritual laws of which they seem but symbols & prophecies. But I will not fatigue you with guessing any longer in the dark at your inclinations & pursuits. Explain them yourself. They cannot be uninteresting to me. Most of all would it please me if you would take the occasion of your first liberty (I know not your occupation if you have withdrawn from the school) in paying me a visit in old Concord here. My mother & myself are boarding with Dr Ripley & have a capital spare chamber

---

with a letter, encouraging him to visit America. Perhaps, the friendly notice in the N. A. may inspire the Booksellers with courage to reprint the Sartor. F. H. Hedge told me that he had almost concluded to put it to press on his own risk. It will be a curious fact, if Carlyle, as well as Coleridge & Wordsworth should find his warmest admirers in old Massachusetts, but according to all appearance this is likely to be the case.

"Ever, your's sincerely
"Geo: Ripley."

13. Emerson had sent Carlyle a copy of Sampson Reed's book with the letter of May 14, 1834, which began the long correspondence. Carlyle had answered on Aug. 12 of the same year (*C–E Corr.*) that Emerson's Swedenborgian druggist was a "faithful thinker."

14. In the following passage Emerson makes perhaps his most forthright statement of the important connection between the Quaker doctrine of the inner light and his own ideas as later developed in "Self-reliance" and "The Over-soul." Then come in succession, in this remarkable letter, new proofs of the depth of Emerson's interest in science and in the Swedenborgian doctrine of correspondences, which was to make itself strongly felt in *Nature,* published the following year. Science, it is clear, always interested him primarily because it was a book of the laws which it was the business of the thinker to link, like footnotes, to "higher laws."

for prophet[15] or scholar. Fail not to acquaint me with your doing & being. Your old friend & servant

R. Waldo Emerson.

To Lydia Jackson, Concord, February 1, 1835[16]

Concord, 1 February —

One of my wise masters, Edmund Burke, said, 'A wise man will speak the truth with temperance that he may speak it the longer.'[17] In this new sentiment that you awaken in me, my Lydian Queen, what might scare others pleases me, its quietness, which I accept as a pledge of permanence. I delighted myself on Friday with my quite domesticated position & the good understanding that grew all the time, yet I went & came without one vehement word — or one passionate sign. In this was nothing of design, I merely surrendered myself to the hour & to the facts. I find a sort of grandeur in the modulated expressions of a love in which the individuals, & what might seem even reasonable personal expectations, are steadily postponed to a regard for truth & the universal love. Do not think me a metaphysical lover. I am a man & hate & suspect the over refiners, & do sympathize with the homeliest pleasures & attractions by which our good foster mother Nature draws her children together. Yet am I well pleased that between us the most permanent ties should be the first formed & thereon should grow whatever others human nature will.

My Mother rejoices very much & asks me all manner of questions about you, many of which I cannot answer. I dont know whether you sing, or read French, or Latin, or where you have lived, & much more. So you see there is nothing for it but that you should come here & on the Battle-Ground stand the fire of her catechism.

15. *Cf.* a note on Oct. 8, 1834.

16. MS owned by Mrs. Eric Schroeder; ph. in CUL. Excerpts I–II are in Cabot, I, 236–237. This seems to be the earliest extant letter to Lydia Jackson, to whom Emerson was married in the following September. Charles wrote to William, Jan. 22 (MS owned by Dr. Haven Emerson), that "Waldo . . . went to Plymouth to lecture on Tuesday," and on the 23d Emerson recorded (*Journals*, III, 445) that he was "Home again from Plymouth, with most agreeable recollections." Again, under date of Jan. 30, he wrote (*ibid.*, III, 446) that he had spent that day with Lydia Jackson. He reported his engagement in the letter of Feb. 5, 1835, to his brother William.

17. Quoted freely from the first of the letters on a regicide peace (*The Works*, Boston, 1826, IV, 380). Emerson had been reading, no doubt, in preparation for the last lecture of the course he had just begun in Boston.

Under this morning's severe but beautiful light I thought dear friend that hardly should I get away from Concord.[18] [I]I must win you to love it. I am born a poet, of a low class without doubt yet a poet. That is my nature & vocation. My singing be sure is very ' husky,' & is for the most part in prose. Still am I a poet in the sense of a perceiver & dear lover of the harmonies that are in the soul & in matter, & specially of the correspondences[19] between these & those. A sunset, a forest, a snow storm, a certain river-view, are more to me than many friends & do ordinarily divide my day with my books. Wherever I go therefore I guard & study my rambling propensities[I] with a care that is ridiculous to people, but to me is the care of my high calling. [II]Now Concord is only one of a hundred towns in which I could find these necessary objects but Plymouth I fear is not one. Plymouth is streets;[II] I live in the wide champaign.

Time enough for this however. If I succeed in preparing my lecture on Michel Angelo Buonaroti this week for Thursday,[20] I will come to Plymouth on Friday. If I do not succeed — do not attain unto the Idea of that man — I shall read of Luther, Thursday & then I know not when I shall steal a visit. —

Dearest forgive the egotism of all this letter Say they not ' The more love the more egotism.' Repay it by as much & more. Write, write to me. And please dear Lidian take that same low counsel & leave thinking for the present & let the winds of heaven blow away your dyspepsia.

Waldo E.

18. Later letters show that the comparative virtues of Concord and Plymouth were debated for some time, with Emerson inflexible in his preference for Concord as a town fit for a poet.

19. *Cf.* Jan. 23, 1835.

20. Charles Emerson wrote to William Feb. 5, 1835 (MS owned by Dr. Haven Emerson): " Waldo lectures tonight on Michel Angelo. A grand subject & he will do worthily by him I doubt not." The *Boston Daily Advertiser,* Jan. 29–Feb. 26, 1835, announces the introductory lecture, with no title, for Jan. 29, and the lectures on Michelangelo (Feb. 5), Martin Luther (Feb. 12), John Milton (Feb. 20), and George Fox (Feb. 26) — all given in Boston before the Society for the Diffusion of Useful Knowledge. For the final lecture, on Burke, see the letter of Mar. 2, 1835. Cabot, II, 712–714, notes the date on which the course began, outlines the unpublished lectures, and shows where the others first appeared in printed form. Cabot's valuable " Appendix F " attempts also to give similar information for Emerson's other lecture courses year by year, but is limited, in general, to the first delivery of each lecture and is, naturally, not complete even within this limitation.

To William Emerson, Boston, February 5, 1835 [21]

Boston, 5 February, 1835

Dear William,

May not my tardiness make me a teller of stale news & may not my news be strange or unwelcome if I say that I am engaged to marry Miss Lydia Jackson of Plymouth. I announce this fact in a very different feeling from that with which I entered my first connexion This is a very sober joy. This lady is a person of noble character whom to see is to respect. I find in her a quite unexpected community of sentiment & speculation, & in Plymouth she is dearly prized for her love & good works. So be glad with & for me & as soon as possible let me make you & Susan personally acquainted with her. Love to Susan. Yours affectionately

Waldo E

To Charles Chauncy Emerson, Concord? February? *c.* 8? 1835

[Charles Emerson, addressed to Concord and dated Tuesday night (endorsed Feb., 1835, in Emerson's hand), says, "I have your letter & Cuvier," asks for Mason's letter "prescribing dimensions of tablet," shows that he has definitely decided to move to Concord, and urges Emerson to choose Concord rather than Plymouth as his own home. The Tuesday of Charles's letter is clearly earlier than Feb. 12, when Charles wrote to William, quoting Mason's specifications regarding the size and fashion of the tablet for Edward (MS owned by Dr. Haven Emerson), and so, if the endorsement is correct, was Feb. 3 or 10.]

To Lydia Jackson, Concord, February 13, 1835 [22]

Concord 13 Feb

Dear Lidian, Days have I not to give, I heartily wish I had. Pride as well as love tell me that none but I should bring my betrothed into Boston but the spirit by which we live is despotic or at least I am yet far from that discipline of my powers or powerules [23] that shall enable

21. MS owned by RWEMA; ph. in CUL. The "5" at the end of the date line was apparently written over a "6." Charles Emerson to William, Feb. 12 (1835), mentions the engagement here recorded and adds: "The lady is a sort of Sybil for wisdom — She is not beautiful anywise that I know, so you look at the outside alone. Mother is pleased, & everybody." (MS owned by Dr. Haven Emerson.)

22. MS owned by Mrs. Ward I. Gregg; ph. in CUL. The year 1835, which is obviously correct, has been added in another hand.

23. Apparently a diminutive of Emerson's own coinage.

me to control by my will what we call (fondly) the moment of inspiration. O no I am its reverent slave. I watch & watch & hail its aurora from afar. Great words you will think for little works. Be it so. We must make much of our all, be it ever so little. And the knowledge of very unfit preparation for my three last Lectures [24] made me say at Plymouth that I could not come again till they were done. Then as to your deliberate visit to Concord could you not most wise Lidian defer it until December! I deny that it will take any horse from the first of March to the first of May to go from Plymouth to Concord. Really my dear friend we live several miles *on this side* the Ohio.

Ah Lidian Lidian go to bed betimes! Do you sit up writing letters till three in the morn? So shall I never have that brave Spartan wife I pray for. This is a poor sign of that philosophy of action that was to be commenced.

And then the dark eyes could not read clearly the sentence about recent love wounds.[25] That word *recent* only respected the long past, it did not touch the present. And whatever I said, referred to some page or pages of my Day Book where is most pompously recorded the homage its author paid to bright village eyes. Will you not honor me, my sibyl, by visiting my lowly study & reading the page. Right welcome shall you be & it is the only way I can think of to reconcile this divided empire which you & my inkstand both claim in me. O if you could hear Inkstand's silent reproaches addressed to me touching you. Inkstand says he will not budge one foot asks how I dare imagine the thing. asks me if I have not the eye to see his roots in this paternal soil whether I know not the voice "There where thou art, there where thou remainest, work." In fine Inkstand concludes that unless Lidian can trundle Plymouth rock a score of miles northward, she must even quit it & come & sit down by Concord Battle-Bridge. In reward of that grace, Inkstand is full of promises of verses & histories writ in & by her love.

Now must I tell Lidian why I play with this question? I never incline to make influence the measure of the fitness of actions. For me to measure my influence would be to deal with infinitesimal quantities & I might commit suicide. God who makes the influence of the great, little, & of the little, great, takes care of that cattle. I seek rather to act simply; to live where I can possess my soul, & considering that where I am put, there I am due, I do not forsake my native corners without manifest

24. See a note on Feb. 1, 1835.
25. This may refer to a letter which I have not found.

reason. For me to go to Plymouth would be to cripple me of some important resources & not so far as I see to do any work I cannot do here. And you, my dear friend, have paid much of your debt there & when you see some souls here that are now "unwillingly deprived of truth" will thirst to come. So do love

Waldo E.

To Lydia Jackson, Concord, February 17, 1835[26]

Concord
17 Feb

Good Lidian for the letter I have got, I shall come & see thee Thursday morn, say at 11 o'clock or possibly at 10. Think not my own eyes so dim that they did not find out the true tint of thine for Mr Goodwin[27] told my mother that L. had black eyes; I declared to her that they were gray. But they make a dark impression, O sibyl! I see I must rehearse to you that conversation upon the future of the affections. I did not say what you have put into my mouth. Thanks for Hectors noble sentiment & Jean Paul's. which far be it from me to gainsay.

Charles has decided to come to Concord the first of March.[28] How soon will you decide to come? and abide? Two houses have been offered me last week on easy terms but neither will serve us. But what signifies a house, my queen! George Fox lived in a tree.[29] But better than house & lands shall follow true love forevermore. So away to John Milton. Goodbye dear Lidian.

W.

26. MS owned by Mr. Elliot Forbes; ph. in CUL. The correct year, 1835, has been added in another hand.

27. Probably Hersey Bradford Goodwin, a native of Plymouth, who had for several years been colleague pastor with Ezra Ripley at Concord (*cf.* Apr. 22? 1830).

28. Charles Emerson had told William on Feb. 12 (MS owned by Dr. Haven Emerson):

"I have written today a letter to Mr. Hoar accepting his proposal to have me remove to Concord. For how long time it will be I do not say . . .

"I go away from Boston week after next. Until I get married the place will be a poor place for me to live in . . . But Waldo I trust will hire or build him a house there & by & by we shall have a country an Arcadia of our own, & you & Susan will cry to come & live with us — "

29. Emerson may have got this from William Sewel, *The History of . . . the . . . Quakers*, Philadelphia, 1823 (I, 40), a copy of which was given to his brother Charles, in 1832, as the inscription shows, and is still in the Emerson House, at Concord; or from Carlyle's "Sartor Resartus" (*Fraser's*, IX, 665). That he knew Sewel is clear from *Journals*, II, 498–499 (July? 1832). For the lectures on both Fox and Milton, see a note on Feb. 1, 1835.

To Lydia Jackson, Concord, March 2, 1835 [30]

Concord
Monday 2 March

Dear Lidian

I am quite impatient of not writing to you but a visit time & strength-consuming to Waltham a heavy cold riding like the night mare my head & throat, & two biographies of Burke with 8 volumes of his works to read mark & inwardly digest, — quite eat up my hours & minutes.[31] Meantime his great Shade stalks round & frowns upon my temerity. Yet I tell him what can avail my pins against his ethereal mail adamantean proof.[32] And if as seems inevitable I only show my own weakness on this occasion I promise him I will atone by hereafter uttering a word truer wiser to his most deserving name. Thursday night, if I am well, will release me from my present strings, & promises me the happiness of more of your company So live well walk much write a little to your friend. And remember me to Mrs Bliss [33] & Miss Russell.[34] I refresh myself between whiles with thinking that you will live with me soon all the time.[35]

30. MS owned by RWEMA; ph. in CUL. The year 1835, added in another hand, is clearly correct.

31. Charles wrote to William, Mar. 3, 1835 (MS owned by Dr. Haven Emerson), that, in spite of a cold, Emerson was working hard at his lecture on Edmund Burke, the last of his series. I have not found a newspaper notice of this lecture. But Elizabeth Peabody heard it delivered (Mar. 5), as well as several others earlier in the course, and wrote her praise of them all to her sister Mary in letters of Jan.–Mar. of this year (owned by Mr. Horace Mann). Emerson, she said, promised to lend her the lectures to read to Dr. Channing.

32. Milton, *Samson Agonistes,* ll. 133–134.

33. *Cf.* a note on Mar. *c.* 4, 1835. On Feb. 25, 1835, Elizabeth Peabody, who was well abreast of most events of social or intellectual interest in the Boston of that day, wrote her sister Mary about going to tea at Mrs. Bliss's on the 24th to meet Lydia Jackson: "I found a Miss Russell from Plymouth there — & Miss Jackson was up stairs finishing a letter to Waldo (who is in Concord writing his lecture for tomorrow evening). — Mrs. B. & Miss R. (who are old friends from babyhood of Miss Jackson) were so earnest that I should like her. . . . By & bye she descended — she looks *very refined* but neither beautiful or elegant — and very frail — & as if her mind wore out her body — she was *unaffected* but *peculiar.* — When she came down I was reading a letter which Thomas Carlyle wrote to Waldo Emerson . . . She sat down by me — and we had a beautiful talk about a variety of most intellectual & spiritual things — And I should think she had the rare characteristic of genius — inexhaustible originality. . . . I stayed with Miss Jackson till ten oclock — & we parted to meet again as friends." (MS owned by Mr. Horace Mann.)

34. Presumably Mary Howland Russell, of Plymouth, who appears frequently in later letters. *Cf.* especially July 3, 1837, to Ruth Haskins Emerson.

35. The letter ends at the bottom of the first page of the MS without signature.

To Lydia Jackson, Concord, March *c.* 4, 1835 [36]

Concord

I hope our poor town whose name I duly superscribe to my epistles will not come to read Discord through Lidians lenses gray. The innocent river flows through the flats under my eye yet unknowing that his friends friend loves the surly sea's roar better than his childish murmuring. Ah he would look me pathetically in the face, did he imagine. that I his almost sole votary, (for I fear he hath not on his banks another watcher of his poetical aspects,) meditated a desertion of his gentle side. I have promised him a song [37] too, whenever the tardy, callow muse shall new moult her feathers. River large & inkstand little, deep & deep would blend their voices.

Magical fitting of our eye to nature, that a few square miles of rocks bushes & water should present us under the changing light with such resplendent pictures & ever new transformations. Is n't it, Lidian? Why, Plymouth's but a seabeach. What can you say for it? Let me hear let me read your sea song.

I send Carlyles letter [38] for Mrs Bliss,[39] & Charles will bring her the 3[d] Vol. of the Friend.[40] Lidian what have you done with my Plymouth sermon. I forgot twice to take it away. All that is important is to keep it out of sight. If you have left it at P. do not let it be lent again & if you have it in Boston seal it up for me. I have a copy of it that I shall presently finish & bring it to more connected & luminous conclusions, I hope, than when at P. I cannot stay next Friday O magnet mine, for, Saturday night I am to lecture at Waltham & Sunday preach there on an old agreement, which abridges my brief week. One thing more among the

36. MS owned by Mr. William H. Forbes; ph. in CUL. The date " March 1835 " has been added to Emerson's undated heading. Mention of the lecture and sermon to be delivered at Waltham on the following Saturday and Sunday seems to prove pretty definitely that this letter precedes that of Mar. 8; and the same passage indicates an earlier day than Friday the 6th, and apparently, than the 5th. On the other hand, if this letter was written in March it must have been later than Mar. 2, when Emerson wrote: " I am quite impatient of not writing to you . . ."

37. It is not clear, I think, whether Emerson was already planning his poem " Musketaquid."

38. Emerson still had only the one letter from Carlyle. *Cf.* a note on Jan. 23, 1835. A note on Mar. 2 shows, however, that the lone letter had a growing circle of readers and admirers.

39. This letter is addressed to Lydia Jackson at Mrs. Bliss's, Winthrop Place. Mrs. Bliss, who had been a girlhood friend of Lydia Jackson, appears in later years as Elizabeth Davis Bancroft (*cf.* her *Letters from England,* 1904, pp. v–vi) .

40. *Cf.* Jan. 4, 1830.

facts, — please never write my name with that prefix *Rev.* Have I not told you, dear Lidian, that I meet much more reverence than I know what to do with? I never asked this of any before, yet Charles & most of my particular friends as if by consent write me simple Mr — And so having despatched this budget of most momentous trifles I pray to be commended to your friends — to Miss Russell first, as my oldest friend, & next to Mrs Bliss, with sad regret that I must lose the kind society she had designed for me. My mother taxed me for not carrying her love to you as she had enjoined me. Your lover,

Waldo E.

To Andrew L. Russell, Concord? March *c.* 8, 1835

[See the letter of Mar. 8, 1835, to Lydia Jackson.]

To Lucia Jane Russell, Concord, March 8, 1835

[Miss Lucia R. Briggs informs me that the original MS of this letter is in her possession; and she has supplied a typed copy (in CUL). Printed, not quite completely, in *The Plymouth Journal and the Antiquarian Record,* July 22, 1925 (ph. in CUL), where it is without date but is described as belonging to the year 1835. Mrs. George R. Briggs, Sr., writes me that she printed the text in *The Plymouth Journal* from a copy. In the letter of the same date to Lydia Jackson, Emerson inclosed this "letter to Lucia whose correspondent I am proud to be." Probably his correspondence with her had commenced earlier, as a letter from a schoolgirl containing comments on her compositions is endorsed in his hand as from Lucia Russell, Apr., 1834. Lucia was a younger sister of Mary Howland Russell (*cf.* a note on July 3, 1837, to Ruth Haskins Emerson, where an account of the family is cited).]

To Lydia Jackson, Concord, March 8, 1835 [41]

Sunday Eve.

My dear friend,

I enclose to your kind care a note to Andrew R [42] acceding to his proposition to go to Plymouth, if he will let me go on the

41. MS owned by RWEMA; ph. in CUL. "March, 1835" has been added to the original heading in another hand. Two letters from Charles Emerson to William (both owned by Dr. Haven Emerson) fix the date definitely as Mar. 8. On Mar. 3 Charles wrote: "Miss Jackson is to come to Concord next week & spend several days with Mother"; and on the 13th of the same month he sent this news: "Miss Lydia Jackson is paying a visit to Mother & returns to Boston tomorrow." The "next week" referred to was the week beginning Sunday, Mar. 8, and the visit was to end, according to Charles, on Saturday, Mar. 14.

42. For Andrew L. Russell, the Plymouth ironmaster and later admirer of John Sterling, see Feb. 26? 1842.

31 March. and enclosing a letter to Lucia whose correspondent I am proud to be. I have returned this eve. from Waltham where Mrs Ripley promises herself to come to C. & see you Wednesday P. M. I grieve that my poor tame little town hath his gentle back & sides covered this day with new fleeces deforming defacing for I would fain show his cleanest morning face to Lidian. Do not depend on me Tuesday evening for I may not get into town till after 9 'o clock & in that case shall not see you till Wednesday morn' at 9, when I will come with horse & chaise. If you wish to bring any trunk or box which you cannot put in the chaise I will see that the stage brings it in the P. M. I trust ere this you are wholly well in heart & head & frame & that you love

Waldo E.

Call, if you can, upon Mrs Ralph Haskins opposite you, for she is to leave town in a few days for her house in Roxbury & tell her that we had not time to see her Friday. Will you not O Lidian?

To Thomas Carlyle, Boston, March 11, 1835 [43]

Boston 11 March 1835

Mr Thomas Carlyle

My dear Sir,

I have much pleasure in making you acquainted with Mr Henry Barnard [44] of Hartford, Conn., who has been induced by his interest in y^r writings to seek an introduction to you. I am happy in rendering Mr Barnard the same good office M. D'Eichthal rendered me.[45] I trust he will be as fortunate in finding you at home.

Your friend & servant

R. Waldo Emerson.

To Thomas Carlyle, Concord, March 12, 1835

[Printed in the *New-York Tribune,* Oct. 22, 1882, p. 3; reprinted in *C–E Corr.,* 1883.]

To William Emerson, Boston, March 14, 1835

[WmE List.]

43. MS copy, not in Emerson's hand, owned by RWEMA; ph. in CUL. On the same small sheet is a copy of the letter of Apr. 26, 1839, also to Carlyle.

44. Barnard was admitted to the bar in 1835 but went to Europe for travel and study before commencing practice.

45. For Gustave d'Eichthal, member of a family of Jewish bankers at Paris, see a note on Carlyle, Aug. 12, 1834 (*C–E Corr.*), and *cf.* Apr. 16 and 21, 1833.

To Thomas Carlyle, Concord? April? 6? 1835

[According to Moncure D. Conway, *Thomas Carlyle,* p. 102, and to Samuel Longfellow, *Life of Henry Wadsworth Longfellow,* n. d. (c. 1891), I, 208, Longfellow carried a letter of introduction from Emerson when he called on Carlyle. He sailed for Europe on Apr. 10, 1835 (James Taft Hatfield, *New Light on Longfellow,* 1933, p. 32). A letter from Robert C. Waterston to Longfellow adds much to the probability that Emerson wrote on Apr. 6 (Irving T. Richards, in *PMLA,* LI, 1127, Dec., 1936). Presumably Longfellow presented the introduction to Jane Carlyle when he made his first call and found her husband absent (*ibid.,* p. 1129).]

To George Champlin Shepard, Concord? April 8, 1835

[Shepard, Apr. 27, 1835, acknowledges this and Emerson's letter of Apr. 25. One or both these letters from Emerson had to do with a note given by his brother Edward to Shepard's wife. *Cf.* Dec. 16 and 18, 1834.]

To William? Ellery? Channing, Concord? April 12? 1835

[Mentioned in the letter of Apr. 12, 1835. Perhaps Emerson wrote to Dr. Channing about the scheme for a new magazine, which, some years later, resulted in the founding of *The Dial* (*cf.* the letters of Mar. 12 and Apr. 30, 1835, to Carlyle).]

To Frederic Henry Hedge, Concord, April 12, 1835 [46]

Concord, 12 Apr.

My dear Sir

I enclose the note for Mr Channing [47] and lo! our Sibyl whom so hardly her own friends can bring to unclose her lips has writ all this long letter to a stranger because I quoted your Thursday's remark to her. The writer, you understand, is my Aunt Mary. I hope you will not go away without coming here, though I shall not press it, knowing the " manysidedness " of a removal. Only come if you can, & remember at Bangor I shall depend much on being one of your correspondents. Incapable as I am of society, I yet grieve very much that you should leave our neighborhood.

Your friend,

R. W. Emerson.

46. MS owned by RWEMA; ph. in CUL. The superscription is to Hedge at Cambridge. The year 1834, supplied by an unknown hand, is an error. In the letter of Apr. 30, 1835, Emerson wrote Carlyle that Hedge was just leaving to settle in Maine, and Hedge did remove to Bangor in that year.

47. See Apr. 12? 1835.

To Lydia Jackson? April? c. 21? 1835 [48]

[We]bster Natures own son [who] a pew, & afterward spoke at the table a few words of truth & soberness, which were like a cup of cold water to a man thirsting amid hogsheads of lavender. I am a great deal more sorry than vexed, for my debt to Everett is great. When a boy I followed him everywhere & drank every word with full delight & cannot but wonder

. . . . .

no more. Now she will respo[nd] sentiment you utter, with the s[implicity of] a c[hild] but Rousseau would not detect so quick the slightest error in sentiment. And so though we flout her, & contradict her, & compassionate her whims, we all stand in awe of her penetration, her indignant eloquent conscience, her poetic & commanding Reason. So much for the old Aunt & did I not tell you that whilst Lidian's

To William Emerson, Concord? April 24? 1835 [49]

Dear William

It is a long time since I have had so much as the pleasure of your signature or superscription much less any letter. But I trust to find at Geo. B. E.'s this eve a [50][large pac]quet waiting. Is it not so? Here

48. MS owned by RWEMA; ph. in CUL. Only a badly mutilated fragment remains — apparently somewhat more than one-third of a leaf, with writing on both sides. The order in which the two sides were written is by no means certain. As for the date, abundant evidence shows it is almost certainly about Apr. 21, 1835. Emerson wrote in *Journals,* III, 470 ff., a similar comment on the speeches of Edward Everett and Daniel Webster at the Lexington celebration on Apr. 20, 1835; and in her letter of Apr. 24, 1835, to William Emerson, his mother wrote: " Last Monday Waldo, & Charles, went to Lexington to hear Mr Everetts oration — but they were not as much delighted as they formerly were with the orator — They were more pleased with Mr Webster, at the dinner, & others." Internal evidence also tends to show that the letter was addressed to Lydia Jackson, to whom the information about Mary Moody Emerson would very naturally have been sent in the spring of 1835. The reference to her in the third person rather adds weight to the evidence, as there is a similar use of her name in the letter of Feb. 13, 1835, and Emerson would not very probably have used the name " Lidian " alone in a letter to any other person at this time.

49. MS owned by RWEMA; ph. in CUL. Excerpt I is in Cabot, I, 229. This letter follows, on the same sheet, a letter to William from his mother dated Concord, Apr. 24, 1835, in the final paragraph of which is this evidence pointing to the 24th as the probable date of Emerson's own part: " Waldo is expecting the stage directly & he is to take this to Boston." That the date of his part could not have been more than a few days later is clear from the New York postmark of Apr. 30.

50. Badly mutilated by the seal. Though parts of nearly all the letters remain, the reading is conjectural.

we live or sleep as well as usual — for Charles says that Concord society seems hastening back to annihilation Yet here have we ourself even [1]hope to hire a house & set up a fireside next September — Perhaps Charles also and a year hence shall we not build a house on Grandfathers hill facing Wachusett & Monadnoc & the setting sun[1] When can we hope to see you? Susan surely cannot omit her vernal visit to her parents the old & the new so give her my love & say we expect her.

Waldo —

To George Champlin Shepard, Concord? April 25, 1835

[See the note on Apr. 8, 1835.]

To Charles Thomas Jackson, Concord? April *c.* 25, 1835

[Described in Jackson, Apr. 26 (1835), as an invitation to pass the night of May 6 with Emerson at Concord.]

To Thomas Carlyle, Concord, April 30, 1835

[MS listed and partly quoted in Anderson Auction Co., Dec. 1–2, 1909; printed in *C–E Corr.,* 1883.]

To Lydia Jackson, Concord? *c.* May? 1835?

[Partly copied in *Journals,* IV, 29–30 (Mar. 21, 1836). A phrase from this letter was printed in Conway, *Autobiography,* 1904, I, 147.]

To William Emerson, Boston, June 5, 1835

[WmE List.]

To Elizabeth Palmer Peabody, Concord? June 12, 1835

[Bluebook List. This is the earliest trace I have found of Emerson's correspondence with the well-known Transcendental teacher, author, publisher, and bookseller. *Cf.* notes on the letter of Aug. 3, 1835, to her.]

To John Gardiner Ladd, Concord? June *c.* 14, 1835

[Charles Emerson to William, June 17, endorsed 1835 (owned by Dr. Haven Emerson): " I had last week the pleasure of receiving your letter forwarded by J. G. Ladd. The youth himself we have not yet seen, although Waldo has written to him to come . . ." John Gardiner Ladd was the son of Emerson's cousin John Haskins Ladd (*cf.* Apr. 18, 1828).]

To Lydia Jackson, Concord? June? 22? 1835

[Mentioned, with statement of a part of the contents, in *Journals,* III, 493 (June 22? 1835).]

To Frederic Henry Hedge, Concord, June 25, 1835[51]

x In my experience 'good society' is such an optical illusion that I think it should be classed with Bacon's Idols of the Cave.[52] Carlyle affirms that it is extinct[53] Charles Emerson affirms that it has just now begun to exist — Greek & Roman knew it not — To me it seems as if the order of things did thwart it so universally & steadfastly by death, sickness, removals, unfitness, ceremony, or what not, that a design to hinder it must be suspected. Everybody is indulged with an opportunity or two of equal & hearty communication; enough to persuade each man of his potential heaven. But it seems also as if none had any more. For the first interview between cultivated persons is commonly the best, & it is surprizing in how few hours the results of years can be exhausted. And besides if it were not ungrateful to wise friends whom the heart knoweth by name, we should sometimes say that this happiness of "waxing wiser than we were" by conversation, did not befal us according to the wisdom of our company but by quite other & indefinable causes affecting our own moods. I think we owe most recreation & most memorable thoughts to very unpromising gossips x x But to utter one word disparaging the chief good of humanity — a perfect friendship, — I hold it blasphemy — x x If Carlyle comes not, we shall all be glad of Mr Buove's project.[54] I hope by the middle of July to hear from the Scot,[55] & if he should come, a Journal must be his main dependence — so that he wishes to settle here. x x Sometime in August

51. MS owned by RWEMA; ph. in CUL. This is an incomplete copy in Cabot's hand. A paraphrase of nearly half of the portion of the letter I print is in *Journals,* III, 496–497, where it is followed by Emerson's statement, "I copied the above from memory."

52. In *Novum Organum,* tr. Peter Shaw, London, 1818, I, 15. This work is mentioned in an entry of May 13, 1835, in *Journals* (III, 477).

53. In "Sartor Resartus" (*Fraser's,* IX, 672).

54. Presumably this Buove had projected a journal to be edited by Hedge or at least to serve the same purpose Hedge had in mind. In the letter of Apr. 30, 1835, Emerson had told Carlyle of a plan for *The Transcendentalist,* or *The Spiritual Inquirer,* or the like, to be edited by Hedge, who, however, was now going to Maine and wished Carlyle to be editor.

55. On June 27 of this year Carlyle wrote that he did not incline to come to America in the near future but was still undecided (*C–E Corr.*).

I am to read a discourse to the Institute on the means of inspiring a taste for English Literature — or some kindred topic.[56] Then in September I am to read an Historical Discourse on the 200th anniversary of the settlement of Concord.[57] And in the winter I must give 8 or 10 lectures before the Diffusion Society.[58] Moreover I please myself with a purpose of publishing by & by a book of Essays [59] chiefly upon Natural Ethics with the aim of bringing a pebble or two to the edification of the new temple whilst so many wise hands are demolishing the old. But our gravest plans look so comical sometimes that we can scarce believe that we ourselves are in earnest & I certainly never have one touching myself whose defeat would much annoy me. Some day, some age yet to be unrolled from eternity, we shall all *be* something. Then to have *done* anything will seem less. x x

To William Emerson, Concord, July 27, 1835 [60]

Concord, [I] 27 July, 1835.[I]

Dear William,

I believe I am in your debt for a letter but not deeply as it was not very long. Mr Ripley [61] shall not go hence without an assurance that we are alive. [II] Has Charles told you that I have dodged the doom of building & have bought the Coolidge house in Concord with the expectation of entering it next September. It is in a mean place & cannot be fine until trees & flowers give it a character of its own. But we shall crowd so many books & papers, &, if possible, wise friends, into it that it shall have as much wit as it can carry.[II] How is the little boy? [62] & how his mother? doubtless they make sunshine enough for your eyes. If you want a beautiful book to read to Susan certain true & yet pleas-

56. See Aug. 3, 1835, to G. B. Emerson.

57. *Cf.* Sept. 17, 1835.

58. The *Boston Daily Advertiser* of Nov. 3 printed the brief official outline of the course on English literature before the Society for the Diffusion of Useful Knowledge; and the same paper, Nov. 5, 1835 — Jan. 14, 1836, contained announcements of the individual lectures for Nov. 5, 12, 26; Dec. 10, 17, 24, 31; and Jan. 7 and 14. "Chaucer" (Nov. 26) was the only title given.

59. Probably Emerson was thinking of *Nature,* which was to be published in the following year.

60. MS owned by RWEMA; ph. in CUL. Excerpts I–III are in Cabot, I, 230.

61. Probably either Samuel Ripley, of Waltham, or George Ripley.

62. As his gravestone, in the Sleepy Hollow Cemetery at Concord, shows, William Emerson, Jr., was born June 18, 1835. The same date is mentioned in Ruth Haskins Emerson, Feb. 11, 1839.

ant as Miss Edgeworth's Tales,[63] read Miss Peabody's "Record of a School" (Mr Alcott's) just published.[64] To the parents of the little Willy I cannot doubt it will be engaging. Coleridges Table Talk [65] is, I think, as good as Spence's or Selden's or Luther's; better.

Your affectionate brother

Waldo

Mother says she cannot write today. She has been inquiring for a woman in vain. Nancy [66] is to live with me 15 Sept. We have seen nothing of Mrs Mason.[67] I spent a fortnight just now in the library at Cambridge & have just returned. [III]My house costs me $3500. & may next summer cost me 4, or 500. more to enlarge or finish. The seller alleges that it cost him 7800.[III] I am quite sure it need not cost so much I give about its value.[68] I can't think of a thing more.

To Charles Sprague, Concord, July 27, 1835

[Sprague, Boston, Aug. 7, 1835, acknowledges "your very flattering letter of the 27 ultimo," and says he cannot furnish the ode for which Emerson has asked him; he is done writing verses, but would gladly give his services as a cashier. I conjecture that Emerson desired the ode for the Concord celebration of Sept. 12. Sprague, cashier of a bank in Boston, appears in several later letters.]

63. Maria Edgeworth's *Novels and Tales,* London, 1832, soon reappeared in a New York edition.

64. Advertised for sale in the *Evening Mercantile Journal,* Boston, July 20, 1835. Emerson recorded in *Journals* a few days later (III, 509) that he had read the book with delight and, on Oct. 21 following, that he had had a visit from Alcott, a "wise man." This meeting must have occurred on Oct. 17 and 18, though Oct. 18 is given, apparently, as the first day in Sanborn and Harris, *A. Bronson Alcott,* 1893, I, 240–241, where Alcott's diary is copied. Emerson had heard of Alcott from George Partridge Bradford as early as July 3, 1835 (see *Journals,* III, 501). But both Emerson and his brother Charles were well informed about the intellectual currents and eddies of Boston and could hardly have failed to hear of the Temple School some months earlier.

65. At least the first volume of *Specimens of the Table Talk of the Late Samuel Taylor Coleridge,* New York, 1835 (the first American edition), is still in Emerson's library at the Antiquarian House, Concord.

66. *Cf.* Nov. 23, 1834, and a note on May 8, 1838.

67. Her death, at Gloucester, Mass., is recorded in the *Boston Daily Advertiser* of Sept. 16 following, where she is described as "Dona Maria Benito Dorado de Mason, wife of Sidney Mason, Esq. U. S. Consul at St. Johns, P. R. aged 33."

68. William Emerson, Aug. 9, 1835, reported a Concordian's opinion that the Coolidge house was the best-built one in the town and was a bargain. It is true, however, that its location on low land makes it still, in spite of the addition Emerson later built, somewhat inconspicuous.

To George Barrell Emerson, Concord, August 3, 1835 [69]

Concord 3 August 1835

Dear George,

Mr Miles's letter to me asking a lecture for the Institute named the 20th Aug. I see by todays paper that I should speak on Saturday 22d The Historical Discourse at Concord, (12 Sept.) & some private engagements about 20 August, make me unwilling to deliver this Lecture one day later than the 20th Can you not crowd me into that day? If not possible, I much prefer the 21 to the 22d

Yours affectionately,

R. Waldo Emerson.

To Elizabeth Palmer Peabody, Concord, August 3, 1835 [70]

Concord 3 Aug. 1835. x x I kept your letter to read it to my brother Charles whom I tried to persuade to answer it as it concerned him as principal me only as proxy in the alleged heresy. But as he affects to

69. MS owned by Mr. Harry F. R. Dolan; ph. in CUL. The *Boston Daily Advertiser*, Aug. 3, 20, and 21, 1835, shows that the date of the lecture by Emerson on "The Best Mode of Inspiring a Correct Taste in English Literature" was changed, as here suggested, from Aug. 22 to Aug. 20, the same day on which William Henry Furness, Emerson's friend, had lectured in the morning. *The Introductory Discourse and the Lectures Delivered before the American Institute of Instruction, in Boston, August, 1834,* Boston, 1835, pp. xiv–xv, shows that George B. Emerson was elected in 1834 as one of the vice-presidents of the Institute and Solomon P. Miles as a corresponding secretary. The similar volume for Aug., 1835, published in 1836, does not print Emerson's address but merely mentions it (p. x). Probably Emerson objected to publication of his lecture, as he often did in later years.

70. MS owned by RWEMA; ph. in CUL. This is an incomplete copy in Cabot's hand. Excerpts I and II are in *Journals,* III, 530–532. It is sometimes stated that Elizabeth Peabody once studied under Emerson. However that may be, his friendship with her seems to have had its effective beginning about the time his attention was called to her part in Alcott's school, presumably not long before June 12, 1835, the date of the earliest letter to her of which I have found any trace, though it is clear from letters she wrote to her sisters (MSS owned by Mr. Horace Mann) that she had for more than a year observed his doings with great interest. In an unpublished entry of a notebook dated 1848 but written over a period of years, Emerson drew her character:

"A wonderful literary head, with extraordinary rapidity of association, and a methodising faculty which enabled her to weave surprising theories very fast, & very finely, from slight materials. Of another sex, she would have been a first-rate academician; and, as it was, she had the ease & scope & authority of a learned professor or high literary celebrity in her talk. I told her I thought she ought to live a thousand years, her schemes of study & the necessities of reading which her inquiries implied, required so much. She was superior, & really amiable, but took no pains to

esteem such speculation out of his cure, I must at least make my own disclaimers, & express my thanks for the letter.

I am afraid I said some yeas & nays at random in the Chapel at Cambridge [71] now that you repeat what you said. [I]I should certainly not have denied, awake, that the spiritual contains the intellectual nature, or that the moral is prior in God's order to the intellectual; which I believe. The two attributes of wisdom & goodness always face & always approach each other. Each when perfect becomes the other. Yet to the moral nature belongs sovereignty, & so we have an instinctive faith that to it all things shall be added, that the moral nature being righted, the circulations of the Universe take effect thro' the man as a member in its place, & so he learns sciences after a natural or divine way. A good deed conspires with all nature, as " the hand sang with the voice " [72] in the angels' concert, but there's a kind of falsehood in the enunciation of a chemical or astronomical law by an unprincipled savant But whilst all considerate persons incline to this general confession, there still stand the uncontested facts that in our experience is almost no proportioned cultivation; the blacksmith has a strong arm, the dancer a strong foot; great proficiency in the mathematics may coexist with extreme moral insensibility, & the splendours of holiness with a contempt for learning, Such lobsided one eyed half men are we now, & such a yawning difference between our esse & our posse. I am content to find these differences. I am content to wait long before many refractory facts. A great tendency I like better than a small revelation & hate to be imprisoned in premature theories. I have no appetite such as Sir Thos. Browne avows for " difficultest mysteries that my faith may have some exercise " [73] but I had rather not understand in God's world than understand thro' & thro' in Bentham's [74] or Spurzheim's. [I] I sympathize with

make herself personally agreeable, & was not neat, — & offended." (Typescript *Journals.*)

It may be, I think, that the present letter continues a discussion inspired by her recently published record of the school, which Emerson had, at any rate, read with delight (see a note on July 27, 1835, to William Emerson).

71. I am uncertain what this occasion was; but in *Journals,* III, 516, Emerson mentions " my own sayings two nights ago at Dr. Willard's " — presumably sometime between July 24 and 28. I conjecture that Willard was Sidney Willard, earlier a professor at Harvard.

72. *Paradise Regained,* I, 171–172.

73. Apparently Emerson had in mind a passage in *Religio Medici:* " As for those wingy mysteries in divinity . . . I desire to exercise my faith in the difficultest point . . ." (*Miscellaneous Works,* Cambridge, Mass., 1831, pp. 19–20).

74. On Bentham and the Utilitarians Emerson was in sympathy with Carlyle's view (*cf.* " Sartor Resartus," *Fraser's,* IX, 673–674), if not influenced by it.

II what you say of your aversion at being confined to Swedenborg's associations[75] & I confirm myself with similar declarations whenever 'my critical acumen' with which you make yourself merry, is at fault in the great Life.

You have studied much the character of Jesus & I read with pleasure every considered expression of praise of him.[76] But perfect in the sense of complete man he seems not to me to be, but a very exclusive & partial development of the moral element such as the great Compensation that balances the universe provides to repair accumulated depravity. The weight of his ethical sentences deserves more than all the consideration they have, & his life is one original pure beam of truth but a perfect man should exhibit all the traits of humanity & should expressly recognize the intellectual nature. Socrates I call a complete universal man fulfilling all the conditions of man's existence. Sublime as he is I compare him not as an ethical teacher to Christ, but his life is more humane.II x x x

To Thomas Carlyle, Concord? August, 1835

[Mentioned in Oct. 7, 1835; an introduction for Lydia Maria Child, who, however, did not make her intended voyage to England.]

To Lemuel Shattuck, Concord, August 31, 1835[77]

Concord, 31 Aug. 1835.

My dear Sir,

Can you not help me to some information respecting the original division of lands? Did not every settler receive some portion of

75. In *Nature,* to be published a little more than a year later, and in other writings, Emerson doubtless owes something to Swedenborg's theory of correspondences; but in *Representative Men* he testifies to his aversion to the narrow theological way in which the mystic worked out his theory.

76. This paragraph points clearly enough toward the Divinity School address. *Cf.* also *Journals,* III, 518.

77. MS owned by Dr. Max Farrand; ph. in CUL. Emerson had promised the committee on June 29 (possibly in a letter I have not found) that he would prepare an address for the celebration of the second centennial of Concord (*Journals,* III, 497). Charles seems to have urged his brother to make thorough preparation and to have brought back to him whatever suggestions he could from a similar celebration at a neighboring town. In his letter to William, July 25 (owned by Dr. Haven Emerson), he wrote: "I hope Waldo will search well the Concord Records for texts to his Commemorative talk in September. He says he shall." And in the same letter he reports his presence, with Rockwood Hoar, at the celebration of the centennial of

land without money on the single condition of his improving it? Yet the Record which you have copied p. 34 of your History seems to show that there were poor men not landholders & no fee of land was granted them. If nothing is known of the first distribution of land in Concord & the principles on which it was divided is not any thing preserved touching the same matter in other towns. Pray tell me if you know any thing on this subject. Respectfully, Your obliged serv^t

R. Waldo Emerson.

To Lemuel Shattuck, Concord, September 17, 1835 [78]

Concord, 17 Sept. 1835.

My dear Sir,

The Committee of Arrangements or rather I believe the town by subscription propose to print the Discourse delivered by me last Saturday.[79] I am to give it next Monday & it will be out in two or

---

the incorporation of Acton, where he was stirred by the reading of some of the votes and resolutions of that town in Revolutionary times.

Emerson's later letters of 1835 to Lemuel Shattuck show pretty fully his dealings with the author of *A History of the Town of Concord,* Boston and Concord, 1835, a work in paged proof, apparently, at the time of the present letter. On Sept. 1 Shattuck answered that he had seen no account showing that land was granted merely on condition of improvement. On p. 34 of *A History* as published Shattuck quoted a regulation granting "pooremen" the use of the "commons," "till they be able to purchase for themselves, or untill the townsmen shall see cause to take it from them." A letter from Shattuck dated July 14, 1835, mentioning the return of the "sheets" of the Concord history and some letters Shattuck had received from various correspondents and was then sending to Emerson, may indicate that there was at least one earlier letter from Emerson; but what it shows clearly is that there had been a conversation between the two men on the subject of Concord historical records. For a detailed sketch of Shattuck, see his own compilation, *Memorials of the Descendants of William Shattuck,* Boston, 1855, pp. 302–312.

78. MS owned by the Henry E. Huntington Library; ph. in CUL.

79. That the people of the town were not unanimous in their approval of the plans made for the program is clear from the *Concord Freeman* of Sept. 12, the day of the celebration. Under the caption "Another '*Lafayette*' Celebration!" a writer who signed himself "A Native-born Citizen of Concord" recalled that when La Fayette visited the town the common people were snubbed, and he predicted that they would get the same treatment at the hands of the "aristocrats" in charge of the second centennial celebration, not one of whom, said he, was a native and citizen of Concord. A refutation of this charge was published in the same paper for Sept. 19 by "*The Wife of a Middlesex Farmer.*" Meantime the *Concord Freeman* had little else about the celebration. But Charles Emerson, always a loyal recorder of his brother's achievements, wrote a full and, doubtless, just account of the occasion in his letter to William (owned by Dr. Haven Emerson):

three weeks thereafter.[80] Pray let the History come out first, & then if in any way my poor Commentary can affect it at all, I think the History

---

" Concord Sept. 14, 1835

" Dear William

" Last Saturday we celebrated our two hundredth municipal birthday. It was a bright day & men & women wore pleased & excited faces. At about ½ past 11 o'clock we found ourselves in the Church. There we had music enough — voluntary, & ode, & psalm, & ode again, & original hymn. The psalm was . . . from the old New England version, written chiefly by John Eliot, & used in the Churches from 1640. It was a noble ancient strain, & had the more effect from being ' deaconed ' out, a line at a time, after the fashion of our grandfathers, & sung by the whole congregation. The orator occupied about an hour & forty five minutes with a discourse which none but the children I think found too long. It was a faithful historical sketch of this Town — honor due was done unto the brave company of First Settlers, Peter Bulkeley, Simon Willard, & their faithful associates; the harmony with which the negotiation was conducted with the Indians suggested the name of the town which it received from Peter Bulkeley. There was much said of the red men the original lords of the soil — of their astonishing physical powers, before the blight of English civilization came nigh them, of their manly friendship toward the whites, & by & by of the prophetic fears of the best among them of the decay & extinction of their race; and these prophetic fears were accomplished to the uttermost.

" ' Their fires are out by wood & shore
Their pleasant springs are dry — '

Then came the record of the doings & counsellings of the good town of Concord down to the epoch of the Revolution; — here the quiet river of its fortunes again opened into a capacious sea, or rather, swollen by tributary waters, rushed over the rocky barriers that would have choked its course, & this triumph achieved, held on its modest noiseless way.

" The wise invention of ' a Town,' an invention which was the daughter of that prolific old mother Necessity, was commended to notice. It is a school wherein men learn how to be sovereigns & legislators.

" But you cannot think how intolerable it is to me to be thus lamely hobbling back through the field which we have all just been borne over so handsomely. I prithee have me excused. Doubtless the Discourse will be requested for publication & you can be satisfied from itself. There was good company here, & the old meeting house showed such a mass of heads as have hardly been crowded under its roof since roof it had. Gov. Armstrong was here, & Winthrop (my class mate) as his aid. This was appropriate — for Gov. John Winthrop was once a land owner in Concord, by grant of the General Court. Alden Bradford too was here, Edward Everett, & Philip Hone of your city, whom we liked, all of us, right well, so hearty a speech did he make us at the Dinner Table.

" The Ladies had a Collation at the Court House, & it was quite elegantly arranged — Thither the gentlemen after dinner repaired, & took from fair hands a cup of coffee or tea."

Further details are given in the much less personal — and less interesting — account contributed by " a friend," and printed on pp. 48–49 of *A Historical Discourse,* Concord, 1835, and, like the discourse itself, reprinted in *Cent. Ed.,* XI.

80. Publication must have occurred about the first of November, for Charles Emerson to William, Nov. 7, 1835 (MS owned by Dr. Haven Emerson), says he has " sent withal, the long expected Historical Discourse of Waldo's " to New York.

might sell a little better for so much attention as the Discourse & the Day have called to the whole subject. Do hasten it for I think now is its very time & much better before the Oration. Do not be in Concord without seeing me for I am now a housekeeper & have many things respecting your book to say. So with hearty thanks for your kindness I am your obliged servant

R. W. Emerson.

To William Emerson, Concord, September 21, 1835 [81]

Concord, 21 Sept. 1835

Dear William

I am ashamed of my long silence toward my brother & sister. But point me to the man in New York that is so busy as idle I. I am compelled to slight & slur all my works so manifold they are — the great nothings. But here we are forming a new house,[82] as mother shall tell you, on the banks of the Musketaquid; and Lidian is getting a smart chamber ready for you & Susan, & baskets of playthings for William the Fourth.[83] As for Mother, you may have her one month — no more — it will be long enough for you & Susan to find out what a benediction and benefaction she has been every day of these long years to your affectionate brother, Waldo.

Send any friends now with confidence to me, as at last we have room bread & broad welcome for friends old or new & lie directly on the stage road 2½ hours from Boston.[84] Lidian rejoices in the hope of knowing you & Susan.

81. MS owned by RWEMA; ph. in CUL.

82. In his letter of Sept. 14 and 18, 1835, to William (owned by Dr. Haven Emerson), Charles, after narrating the events of the Concord celebration, wrote, still under date of Sept. 14: " Waldo went away last night & is to be married tonight, & tomorrow night is to be at home — " The *Boston Daily Advertiser,* Sept. 22, 1835, recorded the event: " MARRIED. . . . In Plymouth, 14th inst. by Rev. Dr. Kendall, Rev. R. Waldo Emerson to Miss Lydia Jackson, daughter of the late Charles Jackson, Esq." For a picture of the Winslow mansion in Plymouth, where the wedding was performed, see *The Bookman,* New York, XVII, 338 (June, 1903). On Oct. 10 Charles wrote to William (MS owned by Dr. Haven Emerson): " Waldo & Lidian will, by next week, be all in apple pye order — ; that is, if the worker in stone & mortar, even Mr. Dennis, shall be as good as his word."

83. See July 27, 1835, to William Emerson. " William the Fourth " is the " Willie " and " William, Jr." of many later letters.

84. Stages now left Boston every morning for Keene and Walpole, N. H., by way of Concord and Groton; and there were also Lexington and Concord accommodation stages (*Daily Evening Transcript,* Sept. 20, 1835).

To Lemuel Shattuck, Concord, September 27, 1835 [85]

Concord 27 Sept. 1835

My dear Sir,

I sent you a letter by mail about a week since [86] informing you of my purpose to print my Discourse at the request of the Committee. I judged from your note, received this morning, that you have not received that line from me. I am truly sorry to perceive from the tone of your note, that my quotations from your book in my discourse, have occasioned you some uneasiness. I certainly am very much indebted to your researches, your extracts, & your tables; yet by no means so much indebted, as you seem to imagine. I am afraid you suppose me indebted to you for much that I have taken, in common with you, from the original authorities. I have now on my table the seven first volumes of the Town Records, and the Volume of Church Records; all which books I have examined with great attention; I have Johnson's Wonder Working Providence in the Historical Collections.[87] I have here also Hubbard's Indian Wars, Mathers Magnalia, Winthrops Journal Hutchinsons History & his Collection; Minot; & Bradford; Bancroft's U. S. Peter Bulkeleys Gospel Covenant. Allens Biog. Dictionary. Dr Ripley's Half Century Sermon & History of ye Fight; Phinney; & the Lexington Sermons; Brigham's Discourse at Grafton; &c — These books are & have been before me. At Cambridge in August I made written extracts from Neal's New Eng^d^; Shepards Clear Sunshine &c; Mourt; Higginson; Josselyn; Underhill; Shepards Lamentation, &c. And I believe I have several extracts which might interest you.

There are only two passages in my discourse of any length for which I am indebted solely to you, and I confess I felt some scruple about introducing them into it; and it was these I referred to when I told you on the day of the Celebration 'that I had resisted the temptation of quoting from you whenever I could but these stories were so excellent you must forgive me.' — I refer to the story of Mary Shepard, which, if it is in Hubbard, I overlooked it there; & the other, the story of Mr Hoar, & the friendly Indians, which you quote from MSS. The last, on

85. MS owned by the Henry E. Huntington Library; ph. in CUL.

86. Letter of Sept. 17, 1835.

87. *Coll. Mass. Hist. Soc.,* 2d series, II, III, IV, VII, and VIII. The titles of early editions of Edward Johnson and the many other authorities cited in this letter are given in the index. The letter is a notable proof of Emerson's ability, on occasion, to carry his researches into considerable detail.

writing off my papers for the press, I have struck out. You will find I believe in my Discourse which I shall send you as soon as it appears, that I have given you credit for every fact in particular that I owe to your book, besides a general acknowledgment,[88] which I intended to be at least as ample as my debt. Meantime, I hope you are mistaken in thinking that I can at all hurt the sale of your book. I conceive that my sketches, if they should have any effect, would serve as an advertisement to your History. It was so liberal in you to lend it, that I should be extremely grieved, if, so, you should come to any loss. I had already undertaken to prepare a notice of it, which is to appear in the next Yeomans Gazette.[89] I wish you to send me, at the subscription price, ten copies. You intimate that I have made some erroneous statements in my discourse. It is altogether probable; & I shall be very thankful to have them corrected.

Your obedient servant
R. Waldo Emerson.

To George Partridge Bradford, Concord? September? 1835

[Described in Bradford, Sunday eve and Monday (endorsed Sept., 1835, by Emerson), as "your letter about the seal." Bradford wrote of a device Emerson wished to have engraved.]

To Ruth Haskins Emerson, Concord? October 3? 1835

[Acknowledged in Ruth Haskins Emerson, New York, Oct. 8 and 11, 1835; mentioned in William Emerson, Oct. 10, 1835, as "Your favor of the 3d (as I think) addressed to mother."]

To George Partridge Bradford, Concord? October? *c.* 5? 1835

[Described in Bradford, Oct. 10 (endorsed 1835 by Emerson), as "your few lines in token of kindly remembrance" and "invitation to me to write you a long letter."]

88. Emerson says in *A Historical Discourse*, 1835, pp. 40–41: "I have been greatly indebted, in preparing this sketch, to the printed but unpublished history of this town, furnished me by the unhesitating kindness of its author, long a resident in this place. . . . Meantime, I have read with care the town records themselves." And in many footnotes he cites Shattuck by name and page. He seems to have given full credit, as he had promised to do.

89. The file of the *Yeoman's Gazette* in the Concord Free Public Library lacks the issues for Sept. and Oct., 1835; and I have not found them elsewhere. Apparently a minor item in Emerson bibliography is to be credited to the paper which later published the famous letter to Van Buren.

To Thomas Carlyle, Concord, October 7, 1835

[MS owned by RWEMA (a rough draft, incomplete). Printed in *C–E Corr.*, 1883, from the rough draft.]

To Charles Wentworth Upham? Concord, November 2, 1835

[MS listed and partly quoted in Merwin-Clayton Sales Co., June 6, 1907; Emerson refers to "a Lecture at Salem" and asks whether his correspondent will come to the Concord Lyceum on Dec. 23. According to the MS records of the Lyceum (in the Concord Free Public Library) the lecture of Dec. 23, 1835, was delivered by the Rev. John A. Williams, of Billerica, Mass. But it seems probable that the person Emerson addressed in the present letter was his college classmate Upham. *Cf.* Apr. *c.* 3, 1836.]

To Ruth Haskins Emerson, Concord? November? *c.* 7? 1835

[Ruth Haskins Emerson, New York, Nov. 15, 1835, acknowledges this "letter a week since received."]

To Ruth Haskins Emerson, Concord? November *c.* 20? 1835

[Ruth Haskins Emerson, New York, Nov. 26, 1835, says she has neglected writing in answer to her son's last letter. Probably Emerson wrote another letter I have not found as an answer to a letter from his mother dated New York, Dec. 7, 1835.]

To William Emerson, Concord, November 28? 1835 [90]

Concord, Nov 1835.

My dear brother,

I was grieved to hear of the death of your young friend & inmate of whose pleasant society to Susan & to Mother we had heard so much & certainly you suggest a painful disclosure when the death is made known to her mother. Familiar as is this event, we shall never get wonted to it — it always astonishes, & when it comes into the circle of these affections it wounds & mangles — to good & great ends, however I hope & believe. Present my condolence and affetionate regards to Susan & to mother. Lidian begs me to say to Mother that she feels sore & dis-

90. MS owned by RWEMA; ph. in CUL. William Emerson endorsed "Nov. 28/35," and there is no reason to suppose that this was not the actual date of writing, for he was habitually accurate and he could probably have learned the date of his brother's writing from Samuel Hoar (see note below). Thanksgiving Day, referred to as still in the future, was observed in Massachusetts on Dec. 3 that year (*Boston Daily Advertiser*, Nov. 6 and later, 1835).

appointed at the prospect of not seeing her for a great length of time and she must come as soon as she can. At the same time we will not interfere with your comfort & rights, specially those of affliction.

We are all very well but can make up no large family party for Thanksgiving but shall have Eliz. & Charles — Mr Hoar is so obliging as to promise to see mother if he have two hours in N. Y.[91] which he may not have Bulkeley is at Chelmsford & unusually well. Yours affectionately

Waldo

May I trouble you with the care of these two Discourses.[92]

To Henry Ware, Jr., Concord, December? 12? 1835

[MS listed and partly quoted in Goodspeed's, Nov., 1935; Emerson says he had congratulated himself that he was not to speak for "the Society" but that if he must choose a topic, "the fourth in your list comes nearest mine, viz., 'The circumstances which favor a tendency toward the abolition of war.'" Goodspeed's gives only the year of the date line and does not name the person addressed; but this is obviously the letter to Ware mentioned, with some indication of the contents, in *Journals,* III, 574 (Dec. 12, 1835). Ware was a member of a committee of the Massachusetts Peace Society and had outlined a course of lectures on war and peace, which, however, could not be given till a few years later (John Ware, *Memoir of the Life of Henry Ware, Jr.,* Boston and London, 1846, p. 379).]

To Obadiah Rich, Concord? *c.* 1835

[Described in Sept. 13, 1837, as a request that Rich send a bill for some books he had sold to Emerson "two or three years ago." The other letters to Rich mentioned *ibid.* seem not to have been written by Emerson.]

91. The superscription shows that this letter was sent by Samuel Hoar, of Concord.

92. Copies of *A Historical Discourse,* which had been printed by Nov. 7 (see a note on Sept. 17, 1835).